SMITHSONIAN

CONTRIBUTIONS TO KNOWLEDGE.

VOL. VIII.

EVERY MAN IS A VALUABLE MEMBER OF SOCIETY, WHO, BY HIS OBSERVATIONS, RESEARCHES, AND EXPERIMENTS, PROCURES KNOWLEDGE FOR MEN.—SMITHSON.

1856.

CITY OF WASHINGTON:
PUBLISHED BY THE SMITHSONIAN INSTITUTION.
MDCCCLVI.

ADVERTISEMENT.

THIS volume forms the eighth of a series, composed of original memoirs on different branches of knowledge, published at the expense, and under the direction, of the Smithsonian Institution. The publication of this series forms part of a general plan adopted for carrying into effect the benevolent intentions of JAMES SMITHSON, Esq., of England. This gentleman left his property in trust to the United States of America, to found, at Washington, an institution which should bear his own name, and have for its objects the "*increase* and *diffusion* of knowledge among men." This trust was accepted by the Government of the United States, and an Act of Congress was passed August 10, 1846, constituting the President and the other principal executive officers of the general government, the Chief Justice of the Supreme Court, the Mayor of Washington, and such other persons as they might elect honorary members, an establishment under the name of the "SMITHSONIAN INSTITUTION FOR THE INCREASE AND DIFFUSION OF KNOWLEDGE AMONG MEN." The members and honorary members of this establishment are to hold stated and special meetings for the supervision of the affairs of the Institution, and for the advice and instruction of a Board of Regents, to whom the financial and other affairs are entrusted.

The Board of Regents consists of three members *ex officio* of the establishment, namely, the Vice-President of the United States, the Chief Justice of the Supreme Court, and the Mayor of Washington, together with twelve other members, three of whom are appointed by the Senate from its own body, three by the House of Representatives from its members, and six persons appointed by a joint resolution of both houses. To this Board is given the power of electing a Secretary and other officers, for conducting the active operations of the Institution.

To carry into effect the purposes of the testator, the plan of organization should evidently embrace two objects: one, the increase of knowledge by the addition of new truths to the existing stock; the other, the diffusion of knowledge, thus increased, among men. No restriction is made in favor of any kind of knowledge; and, hence, each branch is entitled to, and should receive, a share of attention.

The Act of Congress, establishing the Institution, directs, as a part of the plan of organization, the formation of a Library, a Museum, and a Gallery of Art, together with provisions for physical research and popular lectures, while it leaves to the Regents the power of adopting such other parts of an organization as they may deem best suited to promote the objects of the bequest.

After much deliberation, the Regents resolved to divide the annual income into two equal parts—one part to be devoted to the increase and diffusion of knowledge by means of original research and publications—the other half of the income to be applied in accordance with the requirements of the Act of Congress, to the gradual formation of a Library, a Museum, and a Gallery of Art.

The following are the details of the parts of the general plan of organization provisionally adopted at the meeting of the Regents, Dec. 8, 1847.

DETAILS OF THE FIRST PART OF THE PLAN.

I. To increase Knowledge.—*It is proposed to stimulate research, by offering rewards for original memoirs on all subjects of investigation.*

1. The memoirs thus obtained, to be published in a series of volumes, in a quarto form, and entitled "Smithsonian Contributions to Knowledge."

2. No memoir, on subjects of physical science, to be accepted for publication, which does not furnish a positive addition to human knowledge, resting on original research; and all unverified speculations to be rejected.

3. Each memoir presented to the Institution, to be submitted for examination to a commission of persons of reputation for learning in the branch to which the memoir pertains; and to be accepted for publication only in case the report of this commission is favorable.

4. The commission to be chosen by the officers of the Institution, and the name of the author, as far as practicable, concealed, unless a favorable decision be made.

5. The volumes of the memoirs to be exchanged for the Transactions of literary and scientific societies, and copies to be given to all the colleges, and principal libraries, in this country. One part of the remaining copies may be offered for sale; and the other carefully preserved, to form complete sets of the work, to supply the demand from new institutions.

6. An abstract, or popular account, of the contents of these memoirs to be given to the public, through the annual report of the Regents to Congress.

II. To INCREASE KNOWLEDGE.—*It is also proposed to appropriate a portion of the income, annually, to special objects of research, under the direction of suitable persons.*

1. The objects, and the amount appropriated, to be recommended by counsellors of the Institution.

2. Appropriations in different years to different objects; so that, in course of time, each branch of knowledge may receive a share.

3. The results obtained from these appropriations to be published, with the memoirs before mentioned, in the volumes of the Smithsonian Contributions to Knowledge.

4. Examples of objects for which appropriations may be made:—

(1.) System of extended meteorological observations for solving the problem of American storms.

(2.) Explorations in descriptive natural history, and geological, mathematical, and topographical surveys, to collect materials for the formation of a Physical Atlas of the United States.

(3.) Solution of experimental problems, such as a new determination of the weight of the earth, of the velocity of electricity, and of light; chemical analyses of soils and plants; collection and publication of articles of science, accumulated in the offices of Government.

(4.) Institution of statistical inquiries with reference to physical, moral, and political subjects.

(5.) Historical researches, and accurate surveys of places celebrated in American history.

(6.) Ethnological researches, particularly with reference to the different races of men in North America; also explorations, and accurate surveys, of the mounds and other remains of the ancient people of our country.

I. To DIFFUSE KNOWLEDGE.—*It is proposed to publish a series of reports, giving an account of the new discoveries in science, and of the changes made from year to year in all branches of knowledge not strictly professional.*

1. Some of these reports may be published annually, others at longer intervals, as the income of the Institution or the changes in the branches of knowledge may indicate.

2. The reports are to be prepared by collaborators, eminent in the different branches of knowledge.

3. Each collaborator to be furnished with the journals and publications, domestic and foreign, necessary to the compilation of his report; to be paid a certain sum for his labors, and to be named on the title-page of the report.

4. The reports to be published in separate parts, so that persons interested in a particular branch, can procure the parts relating to it, without purchasing the whole.

5. These reports may be presented to Congress, for partial distribution, the remaining copies to be given to literary and scientific institutions, and sold to individuals for a moderate price.

The following are some of the subjects which may be embraced in the reports:—

I. PHYSICAL CLASS.

1. Physics, including astronomy, natural philosophy, chemistry, and meteorology.
2. Natural history, including botany, zoology, geology, &c.
3. Agriculture.
4. Application of science to arts.

II. MORAL AND POLITICAL CLASS.

5. Ethnology, including particular history, comparative philology, antiquities, &c.
6. Statistics and political economy.
7. Mental and moral philosophy.
8. A survey of the political events of the world; penal reform, &c.

III. LITERATURE AND THE FINE ARTS.

9. Modern literature.
10. The fine arts, and their application to the useful arts.
11. Bibliography.
12. Obituary notices of distinguished individuals.

II. TO DIFFUSE KNOWLEDGE.—*It is proposed to publish occasionally separate treatises on subjects of general interest.*

1. These treatises may occasionally consist of valuable memoirs translated from foreign languages, or of articles prepared under the direction of the Institution, or procured by offering premiums for the best exposition of a given subject.

2. The treatises to be submitted to a commission of competent judges, previous to their publication.

DETAILS OF THE SECOND PART OF THE PLAN OF ORGANIZATION.

This part contemplates the formation of a Library, a Museum, and a Gallery of Art.

1. To carry out the plan before described, a library will be required, consisting, 1st, of a complete collection of the transactions and proceedings of all the learned societies in the world; 2d, of the more important current periodical publications, and other works necessary in preparing the periodical reports.

2. The Institution should make special collections, particularly of objects to verify its own publications. Also a collection of instruments of research in all branches of experimental science.

3. With reference to the collection of books, other than those mentioned above, catalogues of all the different libraries in the United States should be procured, in order that the valuable books first purchased may be such as are not to be found elsewhere in the United States.

4. Also catalogues of memoirs, and of books in foreign libraries, and other materials, should be collected, for rendering the Institution a centre of bibliographical knowledge, whence the student may be directed to any work which he may require.

5. It is believed that the collections in natural history will increase by donation, as rapidly as the income of the Institution can make provision for their reception; and, therefore, it will seldom be necessary to purchase any article of this kind.

6. Attempts should be made to procure for the gallery of art, casts of the most celebrated articles of ancient and modern sculpture.

7. The arts may be encouraged by providing a room, free of expense, for the exhibition of the objects of the Art-Union, and other similar societies.

8. A small appropriation should annually be made for models of antiquity, such as those of the remains of ancient temples, &c.

9. The Secretary and his assistants, during the session of Congress, will be required to illustrate new discoveries in science, and to exhibit new objects of art; distinguished individuals should also be invited to give lectures on subjects of general interest.

In accordance with the rules adopted in the programme of organization, each memoir in this volume has been favorably reported on by a Commission appointed for its examination. It is however impossible, in most cases, to verify the statements of an author; and, therefore, neither the Commission nor the Institution can be responsible for more than the general character of a memoir.

The following rules have been adopted for the distribution of the quarto volumes of the Smithsonian Contributions:—

1. They are to be presented to all learned societies which publish Transactions, and give copies of these, in exchange, to the Institution.

2. Also, to all foreign libraries of the first class, provided they give in exchange their catalogues or other publications, or an equivalent from their duplicate volumes.

3. To all the colleges in actual operation in this country, provided they furnish, in return, meteorological observations, catalogues of their libraries and of their students, and all other publications issued by them relative to their organization and history.

4. To all States and Territories, provided there be given, in return, copies of all documents published under their authority.

5. To all incorporated public libraries in this country, not included in any of the foregoing classes, now containing more than 7000 volumes; and to smaller libraries, where a whole State or large district would be otherwise unsupplied.

OFFICERS

OF THE

SMITHSONIAN INSTITUTION.

THE PRESIDENT OF THE UNITED STATES,

Ex officio PRESIDING OFFICER OF THE INSTITUTION.

THE VICE-PRESIDENT OF THE UNITED STATES,

Ex officio SECOND PRESIDING OFFICER.

ROGER B. TANEY,

CHANCELLOR OF THE INSTITUTION.

JOSEPH HENRY,

SECRETARY OF THE INSTITUTION.

SPENCER F. BAIRD,

ASSISTANT SECRETARY.

W. W. SEATON, TREASURER.

ALEXANDER D. BACHE, JAMES A. PEARCE, JOSEPH G. TOTTEN,	EXECUTIVE COMMITTEE.
RICHARD RUSH, WILLIAM H. ENGLISH, JOSEPH HENRY,	BUILDING COMMITTEE.

REGENTS.

—— ———	*Vice-President of the United States.*
ROGER B. TANEY, ...	*Chief Justice of the United States.*
WILLIAM B. MAGRUDER, ...	*Mayor of the City of Washington.*
JAMES A. PEARCE, ...	*Member of the Senate of the United States.*
JAMES M. MASON, ...	" " " " " "
STEPHEN A. DOUGLAS, ...	" " " " " "
WILLIAM H. ENGLISH, ...	*Member of the House of Representatives U. S.*
BENJAMIN STANTON, ...	" " " " " "
HIRAM WARNER, ...	" " " " " "
GIDEON HAWLEY, ...	*Citizen of New York.*
RICHARD RUSH, ...	" *of Pennsylvania.*
JAMES E. BADGER, ...	" *of Georgia.*
ALEXANDER D. BACHE, ...	*Member of Nat. Inst. Washington.*
JOSEPH G. TOTTEN, ...	" " "

MEMBERS EX OFFICIO OF THE INSTITUTION.

Franklin Pierce, ...	*President of the United States.*
——— ———	*Vice-President of the United States.*
William L. Marcy, ...	*Secretary of State.*
James Guthrie, ...	*Secretary of the Treasury.*
Jefferson Davis, ...	*Secretary of War.*
James C. Dobbin, ...	*Secretary of the Navy.*
James Campbell, ...	*Postmaster-General.*
Caleb Cushing, ...	*Attorney-General.*
Roger B. Taney, ...	*Chief Justice of the United States.*
Charles Mason, ...	*Commissioner of Patents.*
William B. Magruder, ...	*Mayor of the City of Washington.*

HONORARY MEMBERS.

ROBERT HARE,	ALBERT GALLATIN,*
WASHINGTON IRVING,	PARKER CLEAVELAND,
BENJAMIN SILLIMAN,	A. B. LONGSTREET.

(*Deceased.)

TABLE OF CONTENTS.*

* Each memoir is separately paged and indexed.

APPENDIX.

SMITHSONIAN CONTRIBUTIONS TO KNOWLEDGE.

ARCHÆOLOGY

OF THE

UNITED STATES.

OR

SKETCHES, HISTORICAL AND BIBLIOGRAPHICAL, OF THE PROGRESS OF INFORMATION AND OPINION RESPECTING VESTIGES OF ANTIQUITY IN THE UNITED STATES.

BY

SAMUEL F. HAVEN.

[ACCEPTED FOR PUBLICATION, JANUARY, 1855.]

COMMISSION

TO WHICH THIS PAPER HAS BEEN REFERRED.

PETER FORCE,
BRANTZ MAYER.

JOSEPH HENRY,
Secretary S. I.

T. K. AND P. G. COLLINS, PRINTERS,
PHILADELPHIA.

CONTENTS.

ERRATA.

Page 143, line 3d from bottom, *for* east to west, *read* west to east.
" 145, line 3d from top, *for* parallel, *read* principal.

INTRODUCTORY NOTE.

THE adventurous activity of the people of the United States, joined to a wandering propensity, partly national and partly characteristic of the age, has left few, if any, considerable portions of the country unexplored. The emigrant overtakes the government surveyor, and railroads and other improvements advance with equal rapidity in the steps of the latter. It would be difficult to point out upon the map a section of much extent, however secluded, that has not been traversed by intelligent observers, taking note of the quality of its soil, its vegetable and mineral productions, and whatever else would contribute to an appreciation of its resources. In these expeditions, often conducted by topographical engineers, and accompanied by naturalists constantly looking out for objects of interest, it is hardly to be supposed that vestiges of ancient art would fail to attract attention. We can therefore anticipate little of novelty hereafter in that class of discoveries, and now that the peculiar earthworks of Wisconsin have been carefully investigated, it may reasonably be inferred that all the prominent varieties of aboriginal remains, which are found in the United States east of the Rocky Mountains, have been more or less minutely described.

The memoir of Messrs. Squier and Davis, constituting the first volume of the "Smithsonian Contributions," although entitled "Ancient Monuments of the Mississippi Valley," and mainly devoted to the antiquities of that extensive region, yet aimed to embrace within its scope all that was known of similar vestiges north of the Gulf of Mexico. Hence, the writers added to their own materials the results of previous and contemporary researches in other parts of the United States, as well as that to which their personal observations were confined. Their treatise contains a faithful and able exposition of the subject, corrects many errors previously entertained, and defines and classifies the information collected with great clearness and particularity.

In the second volume of the "Contributions," again under a limited title, that of the "Aboriginal Monuments of the State of New York," Mr. Squier has extended his private explorations to the aboriginal relics of that State, and, in an ample appendix, has once more gone over the whole ground, for the purpose of presenting a general view of the characteristics of such antiquities in the United States, and comparing them with analogous remains in other countries. Some of his former opinions respecting the earthworks in that section are changed or modified, and the fruits of much inquiry and mature study are brought to bear upon the question of the origin and use of the various structures.

Thus, without looking beyond the publications of this institution, we have a fund of materials, of recent compilation, for a clear understanding of the nature of these remains, and a proper estimation of the kind and degree of archæological interest attached to them.

We have also other and distinct sources of information and opinion not comprehended, or only partially considered, in those volumes; some relating to the character and design of existing monuments, and others to the origin and peculiarities of ante-Columbian population in the country. Among the latter are vocabularies of the native languages, analyzed and compared by able philologists. Mr. Gallatin, especially, in his elaborate essay published by the American Antiquarian Society, and in later communications to the American Ethnological Society, has enlarged the range of that branch of inquiry, and poured a flood of light upon the subject by an acute and philosophical analysis of the subtleties of grammatical construction; the late eminent physiologist, Dr. Morton, has, in his speciality, examined the analogies belonging to the physical attributes of the American races; Mr. Schoolcraft has collected the miscellaneous results of his protracted study of the past and present history of the aborigines into the magnificent quartos published at the expense of our national government; and these are only some of the prominent writers who have studied the subject in one or another of its aspects. A mass of information has thus accumulated, gathered from our whole territory by intelligent and comparatively recent observers.

The present may therefore be a favorable occasion for introducing a retrospective view of the progress of opinion and information concerning the ethnological position and social advancement of the people by whom our soil was occupied in ages beyond the reach of history. The way would then be prepared for an estimate of the real knowledge, thus far obtained, of the customs, arts, and civil condition of those mysterious races.

This inquiry involves the necessity of referring to early hypotheses concerning the origin of American population which embrace the whole of both continents, although little beyond a mere allusion to the prolific themes of controversy they have generated is permitted by the limits to which this paper is restricted.

CHAPTER I.

GENERAL OPINIONS RESPECTING THE ORIGIN OF POPULATION IN THE NEW WORLD.

After the discovery of America, the minds of the learned and ingenious were much exercised to account for its habitation by men and animals. On the presumption that all the varieties of the human race were descended from a single pair, and that after the flood the earth was indebted solely to the ark of Noah for the replenishment of man and beast, the manner in which these reached the western world became to scholars and divines a subject of anxious inquiry. The complete isolation of the newly-discovered land was not, it is true, immediately suspected; and Columbus and Vespucius both died in the conviction that they had only touched on portions of Asia. Indeed, so late as 1533, it was maintained, by the astronomer Schöner, that Mexico was the *Quinsai* of Marco Paulo. But when this was ascertained to be a vast continent by itself, separated by broad oceans or by frozen barriers from the rest of the globe, the solution of the mystery of population became a matter of intense philosophical interest; and the materials relied upon for such a solution, drawn from sacred and profane history, and the writings of ancient philosophers, poets, and geographers, were employed to sustain a great diversity of opinions. As these materials have continued to be reproduced in various combinations, and the hypotheses they suggested are constantly repeated by modern theorists, it becomes essential to an understanding of the subject, not only as formerly regarded, but in its existing position, that they should be succinctly enumerated.

While most authors have been content to go no further back in their speculations than the period of the division of the earth among the descendants of Noah, there are others who take a less limited flight, and assume a still earlier date for the peopling of America. It has been held that the earth before the flood was one mass of land, and that, when this was broken at the deluge, Providence made provision to save a remnant of people in every country, although we have accounts of what happened in one continent only.[1] It has been argued, from differences in the animal kingdom, many of whose species would not survive transportation, that they must have been originally bred where they are found; and it has been maintained that, according to the prevailing traditions of antiquity, Paradise was without the eastern continent, and beyond the ocean.[2]

---

[1] Burnett's "Theory of the Earth," Lond., 1684.

[2] Ibid.

What the prolific fancy of Paracelsus suggested, among the bold assumptions of his peculiar genius,[1] and Voltaire, Lord Kames, and others, have argued upon general philosophical principles, some naturalists are now attempting to deduce from observation, viz: that the races of men and animals were severally created in the regions which they inhabit. A distinct and intimate connection is asserted to exist between the *fauna* of different latitudes and the races of men associated with them. The diversity and distribution of men and animals were a stumbling-block to early writers, which but few ventured to overleap by explanations deemed inconsistent with sacred history. If we may judge from the tendency of recent publications, we must be prepared for the readvancement of an ancient theory, now based upon geological phenomena, the structure of native dialects, and other scientific data, which would give the New World precedence of the Old one, as sooner prepared for the occupancy of human and brute creation, and as actually inhabited at a more remote period.[2]

The plausible theory of an original communication between the two continents by means of lands now submerged in the Atlantic, has always found numerous supporters. A belief has also prevailed that without such means of transmission, emigration took place from Africa to America before the flood.[3]

Passing from the question of an antediluvian population on the American Continent, supposed, moreover, to be indicated by Mexican traditions, we meet with writers who imagine they discover evidences of settlement in this country by the immediate descendants of Noah. For example, it has been advanced by biblical critics that Juctan, or Joctan, son of Heber, founded a city in Peru; and that colonies were planted by Ophir and Johab his sons. It was a belief entertained by distinguished Hebrew scholars, that Ophir, to which land of gold the ships hired of the Tyrians by Solomon, sailed on a three years' voyage, must be in America.

Tornielli, the annalist, was of opinion that the descendants of Shem and Ham passed to America by way of Japan.

From some supposed resemblance of religious rites, Gomara, De Lery, and Lescarbot,[4] who had opportunities of personal observation in America, and in different regions, concluded that the natives were descended from the Canaanites whom Joshua compelled to seek a new habitation; a theory which, in later times, and upon different grounds, seemed to President Stiles, of Yale College, the most probable of any that had been advanced.

---

1 "Omnium Stultitiam Theophrastus Paracelsus exhausit, qui duplicem Adamum, alium in Asia, in America alium creatum asserit."—*Hornius de Originibus Americanis*, Lib. I., Cap. 2.

2 "Types of Mankind," by Messrs. Nott and Gliddon, Ch. IX., p. 271, *et seq.*

3 "Opus Chronographicum ab orbe Condito" of Peter Opmeer, Anvers, 1611.

4 Francesco Lopez de Gomara, professor of rhetoric, who came to Mexico to prepare his history of its conquest. Jean de Lery, a French Calvinist, who was sent to aid Villegnanon in establishing a protestant colony in Brazil, in 1556–7. An English translation of his account of Brazil was printed in 1611. Mark Lescarbot, advocate of the parliament of Paris, who aided in forming the first French establishment in Canada, and wrote "Histoire de la Nouvelle France," Paris, 1609.

But of all opinions having their foundation in sacred history, that which traces the origin of our Indian tribes wholly, or in part, to the lost ten tribes of Israel, has found the warmest and most numerous supporters. It is among the oldest hypotheses, has been supposed to find the strongest corroboration in the customs and traditions of the Indians, and has been continually discussed to the present time. The four principal grounds on which the argument in its favor rests, are: 1st, that the ten tribes, on being carried into captivity by Psalmanazar, were established in the northeastern provinces of the Assyrian Empire, from whence they disappeared in a direction towards that part of Asia which is nearest to America, the point from whence some kind of emigration is commonly believed to have taken place; 2d, that the book of Esdras, classed among the Apocryphal Scriptures, but regarded as possessing claims to historical authenticity, speaks of the tribes as having resolved to go forth *into a further country where never man dwelt*, and as *passing over the waters into another land, &c.*; 3d, that many of the customs of the Indians indicate a Hebrew origin; 4th, that numerous Hebrew words and idioms are found in the languages of the latter. Genebrard and Andrew Thevet were among the early writers who traced the lost tribes in America. But a new and more vigorous impulse was given to this course of investigation in the succeeding century, when the labors of Mayhew and Eliot for the conversion of the natives in New England began to excite much interest abroad, where a belief prevailed that the restoration of the Jews was at hand. Thomas Thorowgood, a member of the Assembly of Divines, published in 1650 a book entitled "Jews in America, or probabilities that the Americans are of that race." This was first circulated in manuscript, and attracted the attention of John Dury, a divine of some celebrity, who wrote urging its publication, and communicated two remarkable stories he had heard in Holland, that were printed with it. The first story was of a messenger from the ten tribes, who had made his appearance in Palestine to inquire after the remnant that remained when they themselves were carried into captivity. The other was the narrative of Antonie Monterinos, who professed to have found a community of Jews in Peru, by whom he had been entertained for several days. This had been sworn to before Manasseh Ben Israel, the chief Rabbi, at Amsterdam, who testified to the good character of Monterinos. The inquiries of Dury induced Manasseh Ben Israel to write his well known treatise, "The Hope of Israel," in which he endeavored to prove that the Israelites were "the first finders out of America." It appears to have been from these sources that Mayhew, Eliot, Roger Williams, and other New England preachers of Christianity to the children of the forest, received impressions concerning the descent of the Indians from the Jews, which their own observations tended to confirm.[1] The Mathers, Samuel Sewall, and most of the prominent scholars and theologians of Massachusetts, were inclined to the same opinion, which has never failed to find supporters. The Earl of Crawford and Lindsay, who, as

---

[1] Dury was a friend and correspondent of the New England Clergy, and when the letters from Eliot and others, giving an account of the progress of the gospel among the Indians, were printed in London, he added an appendix, in which he gives some reasons for believing the Indians to be descended from the Jews. This was previous to Thorowgood's publication.

an officer of the British army during the war of the Revolution, was much among the Indians, wrote a tract on the subject. Adair, the distinguished Dr. Elias Boudinot, Rev. Ethan Smith, the late M. M. Noah, Lord Kingsborough, and Mrs. St. Simon, continue the series of persevering advocates of that view of the question.

Profane history and the ancient classics, have suggested more numerous, if not more plausible conjectures, respecting the origin of the Americans. Vague intimations derived from that mysterious repository of primeval lore, the Egyptian Priesthood, have been supposed to warrant a belief in the former existence of a seat of arts and empire now buried beneath the Atlantic Ocean. Of these the most distinct is recorded in the Timæus of Plato as having been related to Solon, about six hundred years before Christ, by a priest of a temple in the Delta. This keeper of the secrets of the past, looking down, as it were, from a superior antiquity, tells Solon that the Greeks are ever children; that an air of youth is visible in all their histories; while in the Egyptian temples are the records of ages and nations long buried in oblivion. He proceeds to inform him that there have been innumerable deluges and conflagrations of the regions of the earth; some of them faintly shadowed in the fables and mutilated traditions of the Greeks. In one of these the great Island of Atlantis, larger than Lybia and Asia together, was submerged in the ocean that inherits its name. This island was stated to be opposite the Straits of Gades (Gibraltar), and its inhabitants extended their sway over all the adjoining regions, until checked by some ancestors of the Athenians.

Allusions to this lost island, or continent, are frequent in Greek and Roman authors, and it is not supposed to be a fiction of Plato's devising. Buffon believed in the probability of the story; and Bailly, in his "Lettres sur l'Atlantide de Platon," maintains its reality by the additional authorities of Homer, Sanchoniathon, and Diodorus Siculus. Whether the island was in fact submerged, or simply the means of communication with it lost, has been a question much discussed. Various islands have been assigned as its locality, and even regions in the north of Europe connected with the main land. Many supposed it to be America. According to Plato, there were first smaller islands from which there was an easy passage to the larger one, or continent, beyond. The theory of a chain of islands, with slight intervals, if not a solid body of land, quite across both the Atlantic and Pacific Oceans, is supposed, by some modern writers, to be geographically sustained.

The celebrated lines in the "Medea" of Seneca, who lived about the time of our Saviour, have been received as indicating either a ray of traditionary light or a prophetic inspiration.[1] Humboldt and Bishop Horsley have shown how slight are

---

[1] Venient annis sæcula seris
Quibus Oceanus vincula rerum
Laxet, et ingens pateat tellus,
Tethysque novas detegat orbes,
Nec sit terris ultima Thule."

their claims to the latter construction.[1] They were doubtless an accidental, and not unnatural, though very felicitous stretch of a poet's fancy.

Another remarkable passage is in the "Varia Historia" of Aelian, where Silenus is represented as saying to Midas, King of Phrygia, that Europe, Asia, and Africa are surrounded by the ocean; and that beyond there is a great continent sustaining huge animals, and men larger and longer lived than their own. There were, he said, great states, various institutions and laws, unlike those of Phrygia, and the land possessed an abundance of gold and silver, which the people regarded less than the Phrygians did iron.

To these ancient references to lands in the Atlantic, far removed from the European shores, may be added the story of the mythological Hesperides, which Lescarbot believed to be the Antilles of the Gulf of Mexico; the island called Antilla, mentioned by Aristotle as having been discovered by the Carthaginians; the very large island described by Diodorus Siculus as many days' sail from Africa, abounding in mountains and navigable rivers, which the Carthaginians wished to conceal from the rest of the world, as a place of retreat in case of misfortune to their city; and the story of Pomponius Mela of certain Indians being cast on the German coast, who were given to Metellus Celer by the King of the Suevians.[2] Nor must the tradition of the island of the Seven Cities be omitted, where, on the conquest of Spain and Portugal by the Moors, seven bishops, and a multitude of followers, escaping in ships, accidentally landed, concerning whom rumors reached Portugal in the time of Prince Henry.

There are records, bearing marks of authenticity, of voyages made by the commercial inhabitants of the African shores of the Mediterranean, that are deemed to indicate a degree of maritime skill and enterprise rendering possible a knowledge on their part, not only of the Canaries, the Cape Verde Islands, and the Azores, but also of the Antilles, and even the continent of America; and many theories of the origin of population here have been based upon them which are adhered to by various recent writers.

The first in order of time is that, so celebrated, of Hanno, the Carthaginian, many centuries before Christ, and related by himself in what is called "the Periplus of Hanno." Efforts have been made to prove the Periplus a spurious production; but Robertson considers its authenticity established by unanswerable arguments.[3] According to Pliny, Hanno sailed from the Straits of Gibraltar around Africa to Arabia. Bougainville, Gosselin, and other commentators, have endeavored to trace his course, step by step; and the latter affirms that all the authorities, not-

[1] Examen Critique, I. 162, *et seq.;* Horsley's Sermons, II. 44. Yet Humboldt says:—

"When Strabo tells us that in the Atlantic Ocean, in that part of the northern hemisphere which is not occupied by our habitable land, there may exist another habitable earth, or even many, above all in the parallel of Thinæ, which is that of the widest part of the continent of Europe and Asia, he prophesies, that is to say he divines, as seems to me, the discovery of America, and the Isles of the South Sea."—*Humboldt, Examen Critique*, I. 165.

[2] Aristotle De Mirabiles Auscultationes, Cap. 84, p. 836; Diodorus Siculus De Fabulosis Antiquorum Gestis, Cap. 84, Lib. 6, p. 331; Humboldt, Exam. Critique, I. 130–131.

[3] Hist. of America, I., note to p. 13.

withstanding apparent contradictions, bring us to the same result, and fix the limit of his voyage near Cape Non, or Cape Bajador.[1]

The next expedition is that of some Phœnicians, whom Pharaoh Necho, about 604 B. C., dispatched from a port in the Red Sea, with orders to return through the Pillars of Hercules. This they are said to have accomplished in somewhat less than three years. The account in Herodotus is quite circumstantial, and, although much controverted, is received as correct by Humboldt, who cites Rennell, Heeren, Sprengel, and a more recent writer of great repute, Etienne Quatremére, in its favor, and adds that the command of Necho implies a previous knowledge of the possibility of such a navigation.[2] It is stated, moreover, by Pliny, from Cornelius Nepos, that one Eudoxus, a great sailor, in the reign of Cleopatra, "at the time he fled from King Lathyrus, departed out of the Arabian Gulf, and held on his course as far as Gades" (Gibraltar). Not much weight, however, is given to this story by reliable authorities.[3]

It will be seen that, if it is once admitted that Phœnicians, Carthaginians, or Tyrians, actually sailed around Africa, their knowledge of the islands opposite to its western shores may be presumed, as they would almost of necessity be driven near them by the well-known courses of the winds. By the same means, in case of a tempest, they might be carried still further to the westward, and to the American coast. It was thus that Brazil was discovered in A. D. 1500, by Pedro Cabral, while on his way from Portugal to the East Indies. A fact, which, like the wreck of a Japanese junk at the mouth of the Columbia River in 1833, substantiates the possibility of such occurrences in more ancient times.[4] It was on the coast of Brazil that the Pilot, who is alleged to have preceded Columbus in the passage of the Atlantic, was by some reported to have been cast.

And this brings us to the last class of narratives, viz: those which are adduced to show that Columbus was not entitled to the credit of original discovery, but may have been indebted to other navigators who preceded him for a knowledge of the existence of western lands far beyond the limits of ordinary communication.

Many persons find it difficult to realize that things so simple, as great truths uni-

---

[1] Irving's Columb. III., Appendix No. 14.

[2] Cosmos, II. 127, note.

[3] Reinholdt Foster says: "The Phœnicians sent out for the purpose, by the Egyptian king and conqueror, *Sesostris*, and his father, Amasis I., gradually discovered the coasts of all Africa.

The third epocha of the circumnavigation of Africa fell in the time of Solomon, nearly five hundred years later. Three hundred and eighty years after this Necho gave orders for the circumnavigation of Africa to be performed; and, in the reign of Ptolemy Euergetes II., one Eudoxus sailed once more round Africa, which is four hundred and fifty years later than the voyage of Necho; and yet, in Strabo's time, many people doubted of the possibility of making the tour of Africa by sea."—*Voyages and Discoveries in the North*, p. 7, n.

See also Jeremy Belknap's Dissertation on the Circumnavigation of Africa by the Ancients, attached to his Discourse in Commemoration of the Discovery of America by Columbus, before the Massachusetts Historical Society, Oct. 23, 1792.

[4] Gumilla, in his History of Orinoco, states that, in December, 1731, a batteau, from Teneriffe, bound for the Canaries, was driven upon the South American coast, near the mouth of the Orinoco. Tome II. p. 208.

versally are, should remain for ages entirely concealed from mankind; and a successful enterprise is often reluctantly admitted to have proceeded from the original conceptions and intuitive sagacity of its author.[1]

Partly perhaps upon this principle, and it may be somewhat stimulated by national jealousy, statements prejudicial to the claims of Columbus were early circulated, and have been since repeated as entitled to belief, or have undergone investigation as questions of scientific interest.

Thus Oviedo, in his history of the Indies, printed A. D. 1535, mentions, but as a rumor merely, that about the year 1484, a certain pilot, in one of his customary voyages, was driven by a violent storm to an unknown land, and on his return was received, with a few survivors of his crew, into the house of Columbus, where they died, leaving their papers in his hands. This, although disregarded by contemporary authors, was brought forward against Columbus, in 1552, by Gomara, a writer not esteemed entirely trustworthy;[2] and, one hundred and twenty years after the event, was seriously narrated by Vega, in his commentaries of Peru. Vega gives the name of the pilot and the number of his crew, with many other details, which he professes to have heard when a child. He refers for confirmation to Gomara, and also to Acosta, who, in 1591, slightly noticed the circumstance. It is a good illustration of the manner in which a tale expands and develops itself in the process of transmission. The fact that Columbus communicated his idea of discovery ten years before the assigned date of the occurrence is believed to be well established.[3] The same tendency to expansion is exhibited in the case of the claim that, at a still earlier period, about 1464, John Vaz Casta Cortereal, a gentleman of the royal household of Portugal, explored the northern seas by order of Alphonso 5th, and discovered the Terra de Baccalhaos, or land of codfish, afterwards called Newfoundland. The descent of this remarkable statement is traced, by the author of a memoir of Sebastian Cabot, from Cordeyro, an obscure Portuguese writer, of the date of 1717, to "Barrow's Chronological History of Voyages," and from thence to "Lardner's Encyclopedia," as a reliable fact, and to the "Edinburgh Cabinet Library," where the event is spoken of as happening "*nearly a century* before the celebrated voyages of Columbus and Cabot"![4]

The uncertain expedition of the eight Arabian brothers, who, it is related, some time previous to 1147, sailed from Lisbon, and "swore they would not return till they had penetrated to the farthest bounds of the DARK SEA,"—which resulted in the discovery of an island inhabited by a people of lofty stature and a red skin—has by some writers been extended to the Coast of America; but the better opinion seems to be that the island referred to was one of the Canary group.[5]

---

[1] En un mot, Colomb n'est point du tout un génie transcendant, une espèce de prophète, qui ait deviné le noveau monde, c'est tout bonnement un navigateur instruit et courageux, c'est le Cook de son siècle. Son mérite réal est trop grand pour qu'il ait besoin d'une gloire imaginaire.—Géographie Mathématique de Mentelle et Malte Brun. Tome XIV. p. 8, n.

[2] Irving's Life of Columbus, III. Appendix, No. 11.

[3] Humboldt's Examen Critique, I. 12.

[4] Biddle's Memoir of Sebastian Cabot, Book ii. ch. xi.

[5] N. A. Review, XLVII. 178.

In the History of Wales, translated by Dr. Powell from the original British of Caradoc of Lhancarvan, is the foundation of the story of Madawk ap Owen Gwynedh, who, about 1170, as it is represented, sailed westward with a small fleet of ships, and leaving Ireland on the north, came at length to an unknown country, where he left a part of his followers, and returning home for more, bade a final adieu to his native land, and sailed again with ten ships.

Concerning this country, Humphrey Lloyd, the first translator of Caradoc, says (and from him Hakluyt has adopted the expression): "It must of necessity be some part of that vast tract of ground of which the Spaniards since Hanno's time boast themselves to be the first discoverers." Lloyd supposes it to be New Spain or Florida; but Powell is inclined to consider it a part of Mexico.[1] Here is really all that is known in history respecting the voyage of Madoc, which has been the basis of so many theories, supported by the imagined detection of Welsh words and a Celtic race in America.[2]

The assertion that Columbus may have derived his knowledge of a western continent from the Scandinavians, during his voyage to the north, in 1477, or from a map representing the discoveries of the Zeni, is invalidated by a comparison of dates. The claims of Martin Behem, the German contemporary of Columbus, ingeniously presented by M. Otto in the Transactions of the American Philosophical Society for 1786, are also disposed of by similar scrutiny.[3]

That the NORTHMEN planted themselves in Greenland, and, about A. D. 1000, coasted the North American shores as far south as 41° 30′ N. latitude, seems to be established by documentary proof. A greater extent of discovery is claimed for them by Scandinavian writers upon similar testimony; and wonderful tales are told of what they heard from the natives, of white men, supposed to be from Ireland, who had preceded them, and occupied the country as far south as Florida. Moreover, an Icelandic chief, Are Marson, was said to have been driven by a storm among the same white men as early as A. D. 982; who being detained, was baptized in the Christian faith, and was recognized subsequently by some sailors from the Orkney Islands and Iceland.[4]

Belonging to the same region of mystical adventure, although its heroes were natives of Venice, is the marvellous tale of the Zeni. These brothers, Nicolo and Antonio Zeno, were of a distinguished family in Venice, and, according to the narrative, Nicolo, the elder, having a strong desire to see the world, about A. D. 1380, equipped a vessel at his own expense, and passing the Straits of Gibraltar sailed towards the north. The incidents of the story are that he was wrecked upon an island north of Great Britain, called Friseland; and being rescued from

---

[1] Hist. of Wales, p. 196. Price's Edition.

[2] For a summary of evidence supposed to indicate the emigration of a Welch colony to this country, and a knowledge of the language by certain tribes of Indians at the south and west, see "Enquiry into the truth of the tradition concerning the Discovery of America by Prince Madog," by John Williams LL. D., London, 1791, and Carey's American Museum for April and May, 1792.

[3] Irving's Columbus, III. Appendix.

[4] "Antiquitates Americanæ," Transactions of the Royal Society of Northern Antiquaries.

the natives by a powerful chief who happened to arrive just then for the purpose of making a conquest of the island, was received into his favor, knighted, and became the commander of his navy. Antonio having been sent for, the brothers engaged in various enterprises together, and founded a monastery and church in Greenland. Nicolo dies, but Antonio remains in the service of the chieftain, Earl Zichmni, fourteen years. At some time during this period he obtained, from a mariner who came to Friseland, the following statement: That twenty-six years before, the mariner was one of a party which was cast upon an island called Estotiland, a thousand miles distant, a populous and civilized country, there being Latin books in the King's library; that being sent by the King to visit a country to the south called Drogeo, they narrowly escaped being devoured by the inhabitants, who were cannibals; but learned that far to the southwest was a more civilized region and temperate climate, where the people had a knowledge of gold and silver, erected splendid temples to idols, and sacrificed human victims; and that after a long time, having acquired wealth in Estotiland, the mariner fitted out a bark of his own and made his way back to Friseland.

Stimulated by this story Earl Zichmni sent Antonio in search of the countries described. The mariner died before Antonio sailed; but some of his companions from Estotiland were taken as guides. The voyage proved unsuccessful; and there the matter appears to have ended.

These particulars are said to be derived from the letters of the Zeni to their friends in Venice. They were first published in 1558, by a descendant of the family who represented that, when a child, he had mutilated the manuscript, not knowing its value, but afterwards collected the fragments and disposed them in the best possible order. Some able writers and candid judges have considered the account as authentic and credible. It was rather difficult to find a locality for Friseland, which was described as larger than Ireland; but the name was decided to be a corruption of Ferrisland, or Faro Islands. Zichmni was supposed to be a Scottish chieftain named Sinclair, known as the Earl of the Orkneys. In construing the tale of the mariner, Estotiland is determined by Malte Brun, to be Newfoundland, Drogeo the country intermediate between that and Florida; while Mexico is considered as the civilized region spoken of as lying far to the southwest.[1]

To this list of sources from whence the ante-Columbian population of America may have been derived, should be added the supposition that the fleet of Kublai Khan, first emperor of the Moguls, which, being sent to conquer Japan, disappeared in a storm, about A. D. 1294, may have been driven to this continent. It has been remarked that the two empires of Mexico and Peru, about that time, sprang up in the midst of savage and rude nations; a circumstance which has been thought to favor the supposition that the founders of those empires came to their respective localities by sea, and may have belonged to the missing ships.[2]

---

[1] For a favorable view of the narrative of the Zeni, see an article in the North American Review, for July, 1838, written by Hon. George Folsom.

[2] Foster's Hist. of Voyages and Discoveries in the North, p. 43. n.

It remains to mention, with great brevity, the manner in which the various hints from history have been used in accounting for the population of the new world.

Many writers upon this subject, particularly those of ancient date, refer to numerous authors, whose works, however famous in their time, are now seldom perused, and whose names, to most persons, will convey no definite idea of the value of their opinions. Among those who were supposed to be able to throw light upon the subject, out of the abundance of their learning, were celebrated hebraists, biblical critics, and professors of history, the expression of whose views is often quite incidental, and founded upon facts or analogies which happened to strike them while pursuing investigations but indirectly connected with it. Annalists, geographers, and chronologists, who made a special study of cosmogony, are more legitimate authorities; and authors who wrote concerning any portions of this country from personal observation, or as compilers of the narratives of others, are entitled to a due consideration of their impressions in regard to the probable sources of its population.

It would be too wide a departure from the object of this cursory review to attempt a scrutiny of the circumstances under which opinions were formed, or the grounds on which they were based, beyond such allusions as in the course of a rapid summary have been, or may be, casually introduced.

The theory of an indigenous origin of men and animals in America, goes behind all others, of course, whether relating to a part only, or to the whole of the continent. This view has not been uncommon among writers of a certain school. Cornelius de Pauw, one of the philosophic coterie of Frederic the great, argued that life in the New World was not only distinct in its origin but of inferior quality, the men having less vigor of mind and body, and animals less of spirit and strength than their congeners elsewhere.[1]

Count Carli, an Italian of distinguished scientific attainments, undertook a refutation of the opinions of de Pauw, and at the same time endeavored to establish his own in favor of the former existence of the island or continent of Atlantis, five or six thousand years before our era; which he supported by a learned analysis of mythological and historical traditions, geological phenomena, and astronomical calculations.[2]

The hypothesis of submerged land in the Atlantic Ocean is, in fact, that which is most generally resorted to by those who suppose the western continents to have been peopled anterior to the flood of the Scriptures.

Peter Martyr d'Anghiera, whose history of the discovery of the New World was compiled from the manuscripts of Columbus, held that the inhabitants of Yucatan were descended from Ethiopians. Oviedo, under whose administration as Director of the mines of St. Domingo, the natives melted away beneath the severity of their taskwork, in his History of the Indies affirms, that the Antilles are the Hesperides of the ancients. Andrew Thevet, a Frenchman of great learning, but accused of

---

[1] Recherches Philosophiques sur les Américaines, &c.

[2] A French translation of Carli's American Letters, with notes and additions by Lefebre de Villebrune, was published in Boston and Paris simultaneously, in 1788.

credulity, who came to Brazil in 1555, charged with the establishment of a religious colony, believed in the transatlantic migration of the Israelites. Gomara and de Lery, with similar opportunities of observation, as already stated, made the Americans to descend from the Canaanites.

William Postel, an ingenious ethnological writer and oriental scholar, sometimes called a visionary,[1] maintained that all North America was peopled from Mauritania. He is the first who made a distinction between North and South America, supposing them to have nothing in common in their origin. The Peruvians and Chilians, he traced to the Gauls; in which conjecture he is sustained by Jaques Charron author of a history of the Gauls. Paolo Giovio, an Italian historian of great repute, imagined that the Mexicans derived from the Gauls their practice of human sacrifices. Edward Brerewood, an English antiquary of the sixteenth century, deduced the whole population of the New World from the Tartars. Martin Hamkema (Latinized Hamconius), and Suffrid Petri, two historians of Dutch Friseland, agreed in deriving the occupants of Peru and Chili from the Frisians. Acosta and Garcia, Jesuit Missionaries long in Spanish America, thought the country was peopled by degrees, and from various sources. The former, deeming it not improbable that vessels might, from time to time, have been cast upon these shores, inclined to credit the story from Aristotle, of a Carthaginian ship driven far to the westward, which discovered lands till then unknown, that might have been America. He was at a loss to determine how animals were transported. Athanasius Kircher, a German mathematician and antiquary, who wrote several works concerning Egypt, traced the Americans to the Egyptians, and thought the Atlantis extended from the Canaries to the Azores. Arius Montanus, a Spaniard very learned in Jewish antiquities, Francis Vatable, and Gilbert Genebrard, both eminent professors of Hebrew, at Paris, Anthony Possivin, a learned Jesuit of Mantua, and Martin Becan, a German professor of theology and philosophy, concurred in the belief that the Ophir of Solomon was in America.

Among the most prominent of those who, at an early period, wrote expressly upon the question of the origin of the American nations, are the learned Grotius, the Flemish geographer John De Laet, and the Leyden Professor Horn. Grotius supposed that the Isthmus of Panama was an impenetrable barrier between the two divisions of the continent. With the exception of Yucatan and its neighborhood, he makes the whole of North America to have been peopled by the Norwegians, by way of Iceland, Greenland, Estotiland, &c., who were followed, some ages after, by Danes, Swedes, and other German nations. He believes, with Peter Martyr, that some Ethiopians, who were Christians, may have been cast on the shores of Yucatan. He would derive the Indians of South America, near the Straits of Magellan, from the Moluccas and Java. The Peruvians, he doubts not, are a Chinese Colony. The Tartars, or Scythians, he excludes entirely.

Upon the dissertation of Grotius, De Laet published a sharp criticism, and a warm controversy arose between them. Having disposed of most of the theories of Grotius,

---

[1] "Célèbre visionaire, et l'un des plus savants hommes de son siècle."—*Biog. Universelle.*

successfully, as Charlevoix thinks, whose convenient summary of their views is here abbreviated, and having also reviewed the positions of other writers, De Laet expresses his own, viz: that the ancient inhabitants of the Canaries, whose deserted edifices were seen, according to Pliny, by the first Europeans who discovered those islands, had passed over to America, and that, with equal probability, passages might have been effected from the Cape Verdes to Brazil. Great Britain, Ireland, and the Orcades, are also admitted as probable sources of emigration, and the story of Madoc is received with favor. He thinks colonies might have come from the Scythians, and that South America was peopled from New Guinea. He concludes with an examination of the opinion of Emanuel de Moraes, that the whole country was peopled by the Carthaginians and Israelites.

Prof. Horn, who had the advantage of coming after most of the authors already referred to, discusses the subject in a Latin treatise of two hundred and eighty-two pages, 12mo, printed in 1652. Having reference to previous opinions, he excludes from the New World, as original colonists, Ethiopians, Norwegians, Danes, Swedes, Celts, Samoides and Laplanders, Greeks and Latins, Hebrews, Christians and Mahometans. He supposes that the country began to be peopled from the north by the Scythians; that the Phœnicians and Carthaginians afterwards got footing by the Atlantic Ocean, and the Chinese by the Pacific; that other nations might from time to time have landed here; and, lastly, that some Jews and Christians may have arrived, but not till the land was already peopled. He considers it probable that the Atlantis of Plato was part of America, and was submerged in the deluge of which traditions remained among the Mexicans.

The relation of Diodorus Siculus, respecting the large island visited by the Phœnicians, he regards as indicating their second emigration to America; their third and last being in the service of Solomon to Ophir, which is Hayti. The later emigrations he would make out to be of three sorts of Scythians, viz: the Huns, the Tartars of Cathay, and the Chinese. The following are some of his fanciful derivations. The Apalaches of Florida from the Apaleans of Solinus; the Tombas of Peru from the Tabians of Ptolemy; the northern Hurons from the Huyrons, neighbors of the Moguls; the Iroquois from the Yrcas, or Turks.

These references might be very much extended; but the foregoing are perhaps sufficient to indicate the principal varieties of opinion, and the more prominent among early authors by whom they have been entertained. Other writers appear to have added little to their facts or their arguments, although many changes have been rung upon these in their application.

The sources of derivation that appear to have been regarded as possessing the strongest claims to consideration, are the Hebrews (by whom the lost tribes are most commonly signified); the Phœnicians under various names, as Carthaginians, Tyrians, Canaanites, &c.; the Scythians, and the Scandinavians. Analogies in arts and customs have led to the supposition of Greek, Roman, Etruscan, Chinese, Hindoo, and other colonies in America; but the four sources above mentioned seem to have found the most numerous advocates.

Some of the later supporters of the Hebrew origin of the Indian tribes have already been mentioned. The Phœnician emigrations are presented under a new aspect in the work of Dr. Cabrera, published in 1822;[1] and the somewhat peculiar production of George Jones, printed in 1843,[2] not only maintains the advent of the Tyrians, but also the arrival of St. Thomas and the introduction of Christianity, a notion to which certain supposed Christian symbols in Central America gave rise at a very early period.[3]

In the work of Rivero and Von Tschudi, on Peruvian antiquities, recently translated by Rev. Dr. Hawks, the Scandinavian tale of Whitemen (Irish), established in the Carolinas, and perhaps in Florida, who had *horses*, is admitted as a *certainty*, while credit is also given to various ancient speculations; and the translator states that the hypothesis of a Phœnician origin for that body of settlers who peopled Guatemala, has, within the last two or three years, been invested with fresh interest by the new discoveries of the Abbé de Bourbourg, whose work was said to be in the press at Paris.

With regard to the maritime skill and enterprise of very early periods, it may be remarked that the tendency at present is to ascribe to those periods a wider knowledge of the form and surface of the earth, and of the arts of navigation, than has sometimes been deemed warrantable; and this tendency is the result of enlarged information upon cosmical questions.

Humboldt not only yields a belief to the circumnavigation of Africa at a very remote era, but expresses the opinion, founded upon careful investigations, that the Canary Islands were known to the Phœnicians, Carthaginians, Greeks, and Romans, and, perhaps, even to the Etruscans.[4] This admission, of course, implies a

---

[1] Translation of Del Rio's Description of an Ancient City near Palenque; to which is added a Critical Investigation and Research into the History of the Americans, by Dr. Paul Felix Cabrera, Lond. 1822.

[2] An Original History of Ancient America, founded upon the Ruins of Antiquity, the Identity of the Aborigines with the People of Tyre and Israel, and the Introduction of Christianity by the Apostle St. Thomas, by George Jones, R. S. I: M. F. S. V., &c., London and New York, 1843.

[3] Clavigero's Mexico, pp. 13 and 14, Cullen's translation.

Madame Calderon de la Barca inserts the following account of these emblems of Christianity in her "Life in Mexico," 1843:—

"It is strange, yet well authenticated, that the symbol of the cross was well known to the Indians before the arrival of Cortez. In the Island of Cozumel, near Yucatan, there were several, and in Yucatan itself there was a stone cross. And there an Indian, considered a prophet among his countrymen, had declared that a nation, bearing the same as a symbol, should arrive from a distant country! More extraordinary still was a temple, dedicated to the *holy cross* by the Toltec nation, in the city of Cholulu. Near Tulansingo, there is also a cross engraved on a rock with various characters, which the Indians, by tradition, ascribe to the Apostle St. Thomas. In Oajaca, also, there existed a cross, which the Indians, from time immemorial, had been accustomed to consider as a divine symbol. By order of the Bishop Cervantes, it was placed in a sumptuous chapel in the cathedral. Information concerning its discovery, together with a small cup cut out of its wood, was sent to Rome by Paul V., who received it on his knees, singing the hymn 'Vexilla Regis,' &c."

[4] Cosmos, N. Y. ed., II. 135, n.

considerable degree of maritime skill on the part of those nations, and the probability of more extended voyages by chance or design.

It is difficult to say anything on a subject like this without saying either too much or too little. It seemed desirable to present a view of the influences under which the investigation of ancient remains in the United States began, and which have continued to affect its progress; but, unless restrained within the limits of a special and well-defined purpose, the theme would expand beyond the compass of a preliminary chapter, and demand a volume for its proper consideration. Too little is, on the whole, better than too much for the object intended. Few persons have undertaken to treat of American antiquities without being seduced into speculations upon their origin founded upon analogies which appeared to them evidences of connection with some nation or race of the eastern continent; yet nothing is more deceptive than are such superficial resemblances. Proof of this may be seen in the fact that all the learned discussions that have taken place, and all the ingenious theories of this nature that have been suggested, have left the questions in their original perplexity; at least have made no advances towards their solution that are satisfactory to the public mind. In most cases, analogies of customs, of arts, and of terms in language, if they prove anything, prove more than can possibly be admitted, as researches into that field of inquiry abundantly show. If trusted implicitly, there is hardly a people on the globe that may not be supposed to have left traces of occupancy or communication in some section of our continent. Whether an examination of the physical characteristics of the native tribes, and the grammatical structure of their dialects, to which scientific men have turned with the hope of detecting reliable tokens of national lineage, has been productive of more certain conclusions, succeeding inquiries may disclose.[1]

---

[1] Morton, in "Crania Americana;" Morton's "Inquiry into the Distinctive Characteristics of the Aboriginal Race of America;" "The Physical Type of the American Indians," in Schoolcraft's large work; the "Mithridates" of Adelung, Vater, &c.; Vater's "Untersuchungen über America's Bevölkerung;" Duponceau and Heckewelder, in "Trans. of the Historical and Literary Committee of the Am. Phil. Society;" Duponceau, in "Mémoire sur les Langues de L'Amérique du Nord;" Gallatin, in "Trans. of the Am. Antiquarian Society," and "Trans. of the Am. Ethnological Society;" "Types of Mankind," by Messrs. Nott and Gliddon; &c. &c.

CHAPTER II.

PROGRESS OF INVESTIGATION IN THE UNITED STATES.

In passing from general opinions and speculations to such as relate to that portion of the continent which alone is now the subject of consideration, the attention is first directed to a class of authorities from which we might reasonably expect to derive much valuable information. To this class belong the narratives of those early adventurers who saw its inhabitants in their natural condition, occupying their original seats, and in the exercise of their hereditary customs and habits. The Atlantic shores of the United States do not, indeed, present such remains of ancient art as would be likely to attract the observation of those who first visited them; but, in the records of the Spanish expeditions to Florida and Louisiana, we should look for some descriptive recognition of the extensive earthworks that are found in those regions. More especially should we anticipate that the French priests, Franciscans, and Jesuits, who, very early in the 17th century, penetrated to the upper lakes, and thence worked their way through the Valley of the Mississippi to the Gulf of Mexico, would have seen the mounds and inclosures there so frequent, and have been impressed by their numbers and magnitude.

The followers of Narvaes and Soto passed through the sections of country that contain the largest and most imposing of the southern earthworks. The French emigrants that succeeded to the Spaniards, accompanied by missionaries who rendered to ecclesiastical authorities at home periodical accounts of their operations, were in the midst of those structures. At the north, the same class of learned and devoted men were historians of the progress of discovery. In the narrătives of the Franciscan Friars, and in the reports of the Jesuits to their Superiors, we have elaborate notices of the natural history of the country, the manners, customs, and dialects of the natives, and their faculties and dispositions.[1] At a later period,

---

[1] These Reports, commonly termed *Relations*, "Relations de ce qui c'est passé, &c.," are not only very valuable, as sources of important and peculiar information, but they are, unfortunately, very rare. They are printed in small volumes, 12mo or 8vo, in number about forty, extending, with some intervals, from 1611 to 1671, and perhaps later. It is said that a complete series is not to be found even in the Royal Library at Paris. Dr. O'Callaghan prepared an account of them, which was printed with the Proceedings of the New York Historical Society for November, 1847, and contains a table showing what volumes are in this country, and where they may be found. This account was printed in French in 1850, with notes, corrections, and additions, by the Superior of St. Mary's College, Montreal. Mr. James Lenox, of New York, has recently caused to be reprinted fac-simile copies of the letters of Father Le Mercier, written in 1655, and those of Jerome Lallemant, written in 1659, and has added to them the Relation for the years 1676 and 1677, which had not before been published.

similar returns, published under the title of "Lettres edifiantes et curieuses," contain much of the same kind of information. But, from all the explorations of these educated men, apparently observing as well as learned, very little is to be derived illustrative of the antiquities of the country, or even referring to their existence. It is remarkable how completely monuments, now viewed with surprise, were unobserved or disregarded by French and Spanish adventurers and travellers. Not only the pictorial mounds of Wisconsin, whose slight elevation and large dimensions might in uncleared lands conceal their forms, but the massive and regular parapets and lofty tumuli of the middle and southern portions of the west, seem to have been unheeded, at least as antiquities, or not esteemed worthy of special examination.

La Hontan, in one of his letters, dated May 16, 1689, gives a drawing and description of a medal that he professes to have found among the savages west of the Mississippi, and which he calls a modern antique (*antique moderne*). It is represented as of copper, with figures of animals on one side, and characters on the other. But the whole story of his expedition in that quarter is held to be apocryphal.

It may be that minds preoccupied with the grandeur of Mexican structures would be likely to consider the inferior elevation and extent of earthworks north of the gulf as rendering these undeserving of notice; and, in Florida and Louisiana, they may have been so far used, and even formed, by existing tribes, as to create no impression of an ancient or other than contemporaneous origin.

In the letters of Charlevoix and Father le Petit, and in the "History of Louisiana," by Du Pratz, we have very minute accounts of the Natchez Indians, who, with the Arkansas, were the most civilized of the North American aborigines. We learn that they worshipped the sun, had temples in which was kept the "eternal fire," and a despotic government; that their chiefs were the high priests, and were called suns, or children of the sun; and that the temples and the dwellings of the chiefs were raised upon mounds, and for every new chief a new mound and dwelling were constructed.[1] Thus, a civil and religious system, with customs and ceremonials pertaining to it, is described, which explains the use of some of the artificial elevations, and may indicate the purpose of others. But parapets and tumuli, and other structures of earth, are found in that region, which seem to imply the existence of more cultivated or more populous nations, and a larger scale of ceremonial observances, than these writers have represented. A mere diminution of numbers, and consequently of power, without any material difference of customs or capacities, may perhaps be sufficient to explain the diminution of grandeur in the ceremonies and structures of the later inhabitants. The decay of energy and enterprise, rather than of arts—the result, probably, of a decrease of population—which, in other parts of the country, led to a discontinuance of the construction of works consecrated to religious rites, or intended for permanent defence—may have been less advanced in its influence at the south. Hence the contrast between the monuments of the past and the productions of the living inhabitants would be less striking. Still, the absence of archæological discoveries and speculations, on the part of the intelligent

---

[1] See also Garcilazo de la Vega's Account of Soto's Expedition, I, 218.

and well-informed men who first visited the interior parts of the present United States, is somewhat singular, in view of the fact that so much has since been brought to light in the very paths on which they trod.[1]

We therefore advance to the period when investigations may be said to have commenced; and it is proposed to refer, in chronological order, to the observations and opinions of which the antiquities of the United States have been the subject, since they were noticed as such, and regarded as objects, not of curiosity merely, but of mystery and wonder.

It is not to be expected that every allusion which may have been made by travellers or others to the existence of such remains will be included in these references; but it is hoped to embrace those which are of most importance, and which represent the nature and degree of knowledge possessed at the time.

In the years 1748, 1749, and 1750, Peter Kalm, Professor of Economy in the University of Abo, in Swedish Finland, made a tour of scientific observation in this country, and was careful to record everything that seemed to him worthy of attention.[2] After speaking of the entire absence of ruins or evidences of ancient habitations that give interest to travels in other countries, he says: "There have, however, been found a few marks of antiquity, from which it may be inferred that North America was formerly inhabited by a nation more versed in science and more civilized than that which the Europeans found here on their arrival; or that a great military expedition was undertaken to this continent from those known parts of the world." He then states that, some years before he came into Canada, the Governor-General sent M. de Verandrier, with a number of people, across North America to the South sea. From Montreal they went as due west as the lakes, rivers, and mountains would permit. In a far country, beyond many nations, they met with large tracts free from wood, many of which were everywhere covered with furrows, as if they had formerly been ploughed and sown. "When," says Kalm, "they came far to the west, where, to the best of their knowledge, no Frenchman or European had ever been, they found in one place in the woods, and again on a large plain, great pillars of stone leaning upon each other. The pillars consisted of one single stone each, and the Frenchmen could not suppose that they had been erected by human hands. * * * * At last they met with a large stone, or pillar, in which a smaller stone was fixed that was covered on both sides with unknown characters. This stone, which was about a French foot in length, and

---

[1] Brackenridge, in his "Views of Louisiana," remarks, in relation to the remains of supposed fortifications there: "The French writers, who most probably observed them, do not speak of them; a proof that they had no doubt as to their origin, nor thought of attributing them to any other than the natives of the country." p. 183.

[2] The expenses of Professor Kalm's scientific tour were defrayed in part by contributions from the universities of Sweden, and in part by the king. One of the points to which his curiosity was directed he states to be, "whether any other nation possessed America before the present Indian inhabitants came into it; or whether any other nations visited this part of the globe before Columbus discovered it." The question of discoveries and settlements in the United States by the *Northmen* had not then been agitated.

between four and five inches broad, they carried to Canada, from whence it was sent to France, to the Secretary of State, Count de Maurepas. Several Jesuits, who have seen and handled this stone, unanimously affirm that the letters on it are the same with those which, in the books containing accounts of Tartaria, are called Tartarian characters." The places where the pillars were found were estimated to be near nine hundred French miles westward of Montreal. We believe that such monolithic pillars as are here described have not attracted the attention of later explorers; but the "garden-beds" (as they are now called) exist in Michigan and Wisconsin, and are regarded with wonder at the present day, as differing altogether in form and arrangement from the usual remains of Indian agriculture. The mention of them imparts an air of authenticity to Verandrier's narrative.

Prof. Kalm draws his own inference from the account, and believes that the pillars and the Tartarian inscription indicate the presence of the followers of Kublai Khan.[1]

In another part of his work he mentions having been informed, by an aged Swede in New Jersey, that when the Swedes settled on the Delaware, near where Salem is now situated, they found, at the depth of twenty feet, some wells inclosed with walls of brick. Since that period the river had so far encroached upon the land, by washing away its banks, that the wells were then covered with water, which was seldom low enough to admit of their being seen. From these and other evidences of the use of bricks discovered in that neighborhood, he infers the existence of an ante-Columbian settlement at that place.

In November, 1766, Jonathan Carver was at Lake Pepin on the Mississippi; and in the journal of his travels mentions the embankments he saw in that neighborhood, which appeared to him of a military character, and sufficient to cover five thousand men. This is usually considered the earliest mention of western earthworks as indicating a higher degree of art than existing races of aborigines were supposed to possess. James Adair, whose History of the American Indians was published in 1775, began his acquaintance with Indian life as early as 1735, and most of his book was written among the Chickasaws, with whom he first treated in 1744. He says that, from the most exact observations he could make, in the long time that he traded among the Indians, he was forced to believe them lineally descended from the Israelites; and the main object of his book seems to be to demonstrate that proposition. His references to vestiges of antiquity are few and rather indefinite. He speaks of traces of the ancient warlike disposition of the people as being found, "through the whole continent and in the remotest woods," that, "great mounds of earth, either of a circular or oblong form, having a strong breastwork at a distance around them, are frequently met with," but does not give the details of configuration or measurement.

The celebrated botanists, John and William Bartram, father and son, may be regarded as the first by whom a careful and intelligent observation of these structures has been recorded. They were in Florida together in 1765; and in

[1] "Travels into North America," III, 123, et seq.

January, 1766, discovered the remarkable works at Mt. Royal near Lake George. Eight years later William visited the same scene, and found it much changed by the whites who had begun to occupy and cultivate the land. He describes Mt. Royal as a magnificent Indian mound, from which a noble Indian highway fifty yards wide, sunk a little below the common level, and with a slight embankment on each side, led in a straight line three-quarters of a mile to an artificial lake.

William Bartram commenced his journey in the spring of 1773, and passed through the Carolinas, Georgia, East and West Florida, and as far west as the Mississippi river. He gives an account of "many very magnificent monuments of the power and industry of the ancient inhabitants" visible near Wrightsborough, Columbia Co. Georgia, "the work of a powerful nation whose period of grandeur perhaps long preceded the discovery of this continent."

A fortification on the Altemaha, opposite the town of Darien, he mentions as supposed to be of Spanish origin; and he takes note of mounds, terraces, embankments, &c., at the junction of the Ocmulgee and the Oconee rivers; at Charlotia on the river St. Johns; at the junction of the Broad and Savannah rivers in Georgia; at fort Prince George, Pickens Co., South Carolina; and at Taensa and Apalachicola. At the close of his narrative he remarks: "To conclude this subject concerning the monuments of the Americans, I deem it necessary to observe as my opinion, that none of them that I have seen discover the least signs of the arts, sciences, or architecture of the Europeans, or other inhabitants of the old world; yet they evidently betray every sign and mark of the most distant antiquity."[1]

It is singular that Captain Bernard Romans, who in 1771–2 travelled through the same regions, and, in 1776, published "A Concise Natural History of East and West Florida," should have paid no attention to the remains of ancient labor that he must have seen. He mentions, in one instance, a large *tumulus* as the only remarkable thing in a certain place, but it did not seem to excite his curiosity. His decided views respecting the aborigines may have influenced his mind in this regard; as he expresses his belief that "from one end of America to the other, the red people are the same nation, and draw their origin from a different source than either Europeans, Chinese, negroes, Moors, or any other different species of the human genus." Again he says: "I am firmly of opinion that God created an original man and woman in this part of the globe, of a different species from any in the other parts," p. 38. He speaks of having noticed some stones deeply marked with lines straight and crossed, which "do not ill resemble inscriptions;" but conjectures that they are made by the savages in grinding their awls, p. 327.

In 1772–3, the Rev. David Jones, of Freehold, N. J., spent some time among the Indians west of the Ohio, and in his journal notices the "Old Fortifications" near Chilicothe and on the Scioto.

---

[1] In a MS. work on the Creek Indians, left by Bartram, that came into the possession of Dr. Morton, he describes "public squares," alluded to by Adair, which were used by the Indians for religious ceremonies and deliberative councils, and states that ancient inclosures and other remains, concerning the origin of which they professed no knowledge, were also sometimes appropriated to such purposes.—Smithsonian Contributions, II, page 135 of Mr. Squier's Memoir.

A plan and description of the earthworks at Circleville, Ohio, were communicated anonymously to the Royal American Magazine, printed in Boston, and were inserted in the number for January, 1775. The plan was taken on horseback, by computation only, Oct. 17, 1772.

During the struggle of our revolution, the minds of all classes of people were absorbed in the exciting political and military events of the time, and little inclination or opportunity existed for archæological investigations. Near the conclusion of the war, Mr. Jefferson gratified his taste for such pursuits, by preparing his "Notes on Virginia," which were written in 1781–2, though not fully published till 1787.[1] His opinions there expressed in regard to the great antiquity of the American races are well known. He was uncertain whether to believe that the Americans were derived from the northern Asiatics, or the Asiatics from the Americans, but saw positive indications of a common origin. Our community was less prepared than now for the reception of views opposed to the usual interpretation of scripture history, and when Mr. Jefferson was a candidate for the presidency, his supposed sceptical sentiments upon this question were strongly urged against him. Of the great earthworks at the west and south he appears to have known little or nothing. He says: "I know of no such thing as an Indian monument." "Of labor on a large scale I think there is no remain so respectable as would be a common ditch for the draining of land." He refers to the barrows found all over the country as possible exceptions, but had in his mind only the small burial mounds of modern date, such as he had seen in Virginia. William Bartram's work had not then been published. Mr. Jefferson's speculations manifest the philosophical acuteness of his mind; and his remarks on a study of the aboriginal languages, as affording the best evidences of derivation, and as most likely to lead to a true solution of the question, indicate the ability and relish with which he would have examined the subject, if the duties of a statesman had left him leisure to devote to it.

No sooner were our citizens relieved from the cares and restrictions of war, than they began to explore and occupy the western country. From Fort Pitt, as a centre of operations, military and surveying parties were sent in different directions to prepare the way for emigration, and to secure the protection of the frontiers. Pioneer settlements had already been made in Kentucky; of which an account was printed by John Filson in 1784, containing a brief notice of two "ancient fortifications," with ditches and bastions, near Lexington.

The design of making an organized settlement northwest of the Ohio, appears to have been first publicly suggested by the soldiers of the revolution in June 1783. A grant had been solicited from the British government as early as 1772, on behalf of the provincial officers and soldiers who had served in the war against France; and on receiving a favorable reply, Israel Putnam and Rufus Putnam, the first afterwards the celebrated general of the revolution, the other, also, subsequently, a

---

[1] Jefferson distributed to his friends in Paris, copies of his "Notes," bearing the date of 1782, but supposed to be printed in 1784. A more complete edition was printed in 1787.—*Rich. Bibliotheca Americana.*

general officer, but better known as the pioneer of settlements in Ohio, went with one or two more to the southwest, and spent some months in exploring and locating townships on the Big Black river near its junction with the Mississippi, about latitude 33° north. Several hundred families are said to have left Massachusetts and Connecticut to make the settlement; but the grant was revoked by the king, many of the emigrants sickened and died, and war breaking out soon after, the enterprise was abandoned.[1] It would be a matter of curious speculation to determine what might have been the results if a New England colony had then been planted so far to the southwest. We may at least suppose that one of the Putnams would have been lost to the army of the revolution, and the other have given priority in prominence to the antiquities of the Yazoo country, instead of to those of the Muskingum.

It was not till April 7, 1788, that the company organized by General Rufus Putnam, after the Revolution, arrived at the mouth of the Muskingum to take possession of lands they had purchased of the United States Government. That day is commemorated by the Historical Society of Ohio, as introducing the first organized white settlement in the region northwest of the Ohio river.

The remarkable earthworks of Marietta are doubtless the first that were carefully surveyed, and of which drawings were presented to the consideration of scientific men. Dr. Mannasseh Cutler, and General Rufus Putnam, are usually cited as original observers of the remains among which the new village was located. The precedence of discovery and description is, however, due to other persons, as a comparison of dates will show.[2] During the years 1785 and 1786, letters from officers in the army to their friends at home, containing allusions to Indian antiquities, were published in the newspapers of the day. The accounts were often highly exaggerated, and gave rise to burlesque descriptions of wonderful adventures and discoveries that affected the credit of well-founded narratives. General Samuel H. Parsons, an officer of standing and character, from Connecticut, gave to these observations an authentic character, in a communication addressed to President Willard, of Harvard College. In his letter, dated Oct. 2, 1786, the mound at Grave creek is described, and the works at Marietta are referred to, and mention is made of a plan of the latter, which the writer had previously sent to President Stiles, of New Haven. This communication was afterwards published in the Memoirs of the American Academy of Arts and Sciences, Vol. II, 1793, but without the plan. There is good reason to believe that the plan forwarded by General Parsons to President Stiles is the same that may be found in the Columbian Magazine of May, 1787. This was drawn by Captain, afterwards Major Heart, and is accompanied by an elaborate description. In the winter of 1786, President Stiles had written to Dr. Franklin, requesting his opinion of the fortifications at Muskingum, &c., described by General Parsons and others. It may

---

[1] MS. Autobiography of Gen. Rufus Putnam.

[2] Dr. Cutler, who with Winthrop Sargent had negotiated the purchase of the land for the Ohio company, did not arrive at Marietta till August, 1788.—*Historical Disc. of Rev. Thomas Wickes,* at Marietta, Dec. 6, 1846.

be presumed that the drawing was sent at the same time, as it would be required, of course, to enable Franklin to form a judgment of the nature and object of the structures. Franklin might naturally transfer it to the editors of the magazine in Philadelphia for publication, as a matter of general interest and curiosity. It does not appear as a communication *from* Captain Heart, and is inserted without note or comment. General Parsons, who was but two days at Marietta,[1] on his way down the river, speaks of having left at that place, a request with an officer of learning and great curiosity in his observations of the natural world, to inform him of his discoveries, from whom it would appear that much of his information had been derived. Captain Heart was stationed at Fort Harmar, on the opposite bank of the Muskingum, and subsequent papers written by him manifest the qualities attributed to the officer alluded to.

We may justly conclude that the plan in the Columbian Magazine, is the one referred to by General Parsons, and that, next to the sketch of the works at Circleville in 1772, before mentioned, it is the earliest diagram made of western antiquities. Captain Heart was not only one of the earliest observers in this field of investigation, but manifested a zeal, intelligence, and comprehensiveness of research, that promised the most satisfactory results. A few years later (Jan. 1791), in reply to inquiries of Dr. Benjamin Smith Barton, he wrote a paper, embodying much valuable information, that was read before the American Philosophical Society, and is included in the third volume of the transactions of that body. In this communication, he refers to a large number and variety of earthworks observed by himself and others in the western country, at the mouth of the Muskingum, at Grave creek, at Paint creek, and along the Scioto, on the Kentucky side of the Ohio opposite the mouth of the Scioto (the last said to have been accurately traced by Col. George Morgan), and on the Great and Little Miami. He mentions that others have been described to him as situated on the Big Black river (the intended site of the colony from New England before the Revolution), at Bio Pierre on the Mississippi, and on the head waters of the Yazoo and Mobile rivers. This was an extensive range for that period, and includes remains whose discovery has been ascribed to later explorers. Contrary to the general tendency of the time, the writer indulges in no visionary speculations, but simply gives his opinion that the earthworks were not constructed by De Soto, because he did not visit the regions where they are principally found, and had no time for such labors anywhere; that the state of the works and the trees growing on them indicated an origin prior to the discovery of America by Columbus; that they were not due to the present Indians or their predecessors, or some tradition would have remained of their uses; that they were not constructed by a people who procured the necessaries of life by hunting, as a sufficient number to carry on such labors could not have subsisted in that way; and, lastly, that the people who constructed them were not altogether in an uncivilized state, as they must have been under the subordination of law, with a strict and well-governed police, or they could

[1] Then called "Muskingum," from the river at whose mouth it is situated.

not have been kept together in such numerous bodies, and been made to contribute to the execution of such stupendous works.

It is evident that, with the aid of persons so competent and so well disposed to pursue such investigations as Captain Heart and General Parsons, a rational development of the nature, extent, and probable origin of our aboriginal antiquities, need not have been postponed for thirty years, which actually elapsed from this period before any detailed and connected view of them was given to the public. Unhappily both met with a premature and violent end. General Parsons was drowned in the Ohio, in December, 1789; and Heart, then a major, was slain at the disastrous defeat of St. Clair, in November, 1791, when the flower of the western army were involved in the same destruction.

In reply to the inquiry of President Stiles, Franklin would undertake to give no explanation of the works described, but suggested that they might possibly have been constructed by Ferdinand De Soto as a defence against the savages. Upon this hint, Noah Webster addressed a series of letters to Dr. Stiles, in which he attempted to trace the route of the Spanish adventurer, and to show that the embankments at Marietta might have been erected by his followers. These were written in 1787, and first published in the "American Magazine," of which Mr. Webster was editor, and reprinted two years later in the "American Museum."

Col. Winthrop Sargent, who afterwards occupied high official positions at the West, was among the earliest to collect information on matters of antiquarian and scientific interest there. In March, 1787, he wrote to Governor Bowdoin, President of the American Academy of Arts and Sciences, inclosing a plan and description of the remains at Marietta, discovered (he says) by the garrison at Fort Harmar the year previous. For some reason this communication was not published at the time; but, having been brought to the notice of the Academy by Dr. Bowditch, the librarian, so recently as 1850, was first printed in 1853.[1] The sketch is a more

[1] Memoirs of Am. Acad., Vol. V, Part I. Dr. Bowditch remarks that the plan bears a date four years earlier than any documents mentioned by Messrs. Squier and Davis. He also refers to the plan alluded to in the letter of Gen. Parsons to President Willard, of which he says he has no knowledge; and, supposing the latter to be lost, would be right in considering that of Col. Sargent as the earliest now extant. In Part IV. of Mr. Schoolcraft's history of the condition and prospects of the Indian tribes, under the head of "Epoch of the Discovery of the Western Tumuli," it is said, "Accounts of these antiquities at Marietta were first published by Dr. Manasseh Cutler and the Rev. Thaddeus M. Harris, with diagrams of the antique works drawn by Gen. Rufus Putnam, made immediately after the settlement of the town." This statement is evidently taken from Mr. Atwater's treatise in the first volume of the Transactions of the American Antiquarian Society. The facts are, that Dr. Cutler's very brief account is in a note to his charge at the ordination of Rev. Joseph Story, at Marietta, August 15, 1798, which was printed the same year; while Dr. Harris's "Tour" was not published till 1805. The error has so often been repeated that a specific correction is desirable.

In this connection it may be well to refer to another misapprehension in the same volume of the work of Mr. Schoolcraft, viz: that "assertions of a Celtic element in the Indian languages first originated in America in 1782, in certain accounts given by Isaac Stuart, of South Carolina, an early Western trader." The letter of Morgan Jones, "Chaplain to the Plantations of South Carolina," dated New York, March 10, 1685-6, and published in March, 1740, in the "Gentleman's Magazine," London, X, 104, is probably the most remarkable "assertion" that has appeared. The letter affirms that, being taken prisoner by the Tuscaroras in 1660, the writer found himself able to converse with them in the British (Welsh) language, and actually preached to them several months in the same tongue.

elaborate one, and more highly finished than that of Captain Heart, from which it differs in a few slight particulars, being evidently drawn from a subsequent survey.

A few years later, Col. Sargent forwarded to Rev. Dr. Belknap, the historian, and also to the American Philosophical Society, a paper, with drawings of ornaments and implements taken from the mounds at Cincinnati; which formed the text of an elaborate treatise on the subject of western antiquities, read before the Philosophical Society by Dr. Benjamin Smith Barton.[1]

In 1787, Dr. Barton, then a student of medicine at Edinburgh, commenced the publication of a work entitled "Observations on Some Parts of Natural History." The first part, which alone was printed, relates to antiquities, and contains an account of the discoveries at Muskingum, and remarks on the first peopling of the country. This was noticed the same year in the London "Critical Review," where the writer, differing from what he supposes to be the opinion of the author, viz: that America derived its inhabitants from the north of Europe, is disposed to regard the *south* of Europe as the source of their origin. Dr. Barton intended merely to assume, as an hypothesis, that the Danes were the ancestors of the race that built the mounds and fortifications, while the country at large had probably been peopled from a thousand sources.[2]

In 1788, Rev. Samuel Kirkland, missionary to the Senecas, of New York, observed the remains of embankments and inclosures in Monroe and Genesee Counties, in that State.

Notices of earthworks are not infrequent, about this period, in the journals of travellers, and persons connected with the army at the West. The third volume of the Collections of the Massachusetts Historical Society contains an extract from the MS. journal of a gentleman connected with the forces under the command of Gen. St. Clair, in which the vestiges of ancient "fortifications" are spoken of as "ever presenting themselves to the view." The writer says he has been told that they owe their origin to the Welsh; referring evidently to the statement of Isaac Stuart, of what he professed to have learned from certain Indians respecting their origin from a foreign country, supposed, from their knowledge of the Welsh language, to be Wales; which statement was printed in some of the newspapers, in October, 1785.[3]

---

[1] See "Massachusetts Magazine," July, 1795, and "Transactions of Am. Phil. Society," IV, 1799. Dr. Barton's paper was in the form of a letter to Rev. Joseph Priestley.

[2] Letter to Dr. Priestley, Trans. of Am. Phil. Society, IV.

[3] The circumstances that may be adduced to prove the former existence of a Celtic colony in the southern regions of the United States are certainly curious, and exhibit some remarkable coincidences.

The Scandinavian tales of an "Irish Christian people," somewhere south of the Chesapeake, relate to a period nearly two centuries prior to the alleged expedition of Madoc, but deserve to be noticed in this connection. The same localities, near the Gulf of Mexico, have been assigned to them that are designated as the original abode of the followers of the Welsh chieftain. Then we have the story of the Rev. Morgan Jones, that the Tuscaroras understood his preaching "in the British tongue," about A. D. 1660; and the less definite accounts of "one Stedman," and "one Oliver Humphreys," respecting natives, somewhere near Florida, who spoke Welsh. To these are to be added the statement of Mr. Charles Beatty, a missionary, who visited the interior in the year 1766. Benjamin Sutton, a captive, informed him that he had been with the Choctaws to an Indian town, a very considerable

In the American Museum for May, 1792, and also in the Massachusetts Magazine for August, 1792, is an article that purports to be "an extract from the MS. of a late traveller," which is of interest as showing how far west and north the antiquities of the interior had already been observed. The writer refers to the "ruins," in the Illinois and Wabash countries, and adds, that there are others no less remarkable many hundred miles further west, and particularly about the great falls of the Mississippi. He speaks of pyramids from thirty to seventy or eighty feet high, some of which were examined, and a stratum of white substance like lime generally found in them; and of circular fortifications inclosed with deep ditches and fenced with a breastwork.

The attention of literary and scientific men in the eastern States was now fairly roused, by the well authenticated descriptions of remarkable antiquities which had been transmitted from the West. The presidents of the colleges at New Haven and Cambridge, and the members of learned societies in Boston and Philadelphia, were called upon to express an opinion respecting their purpose and origin.

The celebrated discourse delivered by President Stiles, before the general Assembly of Connecticut, in 1783, upon the past, the present, and the future of the United States, gave him distinguished prominence as a curious student of American history, as well archæological as civil and political. In that discourse he assumed as "certain conclusions," 1st, that all the American Indians are one kind of people; 2d, that they are the same as the people of the northeast of Asia. With regard to their origin, he considered them as "Canaanites of the expulsion of Joshua," some

---

distance from New Orleans, whose inhabitants were of different complexions, not so tawny as the other Indians, and who spoke Welsh, and that they had a book among them wrapped in skins, but could not read it; that he heard some of these afterwards in the lower Shawanaugh town speak Welsh with one Lewis, a Welshman, a captive; and that this Welsh tribe now live on the west side of the Mississippi, a great way above New Orleans. Levi Hicks, another captive, told Beatty that he had been in a town of Indians, on the west side of the Mississippi, who talked Welsh, as he was told, for he did not understand them. The account given by Captain Isaac Stuart, said to be taken from his own mouth in 1782, and inserted in the Public Advertiser, Oct. 8, 1785, is in substance as follows: That eighteen years before, he was taken prisoner about fifty miles west of Fort Pitt, and carried by the Indians to the Wabash. After two years of bondage, he, and a fellow captive named John Davy (or David), were redeemed by a Spaniard, and accompanying him they crossed the Mississippi, near Red river, up which they travelled seven hundred miles, when they came to a nation of Indians remarkably white, and whose hair was mostly of a reddish color. The day after their arrival, the Welshman (David) declared his intention of remaining with that people, as he understood their language. Stuart's curiosity being excited by that information, he questioned the chiefs with the aid of his companion, and learned from them that their forefathers came from a foreign country and landed on the east side of the Mississippi, the chiefs describing particularly the country of Florida; and that, on the Spaniards taking possession of Mexico, they fled to their then abode. As a proof of their story they exhibited rolls of parchment carefully tied up in otter's skins, on which were large characters written with blue ink, which the Welshman, being ignorant of letters, was unable to read.

If these statements are compared with Mr. Catlin's account of the Mandans, they will be found to correspond remarkably with his convictions respecting the physical differences between them and other tribes, their probable descent from the followers of Madoc, and the course of their migrations. He would doubtless have employed them to strengthen his argument had he been aware of their existence. Antiquitates Americanæ, p. XXXVII. Williams's "Inquiry," &c., Am. Museum for April and May 1792. Catlin's North American Indians, 6th Lond. Ed. I, 206, II, Appendix A.

of whom, in Phœnician ships, coasted the Mediterranean to its mouth; as appears from the inscription they left there in the ancient Phœnician letter, viz: "*We are they who fled from the face of Joshua the robber, the son of Nun.*" From thence he supposes they crossed the Atlantic, driven by the trade-winds, and commenced the settlement of Mexico and Peru. Another branch of the same people, he inferred, might travel northeastward, become the Tartars of that part of Asia, and finally, passing over to America, constitute the sachemdoms of the northern regions of this continent.[1]

This appears to be an independent opinion of President Stiles, as he does not refer to those early writers (Gomara, De Lery, Lescarbot, &c.) who derived the population of certain portions of this country from the Canaanites, though upon different grounds; but he strengthens his view with the judgment of M. Gebelin, of the Paris Academy of Sciences, who had pronounced the characters on the Dighton rock to be Punic (as M. Jomard has since decided those on the Grave creek stone to be Lybian), and interpreted them as denoting that the ancient Carthaginians once visited these distant regions.

Aboriginal monuments are rare in New England; but her scholars did not fail to observe and investigate such as were found. A copy of the inscription on the Dighton rock was made by Rev. Mr. Danforth, as early as 1680. In 1712, Cotton Mather sent a very rude and incorrect drawing of the same to the Royal Society. The Professor of Hebrew in Harvard College, Stephen Sewall, made, in 1768, the first copy that bears any near resemblance to those of recent date; and another was taken, with special care, by Professor James Winthrop, in 1788. The last two delineations are those which reminded Washington of what he had seen in his youth, while carrying the surveyor's chain through western forests.[2]

President Stiles was active in the examination of American inscriptions. He visited an inscribed rock at a place in Connecticut called by the Indians Scaticook, took full sized drawings of some of the characters, and wrote an account of it in 1789. He also collected accounts of sculptures that had been noticed in other parts of the country, viz: on the south shore of Lake Erie, observed by the missionary Kirkland; on the Alleghany river, below Venango, visited in 1789 by Mr. Frothingham; and others in Brattleboro' Vt., on the Alatamaha in Georgia, and on Cumberland river in Kentucky. In 1790, he prepared an account of a stone bust, supposed to have been an Indian god, which had been found the year before,

---

[1] The story of the inscription is derived from Procopius, the Greek historian, a native of Palestine, who says that he saw and read it at Tangier, on two marble pillars, in the *ancient* Phœnician character.

[2] An account of the Dighton rock, and the various conjectures and speculations to which it has given rise, would fill a volume by itself. Since 1680, copies have continued to be taken by different methods, each aiming to be more accurate than others. These are often widely diverse from one another, and no two of them are precisely alike. The construction given to the inscription by the Scandinavian antiquaries is well known. It is not as well known, perhaps, that the now commonly received opinion, that it is the work of the native Indians, was expressed by Gen. Washington, at Cambridge, in 1789. He remarked to Dr. Lathrop, who visited the college with him, that he had repeatedly noticed similar inscriptions in the Indian country, in early life, which were unquestionably executed by the natives.—*Memoirs of Am. Acad. of Arts and Sciences*, III, 205.

at East Hartford, Conn., and deposited in the museum of Yale College. Other remains of aboriginal art and labor, little conspicuous as they were, also attracted attention.

Rev. Gideon Hawley, who about A. D. 1754, was among the Indians of western Massachusetts and eastern New York, as a missionary, on one occasion saw his Indian guide near Schoharie, looking for a stone, which, when found, he carefully added to an ancient pile. Being pressed for a reason the Indian was reluctant to speak on the subject, but stated that his father had done so before and enjoined the same duty on him. Mr. Hawley remarks that he observed such heaps of stones in every part of the country; the largest being on the mountain between Stockbridge and Great Barrington, in Massachusetts. He says, moreover, "we have a sacrifice rock, as it is termed, between Plymouth and Sandwich, to which stones and sticks are cast by Indians who pass it. This custom, or rite, is an acknowledgment of an invisible God whom this people worship. This heap is his altar. The stone that is collected is the oblation of the traveller."[1]

A similar heap, or mound of stones, was described by Noah Webster, in 1789, as situated about seven miles from Hartford, on the road to Farmington, Conn., where, according to the tradition of the inhabitants, an Indian was buried, and every one of his race on passing by was accustomed to add a stone to the pile.[2]

In 1795, Rev. Jacob Bailey communicated to Jeremy Belknap, the historian, then Corresponding Secretary of the Massachusetts Historical Society, an article entitled, "Observations and conjectures on the antiquities of America." In this, as proving the existence of works which exceed the contrivance and ability of the existing generation of Indians, he describes a mound upon an extensive plain, near the mouth of the Kennebec river, in Maine, which he states to be six hundred feet in circumference, and perhaps fifty feet high, and composed of stones intermingled with earth and sand—the summit being a flat surface, nearly twenty feet in diameter, and exhibiting a kind of pavement of large smooth stones. Thus it had appeared twenty-five years before; and its artificial character was supposed to be indicated by the fact that the surrounding lands, for some distance, were entirely destitute of stones—excepting on the beaches of the river, where they resembled those forming the mound.[3]

Rev. Jonathan Edwards, of New Haven, afterwards President of Union College, at Schenectady, a son of the celebrated metaphysician, communicated to the Connecticut Society of Arts and Sciences, in 1788, his important "Observations on the language of the Muhhekaneew (Mohegan) Indians." This treatise was reprinted in 1823, in the collections of the Massachusetts Historical Society, with great additions by Mr. Pickering, and may fairly be considered as the foundation of the significant philological discovery of a radical connection among Indian languages, notwithstanding a wide local separation, and great diversities of dialect. The author had remarkable qualifications for detecting and developing the most delicate grammatical peculiarities; having begun to learn the language of the Mohegans at six

---

[1] Mass. Hist. Coll., 1st se. IV. 59.

[2] Am. Museum, VI. 234.

[3] Mass. Hist. Coll., 1st se. IV. 104.

years of age, and having lived with them till it became "more familiar than his mother tongue."

Dr. Barton's "New Views of the Origin of the Tribes and Nations of America," printed at Philadelphia in 1797, and much enlarged the following year, is wholly devoted to the subject of language, and the comparison of vocabularies. A reference to philological studies, so intimately associated with inquiries into the origin and affinities of population, is deferred to a later period of our narrative, when these may appropriately form a distinct topic of consideration; hence, no notice has been taken of the efforts of travellers and writers to procure comparative tables of words and phrases. The principal and most trustworthy compilers of vocabularies were the missionaries, who could not communicate theological doctrines to the untutored savage without a more careful study of the shades of meaning in words than ordinary intercourse would require. Much is due to the Jesuit and Franciscan priests; more to Mayhew, Eliot, Roger Williams, and their associates. Some useful additions were also contributed by traders, and other casual residents among the natives. Enough had been collected when Dr. Barton wrote to furnish attractive materials for study to philologists, not only in this country, but in Europe.[1]

From what has been said it will be seen that, before the close of the last century, men of science in the United States had become warmly interested in the vestiges of ancient art which had been discovered; and, supposing the amount of knowledge of the subject possessed by learned men in 1787, to be indicated by Jefferson's opinion that there existed "no remain as respectable as would be a common ditch for the draining of lands," a few succeeding years had certainly witnessed rapid advances of information, derived from nearly every portion of our national territory, and relating to extraordinary and mysterious monuments of antiquity. It is undoubtedly true that, before 1800, the existence of tumuli and inclosures in great numbers, and of imposing magnitude, throughout the valley of the Mississippi, at least on its eastern side, and from the Gulf of Mexico to the Lakes, was well known to the public; and, moreover, that many of the principal localities had been pointed out, some of the works had been described with great particularity, and collections had been made of the curious contents of the mounds. The inclosed works were generally regarded as *fortifications*, and were supposed to demonstrate the former possession of the country by a people skilled in the means of military defence.

In 1803, two well educated gentlemen, of observing habits of mind, were examining these structures at no great distance from one another, but on opposite sides of the Ohio River, and came to very different conclusions respecting their original purpose. One of them, Bishop Madison, of Virginia, became satisfied that the parapets and inclosures were never intended for military uses; and gave his reasons at length in a letter to Dr. Barton, which was read before the Philosophical

---

[1] Among the foreign correspondents of Dr. Barton, was Sir Joseph Banks, President of the Royal Society. In 1795, Sir Joseph sent over some specimens of earthenware found near Lake Huron, in "the ruins of an ancient town," by Dr. Nooth, of Quebec.—*Massachusetts Magazine of Oct.* 1795.

In 1796, the celebrated French philosopher, Volney, travelled through many of the Western States, and collected a vocabulary of the language of the Miamis. He saw mounds at Cincinnati, and in Kentucky; and, from the account of the works at Muskingum, did not think they exhibited evidence of military art.—*Volney's* "View," &c., *translated by C. B. Brown, Phil.*, 1804.

Society, and published a few years later in one of its volumes. The other, Rev. Thaddeus Mason Harris, of Massachusetts, was disposed to agree with the prevailing opinion, that they must have been places of defence.

It appeared to Bishop Madison that such remains were too numerous, too various in form and dimensions, and often too unfavorably situated to be regarded as fortresses; while certain striking features, in which they all agreed, indicated one common origin and destination. The lowness of the walls, the fact that the ditch was generally within, the whole being usually commanded by natural or artificial elevations without, were circumstances that, in his judgment, pointed to some very different design. The mounds he considered as burial-places, raised by the gradual accumulation of deposits. He does not allude to the conjecture which had been ventured by some, that the supposed forts were *sacred inclosures,* and the elevated squares areas of temples, or *places of sacrifice.*

Mr. Harris, on the other hand, adopting from Clavigero his account of the emigration of the Toltecs from the North, ascribed to them the construction of the "fenced cities," whose walls of earth he imagined to have been surmounted by palisades, and to have been intended for protection in the gradual progress of that people through the territories of less civilized tribes.[1]

These gentlemen are often cited as pioneers in this field of investigation. They are among the first who, uniting opportunities of personal observation to the advantages of scientific culture, imparted to the public their impressions of western antiquities. They represent the two classes of observers whose opposite views still divide the sentiment of the country; one class seeing no evidences of art beyond what might be expected of existing tribes, with the simple difference of a more numerous population, and consequently better defined and more permanent habitations; the other finding proofs of skill and refinement, to be explained, as they believe, only on the supposition that a superior native race, or more probably a people of foreign and higher civilization, once occupied the soil.

The official expedition of Capts. Lewis and Clark to the sources of the Missouri, in the years 1804, 1805, and 1806; and that of Lieut. Pike to the sources of the Mississippi, and through the western parts of Louisiana in the years 1805, 1806, and 1807, were productive of very little increase to the stock of archæological information; although Allen's narrative of the former contains a drawing of earthworks observed on the Missouri, near Bon Homme Island.

Robin, a French naturalist, who was in Louisiana in 1805, described the remarkable tumuli near the junction of the Washita and Tœnsa rivers.[2] The account of these in the memoir of Messrs. Squier and Davis, is derived from Major Stoddard's "Sketches of Louisiana," published in 1812. In his brief chapter on the remains of antiquity at the West, that author expresses the opinion that "Till we are better informed, it seems fair to attribute them to the Welsh."[3]

---

[1] "Journal of a Tour in the Territory Northwest of the Alleghany Mountains in 1803, &c."

Rev. Dr. Harris was subsequently an active and distinguished officer of the American Antiquarian Society, and contributed to that institution many valuable relics, and some MS. notes of observations.

[2] "Voyage dans Louisiane, &c., par C. C. Robin, Paris, 1807."

[3] Stoddard's Sketches, p. 347.

The Portfolio, in 1810, furnished an excellent plan of one of the most unquestionable works of defence to be found in the country, and also the most elaborate and extensive, situated on the east bank of the Little Miami, in Warren County, Ohio. In 1814, the same periodical contained other accounts and drawings of remains found in different localities, and in that year Mr. Brackenridge published his "Views of Louisiana," with a sensible chapter, and some notes, devoted to the subject of antiquities.

In 1812, an organization was first adopted for promoting the study of antiquities, and collecting and preserving the materials of our national history. The need of such a measure had become apparent; objects of archæological interest were known to exist in great numbers; but in the crude and defective state of information respecting them, no inferences worthy the name of scientific deductions could be derived from the features they presented. Not only accurate delineations and trustworthy descriptions, but aggregation and classification, were wanting to a development of their real nature and probable origin. Generations of forests, it was asserted, had flourished and decayed over curious relics and surprising works of art. Gigantic bones had been disinterred from the morasses of the West. Vestiges of human forms of unnatural dimensions, were supposed to have been discovered. The valley of the Mississippi was like a wonder-book, full of marvels and mysteries, and productive of vague and dreamy lucubrations. While men of education were reviving one or another of the many theories of colonization from the old world, at some dim and distant period, faintly indicated by history or tradition, another class convinced themselves that giants and pigmies had, in turn or together, inhabited that region.

Among those who were impressed with the importance of subjecting these questions to scientific scrutiny, and seasonably securing facts of every kind, necessary to the completeness of American history, in its relation both to the past and the future, was Isaiah Thomas, an eminent printer and publisher, of Worcester, Massachusetts. He did not confine himself to personal influence and exertions, but, as a literary nucleus to the proposed institution, offered the gift of his private collection of rare and curious books, valued at not less than five thousand dollars. The design found favor with many gentlemen of literary and political prominence; and, in October, 1812, the American Antiquarian Society was established, with an act of incorporation from the Legislature of Massachusetts. It was supposed that the United States Government had not constitutional power to grant charters to public societies without the District of Columbia. For some reasons of convenience, to which pecuniary inducements were afterwards added, the institution was located at Worcester, the residence of Mr. Thomas, who had been chosen its President.

The war with Great Britain, and the Indian hostilities which had been excited throughout the West, rendered the period an unfavorable one for active researches. Immediate measures were, nevertheless, adopted to awaken public attention, and prepare the way for future success. Meetings were held at which addresses were delivered that were afterwards printed and circulated. Members were selected from all parts of the Union, and the correspondence of persons who had manifested an interest in historical and antiquarian studies, was earnestly solicited. Valuable communications were from time to time received, some of which are inserted in the first volume of the Society's Transactions.

When peace was restored, and the interior of the country tranquillized, a lively spirit of inquiry sprang up in the midst of the antiquities to be investigated. Men of intelligence at Lexington, Ky., at Cincinnati, and in other parts of Ohio, resorted to accurate measurements of works in their neighborhood, and to excavations for the purpose of ascertaining the contents of the mounds. Among the most enterprising of these was Caleb Atwater, of Circleville, Ohio, a village deriving its name from a remarkable aboriginal structure that occupied its site, and which it destroyed.

At the request of the President of the Antiquarian Society, and assisted by him with pecuniary means, Mr. Atwater undertook to prepare a comprehensive account of the antiquities of the Western States, with plans of the principal earthworks, and drawings of the most characteristic relics. This was published by the Society in 1820, and occupies the greater part of the first volume of "ARCHÆOLOGIA AMERICANA."

Thus, a connected and authentic representation of these objects of interest and curiosity was at length accomplished; and in a manner that, under the circumstances, must be regarded as highly creditable, both to the author, and the institution under whose auspices it was effected. Considering the difficulties that were to be surmounted in tracing lines often buried in forests, and otherwise obscured by time, before repeated observations had assisted the judgment, the surveys are more accurate than could reasonably be anticipated. When we take into view the fact that almost every writer on the subject, thus far, had been engaged in determining by what foreign people the mounds and fortifications might have been reared, rather than in seeking in the works themselves to find their true significance and history, the treatise of Mr. Atwater is entitled to the praise of being more than ordinarily practical, and free from visionary tendencies; while its claims to the general merit of faithful and comprehensive research have not been impaired by later investigations.

It is not surprising that Mr. Atwater should indulge to some extent in the seductive practice of premature speculation, instead of confining himself to a simple exhibition of facts; but he did not arrange or employ the latter for the support of any peculiar theory or private opinion. If the literary merits of his narrative are not of a high order, he escaped the dangers of an ambitious and imaginative style of description. He was greatly assisted by other gentlemen at the West, whose attention had been directed to particular localities. From many he received drawings and useful information acknowledged in his work. Great credit is due to Dr. Daniel Drake, for the sensible account of the antiquities of the Miami country, contained in his "Picture of Cincinnati," published in 1815.

The "Western Gazetteer," compiled by Samuel R. Brown, in 1817, embraced in its statistics the known antiquities of the States to which it refers; and in the same year, De Witt Clinton read before the Literary and Philosophical Society of New York, his memoir on the antiquities of that State, having previously touched upon the subject of aboriginal remains in a discourse before the Historical Society, in 1811.

By these publications, and others of a more limited and incidental nature, near the same period, the preparation of Mr. Atwater's summary was doubtless facilitated.

The first volume of the Archæologia Americana contains, besides the principal memoir, communications from various correspondents of the Society, relating to the same subject, and bearing different dates, from 1815, to 1820.

Among these is a series of characteristic papers by the learned Dr. Samuel L. Mitchell; who, as chairman of the Committee on Indian affairs in the United States Senate for several years, had been accustomed to a good deal of intercourse with the aborigines.

The work, as a whole, may probably be regarded as an exponent of the opinions of investigators at that period, as well as an embodiment of facts which had then been ascertained.

Mr. Atwater assumes that the *present* race of Indians was most numerous near the sea, and in the northern and eastern portions of the United States, as shown by the greater quantity of arrow-heads, and other implements of war and peace, found in those regions; that of the few *earthworks* discovered east of the Alleghanies, the most northerly is near Black River, south of Lake Ontario, in New York, and the most easterly at Oxford, on the Chenango river, in the same State; while west of the Alleghanies, and as far as the Rocky Mountains, tumuli are numerous; and in the eastern valley of the Mississippi, remains of a more remarkable character are met with, from the Lakes to the Gulf of Mexico, that gradually increase in size and frequency towards the south. Some of these structures he believes to have been fortifications; others sacred inclosures, with their mounds of sacrifice, or sites of temples; others places of diversion; and others mounds of burial.

The contents of the tumuli are described as articles of pottery, implements and ornaments of stone, similar to those of modern Indians; figures wrought in stone; carved pipe-bowls; articles of copper, such as tubes, bracelets, arrow-heads, pipes, &c., of rude workmanship; beads of bone or ivory; mirrors of mica; marine shells; and, in a few instances, ornaments *plated with silver*. Knives and swords of iron were also supposed to be indicated by their oxidized remains.

The skeletons from the mounds are represented as those of a people unlike our present Indians—the latter being tall, slender, and straight-limbed; the former short and thick, rarely over five feet in height; their faces short and broad, with rather high cheek bones; their foreheads low, their eyes very large, and their chins broad.

The relics were said to be found, in some instances, at the bases of excavated mounds, in connection with one or more skeletons lying upon hearths or altars of burnt clay; the whole having been subjected to the action of fire, implying a ceremonial of sepulture or sacrifice, followed by the heaping of earth upon the remains.

Plans are given of the most prominent works in Ohio; where are found nearly all the varieties of form and construction which had then been recognized, except such as belong to the States bordering on the Gulf of Mexico. Concerning the latter, Mr. Atwater's information was limited to general accounts of inexact observations; and he does not undertake to exhibit their figures or dimensions, although some relics from that section are engraved with those of other parts of the country.

The growth of generations of forests over these remains, and the changes in the levels and courses of streams on whose ancient banks they are situated, are applied as tests of their antiquity. The mathematical accuracy of squares and circles inclosing large areas, often many acres in extent, is adduced as evidence of scientific culture. The indications of improvement in art, and apparent increase of population, observable in following the courses of the streams towards the south, are received as proofs of migration from the north, protracted, perhaps, and with long intervals of interruption, but still ever progressive in one direction.

These data, and others of a similar character, were naturally made the basis of conjectures respecting the people to whom the vestiges of ancient residence and ultimate removal should be ascribed.

On this point there appears to have been a general coincidence of opinion among those who occupied the position of authorities at the time of Mr. Atwater's publication.

That the inhabitants of America were chiefly descended from two branches of the same Asiatic family, was a doctrine advocated by the learned Dr. Hugh Williamson in 1811 and 1812—the arts of civilization being, in his judgment, traceable to the Hindoos.[1] Dr. Mitchell, whose multifarious erudition sometimes impaired the definiteness and consistency of his reasoning, had taken the ground, in 1815, that "the original inhabitants of America consisted of the same races with the Malays of Australasia, and the Tartars of the North;" that the former landed in North America, and penetrated across the continent to the region lying between the Great Lakes and the Gulf of Mexico, where they constructed the fortifications, mounds, &c.; and that they were probably overcome by the more warlike and ferocious hordes that came from the northeast of Asia, and were the ancestors of the present race. In 1816, he claimed to establish these hypotheses "by a process of reasoning not hitherto advanced," and, at the close of his argument, declares: "I forbore to go further than to ascertain by the correspondences already stated, the identity of origin and derivation of the American and Asiatic nations, avoiding the opportunity that grand conclusion afforded me of stating that America was the cradle of the human race. I had no inclination to oppose the current opinions relative to the place of man's creation and dispersion, and thought it scarcely worth while to inform a European that on coming to America he had left the *new* world behind him, for the purpose of visiting the OLD." At a later period of the same year he gave another exposition of his views, repeating his assertion that the physiognomy, manufactures, and customs, of the North American tribes of the middle and low latitudes, and of the South Americans, show them to be nearly akin to the Malay race of Australasia and Polynesia. But a new element had entered his calculations, from a suggestion of De Witt Clinton, that some of the "old forts" in New York were of a *Danish* character. "In the twinkling of an eye," he says, "I was penetrated by the justness of his remark. An additional window of light was suddenly opened to me." He then proceeds to the supposition, that the Danes, or Finns, and the Welshmen (for he puts the followers of Madoc and the Scandinavians together) performed their migration gradually to the southwest, and fortified them-

[1] Some account of the aborigines of America, in his "Observations on the Climate," &c. Hist. of North Carolina, I, appendix B.

selves in the country south of Lake Ontario. There the Tartars or Samoiedes found them; and having first exterminated the Malays, who had advanced along the Ohio and its tributaries, had a harder task to subdue the warlike Europeans entrenched and fortified in the country. The Scandinavians, he thinks, were ultimately overpowered in New York, and finally retreated to Labrador.

The theory that the mound-builders came from India, or were of a common origin with the Hindoos, was greatly strengthened by the discovery in Kentucky of a piece of pottery, fashioned in the form of three human heads united at their backs with a vase, which they supported. It was commonly called the "Triune idol, or vessel." "Does it not represent the three chief gods of India—Brahma, Vishnoo, and Siva?" is the exclamation of Mr. Atwater. Moreover, no less than nine murex shells had been found in the same State, within twenty miles of Lexington. Shells so highly esteemed in India, and consecrated to the god Mahadeva, corresponding to the Neptune of the Greeks and Romans.

These articles had been collected by Mr. John D. Clifford, of Lexington, a rival, and sometimes antagonist of Mr. Atwater, in the field of archæological research; who, while the latter was preparing his notes for the press, was aiming, in a series of articles in the "Western Review," to demonstrate the proposition that the mound-builders were the ancestors of the Mexicans, and descended from the ancient Hindoos.

Mr. Clifford's argument, and his investigations, were both suddenly arrested by his death; yet they doubtless had an influence in strengthening the views of his contemporary.

Mr. Atwater's opinions are expressed in the following extracts:—

"The Scythians, from whom the Tartars are descended, in all probability first peopled the British Isles. The fact that our works are in all respects like those in Britain, and that similar works may be found all the way from this part of America to Tartary, furnishes no contemptible proof that the Tartars were the authors of ours also. But were the ancestors of our North American Indians the authors of our works? Had not such an opinion been advanced by some great and good men in the United States, the foundation on which it rests is so frail, that I certainly should not trouble myself or my readers to refute it."

"Have our present race of Indians ever buried their dead in mounds? Have they constructed such works as are described in the preceding pages? Were they acquainted with the use of silver, or iron, or copper? All these, curiously wrought, were found in one mound at Marietta. Did the ancestors of our Indians burn the bodies of distinguished chiefs on funeral piles, and then raise a lofty tumulus over the urn that contained their ashes? Did the North American Indians erect anything like the 'walled town' on Paint creek? Did they ever dig such wells as are found at Marietta, Portsmouth, and above all such as those on Paint creek? Did they manufacture vessels from calcareous breccia, equal to any now made in Italy? Did they ever make and worship an idol representing the three principal gods of India?"

"An idol found in a tumulus near Nashville, Tennessee, and now in the museum of Mr. Clifford, of Lexington, Kentucky, will probably assist us in forming some idea as to the origin of the authors of our western antiquities. Like the 'Triune vessel' hereafter mentioned, it was made of a clay peculiar for its fineness, which is quite abundant in some parts of Kentucky. This idol represents a man in a state of nudity, whose arms have been cut off close to the body, and whose nose and chin have been mutilated; with a fillet and cake upon his head. In all these respects, as well as in the peculiar manner of plaiting the hair, it is exactly such an idol as Professor Pallas found in his travels in the southern part of the Russian empire.

"The idol discovered near Nashville, shows from whence its worshippers derived their origin and religious rites. The 'Triune idol, or vessel,' shows, in my opinion, that its authors originated in Hindostan, and the one now under consideration induces a belief that some tribes were from countries adjacent.

"If the ancestors of our North American Indians were from the northern parts of Tartary, those who worshipped this idol came from a country lying further to the south, where the population was dense, and where the arts had made great progress. While the Tartar of the North was a hunter and a savage, the Hindoos and southern Tartars were well acquainted with most of the useful arts. The former (the Tartars of the north), lived in the vicinity of our continent, and probably found their way hither at an early day, while the latter came at a later period, bringing along with them the arts, the idols, and religious rites of Hindostan, China, and the Crimea. The ancestors of our North American Indians were mere hunters; while the authors of our tumuli were shepherds and husbandmen. The temples, altars, and sacred places of the Hindoos were always situated on the bank of some stream of water. The same observation applies to the temples, altars, and sacred places of those who erected our tumuli. At the consecrated streams of Hindostan devotees assembled from all parts of the empire, to worship their gods, and purify themselves by bathing in the sacred water. In this country, the sacred places were uniformly on the bank of some river; and who knows but that the Muskingum, the Scioto, the Miami, the Ohio, the Cumberland, and the Mississippi, were once deemed as sacred, and their banks as thickly settled, and as well cultivated, as are now the Indus, the Ganges, and the Burrampooter!

"Ablution, from the situation of all the works which appear to have been devoted to sacred uses, was a rite as religiously observed by the authors of our idols, as it was neglected by our North American Indians. If the coincidences between the worship of our people and that of the Hindoos and southern Tartars furnish no evidence of a common origin, then I am no judge of the nature and weight of testimony."

Mr. Atwater assigns a very early period for the migration of these people into the territory now included in Ohio, as indicated by the rude state of many of the arts among them, and the proofs of primitive times seen in their manners and customs. He thinks the numerous cemeteries are evidences of long residence; and that, while contending against foes from the northeast, they moved gradually down the streams towards the country where they finally settled.

As this work was the first in which a consideration of North American antiquities was based upon elaborate explorations, and as it was prepared at the instance, and published under the sanction of a scientific association, the conclusions it seemed to justify deserve to be carefully stated. They doubtless exerted an important influence upon subsequent speculations, but cannot be held answerable for the vagaries of enthusiastic and visionary writers. The points in whose favor the "Archæologia Americana" gives the weight of its opinion, are 1st. That the vestiges of antiquity in the United States are indicative of the former occupation of the country by a people having a regular government and laws, and possessing many of the customs, arts, and institutions of civilized communities. 2d. That they were not the ancestors of the modern tribes of Indians; but probably retired to Mexico and Peru, and founded the semi-civilized empires that were encountered and overcome by Cortes and Pizarro. 3d. That, with some exceptions of insufficient magnitude and permanency to affect the general characteristics of the people, the American races, ancient and modern, were derived from different portions of Asia. 4th. That the early inhabitants were very numerous, and occupied fixed abodes for long periods of time.

These are a sufficient foundation for the support of many visionary hypotheses, and were susceptible of indefinite enlargement and extension from the same materials, and such others as might from time to time be added to them.

It may be well to leave, for a moment, the chronological order of narration, for the purpose of introducing together the most remarkable instances of fanciful deduction, resulting from this stage of discovery, and the prevailing tendency of public sentiment.

In 1823, Mr. John Haywood published an 8vo. volume of 450 pages, entitled "The Natural and Aboriginal History of Tennessee, up to the first settlements therein by the White People." A small portion of the work only is devoted to the natural or physical history of the State. The aboriginal history commences with a comparison of the Mexicans and Peruvians with the Hindoos and Persians, the Natchez Indians with the Mexicans, and the ancient inhabitants of Tennessee with both the latter. Not only are all admitted discoveries of an archæological nature, pressed into the service of this examination, but many of doubtful authenticity, and circumstances irrelevant as well as unverified, are made to swell the mass of analogies which the writer has accumulated. With the aid of these he undertakes to compile a history of the ancient Tennesseeans, applicable also to other Western States, describing the ceremonies and superstitions of their religious faith, their civil polity, their sciences and arts, their games and pastimes, &c. &c., with a particularity that could hardly be surpassed in a history of a living and familiar people. We are told, among other things, that they burnt incense on their high places, to the sun, moon, and planets, and to the host of heaven; that they placed altars on their mounds, and sacrificed human beings; that in worshipping, they stood towards the east, and lifted up their hands towards heaven, and towards their idols; that they venerated the number three, and worshipped *triune idols;* that they deemed the cross a sacred symbol; that they used the conch-shell as emblematic of the properties of their god of the ocean; that they made wells, walled up with stone from the bottom; that they had swords of iron and steel, and steel bows, and mirrors with iron backs; knives of iron, with ferules of silver, and iron chisels and spades; that they buried their sacred animals; that they made bricks and burnt them, and used both them and stone in their buildings; that their complexion, hair, and eyes were like those of the Baroans of Chili;[1] that their stature was of the common size; but that of their exterminators—a new and modern race, like the Gauls in the time of Lucullus—was frightfully gigantic; that those same marauders, who, from the 7th to the 11th centuries of the Christian era converted the cultivated fields of Italy into a wilderness, came hither also, searching through all the corners of the world for plunder and subsistence; and that the new comers into America worshipped a spiritual God, without mounds, idols, or human sacrifices.

All these things, and much more, the author claims to be able to prove respecting the primitive inhabitants of the country watered by the Ohio and its branches; who came, as he believes, from the *South*, and had intimate connections with the people of Mexico, and some intercourse with the Peruvians and Chilians. Anticipating that the reader may regard his programme as somewhat conjectural, he declares that "it will soon be converted into real history."

The writer's facility of belief is not limited to the necessary support of his principal theory; but is extended to the accounts of pigmies, whose remains had been disinterred in large numbers, and to the discovery of Roman coins, that must have been buried before the age of Columbus, and to vestiges of the sanctity of the number seven.

Of a somewhat similar character, and not less remarkable, are the "Ancient Annals of Kentucky," by Prof. C. S. Rafinesque—prefixed to Marshall's History of that State, printed in 1824.

Beginning with the origin of the human race, the learned Professor accepts the tradition that mankind was created in Asia, and follows down the course of generations and migrations with surprising minuteness. Having reached the proper period, he informs us that "the principal nations of the eastern continent, which have contributed to people North America and Kentucky, were the Atlans and Cutans, who came easterly, through the Atlantic Ocean; and the Iztacans and Oghuzians, who came westerly, through the Pacific Ocean."

The history of those two nations, and of their settlements in America, he divides into five periods: "1st. From the dispersion of mankind to the first discovery of America, including several centuries. 2. From the discovery of America (by the Atlans, Cutans, &c.) to the foundation of the Western empires, including some centuries. 3d. From the foundation of those empires to the Pelagian revolution of nature, including several centuries. 4th. From the Pelagian revolution to the invasion of the Iztacan nations, including about twelve centuries. 5th. From the Iztacan invasion to the decline and fall of the Atlan and Cutan nations in North America, including about thirty centuries to the present time."

The details of incidents in these periods are so fully recorded as to leave little to be desired in the way of precise information. A chronological chart of events happening in North America from the beginning, presents the succession of peoples and empires, with a lavish profusion of names and pedigrees, and an air of intimate

---

[1] *i. e.* that is comparatively light, and of variable tints.

acquaintance with their civil and religious customs, and the motives and results of military operations, which seem to imply the possession of an insight the reverse of prophetic, but equally supernatural. He informs us that several other nations, besides the Atlans, Cutans, Iztacans, and Oghuzians, had reached various parts of America before the modern Europeans; such as the Mayans or Malays, the Scandinavians, the Chinese, the Ainus of Eastern Asia, the Nigritians or African negroes, &c.; but, as they did not settle in or near Kentucky, they did not fall under his present scope. He states that the country watered by the Ohio and its branches was the centre of the Atalan empire, which was divided into several provinces, and was ruled by a powerful monarch of the Atlas family; that an intercourse was kept up, more or less regularly, between all the primitive nations and empires, from the Ganges to the Mississippi; and that Chrishna or Hercules, and Ramachandra, two heroes of India, visited Atala and the court of the western monarchs, which is called one of the heavens on earth by the holy books of the East. But, he says, the Atlantes of the interior of America were separated from the rest of the Atlantic empire by that dreadful convulsion of nature which is recorded in the oldest annals of many nations. In this cataclysm, which is signified by the division of the earth under Peleg, the flood of Ogyges or Ogug, and the Sanscrit convulsion of the White sea, or Atlantic ocean, many countries were destroyed or changed; and the eastern Atlantes thought the whole American continent had sunk, like the Atlantic and many Antillan islands. After this event, the history is of necessity, for awhile, more exclusively American. But, he tells us, in the lapse of centuries, a casual intercourse was restored between the two continents. The Caribs, who appear to be of Cantabrian origin, came to South America. The great nation of Guarini, of Daran derivation, had arrived earlier, and extended itself over Guiana, Brazil, and Paraguay. When the Arcutans or Femurians of Ireland were expelled by a tribe of the Gaels, they fled to Hayti, and became probably the Arohuac nation. Before the Christian era the Phœnicians traded to America. The Numidians and the Celts frequented Hayti 2000 years ago; and the Etruscans attempted to settle colonies in this country, but were prevented by the Carthaginians. Owing to numerous shipwrecks, and the warlike habits of the Caribs, Iztacans, and Oghuzians, this intercourse gradually declined, till the knowledge of America became almost lost or clouded in fables and legends.

The annals of Kentucky, however, are by no means interrupted; but continue to flow through intricate revolutions, which the author is fortunately able to describe, briefly, to be sure, but with great exactness, until the history is broken in upon and obscured by the arrival of the present race of Caucasian interlopers.

So perfect a revelation necessarily removes all mystery from the origin and purpose of the ancient remains of the Mississippi valley.

Mr. Rafinesque was a man of very considerable scholastic and scientific attainments. He was connected with Transylvania University as professor of Historical and Natural Sciences, and subscribes himself a member of many learned societies in Europe and America. He had been actively engaged in researches among the antiquities of the West, and left, at his decease, a manuscript work on the subject, illustrated with drawings, which proved very serviceable to Messrs. Squier and

Davis in the preparation of their memoir. A list of seats of ancient population in North America, ascertained by him, is attached to his "Annals," of which he says, that out of 541, 393 are in Kentucky; and of 1830 monuments observed by him, 505 are in the same State. In 1836, he commenced at Philadelphia, the publication of "A General History, Ancient and Modern, of the Earth and Mankind in the Western Hemisphere; including the philosophy of American History, the Annals, Traditions, Civilization, Languages, &c., of all the American Nations, Tribes, Empires, and States." It was to be comprised in twelve volumes, of 300 pages each, and was dedicated to the Society of Geography of Paris, as a homage due to the public approbation given by that body to his first analogous labor, a series of researches on the origin of mankind.

Two volumes only, it is believed, were printed, which are far from being intelligible to a common capacity, or to ordinary erudition.[1]

With the productions of Haywood and Rafinesque, may be associated that of Josiah Priest, upon "American Antiquities and Discoveries in the West," published in 1833. We are informed, in the title page of the fifth edition of this book, that twenty-two thousand copies had been printed within thirty months, for subscribers only. It must therefore have had a wide circulation, and perhaps a corresponding degree of influence on the opinions of certain classes of readers. It is a collection of odds and ends of theories and statements, relating, more or less directly, to American antiquities, many of them derived from Rafinesque—a sort of curiosity-shop of archæological fragments, whose materials are gathered without the exercise of much discrimination, and disposed without much system or classification, and apparently without inquiry into their authenticity. It is not strange that references should sometimes be rather confused, and labels be occasionally misplaced. It must be in some such way that Prof. Horn, whose treatise "De Originibus Americanis" we have had occasion to mention, comes to be represented as "a son of Theodosius the Great, Emperor of the West, who lived in the third century!"[2]

To return from these eccentricities to the period of Mr. Atwater's publication,

---

[1] Mr. Rafinesque was a laborious student in almost every conceivable department of knowledge, and only wanted the faculty of judicious discrimination to secure him a distinguished name among men of science. He was of foreign birth, and had been a resident in Sicily, and first travelled in the United States in 1802, 1803, and 1804. Before 1815, he had published a very considerable number of treatises, chiefly upon natural history, from observations in this country and in Sicily, with others of a more general character. In 1815, he returned to America, and had the misfortune to be shipwrecked on the coast; losing, according to his own statement, all his "books, manuscripts, plates, drawings, maps, herbarium, collections, minerals, &c., the fruit of twenty years' labors, exertions, and travels." Some of his lost MSS. on botany, zoology, mineralogy, &c., he undertook to re-write, and endeavored to obtain subscriptions for their publication here. In 1838, he printed an essay introductory to a proposed work, to be entitled "Researches on the Antiquities and Monuments of North and South America." He died at Philadelphia, in 1840.

[2] Rafinesque, who did not relish the use made of his own theories, charged Priest with asserting that Noah's ark rested in America, and that he had three sons—one white, one red, and one black! This statement does not appear to be quite correct, unless Mr. Priest's expressions were modified in the later editions of his work.

we find the field of research gradually extending its limits, and the results of investigation discussed in various connections.

In 1819, Professor Silliman, of Yale College, established his "American Journal of Science," which, associated with geological and other scientific observations, contains many interesting notices of antiquarian discoveries. The first volume has an account of remarkable remains on the Etowee (or Hightower) river, in Georgia, by Rev. Elias Cornelius, afterwards a distinguished clergyman of Massachusetts; and another of mounds in East Tennessee, by Mr. John H. Kain, of Knoxville.

The same year, David Thomas printed his "Travels through the Western Country, in the Summer of 1816," with notices of antiquities, and a dissertation of more than twenty pages on the ancient inhabitants of the United States.

In 1820, Sir Gilbert Blane, Bart., communicated to the "London Quarterly Journal of Science and Arts," a letter addressed to Dr. Mitchell, on the antiquities of New York.

Nuttall's "Journal of a Tour in Arkansas," appeared in 1821; and in 1822, Jacob B. Moore, Esq., of New Hampshire, made known to the Antiquarian Society the very interesting and important fact of the former existence in that State of an extensive fortification in Sanbornton, near Lake Winnipisiogee. It was represented as a double inclosure, perfectly symmetrical in form, having mounds at the entrances, and a large one without the walls, in the manner so common at the West. The walls were of stone externally, filled in with clay, shells, and gravel; and, when first discovered, about eighty years before, were breast high, and six feet in thickness, and had evidently diminished considerably in height since their erection.[1] Unless certain traces of regular embankments on the Merrimack, near Concord, also mentioned by Mr. Moore, are to be excepted, this is believed to be the only instance, east of New York, of an inclosure like those so common beyond the Alleghanies.

During a few succeeding years, we are not aware that the archæology of the United States was advanced or elucidated by the development of new features, or the conception of new hypotheses deserving consideration. Mr. Atwater's Memoir was received with much favor, and read with great interest both at home and abroad. The celebrated Dr. Adam Clark wrote to Mr. Duponceau, expressing the delight and instruction with which he perused it. After referring to the mounds, forts, and gigantic rings or stone circles of Ireland, as not unlike those on the Ohio, and as little understood, but which, with certain customs and habits of the Irish, he supposes to be of Asiatic derivation, he declares himself particularly struck with what in the memoir is called the "Triune Vessel," as telling a more direct tale of Asiatic origin than anything else in the volume.[2]

In local histories, gazetteers, &c., the subject was sometimes discussed at considerable length, and with occasional additions to the list of remains. Thus, Beck's "Gazetteer of Illinois and Missouri," published in 1823, Yates and Moulton's

---

[1] Belknap, Hist. of New Hampshire, III, 89, speaks of "the appearance of a fortress at Sanbornton, consisting of *five distinct walls.*"

[2] The letter is in the 2d vol. of the Transactions of the American Antiquarian Society.

History of New York," in 1824; "Flint's Recollections of the Mississippi Valley" in 1826; and "Macauley's History of New York," in 1829, are often referred to. In the two histories of New York above named, the subject of American antiquities is treated of at considerable length. In the *American Journal of Science and Arts*, (Vol. III, p. 37) is an account of a fortification on the Arkansas River, 320 miles from its mouth, inclosing about twenty-five acres, with a wall eight feet high, and a ditch twenty-five feet wide; and having in the centre two mounds about eighty feet in height.[1]

Although the general sentiment was in favor of attributing the ancient monuments of the United States to a race or races entirely distinct from our Indian tribes, there were those who, with unusual means and opportunities of forming an enlightened judgment, adopted a different opinion, and upon grounds entirely aside from those philological and physiological considerations that will presently be adverted to.

A prominent argument opposed to the descent of the Indians from the mound-builders, had been the absence of traditions among the savages, pointing to such a connection, and their entire ignorance of the purposes for which the structures were designed. Yet it is not true that real or pretended traditions are entirely wanting. The Senecas related to the missionary Kirkland, that the fortifications in their territory were raised by their ancestors in their wars with the western Indians, three, four, or five hundred years before—they having no very definite idea of the time;[2] and Indian Legends have been more common than faith in the sincerity of the narrators.

The most particular and pertinent traditions referring to ancient fortifications, are those collected from the Delaware Indians (Lenni Lenape) by Rev. John Heckewelder, the Moravian missionary.[3]

According to these, the ancestors of the Delawares resided many hundred years ago far away in the western part of the American continent. For some reason, they determined on migrating to the eastward, and set out together in a body. After a long journey, they came to the Mississippi, where they fell in with the Mengwe or Iroquois, who had likewise emigrated from a distant country, and were also proceeding eastward until they should find a land that pleased them. The spies sent forward by the Delawares had already discovered that the region east of the Mississippi was inhabited by a powerful nation having many large towns built on the rivers flowing through their land. These people called themselves Tallegewi or Allegewi. They were remarkably tall and stout, and had regular fortifications or entrenchments.

The Delawares sent a message to the Allegewi, asking permission to settle in their neighborhood. This was refused, but leave was given them to pass through the country in search of a residence beyond. But when they began to cross the river the Allegewi, alarmed at their numbers, attacked them with great fury, and threatened them with destruction if they persisted in their attempt.

---

1 Letter from L. Bringier, Esq., to Rev. Elias Cornelius.

2 Mass. Hist. Coll., 1st se., IV., 106. See also Cusic's "Ancient Hist. of the Six Nations."

3 "Account of the History, Manners, and Customs of the Indian Nations who once inhabited Pennsylvania and the Neighboring States," in Trans. of Hist. and Lit. Committee of the Am. Phil. Soc'y, I., 1819.

Indignant at such treachery, the Delawares and the Mengwe united their forces and declared war against the Allegewi. The enemy fortified their large towns, and raised entrenchments on large rivers and near lakes, which were attacked and sometimes stormed by the allies. No quarter was given; and after the war had lasted many years, the Allegewi at last abandoned the country to the victors, and fled down the Mississippi river, from whence they never returned.

The Delawares charged the Mengwe with hanging back always and leaving them to face the enemy. But in the end they divided the conquered land between them, the Mengwe choosing the vicinity of the Great Lakes, and the Delawares taking possession of the country further south.

The tradition continues, giving an account of subsequent wars with the Mengwe, (better known as the Iroquois), and the ultimate confederacy of the Five Nations.

This is a simple story, viewed by itself, containing nothing marvellous or incredible. Yet the traditions recorded by Heckewelder, taken together, have not been regarded as entitled to confidence. He has been charged with credulity, and even suspected of a desire to embellish his narrative. It is also declared that no reliance can ever be placed on the legends of the Indians, as they are usually invented to amuse or mystify the inquirer.

Admitting this to be the case as a general rule, still the statements of the Moravians should be fairly considered in connection with the circumstances under which their information was obtained.

These "United Brethren," as they best liked to be called, who sought, in their system of organization, to combine the simple social habits and the apostolic office of the primitive Christians, came to Pennsylvania about the year 1740.

Their communities had been driven from Bohemia to Moravia, and were everywhere persecuted. Under the guidance of Count Zinzendorf, at once their protector and their leader, they found a partial security at home, just enough to enable them to become the nurseries of missionary enterprise abroad. Seeking opportunities to spread the gospel among the heathen wherever they might be found, their first mission in this country was with the Indians of Georgia. The hostilities of the English and Spanish claimants of jurisdiction, between whom they were not permitted to retain a position of neutrality, compelled them, after a few years' residence, to remove from that section of the United States.

Their efforts were then directed to the conversion and civilization of the Delawares, the Iroquois, and the Mohegans, among whom they labored with great perseverance for many years. Their influence over the natives even exceeded that of the Jesuits and Franciscans of an earlier period; and communities of converts grew up around the solitary posts of the preachers far in the wilderness. Constantly pressing towards the interior, in 1772 they had villages beyond the Ohio, where the savage assumed the habits and adopted the worship of civilized men. Living in the midst of their pupils, directing their agricultural labors, and working with them, the missionaries gained their affections while they studied their habits and mental peculiarities, and prepared dictionaries and grammars of their language. To Zeisberger, Pyrlæus, Schultz, and Heckewelder, philologists have been indebted for some of the most important materials used in their investigations.

However simple and credulous these men might be, they were not without intelligence and culture; and their sincerity was attested by their toils and sufferings. Their knowledge of Indian character and languages was of wide extent, and in Heckewelder's case of forty years' duration. If deceived by fictitious tales, it was not as inquisitive strangers that deception was practised upon them, but they were imposed upon by neighbors and familiar friends.

What Mayhew and Eliot had been to the aborigines of New England, the Moravians were to the Delawares and Iroquois; but with more protracted and more perfect intimacy. As the villages of Christian Indians in Massachusetts were broken up, one after another, as, in time of war, their occupants fell under suspicion, now of their own people, and now of the whites, and were massacred in turn by both; so the "Tents of Grace" of the Moravian converts were destroyed, and their "Beautiful Prospect" laid waste and made desolate. No enduring monument of the toils of those missionaries remains, except the vocabularies they collected, and the narratives they compiled; save that, in the names of some of their settlements which have been preserved, the memory of their pious endeavors may be transmitted.

Heckewelder's narrative, and even his linguistic accuracy, were, many years ago, subjected to severe criticism by one of our prominent statesmen, Hon. Lewis Cass.[1] Few men of education have had better opportunities than Governor Cass, of acquiring a knowledge of the characteristics, customs, and capacities of the Indians. He has lived among them, explored their distant abodes, and dealt with them in many different relations; and his opinion is entitled to great weight on all points connected with their history. It is proper, however, to remark that he belongs to that class of writers who are careful to divest the character of the aborigines, as well as their history and antiquities, of all romantic and poetical coloring.

In the article referred to, Governor Cass describes Heckewelder as a worthy missionary, of moderate intellect, and still more moderate attainments, of great credulity, and strong personal attachments to the Indians, who had passed almost his entire life among the Delawares, and derived his knowledge of the natives wholly from them. Even the correctness of his interpretations is questioned; and it is said of him: "Every legendary story of their former power, and of their subsequent fall, such as the old men repeat to the boys in the long winter evenings, was received by him in perfect good faith, and has been recorded with all the gravity of history. It appears never to have occurred to him that these traditionary stories, orally repeated from generation to generation, may have finally borne very little resemblance to the events they commemorate; nor that a Delaware could sacrifice the love of truth to the love of his tribe. To those who know something about Indian traditions, nothing can be more unsatisfactory than these details, unless they are corroborated by the accounts of the early travellers, or by concurrent circumstances." Governor Cass also speaks of having listened to Heckewelder in his own house, "as anxious to hear as he was to relate the marvellous events of his intercourse with

---

[1] North American Review, for January, 1826.

the Indians; and when both narrator and hearer believed all that was told, and frequently in an inverse proportion to its probability."[1]

If the fact is admitted, as intimated above, that the tales communicated to Heckewelder were "traditionary stories, orally repeated from generation to generation by the old men to the boys," they would seem to be entitled to all the faith that is ever due to merely traditionary evidence. But it has been generally denied that the Indians possessed any such system of transmission. Major Long, to whose observations Governor Cass refers, as according entirely with his own, says: "The knowledge they have of their ancestry is very limited; so much so that they can seldom trace back their pedigree more than a few generations; and then know so little of the place whence their fathers came, that they can only express their ideas upon the subject in general terms, stating that they came from beyond the lakes, from the rising or setting sun, from the north or south," &c.[2]

Governor Cass's experience of savage life, as viewed by him, if it might "point a moral" would hardly "adorn a tale." He says: "The effect of Mr. Heckewelder's work, upon the prevailing notions respecting Indian history, is every day more and more visible. It has furnished materials for the writers of periodical works and even of *history;* and in one of those beautiful delineations of American scenery, incidents, and manners, for which we are indebted to the taste and talent of our eminent novelist (Cooper), 'the last of the Mohegans' is an Indian of the school of Mr. Heckewelder, and not of the school of nature."

We may reply that, romance is seldom a positive attribute of circumstances or things, but rather a quality in the mind of the observer. The very time and people from whence the term was derived, the age of chivalry itself, and the characters and habits of knights and troubadours, would hardly bear the test of a literal and unpicturesque delineation.

With regard to the possession of hereditary information by the Indians, respecting the origin or migrations of their ancestors, it is probably true, that their legends are too indefinite, and often too contradictory, to serve any useful purpose in the solution of archæological questions. They seldom relate to very remote periods of

---

[1] Governor Cass's estimate of the capacity and information of Heckewelder does not accord with that of other persons who cannot be regarded as incompetent judges. The Historical and Literary Committee of the American Philosophical Society, in their Report of 9th January, 1818, say: "The intimate knowledge which this respectable missionary (Heckewelder), is known to possess of the languages and manners of various Indian nations, among whom he resided more than forty years, pointed him out to us as a person from whom much information could be obtained; nor were our hopes deceived. In answer to the inquiries of your committee, he laid open the stores of his knowledge, and his correspondence gives us a clear insight into that wonderful organization which distinguishes the languages of the aborigines of this country from all the other idioms of the known world. Mr. Pickering, in his preface to Eliot's Indian Grammar, describes him as "the venerable Mr. Heckewelder, whose fidelity, and intelligence, and skill (in the Delaware dialect in particular), are beyond all question." A reviewer of his Indian History in the "Portfolio" of September, 1819, calls him "a learned and inquiring man, doing good among this people, and possessing their confidence. His opportunities have been better than those of any person living to give the views which he has now presented to the public; and his character is a sure pledge for the fidelity of his work."

[2] Expedition from Pittsburg to the Rocky Mountains, II, 371.

time; and the events to which they refer are often found, on examination, to have occurred since the arrival of the whites.

Although rejecting the traditions of the Delawares, which ascribe the defensive structures of the west to the Allegewi, Governor Cass is by no means disposed to attribute them to a foreign race, now removed or extinct. His opinion is expressed in the following paragraph from the same article to which we have been referring.

"The ancient fortifications scattered through the United States, and attributed by Mr. Heckewelder to these Allegewi, have been the fruitful source of abundant speculation. We have no doubt that they were erected by the forefathers of the present Indians, as places of refuge against the incursions of their enemies, and of security for their women and children when they were compelled to leave them for the duties of the chase. And much of the mystery in which this subject has been involved owes its origin to a want of due consideration of the circumstances and condition of the Indians. We do not reflect on their almost infinite division into petty tribes, and on their hereditary and exterminating hostilities. Nor have we reflected that the stone tomahawk is a very inefficient instrument for cutting timber into palisades; nor that, if fire be adopted as a substitute, the process is tedious and laborious. Their transportation too, must have been a serious objection to their use, and in a few years they required renewal. Even when otherwise proper, they were always liable to be burned by the enemy. These circumstances render it probable that the erection of earthen parapets was the most economical and desirable mode in which the Indians could provide for the security of themselves and those most dear to them. And their migratory habits will sufficiently account for the number of these works, without resorting to the existence of a dense population utterly irreconcilable with the habits of a people who have not yet passed the hunter state of life."

This theory is at an opposite extreme from most of those which have thus far been considered. Neither the introduction of arts from other continents, nor the supposition of higher civilization here, nor even the probability of a denser population and more stationary habits of life, are deemed essential to explain the origin of those numerous and extensive structures. Their erection is held to be entirely consistent with the civil condition, the degree of mechanical skill, the manners and the wants of the savage, as these have been known to us since the settlement of the country.

A reaction of sentiment respecting the antiquities of the United States naturally followed the excessive credulity of which they were sometimes the subject, and the absurd theories often founded upon them. Other circumstances also materially affected the aspect of archæological questions, and gave a new direction to scientific inquiry. The most important of these was the progress now making in the analysis and comparison of the words and idioms of American languages. But before proceeding to speak of that branch of investigation, which deserves to be considered by itself, it is proper to notice a very elaborate and highly valuable work that appeared in 1829.

This was entitled "Researches, Philosophical and Antiquarian, concerning the Aboriginal History of America, By J. H. McCulloh, Jr., M. D." It was the completion of a labor commenced by the author many years before, of which some partial results were printed in 1816. No more perfect monument of industry and patient research connected with this subject has been published. The author's field of inquiry was the whole American continent. He made no personal explorations, but contented himself with collecting under different heads the facts related by those who wrote from observation, and arranging with them analogies derived from every historical and literary source within his reach; thus forming a convenient cyclopedia of that kind of information. All that relates specifically to the mounds and fortifications of North America is contained in a brief appendix; but much of the entire work has a pertinent bearing upon the questions of their nature and history. It demonstrates with how little safety affinities of race, or an identity of origin, can be deduced from partial similarities of customs, arts, or superstitions; which often proceed from the instincts of a common human nature; and even for practices apparently the most anomalous the author finds parallels elsewhere. He pursues his search for definite conclusions, through the complexity of his accumulated facts and illustrations, with untiring patience; and his opinions have this claim to deference, if no other, that they are the result of painful and protracted study. They are liable, however, to whatever diminution of weight is due to the mistakes and misrepresentations of the authorities on whom he relies; a source of error to which such a compilation of miscellaneous evidence is peculiarly exposed.

In his chapter on the complexion and appearance of the American Indians, after rejecting, for reasons shown, the term *copper colored* applied to the Americans, as not being either correct or distinctive, and adopting that of *brown* as more generally accurate, he finds described by different writers, three classes of complexion among the aborigines, viz: white, brown, and black; not to mention the intermediate shades. The existence of a white class is supported by extracts from the journals of travellers who profess to have observed in certain tribes the complexional characteristics of the races to which that term is usually applied—red and white cheeks, a fair skin, and varied shades of color in the hair, some chestnut, some auburn, some flaxen, as well as some black and curling. The Mandans and Gros-ventres of the United States, the Guayanas of Brazil and Paraguay, the Eskimaux, and the Greenlanders, are adduced as instances of this peculiarity. The light complexion of the Eskimaux led Dr. Robertson to conjecture that they were descendants of the Norwegian discoverers. Captain Lyon and Captain Parry had remarked that their skins, when washed, and such portions as were kept covered by clothing, were clear and transparent, and not darker than that of the natives of southern Europe. Captain Dixon is still more explicit in his statement to that effect; and La Peyrouse, Marchand, Cook, and sundry others whom he mentions, testify to the whiteness of the children at their birth. Baron Humboldt, the Abbe Molina, Herrera, Dobrizhoffer, &c. &c., are quoted as authorities for the existence of tribes in South America that may more probably be called white than copper colored or brown.

Dr. McCulloh's opinion, that aboriginal *blacks or negroes* had been found on this continent, was grounded on the statements of Torquemada, La Peyrouse, and Langsdorf, that some tribes of Indians in California were black, and, as asserted by the latter, with "large projecting lips, and broad, flat negro noses;" and upon Peter Martyr's account of Balboa's journey across the Isthmus of Darien, where, it is said, "There is a region, not above two days' journey from Quarequa, in which they found only blackamoors, &c." Stevenson's Travels in South America, and Juarros' History of Guatimala, are quoted as confirming this story by collateral evidence.

If the country had been as thoroughly explored when Dr. McCulloh wrote as it has been since, he would hardly have considered the admitted diversity of shades of complexion as justifying so distinct a classification as he has adopted.[1]

At the close of his chapter on the "social and moral institutions of the barbarous tribes," his views of their traditions are thus expressed:—

"The ancient histories of the migrations of the barbarous tribes are equally confused with those they relate concerning their origin, and in no instance can be presumed to extend back beyond a century of years anterior to the immediate inquiries of the Europeans.

"After a deliberate examination of their respective traditions of emigration, I cannot consider them as throwing the least degree of light upon the history of their origin. They certainly only relate to the partial removals or emigrations of these people from one to another part of the American continent. This belief is in strict conformity with everything we know of their actual condition when we first became acquainted with them. They were continually engaged in war with each other, and, according as they were fortunate or unsuccessful, they either enlarged their country, or abandoned it, to be incorporated with another people.

"Every change of political circumstances, therefore, altered the limits of an Indian territory; which would, in the course of a single century, leave but an indistinct impression on their minds as to any former country from which they may have emigrated. A vague idea of a previous removal might be retained by their oldest people, which they might state to be from some particular point of the compass; but beyond this they seem to have retained no precise information."

As native traditions have not been without their believers, and are blended with the progress of information and opinion, it may be well, before leaving the subject, to illustrate them further.

In a manuscript history of the western country, by Rev. John P. Campbell, of Chillicothe, who died near the close of 1814, it is said:—

"Mr. Thomas Bodley was informed by Indians of different tribes northwest of the Ohio, that they had understood from their old men, and that it had been a tradition among their several nations, that Kentucky had been settled by *whites*, and that they had been exterminated by war. They were of opinion that the old fortifications, now to be seen in Kentucky and Ohio, were the productions of those *white inhabitants*. Wappockanitta, a Shawnee chief, near a hundred and twenty years old, living on the Anglaze river, confirmed the above tradition.

"An old Indian, in conversation with Col. James F. Moore, of Kentucky,

---

[1] See Dr. Morton's remarks on the complexion of the American Indians, in Schoolcraft's History, Condition, and Prospects of Am. Indians, II, 320.

informed him that the western country, and particularly Kentucky, had once been inhabited by white people, but that they were exterminated by the Indians; that the last battle was fought at the falls of the Ohio; and that the Indians succeeded in driving the aborigines into a small island below the rapids, where the whole of them were cut to pieces. He said it was an undoubted fact, handed down by tradition, and that the Colonel would have ocular proof of it when the waters of the Ohio became low. This was found to be correct on examining Sandy Island, when the river had fallen, as a multitude of bones were discovered.

"Col. Joseph Daviess, when in St. Louis, in 1800, saw the remains of an ancient tribe of the Sacs, who expressed some astonishment that any person should live in Kentucky. They said the country had been the scene of much bloodshed, and was filled with the manes of its butchered inhabitants. They stated, also, that the people who inhabited this country were *white*, and possessed such arts as were unknown by the Indians.

"Col. McKee, who commanded on the Kenhawa when Cornstalk was inhumanly murdered, had frequent conversations with that chief, respecting the people who constructed the ancient forts. He stated that it was a current and assured tradition, that Ohio and Kentucky had been once settled by white people. That, after many sanguinary contests, they were exterminated. Col. M. asked him if he could tell who made those old forts, which displayed so much skill in fortifying. He answered that he did not know, but that a story had been handed down from a *very long ago people*, that there had been a nation of white people inhabiting the country, who made the graves and forts."

In the Portfolio, of June, 1816, from which the above extracts are taken, it is said that the MSS. of Rev. Dr. Campbell had been placed in the hands of a friend of the family to be prepared for publication. It is believed, however, that they were never printed. The *white men* spoken of, in the traditions recorded by the author, may possibly have been the early Spanish and French adventurers; the want of conformity to facts, in regard to events and localities, being explained by the usual absence of consistency in the legendary tales of the natives.

The Kaskaskia chief, Baptist Ducoign, told Gen. George Rogers Clark, that the works on the Kaskaskia river were the palaces and fortifications of his forefathers "when they covered the whole country and had large towns."[1]

The traditions related by Cusic, an educated Tuscarora, in his Ancient History of the Six Nations, may be compared with the statement of the Iroquois to the missionary Kirkland, that the defensive inclosures of New York were erected in their wars with the southern and western Indians, three, four, or five centuries ago. Cusic refers to the mounds and fortifications of the west, as the works of ancient southern and western tribes, who had penetrated and occupied the country nearly to the banks of Lake Erie. They were, he says, opposed by the northern tribes, who were more skilled in the use of bows and arrows; and after long and bloody wars, which are conjectured to have lasted for centuries, the Algonco-Iro-

---

[1] Schoolcraft's Cond. and Prosp. of Am. Indians, IV, 135.

quois confederacy of the tribes prevailed. The towns and forts in the Mississippi valley fell before these conquering tribes, and were left in ruins.

Mr. Gallatin says: "The evidently fabulous annals of the Iroquois were invented by a pure Indian (Cusic). They (the Indians) have no scruple in telling what are called white fibs. If any inquiry is made on any subject, they have considerable tact in discovering the answer which would please the inquirer, and immediately invent a tale for that purpose. I have traced some, evidently of that character, in reference to the supposed Welsh Indians. Yet some of the traditions may be founded on a true fact, though altered, as is so generally the case, in order to answer some immediate purpose. Thus, the assertion of the Delawares that they came from beyond the Mississippi has been confirmed by the affinities of their language with that of the Black Feet. But the story of their having come with the Iroquois, and the recital of their subsequent relations, have evidently been invented."[1]

In his chapter on the Natchez and other Indians of Florida, Dr. McCulloh regards the evidence as conclusive that those tribes were competent to the erection of all the earthworks found in that region; as they are known to have constructed similar ones, and to have had customs that indicate their use.

It has been remarked already, that in the accounts of early Spanish and French occupation of the country, no notice is taken of mounds or parapets, except such as were then formed or used by the natives. By reference to Smithsonian Contributions, Vol. I, Ch. IV, it will be seen that the characteristic monuments of Florida and Louisiana are pyramidal elevations, often of large horizontal dimensions, but not lofty in proportion, with a flat surface at the top, and a graded way of easy ascent on one side. These are sometimes surrounded, at a little distance, by ditches or parapets.

Now, it happens, that Garcilazo de la Vega, in his history of Florida, describes the formation and purpose of such structures, with a particularity that seems to admit of no misapprehension.

"The town and house of the Cacique of Osachile are similar to those of all other caciques in Florida, and, therefore, it seems best to give one description that will apply generally to all the capitals, and all the houses of the chiefs in Florida. I say, then, that the Indians endeavor to place their towns upon elevated places; but because such situations are rare in Florida, or that they find a difficulty in procuring suitable materials for building, they raise eminences in this manner. They choose a place to which they bring a quantity of earth, which they elevate into a kind of platform two or three pikes in height (from eighteen to twenty-five feet), of which the flat top is capable of holding ten or twelve, fifteen or twenty houses, to lodge the cacique, his family, and suite. They trace around the foot of this mound a square place, conformable to the extent of the town they intend to build, and around this square the more considerable people erect their dwellings. The commonalty build around them in the same manner, and the whole population thus surround their chief. The mound upon which the cacique lives has its sides made

[1] Trans. of Am. Ethnol. Soc., II, cxlvii.

so steep that it is impossible to ascend it but by the artificial steps or way that is fixed alone on one side."

From this and other notices, less particular but equally distinct, of mounds as the sites of temples, and as fortresses, and of fortified inclosures, found in the early narratives as well as from the arts, religious system, and despotic government of those tribes, and from all we know of their history, Dr. McCulloh felt himself justified in maintaining that they and their ancestors were the authors of all the works whose remains exist in that portion of the country. He inferred, too, "that other tribes, also of a certain degree of civilization, inhabited the shores of the Mississippi and Ohio, even up to Pennsylvania, who were fully able to construct any monument hitherto discovered north of Mexico." These he supposed might have been exterminated by the barbarian nations around them, or compelled to migrate elsewhere, perhaps pressed down towards Florida, where they were incorporated with a people of congenial disposition.

He might have added to his references what Ribault says of the great chieftain Chiquola. "They (the Floridians) gave me to understand that they would bring me to see the greatest lord of this country, which they called Chiquola, which exceeded them in height (as they told me) a good foot and a half. They said unto me that he dwelt within the land, in a very large place, and *inclosed exceeding high*, but I could not learn wherewith. * * * I began then to show them all the parts of the heaven, to the intent to learn in which quarter they (Chiquola's people) dwelt. And straightway one of them stretching out his hand showed me that they dwelt towards the north. * * * Besides this proof, those which were left in the first voyage have certified me, that the Indians showed them by evident signs, that further within the land, toward the north, there was a great inclosure or city where Chiquola dwelt."[1]

Dr. McCulloh's conclusions respecting the mounds and fortifications of North America may be embraced in a few sentences.

He was decidedly of opinion, in opposition to the views held by him at the commencement of his researches, that they were erected by Indian tribes; the more eminent monuments, probably by nations kindred with the Natches, Tœnsas, Mobilians, &c., if not by the ancestors of those very people, whose traditions point to some ancient establishments in the western country.

The fortifications, as they were usually termed, he regarded as simple walls, which surrounded towns and villages, including also cultivated grounds, thrown up for protection against surprisals, but without reference to any general system of military defence. The mounds within the inclosures he considered as sites for the dwellings of the chiefs, for council halls, or for temples, the conical mounds being generally for sepulchral purposes.

He thought he had been able to show that, on opening the mounds, nothing had been discovered indicating a state of civilization materially different from that of ordinary Indian society; and certainly nothing surpassing the demi-civilization of

---

[1] Ribault's account of Florida, in Hakluyt, III, 376.

the Florida Indians. All articles of a higher order of manufacture, said to have been occasionally met with, he believed to have been derived from the early Spanish or French adventurers, or from other external sources.

Although Dr. McCulloh's deductions are usually sensible and discriminating, the plan of his work is open to serious objections. It may serve for a dictionary of reference, but as a method of reasoning it is unsound and deceptive. Detached quotations need not of necessity mislead the compiler, provided he carefully studies the connection in which they are found, but they are liable to have in their separate position, or when combined with other extracts, a force and signification their authors by no means intended. They can never be admitted as evidence, or made the basis of a solid judgment, without a knowledge of the circumstances in which they were written. Dr. McCulloh's work has this great merit and interest: It contains the first clear and definite statement, upon evidence, of opinions that have since been adopted by some of the latest and most influential writers. Dr. Morton employs the term *brown*, suggested by him, to express the general color of the Indians, recognizing also the various shades of complexion which Dr. McCulloh has described, without, however, regarding them as indicative of distinctions of race. Mr. Schoolcraft confirms his views respecting the southern origin of the mound-builders, and the probable history of those remains, and apparently concurs with the general conclusions of his research.[1]

It is time to notice more particularly a department of research, thus far but indirectly referred to, which is destined to exert a prominent, if not decisive influence, upon archæological questions.

An examination of American languages, as a means of determining from what branch of the human family the original inhabitants of the country were descended, was suggested at an early period. Efforts have never been wanting, since vocabularies began to be collected, to trace affinities with the languages of the Old World, through words having a similarity of sound and signification; yet, although many striking cases of apparent resemblance between single words of various Indian dialects and those of parallel import in other tongues were detected, philological inquiries produced no satisfactory fruits, because the proper principle on which they should be conducted was not understood.

When Psammeticus, king of Egypt, caused two children to be brought up without an opportunity of hearing speech, in order, by the first words they should utter, to settle a dispute between the Egyptians and Phrygians, as to which was the most ancient language, he acted under the same philosophical misapprehension. The first word spoken happened to be *beccos;* and the Phrygians claimed the victory, because beccos in their tongue signified *bread.*

If Psammeticus had prolonged his experiment until the children sought to communicate their ideas to one another, and, after having given names to things, endeavored to combine and modify them to express relation, quality, and action, he might, perhaps, have ascertained in what manner the human mind, governed solely by instinctive impulses, would proceed to the construction of language.

---

[1] Hist. Cond. and Prosp. of the Ind. Tribes, II, 84 and 320. Ib., IV, 115.

It is in the forms of grammatical structure, the modes of associating and expressing ideas, without regard to the meaning of particular words, that modern philologists have found the true key to the origin and connection of the varieties of human speech.

This is claimed to be a discovery so newly made as to be known and practised on only by scholars of the present generation. It is to Frederic Schlegel that Chevalier Bunsen attributes the establishment of this principle, and so recently as 1808.[1] It is relied upon to solve the question of the relative antiquity of nations, and to elucidate some of the mysteries connected with the descent and distribution of races. The proposition is, simply, that names of things, and terms of expression, are transitory, and in the course of time may be wholly replaced by others; but the system of grammatical construction is permanent, assimilating to itself, and distributing, according to its own laws, whatever new material is acquired; and, unless overwhelmed by the irruption of a new system, sustained by the dominating force of numbers and conquest, maintains its vitality through all changes.

As applied to American languages, the results of this rule of exegesis have been most remarkable. No theories of derivation from the Old World have stood the test of its alchemy. All traces of the fugitive tribes of Israel supposed to be found here, are again lost.[2] Neither Phœnicians, nor Hindoos, nor Chinese, nor Scandinavians, nor Welsh, have left an impress of their national syntax behind them. But the dialects of the Western Continent, radically united among themselves, and radically distinguished from all others, stand in hoary brotherhood by the side of the most ancient vocal systems of the human race. "It deserves notice," says Mr. Gallatin, "that Vater could point out but two languages that, on account of the multiplicity of their forms, had a character, if not similar, at least analogous to those of America. These were the Congo and the Basque. The first spoken by a barbarous nation of Africa, the other now universally admitted to be a remarkable relic of a most ancient and primitive language found in the most early ages of the world."[3]

The science of comparative philology is yet in its infancy, and investigators are constantly pointing out new analogies, and as often invalidating those which had before been suggested. The subject is one of great complication and difficulty; and it is not always easy to draw the line of distinction between resemblances incident to the attributes of a common human nature, and affinities upon points of structure that constitute the original and peculiar genius of a language. With whatever primordial forms of speech the American languages may be associated by different writers (and on this point they are by no means agreed), their primitive unity and long separation from those of other countries seem to be generally admitted.

There are three epochs in the progress of information respecting the languages

---

[1] Bunsen's "Outlines of the Philosophy of Universal History, applied to language and religion." Lond., 1854, I, 50.

[2] The essential diversity between the Indian languages and the Hebrew, is learnedly exhibited in the Discourse of Rev. Dr. Jarvis before the N. Y. Hist. Soc. in 1819, on the Religion of the Indian tribes.

[3] Trans. of Am. Antiquarian Soc., II, 203.

of America. In the first, the study of words was the principal object of attention, for the purpose of detecting similarities of sound and sense with those of other nations. In the second, the radical connection subsisting between the native dialects of the whole continent excited the special interest of inquirers. In the third, the modern linguistic system was adopted, and the philosophy of organization, the grammatical machinery by which ideas are combined, and quality, relation, and action, are indicated, became the prominent subject of investigation.

Vocabularies were not collected at first with a view to comparison, but to facilitate communication with the natives. Tables of Mexican words with a Spanish translation were printed in Mexico as early as 1571; and there are few early travellers and missionaries who did not preserve similar specimens in their journals, from the different regions they visited.

When terms and phrases were analyzed for grammatical purposes, the object was still limited to the convenience of intercourse, or the conveyance of religious instruction. Roger Williams, who preceded Eliot in this kind of labor, prepared his "key," "as a help to the language of the natives;"[1] and Eliot's "Grammar begun,"[2] was "for the help of such as desired to learn, and for the furtherance of the gospel among the Indians." Father Rasle's copious MS. dictionary, commenced in 1690, had no other design. The same may be said of Josiah Cotton's Vocabulary, compiled in 1707–8.

It is not until the treatise of Jonathan Edwards appeared, in 1788, that we find the recognition of a different purpose; and in this the same principles of investigation are declared and practised that have given to Schlegel the reputation of establishing a new school of comparative philology.[3] The title of Dr. Edwards's tract deserves to be inserted at length, as significant of the nature and scope of a plan which he suggested and illustrated, but did not attempt to execute upon any extensive scale.[4] The principal merit of Edwards undoubtedly consists in the detection of a prevailing identity of language among tribes widely separated, and employing words apparently dissimilar.

Although not fully aware, it may be, of the ethnological importance of a study of the mechanism of language, it must have always been regarded with interest by men of philosophical minds. Maupertuis, the celebrated mathematician, in his "Reflections on the origin of language," first printed about 1750, recommended the study of barbarous languages, "because we may chance to find some that are

---

[1] Printed in 1643. [2] Printed in 1666.

[3] Schlegel's Essay is thus referred to by Bunsen: "In 1808 a book appeared, small in extent, and on the whole a mere sketch, but possessing all those properties which constitute an *epoch-making* work. I mean Schlegel's Essay on the language and philosophy of the Hindoos. It fully established the decisive importance and precedence which grammatical forms ought to have over single words in proving the affinities of languages. To the impulse given by Schlegel's work we are indebted in a high degree, for the ideas on which the new linguistic school of Germany has proceeded." Phil. of Universal Hist., I, 50.

[4] "Observations on the language of the Muhhekaneew Indians. In which the extent of that language in North America is shown; its genius is grammatically traced; some of its peculiarities, and some instances of analogy between that and the Hebrew, are pointed out."

formed on *new plans of ideas*." His contemporary, Turgot, professed not to understand what was meant by "plans of ideas;" but he was then a youth, a little over twenty years of age, and aiming to write a smart criticism on the essay of Maupertuis.

Jefferson's remarks in his Notes on Virginia, Quere IX, contain the idea that Schlegel subsequently made productive. "Were vocabularies formed of all the languages spoken in North and South America, with *the inflections of their nouns and verbs, their principles of regimen and concord*, it would furnish opportunities to those skilled in the languages of the Old World to compare them with these, and hence to construct the best evidence of the derivation of this part of the human race."[1]

The labors of Dr. Barton are entitled to the highest praise; but they were in a path which had been travelled before. His comparisons related almost exclusively to words, their sense, and etymology, and did not penetrate to the vital principle that controls their regimen, as the vital principle of a plant determines the form of its growth. Pursuing the same line of investigation, he advanced further than his predecessors, and having, with great patience and industry, accumulated a larger stock of materials, he very much extended the field of inquiry.

As early as 1708, Adrian Reland, distinguished as an oriental scholar and a philological writer, published, at Utrecht, a dissertation on the languages of America. The dialects he had examined were, as enumerated by him, the Brazilian, the Peruvian, the Chilian, the Poconchi or Pocoman, the Carib, the Mexican, the Virginian, the Algonkin, and the Huron. That which he called the "Virginian" was the language of Eliot's Bible and Grammar, and his specimens of the Algonkin and the Huron were derived from the vocabularies of Baron de la Hontan. He states, as the result of his observations, that, while most of the languages of Europe, Asia, and Africa, can easily be traced to their origin, it is very different with those of America; as, on comparing the latter with others, it is almost impossible to discover sufficient resemblance to excite even a suspicion of what people took possession of this vast continent. Yet, supposing that the New World must have received its population from the Old, he seeks an explanation for the radical changes of speech in the known fact, that the priests and chiefs of some tribes created a language for themselves, purposely unintelligible to the lower orders, which, from being exclusively a court language, might gradually be communicated to the people, and supersede their own. To this he adds the fluctuating tendency of all speech, in the absence of written symbols to give permanency to sounds. If any relation is to be found between the tongues of the two hemispheres, he thinks it must be looked for among the languages of Asia. He inserts an Icelandic vocabulary, by which, he says, "they who imagine there is any affinity between the languages of the North and those of America may be undeceived." Even Clavigero, the contemporary of Jefferson and Barton, was somewhat in advance of them in express-

---

[1] It is stated that President Jefferson had himself gathered vocabularies which, at some interval of leisure from public employments, he intended to digest and publish; but in 1801 his MSS. were destroyed by fire, and he had not the heart to commence his work anew. Schoolcraft's Hist. of the Cond. and Prosp. of the Indians, II, 356.

ing the opinion, based upon his own philological researches, that the Americans do not derive their origin from any people now existing in the ancient world.[1]

The great names that have given lustre to the modern school of comparative philology are mostly German; and the number of American dialects collected and analyzed by the two Adelungs, Vater, and William Von Humboldt, caused our own distinguished philologists, Duponceau and Pickering, to unite in an expression of astonishment and admiration towards them as their masters in a knowledge of the customs, manners, and languages of the aborigines of this country.[2]

Frederic Adelung ascribes to the Empress Catharine II, of Russia, the honor of commencing, personally, the solid foundation on which philological science now rests. For her private gratification and amusement, she had formed the plan of procuring vocabularies of all the languages in the world; and directed her Secretary of State to write for that purpose to the powers of Europe, Asia, and Africa. Application was made to President Washington for our Indian languages, and several specimens were furnished. The empress pursued her studies of comparison in solitude for many months; but at length growing tired of this hobby, she sent for Professor Pallas, and "after a full confession" (as she says in a letter to a friend) of the manner in which she had been occupied, it was agreed between them that the translations she had made of a list of Russian words into more than two hundred languages or dialects, should be printed for the benefit of those who were willing to engage in such labors.[3]

---

[1] Hist. of Mexico, first printed in 1780.

[2] Mass. Hist. Col., 2d se., IX, 232.

[3] Catherinens der Grossen Verdienste um die Vergleichende Sprachenkunde. Mem. of Am. Acad., IV, 321.

The Russian Empress and Eugene Aram are singular persons to be brought together in this connection; yet they both appear to have entertained views upon philological subjects somewhat in advance of their contemporaries. The following note, received through Professor Henry, from Col. C. A. Alexander, of Washington, will be found to possess more than a merely scientific interest. It will increase the regret that the eminent abilities of Aram could not have been employed in pursuits that might have proved honorable to himself, and useful to mankind.

"In any work treating of the affinities of language, it would seem to be unjust to overlook the claims of the remarkable but unfortunate *Eugene Aram*, to be considered as an early (if not the earliest) cultivator of this branch of philological science, upon the right principle, and with anything like an adequate comprehensiveness of purpose. Some account of his labors may be found in the *Annual Register* (Dodsley's) for 1759, page 360, where we are told that having discovered a surprising affinity throughout the Latin, Greek, Hebrew, French, Chaldee, Arabic, and Celtic languages, 'he resolved to make a Comparative Lexicon, and, at the time of his trial and death, had collected for that purpose above one thousand notes.' He had observed that all previous lexicographers had limited their views to tracing such accidental derivations as might have sprung from commerce or occasional intercourse, without adverting to the radical affiliation which a more profound inquiry discloses. 'Yet,' as he well remarks, 'it is not to be thought of, much less concluded, that the multitude of English words which are certainly of Latin, Greek, and Phœnician origin, are all the relics of the Roman settlements in Britain, or the effects of Greek or Phœnician commerce; on the contrary, the resemblance was coeval with the primary inhabitants of the island. How nearly related is the Cambrian, how nearly the Irish, in numberless instances, to the Latin, the Greek, and even the Hebrew, and both possessed this consimilarity long ago, before Julius Cæsar and the Roman invasion. I know not but the Latin differed more from itself in the succession of six continued centuries, than the Welsh and Irish at this time

From Pallas to the compilers of the "Mithridates" the transmission of the design of the empress is direct. That great work, commenced by Professor John Christopher Adelung, and continued by Professor Vater, the Hon. Frederic Adelung, and Baron William Von Humboldt, was published at Berlin, gradually, from 1806 to 1817. Two volumes, containing together no less than eight hundred and seventy-four pages, are exclusively dedicated to the languages of the Indians of North and South America, and were written almost wholly by Professor Vater.

We are, without question, indebted to the fruits of the labors of those learned men, for the active proceedings of the Historical Committee of the American Philosophical Society, in 1816.

In that year, Mr. Duponceau commenced a correspondence with Mr. Heckewelder, the object of which was "to ascertain the structure and grammatical forms of the languages of the aboriginal nations of America."

To facilitate this investigation, the library of the society was enriched with a collection of valuable MS. dictionaries, grammars, and vocabularies, prepared by the Moravian missionaries, a series of vocabularies presented by Mr. Jefferson, and various tables obtained from different quarters. Thus, in addition to the resources provided by professor Vater, the society had become possessed of new materials of an important character, with the advantage of having at hand an experienced interpreter, able, from personal knowledge, or by correspondence with his brethren at different missionary stations, to supply the most exact and pertinent information.[1]

The duty of the Historical Committee, begun by Dr. Wistar and Mr. Duponceau, was continued by the latter alone, in consequence of Dr. Wistar's death; and the results were published in 1819, in connection with Mr. Heckewelder's "Historical Account of the Indian Nations." Their report describes the peculiar characteristics of the American languages, thus: "We find a *new* manner of compounding words from various roots so as to strike the mind at once with a whole mass of ideas; a *new* manner of expressing the cases of substantives by inflecting the verbs that govern them; a *new* number (the particular plural), applied to the declension of nouns and conjugation of verbs; a *new* concordance in tense of the conjunction with the verb; we see not only pronouns, as in the Hebrew and some other languages, but adjectives, conjunctions, adverbs, combined with the principal part of speech, and producing an immense variety of verbal forms. When we consider

---

from the Latin. We find pure Greek in the Peak (of Derbyshire) itself, whither foreigners can scarcely be supposed to have come, there having been but few invitations to it twice ten centuries ago, and perhaps not many now.'

"In the work quoted from, an example of his method is given in the word 'beagles,' which he traces from its Celtic root, *pig, id est, little*—through the Greek (πυγμαίος, *i. e.*, a dwarf), the Irish (*beg aglach, i. e.*, little fearing, &c.), the Scotch (philibig, *i. e.*, a little petticoat), as well as in several English provincialisms. Thus, *beagle* is not only a *little* dog, but also a *cowslip*, from the littleness of its flowers, and the appellation *Peggy*, is properly applicable to no female as a Christian name, but is merely an epithet of size, and a word of endearment only."

[1] The Moravians had paid great attention to Indian lexicography. Zeisberger prepared a dictionary and grammar of the Irōquois, and a copious vocabulary and grammar of the Delaware language; Pyrleus, a collection of Iroquois words and phrases, grammatically arranged; and Schultz, a dictionary and grammar of the Aruwack language.

these and many other singularities, which so eminently characterize the American idioms, we naturally ask ourselves the question: Are languages formed on this model to be found in any other part of the earth?"

Mr. Duponceau gives the following summary of the products of philological research at that period, in his notes on Eliot's Grammar, printed by the Massachusetts Historical Society, in 1822.

"Before I proceed to the language of the Massachusetts Indians, I may be permitted to show what fruits have been derived from our science, since it has begun to be considered an interesting object of study.

"By the labors of the illustrious Adelung, a census, as it were, has been taken of all the languages and dialects (that are known to us) existing on the surface of the earth; they have been all registered and enumerated, and it is now ascertained, as nearly as possible, that their aggregage number amounts to 3,064; of which Africa has 276; Europe, 587; Asia, 987; and America, 1214—being more than Asia and Africa together, and nearly as many as the whole of the old continent, Africa excepted."

"It is ascertained, at least nothing has yet appeared to the contrary, that the languages of our American Indians are rich in words and grammatical forms; that they are adequate to the expression of even abstract ideas; and that they have a mode (different from our own), by which they can easily combine their radical sounds with each other, so as to frame new words whenever they stand in need of them. What is still more extraordinary, the model of these languages has been found to be the same from north to south; varieties being only observed in some of the details, which do not affect the similarity of the general system; while, on the eastern continent, languages are found, which, in their grammatical organization, have no relation whatever with each other. And yet our American idioms, except where they can be traced to a common stock, differ so much in point of *etymology*, that no affinity whatever has been yet discovered between them."

"It has been, moreover, ascertained, that one nation at least, on the eastern continent of Asia, the *Sedentary Tschuktschi*, speak an *American* language (a dialect of the Eskimaux). On the other hand, no nation has yet been discovered on this continent that speaks an Asiatic language."

"It has been also ascertained that from the peninsula of Malacca, in Asia, to the Cocos Island, and through the various clusters in the South Sea, and also in the island of Madagascar, dialects of the same language (the Malay) are spoken. No traces of this language have been yet discovered on the coast of the American continent; but they may appear on further research."

One of the greatest obstacles to a successful and satisfactory comparison of Indian vocabularies, was caused by the capricious and ever varying orthography adopted by writers of different nations. The elementary sounds were often so variously represented that the same word could not be recognized in the dissimilar combinations of letters employed to express it. Thus, for example, if the letter *j* was used by an Englishman, to a German or Italian it would represent the sound of our *y*; to a Frenchman or Portuguese, that of *zh* or *s* in pleasure; while a Spaniard would give it the strong guttural accent of his country. As the tables of words were collected by persons of all these different nations, it is evident that they could not be compared, with any reasonable expectation of determining their affinities, without a careful reduction to some common standard of orthography. Dr. Barton attempted it in his own researches; other philologists were less careful; and even Vater was led into many mistakes arising from this difficulty.

The investigations of the Committee of the Philosophical Society were no sooner published than they excited a deep interest in that able scholar and lexicographer, Mr. John Pickering, of Massachusetts, and led him to prepare a treatise on the orthography of the Indian languages of North America, with a view to obviating the embarrassments that had been experienced. This was printed by the American Academy, in the 4th volume of its Memoirs.[1] Becoming more engaged in the subject, Mr. Pickering wrote a valuable introduction to Eliot's Grammar, republished by the Massachusetts Historical Society in 1822, with elaborate notes by Mr. Duponceau; and, the year following, prepared his edition and extension of the work of Dr. Edwards, which was printed by the same Society. The able and learned article on Indian languages, in the appendix to the sixth volume of the Encyclopædia Americana, was also written by him.

In that article, Mr. Pickering refers to Mr. Duponceau as "the first to discover and make known to the world the remarkable character which pervades the aboriginal languages of America from Greenland to Cape Horn," and states that it is from his writings we derive nearly all that is known of the general characteristics of those dialects, while his theory has been confirmed by all subsequent observations.

Mr. Duponceau attributed the origin of his own interest in this subject to his undertaking a translation of Zeisberger's Delaware Grammar on behalf of the Committee of the Philosophical Society, and to his correspondence with Heckewelder, of whom he always spoke in terms of the highest respect and regard. He continued to promote inquiry by various contributions to the transactions of the Philosophical Society, and crowned his labors in this department of science by his elaborate memoir on the grammatical system of the languages of the North American Indians, to which the Royal Institute of France awarded the prize founded by Volney for the encouragement of philological studies.[2] That work was published by the Royal Institute, in 1838, and constitutes a volume of four hundred and sixty-four pages, embodying the substance of the author's information scientifically arranged, and the views that had resulted from his investigations. These views differ from those already presented in a single particular. An apparent exception to the rule of uniformity in the structure of the American languages was pointed out to Mr. Duponceau by Don Manuel Najera, a Mexican. This was in the case of the Otomis, a rude tribe of central Mexico, whose language is monosyllabic, like the Chinese. Najera demonstrated that peculiarity in a Latin treatise,

---

[1] Mr. Pickering's system of orthography was adopted by the American Board of Commissioners for Foreign Missions, and has been used in their numerous publications.

[2] "Mémoir sur le système grammatical des langues de quelques nations Indiennes de l'Amérique du Nord."

in the fifth volume of the new series of the transactions of the American Philosophical Society.[1] The fact was not made known to Mr. Duponceau until his memoir was in the possession of the French Institute, and is first mentioned in the preface attached to it when printed, accompanied with the reflection that "in science, especially in metaphysical science, it is not well to be in haste to generalize."[2]

When Mr. Gallatin prepared his "Notes on the semi-civilized nations of Mexico, Yucatan, and Central America," in 1845, he examined Najera's treatise with a good deal of care. Some exceptions or objections were found to his theory, and some affinities to other dialects were detected, yet the theory appeared to him to be substantially correct; and he drew from thence a moral similar to that of Mr. Duponceau. "The distinct character of the Otomi, teaches us we must be cautious in drawing too general conclusions. It appears certain that almost all the Indian languages are similar in their grammatical forms, structure, and general character. But it does not follow that there are no exceptions."

Mr. Gallatin commenced his labors in this field of inquiry, in 1823, with an attempt to classify the Indian tribes of North America in families according to their respective languages, at the request of his friend Baron Alexander Von Humboldt. That essay having been communicated by Humboldt to M. Balbi, was noticed by the latter in the Introduction to his "Atlas Ethnographique," and there attracted the attention of the American Antiquarian Society, whose officers applied to Mr. Gallatin for a copy. As he had kept none, but had collected many additional materials, the essay was re-written and much enlarged, and occupies the greater part of the second volume of "Archæologia Americana," published in 1836.

The synopsis was originally intended to embrace all the tribes north of the semi-civilized nations of Mexico; but the want of materials confined the inquiry towards the south to the territory of the United States. Within that territory, east of the Rocky Mountains, nearly all the dialects were ascertained, as well as most of the *families* of languages north of the United States.

Mr. Gallatin's general conclusions were not dissimilar to those of Mr. Duponceau. Being less imaginative, and less under the influence of excitement produced by the development of unexpected and extraordinary characteristics in the American languages, he employed a cooler and stricter logic in their examination. He had the advantage also of a wider scope, and a field of observation prepared, to a considerable extent, by previous labors. Hence, his view is more comprehensive, and his exposition of details more complete.

His own account of the result is that "it appears to confirm the opinions already entertained on that subject by Mr. Duponceau, Mr. Pickering, and others; and to prove that all the languages, not only of our own Indians, but of the natives of America from the Arctic Ocean to Cape Horn, have, as far as they have been investigated, a distinct character, common to all, and apparently differing from any of those of the other continent with which we are most familiar."

---

[1] In the title to that treatise, the name is written Naxera; but the author usually employed the other form of Na*j*era, the sound in Spanish being the same in either case.

[2] Dans les sciences, et surtout dans les sciences métaphysiques, il ne faut pas se hâter de généraliser.

"Those of America seem to me to bear the impress of primitive languages—to have assumed their form from natural causes, and to afford no proof of their being derived from a nation in a more advanced state of civilization than our Indians. Whilst the unity of structure, and of grammatical forms, proves a common origin, it may be inferred from this, combined with the great diversity, and entire difference in the words of the several languages of America, that this continent received its first inhabitants at a very remote epoch, probably not much posterior to that of the dispersion of mankind."

"I rather incline to the opinion, that the civilization of Mexico, and some portions of South America, grew out of natural causes, and is entirely of American origin."[1]

While declaring that the languages of America attest the antiquity of its population, Mr. Gallatin is careful not to be understood as expressing views "inconsistent with the opinion of an Asiatic origin, and with the received chronology."

"Assuming the central parts of Asia to have been the cradle of mankind, since three couples would, in thirty periods of duplication, increase to more than six thousand millions of souls, we may fairly infer, not only the possibility, but even the probability, that America began to be inhabited only five or six hundred years later than the other hemisphere."

"On the probable supposition, that the whole continent of America was inhabited one thousand years after the flood, or near four thousand years ago, the faculties of man, gradually unfolded and improved, may, in the course of so long a period, have produced, without any extraneous aid, that more advanced state of society and knowledge, which existed in some parts of America when first discovered by the Europeans."

In regard to the monuments of the United States, he remarks: "It is not necessary to refute the opinion of those who would ascribe these works to European emigrants. There is nothing in them which may not have been performed by a savage people. The Scandinavian colony of Vinland is out of the question. The Norwegians might, indeed, have penetrated through the Straits of Bellisle to the St. Lawrence; but, if not destroyed by the savages, a considerable time must have elapsed before they could, in their subsequent progress, have reached the Mississippi and ascended its western tributaries. The well ascertained age of trees growing on those ramparts in the lower part of the valley of the Ohio, proves that some of those works were erected before the thirteenth century; and we know that the insignificant colony of Vinland had not left its original seats in 1120. Ignorant as we are, and shall ever remain, of the internal revolutions which may have formerly taken place among the uncivilized tribes of North America, it is not probable we can ever know by whom the works in question were erected."

In 1845, Mr. Gallatin communicated to the American Ethnological Society his "Notes on the semi-civilized nations of Mexico."

In that valuable paper he not only extended his philological comparisons to the languages of those nations, but reviewed their history and chronology, and their

---

[1] Prefatory letter.

astronomical system; devoting a chapter to conjectures on the origin of American civilization.

After the lapse of nine years from the period of his first publication his opinions were not materially changed. Referring to his previous essay, he says: "Taking into view the words or vocabularies alone, although seventy-three tribes were found speaking dialects so far differing, that they could not be understood without an interpreter by the Indians of other tribes; yet the affinities between the words of many of them were such, as to show clearly that they belonged to the same stock. Sixty-one dialects, spoken by as many tribes, were thus found to constitute only eight languages, or rather families of languages, so dissimilar, that the few coincidences which might occur in their words appeared to be accidental. But it was, on the other hand, ascertained that all the languages of which partial grammars could be obtained, however dissimilar in their words, were in their structure of the same character."

"As a general result, it appears to me indubitable that, however dissimilar in their words, the grammar proper and general structure of all their languages is, with the exception of the Otomi, founded on the same principles."

His remarks upon the Eskimaux are worthy of particular notice, on account of the contradictory opinions held respecting that people.

"Several writers have taken it for granted that the Eskimaux were a different race from the other Indian nations of America. Their language is eminently polysynthetic, and, in that respect, in its mode of forming other derivative or compounded words, as well as in its grammatical forms, it is perfectly similar to the other Indian languages, and evidently belongs to the same family. The physical type seems to be essentially the same, and no further varied than might be expected from the excessive severity of the climate. There is not in their size a greater difference between them and the Algonkins, than between the Laplanders and the Finns. With respect to their true color, not easily discernible, Captain Clavering, who reached the most northerly inhabited parts of the eastern coast of Greenland, having thoroughly washed a boy, found that he was copper colored."[1]

After stating that the most striking points of resemblance between the Americans and the inhabitants of the other hemisphere, refer almost exclusively to Asiatic countries; and that, as our knowledge of the languages of northeastern Asia is as yet limited, further investigations are necessary before any legitimate inference can be drawn, he says:—

"From whatever quarter America may have been peopled, the first important question is that of the time at which that event must have taken place."

"We find in America more than one hundred languages, which, however similar in structure, differ entirely in their vocabulary, or words. This difference must have originated either before or after America was inhabited. The first supposition implies that of America having been settled, not by a few distinct nations, which is very possible, but by more than one hundred distinct tribes and nations of different origin, and speaking entirely different languages. This supposition, so utterly

---

[1] See *ante*, p. 48, respecting the supposed color of the Eskimaux.

improbable in itself, is, moreover, inconsistent with the great similarity in their physical type, and the structure of their languages, between almost all the several nations and tribes which inhabited America when discovered in modern times by the Europeans. If, as is highly probable, the prodigious subdivision of languages took place in America, after making every allowance for the greater changes to which unwritten languages are liable, and for the necessary subdivision of nations, in the hunter state, into separate communities, yet, for producing such radical diversity and great multiplication of languages, we want the longest time we are permitted to assume. There is the highest probability that America was inhabited at a date as early as is consistent with the laws which govern the multiplication of the human species, and with the time necessary for the spreading of men to the extreme shores of the other hemisphere."

"I beg leave once more to repeat that, unless we suppose that which we have no right to do, a second miraculous interposition of Providence, in America, the prodigious number of American languages, totally dissimilar in their vocabularies, demonstrates, not only that the first peopling of America took place at the earliest date which we are permitted to assume; but also that the great mass of the existing Indian nations are the descendants of the first emigrants; since we must otherwise suppose that America was peopled by one hundred different tribes, speaking languages totally dissimilar in their words."

After expressing his opinion that, if the articles from the mounds do not afford evidences of a much greater progress in the arts than the Indians had attained when first visited by the Europeans, the monuments themselves are proofs, not only of a more dense, and therefore agricultural population, but also of a different social state, he proceeds to say:—

"As now informed, there is but one leading fact which may aid us in forming any conjecture respecting that extinct race. Their monuments are found exclusively in the valley of the Mississippi, and they are not even seen on the upper or northwestern branches of the Missouri. Not a single one has ever been found either east of the Alleghany, or west of the Rocky Mountains. It seems impossible that, if coming immediately either from Europe or Asia, they should have left no traces whatever of their existence in the regions where they must have landed. There seem to be but two alternatives. Either they were a colony from Mexico; or some of the savage tribes must by conquest, or by some other means unknown to us, have converted themselves into an agricultural nation. The first supposition seems to me the most probable; and, at all events, their agriculture must have been derived from Mexico. In either case, and whatever opinion may be entertained respecting their origin, or their apparent progress in agriculture, it appears that they were not numerous or strong enough to maintain their position; and they must have been ultimately either exterminated or driven away by the savage tribes which surrounded them."

Mr. Gallatin had previously gone into an argument to prove the domestic origin of the astronomical knowledge possessed by Peruvians and Mexicans. He had, also, endeavored to show that the *cereals* of the eastern hemisphere (millet, rice, wheat, rye, barley, oats), were entirely unknown to the Americans; and that maize, which was the great and almost sole foundation of American agriculture, was exclusively of American origin, indigenous in Mexico and other tropical regions, from whence it spread in different directions.[1]

A few years later he had an opportunity to give a degree of completeness to his philological observations, and to mature his views upon the general subject of American archæology. The results of studies continued through a period of more than twenty-five years, are given in his most copious and elaborate introduction to the principal article of the second volume of the Transactions of the Ethnological Society, printed in 1848. The article is entitled "Hale's Indians of Northwest America, and Vocabularies of North America," being composed of ethnological materials collected by Mr. Hale, while attached, in the capacity of Philologist, to the United States exploring expedition of 1838–42.

Mr. Gallatin's Introduction occupies one hundred and sixty-four closely printed 8vo. pages; and, when we reflect that, at the time of its publication, he was eighty-seven years of age, we cannot but be surprised at the clearness of his ideas and the youthful vigor of his style. To any one else, the labor of analysis and comparison involved in his essays, would, at almost any period of life, be fatiguing, however agreeable; but to him it seemed only a source of amusement and recreation. His mind was well adapted by nature to such investigations; the subject was one with which he had become familiar; and his latest efforts indicate no diminution of activity or interest.

In this, his last important work, most of his previous conclusions are repeated, as confirmed by enlarged observation. A table is given of thirty-two distinct families of languages in and north of the United States; but care is taken to explain that this division is made without any reference to their grammar, or structure; "as, however differing in their words, the most striking uniformity in their grammatical forms and structure appears to exist in all the American languages, from Greenland to Cape Horn."

As a fact bearing upon the antiquity of American dialects, which, from an original identity of nomenclature, have by some means become so diversified, it is stated that the tenacity of even unwritten languages has been proved by a multitude of instances; and that those of the same tribes cannot have materially altered during the last three hundred years—the vocabulary taken by Cartier, in the middle of the sixteenth century, being still recognized as belonging to the Iroquois family, while, with the aid of a few words found in the narrative of De Soto's expedition, Mr. Gallatin had been able to trace his march as far west as the Mississippi. Mr.

---

[1] Dr. Bachman doubts whether the native country of *maize* is positively determined. He says: "We have as yet been unable to find any spot, either in North or South America, where it may be said to be indigenous. In every locality where it has been found, it had been planted by the Indian tribes, and was only preserved from extermination by artificial culture. Linnæus, Willdenow, Pursh, &c., regarded it as a native American production; on the other hand, Crawford, and several other botanists, who travelled extensively in India, have expressed an opinion that it was a native of the warmer parts of Asia."—*Doctrine of the Unity of the Human Race Examined*, &c., p. 281.

Duponceau also made himself intelligible to the Wyandots, with no other assistance than the imperfect vocabulary taken in the year 1625, by the Franciscan Sagard.

In Bradford's "American Antiquities," published five years before, arguments had been brought forward tending to show an affinity between the Polynesian and American languages. Mr. Gallatin's opinions on this point are very decided. He admits that there are some analogies of structure between the two, inviting further investigation, which he proceeds to bestow upon them, but says: "No traces of the Malay language are found in the vocabularies of any of the American languages which have been investigated. On the other hand, all the languages of the Polynesian Islands (not including among these either Australia or the black Papuan race) were at once recognized as belonging to the great Malay family, as soon as vocabularies of their various dialects had been published. The supposition that this language had its origin in Polynesia, and was transferred thence to the Asiatic Islands and Continent, is inadmissible. The fact that the connection between the Polynesian and Malay languages is still so visible, proves that the migrations from Asia, by which Polynesia was colonized, are of a comparatively recent date. If any portion of the Continent of America was ever settled by Malay emigrants, which is extremely improbable, it must have been at a very early and remote period."[1]

In 1846, Mr. Gallatin wrote to Mr. Schoolcraft for certain vocabularies that he wished to possess, and in his letter, remarks: "I am preparing for the press—1st, a general, but still very imperfect, view of the grammar or structure of the several languages of the aborigines of America; 2d, a comparative vocabulary of the languages of the tribes within the United States, and north of their northern boundaries."

"As this, if I live long enough to complete it, will be my last contribution to that object, I naturally feel anxious to make it as full, and as useful to those that may succeed me, as possible."[2]

He mentions that he shall publish the work at his own expense. But, with the exception of such portions as are used in the Introduction to Mr. Hale's essay, it is presumed that the materials were never fully arranged for publication.

No one appears to have caught the mantle of Mr. Gallatin, and sought to fulfil his mission. Many valuable contributions have been added to the means of effecting his purpose; but the purpose itself, the completion of a full and well digested analysis of the American languages, exhibiting their peculiarities, and their affinities with one another, and with those of other parts of the world, has never been accomplished.

We are not unmindful of what Mr. Schoolcraft has written at various periods,

---

[1] In Dr. Lieber's brief essay on the "Plan of Thought of the American Languages," in the second volume of Mr. Schoolcraft's large work, the author states that, in 1843, he addressed a letter to Mr. Gallatin, calling his attention to certain points of similarity between American idioms and those spoken by the Islanders of the South Pacific Ocean. This had reference apparently to Mr. Bradford's hypothesis that the American red race is of Mongolian origin, and reached this continent by the islands of the Pacific. Mr. Gallatin's observations may, therefore, be regarded as a reply to those gentlemen.

[2] Schoolcraft's Hist., &c., of the Indian Tribes, III, 397.

and collected in his summary of Indian history, in course of publication by the United States Government. His philological treatises contain rich stores of information; but they do not aggregate the materials in a manner to admit of conclusions that are well defined, and at the same time so universal as to be free from important exceptions.

A series of essays upon the languages of the Indians, some of them accompanied with vocabularies, was commenced in the second part of his general history, and has been continued in subsequent volumes; but the facts and views presented are either partial, being derived from an investigation of particular dialects, or, if general, are brief, and by no means intended to be absolute or conclusive. The article entitled "Plan of Thought of the American Languages," by Dr. Lieber, occupies but four pages, and is chiefly devoted to the suggestion and recommendation of a new term for expressing a prominent idiomatic feature.

Mr. Schoolcraft's prolonged and familiar acquaintance with various Indian tribes, and his connection with the race, seem to give him almost unequalled advantages for such investigations, and the fruits of his local studies are of superior importance. It remains to be seen whether the state of his health will permit him to prepare, for a future volume, a comprehensive view of the whole subject, from which may be deduced some formulæ exhibiting, with satisfactory clearness, the principles of organization that constitute the distinctive genius of American speech. The idea is held up, however, throughout his work, that the time has not yet come for that most desirable consummation.

Mr. Gallatin commenced his latest endeavor to point out some striking features common to all the numerous dialects, with the following disclaimer of qualification:

"The process by which languages are gradually formed, and a clear conception of the fundamental principles which distinguish those of America from those of other parts of the world, are subjects beyond my competence. Although I perceive, and am satisfied of, the similarity of character in the structure of all the known American languages, I cannot define with precision the general features common to all. I can only state those which, on a very superficial view of the subject, have struck me as characteristic; and it is with unfeigned diffidence that I submit some general and desultory observations."[1]

The peculiarity most frequently mentioned, as characteristic of the Indian idioms, is a tendency to accumulate a multitude of ideas in a single word. This process was called by William Von Humboldt, and by other philologists after him, *agglutination*. Mr. Duponceau preferred the term *polysynthetic*. Dr. Lieber suggested *encapsulated* (which is explained by Mr. Schoolcraft as applicable to those cases that are "clustered or botryoidal, thought exfoliating thought, as capsule within capsule, or box within box"), but endeavored to show that *holophrastic*—from two Greek words, signifying to speak or express the whole—best conveys a correct idea of the principle.[2]

---

[1] Trans. of Ethnol. Soc., II, 120.

[2] "*Coalescence*" is the word employed by Governor Cass. "The power of coalescence, if it may be so termed, possessed by the Indian languages, is one of their most extraordinary features. Words,

The process, in fact, is simply that of condensing a sentence into a single word; it may be by running the several words together, somewhat clipping a portion or all of them; or by using their most emphatic and expressive syllables, and inserting vowels or consonants when required for euphony. The Delaware word "*nadholineen*," is composed of the first syllable of the verb *naten*, to fetch, of the last syllable of the noun *amochol*, a boat, and of *ineen*, a termination giving a personal application to any word or phrase, and corresponding in sense to the English *us*. A free translation of the compound is, "Come and fetch us across the river in a canoe." In the condensed form it becomes a verb, that is conjugated through all the moods and tenses. The third person singular, indicative, is *nadholawall*—"He is fetched over the river in a canoe." In like manner, "*Wunaquim*," an acorn, is formed from *wunipach*, a leaf, *nach*, a hand, and *quim*, a nut. Thus it signifies the nut of a tree whose leaves are in the form of a hand.[1]

The Indian seldom makes use of terms that are either abstract or arbitrary. He does not say *a* tree, *a* man, or *a* horse; but the word employed indicates some particular tree, man, or horse, identified by certain qualities or circumstances connected with it, and often by the gender to which it belongs. Thus many ideas are embraced in a name; and a combination of words, or parts of words, suggesting all of them, is required in its construction.

Mr. Gallatin adduces, from the English, such words as "incompatibleness, incommunicableness, congregationalist, &c.," as not differing essentially, either in the number, nature, or arrangement of the elements of which they are composed, from a large portion of the Indian compounded words. But words derived from other languages, with changes to adapt them to English idioms, cannot be regarded as perfect analogies. There is a fine illustration of holophrasm in the perhaps fanciful derivation, that we have somewhere seen, which, from the Latin "*caro data vermibus*, deduces *ca-da-ver*, a dead body, or corpse.

The want of general and abstract terms would necessarily give rise to a polysynthetic method of expression, as the characteristics of every object of thought or observation must be included in the term that denotes it. The habit may have

---

and parts of words, are detached and attached so as to form others, conveying simple or complex ideas, and sometimes without any apparent connection between the new word and its roots."

The above is from an article in the *North American Review* of July, 1828, said to be written by Governor Cass. It is, professedly, a notice of one of Mr. Schoolcraft's publications, and also of a vindication of Heckewelder's Indian History communicated to the Historical Society of Pennsylvania by its President, William Rawle. It is, however, principally devoted to a repetition and justification of the doubts the writer had formerly expressed of the accuracy of Heckewelder's philosophical investigations and knowledge of the Delaware language, and to an exposition of his own views of the idioms of that and other Indian dialects. He differs from Edwards and Duponceau on some points of grammatical construction (perhaps it would be more correct to say, points of grammatical *definition*), but concurs in the general ethnological principle that, except in those elements of universal grammar which are common to all tongues, these languages have no affinity, either in etymology or construction, to any others that are known to us.

[1] These examples are taken from Heckewelder's Illustrations of Delaware Idioms, in his correspondence with Mr. Duponceau, Letter XVIII.

commenced with the names of persons and things, where, to some extent, it is common to all languages, and have been gradually extended to other parts of speech, in which its chief peculiarity consists.

Another feature of American languages, pronounced by Mr. Gallatin to be the most remarkable one, may, possibly, be attributed to the absence of the substantive verb *to be*, as an auxiliary. It is a controverted question, whether a true substantive verb—that is to say, one that conveys the abstract idea of existence—can be found in the American languages. But it is certain that, where we use the verb *to be* in connection with an attribute or a noun, that verb is omitted by the Indians, and the attribute or noun is converted into an intransitive verb. Instead of saying, I *am* cold, I *am* a man, the Indians say, "I cold," "I man," and the nouns "cold" and "man" become intransitive verbs, and are conjugated through all the persons, tenses, and moods, like other verbs; number and person being expressed by variations of the pronoun, while other distinctions are produced by inflexions of the word itself.

Nearly all parts of speech are, in like manner, convertible into verbs; and very nice varieties of action are indicated by the insertion of particles having the effect of adverbs, but having no separate existence as such. Thus, an action may be in contemplation, or on the point of execution; it may be done well or ill, quickly or otherwise, jointly, rarely, repeatedly, habitually, &c.; or doubt, denial, and various degrees of assertion, may be expressed—whether it rains hard, by showers, steadily, &c.—whether you see near, or far off, &c. &c.

By the joint means of agglomeration, and the use of particles and inflections, it will be seen that very delicate shades of meaning may be attained; but they are applicable only to the case in hand, and the expression cannot be made to serve a general or abstract purpose.

In some dialects, a form of plural has been noticed, that distinguishes between a particular number and an indefinite number of objects, and by some writers this has been termed "the American plural."

Extreme precision is, indeed, a general characteristic of American languages; and yet the masculine and feminine genders are not always clearly distinguished. The distinction made by most of the northern Indians is whether the object is animate or inanimate; and this is indicated with great care. A remarkable peculiarity, however, in relation to sex, may be mentioned, as a feature said to be common to all the American nations. While the terms for younger brother and younger sister are identical (except among the Iroquois), in expressing the various degrees and modifications of kindred, such as elder or younger brother or sister, paternal or maternal uncle or aunt, &c., the women use different words from the men; a habit that seems to be confined to that subject, or analogous ones.

We shall venture to specify no more peculiarities. It is only in its bearings upon ethnological questions that the philosophy of language has any connection with our purpose. Mr. Bancroft has undertaken to explain the characteristic features of the American languages in the third volume of his history. His description is at once elaborate and felicitously graphic. If not universally applicable in all its details, it is probably a correct analysis of the most prominent dialects of the United States. Speaking of the practice of agglutination, or synthesis, he says:

"If we search for the distinguishing traits of our American languages, we shall find the synthetic character pervading them all, and establishing their rules. The American does not separate the component parts of the proposition which he utters; he never analyzes his expressions; his thoughts rush forth in a troop. His speech is as a kindling cloud, not as radiant points of light. This absence of all reflective consciousness, and of all logical analysis of ideas, is the great peculiarity of American speech. Every complex idea is expressed in a group. Synthesis governs every form; it pervades all the dialects of the Iroquois and the Algonkin, and equally stamps the character of the language of the Cherokee."

"It has been asked if our Indians were not the wrecks of more civilized nations? Their language refutes the hypothesis; every one of its forms is a witness that their ancestors were, like themselves, not yet disenthralled from nature. The character of each Indian language is one continued, universal, all-pervading synthesis. They to whom these languages were the mother tongue, were still in that earliest stage of intellectual culture where reflection has not begun."[1]

Mr. Schoolcraft, in his Essay on the grammatical structure of the Algonkin language, one of the most extensive of Indian forms of speech, has intimated an opinion that it was built up from monosyllabic roots.[2] It is very probable that the same may have been the case with all American dialects; and, while they exhibit different degrees of advancement from that primitive condition (the Otomis, a rude and inferior tribe, retaining most of the original form) to whatever stage of refinement they may have attained, the system of progression has been determined by the laws of intellectual and physical organization peculiar to the race; hence the radical unity observable throughout the continent.[3] It may be, therefore, that the philosophy of American speech, the phenomena constituting its genius, will not be fully comprehended until the metaphysical, physiological, and possibly phrenological traits of the aborigines are accurately determined. The acuteness of the senses, especially that of hearing, exerts a material influence on the structure of language. Many compounded words of the Indians require a delicate articulation, and a very nice discrimination of tone, assisted by signs addressed to the eye. The predominance of certain faculties of mind, and the absence or inactivity of others, by which different families of men are distinguished, a prevailing temperament, and purely physical habits, all combine to constitute the mould in which the forms of speech are modelled; and where these attributes are the same, a similar linguistic system will be generated.

It is by no means improbable that the aspect of the question concerning the

---

[1] See also Mr. Prescott's "Conquest of Mexico," III, 393, *et seq.*

[2] Gov. Cass, N. A. Rev., XXVI, before referred to, makes a similar suggestion.

[3] The supposed grammatical isolation of the Otomi language has been questioned by Dr. Latham, "Varieties of Man," p. 408.

abnormal character of American forms of speech may be much modified hereafter, that the number of distinct dialects may be reduced, and that their apparent contrast to the grammatical systems of other nations may prove to be less marked than has been imagined.

It was suggested by Alexander Von Humboldt (who, although devoting less attention to philological studies than his brother William, shared with the latter his interest in American languages, and supplied a portion of his materials), that the rigid distinction between development by inflexion and the combination of agglutinated particles might not always bear the test of scrutiny.[1]

There are recent indications that the verb substantive, even as an auxiliary, may be discovered to exist in effect where it has been believed to be wanting. The indefinite article, and the masculine and feminine genders, are also claimed for some dialects.[2]

There are very few points asserted by any one philologist that are not questioned by some other. Mr. Gallatin's illustration of the permanency of dialects, derived from the supposed fact that the earliest vocabularies could still be used in communicating with the Indians, is opposed to the observation of Colonel Smith, who mentions having learned on the spot that the catechisms printed in the Huron and other languages, not quite a century ago, are now understood only in consequence of daily repetition and careful explanation.[3]

But notwithstanding contrarieties of opinion and testimony, the archæological inferences of principal importance that have been drawn from such inquiries are not materially disturbed. These are that the ancestors of the present Indians must have occupied this country, or have been separated from other nations, at a very remote—perhaps the remotest—period of history, and that proofs of connection with more civilized races are not manifest in their dialects.

Whatever discoveries may be claimed, or suggestions ventured, by partial observers, at variance with the judgment of those who have made the whole subject a matter of study, they cannot be regarded as entitled to similar confidence until they have received the sanction of investigations equally prolonged and extended.

A greater reliance may be placed upon the general uniformity of structure among the American languages, and a general diversity from those of the eastern hemi-

---

[1] Personal Narrative, 2d Lond. ed., III, 263–4.

[2] See "Grammar of the Dakota Language," by Rev. S. R. Riggs, Smithson. Contrib. IV.

Rev. Dr. Hawks, whose translation of the work of Rivero and Von Tschudi on Peruvian antiquities was published in 1853, says, in a note to the chapter on American languages, where the writers adopt and confirm from their own observations the conclusions of Duponceau and Gallatin: "He who has studied these most carefully will be most cautious in making general conclusions." And he cites, in confirmation of this view, the opinion of Mr. Wm. W. Turner, who has devoted a good deal of attention to the subject of American languages, and according to whose suggestions the Dakota grammar of Rev. S. R. Riggs was entirely remodelled before publication.

In another place, Dr. Hawks informs the reader that he is himself engaged in researches for "a work on the antiquities of America generally." Its completion will be looked forward to with interest.

[3] Nat. Hist. of the Human Species, p. 259.

sphere, than upon any exceptional instances that may be detected.[1] Thus while the question of foreign derivation may be left to stand or fall with that of the unity of the human species, the philological indications of extreme antiquity claimed for the American race as a variety of mankind will hardly be disputed.

There is a curious circumstance which deserves to be mentioned before leaving this subject. It is that the European language which has been pointed out as most nearly resembling those of the American aborigines, in its employment of the principle of agglutination, is the Basque or Euskarian; and this is supposed to have been a language of the *aborigines of Europe*, who, by the irruption of the Celts and Indo-Germanic races from the East, were either exterminated or driven to inaccessible regions. Of these the Lapps and Finns, and the Euskarians of the Biscayan provinces, have been regarded by some writers as the remnant.[2]

The physical attributes of aboriginal Americans have furnished arguments in favor of the unity and antiquity of the race, subject to an equal want of harmony of sentiment in regard to matters of fact.

As in what has been said of native languages the object has been to present the American view of the subject almost exclusively, for similar reasons the archæological deductions of the physiologist will be examined chiefly from the same point of observation.

The inquiry is not what opinions Buffon, Cuvier, Blumenbach, Prichard, Lawrence, Smith, and other writers on the natural history of man in general, have entertained concerning the origin and varieties of the human species—and reference to these must be brief and incidental—but the aim is to ascertain what impressions have been interwoven with ethnological studies and discussions here; what special comparisons have been instituted; and what substantial results, if any, have been reached by the scientific men of our own country.

There has been great unanimity among writers usually regarded as authorities, in considering the American race—not including the Eskimaux—as a distinct variety of human kind; and whatever deviations have been made from the systems of Linnæus, Buffon, and Blumenbach, this division has generally been retained by their successors.

The propriety of distinguishing between the occupants of the polar regions and other inhabitants of the continent has also been commonly recognized.[3]

---

[1] "Neither the analogy nor the diversity of language can suffice to solve the great problem of the filiation of nations."—*Humboldt, Personal Narrative,* III, 285.

"Humanity has a common character. The ingenious scholar may find analogies in language, customs, institutions, and religion, between the aborigines of America and any nation whatever of the Old World."—*Bancroft, Hist. of U. S.,* III, 312.

[2] Prof. Carpenter, in "Cyclop. of Anat. and Physiol.," p. 1349. Latham, in "Varieties of Man," p. 551, who quotes Arndt and Rask, distinguished Scandinavian ethnologists.

[3] "The Eskimaux are manifestly a race of men distinct from all the nations of the American continent, in language, in disposition, and in habits of life. But among all the other inhabitants of America there is such a striking similitude in the form of their bodies, and the qualities of their minds,

The physical resemblance of the residue of the original population to each other has impressed the observer more forcibly than any variations of form and color. It is mentioned by Robertson as remarkable, that there is less variety in the human form throughout the New World than in the ancient continent; and that the varieties in any single race of the Old World are greater than in the widely scattered inhabitants of the two Americas.

With this general uniformity among themselves, the striking similarity of the Americans to two other classes or varieties of the human species has been not less universally noticed.

Aside from the theories of multifarious origin, and of colonial settlements by civilized nations at different periods, the belief has prevailed, as stated in previous pages, that the physical, moral, and intellectual traits, as well as the arts and customs of the various tribes, were to be explained by tracing their descent from either the Northern or Southern Asiatics. These were often confounded under a common name, as Tartars or Scythians, but correspond to the separate divisions of Mongolian and Malay in Blumenbach's classification.

When opportunities of comparison were more rare than they have been since, it was customary to refer to the testimony of Smibert, the portrait painter, and Ledyard, the traveller, as having somewhat of the authority which in our courts of law is given to the evidence of *experts*. The first had painted several Tartars for the Duke of Tuscany; and when he arrived with Bishop Berkley at Newport, in 1739, and saw our Indians, he pronounced them to be the same people. The other, who had been familiar from boyhood with the Indians of Connecticut, declared the Mongolians of Siberia to be universally and substantially like the American natives.

Governor Pownal stated, in 1766, that "the American inhabitants are the same race of people from one end of the continent to the other; and are the same race

---

that, notwithstanding the diversities occasioned by the influence of climate, or unequal progress of improvement, we must pronounce them to be descended from one source."—*Robertson's Am.*, Lib. iv. p. 41.

"We ought to admit, as an established fact, that the Americans, whatever their origin may be, constitute, at the present day, a race essentially different from the rest of mankind. The truth of this proposition has been demonstrated by a long course of physiological observations."—*Malte Brun, Geog.*, Lib. lxxv.

"The nations of America, except those which border the polar circle, form a single race, characterized by the formation of the skull, the color of the skin, the extreme thinness of the beard, and the straight glossy hair."—*Humboldt's Researches*, Preface, p. 14.

"The fourth, or American variety, includes all the Americans, excepting the inhabitants of the northern parts of the Continent, which I have placed in the Mongolian division."—*Lawrence's Lectures*, p. 313.

"The aborigines of America, or those nations whose abode in the Western Continent dates from a period antecedent to history, may be said to form a well-marked division of the human family; from which, however, we ought to except the Esquimaux, and some other tribes."—*Prichard's Researches*, I, 268.

"The American race includes all the aborigines of the New World, except the Esquimaux."—*Wiseman's Lectures*, I, 167.

or family as the Tartars, precisely of the same color, of the same form of skull, of the same species of hair, not to mention the language and their names."[1]

Jefferson says, in his Notes on Virginia, "The resemblance between the Indians of America and the eastern inhabitants of Asia, would induce us to conjecture that the former are descendants of the latter, or the latter of the former; excepting, indeed, the Esquimaux, who, from the same circumstances of resemblance, and from identity of language, must be derived from the Greenlanders, and these, probably, from some of the northern parts of the old continent."[2]

Still, notwithstanding that kind of similitude which is best expressed by the phrase *tout ensemble*, a decided difference of particular features has been evident to careful observers. While pointing out the remarkable resemblance between the Americans, Mongols, and Malays, Alexander Von Humboldt refused to admit a necessary identity of race, asserting that, in fact, osteology teaches us that the cranium of the American differs essentially from that of the Mongol.[3]

In the very difficult operation of drawing lines of demarcation between the assumed varieties of mankind, some test more certain than color, or any merely external attribute, has been regarded as necessary. Camper and Blumenbach advanced the idea more than half a century ago that a comparison of *crania* was a principal requisite in such inquiries. But, according to Cardinal Wiseman, this conception of deriving from cranial peculiarities a basis of classification originated with our Provincial Governor, Thomas Pownal, who was equally remarkable for political sagacity and a love of philosophical research.[4] Camper has the merit of devising a rule by which the crania of different nations might be mutually compared, so as to give definite results, and his system of observation was matured and

---

[1] Knox's New Coll. of Voyages, II, 273.

[2] Notes on Virginia, p. 148.

In the Boston News Letter of June 29, 1749, is a notice of a meeting between three Indians from Greenland and two from Surinam, and some Delawares and Mohegans, at Bethlehem, in Pennsylvania, they being all converts of Moravian missionaries. Though their native lands were so wide asunder, "what they observed of each other's hair, eyes, and complexion, convinced them that they were all of the same race."

[3] "What we have been stating as to the exterior form of the indigenous Americans, confirms the accounts of other travellers of the striking analogy between the Americans and the Mongol race. This analogy is particularly evident in the color of the skin and hair, in the defective beard, high cheek bones, and in the direction of the eyes. We cannot refuse to admit that the human species does not contain races resembling one another more than the Americans, Mongols, Mantchoux, and Malays. But the resemblance of some features does not constitute an *identity* of race. In fact, osteology teaches us that the cranium of the American differs essentially from that of the Mongol; the former exhibits a facial line more inclined, though straighter, than that of the negro; and there is no race on the globe in which the frontal bone is more depressed backwards, or which has a less projecting forehead. The cheek bones of the American are almost as prominent as those of the Mongol; but the contours are more rounded, and the angles not so sharp. The under jaw is larger than the negro's, and its branches are less dispersed than the Mongol's. The occipital bone is less curved (bombé), and the protuberances which correspond to the *cerebellum*, to which the system of M. Gall attaches great importance, are scarcely sensible."—*Political Essay*, Black's trans., I, 153–155.

An equal difference in the form of the nose is noted in his Personal Narrative, III, 224, 2d Lond. ed.

[4] Wiseman's Lectures, 5th Lond. ed., I, 158.

materially improved by Blumenbach; while to the methods of these naturalists important additions have been suggested by Professor Owen.

Very high expectations were formed that more trustworthy conclusions would be derived from osteological comparisons than other methods of examination had yielded; and an eager desire was manifested to obtain from this country the means of tracing anatomically the affiliation of its people.[1]

Although the attention of scientific Americans was particularly called to this department of inquiry by the philosophers of Europe, its prosecution was attended with difficulties which only the most persevering zeal could overcome. Not only were cabinets of foreign crania beyond the reach of our students, but skulls of our aborigines, well authenticated with regard to the period and the tribe or race to which they belonged, were by no means easy to be obtained; yet a response creditable at once to the enterprise and the ability of American scholars has not been wanting.

In September, 1837, Dr. John C. Warren, of Boston, read before the British Association for the Advancement of Science a paper on crania found in western mounds. After stating that these crania differed from those of the present Indians, from the Caucasian or European, and from all existing nations so far as they are known, but had an exact resemblance to the ancient Peruvian heads, he remarked upon a degree of similarity shown by anatomy between the crania spoken of and those of the modern Hindoos. From all the facts he had observed he drew the following inferences:

"1st. The race whose remains were discovered in the mounds were different from the existing North American Indians. 2d. The ancient race of the mounds is identical with the ancient Peruvians." To these conclusions he thought others might be added tending to support existing opinions, but which are hypothetical:— "1st. That the ancient North American and the Peruvian natives were derived from the southern part of Asia. 2d. That America was peopled from at least two

---

Governor Pownal appears to have possessed a very suggestive mind, and one unusually quick and prospective in its perceptions. His political anticipations are among the most striking instances of foresight to be found on record. Cardinal Wiseman's reference is to a passage in Knox's "New Collection of Voyages," printed in 1766. In 1782, Governor Pownal published a treatise on the study of antiquities as the commentary to historical learning; with an appendix on the elements of speech, and the origin of written language. In 1787, appeared his "Hydraulic and Nautical Observations on the Currents in the Atlantic," in some measure anticipating the idea since realized by modern research. In 1795, he printed what he called "An Antiquarian Romance; endeavoring to mark a line by which the most ancient people, and the processions of the earliest inhabitant of Europe may be investigated," &c.

It is to be regretted that only a portion of his philosophical and ethnological treatises (which were numerous) are known to be in this country.

[1] "Let us hope," said Humboldt, "that the learned men who now honor the United States will hasten to convey the skeletons of the tumuli, and those of the caverns, to Europe, that they may be compared together, and with the present inhabitants of native race, as well as with the individuals of Malay, Mongol, and Caucasian race, found in the great collections of MM. Cuvier, Sœmmering, and Blumenbach."—*Personal Narrative*, VI, 319.

different parts of Asia; the ancient population having been derived from the south, and the present Indian race from the more northern part of the same continent."[1]

It will be noticed that these views, so far as they relate to the origin of population, are simply in accordance with such as had been long entertained, although previously founded on other than anatomical facts.

Dr. Warren's examinations, however carefully and scientifically conducted, were limited to a small number of crania; but a collection was then in progress, intended to be sufficiently numerous and varied to insure reliable results.

In 1830, Dr. Samuel G. Morton, of Philadelphia, already distinguished as a naturalist, having occasion to lecture on the form of the skull as exhibited in the five races of man, found himself unable to procure specimens of each for his illustrations. Impressed with this great scientific deficiency, he resolved upon making a collection himself.

By the most indefatigable exertions, and a large expenditure of time and money, he succeeded in obtaining a cabinet of crania superior to any in the world.[2] With these means he prepared his *Crania Americana*, which has been received by common consent into the highest ranks of that department of literature.[3] In 1842, he read before the Boston Society of Natural History an essay which was afterwards printed with the title of "An Inquiry into the Distinctive Characteristics of the Aboriginal Race of America." A second edition appeared in 1844, and in that year his *Crania Ægyptiaca* was published with the Transactions of the American Philosophical Society.

As having more elaborately than any predecessor investigated the comparative physiology of our aborigines, and applied to a greater extent those anatomical tests supposed to be most conclusive in determining national affinities, he must be regarded as representing the highest advance which that branch of science has made in this country. And more than this, his reputation abroad and at home as an able and learned ethnologist has given to his views a position of authority that

---

[1] Am. Journal of Science, XXXIV, 47.

[2] The cost to Dr. Morton was estimated at from ten to fifteen thousand dollars, and at the time of his death he had accumulated nearly a thousand human skulls, derived from all quarters of the globe.—*Dr. Patterson's Memoir of Morton, in "Types of Mankind."*

[3] "Crania Americana, or a Comparative View of the Skulls of the various Aboriginal Nations of North and South America. To which is prefixed an Essay on the Varieties of the Human Species." Philad. and Lond., 1839.

Alexander Von Humboldt addressed a complimentary letter to Dr. Morton in January, 1844, containing these expressive words:

"Les richesses craniologiques que vous avez été assez heureux de réunir, ont trouvé en vous un digne interprète. Votre ouvrage, Monsieur, est également remarquable par la profondeur des vues anatomiques, par le détail numérique des rapports de conformation organique, par l'absence des rêveries poétiques qui sont les mythes de la physiologie moderne, par les généralités dont votre 'Introductory Essay' abonde. Rédigeant dans ce moment le plus important de mes ouvrages, qui sera publié sous le titre imprudent de Kosmos, je saurai profiter de tant d'excellents aperçus sur la distribution des races humaines qui se trouvent épars dans votre beau volume. Que de sacrifices pécuniaires n'avez vous pas dû faire, pour atteindre une si grande perfection artistique, et produire un ouvrage qui rivalise avec tout ce que l'on a fait de plus beau en Angleterre et en France."

is not merely national, and one that can be yielded only to advantages and talents that are shown to be superior.[1]

Dr. Morton undertook to furnish for Mr. Schoolcraft's national work an article on the Physical Type of the American Indians; but his death occurring before the paper was completed, it was brought to a conclusion by his friend, John S. Phillips, Esq., to whom the *Crania Americana* was dedicated.[2]

The Inquiry into the Distinctive Characteristics of the Aboriginal Race contains a compendious view of the author's deductions in reference to the archæological points of which we are treating; and from that our condensed summary will be mainly, but not exclusively drawn.

Dr. Morton adopts the general divisions of mankind assumed by Blumenbach, simply substituting the word *race* for the term "variety" of the German author. While he admits the unity of the human species, he conceives that "each race was adapted from the beginning (by an all-wise Providence) to its peculiar local destination;" in other words, that "the physical characters which distinguish different races are independent of external causes." He regards the American race as possessing certain physical traits that serve to identify it in localities the most remote from each other. He divides the race into the "*Toltecan* family," or demi-civilized nations, and the "*American* family," which embraces all the barbarous tribes of the New World, excepting the Polar tribes, or Mongol Americans. The Eskimaux, and especially the Greenlanders, are held to be a partially mixed race, among whom the physical character of the Mongolian predominates, while their language presents obvious analogies to that of the Chippewas who border them on the south. The two "families" above mentioned are regarded as similar in physical, but less alike in intellectual attributes.

He says it is an adage among travellers that he who has seen one tribe of Indians has seen all, so much do individuals of this race resemble one another. All possess alike the long, black, lank hair, the brown skin, the heavy brow, the dull, sleepy eye, the full, compressed lips, and the salient, but dilated nose. Although physical diversities do occur, they are mere exceptions to a general rule, and do not alter the peculiar physiognomy of the Indian, which is as undeviatingly characteristic as that of the negro, and cannot be mistaken for that of any other race. This remark, he maintains, is equally applicable to the ancient and modern nations of our continent; for the oldest skulls from the Peruvian cemeteries, the tombs of Mexico, and the mounds of the United States, are of the same type as the heads of the most savage existing tribes. Their physical organization proves the origin of one to have been equally the origin of all. The various civilized nations are to this day represented by their lineal descendants, who inhabit their ancestral seats, and differ in no respect from the wild and uncultivated Indian. He had been of opinion that the ancient Peruvians who inhabited the confines of Lake Titicaca

---

[1] "The magnificent publication of Dr. Morton, which far exceeds in its comprehensiveness, and in the number and beauty of its engravings, any European work that has yet appeared on national varieties of the skull, comprises nearly the sum of our information on the distinctive characters of the head and skeleton in the several tribes of the New World."—*Prichard, Nat. Hist. of Man*, 4th ed. II, 502.

[2] Hist. and Prosp. of the Indian Tribes, II, 315.

presented a congenital form of head entirely different from that which characterizes the great American race, but believed it to have been fully established by the observations of M. D'Orbigny that the peculiarities of shape were wholly artificial, and the result of pressure in infancy.[1]

The osteological characters are thus detailed in Dr. Morton's latest production: "The Indian skull is of a decidedly rounded form. The occipital portion is flattened in the upward direction, and the transverse diameter, as measured between the parietal bones, is remarkably wide, and often exceeds the longitudinal line. The forehead is low and receding, and rarely arched as in the other races; a feature that is regarded by Humboldt, Lund, and other naturalists, as a characteristic of the American race, and serving to distinguish it even from the Mongolian. The cheek bones are high, but not much expanded; the whole maxillary region is salient and ponderous, with teeth of a corresponding size, and singularly free from decay. The orbits are large and squared, the nasal orifice wide, and the bones that protect it arched and expanded. The lower jaw is massive, and wide between the condyles; but, notwithstanding the prominent position of the face, the teeth are for the most part vertical."[2]

Such are the traits indicated by a comparison of upwards of four hundred crania of tribes inhabiting almost every region of North and South America. It is stated that the acute angles of the eyes seldom present the obliquity so common in the Malays and Mongolians; that the color of the eye is almost uniformly between black and gray; and that, even in young persons, it seldom has the brightness, or expresses the vivacity, usual in the more civilized races.

The *moral* constitution of the Americans is regarded as not less specific than the physical, and as equally pervading the entire race. The *intellectual* appears to exhibit greater diversity, and Dr. Morton has arbitrarily grouped the aborigines into two families: one embracing the tribes which had made advances in civilization, and termed by him *Toltecan;* the other, a more numerous division, consisting of those remaining in a barbarous condition, which he calls *American.* These appellations are by no means satisfactory or distinctive, unless the Toltecans are

---

[1] It will be seen, on subsequent pages, that this curious question continues to be involved in its original obscurity. Humboldt wrote, in 1808, "This extraordinary flatness is found among nations to whom the means of producing artificial deformity are totally unknown, as is proved by the crania of Mexican Indians, Peruvians, and Atures, brought over by M. Bonpland and myself, of which several were deposited in the Museum of Natural History at Paris. I am inclined to believe that the barbarous custom which prevails among several hordes of pressing the heads of children between two boards, had its origin in the idea that beauty consists in such a form of the frontal bone as to characterize the race in a decided manner."—*Political Essay,* I, 154.

Dr. Morton, when he published his *Crania Americana,* concurred in this view, but was led to change his opinions by the statements of D'Orbigny, who was supposed to have proved, by an examination of the tombs of the ancient race, that the greater number of crania were not flattened; that the peculiarity was confined to the men; and, as the most ill-shaped heads were found in the largest and finest tombs, that the deformity was a mark of distinction. Traces of the bandages and the mode of their application were also believed to be clearly discernible.—*L'homme Américain considéré sous ses Rap. Phys. et Mor., par Alcide D'Orbigny.* 1839.

[2] Schoolcraft's Hist. and Prosp., &c., II, 316.

regarded as a different race from the Americans, which is expressly denied. It is remarked that the civilized states do not stand isolated from their barbarous neighbors, but that these gradually merge into each other, so that some nations are with difficulty classed with either division, and that the diversity is not greater than has been known to exist between the same people, in other parts of the world, at different periods of their history. The intellectual disparity that is pointed out as existing between the Mongolians and Malays, and the more barbarous Americans, would seem to admit of some qualification. The latter are regarded as decidedly of an inferior nature; as not only averse to the restraints of education, but, for the most part, incapable of a continued process of reasoning upon abstract subjects; as wanting mechanical ingenuity, and as possessing but an humble grade of the imitative faculty. "Savage or civilized, the sea has had few charms for the American, and his navigation has been almost exclusively confined to lakes and rivers, and a canoe, excavated from a single log, has been his principal vessel. On the other hand, the Mongolians and Malays are proverbially aquatic in their habits, and exhibit a considerable degree of mechanical contrivance. Their greater constructiveness is exhibited in their dwellings, as well as in their implements and utensils, while an absence of the courage, cunning, cruelty, and improvidence, that are so habitual in the red man, is characteristic of the moral nature of the Eskimaux. These people, too, are remarkable for a large and rather elongated head, which is low in front and projecting behind; great width and flatness of the face; eyes small and black; mouth small and round; and nose so diminutive and depressed that, on looking at a skull in profile, the nasal bones are hardly visible. Their complexion, moreover, is comparatively fair, and there is a tendency throughout life to fulness and obesity. It is stated by the traveller Hearne that the Indian tribes who are their proximate neighbors on the south once excused an unprovoked massacre of Eskimaux men, women, and children, by asserting that they were a people of a different nature and origin from themselves."

Dr. Morton adverts to the opinion of Gallatin, that analogies of words and grammatical forms prove the cognate relation of the Eskimaux and other Indians. This he pronounces a mere postulate. "For, from the evidence adduced in respect to the ethnographic difference between these people, we have a right to infer that the resemblance in their respective languages has not been derived by the greater from the lesser source—not by the Americans from the Eskimaux—but the reverse; for the Asiatics, having arrived at various periods, and in small parties, would naturally, if not unavoidably, adopt more or less of the language of the people among whom they settled, until their own dialects finally merged in those of the Indians who bound them on the south."[1]

In addition to what has been said of the Mongolian features, as seen in the Eskimaux, it is remarked that there are some characters so prevalent as to pervade all the ramifications of the great Mongolian stock, from the repulsive Calmuck

---

[1] Latham seems to accord with Morton on this point. "Physically, the Eskimaux is a Mongol and Asiatic; philologically, he is an American, at least in respect to the principles upon which his speech is constructed."—*Varieties of Man*, p. 288.

to the polished and more delicately featured Chinese. These are, the small, depressed, and seemingly broken nose; the oblique position of the eye, which is drawn up at the external angle; the great width between the cheek bones, which are not only high but expanded laterally; the arched and linear eyebrow; and, lastly, the complexion, which is invariably some shade of yellow or olive, and almost equally distant from the fair tint of the European and the red hue of the Indian. "In fine," says Dr. Morton, "we are constrained to believe that there is no more resemblance between the Indian and Mongolian, in respect to arts, architecture, mental features, and social usages, than exists between any other two distinct races of mankind."

In reference to the idea that America has been peopled by the Malay race (which, in the ordinary classification, includes the Malays proper of the Indian Archipelago and the Polynesians in all their numberless localities), it is said: "These people have so much of the Mongolian character, that nearly the same objections arise to both. The head of the Malay proper is more like that of the Indian, because it not unfrequently presents something of the vertical form of the occiput, and the transverse diameter, as measured between the parietal bones, is also remarkably large. But, excepting in these respects, the osteological development coïncides with that of the Mongolian; while the category of objections urged against the latter people is equally valid in respect to the whole Malay race."

The various points alluded to in the above summary, are discussed by Dr. Morton with force and ability, and his essay closes with the following comprehensive declaration:

"Our own conclusion, long ago deduced from a patient examination of the facts thus briefly and inadequately stated, is, that the American race is essentially separate and peculiar, whether we regard it in its physical, its moral, or its intellectual relations. To us, there are no direct or obvious links between the people of the Old World and the New; for, even admitting the seeming analogies to which we have alluded, these are so few in number, and evidently so casual, as not to invalidate the main position. And, even if it should be hereafter shown that the arts, sciences, and religion of America can be traced to an exotic source, I maintain that the organic characters of the people themselves, through all their endless ramifications of tribes and nations, prove them to belong to one and the same race, and that this race is distinct from all others."

These are the views that have, in substance, been repeated by Dr. Morton in various connections, and at different periods. In one place he says: "I can aver that sixteen years of almost daily comparisons have only confirmed me in the conclusions announced in my *Crania Americana,* that all the American nations, excepting the Eskimaux, are of one race, and that this race is peculiar and distinct from all others."[1]

In one of his papers he observes: "I regard the American nations as the true *autochthones*—the primæval inhabitants of this vast continent—and when I speak of their being of one race and of one origin, I allude only to their indigenous

[1] "Ethnography and Archæology of the American Aborigines," p. 9. New Haven, 1846.

relation to each other, as shown in all those attributes of mind and body which have been so amply illustrated by modern ethnography."[1] He admits that there might have been, in ancient times, occasional or accidental immigrations from the Old World, though too small to affect materially the language or the type of the Aborigines.[2]

The subject of American ethnology passes so insensibly into the general question of the original unity or diversity of mankind, that it is not easy to refer to the various forms and shades of opinion pertaining to a consideration of the former without an appearance of entering a field of contention which it is desirable to avoid. Yet the convictions of men of science, that may be supposed to influence, more or less directly, the manner of regarding the archæological problem of primeval population in this country, cannot be entirely excluded from these pages on account of the polemical associations they have acquired. Whether man was created in one pair, or in many pairs, in one locality or in many localities, is an inquiry that forces itself into the study of any division of his history. Its discussion has added to the interest of philological and physiological investigations, but has no other necessary bearing upon the proper theme of this memoir, than as it affects the question of the derivation of the American aborigines from any other people within the historical period. In alluding briefly to these collateral elements of opinion, it is intended to observe strictly the rule of the Ethnological Society of Paris, in relation to the vexed point of dispute: "Dans l'état actuel de nos connaissances, la question est insoluble au point de vue scientifique et ne peut être utilement débattue. Or telle a toujours été a cet égard l'opinion adoptée et la ligne de conduite suivie par la Société Ethnologique."[3]

Dr. Morton endeavored to avoid the topic in his principal work; but as his sentiments were freely declared in subsequent publications, they are usually blended with his purely technical exposition of American physiology. They have been made more prominent by the authors of "Types of Mankind" in connection with a "*Sketch of the natural provinces of the animal world, and their relation to the different types of man,*" contributed by Professor Agassiz.[4] The elevated standing of these

---

[1] Trans. of the Am. Ethnol. Soc., II, 219.

[2] In noticing a few of the hypotheses that have been formed to solve the problem of the origin of the monuments of America, independently of any agency of the aboriginal race, Dr. Morton refers to the opinion which has been advanced, that they are the work of a branch of the great Cyclopean family of the old world, known by the various designations of the Shepherd Kings of Egypt, the Anakim of Syria, the Oscans of Etruria, and the Pelasgians of Greece. *Wandering Masons* they were also called, and are supposed to have passed from Asia into America at a very early epoch of history, and to have built the more ancient monuments which are attributed to the Toltecan nation.

It is probable that he had in his mind an article on Mexican antiquities in the *Foreign Quarterly Review* for October, 1836, where the proposition is maintained that the Toltecans were a branch of the Shepherd Kings, or Cyclopeans—that is, they were Canaanites. "The builders of the Cyclopean monuments of Palenque, &c. &c., were the Anakim or Cyclopean family of Syria, who, with their brethren the Canaanites, were vanquished or expelled by Joshua"—thus reviving the theory of President Styles.

[3] Bulletin de la Société, 1846, p. 81.

[4] TYPES OF MANKIND, or Ethnological researches, based upon the ancient monuments, paintings,

prominent naturalists gives great weight, and a high degree of scientific interest, to whatever conclusions have resulted from their researches.

They both disavow any inconsistency between their theories and a rational interpretation of Scripture, and they claim that these involve no greater latitude of construction than geologists require for their material systems. They assert the moral and physical unity of the human species, which they do not imagine to be dependent on a common parentage, but regard as possessing a common and indivisible nature under whatever varieties of aspect and manifestation it is acknowledged to be found.

The deductions from natural science of Professors Morton and Agassiz, as applied to both local and general ethnology, are materially relied on in the work of Messrs. Nott and Gliddon; and those of Dr. Morton, in particular, are represented as the basis of that extended dissertation.[1]

Without attempting an analysis of the doctrines there maintained, or aiming to follow the order of their discussion, we may state, in a condensed form, some of the leading paleological propositions which relate to this continent, as follows:—

"There exists no data by which we can approximate the date of man's first appearance upon earth; and for aught we yet know, it may be thousands or millions of years beyond our reach."

"*Human Fossil Remains* have now been found so frequently, and in circumstances so unequivocal, that the facts can hardly be denied."

"Geology finds the oldest landmarks in America."

"The human fossils of Brazil and Florida, carry back the aboriginal population of this continent far beyond the necessity of hunting for American man's foreign origin through Asiatic immigration."

"The form of these (fossil) crania, moreover, proves that the general *type* of races inhabiting America at that inconceivably remote era was the same which prevailed at the period of the Columbian discovery."

"There are natural relations between the different types of man and the animals and plants inhabiting the same regions."

"The laws which regulate the diversity of animals, and their distribution upon the earth, apply equally to man, *within the same limits, and in the same degree.*"

"Not a single animal, bird, reptile, fish or plant, was common to the Old and New Worlds."

---

sculptures, and crania of races, and upon their natural, geographical, philological, and biblical history: Illustrated by selections from the inedited papers of Samuel George Morton, M. D., and by additional contributions from Prof. L. Agassiz, LL. D.; W. Usher, M. D.; and Prof. H. S. Patterson, M. D. By J. C. Nott, M. D., and Geo. R. Gliddon. 1854.

[1] Dr. Nott, in his *Introduction*, says: "It will be observed that, with the exception of Morton's, we seldom quote works on the Natural History of Man, and simply for the reason that their arguments are all based, more or less, on fabled analogies, which are at last proved by the monuments of Egypt and Assyria to be worthless. The whole method of treating the subject is herein changed. To our point of view, most that has been written on human natural history becomes obsolete; and therefore we have not burdened our pages with citations from authors, even the most erudite and respected, whose views we consider the present work to have, in the main, superseded."

These passages, taken almost at random, indicate the bearing of the argument upon the archæology of this continent.

The writers have aimed to construct a theory of human natural history from purely scientific facts and archæological discoveries.

The monuments of Egypt and Assyria, as explained by Belzoni, Champollion, Rossellini, Wilkinson, Lepsius, Layard, and others, are regarded as sources of reliable chronology, and, under the physiological expositions of Morton, as illustrating the original types of man. The geological and palæontological revelations of nature are studied, in preference to records and traditions, for light upon human origins; and in the general harmony, consistency, and uniformity of physical laws, and the mutual relations of the phenomena of the natural world, are professedly sought the means of solving the mystery of the creation and distribution of all organized beings.

Considered from this point of view, and without reference to any theological speculations or controversial disquisitions, in which the authors have indulged, their work is an exponent of a method of inquiry which might be expected to yield interesting results.

Professor Agassiz, in his contribution to this work, points out the manner in which the physical and organic features of the American continents vary from those of the Old World. In the Old World, the tropical realms are in strong contrast to the temperate zone; tropical Africa has hardly any species of animals in common with Europe; tropical Asia differs equally from its temperate regions; and Australia forms a world by itself. On the contrary, the range of mountains which extends in almost unbroken continuity from the Arctic zone to Cape Horn, establishes a similarity between North and South America, which may be traced also to a great extent in its plants and animals. Entire families, which are peculiar to this continent, have their representatives in both Americas. "Thus, with due qualification, it may be said that the whole continent of America is characterized by a much greater uniformity of its natural productions, combined with a special localization of many of its subordinate types, which will justify the establishment of many special faunæ within its boundaries." "With these facts before us, we may expect that there should be no great diversity among the tribes of man inhabiting this continent. At the same time it should be remembered, that in accordance with the zoological character of the whole realm, this race is divided into an infinite number of small tribes, presenting more or less difference one from another."

In the chapter on *The Aboriginal Races of America*, by Dr. Nott, it is remarked that, in treating of American races, the purpose is "simply to bring forward such facts as may be sufficient to establish their origin and antiquity," without going into details "respecting the infinitude of types which compose them." Having shown, as he thinks, "that the major divisions of the earth, or its different zoological provinces, were populated by groups of races bearing to each other certain family resemblances, notwithstanding that, in reality, these races originated in nations, and not in a single pair—thus forming proximate but not identical species"—he adduces the Mongols, the Caucasians, the Negroes, the Americans, as each constituting a group of this kind. He considers it as acknowledged by all travellers that there is among the latter people a pervading type, a family resemblance, quite as strong, for example, as that seen at the present day among the full-blooded Jews; yet, although every tribe has some characters that mark it as *American,* there are certain sharply drawn distinctions among some of these races which cannot be explained by climatic influences. The two divisions adopted by Morton (viz: the Toltecan and the Barbarous tribes) are taken as illustrations. The first (says Dr. Nott) "comprising all the semi-civilized nations of Mexico, Peru, and Bogota, who, there is every reason to believe, were the builders of the great system of mounds found throughout North America," possessed certain cerebral peculiarities distinguishing them from the savage tribes by whom "the semi-civilized communities of America seem at all times to have been hemmed in and pressed upon as they are at the present day." Mr. Phillips's *Appendix* to Morton's memoir on *The Physical Type of the American Indians,* in the second volume of Mr. Schoolcraft's large work, and Mr. George Combe's phrenological remarks in the *Appendix* to Morton's *Crania Americana,* are quoted in explanation of this difference. According to these writers, the barbarous tribes have larger brains than those races capable of considerable progress in civilization, but the animal propensities outweigh and subordinate the intellectual portion of the character; while in the Mexicans and Peruvians, "the intellectual lobe of the brain is at least as large, and the intellectual and moral qualities being not so subordinate to the propensities and violent passions, are left more free to act."

This attempt to explain why races possessing an apparently inferior phrenological organization should exhibit superior reflective and inventive capacities, is accompanied by the following corollary:—

"These facts afford very instructive material for reflection. We here behold one race, with the larger though less intellectual brain, subjugating the unwarlike and half-civilized races; and it seems clear that the latter were destined to be either swallowed up or exterminated by the former. Who can doubt that similar occurrences had been going on over this continent for many centuries, or even thousands of years? There are scattered over North America countless tumuli, which it is believed were built by races different from the savage tribes found around them on the advent of the whites, and an impenetrable oblivion rests upon these earth-works. There are many reasons for supposing that these mound-builders were either identical with, or closely allied to, the Toltecs; and that they were driven south, or exterminated by more savage and bellicose races."

Dr. Nott expresses the opinion that the opposite intellectual and physical characters in the two great American families cannot be explained "except by primitive cranial formations, each aboriginally distinct;" and regards it "as more probable that each of these families, instead of springing from a single pair, have originated in many."

After quoting from the *Christian Examiner* of July, 1850, the views of Professor Agassiz upon the natural origin of speech, in which a parallel is drawn between the analogy in sound and structure of the languages of kindred nations and the similarity of intonation of the notes of closely allied species of birds, he suggests, in explanation of the general uniformity of structure of the American languages, that among races osteologically allied, and possessing physical characters and instincts in common, it is probable that their primitive languages would more or less resemble each other; and that all languages which, in their infant state, come together, would necessarily become fused into one heterogeneous mass, after a period of more than five thousand years, for which, he considers, there is every reason to believe that this continent has been inhabited.

Dr. Nott presents his conclusions respecting the aboriginal races of America in the form of eight propositions, viz:—

"1. That the continent of America was unknown, not only to the ancient Egyptians and Chinese, but to the more modern Greeks and Romans.

2. That at the time of its discovery, this continent was populated by millions of people resembling each other, possessing peculiar moral and physical characteristics, and in utter contrast with any people of the Old World.

3. That the races were found surrounded everywhere by animals and plants specifically different from those of the Old World, and created, as it is conceded, in America.

4. That these races were found speaking several hundred languages, which, although often resembling each other in grammatical structure, differed, in general, entirely, in their vocabularies, and were all radically distinct from the languages of the Old World.

5. That their monuments, as seen in their architecture, sculpture, earth-works, shell-banks, &c., from their extent, dissemination, and incalculable numbers, furnish evidence of very high antiquity.

6. That the state of decomposition in which the skeletons of the mounds are found, and, above all, the peculiar anatomical structure of the few remaining crania, prove these mound-builders to have been both ancient and indigenous to the soil; because American crania, antique as well as modern, are unlike those of any other race of ancient or recent times.

7. That the aborigines of America possessed no alphabet, or truly phonetic system of writing—that they possessed none of the domestic animals, nor many of the oldest arts of the eastern hemisphere; whilst their agricultural plants were indigenous.

8. That their system of arithmetic was unique—that their astronomical knowledge, in the main, was indubitably of cis-atlantic origin; while their calendar was unlike that of any people, ancient or modern, of the other hemisphere."

"Whatever exception," he adds, "may be taken to any of these propositions separately, it must be conceded that, when viewed together, they form a mass of cumulative testimony, carrying the aborigines of America back to the remotest period of man's existence on earth."

The extracts from Morton's inedited MSS., and Dr. Usher's chapter entitled "Geology and Palæontology, in connection with Human Origins," contain a summary of accounts, claiming to be authentic, of discoveries of human bones in a fossilized state.

Omitting the references to those of foreign lands, we find enumerated a human skeleton preserved in the museum at Quebec, that was dug out of the solid schist-rock on which the citadel stands; several skeletons from Guadaloupe, preserved in European cabinets, found in a rock described as "harder under the chisel than the finest statuary marble;" human fossils discovered by Dr. Lund, the Danish naturalist, in eight different localities, among the calcareous caves of Brazil, in connection with those of extinct species of animals—all represented as incorporated with a very hard breccia; and, from the same source, a human skull taken out of a sandstone rock now overgrown with lofty trees. Remains of a similar character, although from positions supposed to be less unequivocal, found in Mississippi and Florida, by Dr. Dickeson and others, are also named. All of these, it is believed, had previously been the subjects of communications to learned societies, with testimony in favor of their geological antiquity, and their cranial conformity to the aboriginal American type, exhibiting, in some instances, as stated, the American peculiarity of configuration in an excessive degree.[1] The concluding passage of Dr. Morton's inedited MSS. contains this prediction: "I have no doubt that man will yet be found as low down as the Eocene deposits, and that he walked the earth with the Megalonyx and Palæotherium."

The following is quoted by Dr. Usher as the language of Professor Agassiz, at Mobile, in April, 1853:—

---

[1] Am. Phil. Soc. Trans., III, 286–296: Communication from C. D. Meigs, M. D., on the human bones found at Santos, in Brazil. Am. Journ. of Science, &c., XXXII, 361: Dr. Moultrie's description of the skull of the Guadaloupe fossil human skeleton. Proceed. of Phila. Acad. of Nat. Sciences, Dec., 1844: Lieut. Strain's letter to Dr. Morton, respecting Dr. Lund's discoveries. Mémoirs de la Soc. Royale des Antiquaires du Nord, 1845–'49, pp. 49–77: Communication from Dr. Lund. Dr. Lund states that the remains examined by him manifested not only the cranial characteristics common to the American and the Mongol, and also those peculiar to the American; but a form of teeth unknown among existing races of men, which, being found alike in young and old, he believed to be natural, although resembling a conformation noticed among Egyptian mummies, and ascribed to attrition. On this point Dr. Morton refrains from expressing an opinion for want of opportunities of personal observation.

Dr. Lund declares his belief that South America was inhabited, not only in remote historical times, but also probably in the geological eras, as many species of animals seem to have disappeared since the existence of man in this hemisphere; and that the race of men occupying this part of the world in ages the most remote, was, as to its general type, the same that was found by European discoverers. He remarks, that the cranial conformation of the Americans, similar but inferior to that of the Mongols, has led to the supposition that the former were Mongolians who had degenerated as a result of emigration; but that this opinion is opposed by the fact that no indication of an ancient superior development is found. Moreover, if we consider that nature habitually advances from the imperfect to the perfect, that this part of the world is, according to geological evidence, of a date anterior to what is commonly called the Old World, and that an examination of the caves referred to leads to an admission of the antiquity of its original inhabitants, while the primitive type has continued without change, there is good reason, he thinks, to entertain an opinion the reverse of that which would establish a relation between the Mongolian and American races. He mentions, in a note, that the interior plateau of Brazil is composed of horizontal strata of the transition period, which are nowhere covered with the secondary or tertiary formations; which proves that the New World was elevated above the sea before the secondary period, so as to form an extensive continent. No part of the Old World, to his knowledge, presented the same phenomenon to such an extent that an equal antiquity could be attributed to it.

"Respecting the fossil remains of the human body I possess from Florida, I can only state that the identity with human bones is beyond all question; the parts preserved being the *jaws with perfect teeth*, and portions of a foot. They were discovered by my friend, Count F. D. Portales, in a bluff upon the shores of Lake Munroe, in Florida. The mass in which they were found, is a conglomerate of rotten coral-reef limestone and shells, mostly *Ampullarias* of the same species now found in St. John River, which drains Lake Monroe. The question of their age is more difficult to answer. To understand it fully, it must be remembered that the whole peninsula of Florida has been formed by the successive growth of coral reefs, added concentrically from north to south to those first formed, and the accumulation between them of decomposed corals and fragments of shells; the corals prevailing in some parts, as in the everglades, and in others the shells, as about St. Augustine and Cape Sable. Upon this marine limestone formation, and its inequalities, fresh-water lakes have been collected, inhabited by animals, the species of which are now still in existence, as are, also, along the shores, the marine animals, remains of which may be found in the coral formation. To this lacustrine formation belongs the conglomerate containing the human bones mentioned above; and it is more than I can do to establish, with precision, the date of its deposition. This, however, is certain, that Upper Florida, as far south as the head-waters of the St. John, constituted already a prominent peninsula before Lake Okeechobee was formed; and that the whole of the southern extremity of Florida extends for more than three degrees of latitude south of the fresh-water system of the northern part of the peninsula.

"If we assume that rate of growth to be one foot in a century, from a depth of seventy-five feet, and that every successive reef has added ten miles of extent to the peninsula (which assumption is doubling the rate of increase furnished by the evidence we now have of the additions forming upon the reef and keys south of the main land), it would require 135,000 years to form the southern half of the peninsula.

"Now, assuming further, which would be granting by far too much, that the surface of the northern half of the peninsula, already formed, continued for nine tenths of that time a desert waste, upon which the fresh waters began to accumulate before the fossiliferous conglomerate could be formed (though we have no right to assume that it stood so for any great length of time), there would still remain 10,000 years during which, it should be admitted, that the mainland was inhabited by man and the land and fresh-water animals, vestiges of which have been buried in the deposits formed by the fresh waters covering parts of its surface. So much for the probable age of our conglomerate."[1]

Dr. Usher says the phenomena of geology "establish not only that South America was inhabited by an ancient people long before the discovery of the new continent, or that the population of this part of the world must have preceded all historical notice of their existence—they demonstrate that aboriginal man in

---

[1] For a general account of bones of man among organic remains, see *Smith's Nat. Hist. of the Human Species*, pp. 93–110.

America antedates the Mississippi alluvia, because his bones are fossilized; and that he can even boast of a geological antiquity, because numerous species of animals have been blotted from creation since American humanity's first appearance. The form of the crania, moreover, proves that the general *type* of races inhabiting America at that inconceivably remote era was the same which prevailed at the period of the Columbian discovery; and this consideration may spare science the trouble of any further speculation on the modes through which the New World became peopled by immigration from the Old."

In the chapter on the comparative anatomy of races, Dr. Nott maintains that the distinctions between the Americans and the Polynesians are marked and decisive; that, with perhaps some very partial exceptions along the Pacific coast, the types of America are entirely distinct from those of Oceanica; and that American languages, civilization, social institutions, &c., are utterly opposed to Oceanic influence. "It is," he says, "from the so-called Polynesian and Malay races, that many writers have derived the population of America; yet in no two types of man do we find cranial characters more widely different." * * * "The American heads differ more widely from all Oceanic crania than they do even from those of the Chinese, or true Mongol races. The Oceanic races, including even the Sandwich Islanders, when compared with our Indians, exhibit crania more elongated, more compressed laterally, less prominent at the vertex, and more prognathous in type. American races are strongly distinguished by the reverse of all these points, in addition to their own greatly flattened occiput."

The suggestions, speculations, and opinions, collected in the volume now under notice, had, for the most part, been previously advanced in some less connected and more incidental shape—in lectures, in papers communicated to learned societies, in essays, prefaces, and casual discussions, but had not been deliberately applied in this country to the construction of an entire ethnological system.

In whatever form the views there combined have heretofore found expression, they have been earnestly opposed in the United States, as elsewhere, by those who have deemed them unsound and objectionable. They are to be regarded as individual sentiments, which, as elements of opinion, are entitled to a place with other materials out of which theories relating to our subject have arisen.

The late Dr. Samuel Forrey, of New York, published in the *American Biblical Repository* of July, 1843, an elaborate essay, entitled "Unity of the Human Race confirmed by the Natural History of the American Aborigines." From this we have desired to select salient passages that might be set against those which have been quoted of an opposite bearing; but the subject is treated in a manner that is unfavorable to such a purpose. The investigation is not a technically scientific one, nor does it aim to add to the existing materials of opinion. Receiving Dr. Morton's statements of facts, but rejecting his inferences, Dr. Forrey's design was to show that the former do not necessarily conflict with the reasoning of Prichard, Lawrence, and other naturalists, who believe in the singleness of human origin. He gives a list of authors on the natural history of man, and of writers on American antiquities, whose works he had carefully studied in reference to his subject, and states his proposition thus: "What we propose to demonstrate is, that revelation and science are both beams of light emitted from the same Sun of Eternal Truth. As truth can never be in opposition to truth, so it has been found that many investigations into the laws of natural science, which were thought at first to conflict with Holy Writ, have been discovered in the end, as will be shown in this inquiry into the *unity of the human family,* to afford confirmation and elucidation of its divine truths."

He maintains that there is nothing in the position of America that forbids the supposition of an exotic origin of its primitive inhabitants, and that Morton's conclusion that there are no direct or obvious links between the people of the Old World and the New, can be successfully refuted. In his argument it is not claimed that his facts are new, or the views original. They are mainly derived from the great authorities upon human history, in whose larger field of reasoning the inquirer can seek a solution of the doubts which partial or local observations may engender. "Any one," says Dr. Forrey, "who allows himself to speculate upon this subject, will, at first view, be inclined to adopt the opinion, that every part of the world had originally its indigenous inhabitants—*autochthones*—adapted to its physical circumstances. By this hypothesis a ready solution is afforded of some of the most difficult questions presented in the investigation of the physical history of mankind. * * But many of these obscurities will be made to disappear before the light of science, like mist before the morning sun; thus reconciling, in many points, science and revelation." We believe Dr. Forrey first introduced, in this connection, that striking illustration of the tendency of physical organization to modify its characters in conformity to external circumstances which is found in the fact that fishes, in the sunless waters of the Mammoth Cave, have no eyes.

The archæological conclusions of his essay are, that all our aborigines, with the exception, perhaps, of the Eskimaux, have the same origin; that the emigration of the Eskimaux tribes is of comparatively recent date, while the arrival of what is considered an aboriginal race dates back to the earliest ages of mankind, and cannot be said to be derived from any nation, or variety of mankind, now existing; but it is assimilated by so many analogies to the most ancient type of civilization in the eastern hemisphere, that the character of its civilization cannot be regarded as wholly indigenous.[1]

In 1850, public attention was particularly drawn to these questions, not only by reviews and debates at scientific meetings, but by more elaborate efforts to meet and overcome whatever objections had been started to the commonly received doctrine of human descent. The treatises of Drs. Bachman and Smyth, having imme-

[1] A brief article by Dr. Forrey, under the title of "Considerations on the Distinctive Characteristics of the American Aboriginal Tribes" is inserted in Vol. IV of Mr. Schoolcraft's general work. The American *variety* is there regarded as having a relation to the Caucasian and Mongolian, as the Malay variety has a relation to the Caucasian and the Ethiopian, they being merely intervening shades of those leading types.

diate reference to the conclusions of Morton and Agassiz, appeared in that year.[1] They both emanated from Charleston, South Carolina, a city which has been distinguished for the attention given to natural science by its literary men, and in some branches (that of herpetology, for example), has taken the lead in this country. Dr. Bachman's argument is based, to a great extent, upon his personal observations and researches as a naturalist; whilst that of Dr. Smyth is chiefly historical and theological. Neither of them alludes, except incidentally, to the origin of American population, and they do not profess to have given special attention to that inquiry.

Dr. Bachman, however, places his private observations in opposition to Dr. Morton's belief of a physical diversity between the Americans and the Mongolians. He says: "The early writers on the history of the aboriginal races of America, were of opinion that these people descended from the Mongols on the north of the eastern continent, and others that they originated from the Malays of the Indian Archipelago. The writings of Dr. Morton, however, appear to have silenced, for a time, the advocates of the old theory.*** The opinions of an intelligent naturalist, possessing so many materials to direct his judgment, are entitled to much weight on a subject with which he has long been familiar. We readily admit that in this he possesses superior claims on public confidence, and it would, therefore, appear presumptuous in us to express a contrary opinion. We regard this, however, as still an open question; and, as all men are entitled to an honest expression of their views, so long as they are not injurious to public or private interests, we will proceed without entering into a discussion which, if fully treated, would occupy a volume, to express the grounds of our conviction, that when this whole subject is more fully investigated, it will yet be discovered that the original theory, which at present seems to have few advocates, will, notwithstanding the many erroneous speculations on which it was founded, prove to a considerable extent correct. Nor do we express this opinion hastily, or without due deliberation founded on personal and minute examinations. Opportunities have been afforded us of seeing many individuals in every Indian tribe that existed within the last forty years, in all our Atlantic States, from the Canadas to South Florida. We have never had an opportunity of seeing the Eskimaux, and possess no further knowledge of that race than from the skulls and the many portraits with which the public is familiar; we have not visited Florida, and our only knowledge of those tribes is derived from an examination of the prisoners brought to Sullivan's Island during the late Florida war; but with all the intermediate Atlantic tribes we became acquainted, studied their forms, features, and habits of life, and at one period spent three months in their villages. On the eastern continent we possessed opportunities of examining several individuals from all but one of the families regarded by Professor Morton

[1] The Doctrine of the Unity of the Human Race, examined on the Principles of Science. By John Bachman, D.D., Charleston, S. C. 1850.

The Unity of the Human Races proved to be the doctrine of Scripture, Reason, and Science, with a review of the present position and theory of Professor Agassiz. By the Rev. Thomas Smyth, D.D. New York, 1850.

as belonging to the Mongolian race, viz: the Mongol Tartars, Turkish, Chinese, and Indo-Chinese families. We saw no individuals of the Polar family. Although we did not examine these races of men in regard to the question of unity or plurality of their origin, we were anxious to render ourselves familiar with the different varieties. We became satisfied that the characters so confidently insisted on as pervading all the ramifications of the great Mongolian stock are far from being uniform or permanent in all the varieties of the Mongolian family. In a crew of thirteen Chinese, which we examined at Liverpool, all represented to us by gentlemen who had resided in China, as of unmixed blood, there were only three who possessed any claims to the oblique eye, so generally represented as characteristic of this nation. Among a crew of Japanese, which we examined in London, we sought in vain for the striking peculiarity spoken of by Thunberg, who says, 'the eyelids form in the great angle of the eye a deep furrow, which makes the Japanese look as if they were sharp-sighted.' An impression was left on our minds that several peculiarities ascribed as the invariable characteristics of the Mongolian race were confined to the races existing in the Polar regions, and that the causes might yet be traced to the snow-clad regions which they inhabited. The color was not as uniformly yellow as has been represented, nor have we found that the red man of America is always entitled to the latter appellation. We saw a considerable number of individuals who belonged to several of the Mongolian families on the eastern continent, whom, if we had met with them in America, we should immediately have classed with some of the tribes of our now dispersed and almost extinct aborigines. We observed the same high cheek bones, the same very straight hair with scarcely a tendency to curl, the same beardless face, so very striking and peculiar in every branch of the Mongolian family; a few partial exceptions exist in both countries, but we observed at least as much beard in two of the Japanese as we ever witnessed on the face of an American Indian. We could add many other resemblances in countenance, language, and modes of life, but our only object in this place is to draw the attention of naturalists again to a subject which, we believe, when properly investigated, will once more direct the current of opinion into the original, but now apparently choked-up channel.

"From all the observations we were enabled to make, we have been led to the firm conviction that the descendants of what is called the Mongolian race, are found in a variety of forms and shades of color in America, from Greenland on one side, and Kamtschatka on the other, in the arctic circle, through the Russian settlements and Oregon, down to California in the west; and through the Canadas and the Atlantic United States on the east, down to the southern point of Florida, on the very borders of the tropics; that with occasional admixture of the Malays, which appear to predominate in many tribes of California, Mexico, and South America, and an admixture of the negro in some of the Florida and Cherokee tribes, the same race, with many variations, may be traced through the whole range of the American continent, down to Patagonia and Tierra del Fuego."[1]

[1] Doctrine of the Unity of the Human Race, pp. 268–272.

It is admitted by Dr. Bachman, that every species of animal and plant has its central birth-place, from which it spreads to certain limits, where it ceases to exist, unless removed to other localities by artificial means.

It is also claimed that the native plants, animals, and insects of America, are all of species distinct from those of the other hemisphere, except where the continents approach one another at the north; and the constitutional adaptation of *man* to every part of the world is attributed to superiority of organization.[1]

If naturalists shall be found to agree in considering the zoology and botany of America as distinct from those of all other countries, and indigenous to the soil, a branch of archæological inquiry, originally deemed a troublesome one, will be disposed of, viz: that relating to the manner in which the inferior orders of creation reached this continent.

Dr. Bachman still pursues the discussion with unwearied industry. In addition to articles in the *Charleston Medical Journal*, he has lately printed an examination of the theories in natural history of Professor Agassiz, and has announced that he is preparing for publication, a work on the skulls, the general anatomy, the color of the skin, and the nature of the hair of the varieties that compose the human family.[2]

Dr. Smyth's work may, in some respects, be regarded as an appendix to that of Dr. Bachman, on which it leans for many of its arguments and illustrations, and whose conclusions it follows in reference to the sources of American population.

The influence of the American climate in modifying the physical character of its inhabitants is a point of considerable importance in estimating the possible sources of their origin. One of the most celebrated ethnological treatises which this country has produced, that of President Smith, of Princeton College, was based upon the doctrine of climatic influences. Although adopting the prevalent opinion that the Malays, or Tartars, colonized America, and founded the semi-civilized empires existing at the time of the discovery by Columbus, this author believed it could be shown that a change had already begun to take place in the Anglo-Saxon and other European inhabitants, both in complexion and feature; and that, in the Southern States at least, if the people were thrown like the Indians into a state of absolute "savageism," they would, in no great length of time, be perfectly marked with the same complexion.[3]

This supposition better accords with the views of Blumenbach, Buffon, and Zimmerman, than with those of most phyisologists of a later date. Lawrence and Prichard agree in deciding that the effects of climate and of *habits of life*, &c., are not transmitted from parent to child;[4] and President Smith's general theory has not

[1] Doctrine of the Unity of the Human Species, pp. 250, 266.

[2] Charleston Med. Journ. of July, 1855.

[3] Essay on the Causes of the Variety of Complexion and Figure in the Human Species, &c. By Samuel Stanhope Smith, D. D. Edinb., 1788.

[4] "In all changes which are produced in the bodies of animals by the action of external causes, the effect terminates in the individual; the offspring is not in the slightest degree modified by them."—*Lawrence's Lectures*, p. 436.

"Nothing," says Dr. Prichard, "seems to hold true more generally than that all acquired conditions

found favor with the principal American writers who have subsequently treated of the same or kindred subjects. It was severely criticized by Dr. Caldwell, in the *American Review* of July, 1811, soon after a second edition of the Essay was printed; and more at length in the *Portfolio*, Vol. IV, 1814, by the same writer, who endeavored to show that we are acquainted with no cause, short of the power that first created man, capable of producing "that striking difference which exists between the African and the European, the American Indian and the Hindoo, the Patagonian and the Laplander."

Following up the subject in after years, Dr. Caldwell published a small volume, in which he took more decided ground in favor of a distinct origin for different races; regarding our Indians as fitted and intended to inhabit uncultivated forests, and wild prairies, and destined to disappear, as these are converted into fruitful fields, on the same principle of adaptation that called them into existence.[1]

Kinmont,—who resorted to the hypothesis of an innate tendency in man to give rise, in the progress of generations, to several distinct races, which, separating under Providential influences, were led to distinct quarters of the earth,—remarks in his lectures: "To say that all mankind originally perfectly resembled each other, and that the several natural varieties which now exist have arisen out of local circumstances—the action of external causes—is to adopt a gratuitous explanation, which cannot be shown to have any foundation in fact. To say that the different races have sprung out of separate original pairs, is equally absurd and unsupported."[2]

With similar positiveness it is declared by Van Amringe, that "the differences in the races of men cannot be accounted for by climate, mode of living, or any natural causes now in operation, or which have been in operation within the period of history." He is equally confident that they cannot be explained by the supposition of accidental or congenital varieties springing up in the human family. This American author has sought to establish a new system of human history and philosophy. He regards the zoological classification of man by his animal properties, excluding his *psychical* attributes, as unphilosophical, on the ground that there is no analogy between man and animals which can assist us to classify man, or to understand his history. He assumes that there are at least four distinct species of men, proved by their physical and psychical properties and powers, but a single original centre of distribution, or creation of man, in the neighborhood of the Euphrates; while of animals and vegetables there were several centres of distribution or creation. He considers that specific differences among the races of men are established by the principles of Zoology, and by Anatomy, Physiology, Psychology, and the natural law of sexual love; and proposes a new classification and

---

of body, whether produced by art or accident, end with the life of the individual in whom they are produced."—*Ibid.*, quoting *Prichard's Disp. Inaug.*

[1] Thoughts on the Original Unity of the Human Race. By Charles Caldwell, M.D. Phila., 1831; second edition, with additions. Cincinnati, 1852.

[2] Twelve Lectures on the Natural History of Man, &c. By Alexander Kinmont. Cincinnati, 1839.

nomenclature, adapted to his own compounded physical and psychical theory.[1] And finally, Dr. Bachman disavows the doctrines of Smith in these terms: "While we are willing to allow some weight to the argument of President Smith, who endeavors to account for the varieties of man from the combined influence of three causes—'climate, the state of society, and manner of living;' we are free to admit that it is impossible to account for the varieties in the human family from the causes which he has assigned."[2]

That all forms of life in this country were wanting in vigor, and generally inferior to those of the eastern continent, was maintained by Buffon, De Pauw, and the Abbé Raynal, and partially adopted by Robertson. It was indignantly repelled by Jefferson, and is termed by Morton "an idle theory," and an hypothesis of "closet naturalists," which there is ample evidence to disprove. An explanation of the assumed fact was sought by its supporters in the supposition that this continent emerged from the water at a later period than the other, and had not recovered from the effect of cold and moisture, which exerted an enervating influence upon the inhabitants, whose resemblance and uniformity showed them to be more recent than the people of the other hemisphere, and that time had not been afforded them to become as robust as the latter.

In curious contrast with these persuasions of the older school of European philosophers, we have now the conviction of Dr. Lund, already cited, and of other eminent geologists, that land in America must have emerged earlier than any known portion of the so-called Old World; and the conclusions of Dr. Martius that the natives of the New World are not in a state of primitive barbarism, but are the last remains of a people once high in the scale of civilization and improvement; but now worn out and perishing. Prichard, after testifying to the learning and ability of Martius, and to the ample resources possessed by him for acquiring an accurate knowledge of the American aborigines, avers that the structure of the American languages, and the national customs and institutions, indicate habits of thought and reflection, and cultivation of mind, very different from the state of savages in general; declaring, also, that attentive observers have been struck with manifestations of greater energy and mental vigor, of more intense and deeper feeling, of a more reflective mind, of greater fortitude, and more consistent perseverance in enterprises, and all pursuits, when they have compared the natives of

---

[1] An Investigation of the Theories of the Natural History of Man, by Lawrence, Prichard, and others, founded on Human Analogies; and an outline of a new Natural History of Man, founded upon History, Anatomy, Physiology, and Human Analogies. By William Frederick Van Amringe. New York, 1848.

Mr. Van Amringe's classification recognizes four species, viz: the SHEMITIC, comprehending the Israelites, Greeks, Romans, Teutones, Slavons, and Celts; the JAPHETIC, comprising the Chinese, Mongolians, Japanese, Chin Indians, and probably the *Eskimaux*, *Toltecs*, *Aztecs*, and *Peruvians;* the ISHMAELITIC, comprising most of the Tartar and Arabian tribes, and *the whole of the American Indians*, unless those mentioned in the second species should be excepted; the CANAANITIC, comprising the Negroes of Central Africa, Hottentots, Caffirs, Australasian Negroes, and probably the Malays.—P. 73.

[2] Doctrine of the Unity of the Human Race, &c., p 177.

the New World, with the sensual, volatile, and almost animalized savages, who are still to be found in some quarters of the Old World.[1]

On the other hand, according to Professor Guyot, it is vegetable life alone that receives a favorable development under the moist and warm influences of the American climate. In both the southern and the northern continents, "this luxuriant vegetation, it might be said, seems to stifle the higher life in the animal world. Animal life is, as it were, overruled, enfeebled; it does not occupy here the first rank, which is its due." "Among the superior animals, development seems to be arrested; it is incomplete;" and, with the exception of some superior types in North America, "they have not the strength nor the indomitable courage, nor the ferocity, nor the intelligence, of the similar creatures of the Old World." He pronounces that "man himself, the indigenous man, bears in his whole character the ineffaceable stamp of this peculiarly vegetative nature." "His lymphatic temperament betrays the preponderance in his nature of the vegetative element." "If he sometimes exhibits a display of prodigious muscular force, he is yet without endurance." "The conformation and position of the New World give to it a hot and watery climate; this impresses its own character on all the organized creation."[2]

Instead of perceiving any analogy between the laws that govern the animal and vegetable kingdoms, and control their distribution, and those that affect mankind, Professor Guyot finds a decided opposition in the two. "There is," he says, "a particular law which presides over the distribution of the human races, and of civilized communities taken at their cradles; a different law from that which governs the distribution of plants and animals."[3]

If we may believe Dr. Knox, this climate, which so depresses the energies of the red man, is positively destructive to the European. He maintains that climate has no permanent influence in altering the races of man, but may and does destroy them; that the Saxon decays in Northern America; and were the supplies from Europe not incessant, he could not stand his ground in these new countries; that already the United States man differs in appearance from the European. Not that this indicates the conversion of the Anglo-Saxon into the red Indian, but is a warning that the climate was not made for him, nor he for the climate.[4]

If climate has power to change not only the complexion, but the bony structure of man, the form of his skull, the cast of his features, and the model of his frame, and if association among different races, without intermixture, tends to produce similarity of appearance, all arguments against the European or Asiatic origin of the American Indians, derived from their peculiar physiological conformation are deprived of their force; for, however various the sources, from which they might have sprung, they would become moulded, according to that theory, into uniformity, by a natural proclivity incident to this hemisphere.

A doctrine similar to that of President Smith is advanced by Dr. Carpenter as

---

[1] Nat. Hist. of Man, II, 497, 501.

[2] The Earth and Man. By Arnold Guyot: Boston, 1850. Lecture VIII.

[3] The Earth and Man. Lecture VII.

[4] The Races of Men: a fragment. By Robert Knox, M. D.; Philad. ed., pp. 44 and 57.

an independent conclusion of his own. The following rather startling passage is from his essay on the varieties of mankind:—

"It has not been pointed out, so far as the writer is aware, by any ethnologist, that the conformation of the cranium seems to have undergone a certain amount of alteration, even in the Anglo-Saxon race of the United States, which assimilates it, in some degree, to that of the aboriginal inhabitants. Certain it is, that among New Englanders more particularly, a cast of countenance prevails, which usually renders it easy for any one familiar with it, to point out an individual of that country in the midst of an assemblage of Englishmen; and though this may chiefly depend upon the conformation of the soft parts, yet there is a certain sharpness, and an angularity of feature, about a genuine 'yankee,' which would probably display itself in the contour of the bones. So far as the writer's observation has extended, there is especially to be noticed an excess of breadth between the rami of the lower jaw, giving to the lower part of the face a peculiar squareness that is in striking contrast with the tendency to an oval narrowing which is most common among the inhabitants of the 'old country.' *And it is not a little significant, that the well marked change which has thus shown itself in the course of a very few generations, should tend to assimilate the Anglo-American race to the aborigines of the country; the peculiar physiognomy here adverted to, most assuredly presenting a transition, however slight, toward that of the North American Indian.*"[1]

As an example of the influence of association, the same writer states that, according to the concurrent testimony of disinterested observers, both in the West Indies and the United States, an approximation in the negro physiognomy to the European model is progressively taking place in instances where, although there has been no intermixture of blood, the influence of a higher civilization has been exercised for a lengthened period. He cites Dr. Hancock, as a most intelligent physician of Guiana, who asserts that it is frequently not at all difficult to distinguish a negro of pure blood belonging to the Dutch portion of the colony, from another belonging to the English settlements, by the correspondence between their features and expression, and those which are characteristic of their respective masters. Sir Charles Lyell is also referred to as having informed Dr. Carpenter that he had been assured by numerous medical men in the slave States of the North American Union, that a gradual approximation is taking place in the configuration of the head and body of the pure negro to the European model.[2]

With the cases of assimilation last adduced, climate has of course nothing to do. They would probably be ascribed to the influence of mental habits and associations upon the muscles of expression, gradually extending to the more inflexible parts of the system, as husband and wife are said to grow into a sort of resemblance, and persons of a particular trade acquire an aspect that distinguishes them; or as the favorite dog of the "Ettrick Shepherd" was humorously said to have gained such a likeness to his master as sometimes to occupy his place in the pew at church, without the minister's ever noting the difference.

---

[1] Carpenter on the Varieties of Mankind, in Todd's Cyc. of Anat. and Physiol., p. 1330.

[2] Ibid., p. 1330.

A recent contributor to the *Protestant Episcopal Quarterly Review*, published in New York, gives his countenance to the idea, that the Anglo-American is gradually assuming the physical type of the aborigines, and seems to regard the tendency as varying according to the special influence of particular localities. Thus, he believes that the New Englander is acquiring the craniological formation of the family of tribes to whom he has succeeded as possessor of the soil, whose skulls differed somewhat from those of the Indians in general.[1]

In referring to the various aspects which archæological science, as applied to this country, has from time to time presented, the endeavor has been to maintain the order of progression so far as practicable, while regarding also the natural connection of different theories, and their bearing upon one another.

Advancing from that stage of opinion when the necessity of looking abroad for the origin of our primitive population was almost universally acknowledged, and when the belief prevailed that physical, moral, and traditionary evidence pointed to Asia as the principal source whence that population was derived, we entered upon one in which another class of sentiments predominated. In this, the deductions from an analysis of dialects, the results of physiological and palæontological investigations, and the conclusions of men of science respecting a radical diversity of races, were combined to favor the hypothesis of an independent and indigenous creation of man in America. We have now come out upon a conjunction of theories, claiming a scientific foundation, from which a new series of inferences may be drawn.

Agassiz and Guyot mutually recognize a peculiar homogeneity in the geological structure of the American continent, from which a like homogeneity might be expected to exist, or to be produced in its animal and vegetable kingdoms severally, such as observation has shown to be the case.

Professor Guyot has superadded the conception that vegetative life is here universally paramount over animal vitality, absorbing the elements of growth and vigor, and affecting the development not only of inferior orders, but of the primitive man, whose nature, inert and passive, is held to be deficient in those mental and corporeal energies which have marked and diversified the history of his race in other lands.

Moreover, aside from the deteriorating influence ascribed to the climate, it is alleged, as has been seen, that it possesses the quality of changing the physical, and, as a consequence, the mental characters, of other varieties of man, into those which distinguish the families that constitute the American division.

And while the tendency to this metamorphosis has, by one authority, been considered stronger in the Southern States, others declare it to be now in gradual but perceptible progress among the Anglo-Saxons of New England.

Thus, if the argument rested on these physical propositions alone, all the nations of the earth might, at some former period, have contributed to the population of the western hemisphere, as they are doing now, and in process of time all traces of distinction would have become obliterated in a common and irresistible degeneracy.

---

[1] Prot. Episc. Rev., July, 1855, p. 380.

A prospective consequence of a similar kind would seem to follow from the same premises, unless it is presumed that the immense and continuous immigration of superior races, which has succeeded to the discovery by Columbus, will keep in check the operations of nature until exhalations from the soil are modified by culture, and other unfavorable conditions are overcome by the arts and habits of civilized life.[1]

Here, then, are three distinct modes of reasoning upon the problems of American archæology; the first resting mainly upon historical intimations and superficial affinities of person, habits, and arts; the second based upon philological, physiological, and geological phenomena; the third dependent on a theory of climatic and geographical agencies. By the first, a direct, and not very distant relationship, between Asiatic and American races, is maintained; by the second, either an entire separation from the rest of mankind, or a connection so remote as to be beyond the limits of recorded events, has been supposed to be indicated; by the third, from whatever source or sources, the population of the country has originated, it has been subjected, as alleged, to physical influences here, destructive of all external means of identification.

Happily our task is to record, not to reconcile opinions. It would be as easy to give unity and consistency to a picture made up of sketches taken from different stand-points, under different lights, and at various degrees of perspective, as to project a congruous scheme of ethnology out of materials that writers have collected from different points of observation, often for contrary purposes, and affected by the coloring of opposite prejudices.

Dr. Bachman's conviction that the original theory which designated the Mongols and Malays as the principal sources of primitive population in America, silenced, as he supposed, for a time, by the doctrines of Morton, would ultimately prove correct, is fortified by the judgment of many writers of authority.

Dr. Pickering, and Col. Smith, whose opportunities for comparison have been highly favorable and extensive, both dissent from Dr. Morton's conclusions. The first, while a member of the U. S. Exploring Expedition, examined the natives on the American coasts in nearly every latitude, and included in his general survey, nearly every variety of the human race.[2] The other claims to have personally compared, and drawn from life, many individuals of different tribes, from Canada to the extremity of the southern continent.[3]

---

[1] Dr. Knox does not appear disposed to admit even this possibility, but anticipates the ultimate decadence of the European stock, if not the ultimate restoration of the native race, should the latter escape annihilation in the mean time. He holds that the probable result is exemplified by the condition of the Spanish American provinces, where, since immigration from the parent country has ceased, the Spanish race has progressively declined, while the descendants of the original inhabitants are gaining in numbers, so that in another century, unless both are destroyed by the Anglo-Saxon, their blood will predominate, and the Castilian be all but extinct. A permanent amalgamation of races, even of those most nearly allied, and the permanent duration of any race in an uncongenial climate, he regards as equally impossible.

[2] The Races of Men, and their Geographical Distribution. By Charles Pickering, M. D. 1848.

[3] The Nat. Hist. of the Human Species. By Lieut.-Col. Charles Hamilton Smith, K. H. 1848.

Dr. Pickering's *map*, prepared to exhibit his view of the distribution of the races of men, assigns the whole of the two continents of America to the Mongols, excepting a portion of the western coast of North America, and some islands of the Gulf of Mexico, which he yields to the Malays. In the text of his work he mentions the possibility that the Malay race is more widely extended than is represented in the map; and he is disposed to attribute to that race whatever is authentic in the accounts of "*black aboriginals*," as geographical considerations render it improbable that any *third* race had reached America prior to the European discovery.[1]

At San Francisco, where there were many Polynesians, he found it difficult to distinguish them from the natives of California; the only perceptible difference being in the hair, which among the islanders was wavy or curled, while that of the Californians was uniformly straight. The manufactures, habits, and customs of the latter, in his estimation, notwithstanding "a strong American impress," bore equal indications of Polynesian affinity. He remarks that, while to persons living around the Atlantic shores, the source of aboriginal population seems mysterious, had writers upon the subject made a voyage to the north Pacific, much of the discussion would, in his opinion, have been spared; as it was only on visiting that part of the world, that the whole of the matter seemed to open to his view. For while the facilities of transit along the northern coast of the Pacific, by means of land-locked passages are, perhaps, unparalleled, the climate is genial for the latitude, and the means of subsistence are abundant. In the chain of population he found no break. He also regarded the Polynesian groups and Japan as favorably situated for communication with California, notwithstanding their distance, on account of the winds and currents that tend from them to the latter; exemplified, in the case of Japan, by the chance arrival of tempest-tost junks on our northwest coast.[2]

The circumstances adduced in support of the common idea that the Aztecs came from the direction of Oregon, such as the terminal "tl" so characteristic of the Mexican language, and found also among the Chinnooks and Nootkas, with other resemblances, in costume, modes of dressing the hair, forms of sculptured pipes, &c., are sustained by his testimony; and, in addition to these direct references of original population to particular exotic sources, he advances the scientific opinion that "it could be shown, on zoological grounds alone, that the human family is foreign to the American continent.

Col. Smith considers the decay of the American races, amounting to prospective extinction, a proof that they are not a *typical* people, but are stems, such as are alone liable to annihilation. He holds that there exist sufficient coincidences of manners, practices and language, between the natives of this continent and those of eastern Asia, to overthrow the hypothesis of an exclusively aboriginal species

---

[1] Yet, in another passage, he speaks of having met, in a few instances, in the United States, with a race which was neither Mongolian nor Malay, and which he terms "the Telingan or true Indian." P. 281, Bohn's ed.

[2] See, in this connection, Humboldt's "matured opinions," Views of Nature. Bohn's ed., 1850, pp. 131-3.

of man in America, unless the "*Flathead* type" may be considered an exception. The primitive flatheads, if not constituting a distinct species of man, were, he imagines, "at least the oldest and first wanderers that reached the American continent." In his judgment, an immigration, continuous for ages, from the east of Asia, is indicated by the traditional pressure of nations from the northwest coast, eastward and southward.

Regarding the flatheaded Paltas, and Aturians, or primeval race of South America, as anomalous, though evidently mixed with tribes whose origin is more marked, and admitting that some of them, such as the, so-called, Frog Indians, are still in being about the east side of the Cordilleras, he states that the stock has in fact been supplanted for ages by other nations, whose Malay aspect countenances the supposition of their original arrival from the islands of the Pacific. The tribes on the Sacramento River he derives from the Sandwich Islands; and he thinks that Polynesians, from the direction of the winds and currents, could hardly fail to reach the coast of Chili, whence they might mix with the Brazilian tribes, and form the race of Araucas.

That abnormal configuration of the skull, commonly expressed by the term *flathead*, is undoubtedly the most remarkable phenomenon connected with the human physiology of these continents. The regions of country where its existence has been noted, the extent to which it prevailed, and the evidences of honor and reverence with which it appears to have been associated, from a period of unknown antiquity, render it an object not only of anatomical interest, but of striking historical significance.

From Lake Titicaca, the original seat of the oldest, and perhaps the highest forms of Peruvian civilization,[1] the practice of moulding the head by compression in infancy, has been traced among the Caribs of the continent and islands; in Central America, Mexico, and Yucatan; and along the southern shores of the United States, from the Mississippi River to the Atlantic Ocean; and it appears again among the tribes of the northwest coast, from Columbia River nearly to the 54th degree of latitude. Thus, in the United States, the Attacapas, the Natchez, the Choctaws, the Waxsaws, the Creeks, and the Catawbas, are known to have had the usage among them; but from these it is necessary to pass the Rocky Mountains and approach the Arctic regions, before meeting with it again. The custom was prohibited in Peru, by an ecclesiastical decree, as early as 1585, and was abandoned where the authority of the Spaniards could be enforced; and with the breaking up of native communities, and the decay of the race, it has generally ceased in both continents; but in Oregon it still continues, as essential to the holding of office or rank in the tribes that make use of it, while it is forbidden to those who are in bondage.

A like distinction and social supremacy appears to have attended this strange disfigurement wherever it has been noticed. In Peru, its possessors were interred with the most costly rites, in the largest and finest tombs; and in the sculptures

[1] Prescott's Conquest of Peru, I, 12.

and hieroglyphic memorials of the Mexican provinces they occupy the position of conquerors and divinities. Hence the association of dignity and conventional beauty with a configuration so unseemly has been ascribed to traditional veneration for the dominant power and intellectual superiority of a race with whom the deformity was congenital. Whether such a race ever existed, is a question now at issue among naturalists.

Baron Humboldt and M. Bonpland are believed to be the first who made this anomaly a subject of scientific investigation. The extraordinary configuration, exhibited by the skulls deposited by them in the Museum of Natural History at Paris, was to be found, according to their testimony, among nations to whom the means of producing artificial deformity were totally unknown. Dr. Morton having adopted this view in his *Crania Americana*, regarded the cranial conformation indicated by the specimens referred to as characteristic of a primitive type of the American man. Subsequently, he became convinced that, at least in its excessive forms, it was always the result of mechanical pressure.[1]

Dr. Nott, the friend and commentator of Morton, suggests, as a mode of reconciling these different conclusions, that they arose from an examination of "contradictory materials;" while he himself receives the doctrine of the former existence of an autochthonous race to whom the deformity was natural—a fact which he deems to be established by Dr. Lund's discoveries of fossil crania, as described by Lieut. Strain, and by the developments of Rivero and Von Tschudi.[2]

It is proper, however, to state that Dr. Morton had before him all the means of forming a judgment that are referred to by Dr. Nott, except the *Peruvian Antiquities* of Rivero and Von Tschudi. Lieut. Strain's account was in the form of a letter addressed to him. In the Essay on the Primitive Type of the American Indians, which Morton commenced for Mr. Schoolcraft's work, but left unfinished at his death, he reaffirms the change of opinion that he had avowed ten years before. After mentioning that Pentland, Tiedemann, Tschudi, and Knox deny the application of art in the case of the Peruvian skulls, and attribute their shape to an original and congenital peculiarity, he says that his own views on that point were changed by the acquisition of a very extended series of crania from the Peruvian tombs. "I, at first," he continues, "found it difficult to conceive that the original rounded skull of the Indian could be changed into this fantastic form; and was led to suppose that the latter was an artificial elongation of a head remarkable for its natural length and narrowness. I even supposed that the long-headed Peruvians were a more ancient people than the Inca tribes, and distinguished from them by their cranial configuration. In this opinion I was mistaken. Abundant means of observation and comparison have since convinced me that all these variously formed heads were originally of the same rounded shape."[3]

---

[1] See *Ante*, p. 78, n. n.

[2] Types of Mankind, p. 440.

[3] Schoolcraft's Hist. and Prosp., &c., II, 326. Dr. Morton began to doubt the correctness of his first opinion before he had seen the work of D'Orbigny, and subsequently announced his "matured conclusions" in connection with the facts he had derived from that distinguished naturalist.—See *Am. Journ. of Science*, XXXVIII, No. 2, 1840, and "*Inquiry into the Distinctive Characteristics of the Aboriginal Race of America,*" pp. 40–3.

The shape of head artificially produced has varied in different, and even in the same tribes. Sometimes the bulk of the cranium was thrown backward by pressure in front, the sides being confined to prevent expansion in a lateral direction. This was the common Peruvian form. In other cases, both the forehead and the occiput were compressed, causing the skull to spread laterally. Another form was conical, inclining backwards. The Arrowacks of the larger West India Islands flattened the head downwards, in the direction of the spine; and, in some instances, an irregular constriction occasioned a one-sided effect.

Dr. Morton ascribes his original conclusions to the difficulty of conceiving in what manner the form first mentioned above could be artificially produced from an originally rounded skull; and it was after he had, with the aid of D'Orbigny's suggestions, ascertained how the bandages could be applied for the purpose, that he adopted the theory subsequently retained by him. Other naturalists were probably influenced by the same inability; and it appears to have been on the ground that those forms could not be attributed to pressure, or any external force, that M. Pentland supposed them to be congenital, and that his view was confirmed, as he says, by "Cuvier, Gall, and many other celebrated naturalists and anatomists." Tiedemann's expression is, moreover: "A careful examination of these skulls has convinced me that their peculiar shape cannot be owing to artificial pressure. The great elongation of the face, and the direction of the plane of the occipital bone, are not to be reconciled with this opinion, and therefore we must conclude that the peculiarity of shape depends on a natural conformation." The language of Knox is: "That the Carib and Chinnook, and the ancient Macrocephali, fancied that by pressure they could give to the human head what form they chose, is certain enough; but does it follow that they could do so? The form of the head I speak of is peculiar to the race; it may be exaggerated somewhat by such means, but cannot be so produced." Dr. Morton was able to show how it could be and was produced, and therefore he believed it to be always artificial.

But investigations not alluded to by Morton, and of equal authority with those of D'Orbigny, present other and stronger reasons for admitting the natural origin of these deformities. Sir Robert Schomburgk found, near the sources of the Corentyne, a branch of the Orinoco, the remnant of a race called the Maopityans, or Frog Indians, whose heads were flattened by nature; at least he could not learn, by the most minute inquiries, that artificial means were employed. A child was born while he was with them, which he saw within an hour of its birth, that had, he states, all the characteristics of the mother's tribe; "and the flatness of its head, as compared with the heads of other tribes, was very remarkable."[1]

The national work on Peruvian antiquities, by Rivero and J. J. Von Tschudi, contains an examination of the question; and, as the result of "the numerous and scrupulously careful observations" of Dr. J. D. Von Tschudi, long a resident in Peru, and of the writers' own private researches, it is affirmed that those physiologists are in error, who suppose that the different phrenological aspects offered by

[1] Journ. of the Royal Geograph. Society of London, XV, pp. 53 and 57.

the Peruvian race were *exclusively* artificial." Such an hypothesis they imagine to have been based solely on the crania of adults; whereas the heads of children of the most tender age, exhibiting no vestige of pressure, were of similar conformation, and the same fact was observable in the case of infants yet unborn, which had been discovered among the mummies. The phenomenon is made more remarkable by the statement that in the crania of these children is found a peculiar bone, or division of the occipital portion of the skull, wanting in all other human beings, and corresponding to the *os interparietalis* of Rodentia and Marsupiata. This anomaly was first brought to notice, by Dr. Franklin Bellamy, an English naturalist, in 1842, and subsequently the bone received, from Dr. J. D. Von Tschudi, the name of "*Os Incæ*," in reference to the nation to which it was confined. Messrs. Rivero and J. J. Von Tschudi declare that they can "assert with certainty" that in some departments of Peru remnants of the races whose natural form of head has been imitated by compression may still be found, as they have themselves had occasion to see.[1]

We are not aware that such cranial deformity has been supposed to have ever existed naturally anywhere in the United States; and if the source from whence the practice was derived as an imitation could be determined, it might be the means of solving important archæological propositions.

The inquiry arises, whether these peculiarities, let them be natural or artificial, must have been indigenous to the country, or might have been introduced from abroad. To which it may be answered, that history is not entirely silent on this subject. In that border land between Europe and Asia, which was in earlier ages, as it is again, the seat of great events affecting the world's history—at once the birthplace and the battle-ground of nations—Hippocrates has located a people whom he calls the Macrocephali, or Longheads. Some of them dwelt near the river Phasis, and not far from the recently captured Turkish province of Kars. The shape of their heads, he tells us, "was at first a work of art, because they esteemed those having the longest heads the most noble, but nature had accommodated herself to it. It began in this way. As soon as an infant was born, they moulded the soft and tender head with their hands, and compelled it to grow into the desired form by bandages and other contrivances. In the course of time, this configuration became natural to the people, and the use of means to produce it ceased to be necessary."[2]

On Bactrian coins, in crania from the coast of Yemen, and in the islands of the Indian Archipelago, a similar configuration is reported to have been observed.[3] The former existence of "*Flat-heads*" in Asia Minor has been confirmed by the

---

[1] Peruvian Antiquities, ch. ii., Dr. Hawks' translation, N. Y., 1853. The original edition of this *national* work was printed for the authors at Vienna, in 1851.

[2] Hippocrates, Opera Omnia, ed. 1595, sec. iii. p. 72, freely translated. "If other singularities are transmitted to offspring," Hippocrates asks, "what hinders then that a Macrocephalus should be born of a Macrocephalus?" Though now, he intimates, they are not in like manner so born, because, for want of care, the model has become extinct.

[3] Smith's Races of Men, p. 143, and Plate V. Crawford's Ind. Archipel., I, 218.

discoveries of William Burckhardt Barker, who, in 1845, obtained a large quantity of terra-cotta images from a mound on the site of the ancient Tarsus. Among these were many specimens of flattened or compressed heads, exhibiting, in some instances, the precise contour of the heads upon the monuments of Central America. Others illustrated the form produced by downward pressure in the direction of the spinal column. The whole collection having been submitted to Mr. Abington, a gentleman skilled in artistic pottery, he was led by the resemblance between a portion of the heads and those portrayed by Mr. Stephens in his *Incidents of Travel in Central America and Yucatan*, to the construction of a theory connecting them together. He imagined that the anomalous faces were faithful portraits of Huns, or the Hiongnu, whose inhuman faces and horse-like heads so terrified the inhabitants of the countries they invaded, and one division of whom, after sweeping all before them as far as China, and penetrating the wilds of Siberia, might, as Humboldt has suggested, have crossed to America. In addressing Mr. Barker, he says: "Perhaps you have the gratification of first bringing before the world a true and exact representation of that once terrible but now forgotten race, and that too by an illustration probably *unique;* also of removing the veil which has hitherto concealed the mysterious origin of the men who have left the memorials of their peculiar conformation upon the sculptured stones of America."[1]

With the heads above described, Mr. Barker obtained images of the divinities of classical Greece and Rome in great numbers, and in a high style of art—the "Lares and Penates" which give the title to his book; and, what is very remarkable, the disfigured heads were also crowned with the tokens of divinity, indicating that they also had at some time been objects of worship. These curious facts may be added to the many coincidences that have been supposed to imply an Asiatic derivation for at least a portion of the original population of this country.

The statement that, under the microscope, the hair of the American Indians exhibits a form and structure peculiar to itself, or at least distinguishing it from that of whites and negroes, should not be omitted from this physiological summary. This subject has been elaborately investigated by Peter A. Browne, Esq., of Philadelphia, and the results are given, with illustrations, in the third volume of Mr. Schoolcraft's general work; having before appeared in literary and scientific journals. It is claimed that the hair of the American natives is cylindrical in form, while in the Caucasian races it is oval, and among negro nations it is eccentrically elliptical. These distinctions, if sustained, are expected to have an important bearing upon the affinities and diversities of races. It has, however, been questioned by other naturalists whether the phenomena observed are sufficiently uniform to establish a scientific principle.[2]

---

[1] Lares and Penates; or Cilicia and its Governors, &c. By Wm. Burckhardt Barker, M. R. A. S. Lond., 1853, p. 203, *et seq.*

[2] Dr. Carpenter asserts that the characters specified by Dr. Browne will not stand the test of extensive observation; that the form of the shaft varies greatly in the hairs of the same race, and even in those of the same individual; for not only is it sometimes round, sometimes oval, and more rarely eccentrically elliptical, or nearly flat, but may be even reniform, or channelled on one side.—*Cyc. of Anat. and Phys.*, Part XLI, p. 1338.

While recording the various forms of opinion that have sprung from philological and physiological observations in this country, we hope that sufficient care has been taken to avoid giving any adscititious weight to particular views. If ideas opposed to the original unity of mankind appear anywhere to be relatively prominent, it is owing, perhaps, to the circumstance that whatever conforms to general opinion arrests attention less than that which differs from it. It is only as ideas, which their authors have connected with our subject in a manner not to admit of separation, that they find a place in our pages. As a portion of the bibliography of American Archæology they can neither be omitted with propriety nor be so disguised as to conceal their tendency. The great question of human unity or diversity rests upon a far wider survey of men and nations than the ethnology of this continent comprehends; and all local facts or phenomena require to be associated with researches linguistic, physiological, and historical, as general and thorough as those of Prichard and Bunsen, before they can prudently be made the basis of argument, much less the foundation of faith. The conclusions of Prichard and Bunsen appear not to have been invalidated in their own estimation by any phases of human condition or conformation developed in the New World; Humboldt's personal researches in this hemisphere have not impaired his faith in the singleness of human origin;[1] and one of our historians, at the close of an elaborate survey of the American aborigines in connection with other races, asserts that "the indigenous population of America offers no new obstacle to faith in the unity of the human race."[2]

Having endeavored to present in a connected form the various aspects which philological analysis and physical science have given to the question of the origin or derivation of the Indian race, we may continue the chronological *resumé* of leading publications that relate, either specially or inclusively, to the antiquities of our national territory.

At about the period of 1830, a rage for migration to the West spread like an epidemic through the Eastern States. In New England particularly, under the influence of a depressed condition of manufacturing and commercial enterprise, the feeling was prevalent that the Atlantic States, with a sterile or exhausted soil, must decline in wealth and population before the rising importance of the productive regions of the Mississippi Valley. While the Southern emigrant transferred the movable appurtenances of his plantation to Louisiana or Arkansas, the farmers of Massachusetts, New Hampshire, and Vermont, sought some locality between the Ohio and the Great Lakes. From Illinois and Michigan they soon advanced into the Territory of Wisconsin, and prepared the way for the discovery of a new and curious class of antiquities. At that time, during half a dozen or more succeeding years, the press was prolific of Notes on the Western States, Guide Books, Sketches of Travel, Letters from Emigrants, and other publications descriptive of the country, in which a chapter was often bestowed upon mounds and other ancient

---

[1] See "Cosmos," Vol. I, closing chapter.

[2] Bancroft's History of the United States, III, 318.

remains, and the crude speculations to which the sight of them gave rise. These not unfrequently added to the stock of local information, but did not throw much new light on the general subject.

It was in 1836, that the first knowledge appears to have been gained of the emblematic earthworks of Wisconsin. Mr. Lapham, whose elaborate Memoir respecting them has recently been published by the Smithsonian Institution, claims to have been the original discoverer, and to have described some of them in the newspapers of that date. They were brought more prominently to public notice by Mr. R. C. Taylor in a paper accompanied by illustrations, communicated to the *American Journal of Arts and Sciences* of April, 1838. They will be considered hereafter under the period of their full development by Mr. Lapham.

Indian Biographies, or works relating to native manners, customs, and exploits, which come within the period of our own national history, do not properly belong to the class of publications that are the subjects of notice in this memoir, although they may indirectly elucidate archæological questions. But the comprehensive sketches of Indian history and adventure, compiled by Mr. Drake (which, in successive editions, have, since 1832, continued to expand in bulk and improve in accuracy), contain also an account of North American antiquities, and a summary of theories and speculations respecting the origin of population on this continent. The author's organ of marvellousness is not large, and he is not disposed to attach an unnecessary degree of wonder and mystery to relics of antiquity, or to circumstances that happen not to be easy of explanation. He comments freely upon hypotheses that appear to him irrational or visionary, and is satisfied with referring the erection of the earthworks at the West to the ancestors of the existing native race, under some condition favorable to a more stationary life and a denser population. His book is the result of great industry and careful research, and contains a large amount of interesting and useful information.[1]

When Professor Rafn was engaged, on behalf of the Royal Society of Antiquaries at Copenhagen, in preparing the extensive work on the Discovery of America by the Northmen, published by that institution in 1837, letters were sent to societies and individuals in this country soliciting the communication of facts that would illustrate the subject. There followed a correspondence with the Historical Society of Rhode Island, through its secretary, Dr. Webb, in relation to the celebrated Dighton rock, and other inscribed stones in the same vicinity.

As the Icelandic manuscripts were supposed to point to the precise region where that rock is placed, as having been occupied by Northmen, the characters drawn upon it were naturally studied with anxious interest by the Danish antiquaries. A new transcript of the lines and figures carefully drawn, a sketch of the rock and surrounding scenery, and maps of the neighboring coasts and country, were forwarded by gentlemen of the Rhode Island Society to Copenhagen. These were submitted to scholars familiar with Runic monuments and inscriptions, who pro-

---

[1] Biography and History of the Indians of North America, from its first discovery to the present time; with an Account of their Antiquities, Manners and Customs, Religion and Laws. By Samuel G. Drake: Boston, 1832, 1841.

nounced the rock at Dighton to be a monument of that class, and the characters upon it a memorial of the occupation of the country by the Scandinavian navigators.

It was, therefore, with some elation of feeling, and greatly increased confidence, that the routes of the Northmen were traced along the shores of New England, and the positions determined, where they had stationed themselves. Supported by such tangible evidences of habitation, there was also less hesitation in extending the claim of Scandinavian discovery to the more Southern portions of the United States. Anticipations were indulged in, that the interpretation put upon the Dighton inscription would be confirmed by the development of other vestiges of that people; and when, after the publication of the volume devoted to these proofs, its author received from Dr. Webb a drawing of the circular stone structure at Newport, of whose erection no distinct account had been preserved, and some copper ornaments or implements found with a skeleton at Fall River, much learning was employed to prove by analogies that these also were of Scandinavian derivation.[1]

But if hopes were thus excited that the veil of mystery was to be lifted from any portion of American archæology, they were not sustained by cooler reflection and more careful scrutiny. The great dissimilarity in the different delineations of the forms of the marks on the Dighton stone, impaired confidence in the possibility of assigning to them any positive signification as linguistic characters. The improbability that the structure at Newport could have been in existence when that place was settled by the English without attracting general attention and remark, combined with the fact that both records and traditions referred to it as a *wind-*

---

[1] ANTIQUITATES AMERICANÆ, sive Scriptores Septentrionales Rerum Ante-Columbianarum, in America. Hafniæ, 1837.

Supplement to ANTIQUITATES AMERICANÆ: 1841.

Mémoires de la Société Royale des Antiquaires du Nord: 1840, 1844.

An Advertisement by the Danish Society, of the "Antiquitates Americanæ" after an account of the *Sagas* embraced in the work, contains the following statement:—

"To which are added: 1. A description accompanied by delineations and occasionally by perspective views of several Monuments, chiefly Inscriptions, from the middle ages, found partly in Greenland and partly in the States of Massachusetts and Rhode Island in North America, on the one hand confirming the accounts in the Sagas; and on the other illustrated by them. II. Detailed Geographical Inquiries lately undertaken at the instance of the Society, whereby the sites of the regions and places named in the Sagas are explored, and are pointed out under the names by which they are now commonly known, viz: Newfoundland, Bay of St. Lawrence, Nova Scotia, and especially the States of Massachusetts and Rhode Island, and even districts more to the South, probably situate in Virginia, North Carolina, and in Florida, which is supposed to be the most southerly land mentioned in the most authentic Saga accounts, although sundry of the northern geographers of the middle ages would seem to intimate their knowledge of the easterly direction taken by the continent of South America. They are chiefly based on the accounts in the ancient MSS., and on the explanations of the astronomical, nautical, and geographical statements contained in the same, which besides receive the most complete confirmation from accounts transmitted by distinguished American scholars, with whom the society have entered into correspondence, and who, after several journeys undertaken for that object in Massachusetts and Rhode Island, have communicated accurate illustrations respecting the nature of the countries, their climate, animals, productions, etc., and have furnished the society with descriptions and also with delineations of the ancient monuments found there."

mill, discountenanced the idea that it could have any other than a modern origin; and a more particular investigation of the circumstances connected with the Fall River skeleton showed that little weight could be attached to that relic as a source of reliable evidence.

The narratives of the voyages of the Northmen, and their discovery of this country, are, however, regarded as well attested, leaving the question open as to the distance in a southerly direction to which their observations extended; and many striking coincidences seem to justify the conclusion that the Vinland of these narratives was really in Narraganset Bay.[1]

There is a fact which deserves to be mentioned in connection with the "Fall River Skeleton" that we have not seen anywhere so employed. The articles found upon it which excited the interest of the Danish antiquaries were, as described, a brass breastplate; brass arrow-heads; and a belt made of small tubes of the same metal, a few inches in length, fastened together side by side. These are certainly unusual articles to find associated with the person of a savage who lived before the occupancy of the country by the English. But in Brereton's *Brief and True Relation of the Discovery of the North Part of Virginia* (New England), by Gosnold, in 1602, it is stated that while they were at an island, since identified, and lying off the coast nearest to Fall River, the natives came to them from the mainland, and the articles they brought with them are described as follows: "They have great store of copper, some very red and some of a paler color; none of them but have chains, ear-rings, or collars of this metal; they head some of their arrows herewith, much like our broad arrow-heads, very workmanly made. Their chains are many hollow pieces cemented together, each piece of the bigness of one of our reeds, a finger in length, ten or twelve of them together on a string, which they wear about their necks; these collars they wear about their bodies like bandeliers, a handful broad, all hollow pieces like the others, but somewhat shorter, four hundred pieces in a collar, very fine and evenly set together. Besides these, they have large drinking cups made like skulls, and other thin plates of copper made much like our boar-spear blades, all which they so little esteem, as they offered their fairest collars or chains for a knife or such like trifle."[2]

As Gosnold, according to the same narrative, had just previously found a Biscayan shallop, with mast and sail and an iron grapple, in possession of eight Indians, one of them "apparelled in a waistcoat and breeches of black serge," and another in "a pair of breeches of blue cloth," there is no difficulty in supposing that all these materials came from the wreck of some unfortunate fishing vessel, notwithstanding Brereton says the Indians intimated by signs that they obtained their metal from the earth.

In 1838, the late President Harrison prepared his well-known *Discourse* for the

---

[1] A very lucid synopsis of the contents and claims of the "Antiquitates Americanæ," by Hon. Edward Everett, appeared in the *N. A. Review*, for January, 1838; and a translation of all the most important Sagas, with a critical examination of their authenticity, by Joshua Toulmin Smith, was published at Boston, and also reprinted in London in 1839, with maps; and was again printed in London in 1842, with maps and plates.

[2] Purchas's Pilgrims, Vol. IV; reprinted in Mass. Hist. Coll., 3d ser. Vol. VIII.

Historical Society of Ohio;[1] a dissertation not only creditable to his literary taste and general scholarship, but containing a large amount of valuable information upon points of Indian history, and the result of his observations and reflections respecting the ancient remains of that region. He had been familiar with the latter many years, having accompanied General Wayne in an excursion to examine those at Cincinnati in 1793, and had studied them both as a military man and as an antiquary. Referring to the fact that the country immediately bordering on the Ohio, when first made known to the whites, appeared not only to have been deserted by its more ancient inhabitants, but to be left by recent races of Indians, as a common hunting-ground or battle-field, without permanent occupancy, he seeks an answer to the question why so beautiful and fertile a portion of country had been thus abandoned.

To aid in forming a satisfactory conclusion, we possess, he says, but a single recorded fact, viz: that the pictorial records of Mexico ascribe the origin of that nation to the Aztecs, who are said to have arrived in Mexico about the middle of the seventh century. He quotes Bishop Madison as declaring his conviction, after much investigation, that the Aztecs are the people who once inhabited the valley of the Ohio; and, on the ground that probabilities are in favor of that opinion, he adopts it, and endeavors to explain the cause and manner of their departure. He assumes, from the appearance of the remains, that they were a numerous people, and congregated in considerable cities; that they were essentially agricultural in their habits, and possessed a national religion, marked by imposing and cruel ceremonies; and that they were driven from their seats by the assaults of a ruder and hardier race on both their northern and southern frontiers. These conclusions were founded on an observation of the differing character of their works at different places. The great inclosures at Circleville and Newark, he was persuaded were not of a military nature; while those on the Ohio River were evidently designed for that purpose, and both could never have been created for the same use by the same people. The contest he regards as having been long and bloody, and the retreat, which was gradual, and delayed at positions favorable for defence, he considers to have been along the descent of the Ohio. In a note to his *Discourse*, General Harrison remarks upon some objections that may be suggested to the theory of the identity of this people with the Aztecs.

"The circumstance which militates most against the supposition of the identity of the Aztecs with the authors of the extensive ancient works in Ohio, is the admitted fact that the latter entered the valley of Anahuac from the northwest, that is, from California, which is much out of the direct route from Ohio to Mexico. A strong argument in favor of it is the similarity of the remains which are found in that region (California), as well as in Mexico itself, with those in the valley of the Ohio. I am not informed whether there are any such in the intermediate country between the lower Mississippi and California. If there are none, it will rather confirm and strengthen my opinion that the fugitives from the Ohio were,

---

[1] A Discourse on the Aborigines of the Valley of the Ohio. By William Henry Harrison. Cincinnati, 1838.

like those from Troy, a mere remnant, whose numbers were too small to erect works of so much labor as those they left behind had required; but after their strength had been increased by a residence of some time in California, the passion for such works returned with the ability to erect them."

"If the opinion is adopted that the Aztecs were never in Ohio, but had pursued the direct route from Asia (whence it is believed they all came) to California, along the coast of the Pacific Ocean, and that the authors of the Ohio erections were from the same continent and stock, the question may be asked: Where did the separation take place? Was it before they left Asia, or after their arrival on the American continent?"

If there are no similar works in the northeast of Asia, or on the route thence towards the Ohio, he thinks that fact would go far to show that such works originated in Ohio, and that those who erected them were the same people who afterwards sojourned in California and finally settled in Mexico; but if the opinion is adopted, that these were distinct peoples or different branches of the same Asiatic stock, it must be believed also that each fell into the practice of erecting extensive works of the same form and materials, in a manner not known to be practised by any other people, without any previous knowledge to guide them, and without any intercourse. This he deems very improbable, and adds that: "If the Aztecs were not the authors of the Ohio works, we can only account for the ultimate fate of those who were, by supposing that they were entirely extirpated, preferring, like the devoted Numantians, to be buried under the ruins of their own walls to seeking safety by an ignominious flight."

It will occur to the reader who is aware how wide an extent of country on this side of the Mississippi the remains referred to by General Harrison are now known to occupy, that any hypothesis respecting them must apply not merely to the valley of the Ohio, but to a territory reaching to Lake Ontario, if not to the St. Lawrence on the north, and to the Gulf of Mexico on the south; that, in the State of New York, there are works of defence of a character as distinctly marked as those on the Ohio, and that in Florida are mounds and inclosures as suggestive of religious ceremonials and barbaric pomp as those of Circleville and Newark.

The main portion of General Harrison's discourse is devoted to a correction of the prevalent opinion that the confederacy of "the Five Nations" had subjugated the tribes which formed the Illinois confederacy, and occupied the region between the Ohio and the Mississippi.[1]

---

[1] The argument in favor of the great antiquity of some of the earthworks at the west derived from the nature and size of the forest trees that cover them, is well illustrated by General Harrison in the following passage: "The process by which nature restores the forest to its original state, after being once cleared, is extremely slow. In our rich lands, it is, indeed, soon covered again with timber, but the character of the growth is entirely different, and continues so, through many generations of men. In several places on the Ohio, particularly upon the farm which I occupy, clearings were made in the first settlement, abandoned, and suffered to grow up. Some of them, now to be seen, of nearly fifty years growth, have made so little progress towards attaining the appearance of the immediately contiguous forest as to induce any man of reflection to determine, that at least ten times fifty years would be necessary before its complete assimilation could be effected. The sites of the ancient works on the

The next year a fac simile of one of the pictorial records referred to by General Harrison was published in connection with an essay on American Antiquities, by Mr. Delafield, of Cincinnati.[1] About the year 1780, the Chevalier Boturini, an Italian, visited Mexico for the purpose of obtaining information concerning the ancient inhabitants of America. He there received the polite attentions of the government, and every facility was afforded him of becoming acquainted with the history and customs of the country. He was highly successful in amassing valuable information, and in collecting hieroglyphic paintings, maps, drawings of the temples, idols, &c. From some unknown cause, before he was quite ready to return to Europe, he incurred the displeasure of the government, and was thrown into prison. There the unfortunate gentleman died, and his collections and manuscripts were taken from him and scattered.

Subsequently, Mr. Bullock, of London, went to Mexico with nearly the same views as those of Boturini. He also succeeded in obtaining many articles of

---

Ohio present precisely the same appearance as the circumjacent forest. You find on them all that beautiful variety of trees, which gives such unrivalled richness to our forests. This is particularly the case on the fifteen acres included within the walls of the work at the mouth of the Great Miami, and the relative proportions of the different kinds of timber are about the same. The first growth, on the same kind of land, once cleared and then abandoned to nature, on the contrary, is more homogeneous—often stinted to one or two, or at most three kinds of timber. If the ground had been cultivated, yellow locust, in many places, will spring up as thick as garden peas. If it has not been cultivated, the black and white walnut will be the prevailing growth. The rapidity with which these trees grow for a time, smothers the attempt of other kinds to vegetate and grow in their shade. The more thrifty individuals soon overtop the weaker of their own kind, which sicken and die. In this way there is soon only as many left as the earth will well support to maturity. All this time the squirrels may plant the seeds of those trees which serve them for food, and by neglect suffer them to remain—it will be in vain; the birds may drop the kernels, the external pulp of which has contributed to their nourishment, and divested of which they are in the best state for germinating, still it will be of no avail; the winds of heaven may waft the winged seeds of the sycamore, cotton-wood, and maple, and a friendly shower may bury them to the necessary depth in the loose and fertile soil—but still without success. The roots below rob them of moisture, and the canopy of limbs and leaves above, intercepts the rays of the sun and the dews of heaven; the young giants in possession, like another kind of aristocracy, absorb the whole means of subsistence, and leave the mass to perish at their feet. This state of things will not, however, always continue. If the process of nature is slow and circuitous, in putting down usurpation and establishing the equality which she loves, and which is the great characteristic of her principles, it is sure and effectual. The preference of the soil for the first growth, ceases with its maturity. It admits of no succession, upon the principles of legitimacy. The long undisputed masters of the forest may be thinned by the lightning, the tempest, or by diseases peculiar to themselves; and whenever this is the case, one of the oft rejected of another family will find between its decaying roots shelter and appropriate food; and, springing into vigorous growth, will soon push its green foliage to the skies, through the decayed and withering limbs of its blasted and dying adversary, the soil itself yielding it a more liberal support than to any scion from the former occupant. It will easily be conceived what a length of time it will require for a denuded tract of land, by a process so slow, again to clothe itself with the amazing variety of foliage which is the characteristic of the forests of this region. Of what immense age, then, must be those works, so often referred to, covered, as has been supposed by those who have the best opportunity of examining them, with the second growth, after the ancient forest state had been regained:" pp. 30, 31.

[1] An Inquiry into the Origin of the Antiquities of America. By John Delafield, Jr.: New York, London, and Paris, 1839.

interest, which he took home to London and exhibited in a room fitted up for the purpose. Among other curiosities, he obtained a very long pictorial record, declared by the native Mexicans to be a chart, delineating the travels of the Aztec race through the continent to their resting-place in the valley of Anahuac. This was said to have been among the collections of Boturini, and to have upon it numerical figures and a table of references in his handwriting.

Mr. Bullock afterwards left London and established his residence in Cincinnati, Ohio, bringing with him two copies of the chart, fac similes of the original. From one of them the exact transcript engraved for Mr. Delafield was taken, and that gentleman expressed his "full and unhesitating faith in the genuineness and authenticity" of the document. This chart, or pictorial record, is seven and a half inches wide, and unfolds to the length of eighteen feet. It begins with a representation of an island on which are two human figures, an altar or tumulus (apparently), and the Mexican symbol for *house* six times repeated. From the island a figure is rowing a boat to what appears to be intended for the main land; and a series of human figures—sometimes marching, and sometimes at rest—with symbols of various kinds, and rude drawings of natural objects, continues through the length of the chart. These are interpreted as exhibiting a passage across a strait corresponding to Behring's Strait, and a gradual progress southward, of many years' duration, often interrupted for considerable periods, and diversified by events of a varied nature; all these circumstances being indicated, either by the evident significance of the drawings or by Mexican symbols and characters, whose meaning is well established. It is not claimed that any of the signs point to a residence, or even a transit east of the Mississippi; but coincidences of climate, soil, and natural productions, have been detected, or imagined, with a route nearer the Pacific.[1]

In the text of Mr. Delafield's book, the notice of this document is preceded by his inquiry into the origin of American antiquities. Assuming that, on the discovery of the country, there were two distinct races inhabiting the continent—one civilized, comprehending the Mexicans and Peruvians, the other savage and nomadic, embracing all the families of the North American Indians; and that the civilized race went from the north, where they constructed the remains yet existing—he proposed to trace these races respectively to the source from whence they sprang. He divided the analogical evidence on which he rested his argument into seven classes, viz: I. PHILOLOGICAL. II. ANATOMICAL. III. MYTHOLOGICAL. IV. HIEROGLYPHIC. V. ASTRONOMICAL. VI. ARCHITECTURAL. VII. MANNERS AND CUSTOMS. These branches of inquiry, he fancied, unite in pointing to Egypt and Hindostan as the homes of the ancestors of the Mexicans, while they indicate the Mongolian origin of the barbarous tribes. Then, resorting to the national genealogies of Scripture and history, he followed the descent of the American aborigines from Chus or Chush, also called Cuth, the son of Ham, whose posterity, the Cuthians or Cuthites, were always a disorderly and wandering race; and some of whom, in process of time, were termed Σκυθαι, or Scythians, having the Greek Σ prefixed to their name.

---

[1] For a full exposition of Boturini's Chart, by Mr. Gallatin, see Trans. of Am. Ethnol. Soc., I, p. 120, *et seq.*

The author is able to track a division of the Cuthites, through various incidents of their history, to the northeastern parts of Asia, towards the point whence the Aztec emigration is supposed to have proceeded, as indicated by the Mexican chart.

In the work of Mr. Delafield, the antiquities of the United States are only referred to in connection with his argument, without any drawings, or details of description.

A different view of the introduction of population to this country, is taken in the able and more elaborate treatise of Mr. Bradford, published, under a somewhat similar title, in 1843.[1] This writer made no personal explorations, but, sitting in his study, carried forward his argument under the burden of an immense number and variety of citations from all classes of authorities. Hence his work is entitled to the merit, and is subject to all the disadvantages, attending that method of reasoning. Many of the statements so collected are such as will not bear the test of a rigid verification; and, although the justness of the author's conclusions should not be impaired by them, the erroneous impressions they convey are liable to be received by the incautious reader, and perhaps transferred to narratives and arguments where their influence is less likely to be corrected by the entire body of information with which they are associated.

Thus, a wrong idea of the state of art among the ancient Americans may easily be occasioned by admitting the hasty inferences of travellers and chance observers to the fellowship of better considered relations. A much higher degree of artistic and mechanical skill on the part of the primitive occupants of the regions now embraced in the United States, would be inferred from the summary in this volume than well-authenticated facts will warrant. For example, the passages respecting evidence of the working of gold and silver (including the process of gilding), the manufacture of glass beads, and the unqualified statement that "the inhabitants of New England appear to have possessed and manufactured chains, collars, and drinking cups of copper;" and many other citations, introduced as reliable illustrations of native skill and industry, exhibit the dangers incident to such a compilation.

But, aside from these considerations, Mr. Bradford's treatise is of high value and interest, not only on account of its great store of references, but for the reflections and opinions that are embodied with or deduced from them.

Mr. Bradford thus defines his purpose:—

"To embody and collate the descriptions of the most remarkable of the ancient remains and ruins scattered over the continent; to compare the traditions, manners, customs, arts, language, civilization, and religion, of its aboriginal inhabitants, internally, and with those of other nations; and thence to deduce the origin of the American race and its subsequent migrations—in a word, to attempt the determination of a portion of its unwritten history, is the object of this work."

His subject is treated of in two parts; the first having for its distinctive title,

---

[1] American Antiquities, and Researches into the Origin and History of the Red Race. By Alexander W. Bradford. New York, 1843: pp. 435.

"AMERICAN ANTIQUITIES;" the second that of "RESEARCHES INTO THE ORIGIN AND HISTORY OF THE RED RACE." Four chapters of Part I. are devoted to an enumeration and consideration of the different classes of antiquities in the United States; and two chapters are taken up with the antiquities of Mexico, the Central American States, and South America. Part II. consists of twelve chapters; and the matters embraced in them are discussed under the heads of "Comparison of Ancient Monuments; Ancient Civilization; Aboriginal Migrations; The Routes of Migration; Ancient Navigation, and the Drifting of Vessels; The Physical Appearance of the Aborigines—their Language, Astronomy, and Religion; The Pyramids; The Conclusion.

The whole is characterized by extensive research, and a careful analysis and combination of facts. At the close of the review of the relics and monuments of the United States he deduces from them: "1. That their authors were all of the same origin, branches of the same race, and possessed of similar customs and institutions. 2. That they were numerous, and occupied a great extent of territory. 3. That they had arrived at a considerable degree of civilization, were associated in large communities, and lived in extensive cities. 4. That they possessed the use of many of the metals, such as lead, copper, gold and silver, and probably the art of working in them. 5. That they sculptured in stone, and sometimes used that material in the construction of their edifices. 6. That they had the knowledge of the arch of receding steps; of the art of pottery; producing utensils and urns formed with taste, and constructed upon the principles of chemical composition; and of the art of brick-making. 7. That they worked the salt springs, and manufactured that substance. 8. That they were an agricultural people, living under the influence and protection of regular forms of government. 9. That they possessed a decided system of religion, and a mythology connected with astronomy, which, with its sister science, geometry, was in the hands of the priesthood. 10. That they were skilled in the art of fortification. 11. That the epoch of their original settlement in the United States, is of great antiquity; and lastly, That the only indications of their origin, to be gathered from the locality of their ruined monuments, point towards Mexico."

The results of Mr. Bradford's general inquiry are stated in the following extracts from his final chapter: "The facts adduced in the course of the preceding investigation, tend, it is conceived, to support the following conclusions:—

"I. That the three great groups of monumental antiquities in the United States, New Spain, and South America, in their style and character present indications of having proceeded from branches of the same human family:

"II. That these nations were a rich, populous, civilized, and agricultural people; constructed extensive cities, roads, aqueducts, fortifications, and temples; were skilled in the arts of pottery, metallurgy, and sculpture; had attained an accurate knowledge of the science of astronomy; were possessed of a national religion; subjected to the salutary control of a definite system of laws; and were associated under regular forms of government:

"III. That from the uniformity of their physical appearance; from the possession of relics of the art of hieroglyphic painting; from universal analogies in their language, religion, traditions, and methods of interring the dead; and from the general prevalence of certain arbitrary customs; nearly all the aborigines appear to be of the same descent and origin; and that the barbarous tribes are the broken, scattered, and degraded remnants of a society originally more enlightened and cultivated:

"IV. That two distinct ages may be pointed out in the history of the civilized nations—the first and most ancient, subsisting for a long and indeterminate period in unbroken tranquillity, and marked towards its close by the signs of social decadence; the second, distinguished by national changes, the inroads of barbarous or semi-civilized tribes, the extinction or subjugation of the old and the foundation of new and more extensive empires: and,

"V. That the first seats of civilization were in Central America; whence population was diffused through both continents, from Cape Horn to the Arctic Ocean."

In relation to the question of their origin, it appears:

"I. That the Red race, under various modifications, may be traced physically into Etruria, Egypt, Madagascar, ancient Scythia, Mongolia, China, Hindoostan, Malaya, Polynesia, and America, and was a primitive and cultivated branch of the human family: and,

"II. That the American aborigines are more or less connected with these several countries, by striking analogies in their arts, their customs and traditions, their hieroglyphical painting, their architecture and temple-building, their astronomical systems, and their superstitions, religion, and theocratical governments.

"It has long been a favorite theory, to trace the aborigines to a Tartar or Mongol migration from Siberia, by Behring's straits. But the Mexicans and Peruvians resemble the cultivated nations of oriental Asia even more closely than do the ruder tribes, the Siberian nomades; in fact they are *all* of the same race, and both in Asia and America, a decline into barbarism has produced analogous developments, which in connection with the relics of their ancient religion and customs, nearly assimilate the savages of both continents. It is not to be denied that there are some tribes in North America, which may have proceeded in modern times from Siberia; for example, the Chippewyans, and perhaps the Sioux, the Osages, Pawnees, and some of the northwestern nations; but even in relation to these, the proof depends mainly upon vague and uncertain traditions. But to suppose that the Mexicans, the Toltecs, the Chiapanese, the Mayas, and the Peruvians, were the descendants of such degraded and savage hordes as occupy northeastern Asia; or that they wandered from more southern Asiatic countries through the cold and inhospitable regions of the north, without leaving any vestiges of civilization on their way, appears equally contrary to experience and philosophy. The ancient monuments in Siberia are situated to the west and to the south, those of America are limited in their extent on the northwest; and in spite of the facility of communication afforded by the contiguity of the two continents in that direction, these facts would seem to be decisive of that question. On the other hand, the evidences of an early knowledge of the compass in China, of the great maritime skill of the Malays, and of their navigation, in remote ages, of the Asiatic seas, the facts stated in relation to the peopling of Islands by the accidental drifting of canoes, and more than all, the actual proof of the distribution of population over the numerous and distant islands of the great Pacific, from Asia to Easter Island, render it unnecessary to resort to the violent hypothesis of a northern route. What greater obstacles were there to impede a passage from Easter Island to the American coast, than attended a migration to Easter Island? Indeed this island itself appears to have been successively occupied by different families; and its pyramidical edifices, and its colossal obelisks and statues, are closely analogous to the American monuments."

"The Red race, then, appears to be a *primitive branch of the human family*, to have existed in many portions of the globe, distinguished for early civilization; and to have penetrated at a very ancient period into America. The American family does not appear to be derived from any nation now existing; but it is assimilated by numerous analogies to the Etrurians, Egyptians, Mongols, Chinese, and Hindoos; it is *most closely* related to the Malays and Polynesians; and the conjecture possessing perhaps the highest degree of probability, is that which maintains its origin from Asia, through the Indian Archipelago."

It will be perceived that Mr. Bradford's inferences have many points of originality; and that while his views harmonize with those which derive the Americans from Asiatic races, they are antagonistical to the idea of a connection by way of Behring's Strait, and a gradual advancement thence of emigrating tribes into Mexico and Peru, bearing with them the seeds of their ultimate civilization. He deems it best to employ in his survey the simple classification of mankind into three divisions, the White, the Red, and the Black, that is, the Caucasian, the Mongolian, and the Ethiopian, without taking into account the varieties that have sprung from intermixture; and his comprehensive application of the denomination *Red*, as a distinction of race, enables him to include nearly every people with whom analogies of customs, arts, or physical attributes, have been supposed to be traced in this country.

In 1845, the American Ethnological Society published the first volume of its Transactions, containing an account of mummies from the nitrous caves of Tennessee, and of various images of stone and clay found in that State; from Professor Troost, of the University of Tennessee; and also an historical and descriptive account of the *Grave Creek Mound*, and an inscribed stone, said to be found therein; from Mr. Schoolcraft. Much has been written about that "Grave Creek Stone;" and the characters upon it have been submitted to the judgment of various learned men and learned associations, but its authenticity has not been satisfactorily established. It will be referred to again in another place.

At an early stage of this historical sketch, it was proper to specify the minor efforts to convey information, or solve questions connected with our subject, appearing in the form of communications to literary and scientific journals, or in some incidental way brought to public notice. Whilst a large portion of facts and discussions relating to the archæology of the United States existed in no other shape this course was a matter of necessity. But such particularity would be inappropriate at the present period of the narrative; and only in case of the development of some new variety of antiquities, or a new field of research, is it desirable to enter into so minute a detail. We may mention, generally, that in the *American Journal of Science*, during the years from 1834 to 1844, were printed valuable papers from gentlemen who had examined particular works, or particular sections of country. The official reports of Topographical and Geological Surveyors also record many interesting facts and observations. The substance of these has, however, been mostly transferred to the archæological work of Messrs. Squier and Davis, to which we may next direct out attention.[1]

This was the first publication of the Smithsonian Institution, and was the result of explorations and investigations, commenced by the authors in the spring of 1845, and continued to the summer of 1847.

Dr. Davis had been previously located as a practising physician at Chillicothe, Ohio, which is in the heart of the most interesting remains that are found in the Mississippi basin, and apparently near the centre of the principal seats of ancient population. There he had been led by scientific curiosity, not only to examine the exterior of mounds and mural structures, abounding in the neighborhood, but to excavate in search of buried contents to explain the purpose of their formation. He had thus collected many singular and striking specimens of art, of superior execution, found in positions and connected with circumstances that promised well to repay the labor of more careful and more extended scrutiny; and, so far as his professional engagements permitted, he was devoting his time and his means to the pursuit.

While Dr. Davis was thus engaged, Mr. Squier became a resident of the State, and was soon attracted to the discoveries which his future colleague had commenced. Combining a knowledge of practical surveying, with that readiness of pen which experience in the editorial chair of a daily press was calculated to bestow, and prompted by the energy and ardor that have since characterized his scientific and literary labors, he gave himself up to the prosecution of studies and researches that might enable him to illustrate the nature and origin of those yet mysterious relics.[2]

These gentlemen, having united their exertions and resources for this mutual purpose, endeavored to obtain the co-operation and assistance of scientific institutions in the accomplishment of their design; and were so fortunate as to make an arrangement with the Secretary of the Smithsonian Institution, which encouraged them to proceed, and secured the publication of their work in a manner to give effect to its merits.

It was a little remarkable, considering all that had before been said and done about the same antiquities, how fresh the subject was to the public mind, how few had any intelligent information respecting it, and how generally unprepared was

---

[1] Ancient Monuments of the Mississippi Valley: comprising the results of extensive Original Surveys and Explorations: By E. G. Squier, A. M., and E. H. Davis, M. D. Published by the Smithsonian Institution, Washington, 1848.

[2] The writer visited Chillicothe in 1845, on behalf of the American Antiquarian Society, with reference to the movement for a re-survey of the antiquities of the west; and was made acquainted with the operations and intentions of the gentlemen above named, and the circumstances under which these originated.

the community at large for any correct conception of the nature of the marvels that might be revealed to an explorer. The time had certainly arrived when new efforts were called for to determine with accuracy the nature and extent of those vestiges of a higher social condition than had been transmitted to later races; and, happily, the men and the means were provided for the accomplishment of the object. No national questions of Science were capable of creating equal interest abroad, or were likely to excite more general attention at home. A more active spirit of inquiry upon all points connected with the primeval history of the western hemisphere, has evidently been promoted by the publication of the work of Messrs. Squier and Davis, and more correct ideas have in consequence been attained.

An analysis of this work in detail will not be attempted; but an effort will be made to gather from it the prominent impressions that a new and wider survey of these remains produced, after the lapse of twenty-five years from the time when they were first collectively examined and illustrated.

The authors satisfied themselves that aboriginal monuments in the United States are diffused over a vast extent of country; that they are found on the sources of the Alleghany river, and in the western part of the State of New York, on the east; and extend thence westwardly along the southern shore of Lake Erie, and through Michigan and Wisconsin to Iowa and Nebraska, on the west. They found no account of their occurrence above the Great Lakes. They refer to Lewis and Clarke as reporting their existence on the Missouri, one thousand miles above its junction with the Mississippi, and state that they have been observed on the Kansas and Platte, and other remote western rivers. They are represented as being found all over the intermediate country, and through the valley of the Mississippi to the Gulf of Mexico, and as lining the shores of the Gulf from Texas to Florida, extending, in diminished numbers, into South Carolina. They are declared to exist in great numbers in Ohio, Indiana, Illinois, Wisconsin, Missouri, Arkansas, Kentucky, Tennessee, Louisiana, Mississippi, Alabama, Georgia, Florida, and Texas; and to be found, in less numbers, in the western portions of New York, Pennsylvania, Virginia, and North and South Carolina; as also in Michigan, Iowa, and the Mexican Territory beyond the Rio Grande del Norte. In all these various regions they are said to be mainly confined to the neighborhood of the principal streams, and when occurring far from them to be of small size.

In this wide extent of country, three geographical divisions were apparent to the authors as possessing remains peculiar to themselves, although certain general points of resemblance pervaded them all. Thus in the region bordering the Upper Lakes, particularly in Wisconsin, the earth-works were in emblematical forms, rudely representing animals and other effigies. In the great section watered by the Ohio and its tributaries, very few such structures were to be seen; but fortified elevations, and large enclosures of symmetrical shape abounded; the latter occupying the river bottoms, and appearing from their formal arrangement, their suites of mounds, and their graded avenues, adapted rather to religious ceremonials than to purposes of habitation or protection. Nearer the Gulf of Mexico, the fortifications, the enclosures, and the conical tumuli, became more rare; and truncated pyramidal structures of less height than the mounds of the north, but of greater horizontal dimensions, and connected with systems of dependent works, were spread numerously through those southern districts.

The central or intermediate region, between the northern and southern extremes, was the principal field of investigation by Messrs. Squier and Davis, as it had been that of Mr. Atwater. To this their personal explorations were confined; and notices of antiquities beyond its limit necessarily assume a supplementary position in the work, as derived exclusively from extraneous sources of information, and are not strictly embraced within the descriptive classifications applied to the varieties of remains they had themselves examined.

Although the vestiges of ancient art and labor, in all their forms, usually constitute an associated system, the different earth and stone-works, for convenience of exploration, were resolved into two general classes, viz: ENCLOSURES, bounded by embankments, circumvallations, or walls; and simple tumuli, or MOUNDS. Of these, subordinate divisions were made; as ENCLOSURES FOR DEFENCE, and ENCLOSURES FOR SACRED AND MISCELLANEOUS PURPOSES; MOUNDS OF SACRIFICE, TEMPLE MOUNDS, MOUNDS OF SEPULTURE, &c.

The writers state that "nothing can be more plain than that most of the remains in *northern* Ohio are military works." They are of a slight character, requiring palisades upon their embankments to render them of much service for protection; but they are contiguous to water, usually cutting off the bends of rivers, guarding the space thus enclosed from access by land, or they are on the high bank of some stream, and invariably have no higher land near them from which they could be commanded. The walls are generally double, and the ditch always *without*. The scarcity of mounds, the absence of pyramids of earth, and of rectangular works, and their general difference from the fortified positions nearer the Ohio, are supposed by Messrs. Squier and Davis to indicate that they belonged to a distinct people.

It is mentioned that entrenchments of a similar character occur still further northward and eastward, and also in Kentucky and Tennessee, implying the existence of sparse but warlike tribes around that central region which bears evidence of denser population and more stationary habits of life.

The defensive works of this interior section are described as exhibiting much judgment in the choice of their locations and much skill in their construction. They are usually upon places above the level of the surrounding country, and naturally difficult of access, having on all sides, or all but one, a precipitous descent. The common defence is a simple embankment thrown up along, or a little below the brow of the hill, varying in height and solidity as the declivity is more or less steep; but the parapets, in form and character, are adapted to the nature of the position, which is guarded by a fosse, by double walls, and mounds, or other contrivances, as circumstances require.

These fortresses vary in size, enclosing from five acres to one hundred and forty. The average of twenty-four of them is forty-six acres. Within some of the largest are marks of habitation, as if they had been occupied by communities in some time of prolonged danger. The smaller ones are most numerous. The walls of earth and stone, it is remarked, although often high and heavy, would in themselves furnish very imperfect means of protection and resistance; hence it is obvious that they were surmounted by palisades, or by something equivalent. They also have many gateways, or openings, which must have been defended by perishable or temporary obstructions.

The enclosures whose form, position, and attendant circumstances, indicate that they were erected for other than defensive purposes, are elaborately exemplified. They are termed *sacred* enclosures, on the ground that the supposition of their being designed for religious rites and ceremonies is the most natural and satisfactory one. Some of them prove to be circles or squares of exact proportions; and precisely the same dimensions have been found in separate localities. The characteristics ascribed to them are, that they are often in a position to be commanded by adjacent heights; that when a ditch occurs, it is *within* the embankments; that, although occasionally isolated, they are usually in groups, forming fanciful figures, but evidently the result of a plan or system; that the larger circles are oftenest found in combination with rectangular works, and connected with them either directly or by avenues; that the walls are comparatively slight, from three to seven feet high, seldom accompanied by a ditch, and formed from earth taken evenly from the surface near them, or from large pits in the neighborhood; and that they enclose pyramidal mounds not much elevated, flat on the tops, with graded paths of ascent, and well adapted to be used for altars or for the foundations of sacred edifices.

The greater number of circles are said to have a nearly uniform diameter of two hundred and fifty feet; yet many of the examples given contain from twelve to twenty-five acres, and some include a space of fifty acres.[1]

The broad and graded avenues ascending the plateaus on which the principal structures are situated, as if prepared for the solemn march of a procession; the lines of low parallel embankments uniting in a curve at one end, suggesting no conceivable design of practical utility; and the nature and discovered uses of the tumuli connected with the systems of works designated as sacred, are explained and delineated in a manner which confirms and illustrates their adaptedness to the purposes ascribed to them.

If Messrs. Squier and Davis were enabled thus to corroborate previous opinions respecting the two classes of Enclosures, they were even more successful in exemplifying the characters and designs of the various kinds of Tumuli.

The low conical or dome-shaped tumuli within the enclosures termed sacred, or closely adjoining them, were found to exhibit these peculiarities. At their bases beneath the vertex were raised and concave symmetrical fabrics, usually of clay, that might well be called altars, inasmuch as they had upon them the customary evidences of sacrifice: There were human bones mixed with the articles likely to be most precious to a rude people, viz: beads, pipes, images, and other ornaments and implements; all of which had been subjected to fire of sufficient intensity or duration to bake the fabric of clay on which they were deposited. Then over

[1] The great circle at Newark, enclosing 30 acres, has a wall of 12 feet perpendicular height and 50 feet base; with an interior ditch 7 feet deep and 35 feet wide.

them had been ceremoniously placed a covering of earth in layers, or strata, of different materials, carefully and evenly spread, and adjusted to a conical shape—the first stratum, perhaps, of loam, the next a thin covering of pure sand; earth and sand, or small stones, continuing to alternate, but in different proportions, till the mound was completed. In consideration of their position, and the circumstances attending them, these received the name of *sacrificial mounds.* They were the most fruitful of relics; the richest among them being of slight elevation and unimposing exterior. Some of them contained altars alone, or relics without human remains, showing that they could not be regarded as places of interment.

A more numerous class of mounds, generally removed from enclosures, and often of great height, were found to cover a single skeleton—in very rare instances more than one—enveloped in bark or coarse matting, and surrounded by a rude protection of timber. The great Grave Creek mound, the most striking example of this class, is a double monument of unusual character. At its base were two skeletons, and thirty-five feet (or half the total height of the mound) above them, was another; so that the superior altitude of this tumulus is the result of two interments, probably at different periods of time.

These mounds contain, with the human remains, various ornaments and implements, but no altars, and the remains have not been burned. They are therefore denominated *sepulchral mounds,* and might with equal propriety be styled *monumental* mounds.

The third variety of earthen elevations, termed *temple mounds,* were so named because their place within the enclosures, their rectangular and truncated forms, and the peculiarity of inclined planes of easy ascent attached to them, make them correspond to the Mexican structures on which sacred edifices were situated. In the United States, near the gulf of Mexico, such was also the use of the similarly shaped mounds which characterize that region.

These diversities are clearly defined by Messrs. Squier and Davis, their antiquity well established, and their occasional invasion by later races satisfactorily distinguished from their original and legitimate use.

Another kind of mounds, erected on commanding positions, they believe to have been intended for signal or alarm posts; ranges of them being so situated that by their means signals of fire could be transmitted a great distance in a few moments. These are called *mounds of observation.*

While the authors are confident that the leading purposes of the mounds (at least those in Ohio) have been rightly determined, they admit the existence of many of an anomalous character, conforming to no classification. It appears natural enough that this should be so when we consider that mound building, for some purpose or other, is a common practice with rude nations, and still prevailing to some extent among the aborigines of the country. There are mounds that are composed of bones collected with pious care by recent tribes from the burial places of their fathers; and there are others known to have grown from gradual contributions made by the passing Indian, in recognition of an inherited obligation to mark the spot, for some reason that he may not himself be able to explain. It would be too much to expect that the motive for these varied and multitudinous erections should in all cases be made apparent. If the most prominent and remarkable have been classified, and their single or associated purpose elucidated, it is quite as much as can reasonably be required of an explorer.

The labors of these gentlemen were specially rewarded by the number and quality of the works of art obtained by them from the sacrificial and sepulchral tumuli; and, what is of great importance, they established the principle of discrimination between articles of European origin, or modern manufacture, which have by some means been buried in and about the ancient works, and the true relics of their builders. Many of the hypotheses that have confused in so remarkable a degree the archæology of the United States are due entirely to the carelessness and ignorance which in this particular have heretofore prevailed.

The true relics of the mounds were found to be articles of pottery of delicate material and graceful form, in the shape of vases, pipes, and moulded figures; implements and ornaments of copper, hammered without melting from the native metal; arrow-heads and spear-heads and various ornaments and implements of stone, precisely similar to those of modern use; strings of pearls, and beads of shells, bone, ivory, and the claws of animals; plates of mica, pieces of galena, and small portions of silver, hammered thin and made to cover some of the smaller ornaments; and, with these, sculptured figures of animals and the human head, in the form of pipes, wrought with great delicacy and spirit from some of the hardest stones. The last-named are relics that imply a very considerable degree of art, and, if believed to be the work of the people with whose remains they are found, would tend greatly to increase the wonder that the art of sculpture among them was not manifested in other objects and places. The fact that nearly all the finer specimens of workmanship represent birds, or land and marine animals, belonging to a different latitude, while the pearls, the knives of obsidian, the marine shells, and the copper, equally testify to a distant though not extra-continental origin, may, however, exclude these from being received as proofs of local industry and skill. Whether they can be considered as evidences of commercial relations with remote places and people, as suggested by Messrs. Squier and Davis, or as having been casually obtained through intermediate agencies, must depend upon other circumstances than their mere presence where they are found.

The silver crosses, the glass beads, the plated and gilded ornaments, the iron instruments, that have figured in so many speculations, are shown to be modern deposits whose origin it is not difficult to trace; and the stone medal from the Grave Creek mound, fancied to contain either Libyan or Runic characters, which has excited so much discussion, is pronounced to be wholly unworthy of confidence as a genuine relic.

The account, in this volume, of the pictorial or emblematic earthworks of that district which is chiefly included in the State of Wisconsin, was derived from papers of Messrs. Richard C. and S. Taylor, published in the *American Journal of Science and Arts*, and from a notice by Prof. John Locke, in his *Report on the Mineral Lands of the United States*, presented to Congress in 1840.

The account of the monuments of the Southern States is also compiled from the descriptions and delineations of other writers; but these chiefly in manuscript, and therefore not generally known to the public.

In some respects the earthworks of the South are comparatively of minor interest, because they are less varied in form and less anomalous in character than those of the middle region, and because they are to a considerable extent explained by the usages of the people existing when Europeans entered the country. On the other hand, their numbers, their magnitude, and the necessary labor of their execution, render them equally objects of surprise and curiosity, if they lack, in any degree, the bewildering attraction of vagueness and mystery.

In closing their remarks upon what they have investigated and described, these gentlemen wisely refrain from drawing many general conclusions. They regard the antiquity of the ancient monuments of the Mississippi valley as manifested by their position beyond the latest formed terraces of the river banks, by the exceedingly decayed state of the skeletons in the mounds, and by the age of the trees upon them that are in no way distinguishable from the primitive forests. They think it clear that the population must have been numerous, and essentially homogeneous in customs, habits, religion, and government; that as their remains are almost entirely confined to fertile valleys, or productive alluvions bordering on lakes and streams, that circumstance, in connection with their nature and extent, necessarily implies the derivation of sustenance from agriculture, involving also such particulars of manners and customs as are incident to stationary and agricultural life; and they venture to suggest that the facts collected point to a connection, more or less intimate, between the race of the mounds and the semi-civilized nations of Mexico, Central America, and Peru.

While Messrs. Squier and Davis were completing their general survey of the antiquities of the United States, Mr. Schoolcraft published his "Notes on the Iroquois."[1]

Next to the valley of the Ohio, no other northern section of the Union presents so great a number and variety of aboriginal remains as the State of New York; and no other native race has been found to possess so much of warlike energy, capacity of organization for combined effort, and profound national policy, as the Iroquois. Their celebrated confederacy, first of five, then of six nations, their systematic plans of conquest, their sagacious management of the fruits of victory, their high-toned manliness of character, their eloquence, their decision and tenacity of purpose, have given a peculiar interest to their history. How far the evidences of former conflicts—the fortified enclosures, and defensive parapets, so frequent in western and northwestern New York, and extending even to more interior localities—are to be explained by their warlike and aggressive habits, has always been a matter of uncertainty and debate. Reference has already been made to inquiries that have, from time to time, been directed, sometimes by eminent citizens of the State, towards the materials of archæological information existing within its limits.

Mr. Schoolcraft was at pains to collect the statistics of the ancient and present

---

[1] Notes on the Iroquois; or Contributions to American History, Antiquities, and General Ethnology. By Henry R. Schoolcraft, Albany, 1847.

condition of the Iroquois population; and to gather from facts and traditions whatever information could be obtained of their origin and history, the principles of their government, their religious ideas and ceremonies, their arts and sciences, and their military enterprises. To these he added archæological investigations respecting the structures and relics that are found upon their ancient seats.

Whether the traditionary tales of *Cusic*, the chronicler of his race, or any of the poetical legends preserved by Mr. Schoolcraft, have in them gleams of historical truth, or no, is a point on which opinions are divided. They have, at least, served to fire the genius of one of our most accomplished poets; and the Lay of Hiawatha, "the Iroquois Quetzalcoatl," has been transferred from the cabin of the savage to the drawing-rooms of literature and fashion, like a captive Indian maiden, with as much of native decoration, and as little of artificial costume, as the conventionalities of civilized taste would permit.

"With the odors of the forest,
With the dew and damp of wigwams,
With the rushing of great rivers,
With its frequent repetitions,
And their wild reverberations
As of the thunder of the mountains."

The "Notes" of Mr. Schoolcraft constitute a comprehensive treatise, uniting all the varieties of illustration, historical, topographical, philological, and anecdotical, that might serve to elucidate his subject; while vestiges of former arts and labors receive a prominent share of consideration and representation.

The aboriginal remains of New York were, however, deemed of sufficient importance to justify a more special and thorough exploration; and this was subsequently accomplished by Mr. Squier, under the joint auspices of the Smithsonian Institution and the Historical Society of the State.[1]

Without dwelling on the particulars of his investigation, we may remark that, after examining many, and taking a general observation of others, he estimated the number of works in New York to be two hundred, or two hundred and fifty, all of which he considered to have been intended for defensive purposes. Mounds are not included in this enumeration; and as they are not connected with the mural structures, but are uniformly sepulchral, and similar to the tumuli not unfrequently raised by existing tribes, they were not regarded as deserving special attention. They are said to be far from numerous, and to owe their origin, probably, to the custom, common to many tribes, of collecting, at fixed periods, the bones of their dead, and depositing them together, with solemn ceremonies.

It is stated that the enclosures are marked by great similarity of position, and are, for the most part, small, including from one to four acres, though sometimes embracing as many as sixteen acres; that the embankments are slight, and the ditches shallow, the former varying from one foot to four feet in height; and that

---

[1] Aboriginal Monuments of the State of New York. Comprising the results of Original Surveys and Explorations, with an Illustrative Appendix. By E. G. Squier, A. M. Smithsonian Contributions, Vol. II.

there appears to be entire uniformity in conditions of occupancy, and in remains of art within their walls. It is represented that these relics of art and traces of occupancy are absolutely identical with those which mark the forts and fortified towns occupied by Indians within the period of historical records.

"All the facts and coincidences," says Mr. Squier, "go to show that if the earthworks of western New York are of remote date, they were not only *secondarily*, but *generally* occupied by the Iroquois, or neighboring and contemporary nations, or else—and this hypothesis is most consistent and reasonable—were erected by them. * * * I am driven to the conclusion that they were erected by the Iroquois or their neighbors.

"Except so far as they illustrate the system of defence practised by the aboriginal inhabitants, and show that they were, to a degree, fixed and agricultural in their habits, they have slight bearing upon the grand ethnological and archæological questions of the country."

And yet—and here is food for reflection—we learn from the drawings and descriptions that, while enclosures of a sacred or ceremonial character, with their accompaniments, are wanting, the mural remains of New York bear a striking resemblance to those of Northern Ohio; and, with less of symmetry, less expenditure of labor, and general inferiority of size, do not differ materially in form and structure from works of defence ascribed to the ancient race. Many of them are now covered with heavy forests; and the suggestion of Mr. Squier, that it may not have been essential to the purposes of the builders that the forests should be removed, cannot be more applicable to them than to others, especially as he speaks of trees, from one foot to three feet in diameter, standing upon the embankments, and in the trenches. The relics they yield, though characterized as such as are known to have been common among the Iroquois, exhibit a near affinity to those of the same class from the western mounds. The vases are described as of very good material, and worked and ornamented with considerable skill and taste; the pipes as often fancifully moulded, some bearing the forms of animals, whose distinctive features are well preserved, others in shape of human heads, of fine quality and well burned; some, indeed, so hard, smooth, and symmetrical, as almost to induce doubts of their aboriginal origin. The terra-cottas, other than pipes, are also pronounced to be very creditable specimens of art.

The *Appendix*, in this publication, is of greater length than the memoir to which it is attached; and treats more or less fully, with frequent illustrative drawings, and much evidence of research, upon many points of general archæological interest essential to a comprehensive view of the subject of American antiquities. For the convenience of readers seeking information, the titles of its contents are here subjoined in a note.[1]

---

[1] Contents of Appendix to Aboriginal Remains of New York, viz: Ancient works in Pennsylvania and New Hampshire. Character of Indian defences. Defences of the ancient Mexicans and Peruvians. Comparison of the defensive structures of the American Aborigines with those of the Pacific Islanders, Celts, etc. Construction of mounds by existing Indian tribes. Sepulchral mounds in Mexico, Central America, etc. Sepulchral monuments of the ancient world. Probable funeral rites of the

An opportunity of indulging in comparisons, and drawing inferences from analogies, to which the author and his colleague, Dr. Davis, felt it imprudent to yield while recording their observations, was thus afforded to Mr. Squier; and many interesting collateral facts, as well as many instructive coincidences, are added to their more strictly limited narrations.

The region between Lake Michigan and the Mississippi, now constituting the State of Wisconsin, had hitherto been comparatively unexplored for archæological purposes; although known to present some peculiar features, and to possess remains of a singular and distinctive character.

Works intended for defence, and such as are apparently designed for religious or sacrificial ceremonials, are there seldom found; but structures of no great elevation, though often on a scale of considerable horizontal extent, representing a variety of fanciful forms, are frequent along the courses of the streams, and by the borders of the lakes.

The figures are described as chiefly those of Lizards, Turtles, Birds, Bears, Foxes, and Men; combined with straight lines, angles, crosses, curves, and other simple embankments. Whatever these may have been intended to portray, there is a uniformity in their configuration which manifests that the outlines are not accidental, but possessed to their makers a distinct and definite meaning.

They appear to be confined within a limited territory, between the Mississippi and Lake Michigan; not extending far below the southern line of Wisconsin, nor much beyond the northern extremity of Lake Winnebago; and diminish in numbers and variety as the two last named boundaries are approached.

That they exist there, and there only, is a fact hardly less remarkable than the anomalous nature of the works themselves; and attention is naturally directed to the physical peculiarities of the district where they are found.

Wisconsin is marked by no great or sudden variations of surface. The hills are seldom more than gentle swells or undulations of land; the highest ridges being those that separate the rivers which run to Lake Superior from those that flow into the Mississippi. At certain points the waters of opposite streams sometimes mingle at high floods, and the portages are always short and easy. In general the flow of the rivers is even and sluggish, expanding, especially on the eastern side of the State, into a profusion of shallow basins, or forming lakes of larger dimensions. Yet, springing from cold and limpid fountains, these are free from miasma and exuberant with wholesome animal life. The fishes are of the finest flavor; and the wild rice that chokes the shallower, and lines the borders of the deeper waters, affords sustenance to myriads of aquatic birds and beasts, that fatten upon the abundance of nutritious aliment. Even the most wet and marshy districts are said not to be productive of fogs or humid exhalations. The air is clear,

---

Mound-Builders. The Mounds not general burial-places; Great Indian cemeteries. Aboriginal sacred enclosures; Temples of the North American Indians; of the Mexicans, Central Americans, and Peruvians; of the Polynesian Islanders, Hindus, etc.; Primitive temples of the British Islands; Symbolism of temples. Stone-heaps; Stones of Memorial, etc. Additional monuments in New York. Use of copper by the American Aborigines. Use of silver.

dry, and healthful; the climate milder than that of the interior of New York; both summer and winter are tempered by the vicinity of the great lakes; and the season and the soil are favorable to vegetation.

It may be assumed, therefore, that the seat of these remarkable works is well adapted to the support of a numerous population, supplying, as it does, the means of savage comfort, and even luxury, without the necessity of laborious exertion. A nation so located, sheltered on three sides by great bodies of water, and favored with such facilities for interior communication, we might expect to find maintaining its independence, and cultivating arts or founding institutions which would leave numerous and distinguishable traces behind them. Yet, the emblematic monuments excepted, no prominent relics have been discovered. The remains of protective, and of ceremonial enclosures, the usual evidences of stationary population, are almost entirely wanting; and only the mounds of more recent date appear to contain the ornaments and utensils so commonly placed in the graves of the aborigines.

Though one of the youngest States, Wisconsin is among the oldest historical regions of the Union. Before the Pilgrims landed at Plymouth, the French missionaries ascended the Ottawa River from the St. Lawrence, and advanced towards the Great Lakes; and before Boston was settled they had established posts in the neighborhood of Lake Michigan. In 1639, Nicolet, the interpreter, explored Green Bay, ascended Fox River, and embarked on the Wisconsin. Thirty-four years later, Marquette and Jolliet, following in his steps, completed the discovery and exploration of the Mississippi. Thus the rivers and lakes of Wisconsin were made memorable by first opening the way to the interior of the West.

Another circumstance of antiquarian interest is connected with the territory bounding on Lake Superior. The copper mines, that have recently attracted so much attention, are supposed to have been wrought at some distant period by the natives. It has even been conjectured that they were the source of supply to the whole aboriginal population of the country north of the Gulf of Mexico; and that remote tribes were accustomed to send deputations to these localities, or obtained the metal by traffic with natives nearer the mines. Mr. Schoolcraft has suggested that the region may have been consecrated to neutrality like that of the celebrated pipe-stone quarries, and that parties of different tribes, thus secured from molestation, may have assembled there at certain seasons to procure their supplies of ore.

The reports of Dr. Jackson, Messrs. Foster and Whitney, and others, employed by Congress as topographical and geological surveyors, afford curious accounts of the evidences of ancient operations observed by them. They found not only masses of native copper from which portions had been rudely severed, but excavations in the solid rock, apparently wrought with great labor, with the simple implements of the savage—the tools with which they had worked lying near in large quantities.

There may, however, be some danger of confounding the results of the labors of Europeans at the mines, with those of the natives. As early as 1632, the existence of the mines was known to the French; for they are mentioned in the narrative of Gabriel Sagard, printed at Paris in that year; and they must have been frequently visited by traders, who may have endeavored to detach from their beds some of the masses now bearing the marks of such efforts. As any tools of iron that might be left behind would be eagerly seized by the Indians, it is hardly to be expected that such should be found in the vicinity.

At any rate, at a later period, yet so long ago as 1771, an English company under Alexander Henry, was employed for a time at the forks of the Onontagon river; and it may not always be easy to distinguish the operations of the unassisted Indian, anterior to the arrival of the whites, from those of later date, when the labors of the two races may have been combined or contemporaneous. Still, it is said that excavations bearing marks of extreme antiquity not to be mistaken, are found in several localities; and that great quantities of metal must have been obtained from the surface alone; fully warranting the opinion, strengthened by native tradition, that, from periods of unknown remoteness, the aboriginal inhabitants of a large extent of country obtained their copper ornaments and utensils from that quarter.

When first made known to the whites, Wisconsin was occupied, in part, by two tribes, the Winnebagoes and the Menomonies, not only distinct from one another, but differing materially, in important circumstances, from others in their vicinity. Carver tells us, that while with the Winnebagoes he employed himself in collecting the most certain intelligence of their origin, language, and customs; and, from the information obtained, he came to the conclusion that they originally resided in some of the provinces belonging to New Mexico. Mr. Schoolcraft, in his narrative of Gov. Cass's expedition, describes them as a "savage and bloodthirsty tribe, who came many years ago from the South, and are related to some of the Mexican tribes."

The supposed discovery of the remains of an ancient city in the valley of Rock river, within the territory of the Winnebagoes, gave rise, at one period, to much speculation, which, on the other hand, would make the Mexicans to have been emigrants from Wisconsin. The name of *Aztalan* was given to the imaginary city, in the belief that it must be the place referred to in the traditions of the Aztecs, which represent their ancestors as coming from a country at the north, near large bodies of water, and called Aztalan from that circumstance. Later investigations, however, have not confirmed the original marvellous statements of the discoverers; and the place is chiefly to be regarded as furnishing the only instance, among the numerous works in Wisconsin, of an *enclosure* in some degree analogous to those which in other States are supposed to be intended for religious purposes.

The territory south of Lake Superior, which includes the State of Wisconsin and a small portion of Michigan, certainly possesses no little archæological interest. Its striking physical features are associated with many early incidents of romantic adventure; it is the seat of mineral treasures towards which the desires of a whole continent of barbarous tribes might converge, and may have been rendered sacred by that circumstance; and, moreover, its aboriginal monuments are anomalous and strange, appearing not so much like structures for any sacred or civil purpose, as like hieroglyphic or symbolic characters. If instead of being clustered on the surface of the earth they had been drawn on rocks and stones, efforts would be made to read them as records. They would derive a superior interest from the supposition that they are, as has been suggested, the "totems" of tribes, perhaps memorials of amity or alliance, written upon the ground where adverse nations were accustomed to meet in peace. It must be confessed that pictorial writing on so immense a scale, with a sovereign state for a tablet, is a phenomenon unparalleled in monumental history.

The great horizontal dimensions of these effigies, raised but a few feet above the surface of the ground, was doubtless the reason why they failed to arrest the attention of travellers at an early period, their forms not being always perceptible from a single point of view, and sometimes only developed by the measurements of the surveyor.

It has been remarked that they were observed first by Mr. Lapham, in 1836. In 1850, that gentleman entered into an arrangement with the American Antiquarian Society, and, on behalf of that institution, commenced a thorough archæological survey of the State. His notes and drawings, when completed, were transferred to the Smithsonian Institution, and constitute a portion of the volume of Contributions published in 1855.[1]

The ordinary mounds were found to possess no peculiar interest; except that a few of them, even as far north as Lake Superior, have the pyramidal truncated form, common at the South, and, in the Middle States, confined to sacred enclosures, where they are regarded as altars, or the sites of temples. The emblematic tumuli were seldom seen in isolated positions, but usually in groups, with a mound at some elevated point, commanding a view of the whole. They yielded no relics to illustrate the habits and arts of their builders, or the design of their construction.

We have had frequent occasion to mention the publications of Mr. Schoolcraft, who has been foremost among pioneers in the investigation of Aboriginal History, and is now the chronicler of its ultimate results. A reference to the labors in which he is still engaged will appropriately conclude this bibliographical epitome.

Under an act of Congress, of March 3d, 1847, the Secretary of War was required "to collect and digest such statistics and materials as may illustrate the history, present condition, and future prospects of the Indian tribes of the United States;" and the fulfilment of this duty was committed to the charge of Mr. Schoolcraft.

By the plan of execution adopted, the several points of investigation were divided into numerous heads or titles; and minute questions in relation to each, framed for the purpose of eliciting information, were distributed, in the form of a circular, throughout the country.

The results of these inquiries, combined with documents in possession of the government, and the editor's private stores of experience and observation, have been arranged under a series of distinct titles, that are continued through the published volumes; each title embracing the portion of new matter that falls to its share, while new titles are occasionally created, when required by the nature of the materials.

---

[1] "The Antiquities of Wisconsin, as Surveyed and Described, By I. A. Lapham, Civil Engineer, &c., On behalf of the American Antiquarian Society."

These *collectanea* are necessarily of a miscellaneous, and not always entirely consistent character, and are liable to a good deal of repetition. Whether they are to have no other than their present documentary form, or are to be digested in a future volume, has not been announced. In the mean time, through the various communications and compilations of which the work is composed, a current of editorial opinion is permitted to flow, that, to a careful reader, may sufficiently indicate the general conclusions which the aggregate of information is deemed to justify.

Under the title of ANTIQUITIES, some new surveys have been registered, and fresh information collected, especially respecting remains at the South, and relating to rocks bearing sculptured marks and figures. Implements, utensils, ornaments, and fabrics, are minutely described and illustrated; and, in this and other connections, the number and variety of archæological elements embodied in the volumes are too great to be particularized. They comprehend comparisons of ancient and modern arts and customs; the traditionary legends of the natives; the scientific deductions of naturalists; philological analyses and classifications; and, in brief, whatever else has been supposed in any way to pertain to the subject. Throughout all departments of the work admitting of exemplification, the artist and the engraver have profusely distributed the highest efforts of their illustrative skill.

It has been less necessary, and less desirable, to notice particularly, in previous pages, the numerous publications of Mr. Schoolcraft during his protracted study of Indian history, because the wide range of these national volumes may be presumed to embrace his latest knowledge, and his matured reflections, on all points to which his attention has at any time been directed. We may gather, from the different connections in which his views are expressed, some prominent examples that will disclose their general nature and tendency.

While frequently admonishing the reader of the little reliance to be placed upon Indian *traditions,* they are still received as legitimate, if sometimes deceptive, elements of opinion; and generally, in the hypotheses that are framed, have more or less of weight attached to their evidence. As they have played no part of much importance in our narrative thus far, it is of more interest to observe the degree of consideration they receive from Mr. Schoolcraft.

Speaking of the origin of the natives, he says: "Thus we have traditionary gleams of a foreign origin of the race of the North American Indians; from separate stocks of nations, extending, at intervals, from the arctic circle to the valley of Mexico. Dim as these traditions are, they shed some light on the thick historical darkness which shrouds the period. They point decidedly to a foreign, to an oriental, if not a Shemitic origin." (Vol. I, p. 26.)

On page 199 of Vol. IV. he says, in reference to the *Eries:* "The veil that conceals their history is lifted in a curious, ill-digested, and obscure pamphlet of Indian traditions, by a semi-educated Tuscarora (Cusic), which was printed in the ancient country of the Iroquois in 1825."[1]

In adverting to the Iroquois traditions recorded by Cusic, that refer to the

---

[1] Sketches of the Ancient History of the Six Nations. By David Cusic.

mounds and fortifications of the West as the works of the southern and western tribes—which, "after long and bloody wars, that are conjectured to have lasted for centuries," were overcome by the Algonco-Iroquois confederacy—although remarking that the chronology and dynastic terms of Cusic's pamphlet are believed to be conjectural or faulty, he says: "That the ancestors of the Iroquois had been parties in this ancient war against the southern intruders, or Allegans, may be inferred. . . The epoch of these old and general wars, so obscurely yet certainly pointed to, is deducible chiefly from the state of the archæological vestiges." (Vol. IV. p. 137, and Vol. V. p. 63.)[1]

Again, alluding to western earthworks, he remarks, "The fullest consideration of the Indian history and character denotes these works to have been built by aboriginal hands. That these beginnings of an Appalachian Indian empire were finally frustrated by the surrounding barbarous tribes, is denoted by the few traditions recorded. It fell, we may affirm, by division, anarchy, and mutual distrust, &c." (Vol. IV. p. 148.)

Again: "We may, on the most enlarged view which can be taken on the subject, recognize in the mounds, earthworks, and mural monuments of the Mississippi valley, the results, and final extinguishment of that impulse towards civilization which was commenced by the Toltecs of Mexico. It cannot be inferred, from our present survey of the languages, that large numbers of the Toltecs mingled in this exodus of tribes from the interior of Mexico into the northern hemisphere; but the movement which led to their downfall in the twelfth century, and gave the sovereignty to the Aztecs, appears, from monumental indicia, to have impelled them northward and eastward, disturbing other tribes impinged on in their progress towards Florida and the Mississippi valley, and across the Appalachian range into the Atlantic slopes. The traditions of the tribes, even of central New England, point to such a migration. They came from the southwest. Their traditions place in the southwestern tropical regions the residence of the benevolent god, from whom they affirmed that they had derived the gift of the zea maize. The Leno Lenapes had also a distinct tradition of their origin in the south and west, and of their crossing the Mississippi river. The Shawnees trace themselves to Florida. The Winnebagoes have a tradition that they came from Mexico. The whole Algonkin family, till the mass of continually dividing tribes reached the confines of New England, trace their origin south and west. The Muscogees assert that they came from the Red river valley, west of

---

[1] Considering the limited period to which Indian traditions, when fairly tested, have generally been found to extend, these legends of Cusic might not unreasonably be accounted for without referring their origin to a distant date. The English title to a large portion of the eastern valley of the Mississippi, was founded on a purchase from the Six Nations, who claimed to hold it by right of conquest; and the alleged era of that conquest is fixed at about the year 1664, when the Iroquois are said to have "carried their arms as far south as Carolina, and as far west as the Mississippi, over a vast country, which extended twelve hundred miles in length, and about six hundred in breadth; where they destroyed whole nations, of whom there are no accounts remaining among the English." This claim, which Great Britain was as much interested to sustain as the Six Nations were to make it, General Harrison endeavors to refute in his *Historical Discourse*. See, also, Butler's Hist. of Kentucky, ch. 1.

the Mississippi. The ancient Chigantalgi, whom De Soto found on the east banks of the Mississippi, as high as the Yazoo, had the worship of the sun established with all the fixity and rites of the Toltecs. From these we date the Natches, who still at the period of their overthrow by the French retained the art of mound-building, two of which structures they erected in the Ouichita (Wachita) valley. The large mound developments formerly existing on the Kaskaskia and Cahokia rivers in Illinois, display traits of the Toltecan arts of building, and of their religion and mythological ideas. The ancient displays at Marietta, at the mouth of the Muskingum, the circular walls of Circleville, and the striking remains on Paint creek, the Little Miami, and in the Scioto valley generally, all within the limits of Ohio, have the same air and traits of the southern element worshippers." (Ibid., 147–8. See also Vol. V. p. 61.)

The above citations are selected as serving to illustrate Mr. Schoolcraft's manner of employing native traditions as materials of evidence, and also as in part exhibiting his views on some leading archæological questions. The authority of traditions is in fact recognized incidentally, if not directly, throughout the work; and the inquiry suggests itself whether he does not make, and whether there should not be made, a distinction between traditions that have been long known to be current in tribes and larger divisions of the Indian race, and such as have only the warrant of individual testimony. There are, doubtless, national legends that have been transmitted through generations of savages with a view to the preservation of some historical truth. It is equally true that individuals among them have the habit of inventing tales founded upon questions asked them, and in accordance with what they conjecture to be the expectation of the inquirer, which they are often very quick to discern. It is, therefore, extremely important that careful discrimination should be exercised respecting the sources of traditions, and the nature of the authority on which they rest. If Mr. Schoolcraft would draw the line so that it should be as evident to the reader as it is perhaps to himself, greater justice might be done to the merit of this kind of testimony.[1]

Mr. Schoolcraft has thrown much light on another archæological element of great interest, that of Indian inscriptions, or pictography. The ideographic devices and symbols of the natives are very elaborately explained and illustrated in his volumes; and it is shown that the aborigines have a hieroglyphic and pictorial system of considerable power in the conveyance of ideas. It appears, from his account, that the Algonkins have a form of symbolic characters called "Kekeewin,

---

[1] Even statements like the following are insufficient to guard the reader from the danger of misapprehension:—

"Aboriginal history, on this continent, is more celebrated for preserving its fables than its facts. This is emphatically true respecting the hunter and non-industrial tribes of the present area of the United States, who have left but little that is entitled to historical respect. Without any mode of denoting their chronology, without letters, without any arts depending on the use of iron tools, without, in truth, any power of mind or hand to denote their early wars and dynasties, except what may be inferred from their monumental remains; there is nothing in their oral narrations of ancient epochs to bind together, or give consistency to, even this incongruous mass of wild hyperboles and crudities." (Vol. I. p. 13. See also Ibid., p. 65, Vol. III. p. 314, etc.)

i. e. *teachings*," which prevails among the tribes from the Atlantic to the Mississippi. Having become acquainted with a highly intelligent chief, who was familiar with the use and signification of those characters, Mr. Schoolcraft put himself under his instructions, and subsequently employed him to decipher the inscription on the Dighton Rock.

This chief (Chingwauk) accordingly took the volume containing the various delineations of those figures to his lodge, and studied it with some of his companions. The next day, he appeared with two of his brethren, one of them acting as his principal assistant, and in the presence of an approved interpreter and two members of Mr. Schoolcraft's family, all well versed in the Chippewa and English languages, the explanation was given.

The inscription was determined to be of a kind practised by "an ancient class of seers, and termed "*Muz-zin-na-bik* (*i. e.*, rock writing)," and was attributed to "the ancient Wa-be-na-kies, or New England Indians." It was said to relate to two nations, both Indian, and that none of the figures denoted a foreigner; but the record had reference to a battle, and was made by the triumphant party. The details of this exposition are minutely illustrated, and the force or meaning given to each particular mark explained.

For some reason, which he did not mention, Chingwauk confined himself strictly to the drawing made by Dr. Baylies and Mr. Goodwin, in 1790. There were some characters which he threw out, as having no significancy. Two of these were among the number interpreted by the Danish antiquaries; three others connected with them could be spared from Chingwauk's reading without impairing its sense; and Mr. Schoolcraft inferred, at that time, that these were due to the Northmen, and perhaps had given the hint to the natives, at a later period, to record their own traditions on the same stone. (Vol. I. p. 108, *et seq.*)

In 1853, a new copy was taken from the rock, under his own supervision, by the daguerreotype process; and from this he decided that the inscription was entirely Indian, without those traces of Runic letters and Roman figures which were thought to be discernible in former drawings. (Vol. IV. p. 120.)

An inscribed rock on Cunningham's island, near the southern shore of Lake Erie, described as the most extensive and best preserved inscription that has been found (which we imagine to be the same that the missionary Kirkland noticed in 1788) has also been interpreted by Chingwauk. In this case, the events recorded are explained as having occurred since the arrival of Europeans, whose *hats* are drawn among the figures. (Vol. II. p. 88, Vol. III. p. 85.)

As these pictorial sculptures have a marked family resemblance wherever they are found, throughout the United States, they may fairly be ascribed to the same people, even if they belong to different eras.

Mr. Schoolcraft has, in former times, given his opinion very decidedly in favor of the genuineness of the "Grave Creek Stone," having communicated respecting it with various learned societies abroad and at home. He still regards it as belonging to a class which he denominates "INTRUSIVE ANTIQUITIES." He says, "An inscription, in apparently some form of the Celtic character, came to light in the Ohio valley in 1838. This relic occurred in one of the principal tumuli of western Virginia (the ancient Huitramannaland). It purports to be of an apparently early period, namely 1328.[1] It is in the Celtiberic character, but has not been deciphered. Its archæology appears corroborative of the Cimbrian and the Tuscarora traditions, representing a white race in the Ante-Columbian periods in this part of America." (Vol. IV. p. 118.)[2]

Although Mr. Schoolcraft does not admit that any race, except the true aboriginal one, has erected any of the monuments of the country, he refers, occasionally, to indications of foreign presence that may have left an impression upon the arts of the people. "There may also be forms of art, disinterred from American soil, introduced from Asia, or by early adventurers from the Mediterranean, which have tended to direct the Indian mind to incipient steps of art or civilization. But these vestiges only serve to perplex, without unravelling the subject." (Vol. V. p. 85. See also Ibid., p. 115.)

Vague intimations of this kind are apt to excite the imagination, and to mislead it. We should be glad to see gathered into one chapter, under an appropriate head, all the evidences of art beyond the ability of the natives, that must be assigned to an ante-Columbian period, and all other indications of a foreign people, before that era, in the United States. They cannot be numerous, and the point is of sufficient importance to be distinctly presented, with all the force it possesses. They have hitherto proved unsubstantial whenever we have attempted to grasp them. We have before us the "Alabama Stone," found, some thirty years ago, near the Black Warrior river, which has been described as containing the following inscription in Roman letters—[3]

HISRNEHNDREV.

1232.

To our eyes, it reads, HISPAN. ET IND. REX. as plainly as the same inscription on a Spanish quarter of a dollar that is somewhat worn. The figures may be as above represented, but of course they cannot be intended for a date.

We have seen the "Rutland stone," on which "the strokes, filled with a black composition," resemble remarkably a regular series of literal characters; but they were formed by the same hand that formed the stone, and are only freaks of crystallization.[4]

---

[1] Judging from the age of a tree on the mound. The stone has no date.

[2] This much controverted relic is a hard piece of sandstone in an irregular elliptical shape, an inch and three-fourths in length, and an inch and a half in breadth, having upon it three lines of characters, apparently alphabetic, which M. Jomard thought to be Libyan, while other European archæologists have considered them nearer to the Phœnician, the Old British, or the Celtiberic. No one professes to interpret their meaning. Its claims to notice rest entirely upon the assertion of the owner and excavator of the Grave Creek Mound, that it was found in the heart of that tumulus. It is stated, in opposition to its authenticity, that its discovery was not mentioned at the time of the excavation, nor until the mound and its contents were used as an exhibition. If genuine, it is at least unique, and is unsupported by any similar or analogous relic. Trans. of Am. Ethnol. Soc., Vol. I. Ibid., Vol. II. Articles by Mr. Schoolcraft and Mr. Squier.

[3] Western Messenger, May, 1838.

[4] Antiquitates Americanæ, p. 360.

We received, a year or two since, a careful drawing of a piece of foreign copper money, found, in the interior of Ohio, in digging a well; and happened to have its exact counterpart among a collection of *modern* oriental coins.

We have at hand Jewish phylacteries that were taken from beneath the soil in a country village, where, it was declared, Jews were never known to have been; but a follower of Moses was ultimately traced to the very spot where these were found.

We have the following inscription, discovered, according to most respectable authority, on a plate of mica upon the breast of a skeleton, buried after the ancient manner, in a mound near that at Grave Creek, from whence the more celebrated *inscribed stone* was derived.[1]

> "Trem Nebo, thou who did Dy for me
> and my son Jero and wife peto.
> 1587. William Welch."

Our faith has not, thus far, been strengthened by sight; and we should be at a loss to form a list of evidences pointing to the presence of an ancient people of foreign origin at any mysterious period of time, or to collect a series of traditions worthy to be presented as possessing an historical value. It is not less desirable that all claims of the kind, having a shade of plausibility, should be by some one assembled for investigation, however frequently, in particular instances, they may have proved to be fallacious.

Mr. Schoolcraft's views of the antiquities of the United States are often emphatically expressed—

"The aboriginal archæology has fallen under a spirit of misapprehension and predisposition to exaggeration. The antiquities of the United States are the antiquities of barbarism, and not of civilization. Mere age they undoubtedly have; but it must require a heated imagination to perceive much, if anything at all, beyond the hunter state of arts, as it existed at the respective eras of the Scandinavian and Columbian discoveries." (Vol. I. Introduction.)

"There is nothing, indeed, in the magnitude and structure of our western mounds which a semi-hunter and semi-agricultural population, like that which may be ascribed to the ancestors or Indian predecessors of the existing race, could not have executed. The interior of these earthy pyramids has disclosed nothing beyond a rude state of the arts, or, at best, such arts of pottery and sculpture, shell-work and stone implements, as are acknowledged to belong to the hunter or semi-hunter races before they or their descendants had fallen into their lowest state of barbarism, or that type in which they were found by the colonists between 1584 and 1620. There is little to sustain a belief that these ancient works are due to tribes of more fixed and exalted traits of civilization, far less to a people of an expatriated type of civilization, of either an ASIATIC or EUROPEAN origin, as several popular writers very vaguely, and with little severity of investigation, imagined." (Ibid., p. 62.) "It is a mistake to suppose that the pipe-sculptures of the Scioto valley—the

---

[1] From James E. Wharton, Esq., Editor of the Wheeling Times and Gazette.

ancient capital of Indian power in the Ohio valley—evince a state of art superior to the general aboriginal type." (Vol. IV. p. 141.)

"The birds of prey and reptiles, chiselled chiefly from sandstone, found buried in the small altar-mounds of the Scioto valley, constitute a feature in this forest sculpture which is not at all at variance with other evidences of the sort from the hunter age of America." (Vol. IV. p. 142.)

Of the animal or emblematical mounds of Wisconsin, he says: "Their connection with the existing Totemic system of the Indians who are yet on the field of action, is too strong to escape attention. By the system of names imposed upon the men composing the Algonkin, Iroquois, Cherokee, and other nations, a fox, a bear, a turtle, &c. is fixed upon as a badge or stem, from which the descendants may trace their parentage. To do this, the figure of an animal is employed as an heraldic sign or surname. This sign is called, in the Algonkin, town-mark, or Totem. A tribe could leave no more permanent trace of an esteemed sachem, or honored individual, than by the erection of one of these monuments. They are clearly sepulchral, and have no other object but to preserve the names of distinguished actors in their history." (Vol. I. p. 52.)

"The totemic mounds are the simplest structures of all. Their object seems to be, by raising mounds on the prairies, with a peculiar mineralogic pictography, to create a symbolic record which shall be understood by their countrymen. They constitute a species of symbolic mounds. Nothing could be more characteristic of these people, or within the means and power of being comprehended by the hunter tribes, than those earth-formed pictographs. It is antiquity adding its voice to modern Indian history." (Vol. IV. p. 128.)[1]

The opinion of the editor respecting the uses of the mounds and enclosures of the Ohio valley corresponds very nearly with that of Messrs. Davis and Squier. He connects the sacrificial altars with the religious habits of modern Indians. "That offerings were made by fire by the mound-builders, as well as by the existing race of Indians, is clearly shown. An altar of earth, not very imposing in height or circumference, was made by them from the loose earth. Here the people could freely make their offerings to the officiating jossakeeds, which appeared to have consisted most commonly of the pipe, in which incense had been offered, and which was probably, from its ordinary and extraordinary uses, one of the most cherished objects in the household. It is probable, from the number of these altars in the Scioto valley, that it had a dense population. By long use, the bed of loam or earth composing the altar would become hard, and partake, in some measure, of the character of brick. What circumstance determined its disuse we cannot say. It is certain that, in the end, the fire was covered up, with all its more or less burned and cracked contents, and the earth heaped up so as to bury it most effectually, and constitute a mound." (Vol. I. p. 52.)

---

[1] Whatever explanation of the object of these mounds may be derived from the native custom above referred to, the inquiry remains, Why are they almost wholly confined to a comparatively limited region? They might be expected to exist wherever the totemic custom prevailed. The latest investigations have shown, as stated by Mr. Lapham, that they are *not* sepulchral.

According to his classification, mounds may be considered as tumuli proper, (meaning the larger class of mounds, termed *sepulchral* by Davis and Squier); propylæ, or redoubt mounds, at the gates of enclosures, barrows or small earthen heaps, generally under nine or ten feet in height; the small "sciotic" mounds of sacrifice; the totemic or imitative mounds; and the massive platform mounds of the South.

The purposes to which the latter were applied, he considers as sufficiently shown by the manner in which they were used and occupied within the period of observation, viz: for the dwellings of the caciques and priests. To this is added the testimony of tradition. "With regard to the platform mounds, it is the recorded tradition of the Muscogees, and Appalachian tribes, that these were public works laid out on the selection of a new site for a town, and engaged in immediately by the whole tribe, to serve as the official seat of their chief ruler." (Vol. IV. p. 130, quoting from Pickett's *History of Alabama*, and Vol. II. pp. 83, 84.) The celebrated work at Marietta he believes to have also been of the same character.[1]

"In Oregon and Washington," he says, "there is not a mound or earthwork analogous to those of the Mississippi Valley, or, indeed, of any kind." "The tribes who had reached the Mississippi in their migrations, did not come from the elevated, bleak, and barren deserts stretching at the east of the Rocky Mountains. There are no indications that they crossed that broad and forbidding barrier." (Vol. V. pp. 100, 101, and authorities there cited.) (Ibid., Appendix, p. 662, *et seq.*)

In further limitation of the extent of such remains, he says: "In the highest latitudes occupied by the Algonkins, on and north of the Lake Superior basin, we search in vain for any striking objects of antiquity. There are no artificial mounds, embankments, or barrows, in this basin, to denote that the country had been anciently inhabited. It is something to affirm, that the mound builders who have filled the West with wonder—quite unnecessary wonder—had never extended their sway here." (Vol. I. p. 66.)

Mr. Schoolcraft has, in various passages, expressed an opinion respecting the period when the mounds, &c. were abandoned.

"Could we determine the age of these works, one great object of their consideration would be attained. The opening of the great tumulus at Grave Creek revealed the mode which brought structures of earth of this capacity within the means of the semi-industrial tribes. The cortical layers, counted in the mature and heavy forest trees, denoted the period of its completion to have been at, or soon after, the twelfth century; but there was no proof that it had not been commenced centuries earlier. It appeared, conclusively, that the structure was the result of comparatively trivial sepulchral labors during an immense period; one age and tribe having added to another the results of its easily accomplished and slowly accumulating toils." (Vol. IV. p. 129.)

"The testimony drawn from the cortical layers of trees on an antique fort in

---

[1] Reference is made, Vol. II. p. 127, to a Creek tradition respecting the construction of *mounds of refuge* from sudden inundations.

Adams County, Ohio, denoted the twelfth century as the period of its abandonment." (Ibid., p. 130.)

"The cortical annular layers in the growth of large and mature trees, occupying the walls and interior areas of the abandoned works, tell a tale, of which we must judge from tumuli, and fortified camps and towns. These data indicate parts of the twelfth and thirteenth centuries as the active period of tumult among the Mississippi Valley tribes." (Vol. IV. p. 137.)

"It is true, that data derived from the monuments of the Mississippi Valley and of Florida, denote the early part of the twelfth century to have been an epoch of great changes and disturbances in that quarter. Of these ancient wars, the traditions of the Iroquois, as recorded by Cusic, and by Ducoigne, both native authorities, represent a period of great ancient wars and disturbances in the Mississippi Valley. But a view of Western antiquities denotes that the wars referred to cannot be located further back than about six hundred years." (Vol. V. p. 61.)[1]

It is a theory of Mr. Schoolcraft, that the arrival of the Aztecs in Mexico, about 1190 (as indicated by their pictorial scrolls), and the dispersion of the Toltecans, created a general movement in different directions, and that some of the latter pressed northwardly and eastwardly. "It is most reasonable to suppose," he says, "that the ancient population of the Mississippi Valley, and thence, in process of time, of the Atlantic coast and plains south of the great lakes, was thus derived." Hence the knowledge and general use of the maize, or Indian corn, &c. (Vol. I. p. 63.)

He is disposed to look for the primitive origin of the American race in the remotest periods of time.

"It must be recollected as one of the fundamental points in our antiquities, that the Indian tribes are of an age that is very antique—that they have occupied various parts of the continent, not only for centuries, but, probably, for scores of centuries." (Vol. I. p. 62.) "Where such a race may be supposed to have had their origin, history may vainly inquire. It probably broke off from one of the primary stocks of the human race before history had dipped her pen in ink, or lifted her graver on stone. Herodotus is silent; there is nothing to be learned from Sanconiathus, and the fragmentary ancients. The cuneiform and Nilotic inscriptions, the oldest in the world, are mute. Our Indian stocks seem to be still more ancient. Their languages, their peculiar idiosyncrasy, all that is peculiar about them, denote this." (Vol. I. pp. 16, 17.)

"Considered in every point of view, the Indian race appears to be an old, a very old stock. Nothing that we have in the shape of books, is ancient enough to recall the period of his origin but the sacred oracles. If we appeal to these, a probable prototype may be recognized in that branch of the race which may be called Almogic (from Almodad, son of Joctan), a branch of the Eberites." (Ibid., p. 17.)

---

[1] In his paper on the "Grave Creek Mound," *Trans. Am. Ethnol. Soc.*, Vol. I., Mr. Schoolcraft suggested that the pestilence of the year 1330, which swept from Tartary and China through India into Europe, might have prevailed in America (as did the cholera of 1832, which was also of Eastern origin), and have destroyed entire bands of the Red race. In the same paper, he speaks of being "impressed with the belief that the common trenches, fortifications, and defenced mounds of the Ohio Valley," are of the era of the wars of the ancient Alleghanians with the ancestors of the Iroquois.

"Thousands of years must have elapsed to produce such diversities of languages and character, and general obscuration. Instead of eighteen hundred years, as the apocryphal Spanish pictographs presuppose as the period of their roving in these forests, there is more probability that the period of their abiding on the continent is thrice that time." (Vol. V. p. 69.)

Mr. Schoolcraft has no very high estimate of the value of the picture writings of Mexico, and thinks the loss of those destroyed by the Spanish ecclesiastics not so great as might be expected. He quotes Mr. Gallatin's statement, that those which have been preserved contain but a meagre account of Mexican history for one hundred years preceding the conquest, and hardly anything that relates to prior events. (Vol. V. p. 102.)

The pictographic scrolls often commented upon as betokening an inkling of Christianity among the natives, he regards as undoubtedly of a date since the conquest. The supposed existence of traditions of the Deluge, in both North and South America, he apprehends to be due to the "fervor of imagination, or the enthusiasm of theory." While there are no traces of the Christian scheme to be found among the Indian tribes, and no Hindoo element in their population, no relics of Buddhism or Brahminism, or Mahomedanism, "their manners and customs present some traits which denote them to be the descendants of a more ancient race whose opinions and dogmas once overspread the oriental world." "There are evidences of the ancient prevalence of the worship of the sun throughout America." (Vol. V. pp. 62, 63.)

Elsewhere he says: "Any attempt to fix on local divisions of the oriental world as the probable theatre of the origin of the Indian tribes, in the absence of all history—without even traditions, poor as they generally are—and on the mere basis of suppositions, must prove unsatisfactory. But where history is baffled, conjecture may sometimes plausibly step in." "The only nation, it must be confessed, with which his (the Indian's) origin has been, with some just probability, compared, is the Hebrew, or at least the Shemitic stock. There are not only some striking principles of agreement in the plan of utterance of the Indian with the Shemitic, but some apparent vestiges of the vocabulary." (Vol. V. pp. 86, 87.[1])

---

[1] Some of the preceding sentences have been transposed for convenience of quotation, but without affecting their sense or connection. In a note the writer says, "The Hebraic theory has not been, in my opinion, thoroughly examined. The attempt of Mr. James Adair, in 1774, to prove it, by customs and languages, is an utter failure on the face of it." On p. 82, Vol. V., he refers to the arguments of President Smith, and Boudinot, on this point, as unsatisfactory, and to the Discourse of Dr. Jarvis questioning the theory as "deemed a paper of sound deduction." He directs the attention of the reader to Vol. I. pp. 30 to 43, for a summary of traits which appear to connect the Indian with the oriental world; and to Vol. II. p. 353, and Vol. IV. p. 386, for some evidences for a comparison of the Indian with the Hebrew language. But it is intimated that the subject requires more time, reading, and elaboration, than the nature of this work admitted. He says, in the same connection, "It has likewise, thus far, been impossible, in this volume, to bring forward, in a digested form, the comparison of manners, customs, rites, and opinions, social and religious, which appear to refer the origin of the Indian tribes to an ancient and general epoch of political mutations over a wide surface of the Asiatic continent, affecting the Mongol, Chinese, and their affiliated nations." Vol. V. p. 82.

We are conscious of the difficulty, if not the impropriety, attending an effort to collect from an unfinished work the views of its author. In a compilation like that required of Mr. Schoolcraft by the United States government, a passing commentary may often represent only an impression suggested by the subject as regarded from a particular stand-point; and while anxious to add to our summary the results of his long and varied investigations, there is a risk of error in undertaking to designate his deliberate and ultimate conclusions.

We have therefore merely selected a few passages bearing upon some of the chief points in the history of opinion, and its progress towards a solution of prominent questions, without expecting to give any just idea of the nature or extent of the valuable information and learned discussions comprehended in the archæological portion of his volumes.

CHAPTER III.

CONCLUSION.

In the preceding pages we have endeavored to select and condense, from a mass of miscellaneous notes, such materials as would illustrate the views entertained at different periods, and by various writers, upon subjects relating to the archæology of the United States.

This has been done under whatever disadvantages are incident to the circumstance of having portions of the text printed before other portions were written. Had opportunity and leisure been afforded for revision of the entire paper, changes and additions might have been made that would have been likely to improve the consistency as well as the completeness of the narrative.

After a consideration of statements and speculations that have failed to present a harmonious result, the mind naturally craves the satisfaction of being able to distinguish acknowledged verities from data that are problematical, if it is only for the sake of some solid basis on which to build new theories, or some fixed point from which future investigations may take their departure. The reader will doubtless expect to be assisted in an effort to separate matters of fact from inferences and hypotheses, by a recapitulation of the principal points that have been with reasonable certainty established.

We shall endeavor, while glancing rapidly along the course of inquiry, to ascertain in what direction, and to what extent, the way is tolerably clear and the path tolerably firm.

The comparative geological antiquity of the two hemispheres is accounted by some an element of weight in estimating the probabilities of an indigenous population on this continent. It is a point, however, that cannot be determined in the present stage of geological observations. If we admit that portions of the western continent exhibit appearances of an earlier emergence than is known to be indicated elsewhere, it might still be true that the mass of the eastern hemisphere was sooner developed, and sooner prepared for the habitation of man. But until it is generally accepted as a fact by scientific men that America really has claims to priority of age, the assertion is, at any rate, entitled to no more than the rank of an hypothesis.[1]

The discovery of human skeletons in a fossilized state, might, under the first

---

[1] "There exists no reason for assuming that one side of our planet is older or more recent than the other." Humboldt, "Views of Nature," p. 106.

impression, be received as conclusive evidence of the presence of mankind in what are called the geological periods. The petrified condition of remains whose place in the rocky tablet of the earth's chronology is not beyond the reach of question, is, however, often to be explained by the rapid growth, under certain circumstances, of calcareous, silicious, and other mineral formations; while the great and sudden changes of level, produced by terrestrial convulsions and elemental influences, afford a solution of the mystery of many deep deposits beneath the soil.

The association of human bones with those of extinct species of animals, observed by Dr. Lund in the caves of Brazil, has been attributed to accidental causes. A comparatively modern date has also been assigned for the disappearance of many species of animals that have ceased to exist. The remains of the megatherium and the mastodon are found near the surface of the earth, in the United States, and do not exhibit signs of having been rolled by floods, or seriously disturbed by commotions. From the stomach of a mastodon, disinterred, at no great depth, from the mud of a small pond in Warren County, New Jersey, were taken seven bushels of the vegetable substances on which it fed, resembling the young shoots of the white cedar, still a common tree in our forests. The bones of the nearly complete specimen from Newburg, New York, purchased by the late Dr. John C. Warren, contain a considerable portion of their original gelatine, and are firm in texture. A megatherium, exhumed while digging the Brunswick Canal, was so near the surface that the roots of a pine tree penetrated its bones. Sir Charles Lyell has shown that the fresh-water and land shells, lying, in some cases, *beneath* such remains, are of the species now living in the same region; so that their climate could scarcely have differed very materially from that now prevailing in the same latitudes. In another passage, speaking of extinct quadrupeds, he says: "That they were exterminated by the arrows of the Indian hunter, is the first idea presented to the mind of almost every naturalist."[1]

An account is given of a mastodon found in Gasconade County, Missouri, which had apparently been stoned to death by the Indians, and then partially consumed by fire. The pieces of rock, weighing from two to twenty-five pounds each, which must have been brought from the distance of four or five hundred yards, "were," says the narrator, "evidently thrown with the intention of hitting some object." Intermixed with burned wood, and burned bones, were broken spears, axes, knives, &c., of stone. "The fire appeared to have been largest on the head and neck of the animal, as the ashes and coals were much deeper there than on the rest of the body." "It appeared, by the situation of the skeleton, that the animal had sunk with its hind feet in the mud and water, and, being unable to extricate itself, had fallen on its right side, and in that situation was found and killed, as above described; consequently, the hind and fore-feet, on the right side, were sunk deeper in the mud, and thereby saved from the effects of the fire." "Between the rocks that had sunk through the ashes were found large pieces of skin, that appeared like fresh tanned sole-leather strongly impregnated with the lye of the ashes, and a great many of the

[1] "A Second Visit to the United States," II. pp. 270, 271; I. pp. 234, 258–9.

sinews and arteries were plain to be seen on the earth and rocks, but in such a state as not to be moved, excepting in small pieces, the size of the hand, which are now preserved in spirits."[1]

In a chapter on "Traditions respecting Extinct Species," Col. Smith remarks, that the bones of the megatherium, in Brazil, are on or near the surface, in a recent state. "Now," he continues, "could they have resisted disintegration during four or five thousand years, considering these to have lain exposed to, or at least within, the influence of a tropical sun and the periodical rains? Yet they often occur on the surface, and the bones of the pelvis have been used for temporary fire-places by the aborigines, wandering on the pampas, beyond the memory of man. In North America, there are native legends which indicate traditional knowledge of more than one species. Such is that of the great Elk or Buffalo, which, besides its enormous horns, had an arm protruding from its shoulder, with a hand at the extremity (a proboscis). Another, the *Tagesho*, or *Yagesho*, was a giant bear, long bodied, broad down the shoulders, thin and narrow about the hind quarters, with a large head, powerful teeth, short and thick legs, paws with very long claws, body almost destitute of hair, except about the hind legs; and therefore called 'the Naked Bear.' Further details are furnished by the Indians, which, allowing for inadequate terminology, incorrectness in tradition and translation from the native dialects to English, leave a surprisingly applicable picture to a species of *megatheridæ*, perhaps the *Jeffersonian megalonyx*. The colossal Elk, another name for the mastodon, or *Père aux Bœufs*, points out, that with designations of existing species, the Indians describe extinct animals with a precision which, in their state of information, nothing but traditionary recollections of their real structure could have furnished."[2]

Thus the bones of men and non-existent species of animals may be admitted to be contemporary without supposing that either perished previous to the chronological period.

So great advances have recently been made in Physical Geography, that we are able to determine, with reasonable accuracy, not only the probability of arrivals on the American coasts from the eastern continent, before the age of Columbus, but the points to which vessels would be driven, and the regions from whence they would be most likely to come.

[3]To present in a few words a general idea of the currents and prevalent winds of the ocean, let us suppose the earth at rest, and the equatorial regions continually heated by the sun in his diurnal revolutions. In this condition, a continuous current of air from the north, and another directly opposite from the south, would blow towards the equator, there ascend and flow backward above toward the poles. If we next suppose the earth to be in motion on its axis from east to west and compound the effects of this motion with that of the winds towards the equator on either side, they will not meet directly opposite each other, as in the previous sup-

---

[1] American Journal of Science and Arts, Vol. XXXVI. pp. 199, 200.

[2] Nat. Hist. of the Human Species, pp. 104–5.

[3] This sketch of the currents of the ocean we give on the authority of the Secretary of the Smithsonian Institution.

position, but in an acute angle, and produce a belt of wind from east to west entirely around the earth in the region of the equator. The continued action of this wind on the surface of the water would evidently give rise to a current of the ocean in the belt over which the wind passed. If, now, instead of considering the earth entirely covered with water, we suppose the existence of two continents extending from north to south, so as to form two separate oceans similar to the Atlantic and Pacific, then the continuous current to the west we have described would be deflected right and left at the western shore of each ocean, and would form four immense whirlpools, viz: two in the Atlantic, one north and the other south of the equator, and two in the Pacific similar in situation and direction of motion. The regularity of the outline of these whirls will be disturbed by the configuration of the deflecting coasts, the form of the bottom of the sea, as well as by islands and irregular winds. Such is a very general view of the tendencies in the direction of motion of the principal currents of the ocean.

The great whirl in the north Atlantic, the western and northern portions of which are known as the Gulf Stream, passes southward down the coast of Africa, crosses the ocean in the region of the equator, is deflected from the northern portion of South America and the coast of Mexico along the United States, and recrosses the Atlantic to return into itself at the place where it started. A portion, however, of this current, probably owing to the configuration of the bottom, passes off in a tangent to the circumference of the great whirl, and flows northward along the coast of Ireland and Norway. The great whirl of the south Atlantic may also be considered as starting from the coast of Africa, crossing the Atlantic, passing down the coast of Brazil, and again recrossing the ocean at the south to near the Cape of Good Hope, and then returning to the place of original departure.

In like manner, the primary currents of the north Pacific Ocean may be described as an immense irregular whirl, the longer axis of which is in an easterly and westerly direction. Starting from the west side of Central America, it passes along the tropical region, across the ocean, then flows northerly past Japan, returns in the vicinity of the Aleutian Islands, and down the coast of Oregon and California to the place of starting. A similar, but perhaps less perfectly defined, current may be traced in the south Pacific.

The winds follow the same general law. Their prevailing direction, as we have before stated, is from the east toward the west in a belt of several degrees in width on either side of the equator, while in the northern and southern latitudes, between 40° and 60° the tendency of the wind is easterly.

A slight consideration of the foregoing views of the currents and winds of the ocean will render the fact evident, that bodies floating on the eastern shore of the Atlantic, near the equator, will tend to move in a westerly direction towards the American continent, and that bodies in higher northern and southern latitudes will move in an easterly direction, towards the coasts of Europe and Africa; that in the Pacific the currents near the equator tend to carry floating masses from the continent of America, and, in higher north and south latitudes, to bring them to its shores. For example, if a body be cast into the axis of the Gulf Stream, it will tend to move along the curve of the current towards the Cape De Verd Islands, or to be deflected by the tangential current we have mentioned to the coast of Ireland or Norway.

Besides the parallel currents we have mentioned, there is a narrow polar current from Baffin's Bay passing in part between the Gulf Stream and the American coast, and which probably bore the Icelandic navigators to Labrador and to New England.

"From present knowledge of currents, we can hardly be justified in the supposition that South America was peopled from Asia by vessels being driven south of the Equator to the American shores. The distance by that route (west-wind region south of the S. E. Trades) is not less than 10,000 miles without any islands, except New Zealand, for a resting place. The route by the Aleutian Islands, with the North Pacific 'Gulf Stream' is a much more probable route."[1]

From the foregoing view, it appears that both the winds and the currents favor an approach to this continent; and there seems to be no reason in the nature of things why both oceans may not from time to time have poured their casual and perhaps irreclaimable contributions on our shores.

Not many instances have been recorded of chance arrivals upon the European coasts from the western hemisphere. Some however may be mentioned in connection with a few illustrations of the general tendencies of the ocean currents.

Humboldt says: "There are well authenticated proofs, however much the facts may have been called in question, that natives of America (probably Eskimaux from Greenland or Labrador) were carried by currents or streams from the north-west to our own (the eastern) continent. James Wallace relates that in the year 1682 a Greenlander in his canoe was seen on the southern extremity of the Island of Eda by many persons, who could not, however, succeed in reaching him. In 1684, a Greenland fisherman appeared near the Island of Westram. In the church at Burra, there was suspended an Eskimaux boat which had been driven on the shore." "In Cardinal Bembo's *History of Venice* I find it stated, that in the year 1508 a small boat manned by seven persons of a foreign aspect was captured near the English coast by a French ship. The description given of them applies perfectly to the form of the Eskimaux. Six of these men perished during the voyage and the seventh, a youth, was presented to the king of France."[2]

The men called *Indians* that appeared on the coasts of Germany in the tenth and twelfth centuries, and the stranded dark-colored men given to Metellus Celer by the king of the Suevi (see ante, p. 7) are supposed to have been natives of Labrador. The corpses of men of a peculiar race, having very broad faces, are said to have confirmed Columbus in his belief of the existence of countries situated in the west.

The mainmast of the English ship of war, the Tilbury, which was destroyed by fire near St. Domingo, was carried by the Gulf Stream to the northern coasts of Scotland; and casks of palm oil from the wreck of an English ship on a rock off Cape Lopez, in Africa, were carried to Scotland, having followed the equinoxial

---

[1] Schoolcraft's Hist. and Prosp., &c. I. pp. 23–6.

[2] "Views of Nature," p. 123.

current from east to west between 2° and 12° north latitude, and the Gulf Stream from west to east between the latitudes 45° and 50°, north. Of two bottles, cast out together, in south latitude, on the coast of Africa, one was found on the Island of Trinidad; the other on Guernsey in the English channel. Another bottle, thrown over off Cape Horn by an American master, in 1837, was picked up within a few years on the coast of Ireland.

In A. D. 1500, Pedro Cabral, while on his way from Portugal to the East Indies, was driven to the coast of Brazil, which he thus accidentally discovered. In 1731, a batteau from Teneriffe came ashore near the mouth of the Orinoco. In 1797, the slaves in a ship from Africa rose upon the crew, who leaped into a boat and cut it adrift. At the end of thirty-eight days the survivors were cast upon Barbadoes. In 1799, six men in a boat from St. Helena lost their course, and after being a month at sea, and resorting to cannibalism, as was the case in the previous instance, four of them reached the South American coast alive.

To account for the population of the islands of the Pacific, Sir Charles Lyell has collected examples of the drifting of parties of savages to very great distances in their frail canoes. In one case, eight months are reported to have been passed on the broad ocean, with no other sustenance than the fishes they caught, and the rain water they found means to secure. It is remarked, in the same connection, that "the space traversed, in some instances was so great, that similar accidents might suffice to transport canoes from various parts of Africa to South America, or from Spain to the Azores, and from thence to North America."[1]

It seems necessary to concede that casual passages from the eastern to the western continents have been possible in very rude ages; and at whatever periods human enterprise has ventured to leave the immediate proximity of the land, before the arts of navigation were assisted by the compass, the probability of their occurrence must have been great.

There is within the American continent no deficiency of evidence tending to confirm the presumptions that rest on maritime facts and principles. The natives of Hispaniola are said to have intimated to Columbus that a *black people* lived south and southeast of them.[2] According to Peter Martyr, Balboa, in 1511, found "*blackamoors*" on the isthmus of Darien.[3] Torquemada says the Californians signified to Viscaino, in 1602, that there was a village of negroes not far from their neighborhood.[4] A race of very *white* Indians was said to exist in Brazil.[5] Hum-

---

[1] Principles of Geology, II. pp. 57–58. Mr. Gallatin was accustomed to assert that the Pacific Islands were populated at a far more recent period than the American continent, as evinced by their languages, and hence could not have contributed to the primitive occupation of this country. In one place, he says, "Their colonization is of a date so comparatively recent that the Malay origin of the inhabitants of Otahiti and the Sandwich Islands was immediately recognized when their vocabularies were first brought to Europe. It seems probable that some of these people may have reached the main land of America; but they found the country inhabited, and either were killed or became mixed with the ancient inhabitants. No trace of the Malay language is found on the western shores of America." —*Trans. of Am. Ethnol. Soc.*, I. p. 176.

[2] Herrera, I. 374.

[3] Third Decade, p. 97.

[4] Venega's Hist. of California, p. 239.

[5] Southey's Hist. of Brazil, I. 389.

boldt speaks of "several tribes of a whitish complexion" in the forests of Guiana.[1] Legendary references to bearded men, with a white skin, arriving from the sea, are common to both the northern and the southern continents. Diversities of color and of physical conformation, and traces of foreign influence supposed to be detected in arts, customs, language, religion, and astronomical science, too numerous to mention, are often cited in proof of intercourse with inhabitants of the other hemisphere before the arrival of Columbus.

But all these evidences fall short of sustaining the probability of intentional colonization. They do not even suggest the arrival of men in any considerable numbers, or by other than accidental means. They imply the previous presence in the country of a native population, in whose language, arts, and physical attributes, all foreign traits have been merged almost to extinction. However frequent foreign accessions may have been, they have not had power to affect materially the structural uniformity of speech and physical conformation, and the homogeneous mental type, of the aboriginal inhabitants.

It may be inferred, from observations upon the land, as well as from the phenomena of the sea, that the casual voyagers who, in ancient times, have crossed the breadth of either ocean to our shores, were in small and feeble parties, last survivors of tempest and famine, and without women to perpetuate their race. They appear to have brought no agricultural productions from their native regions, and to have taught none of the useful arts of civilized industry. According to the laws that determine the transmission of hereditary qualities in the crossing of breeds, all traces of foreign ancestry might, under these circumstances, disappear in a few generations.

These remarks are applicable to arrivals that may be supposed to have taken place from the western shores of the eastern hemisphere, and across the middle and southern latitudes of the Pacific; but in the northern regions, where the two continents are brought almost into contact, there are other circumstances to be considered.

The practicability of voluntary passages to America, at an early period, by way of Iceland and Greenland, has been demonstrated by the Northmen; but we are unable to produce any well-established facts going to show that this practicability has ever been followed by results affecting the population of the country. We are, indeed, justified by the present aspect of the question in assuming that the Scandinavians have left no marks of residence, linguistic, physical, or monumental, to prove that they have, primarily or secondarily, been important contributors to the peopling of the New World.

The probability of permanent settlements from the Pacific side of the eastern hemisphere, near Behring's Strait, has the support of more positive indications.

The Aleutian Islands, about fifteen degrees south of the Strait, appearing on the map like stepping-stones from one continent to the other, are admirably adapted to facilitate communication between the two countries. The diminished space to be traversed, the protective proximity of the islands, a climate mild for the latitude,

---

[1] Political Essay, I. 144.

and a plentiful supply of fish and game, are favorable, not to chance passages merely, but to intentional and continuous transits. The opposing shores are in fact occupied by divisions of the same tribe;[1] and the neighboring regions of Asia are held by that variety of mankind whose physical characters are nearly identical with those of the American race. These are circumstances that, of themselves, give plausibility to the theories which point to that quarter as the place where inhabitants were originally, and have been consecutively, transported to this continent. Those theories also derive some confirmation from the traditions and pictorial records of the southern nations, referring to a pilgrimage of their ancestors from the northwest.[2]

There are also some striking ethnological analogies which seem to connect these distant sections. The Peruvian practice of flattening the skull by compression, as a mark of nobility, is a prominent peculiarity of the tribes on Columbia River. There, too, prevails the singular and inconvenient custom of inserting disks of wood in the lips and ears, found again in Brazil;[3] and, in the dialects of the Columbians and Nootkas, may be observed that distinguishing characteristic of Mexican words, the terminal *tl*.[4]

But beyond a few such coincidences, the evidence of connection does not extend. Though often imagined, vestiges of migration from the north to the south have not been satisfactorily traced. Mr. Bartlett, while at the head of the United States Boundary Commission, gave much attention to this subject; an inquiry for which his previous ethnological studies had given him interest and preparation. "I have been unable," he says, "to learn from what source the prevailing idea has arisen of the migration of the Aztecs, or ancient Mexicans, from the north into the valley of Mexico, and of the three halts they made in the journey thither. I confess I have seen no satisfactory evidence of its truth."

"The traditions which gave rise to this notion are extremely vague, and were not seriously entertained until Torquemada, Boturini, and Clavigero gave them currency. But they must now give way to the more reliable results of linguistic comparisons. No analogy has yet been traced between the language of the old Mexicans and any tribe at the North in the district from which they are supposed to have come; nor in any relics, ornaments, or works of art, do we observe a resemblance between them."[5]

---

[1] The sedentary Tchuktchi.

[2] Mr. Prescott, in his treatise on the origin of Mexican civilization, after considering the weight due to various affinities of arts, customs and dialects, remarks: "The theory of an Asiatic origin for Aztec civilization derives stronger confirmation from the light of *tradition*, which, shining steadily from the far northwest, pierces through the dark shadows that history and mythology have alike thrown around the antiquities of the country. Traditions of a western or northwestern origin were found among the more barbarous tribes, and by the Mexicans were preserved both orally and in their hieroglyphic maps, where the different stages of their migration are carefully noted. But who at this day shall read them? They are admitted to agree however in representing the populous North as the prolific hive of the American races."—*Conquest of Mexico.* Appendix, p. 397.

[3] Mr. Ewbank suggests that the term Oregon or Orejones was bestowed by the Spaniards on account of the custom of preternaturally enlarging the ears.—*Life in Brazil.* Appendix, p. 459.

[4] Vater thought he detected words of common origin in the vocabularies of these widely separated peoples.—*Mithridates*, theil III. abtheil. 3. p. 312.

[5] Personal narrative of Explorations, &c., II. p. 283.

There are no antiquities in Oregon.[1] On the route from thence, there are no monuments or other works of art, such as the southern nations have left in their ancient seats, until the northern limits of a reflux influence are attained. And it is equally true that there are none of the traits of Chinese, or Japanese, or Tartarian semi-civilization, which emigrants from those nations might be expected to have brought with them.[2]

Affinities which have no *united* reference to any particular nation, but point now to one people, and then to another totally distinct from the first, and, in a third case, to others equally disconnected, however numerous they may be in the aggregate, tend, by their diversity, to weaken the force of each individual analogy as an evidence of origin, and can only serve to illustrate the possibility of accidental and partial communications. If congruous affinities, of a positive character, should be found in some detached locality, they might seem to indicate descent from a special stock; but claims to distinctive derivation, founded on such evidence, are opposed by the linguistic and physical proofs of a general unity of race throughout the entire continent.

If a feature in the customs, institutions, or dialect, of a particular tribe, or of many tribes, has a resemblance to some feature in the customs, institutions, or language, of any well-known historical people (the Jews for example), before receiving it as a proof of connection, or as an inheritance, a reason may be required why other features, more likely to be retained, are wanting; and even if many such features are adduced, unless a decided national impress accompanies them, adventitious causes may afford an explanation, which, if not entirely satisfactory, will often correspond to the real importance of the problem.[3]

Thus, if able philologists have shown the existence of certain general principles or phenomena in the languages of America, which are peculiar and characteristic, uniting them together, and distinguishing them from other languages; and if able anatomists have become assured of physical traits in the American aborigines which justify their classification as a separate variety of man; exceptions which may be pointed out in either case do not necessarily impair the soundness of their general conclusions. For exceptions may, with plausibility, be attributed to causes that

---

[1] Letter from George Gibbs, Esq., Indian Agent, to Mr. Schoolcraft.—*Hist. and Prosp.*, &c., Vol. V. Appendix, p. 662.

[2] Some minor arts, or handicrafts, may be traced, perhaps, to Asiatic sources. A letter from the "Alta Californian," quoted by Dr. Bachman, states that the writer obtained from Queen Charlotte's Island some specimens of native sculpture, which struck him as resembling the sculptures of the Japanese; and on taking them to Japan, they were claimed at once as Japanese articles, without any remark directing attention to them. (Charleston Med. Journal of July, 1855, p. 527.) As Japanese junks have sometimes been cast on the coast of California, articles derived from thence may have been imitated by the natives.

[3] No practice less likely to have a natural origin can be produced than one that has prevailed among some tribes in Brazil and Guiana. At the birth of a child, the husband is put to bed, and nursed with great care for a certain period, while the mother goes about her ordinary concerns. Yet the custom is alluded to as having existed among the ancient Cantabrians, the people of Congo, certain Tartars visited by Marco Paulo, the ancient Corsicans, and in the southern French provinces.—*McCulloh's Researches*, p. 99.

are accidental, and applicable only to particular instances; and although philological and physiological affinities with other races should be equally well established, the argument drawn from radical peculiarities and idiosyncrasies may still remain unsubverted, so long as the latter are paramount.

If, in the process of reasoning, a lapse of time, whose duration cannot be defined, and an isolation without material interruption, are admitted as probabilities, the comprehensive deductions of leading European ethnologists need not of necessity conflict with those of investigators in this country, which, while claiming that the American aborigines are a distinct and peculiar people, do not deny the primitive unity of the human race.

The Chevalier Bunsen, in his recent *Philosophy of Universal History*, remarks: "It is not yet proved in detail, but it appears highly probable, in conformity with our general principles, that the native language of the northern continent of America, comprising tribes and nations of very different degrees of civilization, from the Eskimaux of the polar regions to the Aztecs of Mexico, are of one origin, and a scion of the Turanian tribe. The similarity in the configuration of the skull renders this affinity highly probable."

Having subsequently to writing the above seen the first three volumes of Mr. Schoolcraft's national work, he adds: "But the linguistic data before us, combined with the traditions and customs, and particularly with the system of pictorial or mnemonic writing (first revealed in that work) enable me to say, that the Asiatic origin of all these tribes is as fully proved as the unity of the family among themselves. According to our system, the Indian languages can only be a deposit of a north Turanian idiom. The Mongolian peculiarity of the skull, the type of the hunter, the Shamanic excitement, which leads by means of fasting and dreams into a visionary or clairvoyant state, and the fundamental religious views, and symbols, among which the tortoise is not to be forgotten, (II. 390.) bring us back to primitive Turanism. As to the languages themselves, there is no one peculiarity in them which may not easily be explained by our theory of the secondary formation and the consequences of isolation. The verity of the grammatical type was long ago acknowledged, but we have now (as I think) the evidence of the material, historical, physical unity. The Indian mind has not only worked in one type but with one material, and that a Turanian one." (Vol. II. pp. 111–13.)

"We thus see that a very considerable part of the inhabitants of America, and the Polynesian Islands, belong to that one great family which we call the Turanian race, and that the former travelled off from the Mongolian, and the latter from Malay tribes." (Ibid., pp. 115.)

"The first, however, to trace with a bold hand the broad outlines of the Turanian, or as he called it, the Scythian philology, was Rask. He proved that the Finnic had once been spoken in the northern extremities of Europe, and that allied languages extended like a girdle over the north of Asia, Europe, and America. In his inquiries into the origin of the Old Norse, he endeavors to link the idioms of Asia and America by means of the Grönland language, which he maintains is a scion of the Scythian or Turanian stock, spreading its branches over the north of America, and thus indicating the antediluvian bridge between the continent of Europe and America. According to Rask, therefore, the Scythian would form a layer of language extending in Asia from the White Sea to the valleys of Caucasus, in America from Grönland southward, and in Europe (as Rask accepts Arndt's views) from Finland as far as Britain, Gaul, and Spain. This original substratum was broken up first by Celtic inroads; secondly by Gothic; and thirdly by Sclavonic immigrations; so that traces appear like the peaks of mountains and promontories out of a general inundation." (Vol. I. p. 272–3.)[1]

As the affinities claimed in the above extracts are not those of verbal signification but grammatical construction, the classification of American languages with those comprehended in the term *Turanian* amounts simply to this; that the structure of the former exhibits that stage of advancement from an inorganic, or monosyllabic dialect, which is indicated by the system of *agglutination;* in other words, it belongs to the oldest *organic* stage.[2]

The admitted order of development in forms of speech appears to be 1st, the *monosyllabic, or inorganic,* of which the Chinese and the "so called Original People," in the Malayan Peninsula, furnish examples;[3] 2d, the *agglutinated*; 3d, the *inflected,* or highest form. But while this division corresponds with the relative antiquity of the three forms, ethnologists do not agree in supposing the last to have necessarily, in all cases, passed through the two previous stages.[4]

According to Prof. Müller's translation of grammatical conclusions into historical language, the first migration from the common centre of mankind proceeded eastward, where the Asiatic language was arrested at the first stage of its growth, and where the Chinese, as a broken link, presents a reflection of the earliest consolidation of human speech. The second dispersion was that of the Turanian tribes, who went in two divisions, Northern and Southern. In the first division are comprehended the Tungusic, Mongolic, Tartaric, and Finnic branches. In the second the Taic, Malaic, Bhotiya, and Tamulic branches. He supposes that these divisions had not attained to any social or political consolidation before they were broken up into different colonies; that they broke up, carrying away each a portion of their common language—and hence their similarity; but they possessed as yet nothing traditional, nothing like a common inheritance in language or thought, and hence their differences. In secluded districts these differences would ultimately "change the whole surface of grammar and dictionary." The American

[1] Prof. Müller, in his "*Last Results of Turanian Researches.*" Bunsen, I. p. 484, says:—

"The Greenland language has been pointed out as showing a transition into American dialects; and the researches of physical science have already indicated the islands east of Siberia as the only bridge on which the seeds of Asia could have been carried to the New World."

Yet neither Rask nor Müller intend to imply that Greenland is to be considered a route of migration from Europe, as the islands referred to were from Asia. The mixed character of the Greenland language is otherwise explained.

[2] The Turanian dialects share one thing in common—they all represent a state of language before its individualization by the Arian and Semitic types.—Max Müller in Bunsen's *Phil. of Un. Hist.*, II. 476.

[3] Pickering's Races of Men, Bohn's edition, p. 305.

[4] Bunsen, Phil. of Un. Hist., I. p. 283.

dialects are adduced as an exemplification of the principle that if the work of agglutination has once commenced, without any literature to keep it within limits, the languages of tribes separated only for a few generations will become mutually unintelligible. (Bunsen, Phil. of Un. Hist., I. 480, *et seq.*)[1]

It thus appears that a common element required by philological theories, whether European or American, respecting the origin of population in this country, is *time*—no less than all the time that history can grant; and while they go back nearly to the most primitive form of human utterance for a matrix in which the American system of speech might have been cast, they demand for the special development of that system, and the peculiar phenomena it exhibits, a protracted term of isolation. (See ante, pp. 63–4.)

A like duration of separate existence would go far to explain the *physical* peculiarities and idiosyncrasies of the American race. A divergence from their kindred types would seem to be the inevitable result of disconnection for ages, under different influences, moral and material; and while changes of conformation might be philosophically anticipated, the fact that a wild and savage life tends to promote physical uniformity, as domestication and civilization tend to produce variety, may suffice to account for the common direction those changes have taken.

And having the element of *time* granted, we may go behind the commencement of Chinese, Japanese, and other forms of Mongolian culture, and imagine the ancestors of our aborigines to have been still mere wanderers, without arts, and with no religious faith save the primitive oriental worship of the Sun. While the parent stock upon the eastern continent would attain to whatever development it might reach under circumstances not entirely excluding it from being acted upon and instructed by other races, the offshoot in America would experience no external

---

[1] The anonymous author of a recent treatise possessing a high degree of literary and scholastic merit, draws the following conclusions from his studies and observations.

"That the first stock of man was created in the equatorial region of Africa; * * or in other words, that the true negro, the aboriginal inhabitant of Nigritia, is the primary variety of our species.

"That from the Nigritian stock, in regions equi-distant from the equator, sprang the Hottentots and the Chinese; whose striking mutual resemblance has been remarked by the accurate Barrow. And that from the Chinese sprang all the Mongolian, or Turanian races, extending from the limits of the Malayan region, through Asia and Europe to the coldest limits of the habitable earth, and through the *American continents*, pervading every zone of climate.

"That the Malayan variety, judging from physical and philological evidences together, sprang from a branch of the Mongolian or Turanian Stock nearly allied to the Chinese.

"That the Caucasian variety was brought into existence after all the other varieties mentioned above had become developed; commencing with Adam, the man created in the image of God." (*The Genesis of the Earth and Man:* A critical examination of passages in the Hebrew and Greek Scriptures, chiefly with a view to the solution of the question whether the varieties of the human species be of more than one origin; &c. &c. Edited by Reginald Stuart Poole, Edin., 1856.)

"Dr. Prichard, Mr. Pickering, and Hamilton Smith, are of opinion that the African was the primitive form and race of man, and that all the others are divergences from this earliest type; while Dr. Bachman thinks the probability in favor of the supposition that the primitive form and color was intermediate between the African and white races; and that these are therefore variations equally removed from the original." (Smyth's "Unity of the Human Races," p. 264.)

influences but those of Nature, and would possess as a basis of advancement only the native instincts, and possibly a few traditions, of its race.

In this manner time and isolation, which are regarded as indispensable to one division of the problem, may be made to answer the exigencies of other divisions; and whatever is wanting to account for exceptional facts or circumstances may be supplied by the supposition of waifs from other nations, occasionally cast upon these shores.

Leaving the question of origin where the latest opinions place it, among the enigmas of immemorial time, we turn to a brief summary of the archæological facts that have been disclosed by investigation within the United States.

The characteristic antiquities of the United States are confined within certain limits. They are scanty through the entire range of the Atlantic States. A mound of some elevation on the Kennebec, in Maine, and vestiges of enclosures at Sanbornton, and near Concord, New Hampshire, are all that can be named in New England, and few of any importance are in the eastern portions of the country elsewhere. In New York they are more numerous, especially towards its western borders. Beyond the Alleghanies, and east of the Mississippi, they extend from the Great Lakes to the Gulf of Mexico; and occupy in greater or less numbers the southern regions towards the Atlantic as far as the Carolinas. They are also found on the promontory of Florida. West of the Mississippi they have been seen on the Missouri 1300 miles from its mouth; and are said to exist on the rivers Kansas and Platte. They are also known to be on some of the principal streams in Louisiana. In Texas they have not attracted attention as prominent features of the country.[1]

The earthworks are of two classes, viz: *enclosures* and *tumuli*. The enclosures are of various sizes and forms. Some are of no greater dimensions than the ordinary circumference of an Indian Council House; others are sufficiently extended to include a village. Some are evidently defensive, occupying positions of natural strength, and adapted to the nature of the ground in a manner to promote security from attack; but, in most cases, requiring the additional protection of palisades, or parapets of timber. Others have the appearance of being intended for ceremonial or religious purposes, or designed for sports and games.

The tumuli are of various forms, conical, pyramidal, dome-shaped, and pictorial, or symbolic.

The largest and loftiest of the conical tumuli are apparently monumental, covering at the base the remains of one person, or in rare instances two; and are sometimes increased in altitude by a second interment on the summit of the original mound. Their inconsiderable numbers indicate that they are special and extraordinary memorials, whose growth may be due to the tributes of generations.

---

[1] Mr. Schoolcraft says that Texas is entirely without aboriginal monuments of any kind; and that neither tumuli, nor remains of ancient ditches, nor attempts at rude castrametation, occur, from the plains of that State and New Mexico, east of the foot of the Rocky Mountains, till the prairie country embraces both banks of the Missouri, and reaches to the plains of Red River, and the Sascatchawine, west of the sources of the Mississippi. (Hist. and Prosp., II. 70, IV. 115. See also respecting the absence of antiquities in Oregon, Washington, and California, Ibid., V. 101.)

The pyramidal tumuli, usually of moderate elevation, but with a broad base and truncated summit, are without remains, and are generally connected with the ceremonial class of enclosures. At the South, temples and the dwellings of chiefs were placed upon them.

Dome-shaped mounds, or *barrows*, tending more or less to a conical form, are very numerous. They may contain a single skeleton, or may be nearly composed of human bones, or they may not have been used for sepulchral purposes. A class of them, within or near enclosures such as have been termed *sacred*, cover altars and sacrificial relics.

The pictorial or symbolic mounds are almost exclusively local, and are nearly confined to the single State of Wisconsin.

All the *relics* which the seats of ancient habitation have yielded are similar in kind to the utensils, ornaments, and implements of existing races.

We may regard it as established, that there are not in the valley of the Mississippi any remains of edifices from which can be inferred a knowledge of the art of working solid materials into permanent and ornamental buildings for religious or secular purposes. There are no ruins of temples or other structures of stone, wrought by the hammer or the chisel, such as abound in Central America. There are no traces of roads and bridges to connect territorial divisions, or facilitate the commerce of an organized state, such as are found in Peru. There are no distinct evidences of arts and manufactures employing separate classes of population, or conducted as regular branches of industry. There are no proofs of the practice of reducing metals from their ores, and melting and casting them for use and ornament—none of a knowledge of chemistry or astronomy. There are no sculptured memorials exhibiting national manners and customs, the religious ideas, or the physical characteristics of the people. In a word, tokens of civil institutions, of mechanical employments, and the cultivation of science and literature however humbly, such as appear among the remains of Mexican and Peruvian civilization, have no positive counterpart in the regions of which we are speaking. Whatever may have been the kind or degree of social advancement attained to by the ancient dwellers in the valleys of the Ohio and Mississippi, those domestic arts and habits of luxury which attend the division of labor and the accumulation of private wealth, had not been sufficiently developed to leave any symbols behind them.

Yet the great enclosures at Newark, at Marietta, at or near Chillicothe, and in many other localities, with their systems of minor embankments, mounds, and excavations, manifest a unity of design, expressive of concentrated authority and combined physical effort. If those structures were produced by a sudden exertion of these agencies, they would require the presence of large bodies of disciplined men, having experience in such labors, and some regular means of subsistence. If they were gradually formed, or brought to completion by labors at various intervals of time, they imply, in addition to unity of power and action, permanent relations to the soil, and habits inconsistent with a nomadic life.

Many of these works are also such as we should expect to see appropriated to the religious ceremonials of a populous community accustomed to meet for the common observance of solemn and pompous rites. Their arrangements correspond to those which are known to be applied elsewhere to that use. The consecrated enclosures, the mounts of adoration or sacrifice, the sacred avenues approaching guarded places of entrance, are recognized as common features of semi-civilized worship, or rather as exemplifications of the manner in which the instinct of religious reverence has everywhere a tendency to display itself.

The number of works of this character, and the scale on which they are constructed, suggest irresistibly the idea of an organized multitude fond of spectacles, and habituated to public displays of an imposing nature.

It is a circumstance of great significancy that the intelligent Spanish and French adventurers and missionaries who first explored (and that pretty thoroughly), the regions where some of the most remarkable of these remains are situated, observed no want of harmony between the social condition of the natives and whatever works of art came to their notice. They evidently regarded the tribes among whom they sojourned as fully capable of producing every form of structure that they saw. It is true they might not have looked with the eyes of antiquaries, or have estimated the age of works overgrown by venerable forests, and therefore their accounts included no archæological problems.

If we proceed according to logical propriety, from the known to the unknown, and compare the historical habits, customs, and arts, of the aborigines, with the vestiges of a more ancient era, we shall at least determine what residuum of mystery is left for future solution.

It has been a common opinion, that articles of ornament and use taken from the mounds manifest a much higher grade of mechanical proficiency than those known to have been made by modern Indians. There is, however, reason to believe that the former are the choicest specimens of art belonging to their period; and because these are found in the tombs of chiefs and upon altars of sacrifice, it does not follow that such were in common use among the people. They do not necessarily indicate any general condition of mechanical or artistic dexterity; but are likely to be the best of their kind, from whatever source they may have been obtained.

In order to estimate correctly the degree of skill in similar handicrafts possessed by the people who were found in occupation of the soil, we must go back to a time antecedent to the decline in all domestic arts which resulted immediately from intercourse with the whites. So soon as more effective implements, more serviceable and durable utensils, and finer ornaments, could be obtained in exchange for the products of the chase, their own laborious and imperfect manufactures were abandoned; and not only their industrial but their military habits underwent essential modifications from the same influence.

All articles of metal wrought or compounded with the aid of fire, whether iron, copper, or silver, and all enamelled or glass ornaments, are now equally regarded as of extraneous if not of recent origin. The highest archæological position assigned to any of them, is that of "*intrusive antiquities*," which may or may not have preceded European settlements in the country.

If from the relics of the mounds are separated those finer sculptures in hard materials, representing tropical quadrupeds, birds, fishes, &c., which, with some mineral substances, must have come from a different latitude, the residue might have belonged to any savage chief of any savage tribe that the first European invaders encountered.

Mr. Schoolcraft has recorded his *matured* opinion that the antiquities of the United States preserve a general parallelism with the condition of manners, customs, and arts of the later tribes, and seldom or never rise above it (Hist. and Prosp., V. p. 115); and, so far at least as minor works of art are concerned, his conclusion appears to be well sustained. The stone axes, hatchets, gouges, chisels, arrow-heads, and other implements from the mounds, cannot be distinguished from the same articles that everywhere through the country have proved to be almost identical in kind and in form. In pipes there is more variety, yet without much departure from a few established patterns. It was upon these that the aborigines expended their greatest ingenuity. From an Indian burial-place in Canada (where there are no earthworks), have been taken shell-beads, pipes, and copper bracelets, precisely like those from the Grave Creek mound, in connection with articles of European manufacture. (Schoolcraft, Hist. and Prosp., I. pp. 103–5.)[1] From whatever source or sources derived, copper seems to have been in use throughout all America. On the Atlantic coasts it was noticed by all the early navigators from Nova Scotia to Patagonia. (McCulloh's Researches, p. 85.) In New France, copper ornaments, pipes, sea-shells, mica, and flint-stones, were objects of traffic. (Schoolcraft, Hist. and Prosp., V. p. 108.) The excellence of the vases and terra-cottas of the Iroquois is attested to by Mr. Squier in his work on the antiquities of New York, even as compared with the best antique specimens. The Natchez are known to have made fine earthenware of various composition and much elegance of shape, which is described by the Portuguese historian of De Soto's expedition, as differing little from that of Portugal.[2] Indeed, the art of pottery, with unequal degrees of excellence, was practised by almost every tribe. Very large vessels were made by the Natchez Indians for the collection of salt by evaporation from saline springs. (McCulloh, p. 153.) There is nearly, if not quite, as much of spirit and power of imitation to be seen in the carvings and mouldings in clay of recent native workmanship as in the specimens collected from the sacrificial mounds of the Scioto Valley; and the origin of those ancient deposits is satisfactorily illustrated by modern examples.

Thus the Chippewas were accustomed, after the shedding of blood, to perform a sacrifice of expiation, by throwing all their ornaments, pipes, &c., into a fire kindled at some distance from their huts. (Hearne's Journey, pp. 204–6.) Winslow, in his "Good News from New England," says, "The Nanohiggansets have a great spacious house wherein only some few (that are, as we may term them, priests) come; thither at certain known times, resort all their people, and offer almost all the riches they have to their gods, as kettles, skins, hatchets, beads, knives, &c., all which are cast by the priests into a great fire that they make in the midst of the house." They

[1] Some of the copper implements delineated by Messrs. Squier and Davis were from Canada. Smith. Cont., I. p. 201.

[2] Conquest of Florida, Paris ed. 1685, p. 242.

attributed their freedom from the plague, which had prevailed in other places, to this custom. (Mass. Hist. Col., 2d series, vol. IX. p. 94.)

The later aborigines have not unfrequently erected mounds and other earthworks. Those formed by collecting the bones of ancestors at certain periods have been in some instances traced to modern tribes. (Jefferson's "Notes on Virginia," pp. 139–43.) A mound was erected over the body of a chief of the Omahas on the Missouri, who died of smallpox in 1800. (Lewis and Clarke, Exp., I. p. 43.) Another was raised, about twenty years since, at Coteau des Prairies, in honor of a young Sioux chief who perished while attempting an exploit of much daring. (Catlin's N. A. Indians, II. p. 170.) In Beck's Gazetteer of Missouri, a large mound is described as having been formed by the Osages within the last half century. It is said to have been gradually enlarged at intervals. (Appendix to Squier's Ab. Mon. of N. Y., p. 107.) The Natchez Indians, after they were driven from their original seats, built a large mound near Nachitoches. (Ibid., p. 108.)

It is among these retreating tribes that we might expect to find the last traces of hereditary customs. Lewis and Clarke mention seeing repeatedly, on the upper waters of the Missouri, villages either occupied at the time, or recently deserted, that were surrounded by earthen embankments, sometimes in the form of a circle. (Exp., I. pp. 54, 92, 94, 97, 112; II. 380, &c.)

Brackenridge, while travelling in the same region, "observed the ruins of several villages which had been abandoned twenty or thirty years, and which, in every respect, resembled the vestiges on the Ohio and Mississippi." (Views of Louisiana, p. 183.) All the numerous and extensive earthworks of New York have been decided by Mr. Squier to be due to the Iroquois. The process of erecting the mounds and enclosures at the South, and the uses to which they were applied, are fully described in the narratives of the early adventurers into that region. The places constructed for the performance of games, or used for such purposes, though the work of earlier generations, are noticed as among the features characteristic of modern habits and practices; and processions, and other public ceremonies, are described as occurring on a scale hardly less imposing than such as we may imagine to have filled the stately avenues and sacred enclosures of the Scioto Valley. (Du Pratz, Hist. of Louisiana, and Bartram's travels in E. and W. Florida.)

We may narrow the circle of unexplained antiquities by tracing the cordon of less mysterious vestiges surrounding that great centre of ancient habitation which is composed of States bordering on the Ohio.

East of the Alleghanies, from the Carolinas to New York, the country is nearly destitute of such remains. In New York they assume a character so nearly resembling those on the Ohio as to have been classed with them, until Mr. Squier decided by exploration that both relics of art and traces of occupancy were "absolutely *identical* with those which mark the sites of towns and forts known to have been occupied by the Indians within the historical period." The earthworks of northern Ohio are described by the same writer as corresponding with those of New York. No higher claim can be asserted for the remains north of the same line (omitting for the present the emblematic mounds of Wisconsin) and east of the Mississippi. Beyond the Mississippi the works on the Missouri, the Platte, and the Kansas, do not differ from the character of Indian structures. Further south, where such remains occur, they are comprehended in the class to which the accounts of early adventurers apply. The same may be said of those in the entire region south of Tennessee. In fact the Natchez, according to Du Pratz, maintained that their nation once extended as far north as the Ohio.[1]

Within the boundaries thus described lies a region from which no voice has come to tell when, why, and by whom, its structures were reared. They differ less in kind than in degree from other remains respecting which history has not been entirely silent. They are more numerous, more concentrated, and, in some particulars, on a larger scale of labor, than the works which approach them on their several borders, and with whose various characters they are blended. Their numbers may be the result of frequent changes of residence by a comparatively limited population, in accordance with a superstitious trait of the Indian nature, leading to the abandonment of places where any great calamity has been suffered; but they appear rather to indicate a country thickly inhabited for a period long enough to admit of the progressive enlargement and extension of its monuments.

What mighty cause of destruction anticipated by a few centuries the mission of the whites it is not easy to conjecture. That the people perished by plague or war is not more improbable than that they transferred themselves and their institutions to some yet undiscovered locality. The terrible appellation of "The Dark and Bloody Ground" applied to Kentucky, may relate to these distant events; and the fact stated by President Harrison, that the attractive banks of the Ohio, on either side, were without permanent occupants at the advent of European settlers, may have been owing to a lingering instinct of apprehension on the part of the native race.[2]

There are two other classes of remains whose origin is involved in equal obscurity—the emblematic earthworks of Wisconsin, and the so called "Garden Beds," found in the same State, and also in Michigan and Indiana. The last have hitherto been but incidentally noticed in this paper.

It is known that the culture of maize, tobacco, and a few kinds of vegetables, was practised by the aborigines throughout the United States, wherever the climate and soil were propitious, though in a careless and irregular manner; but the garden beds referred to are laid out with all the neatness and symmetry of modern husbandry. They cover large surfaces of prairie land, and as they sometimes cross the low mounds and pictorial embankments, they are supposed to have been formed after these had ceased to be objects of reverence. Mr. Schoolcraft and Mr. Lapham have fully described them.

We desire to stop where evidence ceases; and offer no speculations as to the direction from which the authors of the vestiges of antiquity in the United States entered the country, or from whence their arts were derived. The deductions from scientific investigations, philological and physiological, tend to prove that the

---

[1] London ed., 1774, p. 313.

[2] The region in which Kentucky is embraced was known to the Indians by the name of the Dark and Bloody Ground. (Filson's Disc. and Settl. of Ky., p. 4.)

American races are of great antiquity. Their religious doctrines, their superstitions, both in their nature and in their modes of practice, and their arts, accord with those of the most primitive age of mankind. With all their characteristics affinities are found in the early condition of Asiatic races; and a channel of communication is pointed out through which they might have poured into this continent before the existing institutions and national divisions of the parent country were developed. Fortuitous arrivals, too inconsiderable in numbers and influence to leave decided impressions, may at intervals have taken place from other lands; and geographical facts, and atmospherical phenomena, may serve to explain why the New World remained so long a sealed book to the cultivated nations of Europe, or was only known through the vague intimations and rumors alluded to in history, such as the chances of the sea, and indefinite reports from barbarous regions and peoples would be likely to bring to their ears.

INDEX.

E.

F.

G.

H.

I.

J.

K.

N.

O.

P.

PUBLISHED BY THE SMITHSONIAN INSTITUTION,
WASHINGTON, D. C.
JULY, 1856.

SMITHSONIAN CONTRIBUTIONS TO KNOWLEDGE.

ON THE

RECENT SECULAR PERIOD

OF THE

AURORA BOREALIS.

BY

DENISON OLMSTED, LL. D.,

PROFESSOR OF NATURAL PHILOSOPHY AND ASTRONOMY IN YALE COLLEGE.

[ACCEPTED FOR PUBLICATION, JANUARY, 1855.]

COMMISSION

TO WHICH THIS PAPER HAS BEEN REFERRED.

Prof. J. B. Cherriman,
Prof. J. H. Coffin.

Joseph Henry,
Secretary S. I.

T. K. AND P. G. COLLINS, PRINTERS,
PHILADELPHIA.

ON THE

RECENT SECULAR PERIOD OF THE AURORA BOREALIS.

On the evening of the 27th of August, 1827, after a long absence of any striking exhibition of the Aurora Borealis, there commenced a series of these meteors which increased in frequency and magnificence for the ten following years, arrived at a maximum during the years 1835, 1836, and 1837, and after that period regularly declined in number and intensity until November, 1848, when the series appeared to come to a close. The recurrence, however, of three very remarkable exhibitions of the meteor, in September, 1851, and of another of the first class as late as February 19th, 1852, indicates that the close was not so abrupt as was at first supposed; but still there was a very marked decline in the number of great auroras after 1848, and there has been scarcely one of the higher class since 1853.

A review of the history of the foregoing series of Auroras, appears to warrant the conclusion that it constituted a definite period, which I have ventured to call the "Secular Period," having a duration of a little more than 20 years; increasing in intensity pretty regularly for the first ten years, arriving at its maximum about the middle of this period, and as regularly declining during the latter half of the same period.

It has appeared to me incumbent on some one devoted to the studies of nature, who has witnessed this exhibition of the Aurora Borealis, probably among the most remarkable that have ever occurred since the creation of the world, to write its history; to give an accurate description of its varieties; to present at one view a classification of the principal facts, in order, if possible, to ascertain the *laws* of the phenomenon; and finally, to determine the *origin*, or primary cause to which it may be referred. I am the more encouraged to undertake this labor, from having enjoyed peculiarly favorable opportunities for observing these exhibitions from their commencement, and from having amassed, from the accounts published in the periodicals of the day, and from an extensive correspondence, a greater amount of facts, than, so far as I know, any other person has taken the trouble to accumulate.

I know of no other method of successfully investigating a subject of this kind, than, first, to examine all the facts of the case; secondly, to bring together into one view in separate groups, such as are similar, forming a full and accurate classification; thirdly, to inquire what general truths these facts reveal, since these deductions form the proximate laws of the phenomenon; and, finally, to make the laws the groundwork of a general *theory*, which shall assign the true cause of all.

CLASSIFICATION OF AURORAS.

The Aurora Borealis presents itself to us under six different forms.

1. *Auroral Twilight.*—A light in the north resembling the dawn of day, and of various degrees of intensity.

2. *Arches.*—Arcs of circles or zones, formed at various altitudes between N. E. and N. W., being sometimes the mere boundary of a segment, at other times a dense pillar of light, forming a grand columnar arch which spans the heavens from east to west. It frequently moves from north to south, usually advancing but little further than the zenith, but in a few instances, in our latitude, it has been seen to reach within twenty degrees of the southern horizon.

3. *Streamers.*—Acute cones or spindles, usually shooting up from an arch, or from a dark smoky cloud which lies along the northern horizon, or rises a few degrees above it.

4. *Corona.*—A circular zone around the pole of the dipping needle, formed of wreaths of auroral vapor, either of pure white, or of various prismatic colors, with streamers radiating from the circumference.

5. *Waves.*—Undulations which commonly flow upwards towards the centre of the corona, along the line of the streamers, but sometimes course along the line of an arch from east to west.

6. *Auroral Clouds.*—A milky vapory bank in the north, the quantity and apparent depth of which afford a prognostic of the intensity of the approaching aurora. These clouds are sometimes of a smoky hue, especially in front, while the margins are luminous. The term *Merry Dancers* is loosely applied to several different appearances, constituting the more active portions of the phenomenon. Thus rapid coruscations, flickerings, and swift horizontal movements across a forest of streamers, have been, by different writers, severally denominated merry dancers.

In different exhibitions of the aurora borealis, the various forms above enumerated, are sometimes seen single, but commonly more or less combined. In the most magnificent examples they all are seen in company. At first, usually at an early hour of the evening, appears the northern *twilight*, as though the sun after he had set was rising prematurely in the north. If a large bank of luminous vapor (which is so peculiar in its external properties, and so distinct from watery vapor, as to warrant the denomination of *auroral vapor*), rests on the northern horizon, we may expect to see the aurora put on successively more of its higher forms—streamers will begin to shoot upwards; a dark smoky front will cover the auroral vapor, exhibiting here and there changeable and transient white spots, which suddenly swell out, and often as suddenly disappear—then large columns of a clear silvery lustre will form in the northwest and northeast simultaneously, which will sometimes meet and span the heavens with an entire arch; suddenly the columns and clouds of auroral vapor will assume a crimson hue—next, all the columns and streamers will rush towards a point a little southeast of the zenith, corresponding to the pole of the dipping-needle, and wreathe themselves around it in a splendid coronet—and finally auroral waves will begin to flow upward from the horizon towards the same point in surprising undulations, which are often continued a great part of the night. Meanwhile, the magnetic needle is violently agitated, and deflected from its normal position.

It is the occurrence of these great auroras, repeated with unusual frequency, that constitutes a period like that under review, which I have denominated the Secular Period of the aurora borealis; while auroras presenting some of the humbler forms of the phenomenon, as the northern twilight, or the streamers, are of ordinary occurrence.

We shall find it convenient to distribute the different forms of the aurora into four distinct classes, with a description of the characters belonging to each class respectively.

Class I. This is characterized by the presence of at least *three* out of four of the most magnificent varieties of form, namely, arches, streamers, corona, and waves. The distinct formation of the corona is the most important characteristic of this class; yet, were the corona distinctly formed, without auroral arches or waves, or crimson vapor, it could not be considered as an aurora of the first class.

Class II. The combination of *two* or more of the leading characteristics of the first class, but wanting in others, would serve to mark class the second. Thus the exhibition of arches and streamers both of superior brilliancy, with a corona, while the waves and crimson columns were wanting; or of streamers with a corona, or of arches with a corona without streamers or columns (if such a case ever occurs), we should designate as an aurora of the second class.

Class III. The presence of only *one* of the more rare characteristics, either streamers or an arch, or irregular coruscations, but without the formation of a corona, and with but a moderate degree of intensity, would denote an aurora of the third class.

Class IV. In this class we place the most ordinary forms of the aurora, as a mere northern twilight, or a few streamers, with none of the characteristics that mark the grander exhibitions of the phenomenon.

HISTORY OF THE RECENT SECULAR PERIOD.

From about the year 1780 to 1827, striking exhibitions of the aurora borealis were very unfrequent, although, probably, more or less of an inferior description, as those of the third and fourth classes, were seen every year, even in our own latitude, and a still greater number in the regions north of us; but aged people who witnessed the displays of eighteen hundred thirty-five, six, and seven, testified that these were similar to such as occurred in their youth, from 1760 to 1781.

Indeed, in my childhood, nearly fifty years ago, I recollect to have heard very aged people tell of the strange sights which were seen in the air during "the old French war" (which closed in 1763), when, as some of the more ignorant described them, "armies and spearmen were distinctly seen engaged in battle." From 1781, none of equal intensity, it is believed, occurred for nearly half a century. The splendid arch, therefore, and other striking accompaniments of the aurora of August 28th, 1827, took us by surprise, and were viewed with wonder by nearly all the existing generation of the countries where it was visible. Immediately after this great aurora, exhibitions of the phenomenon became more frequent than for a long time before, as is obvious from the catalogue of auroras published by the late John Dalton, and appended to the last edition of his *Meteorological Essays.*[1] The period of seven years, from 1819 to 1826, averaged per annum, in Great Britain, but $1\frac{3}{7}$; whereas from 1827 to 1834, the average was 16. The number recorded by Dalton in 1826 was only two, while the number for 1827 was ten.

I observed the great aurora of August, 1827, with the deepest interest; but having preserved but few notes of it, I avail myself of the accounts published at the time in a paper in the *American Journal of Science*,[2] communicated by Benjamin D. Silliman, Esq., occasionally, however, drawing upon my own recollections.

The appearances of the aurora were found to be nearly uniform in all the Northern States of the Union. It was first observed at New Haven at haf-past nine o'clock, at which time the light resembled that of a fire at some distance, and was by many attributed to that cause. The light, however, soon became more intense, and its outline better defined, gradually assuming a columnar shape, and extending from about N. N. W. to E. N. E. At 9 h. 45 m., *waves* of light, in detached masses, but all in the line of the luminous arch, began to flow from east to west, until the whole were blended, and the heavens were adorned with a beautiful arch, culminating at a point about 15° north of the zenith. The greatest breadth of the arch, at its centre, was 9 or 10 degrees, and it tapered from that point to its western extremity, where the light was much brighter. The eastern segment was at no time so distinct as the western, but was rendered very beautiful by the constant passage of waves of apparently illuminated vapor, the lines of which were at right angles to the line of the arch, and extended from north to south. Their westward motion was contrary to the course of the wind. The whole arch moved with a gradual and nearly uniform motion toward the south, and passed the zenith about 10 h. 45m., presenting to the eye through its whole length, a broad bright band of wavy light, studded with stars which were seen distinctly through it. The color was a shining white. This arch was remarkable for its duration, which was nearly two hours. A great bank of light lay almost constantly above the northern horizon, sometimes surmounted by, and sometimes resting upon, a dark cloud, which was visible during the whole time.[3] This was visible in the same situation at sea,

---

[1] Meteor. Observations and Essays, Ed. 2d, p. 218. [2] Vol. XIV.

[3] It may be doubtful whether this was anything more than the naked sky, which, by contrast with the illuminated portion often resembles a dark cloud. In the aurora of September 29th, 1851, the base of

off Nova Scotia (lat. 42° 12′ N., long. 63° 9′ W.), as reported by the British ship Dalhousie Castle. The dark cloud remained until midnight. It was elevated 12 or 15 degrees above the horizon, and the space below it was occupied by a dense haze. It was said that, at Utica, New York, sounds were heard attended by a sharp snapping noise, like the discharge of an electrical battery. Peculiar sounds referred to the aurora were also said to have been heard at this place (Yale College). One of the students, indeed, was under the impression that he distinctly heard such sounds, but I was unable, either on this or on any subsequent occasion, to detect any sound which in my judgment could be fairly attributed to the aurora borealis. The bow was seen as far south as Norfolk, in Virginia. It was also conspicuous in Cincinnati, and was said in the newspapers published at that place to have been the first occurrence of the aurora borealis in the southern part of Ohio, since the first settlement of the country. At Montreal, on the previous evening, the 27th (when only an aurora of the fourth class was seen at New Haven), the coruscations are represented to have been "awfully grand," extending in broad columns to the zenith, and even beyond it. At Perth, in Scotland, also, there was the same evening (the 27th), a splendid exhibition of the aurora. The account given of it in the *Courier*, a newspaper published at that place, will serve to indicate the similarity of its appearances to those exhibited here on the following evening. "One of the most brilliant and picturesque appearances (says the *Courier*) of the aurora borealis ever seen in this quarter, exhibited itself on the evening of Monday last. The coruscations were very rapid and transparent, and overspread nearly the whole northern hemisphere. Some of the flashes were almost vertical, and latterly they resembled in clearness and motion the undulations of a bright flame. At one time the meteors formed themselves into a narrow belt, crossing the heavens from east to west."

The great aurora of August 28th, afforded to the existing generation the first example they had seen of those flickerings, and rapid coruscations called *Merry Dancers*. These continued until after midnight, and were accompanied by an unusual frequency of shooting stars.

On the 25th September, 1827, a great aurora was seen all over England.[1] It does not, however, appear to have been equal in magnificence to some which were seen here a few years later, and can therefore rank only in the second class. This aurora was visible at Paris, accompanied by striking magnetic effects, although its luminous phenomena were less imposing than in Scotland. According to M. Arago, previous to this, no aurora had been witnessed at Paris for twenty years.[2] Also, a splendid exhibition of the phenomenon occurred at Paris on the 28th of September, described in the *Journal des Debats*, as tinging the sky with so fiery a hue as to resemble a great conflagration, and call out bodies of firemen. According to the

---

the aurora rested on a dark segment resembling a black cloud, but the bright star in the extremity of the tail of the Great Bear (η *Ursæ Majoris*), then only three degrees above the horizon, shone with undiminished lustre.

[1] Brande's Journal, XXIV, 385. Phil. Mag., II, 375, and III, 75.

[2] Amer. Jour. Sci., XIV, 107.

same paper, a beautiful aurora had been seen in every part of Denmark as early as the 8th of September.

From the preceding accounts it appears that after a long period of comparative repose, the aurora borealis suddenly presented itself to the existing generation both in the north of Europe and in the United States, under forms far more imposing than most persons on the stage had ever witnessed before; and if we pursue its history, we shall find that these exhibitions increased, during the following years, in number and intensity. This increase is strikingly shown by *Dalton's Catalogue of Auroras*, extending from the year 1794 to 1834 inclusive, embracing those observed during this period in Great Britain and Ireland. If we compare the seven years previous to 1827, with the seven years following, the numbers are as follows:—

Year	Number	Year	Number
1820	2	1827	10
1821	2	1828	11
1822	0	1829	18
1823	0	1830	32
1824	0	1831	23
1825	1	1832	5
1826	2	1833	12
Total	7	Total	111

In intensity, the increase during the latter period is equally remarkable, as will be evident by descending to particulars.

In 1828, September 29th, there was a grand auroral arch seen in Great Britain and Ireland, and also in the State of New York.[1] Although in 1829, the number recorded by Dalton was 18, yet none occurred above the third class. The following year, 1830, still manifested an increasing series, the number given in the same catalogue being 32, those of April 19th, August 20th, September 7th, September 17th, Oct. 5th, December 11th and 12th, having been more or less splendid, and some of them entitled to rank in the second class. For 1831, only 23 auroras are given, but that of January 7th is characterized as "one of the finest auroras ever seen," and as lasting from sunset till morning. It was observed in England, Scotland, Paris, and Brussels.[2] That of March 7th is said to have been fine; but most of the exhibitions of 1831 were of the ordinary kind. In the *American Journal of Science* for October, 1831, is a paper by General Martin Field, giving an account of auroras observed by him at Fayetteville, Vermont (lat. 42° 58′). He says: "On examining my meteorological journal, which I have kept for many years, I find the occurrence of the aurora borealis has varied from 10 to 28 nights in different years, and that for ten years previous to the last, the average number of evenings when it has been seen is 18 annually. But within the last twelve months, from May, 1830, to May, 1831, the aurora has been visible on 56 nights, which is twice the number of any former year of which I have any record." The

[1] Dalton's Ess., 221; Brewster's Jour., I, 256, X, 146; Phil. Mag., V, 153.

[2] Luke Howard, Meteor. Ess., III, 873; Phil. Mag., IX, 127, 151, 233; Jameson's Jour., X, 381.

same writer has delineated a remarkable arch observed by him on the 9th of March, although an aurora which occurred on the 14th of July, appears to have been the most remarkable of the year.

In 1832, Dalton has recorded only *five* auroras; but at this period the returns of the academies of the State of New York, embodied in the annual reports of the Regents, begin to furnish a more complete list of these occurrences, than had been kept anywhere in this country anterior to that time. The number observed and reported in the State of New York for 1832 was 24, the most remarkable of which occurred on the 10th of April, and the 22d and 23d of August. That of September 25th, which was conspicuous in the State of New York, was also visible at London and Edinburgh.[1]

Twelve only are recorded in Dalton's list for 1833; but in the Regents' report, we find no less than *thirty-six*. The most brilliant were those of May 16th and 17th, July 10th, Sept. 5th, and November 3d. In September alone the phenomenon was repeated no less than ten evenings. The instances which attracted most attention in Great Britain during the year 1833, occurred March 21st, September 17th and October 12th, but none were observed in the State of New York on those evenings.

Dalton's catalogue extends only to February, 1834, a loss the less to be regretted as from that time the phenomenon became more an object of attention to observers on this side of the Atlantic, and the catalogue contained in the Regents' reports becomes yearly more and more complete. During 1834, that report describes *thirty-two* auroras, of which that of November 2d was the only one particularly remarkable.

In 1835, there is an unexpected falling off in the number of auroras, since in the Regents' report the entire number for the year is only *twenty-six;* but the aurora of November 17th of this year, was greatly distinguished for its magnificence and beauty, and constitutes the first in the series of those entitled to rank in the first class. It exhibited itself with very similar phenomena, though with features somewhat varied at points very remote from each other, as at Montreal and New York, at Dartmouth College and Cincinnati.[2]

Although minute descriptions of these grand exhibitions of the aurora borealis, resembling each other as they do in many particulars, may, when repeated, become tedious by their monotony, yet it appears to me a matter of great importance to science, to place on permanent record a full account of such displays of this mysterious phenomenon, in order to furnish data for comparison at successive returns of the secular periods, and thus finally to establish its physical laws. The following description of the great aurora of November 17th, 1835, was published the next morning, by the author of this article, in the *New Haven Daily Herald:*—[3]

"Last night, our northern hemisphere was adorned with a display of auroral lights remarkably grand and diversified. It was first observed by the writer at fifteen minutes before 7 o'clock, when an illumination of the whole northern sky,

---

[1] Phil. Mag., II, 233. [2] Amer. Jour., XXIX, 388. [3] Amer. Jour. Sci., XXIX, 389.

resembling the break of day was discernible through the openings in the clouds. About 18° east of north was a broad column of shining vapor tinged with crimson, which appeared and disappeared at intervals. A westerly wind moved off the clouds, rendering the sky nearly clear by 8 o'clock, when two broad white columns, which had for some time been gathering between the stars Aquila and Lyra on the west, and the Pleiades and Aries on the east, united above so as to complete a luminous arch spanning the heavens a little south of the prime vertical. The whole northern heavens being more or less illuminated and separated from the southern by this zone, was thrown into striking contrast with the latter, which appeared of a dark slate color, as though the stars were shining through a stratum of black clouds. The zone moved slowly to the south, until about 9 o'clock, when it had reached the bright star in the Eagle (Altair) in the west, and extended a little south of the constellation Aries in the east. From this time it began to recede northward, at a nearly uniform rate, until twenty minutes before 11 o'clock, when a vast number of columns, white and crimson, began to shoot up, simultaneously, from all parts of the northern hemisphere, directing their course to a point a few degrees southeast of the zenith, around which they arranged themselves as around a common focus. The position of this point was between the Pleiades and Alpha Arietis, and south of the Bee, having a right ascension of 42°, and a declination of 24°, as nearly as could be determined without the aid of instruments; but this comes so near the pole of the *dipping needle* at the place of observation (which is about 17° from the zenith), and to the magnetic meridian, that we need not hesitate to conclude, that, agreeably to what has been observed of similar phenomena before, the columns arranged themselves exactly in obedience to the laws of terrestrial magnetism. Soon after 11 o'clock commenced a striking display of the *auroral waves.* They consisted of thin horizontal sheets of light, coursing each other upward with astonishing speed, inspiring awe in every beholder, as something unearthly in appearance. Those undulations which play upon the surface of a field of rye or tall grass, when gently agitated by the wind, may give to the reader a faint idea of the auroral waves. One of the crimson columns, the most dense and beautiful of all, as it ascended towards the common focus (the vanishing point of perspective for parallel lines), crossed the planet Jupiter, then at an altitude of 36 degrees. The appearance was peculiarly interesting, as the planet shone through a crimson cloud, with apparently augmented splendor. A few *shooting stars* were seen at intervals, some of which were above the ordinary magnitude and brightness. One that came from between the feet of the Great Bear, at eight minutes after 1 o'clock, and fell apparently near to the earth, exhibited a very white and dazzling light, and, as it exploded, scattered shining fragments, much after the manner of a sky rocket. As early as 7 o'clock, the *magnetic needle* began to show unusual agitation, and it was afterwards carefully observed by Tutor Loomis.[1] Near 11 o'clock, when the streamers were rising, and the aurora forming, the disturbance of the needle was remarkable, causing a motion of 1° 5′ in five minutes of time. This disturbance continued until 10 o'clock next morning, the needle having traversed an entire

[1] Now Professor Loomis, of N. Y.

range of 1° 40′, while its ordinary diurnal variation is not more than four minutes. The *thermometer*, at 11 o'clock, was at 33°; it shortly fell to 31°, and continued nearly at this point during the remainder of the night, a degree of cold considerably below that of the few preceding nights. About 3 o'clock, the sky grew cloudy, and the moon rising shortly afterwards, further observations were prevented; but the continued disturbance of the magnetic needle, would induce the belief that the aurora prevailed through the night, and to a late hour next morning."

On the evening following the above exhibition of the aurora borealis, that is, on the 18th of November, 1835, a fine aurora was witnessed at London, having all the characteristics of the first class except the corona. It is described in the *Arcana of Art and Science, for* 1836, by Dr. Armstrong, as seen at Vauxhall. The writer remarks that the aurora had made its appearance, with greater or less distinctness, on every clear and calm evening from the middle of October; a frequency very unusual for that climate.

On the 11th of December, of the same year, an aurora of the more brilliant kind (2d class) was observed by Captain Bonnycastle, at Toronto, which he has described and figured in the thirtieth volume of the *American Journal of Science.*

The *Regents' Report*, for 1836, contains an elaborate paper by Professor Joslin, then of Union College, Schenectady, on the auroras of 1835, and several preceding years. He had carefully observed and recorded, during the five years ending in 1835, *fifty-six* auroras, of which twelve were of the last year; and he was the first, in *this country*, to describe certain appearances, seen in the daytime, resembling auroral exhibitions, and which, according to him, are truly such. Dr. Joslin's paper also contains valuable records of the state of the weather preceding and following an aurora, from which he deduces the general rule that, "previous to an aurora, the barometer is rising and the thermometer falling; and that the air is much nearer than usual to the point of saturation with moisture."[1]

It may be remarked that each of these circumstances betokens that fair and transparent state of the atmosphere, which is peculiarly favorable to the exhibition of the aurora.

Dr. Gibbons, of Wilmington, in the State of Delaware (lat. 39° 41′), has given a record of all the auroras seen by him during the six years from 1827 to 1833, amounting to 52,—a number which is evidently much greater than the average for that latitude, and, therefore, plainly indicating that the time fell within the secular

---

[1] In *Jameson's Journal* we find the following account of an aurora borealis seen in the daytime, at *Canonmills*, September 9th, 1827. The morning of Sunday, September 9th, was rainy, with a light gale from the N.E. Before mid-day the wind began to veer to the west, and the clouds in the north-western horizon cleared away; the blue sky in that quarter assumed the form of the segment of a very large circle, with a well-defined line; the clouds above continuing dense, and covering the rest of the heavens. The centre of the azure arch gradually inclined more to the north, and reached an elevation of nearly 20°. In a short time very thin fleecy clouds began to rise from the horizon within the blue arch; and through these, very faint, perpendicular streaks of a sort of milky light could be perceived shooting; the eye, being thus guided, could likewise detect the same pale streaks passing over the intense azure arch; but they were extremely slight and evanescent. Between nine and ten in the evening of the same day, the aurora borealis was very brilliant.

period. Dr. Gibbons, like Professor Joslin, took particular note of the state of the thermometer, and infers that the occurrence of an aurora is always attended and followed by a depression of temperature. He shows that the average temperature of the days immediately preceding the auroras was 55°; that of the days following 52°; and that the difference between the second days before and after the auroras was 6°.

In 1836 the number of the exhibitions of the aurora borealis greatly increased; being, as given in the *Regents' Report*, no less than *sixty-one*. The month of April was remarkably productive, the aurora being seen on the 8th, 11th, 12th, 19th, 20th, 21st, 22d, 23d, and 24th. That of the 22d was of the first class, and the description of it, written by the author of this paper at the time, was as follows:—

"Soon after 7 o'clock, near the end of twilight, a thick covering of auroral vapor was seen to overspread the northern hemisphere, and streamers began to shoot up towards the zenith, accompanied by faint undulations, all tending towards the pole of the dipping needle as a common focus. At this period, the color of the aurora was a dull yellow, with a slight tinge of red; but, as the exhibition advanced, the red predominated. The aurora made slow progress, but the firmament was surpassingly beautiful, particularly in the west, where the planet Venus, now approaching its maximum splendor, the planet Jupiter, and the Moon, near its first quarter, appeared one above the other along the zodiac, while the large constellation Orion, with Sirius and Procyon in his train, conspired to adorn the western sky. Saturn also was shining brightly in the southeast. About half past 10 o'clock began the *auroral waves* (which were very remarkable on that night), and increased rapidly until 11 o'clock; after which they continued, with surprising activity, nearly all night, ascending with swift undulations towards the magnetic focus, traversing about half the quadrantal arc in half a second of time. At five minutes after 11, a number of broad stripes of silvery whiteness appeared in the east and west, all tending upwards to the same point. These were soon replaced by sheets of crimson eight or ten degrees broad below, but tapering above. They crossed the constellation Leo in the west. They had a counterpart in the east, though somewhat less splendid. Soon afterwards broad sheets wreathing themselves in serpentine curves, flowed towards the magnetic pole, with astonishing rapidity, on every side, but most abundantly from the N. W. and the N. E. Their margins were fringed with a white light of peculiar softness. They were like crimson billows, separated by horizontal lines, and rolling towards the zenith. During the fifteen minutes, while these crimson sheets were in view, two parallel arches stretched across the southern sky, the lower about 30° in altitude, from both of which streamers arose. From half past eleven o'clock, the auroral waves exceeded everything as they rushed in pallid, filmy sheets towards the zenith, along the line of the streamers, though apparently much below them, increasing their velocity as they ascended.

"The focus changed its position slightly at different times; first moving northwards, and then returning. At 12 o'clock it had a declination of 23½ degrees, and a right ascension of 209 degrees. The barometer remained through the night nearly stationary, and the thermometer fell only 2° after midnight: namely, from 32° to 30°. At half past 2 o'clock clouds (cirro-stratus) came up, and were scattered over a great part of the sky. Although the moon was down, it was still light enough to see the time of night by the watch."

Such were the appearances at Yale College; but it seems to me desirable to place on record the phenomena of these highest exhibitions of the aurora borealis, as they were observed at places remote from each other, in order to see how far they preserved their identity, or how far they were altered by a change of place in the spectator.

At Mount St. Mary's College, at Emmettsburg, Maryland, this aurora was attentively observed by Professor M'Caffrey.[1] The phenomenon is seldom seen at all in that latitude (39°), and especially in any of its more splendid forms. About 7 o'clock in the evening of the 22d of April, a large part of the northern heavens was covered with a thin vapor-like appearance, white at the base, of a pale red at the upper edges, and of a deeper hue, red and yellow intermixed, about the middle. It spread through an arc of 60° near the horizon, and extended half way up to the zenith. Before 9 o'clock it had disappeared, leaving nothing but a bank of white auroral vapor, stretching along the northern and northeastern horizon. At fifteen minutes after 10, on looking towards the north, I perceived a few well-defined columns, shooting up a short distance, each of them appearing and vanishing momentarily; yet so that, to a careless observer, they might seem to remain permanently before the view. Gradually the northern streamers increased, both in number and in length, as new ones sprung up east and west of those obscured originally. Stars could be seen dimly shining through them. The color of the coruscations was of a bluish white near the base; further up, it was of a brighter and more silvery hue. Those nearest the moon, which was then in her first quarter, and gave a strong light, assumed, for a short time, a pale green, then a bright orange color; and one, which shot up to a great length, became particularly remarkable by its redness. The whole scene was still further enlivened by a beautiful play of crimson light gracefully undulating upwards along the streamers. The long rays continued to shoot up higher and higher, until they all converged to a point on or near the meridian, about midway between Arcturus and Beta Leonis. The right ascension was found to be 194° 20′, and its declination 18° N. At this point, the streamers, which magnificently decorated the whole northern hemisphere, reddening as they converged, formed a superb oval crown of deep crimson light. This crown, which seemed like a lake of blood, extended about 15° east and west, and 10° or 12° in the opposite direction. It had such a preternatural aspect, and, viewed in connection with the accompanying phenomena, one of such overpowering sublimity, as to inspire a profound feeling of religious awe. It lasted from five minutes before 11 o'clock until five minutes after. Gradually the redness faded away; the coruscations, which had lately met and mingled in the color of blood, no longer entirely converged; around the focus was left a blank space of very irregular outline; south of it were seen the broken off extremities of the most northern rays; while all the rays near the convergence had a peculiar brushy appearance. At later periods the

---

[1] Amer. Jour. Science, XXXI, 85.

point of convergence, as well as it could be determined, was found nearer and nearer to Arcturus, indicating that the whole meteor moved with the earth.[1] During the more brilliant stages of the phenomena, the stars looked very dim; and the moon, previous to her setting, shorn of more than half her lustre, had a sickly, pallid aspect. For the space of two hours after the disappearing of the auroral crown, the illuminated portion of the heavenly dome exhibited, in great brilliancy and variety, the phenomenon fancifully called the "merry dancers." It was the incessant play of a flickering light, not so bright as the Vespertine, which in some respects it resembled, glancing about in various directions, but chiefly towards the zenith, over the vast expanse. Its motions were far too varied and fantastic to admit of description. In general, one flash seemed to chase another, as they arose in graceful undulations, or rather darted up the sky, along and between the white auroral columns. At half past 11, the spectacle began to lose its attractive brilliancy. Still later, the luminous rays were intersected by two irregular belts of white vapor, which appeared successively in the north and northeast, one of them spanning an arc of about 30, the other about 40 or 45 degrees. About 12 o'clock the "merry dancers" renewed the splendor of their exhibition, and continued it, in less and less brilliancy, for an hour. Between 11 and 12, a dark cloud had arisen in the northeast; before 2, the wind was blowing from the south, and the sky was so far overcast as to hide completely from our view all that remained of magnificence and splendor.

These two exhibitions of the aurora of April 22d (one of the greatest on record), being both minutely described, and taking place at places removed from each other by 2¼° of latitude, or by a rectilinear distance of nearly three hundred miles, present circumstances very favorable for comparison, and we will pause a moment to consider their points of similarity or dissimilarity. In both places the exhibition commenced about 7 o'clock, and was marked by like appearances of the northern sky, although, as might be expected, the elevation of the aurora was less at the southern than at the northern station. At the latter the display made slow but constant progress; while at the former it disappeared before 9 o'clock, leaving nothing but a bank of white auroral vapor. Then, however, soon after 10, the aurora revived, exhibiting abundant streamers. At half past 10, at the north, commenced a grand display of auroral waves, which, at the south, appeared as a beautiful play of crimson light, gracefully undulating upwards along the streamers. At both places the magnificent aurora was formed about 11 o'clock; but in Maryland it lasted only ten minutes, while in Connecticut it was visible until after 12 o'clock. Although the display at the southern station was probably unparalleled in that climate for splendor and magnificence, yet the greater abundance and more sublime evolutions of the sheets of crimson vapor that flowed upward between 10 and 11 o'clock, as well as the more striking display of auroral waves, which lasted all night, rendered the northern exhibition far the more grand and impressive.

---

[1] This merely indicates that the point of convergence was the pole of the dipping needle, and, therefore, maintained a fixed position with respect to the meridian.—O.

The year 1836 was also distinguished on the Eastern Continent for great auroras. That of October 18th was seen all over Europe.[1]

The year 1837 may be called the maximum year of the whole period; for although the number of auroras recorded in the *Regents' Report* is not equal to that of 1836, being only 50, while that of 1836 was 61, yet this year was distinguished above all for three auroras of the first class, which occurred January 25th, July 1st, and November 14th, while no other single year had hitherto presented more than one of this class. The aurora of January 25th was for some time afterwards known among our small corps of observers as the "magnificent." In many respects it resembled that of November 17th, 1835, but its colors were brighter and more diversified, and its columns were arranged with more symmetry around the magnetic pole, supporting a canopy of unrivalled grandeur. My attention was first attracted to the aurora as early as six o'clock, before the twilight was over. At this time the northern sky exhibited a blush not unlike that of the fairest dawn. This was skirted on the east and west by ill-defined columns of crimson light, which moved slowly from north to south. At 7 o'clock these began to send up *streamers*, all of which tended, as usual, to a common focus, situated a few degrees S. E. of the zenith. At 7 h. 10 m., the *corona* was distinctly formed, embracing the Pleiades, which were nearly at its centre. At three different times during the evening, the corona was dispersed and as often re-formed; but the position of its centre at or near the pole of the dipping needle remained invariable. Meanwhile, the twilight of the northern sky had moved slowly southward, its boundary spanning the firmament from west to east in a well-defined zone, until it left only a segment of the southern hemisphere, about 30° in altitude. This portion of the heavens, thrown as it was into striking contrast with the illuminated parts of the sky, appeared of a dark slate color, and exhibited the interesting spectacle of stars seeming to shine brightly through a stratum of black clouds.

These phenomena exhibited various interesting evolutions until 15 minutes after 10 o'clock, when suddenly the meteor rallied all its forces. Innumerable spindles of silvery lustre darted from the crimson folds of light that hung around the sky, all pointing towards the common focus; and sheets of a thin vapor of mingled white and red flowed over them, and wreathed themselves around the same point in wavy folds. A universal stillness reigned; and the ground itself now covered with snow, which exhibited a delicate rosy tint, contributed to enhance the beauty of the scene. It is obvious, also, to one that reflects on the position of the principal constellations at that time, that a large part of all the brightest of the fixed stars were above the horizon. Sirius and Procyon, Castor and Pollux, Capella and Aldebaran, were arranged around the field in striking array, along with the planets Jupiter and Mars, both at the period of their greatest splendor. So delicate was the auroral covering, that the light of the stars was but little obscured by it. The cluster of small stars in the head of Orion, when most enveloped, was distinctly visible; and the two planets appeared through a dense mass of red vapor with seemingly augmented splendor. In these various attributes of grandeur and beauty, the present exceeded all former exhibitions of the aurora; but there were wanting the *auroral*

---

[1] Bibliothèque Univers. for Oct., 1836.

waves which made so conspicuous a figure in the great exhibitions of November, 1835, and April, 1836. Although the moon was shining in the east, and was but little past the full, yet the distinctness of the auroral lights seemed scarcely impaired by it. This is remarkable; perhaps there is not more than one other instance on record where so splendid an exhibition of the aurora borealis was witnessed in the presence of so full a moon.

The *magnetic needle* was watched attentively by Mr. E. C. Herrick, and was observed to undergo extraordinary fluctuations at one time (7 h. 41 m.), deviating a whole degree west of its normal position, and at another time traversing 45 minutes in two minutes of time. The *barometer* had previously been subject to uncommon variations. On the night of the 21st, between 11 and 12 o'clock, it stood at 28.70 inches, a depression seldom equalled at this place. From that time it had steadily risen, and during the aurora it stood at 30.1 inches. Its entire range from December 19th, when it was 30.91, was very remarkable, since its maximum in ordinary years is seldom above 30.70, and its minimum seldom below 29 inches, making the entire annual range 1.7 inches; whereas, during the 24 hours preceding this aurora, the range was 1.4 inches. The *thermometer* early in the evening of the aurora was at 20° (Fahr.), but sank rapidly, and at 10 o'clock was only 4° above zero, and before morning fell quite to zero. The *zodiacal light* was at that time very conspicuous in the S. W. in the evening, and continued through the two or three months, considerably brighter than in ordinary years.

This great aurora called out many good observers in various parts of the United States and in Canada, and the periodicals of the day abound with descriptions of it. At Annapolis (Maryland), lat. 39°, it was accurately observed by President Humphreys, of St. John's College. Instead of the twilight blush in the north, an appearance which it first presented at New Haven, as early as six o'clock, Dr. Humphreys, although abroad and engaged in taking an astronomical observation, discovered nothing of it until 40 minutes after six, when his attention was suddenly arrested by a column of red light which shot up from the southwest. At its maximum, the aurora afforded light sufficient to cast a deep shadow from trees, houses, and other objects, while the snow reflected a rich crimson. The magnetic needle constantly vibrated in the horizontal arc, and was so affected in the dip, as to be brought closely into contact with the glass plate; and, on inclining the needle so as to cause it to traverse, the difference of declination between 9 o'clock that evening and sunrise next morning was more than *ten degrees*.[1] This result is remarkable, not only for the extent of the change of declination, which, I believe, is altogether unprecedented, but from the fact that at New Britain, twenty-five miles north of New Haven, Mr. Burritt, an experienced observer, watched the needle for two hours during the most active period of the same aurora, and could not discern the least change of declination, while the change of declination at New Haven was, as already stated, a whole degree.[2]

---

[1] *Annapolis Republican*, Jan. 28, 1837. We can hardly avoid suspecting either an error of observation, or a misprint, in a result so unparalleled.—O.

[2] Captain Richardson also reports that in his observations on the auroras of the polar regions, he could discover no effect on the needle. Captain Parry says the same.

I have before me minute descriptions of this grand aurora covering a region of six degrees of latitude from N. to S. and extending indefinitely from E. to W.[1] In all those places, the phenomena were remarkably uniform; all observers remarked the early commencement of the display (before the end of twilight)—the predominance of crimson vapor—the broad and splendid arches—the sudden increase of intensity about 7 o'clock, and the formation of the corona soon after around the Pleiades—and the general illumination and fiery appearance of the canopy extending far towards the southern horizon. Numbers also mention the renewal of the principal features with augmented splendor, from half past ten to half past eleven o'clock, although comparatively few observers had the perseverance to follow out their observations through the whole night.

The same year (1837) afforded two other exhibitions of auroras of the first class, namely, on the 1st of July and on the 14th of November. According to Professor Dewey, that of July 1st, as seen at Rochester, N. Y., exceeded in splendor that of January 25th.[2] It followed a sudden depression of temperature. At 2 o'clock P. M. the preceding day, the thermometer was at 86°; a shower ensued, a cool wind set in, and the following evening the thermometer fell to 58°. Soon after twilight the aurora appeared in short, flocculent, cloud-like forms, all across the northern sky. Soon it extended quite round to the east and west points, at both of which broad and bright arches arose, and extended more than half-way to the zenith, while numerous streamers rose all around the northern sky towards the same point. The corona was formed ten minutes after ten o'clock, but the display was more striking at half past ten. The whole expanse except the south was most splendid; and soon afterwards the flashing towards the vertex from all sides was renewed with great power. The maximum of intensity was about 11 o'clock. The colors were constantly changing; from all the northern, eastern, and western parts, the flashing light rose to the vertex and seemed to shoot back again. Often the light would flash through thirty or forty degrees, disappear within twenty degrees of the vertex, and reappear flashing as before, for the last ten degrees, as if it passed in the intermediate space, through some opaque substances. Mr. E. C. Herrick's description of the same aurora,[3] corresponds in most particulars to that of Professor Dewey. At half past ten the action appeared to him most energetic, and the scene eminently beautiful. From east, north, and west, and all points between, streamers shot up from near the horizon in quick succession, with wonderful celerity, and passed beyond the zenith; while others, starting from an elevation of about 30° in the south met the former about the corona. The display began to decline at 11 h. 10 m., and by midnight became quite faint. At 2 o'clock the aurora began to revive, and soon presented a spectacle in many respects surpassing the former. The exhibition

[1] It was accurately observed and described by Judge McCord, at Montreal; by Professor Dewey, at Rochester; by Mr. R. Haskins, at Buffalo; by Mrs. G. S. Silliman, at Brooklyn, N. Y.; by Mr. E. H. Burritt, New Britain, Ct.; by President Humphreys, at Annapolis, Maryland; also, by a spectator, at Norristown, Pennsylvania, and another in Sussex, New Jersey. Also, at Bermuda.

[2] Amer. Journal Sci., XXXIII, 143.

[3] New Haven Daily Herald, for July 6, 1837.

continued with diminishing intensity all night, and streamers were seen until an hour after daybreak.

In this account, the fact is first distinctly enunciated that when the aurora is unusually brilliant, there sometimes occur *two fits of greatest intensity* at an interval of about four hours. The following are given as the successive positions of the corona:

At 2 h. 31 m. centre of corona	75° 25′ alt.—	S. 4° 27′ E. az.
" 39	74° 55′	3.30
" 42	74° 40′	5.07

Dip, at New Haven, 73° 27′; ——— *Declination*, 6° 10′ W.

The magnetic needle was much disturbed. Between 10 h. 44 m. and 11 o'clock, it traversed an arc of 3° 41′. After midnight the range did not exceed 1°.

Of the great aurora of November 14th of the same year, Professor Barnard, of the University of Mississippi, then resident in the city of New York, prepared a full account from the statements of different observers, which was inserted in the *American Journal of Science* (XXXIV, 267).

At New Haven the exhibition was first noticed about 6 o'clock, while a very thin cloud covered the sky from which a light snow was falling. All things appeared as if dyed in blood. The entire atmosphere, the surface of the earth, the trees, the tops of houses, and in short the whole face of nature, were tinged with the same rosy hue. The disturbance of the magnetic needle was quite remarkable, its entire range, according to Mr. Herrick, being nearly *six degrees*. At 6 h. 26 m. it stood at 3° 10′ W.; and 9 h. 10 m. at 9° 7′ W. From a tabular statement, containing 76 observations made between 5 h. 40 m. and 11 h. it appeared that the influence of the aurora was not uniform in producing a deflection of the needle in the *same direction*. At 6 h. 6 m. having returned to its normal place from east to west, it suddenly turned and moved rapidly eastward for five minutes, and thus oscillated continually.

Professor Barnard observed this aurora in the city of New York, where the cloud was thinner than at New Haven, and only a few light flakes of snow were falling, so that the exhibition was recognized as early as a quarter before 6. After several variations of intensity, the phenomenon rallied a few minutes before 9, when Professor Barnard was summoned to witness a new exhibition of auroral magnificence, "the glories of which no tongue could tell." It formed a grand corona, and had the other characteristics of an aurora of the first class. The duration of the maximum state of intensity was very remarkable. For three-quarters of an hour after its formation, which took place about 9 o'clock, the corona continued, with variable brightness, to maintain its position at the magnetic pole. Within a few minutes after 9, the southern sky was as completely filled with auroral columns as the northern. For a long time, therefore, the spectator was overspread by a perfect canopy of glory. Professor Barnard continued his observations the greater part of the night, to see whether, as had been observed before, there would be a recurrence of the display at a later hour. Such proved to be the fact, as the aurora returned, and came again to a period of maximum intensity about half past 2 o'clock. But the display in this case was much inferior to that of the preceding evening.

Numerous accounts of this grand aurora were published in the newspapers in different parts of the Union, as at Buffalo and St. Louis on the west, and at Annapolis and Richmond on the south, and it was observed as far south as Society Hill, in South Carolina, lat. 34° 35′ N. But at this place it only exhibited red streamers and low arches, without the corona, or any other of those magnificent features which rendered it so remarkable in countries further north. Its appearance at the extreme south is thus noted in a letter from W. Darby, of Culloden, Georgia, lat. 32° 45′ N., addressed to Professor Silliman: "Immediately after dark, or about 6 o'clock, the sky, a little to the north of the star Capella, began to appear luminous, and an arch was soon formed of about 6 or 8 degrees in breadth, and extending over to the northwestern horizon, having the pole star at its highest point. The color of the arch was light scarlet. It appeared to be a semicircle, having for its base about 60° of the horizon. It was observed with wonder by many in this region, *and was such as no one had ever witnessed before.*"

This aurora was seen in England, and was described in the *Cambridge Chronicle* published in November, and also in *Loudon's Magazine of Natural History,* for December, 1837; but its splendors seem to have been greatly obscured by clouds. "At half past 12 a patch of the most intense blood-red color was visible, free from the interposition of clouds; the whole of the sky had an awful appearance; for the tinge of red which pervaded the whole expanse assumed, in many points, from the depth of color above, and the density of the clouds below, the dark copper tint which is seen on the disk of the moon in a lunar eclipse."

The year 1838 was less prolific of fine auroras than the preceding year had been, and the whole number recorded in the *Regents' Report,* was 42. The most remarkable occurred February 21st, August 22d, and, in continued succession, the 13th, 14th, 15th, 16th, and 17th of September. The following year, 1839, gave 58 auroras in all, of which the most remarkable occurred January 10th and 14th, and September 3d. The aurora of September 3d, 1839, was, for its extent as well as its splendor, one of the most extraordinary on record, and requires particular consideration. A minute account of it, furnished by Mr. E. C. Herrick, is given in the thirty-eighth volume of the *American Journal of Science;* and various other descriptions may be found in the *Regents' Report,* and in the newspapers of Great Britain, as well as in those of the United States. The appearances at New Haven were as follows: It was first noticed about half an hour after sunset, and of course while the twilight was quite strong. Previous to midnight, there were three or four seasons of maximum energy, during which a large portion of the heavens was covered with a vast assemblage of streamers of various hues, in which crimson and silver-white predominated. Several times in the course of the evening, the corona was distinctly formed, and in all cases at or near the pole of the dipping needle. Before 9 h. 26 m., there was but little undulation; but about this time the waves began to show themselves, and soon flashed up towards the zenith with great magnificence. Low in the north appeared, at the same time, short dark columns rising across the intensely luminous band which lay there, and then almost instantly vanishing.

This was often repeated. The southern part of the heavens was occupied by streamers to a very unusual extent. The arch bounding the aurora on the south gradually descended, so that, at 10 o'clock, its vertex was not more than 10° above the horizon.

The observations made with the magnetic needle, though not very accurate, were sufficient to show that it was greatly affected.

As late as 1 o'clock, the spectacle, after having declined, was renewed with great splendor, and waves and streamers were numerous until daylight.

At *Nashville*, Tennessee, lat. 36°, this auroral exhibition was more striking than any one seen within the memory of the oldest inhabitants; yet the phenomena were far less imposing than at New Haven. No corona was formed. The northern bank of auroral vapor attained its greatest height at 8 h. 40 m., having then an altitude of 25°. It was soon after this period that, at the north, the aurora was putting on its finest forms.[1] Even as far south as *New Orleans*, lat. 29° 58′, the auroral display was so conspicuous that it was mistaken for a great conflagration, and the fire companies were out. On the corresponding evening, London was strikingly illuminated by the auroral lights. At 2 o'clock in the morning, the phenomenon was described as exceedingly gorgeous. It was accompanied by numerous meteors or shooting stars.

The year 1840 was productive of a great number of auroras of the third and fourth classes, but of none of the highest class. The entire number recorded in the *Regents' Report* was no less than 75. That of May 29th was the most remarkable. Those of August 10th, and September 25th, and December 25th, were of superior brilliancy.

The record for 1841 was nearly the same in respect to number, being 72; but only one was characterized as peculiarly splendid, and that occurred Nov. 18th.

The year 1842 shows a great decline in numbers, only 36 being recorded in the *Regents' Report* for that year; and of these only one, that of April 15th, was at all remarkable.

The report for 1843 gives 55, an increase of number, but a diminution of intensity, as none occurred of the first or second class. That for 1844 shows a still further decline, being 30. Again, that for 1845 gives only 25. Neither year was distinguished for any exhibition of the higher orders. The year 1846 indicates a rapid increase, the number being 47; and the following year, 1847, has 46, of which those of March 19th, April 7th, and November 25th, were characterized by some, though not by all, of the features of the highest class. In all three, the maximum of intensity was near 11 o'clock. The year 1848 was, however, distinguished by a larger number, 64, and for two auroras of superior brilliancy, which occurred April 6th and November 17th. Of the former, my note-book has the following passage: "In all the exhibitions of the aurora borealis which I have seen, I have never before been so much struck with the resemblance of the flashes, as they succeeded each other from near the horizon towards the zenith, to the

---

[1] Amer. Jour., XXXVIII, 263.

appearances exhibited by a strong electric spark in traversing a space of rarefied air, in what is called the *auroral tube*." Having very recently performed this experiment, in a dark room, with a powerful electric machine and a tube four feet in length and two inches in diameter, I was well prepared for making the comparison. Although I am not a believer in the hypothesis which ascribes the *origin* of the aurora borealis to electricity, yet the supposition that the aurora derives its *illumination* from the passage of electricity through it, was favored by this remarkable display of the phenomenon.[1] The aurora of November 17th was equally distinguished for its superior brilliancy and great extent. In respect to extent, I know not that it was ever surpassed, being seen in extraordinary magnificence and splendor in Asia, Europe, and America. We have accounts of it from Odessa, long. 31° E., to San Francisco, long. 122° W., through 153° of longitude; and from 46° to 21° of north latitude; making from north to south a breadth of 25°. Nor is there any reason to suppose that these were the actual limits of the exhibition. We should not, perhaps, exceed the truth if we should assert that this aurora was seen in a zone of 30° in breadth, reaching half round the globe. The Rev. Chester S. Lyman, who has described its appearance at San Francisco,[2] was informed by an old Californian that it was the first time he had ever witnessed anything of the kind; and the same was probably the case with most of those who saw it on the Island of Cuba.

Previous to this return of the aurora, splendid exhibitions of the phenomenon had become so unfrequent as to induce the belief that the secular period, which was supposed to have commenced in 1827, was over; and after this exhibition, so long a period of comparative repose followed, that we again supposed that no more of the highest forms of the aurora would be witnessed by the present generation; but the recurrence of three grand displays in the month of September, 1851, on the 3d, the 6th, and the 29th, has again excited doubts respecting the end of this period.[3] But, meanwhile, the most important facts we have assembled, respecting the progress, so far, of the period under review, may be reserved for future use, and it may add to their value to reduce a few of the leading facts to the tabular form.

---

[1] New Haven Palladium, for April 7, 1848.

[2] Amer. Jour., New Series, VII, 293.

[3] The almost total disappearance of auroras of the higher class for several years past, must be obvious to every observer.

Auroras according to Classes, from 1827 *to* 1848, *inclusive.*

Year.	I.	II.	III.	IV.	Total.
1827	0	4	1	5	10
1828	0	1	3	6	10
1829	0	1	8	8	17
1830	1	3	6	21	31
1831	1	1	1	20	23
1832	0	3	2	19	25
1833	1	2	8	25	36
1834	0	0	3	29	32
1835	1	2	4	19	26
1836	1	3	11	46	61
1837	3	1	9	37	50
1838	0	7	13	22	42
1839	1	2	9	46	58
1840	0	3	12	60	75
1841	0	3	11	58	72
1842	0	1	4	31	36
1843	0	0	8	47	55
1844	0	2	4	24	30
1845	0	1	5	19	25
1846	0	0	8	39	47
1847	2	2	10	32	46
1848	1	3	21	39	64
	12	45	161	652	871
1826	0	0	2	0	2
1849	0	0	0	14	14

Remarks.

1. Before 1832, the numbers relate to auroras seen in Great Britain, as given in Dalton's Meteorological Essays, p. 218 (2d edition). After 1831, the numbers relate to those seen in the State of New York, as given in the Regents' Reports.

2. The greatest number in any one year occurred in 1840, and was 75; in 1841, 72; in 1848, 64; in 1839, 57; in 1837, 50.

3. The *average* number for the whole period, per annum, is $39\frac{1}{3}$.

4. The numbers of the respective *classes* are 12, 45, 161, 652; and the sum total for 22 years, is 871. The series is nearly geometrical, increasing in a fourfold ratio.

5. The number for 1826, the year preceding the period, is only 2, according to Dalton, and those of the 3d class, and that for 1849, the year following this period, is only 14, all of the 4th class. The sudden falling off, both in numbers and intensity, after the year 1848, induced the belief that that year terminated the secular period; but the recurrence of three grand auroras as late as September, 1851, of another in February, 1852, and of another still, in September, 1853, renders the length of the period somewhat doubtful.

6. Of auroras of the 1st class, the year 1830 has 1; 1831, 1; 1833, 1; 1835, 1; 1836, 1; 1837, 3; 1839, 1; 1847, 2; and 1848, 1. Of examples of the 2d class, the year 1838 was the most productive, having afforded no less than 7.

7. In 1849, only 14 were observed at New Haven. Nearly 40 were mentioned in the Regents' Report, but most of them were a mere trace.

Auroras of the separate Months, from 1832 *to* 1848, *inclusive.*

[From the Regents' Report.]

Months.	1832.	1833.	1834.	1835.	1836.	1837.	1838.	1839.	1840.	1841.	1842.	1843.	1844.	1845.	1846.	1847.	1848.	Total.
January . . .	1	0	2	5	0	5	5	9	6	2	3	4	1	3	3	2	8	58
February . . .	0	0	2	3	2	2	4	3	5	12	3	8	1	3	0	1	8	57
March . . .	2	1	5	2	1	6	0	6	8	9	2	4	5	0	1	7	6	65
April	5	3	2	0	9	6	4	8	10	6	6	8	3	3	5	6	9	93
May	3	5	1	0	4	3	1	8	10	5	0	3	5	1	9	3	2	63
June	3	2	0	2	10	3	3	2	3	2	3	7	1	0	2	1	2	46
July	0	3	2	2	10	4	4	2	3	8	6	7	1	3	3	3	5	66
August . . .	5	3	2	1	11	5	3	6	9	12	1	3	1	5	6	4	5	82
September . . .	3	10	1	6	3	8	10	5	6	5	3	6	4	2	8	3	1	84
October . . .	2	6	7	1	4	2	1	5	6	5	2	5	3	2	5	3	7	66
November . . .	1	1	2	3	6	5	4	3	5	5	5	0	4	1	2	9	6	62
December . . .	0	2	6	1	1	1	3	1	4	1	2	0	1	2	3	4	5	37
	25	36	32	26	61	50	42	58	75	72	36	55	30	25	47	46	64	780

Remarks.

1. The average, per annum, for the entire period, is nearly 46.

2. The greatest number for any single year, was in 1840—being 75.

3. Average for the *spring* months, $73\frac{1}{3}$; *autumnal* months, $70\frac{2}{3}$; *summer* months, $64\frac{2}{3}$; *winter* months, $50\frac{2}{3}$. The six months on the side of the *perihelion* (October, November, December, January, February, March), $57\frac{1}{2}$; on the side of the *aphelion*,

72⅓. Whence it appears that, during this period, the number of auroras was greater when the earth was in the part of its orbit most distant from the sun than in the nearer part, in the ratio of 72⅓ : 57½, or nearly of 24 to 19. This result is very different from that obtained by Mairan, who found the number for the six winter months greatly to exceed that for the six summer months; but the cases collected by Mairan were those only of the higher classes, or of the greatest intensity. We shall see that there is no fixed relation between intensity and number.

4. The *monthly* average is nearly 4; but that for April is about 5½, and that for September is about 5; while that for December is but little more than 2, and for June is only 2⅔.

Auroras of the two highest Classes.

Months.	1832.	1833.	1834.	1835.	1836.	1837.	1838.	1839.	1840.	1841.	1842.	1843.	1844.	1845.	1846.	1847.	1848.	Total.
January	..	..	..	..	..	1	..	1	..	..	..	..	..	..	..	..	..	2
February	..	..	..	..	..	..	..	..	..	..	..	..	1	..	..	..	1	2
March	..	..	..	..	..	..	1	..	..	..	..	..	..	..	..	1	1	3
April	..	..	..	..	2	..	..	..	..	..	1	..	..	..	..	2	1	6
May	..	1	1	..	1	..	..	..	1	..	..	..	..	..	..	..	..	4
June	..	..	..	..	..	..	..	..	..	..	..	..	..	..	..	..	..	0
July	..	1	1	..	..	1	..	..	..	..	..	..	..	..	..	..	..	3
August	3	..	..	..	1	..	1	..	2	1	..	..	..	..	..	..	..	8
September	..	1	1	1	..	..	5	2	..	1	..	..	..	..	..	..	..	11
October	..	..	..	..	..	..	..	..	..	..	..	..	..	..	..	..	..	0
November	..	1	1	..	..	2	..	..	..	1	..	..	1	..	..	1	1	8
December	..	..	..	..	..	..	..	..	..	..	..	..	..	1	..	..	..	1
	3	4	4	1	4	4	7	3	3	3	1	0	2	1	0	4	4	48

REMARKS.

1. The average per annum for the whole period, is nearly 3.

2. Maximum year, 1838; maximum month, September. The year 1837 was distinguished for three examples of the first class; 1838 was distinguished for a greater *number*, but they were chiefly of the second class. September, 1838, produced no less than 5 of this class.

3. There is no apparent connection between *number* and *intensity*. The year 1835 was the least productive year of the series; but the exhibition of November 17th, of that year, was one of the highest class. In 1836 there were 61 auroras, and in 1837 only 49; yet in the latter year there were three of peculiar grandeur; while in the former there was only one of the highest order.

4. The auroras of the *first class*, during the period under review, occurred at the following dates:—

1833. May 17th.
1835. November 17th.
1836. April 22d.
1837. January 25th, July 1st, November 14th.
1839. September 3d.
1847. March 19th, April 7th.
1848. November 17th.

With the foregoing data before us, compared with such as have been recorded in different countries and in different ages, we now proceed to classify the leading facts appertaining to this mysterious phenomenon, with the view of ascertaining its laws.

LAWS OF THE AURORA BOREALIS.

I. Beginning.—*An aurora of the first class usually commences near the end of evening twilight, in the form of a northern light resembling the dawn.* The greatest exhibitions are always found in their *incipient* and never in their *maturer* states, at this time of the evening. No instance is on record of an aurora suddenly bursting upon the view, as the light of day disappeared, with its corona or its crimson columns, or its magnificent arches, or its waves fully formed, and in complete operation.[1]

Moreover, the beginning at *different places* is nearly at the same instant of *local* time at points widely different in longitude. Thus the exhibition of November 17th, 1835, was first seen at Boston and Cincinnati at 6 o'clock, and in the incipient stage, although these places differ nearly an hour in longitude; and that of November 17th, 1848, distinguished above all others for its extent from east to west, began, arrived at its maximum, and, in short, performed all its evolutions at nearly the same hour of the night, in Western Asia, in Europe, and in the United States, even to the shores of California.

II. Maximum.—*An aurora of the first class commonly arrives at its maximum at all places from* 10 *to* 11 *o'clock, and more frequently a little before* 11.[2] At this period, the columns suddenly increase in size and splendor, the bloody hue becomes most conspicuous, and there is a general rush from the northeast and northwest towards the common point of concourse, forming the corona.

In some cases, the meteor rallies and forms a second maximum, though of inferior intensity to the first, at a later hour of the night, often about 2 o'clock, a fact first remarked by Mr. Herrick, in the auroral display of July 1, 1837;[3] and the same

---

[1] That auroras usually begin at a certain hour of the evening, and that great auroras begin earlier than others, was noticed by Mairan in the following terms: Le commencement du phénomène arrive commencement deux, trois, ou quatre heures tout au plus après le coucher du soleil, c'est-a-dire qu'il arrive presque toûjours le soir, et jamais, que je sache, le matin après minuit, lorsque les nuits sont un peu longues. Les grandes aurores boreales commencent ordinairement de bonne heure, peu de temps après la fin du crepuscule, et quelques fois auparavant.—*Traité Phys. et Hist. du l'Au. Bor.*, p. 115.

[2] Capt. Lefroy (Preliminary Report on the Observations on the Aurora Borealis, made in Canada, in Regents' Rep. for 1850) recognizes this law, and remarks that he had observed it as early as 1843–4. In my account of the great aurora of Nov. 18, 1841, published the next day after its occurrence in the New Haven Daily Herald, I remarked as follows: In all these respects, as well as by the grand display of auroral waves, this exhibition of the aurora resembled that of November, 1835. Indeed, both came to their maximum and formed their corona around the pole of the dipping needle at almost precisely the same time of the night, namely, about 11 o'clock. Nor does this appear to have been a casual coincidence. It was the case, also, with a great exhibition of the aurora seen in France about a century ago, (particularly described by *Mairan*), and with so many others as to constitute a striking and important feature in relation to the true theory of the phenomenon.

[3] Amer. Journal of Sci., XXXIII, 143.

fact has since been observed repeatedly, varying as to the time of night from 1 to 3 o'clock.

III. End.—*Ordinary auroras commonly end before midnight, but those of the first class frequently continue all night.* In the aurora of July 1, 1837, streamers were observed an hour after daybreak. Auroral waves are sometimes the most conspicuous feature of grand exhibitions after midnight; as was particularly the case in the great displays of November 17th, 1835,[1] April 22d, 1836, and November 18th, 1841, in which these impressive phenomena made their appearance after the corona had vanished, but lasted the greater part of the night.

The foregoing propositions relating to the time of the beginning, maximum, and end of auroras of the first class, have been derived from the comparison of a large number of instances, but are especially exemplified in the six greatest of the series, namely, those of November 17th, 1835; April 22d, 1836; January 25th and November 14th, 1837; September 3d, 1839; and November 18th, 1841. Those exhibitions which extend to an unusually low latitude, sometimes arrive at their maximum at an earlier hour than common. Thus, the aurora of September 3d, 1839, is stated in some reports, to have attained its greatest magnificence between 9 and 10 o'clock, and that of September 29th, 1851, formed its first corona as early as 7 o'clock; but, with these exceptions, there is much uniformity in regard to the times of beginning, middle, and end, in most cases the exhibition commencing near the end of twilight, coming to its maximum splendor about 11 o'clock, and continuing, with an increased display of auroral waves, the greater part of the night. Also, if we examine the accounts of great auroras of other times, and of foreign countries, there appears to be much uniformity in these results. Thus Mairan,[2] in his account of the aurora of 1726, that first drew his attention to the subject which he afterwards investigated with consummate ability, states that its maximum occurred a little before 11 o'clock. Indeed, in the polar regions, when the aurora is observed during the period of the year when the sun is constantly below the horizon, the exhibition is not indifferently at all hours of the 24, but, according to the French Commission at Bossekop, consisting of Lottin and others, the usual display is from 10 P. M. to 4 A. M.; and during the short days, the auroras begin there as elsewhere at a certain definite interval after sunset, the hour varying with the time of year.[3] Something of the nature of auroral clouds is occasionally seen in the daytime, but that great exhibitions do not occur by day, may be inferred from the fact that the extraordinary variations of the magnetic needle which attend such displays, are seldom if ever seen in the daytime.

IV. Extent.—*Auroral exhibitions of the higher order are commonly of great extent.* The arch of August 28th, 1827, was seen all over the Northern States of the Union, and also in Scotland. The display of November 17th, 1848, was witnessed with very similar appearances, in Asia, Europe, and America, accounts of it having reached us from Odessa on the east to San Francisco on the west, through 150° of

---

[1] Amer. Journal of Sci., XXIX, 388.

[2] Traité Phys. et Hist. de l'Aurore Boréale.

[3] Voyages en Scandinavie, etc. Par MM. Lottin, &c.

longitude.[1] That of September 3d, 1839, which was very splendid in the Northern States, was also so conspicuous at New Orleans as to be mistaken for a fire, and to call out fire companies with their engines. At places nearly in the same latitude, however widely they may differ in longitude, the exhibition is everywhere nearly the same; or at least has the same leading characteristics, and a similar degree of magnificence. But in different latitudes, especially in places differing widely in latitude, the effect of parallax is plainly discernible. Thus the great aurora of September 3d, 1839, which was described as very brilliant in England, in Connecticut, and in Missouri, exhibited in Tennessee only an auroral bank in the north, and a few brilliant streamers, although it was pronounced to be the most splendid aurora ever seen there by the oldest inhabitants.[2] So that of July 1, 1837, which was magnificent at New Haven, only exhibited streamers for half an hour at Columbus in Georgia.[3] The extraordinary exhibition of September 29th, 1851, which in the Northern States was attended by a gorgeous retinue of columns, arches, and coronas, formed at the city of Washington, but half the corona, and at places farther south scarcely any traces of it.[4] While, about 7 o'clock, the corona was completely formed at New Haven, there were seen at Charleston, S. C., only different cloudy masses of purple light, occupying the region of the sky above the northern quarter of the horizon, extending about 40° to the east, and as much to the west of the north point, and rising nearly to the height of the pole star.[5] At 11 o'clock only a faint gleam of auroral light was visible, and soon after a dark band whose culminating point was only two thirds the altitude of the pole star; yet was it at this time that Hon. A. N. Skinner, of New Haven, then at Staten Island, saw a splendid arch with a dense bank of auroral vapor which sent forth streamers, within 20° of the southern horizon.[6]

V. Auroral Vapor.—*A great aurora is preceded by a large bank, or cloud, of a peculiar vapor, resting on the northern horizon, commonly of a milky appearance, but sometimes of a smoky hue, or of the two mixed together.* This vapor apparently contains the material from which the aurora is fed, and when it is either wanting, or is small in quantity, the exhibition seldom reaches a high order or lasts long. That the auroral vapor has a density extremely low—less than the lightest fog, is evident from the stars being seen through it with little loss of light. It is, however, sometimes so much accumulated and so luminous as sensibly to impair the brightness of the stars, or even to extinguish those of the lower magnitudes.

VI. Auroral Waves.—*These waves, when peculiarly grand, make their appearance later than the streamers and arches, and usually later than the corona; and they continue to a later hour of the night, often presenting a sublime feature after the other leading characteristics of the aurora are over.* They appear at a lower level than

---

[1] It is worthy of remark, that great auroras extend much further from east to west than from north to south. As they are very seldom seen below lat. 30°, we may take 60° from the pole as the maximum in latitude, while in longitude they extend, as in the case of that of November, 1848, at least 150°. Since, however, there is reason for believing that the exhibition which descends as low as 30° does not reach to the pole on the north, probably the extent from north to south is much less than 60°.

[2] Amer. Journ., XXXVIII, 261.

[3] Ib., XXXIII, 144.

[4] National Intelligencer, Oct. 4th.

[5] Professor Gibbes, in Charleston Daily News.

[6] New Haven Journal and Courier, Oct. 6th.

the columns, and flow upwards in the direction of the columns towards the centre of the corona. The velocity of their motions is amazing, the entire progress being such as would carry them from the horizon to the zenith in a second of time, passing over half that distance (their usual track) in half a second. The appearance is that of undulatory rather than of progressive motion, resembling the waves that sweep over tall, fine grass, when gently agitated by the wind. The finest specimens of auroral waves were exhibited in the displays of November 17th, 1835, April 22d, 1836, November 18th, 1841, and in all three of the great auroras of September, 1851.[1]

VII. Magnetic Phenomena.—*The aurora borealis is accompanied by remarkable magnetic phenomena.*[2] During the great exhibition of November 14th, 1837, according to Mr. Herrick, the needle often moved thirty minutes in three seconds, and its greatest deflection was nearly 6°. The disturbances of the dipping needle are also frequently enormous during great auroras. The position of the streamers in directions parallel to the magnetic meridian, and the situation of the centre of the corona at the pole of the dipping needle, are also facts constantly observed. There does not, however, appear to be any established relation between the state of intensity and the effect on the needle; and there are singular local peculiarities in respect to the accompanying magnetic phenomena. Professor Henry detected an increase of horizontal intensity in the needle *before* an aurora, and a diminution of intensity at the *maximum;* and the same fact is noticed by Hansteen (*Kæmtz' Meteorol.*, p. 461).

During the magnificent aurora of January 25th, 1837, while the maximum declination at New Haven, according to Mr. Herrick, was *one degree,* at New Britain, twenty-five miles north of New Haven, the change of declination was nothing, according to Mr. Burritt, who watched the needle attentively for two hours during the most active part of the exhibition. Captain Parry also says that, in no instance was the magnetic influence affected by the aurora borealis during the three winters he passed within the polar circle. Captain Franklin states that, when the aurora was streaming with prismatic colors, it had an obvious effect upon the needle; but when it gave a steady, dense light, without motion, it produced no effect on the needle.[3]

VIII. Geographical Relations.—*The aurora borealis occurs most frequently in the polar regions. It is only in the great periods that it descends much below the latitude of* 40°*; but it descends lower on the western than on the eastern continent, and prevails more in the northern than in the southern hemispheres.* Franklin observed, in the polar seas, 142 auroras in six months; and the French Commission, at

---

[1] Also in the recent exhibition of February 19, 1852.

[2] Dalton supposes that he was the first to discover the relation between the aurora borealis and the earth's magnetism, in his observations on the exhibition of October 13, 1792 (*Essays,* second edition, p. 147). But he seems to have been unacquainted with the fact that their connection had been detected long before, being mentioned by Mairan, in the second edition of his *Traité de l'Aurore Boréale,* published in 1754, p. 450.

[3] Amer. Jour. Sci., XVI, p. 148.

Bossekop (lat. 69° 58′), recorded 143 auroras in two hundred and six days. The greatest number recorded in any one year, in the temperate zone, is believed to be 75, which is given in the Regents' Report as the number for 1840. The auroral arch of August 28th, 1827, which marked the commencement of the period under review, was the first auroral exhibition seen in the southern part of Ohio, after the settlement of the State; and that of September 3d, 1839, was the first ever seen in Tennessee by the generation then on the stage.[1] On comparing the same latitudes on the eastern and on the western continents, it is found that a far greater number occur on the western continent. Indeed, at the latitudes of Spain and Italy, these exhibitions are seldom seen at all, while in the same latitudes in New England, many usually occur every year; and, in the State of New York, from 1832 to 1848, inclusive, the number recorded in the Regents' Reports, is 780—being an average of more than 43 per annum. We have, in fact, many more auroras in New England and New York, than occur in England ten degrees north of us. The greatest number ever recorded by Dalton, in England, in a single year, appeared in 1830, being 30, which was nearly twice the average of auroras from 1827 to 1834, a period which Dalton considers as very extraordinary for these exhibitions, although during this period, the average number, per annum, was 16; while from 1819 to 1826, the average number was only 1⅞. According to a record of auroras kept at Deerfield, Massachusetts, by General Field, the average for 1830 and 1831, was 56.[2]

Although the aurora occurs in the *southern* hemisphere, yet such evidence as we have, indicates that it is less frequent and less magnificent, than in the northern hemisphere. I have conversed with whalers and others, who have been repeatedly around Cape Horn without ever seeing an aurora australis; and, although we find in Commodore Wilkes's Narrative of the United States Exploring Expedition, instances described and delineated sufficient to establish the fact of the existence of these lights around the southern pole, yet the number appears to be far less than in corresponding latitudes of the northern hemisphere. In the year 1750, Mairan addressed a note of inquiry respecting the aurora australis to Don Ulloa, the celebrated navigator who carried out the French Academicians to Peru. The reply of Don Ulloa, who was much conversant with the southern hemisphere, is so curious and instructive, that it appears to me worthy of more general notice than it is likely to receive in the old and rare volume where it was first published, and I therefore subjoin the original form, as given by Mairan.[3]

M. C'est avec bien du plaisir que j'ai reçû la lettre que vous m' avez fait l'honneur de m'écrire, du 24 de ce mois, sur les Aurores de l'hémisphère austral, dont M. Jallabert vous a parlé, d'après l'entretien que j'avois eu avec lui sur ce sujet. Je lui ai dit que j'en avois vû quelques-unes, lorsque le temps étoit favorable, mais non que j'en eusse fait des observations dans tous les formes, comment il auroit été à desirer, parceque le brouillard plus ou moins épais dont notre navire étoit presque toûjours enveloppé ne le permettoit pas. C'est la raison pourquoi je n'en ai point parlé dans la relation de mon voyage. Et il est bon que je vous dise à ce sujet, que tout ce que j'ai pu distinguer, lorsque les brouillards se

[1] In this *classification* of the general facts, we may be permitted to repeat occasionally individual facts which have been mentioned before.

[2] Amer. Jour. Sci., XX, p. 272.

[3] Mairan, Traité de l'Aur. Bor., p. 439.

dissipoient du côté du sud, c'étoit une grande clarté dans le ciel, qui montoit quelquefois jusqu'à 30 degrés au dessus de l'horizon, à peu près comme quand la lune est prête à se lever, quelquefois plus rougeâtre, et quelquefois plus brillante ou plus blanche. Ces entrevûes ne duroient guère au delà de trois ou quatre minutes, parce qu'un nouvel amas de brouillard en reprenoit la place, et si celui-ci venoit à être dissipé par le vent, il en succédoit bien-tôt un autre qui nous empêchoit de voir l'horizon, et même les autres vaisseaux de la compagnie. Et pour vous faire mieux comprendre l'effet de ces brouillards dans la saison où je passai le Cap de Horn, j'aurai l'honneur de vous dire, que quelquefois nous ne nous voyions point réciproquement entre les trois navires, et que d'autres momens, lorsque nous nous croyions le plus éloignés les unes des autres, nous en découvrions les girouettes qui paroissoient assez proches, sans voir le corps du vaisseau, et que quelquefois nous voyions le corps du vaisseau, et une partie de la mâture, sans rien apercevoir de tout le reste. Un moment après nous ne nous voyions plus, et vous devez imaginer que c'est comme par une fenêtre qu'on ỳ découvre les objets, et qu'on les y perd avec la même promptitude qu'on les avoit vûs, et lorsqu'on s'y attend le moins. C'est ce qui arrivoit aussi à l'égard de tout l'horizon, par ce brouillard qui nous accompagna depuis les 40 degrés de latitude sud, en allant vers le Cap de Horn, jusqu'à pareille hauteur après l'avoir doublé. Je passai le Cap dans le mois de Mars et partie d'Avril de l'année 1745. Mais suivant ce que j'appris de ceux qui avoient fait plus tôt la même traversée, c'est-à-dire, aux mois de Janvier et de Février, les brouillards n'y sont pas alors si communs, ou même y sont-ils assez rares. Mais en pareille saison on ne peut guère s'apercevoir de ces aurores, parce que le crépuscule n'a pas le temps de finir, celui du matin se confondant avec celui du soir. Je pense qu'elles doivent être fréquentes dans l'hiver de cet hémisphère, puisque toutes les fois que les nuages le permettoient, et que le ciel venoit à se découvrir du côté du pole, j'en apercevois quelque chose. Pour ne pas m'y tromper, je comparois cette partie où je voyois la clarté, aux autres parties du ciel, en attendant qu'il s'y fit quelque ouverture de côte ou d'autre. Il me falloit quelquefois attendre plus de deux heures, et pour lors je ne me fiois pas à ma comparaison. Quant à l'heure où paroissoit cette aurore, j'aurai l'honneur de vous dire, que je restois d'ordinaire sur la gaillard jusqu'à minuit, et que j'en ai quelquefois vû la clarté jusqu'à pareille heure, mais le plus souvent c'étoit jusqu'à dix heures, et ce ne'est que deux ou trois fois que je l'ai aperçue plus tard. Je faissoit aussi attention à l'état de la lune, et à voir si ce que j'apercevois n'étoit pas plustôt un effet de la réflexion de sa lumière sur le brouillard délié des particules de glace répandues dans l'atmosphère, qu'une véritable aurore, et ce n'est que lorsque la lune étois sous l'horizon, que je la regardois comme telle. Je la fis observer aussi aux officiers du vaisseau, qui jusqu' alors n'avoient pas fait attention à un pareil phénomène. Je serois charmé de pouvoir vous donner de plus amples instructions sur ce sujet, et vous pouvez être persuadé, &c.

From the statements of Don Ulloa we see reasons why the aurora should seldom be seen in the southern hemisphere by navigators, even if they were of frequent occurrence; for the antarctic seas are very seldom visited except at those seasons of the year when the shortness of the nights, and the presence of a strong twilight, would prevent their being seen; and at other seasons, removed more or less from their mid-summer, the prevalence of constant and dense fogs would be very unfavorable for observation. It is not, therefore, conclusive evidence against the occurrence of such exhibitions in the southern high latitudes, that whalers and other navigators, who double Cape Horn, so seldom see any signs of the aurora. But the long continuance in those seas of the several exploring expeditions which have recently visited them, affords better means of determining the character of the aurora australis. In the antarctic cruise of Captains Wilkes and Hudson, during the summer months of 1839 and 1840, namely, the months of December, January, and February, mention is made of auroras, and the accompanying descriptions leave no doubt that the phenomena are similar to those of the aurora borealis. Some of the exhibitions were striking and interesting, showing a very active state of the cause, whatever it may be, although no instance is given where the combination of great features was fully equal to that in an aurora borealis of the first class, or in many of the exhibitions described by the French Commission as seen at Bossekop. If the number reported by the antarctic cruise is small in comparison with those seen at Bossekop, during an equal period, it must be considered that in the southern polar regions it was mid-summer with hardly anything of night, while in the northern polar regions it was mid-winter with hardly anything of day.

IX. SOUND.—*There is no decisive evidence that the aurora borealis is accompanied by any peculiar sound.* Aware that sounds have been attributed to the aurora in different countries and at different times, I have for many years listened attentively, during the greater exhibitions especially, but have never been able to detect any. In one or two instances, a sound was heard which, at the time, I was inclined to ascribe to the aurora, but afterwards ascertained that it proceeded from other sources. Let one unaccustomed to nocturnal observations, be abroad in a still night, and attentively listen, and he will hear a sound which had never before arrested his attention, and which he will be likely to ascribe to any extraordinary phenomenon then prevailing. He will usually liken it to the rustling of the wind through dry leaves, or to a distant waterfall; but either of these sounds may be heard on almost any still night when the ear is on the alert, being nothing else than the resultant of all the minute sounds which nature is ever uttering. A company of my pupils were strongly impressed with the belief that they heard peculiar sounds connected with an aurora borealis; but on taking them abroad on the next clear evening, and bidding them listen, they were forced to acknowledge that they heard the same sound as before. Men of science who have visited countries most frequented by these lights, as Biot, in the Western Isles, Lottin and his associates in Lapland, and navigators of the polar seas, have been nearly unanimous in the statement that they never heard any sound which could be certainly predicated of an aurora. Judge M'Cord, of Montreal, an attentive and accurate observer, informed me that he had, on one occasion, and only one, heard a sound—a "rustling noise," which he attributed to an aurora then prevailing. The possibility, however, that it might have proceeded from some other source is obvious; and perhaps such a conclusion is more probable than that this, among hundreds which he had observed, should alone afford such a token of its presence. The popular belief in peculiar noises attending these exhibitions, is said to have been extensive, particularly among the Western Islands of Scotland; but scientific observers, even those who, like Farquharson, maintain that these displays are often below the clouds, make no mention of any accompanying noise, and I incline to the opinion that the aurora is not attended by any peculiar sound.

X. HEIGHT.—*The exhibitions of the aurora borealis take place usually at a great but variable height above the earth.* On this point different observers have held widely different opinions; some, as Farquharson, Parry, and Richardson, having assigned these phenomena to the region of the clouds; and others, as Dalton, and the greater number of philosophers, to regions of the atmosphere not less than one hundred miles above the earth. On a point of such importance, it may be useful to compare a few of the leading authorities.

Mairan, about the year 1731, by comparing good observations made at Paris and

Rome, on the aurora of 1726, estimated the height at 266¾ French leagues, or about 735 miles;[1] and he concludes that the greater part give an elevation of 200 leagues, but that they range from 100 to 300 leagues.

In 1790, Cavendish published, in the *Philosophical Transactions*, an estimate of the height of an arch observed at different places on the 23d of February, 1784, making it between 52 and 71 miles. Soon afterwards, Dalton wrote his celebrated Essay on the Aurora Borealis, in which he calculated the height of an arch seen in England, February 15, 1793, at 150 miles. But, in the *Philosophical Transactions* for 1828, appears an article by the same author, in which he determined the height of an arch, from what he deemed satisfactory data and more accurate than any before used, to be nearly 100 miles.

But the investigations of Professor Alexander C. Twining, on this subject, contained in the 32d volume of the *American Journal of Science*, appear to me more satisfactory and conclusive than any within my knowledge, and therefore, deserving of particular consideration. He appears to have been equally fortunate in the selection of his instances, and in the definiteness and variety of the observations on which he founded his estimates. Not all the phenomena of an aurora are alike favorable for this purpose. The corona, for example, being merely the effect of perspective, it would be as useless to attempt to determine its height, as that of the rainbow. The streamers, likewise, are objects too indefinite and evanescent for such estimates. We must be sure that different observers are looking at the same object, before we can attempt to determine its parallax. The boundary line of an *arch* is such an object, and moving, as it frequently does, slowly from north to south, the instant of time when it reaches a known star, furnishes to different observers situated nearly in the same meridian an opportunity for marking its position at a given moment, and thus supplies the requisite data for determining its parallax. Another class of objects the most favorable for this purpose, are detached fragments or *patches* of an auroral cloud,[2] which, presenting to observers in different places a single insulated object, leaves no doubt that they are all looking at the same thing; and its position with respect to particular stars at a given instant, affords opportunity for observations of the requisite degree of precision. It was from both these classes of objects seen in the year 1835 and 1836, that Professor Twining deduced

---

[1] Traité de Aur. Bor., p. 62.

[2] My observations on the aurora borealis, continued for many years, leave no doubt on my mind of the existence of clouds composed of a peculiar kind of matter, and properly denominated "auroral clouds," not being formed of aqueous vapor, although, from their resemblance to certain forms of the cirrus cloud, they are sometimes confounded with that, and are adduced by certain writers, not personally conversant with these exhibitions, as proof that the aurora occurs in the region of the clouds. Thus, Professor Secchi, in a late able and comprehensive review of the discoveries in Terrestrial Magnetism (*Phil. Mag.*, June, 1855, p. 445), remarks that, "at Rome, the perturbations of the needle exhibit themselves in that particular state of the atmosphere in which there are slightly phosphorescent clouds, having at night the appearance of the rudiments of the aurora borealis." That these were not ordinary cirrus clouds, composed of aqueous vapor, is evident from the description which he proceeds to give of them, being *from a very unusual quarter*, being *luminous*, and being *magnetic*, while the only proof that they were cirrus clouds was, that they *looked* like them.

the height of the aurora in three different instances, namely, the auroral cloud of December, 1835; the auroral arch of August, 1836, and of May of the same year.[1] In each case there were at least three scientific observers, all much conversant with observations of this kind. The *identity* of the object seen by all was proved by a number of coincidences, such as the *time* of formation and of disappearance—the correspondence of position in *azimuth*—in the peculiar appearances and successive changes of aspect, described by one observer as *parallel fleeces*, and by another as *ridges* into which the arch broke up. These coincidences apply more particularly to the arch of August, 1836, observed by Professor Twining and myself at a distance from each other of twenty-two miles. On comparing notes, no doubt has remained on the mind of either of us that we were both gazing at one and the same object, and our minutes were sufficiently copious and definite to determine the parallax. The calculation was made by Professor Twining, with all possible accuracy, and gave an altitude of 144½ miles. The same authority, in his observations upon the auroral cloud of December, 1835, remarks that it was not his object to determine the exact height, but to find the limit below which it could not have been, and this limit he fixes at 42½ miles; but he still believes this to have been, in fact, an elevation far less than the true one. In regard to the arch of May, 1836, he concludes that the largest parallax which could be assigned, consistently with the observations, made the height *more than* 100 miles; and he supposes that it might have reached the elevation which I had deduced from my observations compared with those of Dr. Ellsworth, of Hartford, namely, 160 miles, although he believes that this was the utmost limit.

On the whole, I think we are authorized to infer from all the foregoing authorities, that the auroral arches seldom, if ever, fall below an elevation of 70 miles above the earth, and that they do not often exceed a height of 160 miles. The probability is that they vary between these extremes. In fixing these limits, however, it may be thought proper to take notice of certain observations on record, which indicate a much lower elevation, descending even to the region of the clouds, or below it. I allude particularly to the views of Rev. Mr. Farquharson, of Scotland, and of Captain Parry, and one or two other navigators of the Polar Seas.

To nearly all who have attentively observed this phenomenon, a difference of stations of a few miles or even of a few degrees, has made but slight changes in the position of an auroral arch; to an inhabitant of Montreal and to one of Washington City, the same exhibition has been still north; but, according to Mr. Farquharson, an aurora changed its place to the view of an observer, from north to south, merely by crossing a hill in the opposite direction. Moreover, according to the same authority, accurate trigonometrical measurements at the extremities of a base line only 6,810 feet long, afforded so great a parallax as to give a perpendicular height above the lower place of observation of only 5,693 feet, or a little more than a mile; and of only 1,500 feet above the summit of the neighboring hills. These results, and other similar ones reported by the same authority, are so

[1] Amer. Jour. of Science, XXXII, p. 217.

different from those obtained by nearly all others who have observed this phenomenon at different ages and in different countries, that, if we admit these observations to be accurate, we are compelled to believe that there exists at that place some local peculiarity which brings down the aurora to a lower level than it is ever known to reach in any other part of the world. Dalton has assigned several reasons for believing that the observations of the reverend gentleman were at fault.[1]

The statement of Captain Parry that when at Port Bowen (lat. 73° 13′ N.), he saw a ray from an auroral cloud dart down between him and the neighboring land, has been considered by many as decisive of the low level of the aurora. His words are as follows: "About midnight on the 27th of January, this phenomenon broke out in a single compact mass of brilliant yellow light, situated about a southeast bearing, and appearing only a short distance above the land. This mass of light, notwithstanding its general continuity, sometimes appeared to be evidently composed of numerous pencils of rays, compressed, as it were, laterally into one, its limits both to the right and left being well defined and nearly vertical. The light, though very brilliant at all times, varied almost constantly in intensity; and this had the appearance (not uncommon in the aurora) of being produced by one volume of light overlaying another, just as we see the darkness and density of smoke increased by cloud rolling over cloud. While Lieuts. Sherrer and Ross and myself were admiring the extreme beauty of this phenomenon from the observatory, we all simultaneously uttered an exclamation of surprise at seeing a bright ray of the aurora shoot suddenly downward from the general mass of light and *between us and the land*, which was then distant only three thousand yards. Had I witnessed this phenomenon by myself, I should have been disposed to receive with caution the evidence even of my own senses, as to this last fact; but the appearance conveying precisely the same idea to three individuals at once, all intently engaged in looking towards the spot, I have no doubt that the ray of light actually passed within that distance of us."[2]

On this statement I remark, first, that the surprise with which the phenomenon was regarded, indicates that it was never seen by the same observers before, and must therefore be an exceedingly uncommon occurrence, while spectators who live on high mountains describe all the appearances of the aurora borealis as similar to those seen at the level of the sea. Secondly, as the auroral cloud appeared only "a short distance above the land," and it appears from other accounts that the land was only about 700 feet high and was distant from the spectators nearly a mile and three-quarters, the land was seen under an angle of only 4°,[3] and must have afforded but a small base on which to project the auroral ray. The fact that it did actually descend below the top of the hill would hardly be conclusive, unless it had come quite down to the surface of the earth and remained in position long enough for the eye to take a deliberate survey of it. Thirdly, the known difficulty of locating a transient light seen in a dark night, the appearance of the spark of a chimney being, as Dalton observes, scarcely distinguishable from a fixed star,

---

[1] Dalton's Ess., p. 231. [2] Parry's Third Voyage, p. 61. [3] Dalton's Essays, p. 239.

throws much doubt and uncertainty upon the accuracy of the observation. Finally, if the case be as supposed by Captain Parry, it will only be an exception, and a very rare one to a general rule, and will by no means prove that ordinary auroras are at a lower level than that assigned them by Dalton, Twining, and others, who have estimated their heights from undoubted parallaxes, on the sure principles of trigonometry.[1]

XI. PERIODICITY.—*Auroras of the higher classes have three distinct forms of periodicity*—a *diurnal* periodicity, commencing, arriving at their maximum, and ending at definite hours of the night; an *annual* periodicity, rarely or never occurring in June, and the greatest number of the higher order clustering together in September and November, these last bearing a striking resemblance to each other; and a *secular* periodicity, the most remarkable of all, recurring in great series.

1. *Diurnal periodicity.*—We have already seen that auroras of the higher orders usually begin near the end of evening twilight, come to their maximum from 10 to 11 o'clock, and more frequently a little before 11, and last nearly or quite through the night, although those of an inferior kind usually terminate before midnight.

2. *Annual periodicity.*—For the period of twenty years, beginning with 1832 and ending with 1851, of 51 auroras of the first and second classes, 14 were in September, 8 in November, 8 in August, and 6 in March; while there were none in June and October, but 1 in December, and but 2 in January and February, respectively. The sum total for August, September, and November, was 30, averaging 10 to each month, while for December, and January, and February, the number was only 5, averaging but $1\frac{2}{3}$ to each. If, however, we regard number merely without reference to intensity, then for the period of seventeen years, from 1832 to 1848 inclusive, out of 780 auroras the sum for each month was as follows:

1.	April	93	7.	May	63
2.	September	84	8.	November	62
3.	August	82	9.	January	58
4.	October	66	10.	February	57
5.	July	66	11.	June	46
6.	March	65	12.	December	38

In respect both to number and intensity, June and December stand at the bottom of the scale, while September stands highest in intensity and next to the highest in number. October is the fourth in respect to number, but at a minimum for intensity. These results, however, do not appear to be uniform for different periods. According to Celsius, out of 384 auroras, observed in the North of

[1] An instance communicated to Captain Lefroy by Mr. Hardisty, showing the low descent of the aurora, is stated as follows: It (the aurora) appeared between me and the trees on the opposite side of the river, which could not have been 40 feet above the level of the stream, *the trees toward the top of the hill being high above it.*—Lefroy's Second Report, 1850–1, p. 14. A similar case is mentioned by Rev. Mr. Cowles in the American Journal of Science, XIII, p. 429. But should it be proved that, in some rare instances, portions of auroral vapor have descended near the earth, this fact will not militate against our views of its cosmical *origin*.

Europe, from 1716 to 1733, inclusive, the number for each month was as follows:—[1]

1. January	40	7. July	2
2. February	44	8. August	23
3. March	59	9. September	42
4. April	25	10. October	57
5. May	11	11. November	46
6. June	1	12. December	36

From a similar table, given by Delisle, of auroras observed at St. Petersburg, from 1726 to 1737, inclusive, we derive the following results:—

1. January	9	7. July	1
2. February	20	8. August	16
3. March	40	9. September	42
4. April	22	10. October	43
5. May	3	11. November	24
6. June	0	12. December	13

A list, digested from the *London Philosophical Transactions*, embracing thirty-five years, from 1716 to 1850, inclusive, gives the following numbers:—

1. January	10	7. July	3
2. February	12	8. August	8
3. March	32	9. September	24
4. April	15	10. October	45
5. May	3	11. November	20
6. June	1	12. December	29

Remarks.

1. Combining the three foregoing lists, and averaging the months, in the order of their respective numbers, we obtain the following *ratios:*—

1. October	145	7. April	62
2. March	131	8. January	59
3. November	90	9. August	47
4. September	88	10. May	17
5. December	78	11. July	6
6. February	77	12. June	2

2. On comparing these results with those obtained for the recent period from 1832 to 1848, we perceive that they agree in some respects, but disagree in others. In both, September stands high on the scale, and June low; but October, which, in the former period, occupied the first rank, stands fourth in the latter period; and it is remarkable that, except June, this month was the only one during this period which afforded no example of an exhibition of either the first or second class.

---

[1] Mairan, pp. 495 and 497.

3. Making a comparison with respect to *seasons of the year*, the case stands thus:—

	Former period.	Latter period.		Former period.	Latter period.
Winter months	71	51	Summer months	18	65
Spring "	70	74	Autumnal "	74	71

In the former period there was a great excess of the winter over the summer auroras, the numbers being as 71 to 18;[1] whereas, in the latter period, the disparity is small, and the advantage on the side of summer in the ratio of 65 to 51. Moreover, the former gave 74 to autumn, and 70 to spring; while the latter gives 71 to autumn and 74 to spring. In regard, however, to *intensity*, the balance has always been in favor of autumn, the greatest auroras having been most numerous in September and November,[2] while they have never occurred in June; but, in respect to *number*, the balance between the seasons, of late years, has been just the opposite of what it was a century ago, the minimum, instead of the maximum number, having of late occurred during the winter months; and this is the more remarkable, since the greater lengths of the winter nights would, of itself, lead us to expect a greater number of auroras at this season of the year.[3]

3. *Secular Periodicity.—The great returns of the aurora borealis, which we have denominated secular periods, occur at intervals of from sixty to sixty-five years, reckoning from the middle of one period to the middle of another, and last from twenty to twenty-five years.* It is, in general, an acknowledged fact, that there are long intervals during which great auroras are seldom seen, and other periods of less duration during which they occur with remarkable frequency and magnificence. Dr. Halley had reached an advanced period of life before he had an opportunity of witnessing a striking display of this phenomenon, when the great aurora of 1716 announced the recurrence of one of the great periods, which afforded this eminent philosopher numerous occasions for seeing the long desired spectacle; and, as has been before remarked, for a long interval, from about the year 1783 to 1827, there was not, perhaps, a single aurora of the highest class, and but few above those of the lowest. We have seen that, in 1827, there commenced a period of unusual frequency, such as to arrest attention both in Europe and in America; that beginning with ten per annum the number increased by a pretty regular gradation to thirty, fifty, and even seventy-five a year, reaching this latter number in the year 1840, and then declining in number and still more in intensity, until, since 1852, scarcely an example has occurred above the lowest forms of the meteor.

Being assured of the fact, that the phenomenon in question is truly characterized by long periods during which it occurs in unusual intensity and frequency, between

---

[1] Mairan institutes a labored comparison, to show that the number of winter greatly exceeds that of summer auroras, and hence argues that auroras arise from the earth's coming within the sun's atmosphere (as he took the zodiacal light to be), being, of course, most within that atmosphere at the perihelion; but, from the above comparison, it appears that this argument has no weight.

[2] Great Auroras about the middle of November, in 1574, 1607, 1835, 1837, 1840, 1841, 1844, 1848.

[3] We may hope that, by the labors of Mr. E. C. Herrick, at New Haven, and of Lieut. Lefroy, in Canada, both of whom have, for some time, been keeping accurate records of all current auroras, we shall soon have the means of determining more accurately than at present the nature of the *annual* periodicity.

which are still longer intervals when it is hardly seen in any of its higher forms, I must regard it as a problem of much interest to ascertain the length of these cycles after which a great return of the aurora borealis may be expected, and the number of years it may be expected to prevail.

The interval from the middle of one secular period to the middle of another, appears, so far as we can judge from imperfect historical data, to be about sixty-five years. Pliny says, "We sometimes see (than which there is no presage of woe more calamitous to the human race) a flame in the sky, which seems to descend to the earth in showers of blood; as happened in the third year of the 107th Olympiad, when Philip was endeavoring to subjugate Greece." He adds, that about the year 641 from the building of Rome, they saw, during the night, a light which shone as the day; that it was nothing uncommon about that time to see the heavens all on fire. He cites examples of those which appeared to meet in conflict from the east and west; and says that they heard the clash of arms and the sound of trumpets; and that the heavens themselves were on fire.[1]

Along with the fabulous accompaniments which usually graced such narrations among the ancients, we recognize in these statements the middle of one of the great returns of the aurora; nor have the same phenomena, at much later periods, been described without a tincture of the marvellous; for it was the popular belief, at least among the more uneducated classes, during the great auroral period which immediately preceded the one under review, namely, that which covered the time of the American revolutionary war, that conflicts of armies were frequently witnessed in the skies.

About the year 400, historians relate that columns were seen suspended in the sky for the space of three days, and that a fire burned behind a cloud which was terrible for its splendor, sometimes overspreading the sky.[2] Comparing the interval between this period and that described by Pliny, we find that eight periods, of 65 years each, would bring us to the year 408, or into the midst of the remarkable exhibition of auroras thus described.[3] In the year 585, occurred the famous aurora recorded by Gregory of Tours, which Mairan considers as resembling the great exhibitions of his time, as that of 1726, most of all those described by the ancients,[4] and this would fall in the third return after that which occurred about the year 400. In the month of September, 1583, there arrived in Paris, in formal procession, and in the habit of penitents, or pilgrims, eight or nine hundred persons, to present their gifts and ask prayers, on account of signs seen in the heavens, and fire in the air. On comparing this date with the period mentioned by Pliny, which was 112 years before the Christian era, we have an interval of 1695 years, embracing twenty-six periods, of 65 years each. In 1607, November 17th, a great aurora occurred, and is minutely described by Kepler, which greatly resembled our auroras of the first class. Since the aurora of 1583 excited great surprise, it was probably the commencement of the period, and that of 1607 near its close, making the duration 24 years.

---

[1] Hist. Nat., l. 11, c. 57.

[2] Mairan, p. 179.

[3] Building of Rome, B. C. 753; and 753—641 × 408=520=8×65.

[4] Mairan, p. 181.

Taking later dates, let us compare the grand aurora described in *Camden's History of the Reign of Queen Elizabeth,* which occurred in November, 1574, with that of November, 1835, which it greatly resembled. We find the interval to be 261 years, and 4 periods, of 65 years each, make 260 years. Finally, if we take 1837 as the middle of the late return, and subtract from it 65 years, we are carried back to 1772, which is about the middle of the next preceding period, which lasted from about 1760[1] to 1783. By a continual subtraction of 65 years backwards from 1837, we fall successively on periods of which we have no records of auroras. As in the case of Halley's comet, auroral returns might have occurred, but passed into oblivion for want of historians. Still, by this process, we fall in with many periods of auroras which did not fail to arrest the attention of contemporary writers; we annex a few examples:—

1837—65=1772, the middle of the last return before the present.

1772—65 1707, one of the *Reprisès* of Mairan.

1707—2×65=1577, the middle of a great period.[2]

From the foregoing and many similar inductions, I think it may be inferred with considerable probability, that the greatest secular periods of the aurora borealis occur at intervals of about 65 years, reckoning from the middle of one period to the middle of another, although returns of a less remarkable character are probably interspersed among these.

The *duration* of one of these great periods appears to be from 21 to 25 years. That which we have just passed through, commenced in 1827; and if we consider it as completed in 1848, when there was almost a cessation of the phenomenon in its higher forms for two years, its duration was 21 years. The occurrence of three exhibitions of the first class, in September, 1851, and of one in February, 1852,[3] throws some doubt on this point. Although the greatly diminished intensity since 1848, would incline me to consider the period as terminating then, yet these later exhibitions indicate a duration of 25 years. If we examine into the duration of

---

[1] A very inconsiderable aurora, which appeared at Philadelphia in November, 1757, is described as a remarkable and an unusual occurrence; which shows that there had been for some time a period of intermission of the phenomenon.—*Bartram's Letter to Dr. Franklin,* Phil. Trans., V, 474.

[2] Mairan, p. 184.

[3] No aurora of the higher classes has appeared at New Haven since that of February, 1852, to the present time, December 21st, 1855. In the *Regents' Report,* for 1854, only four are recorded, all of which, with one exception, were of the humbler forms; whereas, in 1840, near the middle of our secular period, the same publication contained accounts of seventy-five auroras for that year.

I have recently been favored, through the kindness of Mr. M. H. Boyé, of Philadelphia, with manuscript notes, made by himself, by Mr. Charles Bullock, and by Mr. Isaac Lea, containing, severally, interesting accounts of auroras of the higher classes, observed by them at later dates than any of this description observed by myself.

On the 11th June, 1852, Mr. Lea, while on a voyage to England, off Newfoundland, saw an aurora which possessed so many remarkable features as to rank it in the first class. What was quite singular, the exhibition began on the *south,* and streamers ascended finally from the entire circumference of the horizon. It was also remarkable that streamers shot up from *below* the dark segment. As late, also, as Sept. 2d, 1853, Mr. Boyé saw, off Cape Race, a splendid auroral exhibition which covered almost all parts of the sky. From the drawings which he has been so kind as to send me, I infer that this also must have been one of the higher class of auroras.

other similar periods, we obtain corresponding results. Thus the return immediately preceding the recent ones, lasted from 1760 to 1783, a period of 23 years; and the next preceding that lasted from 1716 to 1740,[1] another period of 24 years. On the whole, therefore, I conclude that the aurora borealis is subject to periodical returns, during which it is exhibited in extraordinary frequency, and greatly augmented splendor and magnificence; that these periods are at intervals of about 65 years; that they last for a period not exceeding 25 years; and, consequently, that from the end of one visitation to the beginning of another is an interval of nearly 40 years; during which time the phenomenon is far less remarkable both in frequency and intensity.

Probably similar periods occur in the polar regions, since travellers differ much in their account of the numbers and degrees of splendor of these exhibitions at different times.

While I feel assured of the general fact of the existence of such great returns of the aurora borealis, as those which I have denominated secular periods, yet in this first attempt to determine the intervals between them and to fix the average duration of each, I am sensible of the want of more precise historical data than we at present possess, and therefore submit the foregoing conclusions to the candid inquirer after truth with much diffidence. Philosophers justly regard with some distrust attempts to trace numerical relations, in natural phenomena, since these coincidences are often entirely imaginary. Examples of this are familiar to all who are conversant with the biography of Kepler; but that such attempts sometimes conduct to valuable discoveries, is also evinced in the labors of the same illustrious astronomer.

ORIGIN AND CAUSE OF THE AURORA BOREALIS.

At the next return of the secular period of the aurora (which I anticipate will commence about the year 1890, and be at its maximum about the beginning of the succeeding century), we may justly expect that, from the more advanced state of the natural sciences, and from the accumulation of more accurate data, philosophers will be able to arrive at more correct conclusions respecting the cause of these mysterious exhibitions than we of the present age can attain. The record contained in the preceding pages, of the facts as observed during the recent period, and of the laws as far as they are already ascertained, may nevertheless, should this record endure so long, afford to the observers of that day some useful examples for comparison, and possibly some valuable hints for reflection, even should our main conclusions be set aside for those which are more definite and just. And I entertain the hope that the inquirers after truth will regard with indulgence any efforts to clear up the mystery which environs this subject, even should they fail to acquiesce in the conclusions to which I have been conducted.

The leading inquiries involved in this discussion are the following: What is

[1] Mairan, p. 426.

the *origin* of the vapor, or material itself that forms the basis of the aurora? What causes the *periodicity* of these exhibitions; or why do they occur in certain parts of the twenty-four hours rather than in others? why in certain months of the year more than in other months; and, especially, why do they return in secular periods? Can any explanation be given of their sensible appearances, such as their *luminous* phenomena, of their remarkable motions, of their definite arrangement in columns, arches, and coronas? Can any reason be assigned why the auroral exhibitions take place in the higher latitudes rather than in the equatorial regions, and why they are more intense in the corresponding latitudes on the western than on the eastern continent? A theory of the aurora borealis can hardly be considered as satisfactory unless it can render a full explanation of most of these points, and be not inconsistent with any known facts. Moreover, an explanation that will account for a part only of the facts and render no reason for other facts equally requiring explanation, must be considered as defective and inadequate. Thus a theory which explains merely the luminous appearances, but renders no account of the *origin* of the aurora itself, must be held as very incomplete, since the origin is the main thing to be accounted for. Nor ought we to lose sight of the distinction between an hypothesis and a theory, an *hypothesis* being a principle assumed to account for a class of facts, and having no other claims to be considered the true cause except that it explains the facts, while a *theory* is a deduction from the facts themselves made in accordance with the established laws of nature. We now proceed to consider what causes have been assigned or may be assigned in explanation of the aurora borealis.

In the year 1716 commenced one of those remarkable series of the aurora borealis which we have ventured to denominate *secular periods;* and the men of science on the stage at that time viewed the exhibitions with great attention, and a few of them eagerly inquired into their cause. Of these philosophers, the most distinguished were Halley and Coates in England, and Mairan in France. Halley offered the following explanation. He considered the earth as a great magnet, analogous to an artificial spherical magnet, and supposed that a certain subtile matter or effluvium passing into the pores of the earth near the south pole, and issuing at the north pole, caused both the polarity of the needle and the phenomena of the aurora borealis.[1] This connecting the cause with magnetism was the more remarkable, because the magnetic properties of the aurora itself were then unknown, being first discovered in 1740 by Celsius, and Hiorter, two Swedish philosophers. But with Halley, the idea of such an origin was suggested by his notion that the magnetism of the earth is owing to the circulation of such an "effluvium," which, as he conceived, might be so condensed as to form the palpable vapor of the aurora, and so exalted in intensity as to exhibit the luminous appearances connected with the aurora. Since no such effluvium as that supposed is known to exist, it cannot be made the basis of an explanation, and it seems unnecessary to argue further against the hypothesis of Halley.

Roger Coates has left, in the *Philosophical Transactions*, a very minute description

[1] Phil. Trs., No. 347, or abridged, IV, 138.

of an aurora which occurred in England in 1720, deemed to be exceedingly accurate, from the exact correspondence of the appearances to those now witnessed in the highest class of auroras; but his reasoning on the cause is sufficiently crude. The auroral bank of vapors usually seen acting on the northern horizon at the commencement of a great display, he ascribes to a mixed mass of exhalations; the streamers, to the fermentation of the mass; their inclined direction, to the prevailing wind; and the waves, to irregular gusts of wind blowing upon and shaking the columns. But Coates was an able geometrician, and we find in this paper the first illustration, upon the true principles of perspective, of the mode of formation of auroral arches, by the projection and superposition of parallel columns; a method of illustration afterwards adopted and considerably extended by Dalton.[1]

Other writers of that age, ascribe the auroral lights to a nitro-sulphurous vapor, a mixed mass of nitre and sulphur in a state of comminution, and, therefore, possessing the properties of gunpowder;[2] which vapor was supposed to rise above the clouds, where it was kindled by pressure and motion, and subjected to continued explosions; and hence the agitation, smoky vapor, peculiar sounds, and bright flashes of the aurora.[3]

In the year 1733, was published the great work of Mairan on the aurora borealis.[4] Mairan was a leading member of the French Academy, and one of the ablest philosophers of his time. His work bears internal evidence of great research, guided by superior powers, and a competent knowledge of the laws of nature, so far as they had then been unfolded. It contained a full history of the aurora borealis, as far as it could be gathered from the records of past ages, and proposed an original theory, which the author illustrated and defended with great ability. He ascribed the aurora to the zodiacal light, the outer portions of which, according to him, the earth traverses at certain periods in its revolutions around the sun, attracting to itself the matter of the zodiacal light, which mingles with its atmosphere, and produces the various phenomena of the aurora. Mairan, therefore, appears to have been the first to propose the doctrine of the cosmical origin of the aurora borealis. Respecting the nature of the zodiacal light itself, he adopted the common opinion, that it is the sun's atmosphere; but this hypothesis scarcely affects his conclusions, in assigning it as the cause of the auroral exhibitions, since the existence of the cause assigned is unquestionable, whatever views may be entertained of its relations to the sun. This theory was embraced by some of the ablest philosophers of the day, and opposed by others equally eminent; but on the discovery of the identity between electricity and lightning, and after the agency of atmospherical electricity in the phenomena of thunder-storms was proved, and especially after the resemblance was recognized between the flashes of electricity in an

[1] Phil. Trans., No. 365, or abridged, VI, 82.

[2] Phil. Transactions, No. 395, or abridged, VI, 94.

[3] The most complete and precise description of any of the auroras of that remarkable period, was given by Professor Greenwood, of Harvard University, of an aurora which occurred October 22d, 1730, published in the Philosophical Transactions, No. 418, or abridged, VI, 115.

[4] The first edition was issued in 1733, in 12mo. A second edition, greatly enlarged, was published in 1754, in 4to.

exhausted tube and those of the aurora, the whole scientific world seemed to acquiesce in the belief that the true cause of this phenomenon was at length discovered; and accordingly, for a long time, a quietus was given to any further speculations on the subject.[1] The discoveries recently made in the science of magnetism, have led to some modification of these views; many men of science are still tenacious of the idea that electricity is the beginning and end of all that belongs to the aurora borealis.[2]

Having examined some of the ablest authorities in favor of the doctrine that ascribes the aurora borealis to the agency of electricity, and found that they are very discordant with each other in regard to the modus operandi, and that their explanations are, as appears to me, unsatisfactory, being either erroneous or defective, or both, I am compelled to believe that the aurora borealis does not owe its origin to electricity. This opinion is strengthened by the consideration that, during the prevalence of an aurora, electrometers indicate no unusual amount of atmospheric electricity. This fact was noticed many years ago by Bergman, the Swedish philosopher; and Humboldt says, recent experiments made with very sensitive electrometers, have indicated no change during the finest auroras.[3]

The "currents" supposed by M. De La Rive would not, it is true, be indicated by the electrometer, but only by the galvanometer. Yet it is to be remarked that most of the electrical hypotheses contemplate electricity under such a form as would affect the electrometer.

Those who ascribe the aurora borealis to *magnetism*, seem to argue with more probability, and comprise also names of high distinction in science. No one can doubt that magnetism has *some connection or other* with the aurora, though it may still be uncertain whether it be as cause or effect. The change produced in the needle—the relation of the auroral columns to the magnetic meridian—the formation of the aurora around the pole of the dipping-needle—and the disturbance of the magnetic telegraph sometimes observed during the prevalence of a great auroral exhibition: these facts plainly indicate the existence of such a connection. But it is to be remarked, that none of these facts touch the question of the *origin* of the aurora, and may severally take place alike whether the origin is terrestrial or cosmical. They do not account for the *production* of the matter of the aurora, the auroral vapor; all they prove is that this vapor has *magnetic properties*. Even Humboldt, who has been supposed particularly to favor the magnetic hypothesis, since he was the first to denominate these exhibitions "magnetic storms," plainly indicates in his latest publication on the subject (the third volume of Cosmos) his belief in the cosmical origin of the matter of the aurora. If (says he) we regard falling stars and meteoric showers as planetary asteroids, we may be allowed to conjecture that in the streams of the so-called November phenomena,

---

[1] See Priestley's History of Electricity.

[2] Discussions of contested hypotheses being deemed inconsistent with the object of the Smithsonian Contributions, the writer reserves his discussion of "Electrical Hypotheses of the Aurora Borealis," for some other medium of publication.

[3] Cosmos, I, 186.

when, as in 1799, 1833, and 1834, myriads of falling stars traversed the vault of heaven, and *northern lights* were simultaneously observed, our atmosphere may have received *from the regions of space some elements foreign to it, which were capable of exciting electro-magnetic processes.*[1] If magnetism is inadequate to account for the origin of the aurora and for the *production* of the *material* of which it is composed, no more adequate is it to account for the *phenomena* that attend it, such as the extent, the light, the motions and the periodicity.

After having carefully examined the leading hypotheses which have been advanced to explain the cause of the aurora borealis, they all appear to me to be inadequate and unsatisfactory. It is required of a *theory* that it be a deduction from well-established truths; and of an *hypothesis*, that it explain the leading facts, and that it be not inconsistent with any known facts, although its *application* in certain cases may not be readily perceived. An explanation which unites the characters of both, which is at once an inference from acknowledged truths, and which affords an adequate solution of the leading phenomena, is deemed peculiarly worthy of confidence until a better can be proposed. Such is the explanation which, in conclusion, I shall attempt.

The origin of the Aurora Borealis is cosmical, the matter of which it is composed being derived from the planetary spaces.[2] First, I argue the cosmical origin of the material of these exhibitions from their great *extent.* That of November 17, 1848, was seen under nearly the same appearances, at Smyrna and Odessa, and on the western coast of Asia, in England and Scotland, in Cuba, and throughout the United States as far west as San Francisco,[3] extending over at least 153° of longitude and 40° of latitude, and we know not how much further. Does it seem probable that such an amount of auroral vapor could have been all at once emitted from the earth, or have been precipitated from the atmosphere, like the particles of ice and snow supposed by M. De La Rive, for example; or that the electric or magnetic equilibrium should, in an instant, or within a few hours, have been disturbed over so large a portion of the earth's surface? And if the causes supposed could give such an amplitude to the aurora, are any known exhalations from the earth, or precipitations from the atmosphere, ever found to reach so *high* as the elevation to which the auroral matter sometimes, if not always, attains—a height at least 100 miles above the earth? The very extent of

---

[1] Cosmos, III, 41.

[2] My opinion of the cosmical origin of the aurora, was expressed in my lectures to the students of Yale College, as early as 1835, and soon afterwards at a meeting of the Connecticut Academy. In my account of the great aurora of January 25, 1837, in the *American Journal of Science*, Vol. XXXII, p. 180, the following language is used: "Nor can I add, at present, anything respecting the *origin* of the aurora borealis, except to declare my conviction that it is not satisfactorily accounted for by any existing theory. In assigning it so hastily to *electricity*, a quietus was given to all further attempts at explanation, while yet even the presence of this agent, in any extraordinary degree, has never been proved. *Magnetism* has done more; the auroral vapor is proved to have magnetic properties; but still this fact gives us no information respecting its *origin*. This, I believe, is to be sought for in a source extrinsic to the earth."

[3] Amer. Jour. of Science, N. S., VII, pp. 127, 293.

the phenomenon, therefore, appears to me to remove it from the sphere of terrestrial causes, and leads us to look to the nebulous matter, which is known from the zodiacal light, and from meteoric showers, to exist in the planetary spaces of dimensions sufficiently ample to correspond to the extent of these exhibitions. There is, however, much reason to believe that the nebulous body which affords the auroral matter does not, in fact, cover the entire extent of display from east to west, but that the diurnal revolution of the earth brings successive portions of the earth's surface under that body, or through the portions of it which afford the auroral matter. This view of the *origin* of the aurora is entirely consistent with the fact that its *exhibitions* take place within the atmosphere. The material comes from the planetary spaces, but is visible only when it traverses the atmosphere.

Secondly, we argue the foreign origin of the aurora borealis, from the fact that, *in places differing many degrees in longitude, the different stages of the aurora (the beginning, maximum, and end) occur at the same hour of the night.* When a great exhibition, like that of November 17, 1848, is seen at various places from east to west, as in London and in New York on the same evening, on comparing the hours at which corresponding parts of the display took place, we find the hour of the day the same at both points. At both it began (say) at an hour after sunset, at both it came to its maximum between 10 and 11 o'clock, and ended at both at 3 o'clock. Such a correspondence, at given hours of the night, we have traced in numerous examples, and it will generally be found to hold good. But were the display produced by any cause acting simultaneously over the regions where it prevailed, then these corresponding parts of the display would occur at different hours of the night, corresponding to the longitude. If it began at New York at 7 o'clock, it would begin at London at 12. If it arrived at its maximum at 10 o'clock at New York, at San Francisco the time of maximum would be half past 5. But the maximum was nearly at the same hour at both places. Were the cause of a terrestrial nature, whether exhalations from the earth, or precipitations from the atmosphere, or electricity flashing from the denser portions of the atmosphere towards the rarer, or the circulation of currents from the upper terminations of electrical atmospheric columns from the equator to the poles, after the manner of De La Rive; or from one point to another through the rarefied air of the upper regions, after the manner of Priestley, Morgan, and the elder electricians generally; or were the cause the flashing of electricity along inclined columns of metallic vapor, standing over the whole region through which the aurora prevails, after the manner of Biot; in each and all these cases, corresponding stages in the exhibition, such as the beginning or the maximum, could not happen at the same hour of the night unless the cause operated from east to west at the same rate as that at which the earth turns on its axis; and this would be required, not only in a single instance, but in nearly every instance wherever the phenomenon has been observed. Indeed, the progress of the supposed agent westward, would have to vary in different latitudes, corresponding to the diurnal velocity due to the latitude. But if, as we suppose, the source of the aurora is extrinsic to the earth, consisting of portions of a nebulous body attracted down to the earth from the part of the body to which the earth successively approximates nearest, then as places differing in longitude come up to this point, one after another, they would receive their respective portions of the auroral matter at times corresponding to the diurnal revolution, and have their exhibition everywhere at the same hour of local time, for the same reason that it is now everywhere noon to places coming successively under the meridian.[1]

Thirdly, we urge the cosmical origin of the aurora borealis, from the consideration that the *velocity* of the motions is too great for any terrestrial matter. These motions (as, for example, that of the streamers rushing up to the pole of the dipping needle to form the corona) cannot be considered as the progress of light itself, or of electricity, or of magnetism, since the apparent motion of each of these agents is instantaneous, while this is progressive; nor can they be ascribed to electric or magnetic attractions and repulsions, because they are too rapid to be produced by them, since auroral vapor, estimated at the height of 70 or 100 miles above the earth, is translated from the horizon to the zenith in a few seconds, and auroral waves dart over 90° in a single second. Where do we meet with matter moved by any terrestrial force that is subject to a velocity like this? If indeed the motions of what are called auroral waves are undulatory and not progressive, their appearance is wholly unearthly, and unlike to any other undulations with which we are acquainted. But portions of a nebula, under or through which the earth passes, may easily be conceived to have any velocity relative to the earth, within the limits exhibited by the auroral matter. This matter is present; it has motions too rapid to be produced by any terrestrial forces; we infer, therefore, that it has come to us from a region extrinsic to the earth, endued with a velocity known to exist among bodies, whether solid or nebulous, that revolve around the sun.

Fourthly, we infer the cosmical origin of the aurora borealis from its *periodicity*, especially its secular periodicity. Whether we have succeeded or not in establishing a definite interval of 65 years, from the beginning of one of these auroral visitations to the beginning of another, the general fact cannot be doubted of the occurrence of great periods when, during 20 years or more, these exhibitions return in greatly increased splendor and frequency, and then, for many years, are scarcely seen except in their humbler forms. Now the terrestrial forces assigned, as electricity and magnetism, are not subject to any such periodicity, but are in a state of constant activity. The most delicate instruments indicate no corresponding long periods of activity and repose in these agents. On the contrary, a nebulous body revolving around the sun, may readily be conceived to have its periods so nearly commensurable with those of the earth that the two bodies shall remain for a long

---

[1] Captain Lefroy, an able and assiduous inquirer into the laws of the aurora borealis, has remarked this fact, although he probably would not agree with us in respect to the cause assigned. He says: "It is remarkable that, in many cases, the phenomenon was first seen, in absolute time, at the north-eastern stations, notwithstanding the earlier commencement of darkness at the extreme north, where the difference of latitude in some cases more than compensates for the difference of longitude. It would appear from this, that the aurora does not commonly appear at a station on any meridian until that meridian generally is in darkness; a result which, if established by the whole body of evidence, will be both new and interesting."—*Second Report*, 1850–1.

period, in the neighborhood of each other, and then gradually separating, not return to the same relative position until after a cycle of years. Indeed, it would not be difficult to give to the nebulous body such an orbit as to make it always remain, as is the fact with the zodiacal light, near to the plane of the earth's orbit, and to assign to it such an extent as to render it practicable for extreme portions of it at any time to enter the earth's atmosphere, and produce auroral appearances, on a diminished scale at least, while the peculiar positions relative to the earth, which occur only after certain cycles, are essential in order to exhibit the higher forms of the phenomenon.

The foregoing considerations proceed no further than to show simply that the material out of which the aurora borealis is formed, is derived from the planetary spaces; in other words, that its origin is cosmical and not terrestrial; and this is the main point we have in view, and this conclusion will not be affected by any opinions we may entertain respecting the nature of the material itself, or respecting its mode of existence before it came into the earth's atmosphere. Still, it may be important to the cause of truth, to determine, if we can, what sort of matter the auroral vapor consists of, in what form it existed in space, and what relation it sustained to the solar system.

First, what is the *nature* of the auroral vapor itself? It is exceedingly light and rare, since the stars are seen through it; those of the first magnitude, and the planets with no perceptible diminution of lustre; and though small stars are rendered invisible by it, yet it is difficult to decide whether this is a real obscuration, or merely the loss of contrast. There is often, however, especially in the earlier stages of the exhibition, an accumulation of auroral vapor near the northern horizon, which is so dense as entirely to obscure the stars.

With respect to the specific nature of the matter itself, the idea was long since advanced, both by Dalton and Biot, that it is metallic. Dalton goes further, and considers it ferruginous. This opinion has had but few advocates, and some have thought it not deserving of the least attention.[1] But what inconsistency is there in supposing it ferruginous vapor? Iron, when sublimed by a high heat, as that of the oxyhydrogen blowpipe, assumes the form of an exceedingly attenuated vapor. Moreover, it is a striking fact that the matter which comes to us from the regions of space is, to a great extent, ferruginous, as in the case of meteoric stones; nor does there seem to me any great improbability in supposing that the matter which composes the tails of comets is iron, in a state of extreme diffusion. Although iron is not the only substance susceptible of magnetism, yet an unknown substance exhibiting this property is so commonly ferruginous that, without special evidence to the contrary, it is inferred to be so. Now here is a substance which arranges itself in obedience to all the laws of magnetism: conforming to them in respect to the magnetic pole, the magnetic meridian, and the pole of the dipping needle, and producing the most striking changes in the motions of the compass needle. The inference that the substance is iron is so natural, that it would require special evidence to the contrary to assume that it was anything else.

[1] Becquerel, Vol. VI.

If it be held as proved that the *light* of the aurora is direct and not reflected light, as experiments on polarization made by Arago would indicate, it must be either self-luminous, or be developed in the passage of the auroral vapor through the atmosphere. The latter case is plainly conceivable; for a vaporous matter passing through even the upper regions of the atmosphere, with the immense velocity which the auroral vapor is known to have, would become luminous by the condensation of the air before it, as tinder is set on fire in the air match. A wad, shot from a cannon with such a velocity, would take fire by the heat elicited by condensation; or if it were constituted of some filmy, incombustible substance, that would become red-hot.

Although I am unable to find any evidence that electricity is the *cause* of the aurora borealis, yet that certain of the local appearances it exhibits occasionally may be owing to electricity, is not incompatible with the views I entertain of its origin. Among the various phenomena, there is one which has much resemblance at times to the passage of electricity through rarefied air. I allude to the momentary *flashes* which sometimes constitute a striking feature in auroras of the first class, as was the case in that of April 6, 1848. Respecting this, I find recorded in my note-book the following remark: "The appearances of the luminous flashes more strikingly resemble those of the auroral tube [in which a strong electric spark is transmitted through a long glass tube containing rarefied air] than anything of the kind I ever witnessed before. I had recently been experimenting with a very large auroral tube, and a powerful electric machine, and was, therefore, peculiarly fitted to make the comparison. At 2 h. 20 m. the luminous undulations extended eastward to Aquila, covering the Swan and the Lyre, and the appearances much resembled those of the auroral tube." In the exhibition of February 20, of the same year, at about 4 o'clock in the morning, similar appearances were seen, which possibly might, and perhaps did, result from the passage of electricity through the upper regions of the atmosphere; but I regard these appearances rather as one of the *effects* than as the grand cause of the aurora borealis. They may arise from a disturbance of the electric equilibrium in the auroral columns, but cannot be regarded as *producing* the columns themselves.

The term "nebulous matter" is not well defined, but is applied, in general, to a kind of matter found in the celestial spaces in a state of extreme diffusion, composing a cloud of dust lighter, to any extent, than atmospheric air. Of such a material we conceive to be constituted not only the nebulæ proper, but also comets' tails, and the zodiacal light; and of such a material we have evidence that the aurora borealis is constituted. We deem it, therefore, allowable to call this material nebulous matter, and to denominate a collection of it existing in space a nebulous body. The number of separate nebulæ that have been discovered among the heavenly bodies, and the vast extent which they severally occupy, and the immense volume which comets' tails sometimes fill as well as the zodiacal light, are facts which strongly indicate the great prevalence of nebulous matter in the celestial spaces; nor would it seem a violent presumption to suppose that more or less of this matter may be diffused in the planetary spaces, even were we not assured of its presence there by the zodiacal light, and its descent in the form of meteoric showers.

But we are not to regard the nebulous body, or bodies, from which the auroral matter is derived, as floating loosely in space, but as revolving around the sun, with an orbit and periodic time of its own; subject, however, to perturbations from the action of the planets, and possibly also from the "resisting medium." We can think of no other way in which this nebulous matter can come into the earth's atmosphere, and produce the aurora borealis, than to suppose that the earth, in its revolution around the sun, comes so near to the nebulous body, or bodies, as to bring within its own sphere of attraction some portion of them. The *swiftness of motion* accompanying the auroral displays (by which we mean the motions of translation, and not mere flashes or undulations) may naturally result from the relative motion of the earth and the nebulous matter, or from that motion combined with the effect of the earth's attraction. The *magnetic* phenomena may be referred to the earth, acting as a magnet on ferruginous, or other magnetic matter, of which the auroral vapor gives clear indications of being constituted. The *luminous* appearances, it seems to me most probable, are owing to the evolution of light and heat, due to the sudden condensation of air, and naturally consequent upon the rapid passage through it of such matter as the auroral matter. The great *returns* which we have denominated secular periods, imply that the nebulous body from which they are derived, returns to the same relative position with respect to the earth after a cycle of years, and remains near to it, on account of the near equality of their periods, for a long time. Such a relation between the two bodies may be conceived to produce the great periods of auroras, while the ordinary forms of the phenomenon may result either from a more distant approach of the nebulous body, or from the earth's encountering other portions of the same material, in a more diffusive state. It will readily be perceived that a nebulous body, like that inferred to exist in the neighborhood of the earth's orbit, could not remain stationary, since, without a motion of revolution, it would descend directly to the sun. It must, therefore, have an orbit and a period of its own. The duration of the great periods of the aurora for upwards of twenty years together, and the almost nightly occurrence of the exhibitions in their humbler forms at the higher latitudes, prove that some portions of this body are always hovering near the earth.

The idea of a connection between the aurora borealis and *meteoric showers*, occurred to me as early as April, 1835, according to a record made at that date in my note-book. Many great auroras have occurred about the time of the November meteors, and during a grand auroral display, an uncommon number of shooting stars have frequently been observed. In the great auroral exhibition of August, 1827, they made a very conspicuous figure. In the *Regents' Report of the State of New York*, for 1836, Professor Joslin remarks, that in the great aurora of November 17, 1835, many shooting stars were seen, and he expresses the opinion that shooting stars are intimately connected with the aurora. On this point the illustrious Humboldt thus expresses himself: "The aurora borealis showed itself with great intensity during the occurrence of the most magnificent display of meteors yet observed, that described by Olmsted on the 12th and 13th November, 1833. The aurora was also seen during the periodical phenomenon in 1838, at Bremen, where, however, the fall of meteors was much less striking than at

Richmond, near London. I have noticed elsewhere the remarkable observation of Admiral Wrangel, which he repeatedly confirmed to me verbally, viz: that during the appearance of the aurora on the Siberian coast of the Polar Sea, he frequently saw portions of the sky not previously luminous, which seemed to kindle when a falling star shot across them, and continued bright for some time afterwards."

In a paper which I had the honor to read before the American Association, at their annual meeting, held at Albany, in 1851, on the Zodiacal Light, I stated several *presumptions*, that the meteoric showers of November are derived from that body. After recapitulating some of the reasons I had previously offered, to show that the meteors of November have their origin in a nebulous body revolving about the sun, I submitted the following presumptions in favor of the opinion that the zodiacal light is the nebulous body itself. Such are the following:—

1. The zodiacal light is a nebulous body.
2. It has a revolution around the sun.[1]
3. It reaches beyond, and lies over the earth's orbit, at the time of the November meteors, and makes but a small angle with the ecliptic.
4. In the meteoric showers of November, the meteors are actually seen to come from the part of the heavens covered by the extreme portions of this light.[2]

It may be added that, in the great showers of 1833, this light was remarkably conspicuous; and that soon after this period of the year, it suddenly makes its appearance on the eastern side of the sun, being before seen only on the western side—a change of position which indicates that, at this period, we pass by it, or through it, so as to project it on opposite sides of the sun.[3]

It is well known that Mairan, in his treatise on the Aurora Borealis, first published in the year 1733,[4] ascribed this phenomenon to the zodiacal light, which he supposed to be the atmosphere of the sun. His opinion was embraced by some, and opposed by others of the men of science of that age. Some of its reasonings, the progress of science has clearly shown to be fallacious; but others have great force, and are still deserving of much consideration. After the discovery of the presence of electricity in the atmosphere, and of its identity with lightning, there was almost a universal conviction among philosophers, that electricity is the true cause of the aurora, and all further investigations on the subject were suspended, and the work of Mairan, the most learned of all those hitherto written on the aurora borealis, fell into neglect, and has remained so ever

---

[1] At the meeting of the American Association for the Advancement of Science, August, 1855, Rev. George Jones, Chaplain in the United States Navy, presented a new and elaborate series of observations on the Zodiacal Light, from which he concluded that this phenomenon is owing to a ring around the *earth*, instead of being, as heretofore supposed, an appendage to the sun. Should this opinion prove to be correct, it will not, perhaps, affect unfavorably the doctrine that the periodical meteors and the aurora borealis are both derived from the zodiacal light.

[2] See Trs. American Association for the Advancement of Science, for 1851; or, Amer. Journal of Science.

[3] See this point fully explained in the American Journal of Science, Vol. XXV, p. 168, and Vol. XXXIII, p. 391.

[4] A second edition, embracing additional matter of great importance, was issued in 1754.

since. But it does not appear to me altogether improbable that the zodiacal light is, indeed, the body which affords, at once, the material of the aurora borealis and of meteoric showers. Lying, as it does, nearly in the plane of the earth's orbit, reaching beyond the earth's path around the sun, and having an immense volume; corresponding in constitution, so far as we can judge, with the auroral vapor itself; nothing can be imagined more competent than this to meet all the exigencies of the case. Some portions of it are always near enough to the earth to afford occasional displays of the aurora in its humbler forms, and the known variations of apparent magnitude and brightness to which the zodiacal light is subject, render it competent to meet the most extraordinary exhibitions of the phenomenon.

In conclusion, we will return to the questions with which we started, and state, briefly, the answers to which we have been conducted.

1. *What is the origin of the auroral vapor, or the material itself which forms the basis of the exhibition?* We think it fully proved that the origin of the aurora borealis is cosmical, being derived from the planetary spaces. My meaning is, that the *material* itself comes into the atmosphere from a region beyond, and so remote as not to be influenced by the earth's rotation, although the *phenomena* are exhibited in the atmosphere. It must of course be either terrestrial or cosmical. But we argue that the *extent* of some of the exhibitions is too great to be produced by any terrestrial exhalations or atmospherical precipitations; that in places differing many degrees in longitude, corresponding phases of the exhibition, as the time of arriving at the maximum, for example, occur at the *same hour of local time*—a fact inconsistent with the doctrine of a simultaneous development of the cause over so vast a space, but entirely compatible with that of a nebulous body in space under or through which successive places on the earth are brought in the diurnal revolution; that the *velocity* of many of the motions, where there is evidence of actual translation of material, and where the movements are not due to mere flashes or undulations of light, is too great to arise from any terrestrial forces; that the *periodicity* which attends the phenomenon takes it out of the pale of atmospheric changes and places it within the sphere of astronomical causes, depending on revolutions and the mutual relations of the earth and foreign matter.

2. *What causes the periodicity of these exhibitions;* or why do they occur in certain parts of the twenty-four hours, commencing, for example (in the case of the greatest exhibitions), a little before the end of twilight, and coming to their maximum from 10 to 11 o'clock? why in certain months of the year, as in September and November, while they are seldom seen in June and December? and, especially, why do they return in secular periods?

The occurrence of these exhibitions at certain hours of the night, that is, the *diurnal* periodicity, a circumstance which belongs to auroras of the polar regions, when it is continual night, as well as to lower latitudes[1]—plainly indicates that the phenomenon has *some* relation to the position of the sun, although, after much reflection, I have not been able to satisfy myself as to the precise nature of that relation. The most promising chance of solution of the case which has suggested

---

[1] See Obs. of Lottin, &c., at Bossekop.

itself to my mind, is that which connects it with the zodiacal light, which is known to maintain a nearly constant position with respect to the sun. Mairan, as before remarked,[1] thought he had discovered the true cause of the greater frequency of auroras during the winter than during the summer months, in the fact that in that half of the annual revolution, the earth is on the side of its perihelion, while during the summer months, it is on the side of the aphelion; consequently, it would plunge deeper into the zodiacal light in winter than in summer. But the result of our collation of the exhibitions recorded in the *Regents' Reports*, indicates that in respect to *number* the aggregate for the winter months is less than for the summer, although the balance is in favor of the winter for the *greatest* exhibitions. If the comparison, when instituted from more extensive and more accurate observations, should continue to afford the same result, then the argument of Mairan could not be held as conclusive; but should a more reliable collation of auroras give the same result as that which appeared so uniformly to attend the researches of that distinguished philosopher, then the argument will gain weight and be deserving of much consideration. Since only extraordinary displays of the phenomenon would be recorded in history, probably the comparison of Mairan was instituted in respect to these alone, and of those the balance still appears to be in favor of the winter months. Yet the argument is weakened by the fact that auroras of the first class have sometimes (though rarely) occurred in the summer, as that of July 1, 1837. It is, however, an acknowledged fact that the exhibitions of summer are generally much feebler than those of winter; nor can this be ascribed merely to the shorter duration of the nights, for in winter the displays occur chiefly at hours when they might be seen equally well in summer nights. We are still much in the dark respecting the true cause of the annual periodicity, but shall anticipate a more full and satisfactory explanation of it, when it has longer engaged the attention of philosophers, and afforded more full and accurate data for investigation.

The cause of the *secular* periodicity appears less obscure, since, referring the phenomenon, as we do, to a cosmical origin, and proving, as we think, the existence of a nebulous body in space which affords the material of the aurora, we recognize at once in the necessary astronomical relations of such a body reasons for the recurrence of the secular periods.

3. *Can any explanation be given of the sensible appearances of the aurora, such as the luminous phenomena, their remarkable motions, and definite arrangement in columns, arches, and coronas?* It would not be incompatible with the views I entertain of the origin of the aurora borealis, to suppose that the luminous appearances attending it are due to electricity, since foreign matter through which the earth plunges with immense velocity, might naturally be expected to develop electrical effects in the atmosphere; and I have mentioned a few cases where the auroral flashes did, in fact, look much like those produced by the passage of electricity through rarefied air. But a more general cause of the auroral light is, I think, due to *condensation*, from the rapid transit of the auroral matter through the air, as tinder is ignited in the

---

[1] Vide *supra*.

air match. If the matter is combustible like ferruginous particles, a real combustion would ensue; if incombustible, ignition, simply, would follow.

It may not be easy or possible to explain all the varieties of *motion* which attend auroral displays, but that "rapid motions," in general, should occur, is a natural consequence of the passage of the earth through a nebulous mass revolving around the sun, either in a direction opposite to that of the earth, or in the same direction with a less velocity.

The *magnetic* phenomena accompanying the aurora, imply that the auroral matter has magnetic properties. These make it tend towards the magnetic pole of the earth, cause it to arrange itself in columns parallel to the magnetic meridian, and to form, by perspective, the corona around the pole of the dipping needle. They likewise, for the same reason, produce marked effects on the compass-needle, and cause exhibitions of the phenomenon to be more frequent in the polar than in the equatorial regions, and more abundant and intense on the western than on the eastern continent, since here the principal magnetic pole of the earth is situated.

PUBLISHED BY THE SMITHSONIAN INSTITUTION,

WASHINGTON, D. C.

MAY, 1856.

SMITHSONIAN CONTRIBUTIONS TO KNOWLEDGE.

THE TANGENCIES

OF

CIRCLES AND OF SPHERES.

BY

BENJAMIN ALVORD,

MAJOR UNITED STATES ARMY.

[ACCEPTED FOR PUBLICATION, JANUARY, 1855.]

COMMISSION

TO WHICH THIS PAPER HAS BEEN REFERRED.

Prof. A. E. Church,
Prof. L. R. Gibbes.

The Smithsonian Institution is under special obligations to the above-named gentlemen, for assistance, in the absence of the author, in revising this paper, and carrying it through the press.

Joseph Henry,
Secretary S. I.

T. K. AND P. G. COLLINS, PRINTERS,
PHILADELPHIA.

A GEOMETRICAL SOLUTION

OF THE

TEN PROBLEMS IN THE TANGENCIES OF CIRCLES; AND, ALSO, OF THE FIFTEEN PROBLEMS IN THE TANGENCIES OF SPHERES, BASED UPON THE PRINCIPLE THAT THE TANGENT LINE, OR TANGENT CURVE, IS THE LIMIT OF ALL SECANT LINES OR CURVES.

THE solution herein given to the problems in the tangencies of circles and of spheres, is strictly based upon the principle that *the tangent line, or curve, is the limit to all secant lines or curves.* This principle is frequently employed in descriptive geometry, and in the discussion of tangents in analytical geometry, but I am not aware that it has ever been employed in the manner set forth in this memoir. Solutions are given of most of these problems in the eleventh volume of the *Annales de Mathématique* (par J. D. Gergonne, Paris, 1820), and in the first volume of Crelle's *Mathematical Journal*, Berlin, 1826. But the methods employed are quite different from that herein explained. It is believed that the following is a more complete generalization of this mass of problems than any heretofore published. The classification given of the problems in the tangencies of spheres, and also the classification of all the cases under each problem, both in the tangencies of circles and in the tangencies of spheres, are believed to be novel.

THE TANGENCIES OF CIRCLES.

The following table exhibits the ten problems in the tangencies of circles proposed by a Greek geometer, *Apollonius Pergaeus,* who lived A. C. 200. A translation of his *Geometria Tactionum* (the Geometry of Tangencies), was made by Francis Vieta. An edition of Vieta, in French, was published by M. Herigon, in 1644. Apollonius recorded some complex solutions, but nothing of a general character.

THE TEN PROBLEMS OF APOLLONIUS IN THE TANGENCIES OF CIRCLES.

	No. 1. To draw a circle through three points. Number of solutions, one.
	No. 2. To draw a circle through two points, and tangent to a given right line. Number of solutions, two.
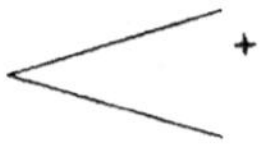	No. 3. To draw a circle through a point, and tangent to two right lines. Number of solutions, two.
	No. 4. To draw a circle through two points, and tangent to a given circle. Number of solutions, two.
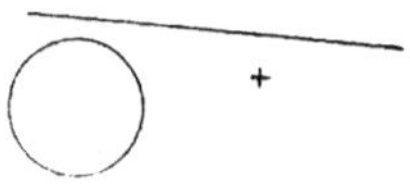	No. 5. To draw a circle through a given point, and tangent to a given right line, and to a given circle. Number of solutions, four.
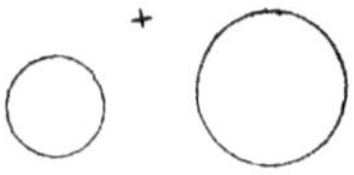	No. 6. To draw a circle through a given point, and tangent to two given circles. Number of solutions, four.
	No. 7. To draw a circle tangent to three given right lines, of which not more than two are parallel. Number of solutions, four.
	No. 8. To draw a circle tangent to two right lines and a given circle. Number of solutions, four.
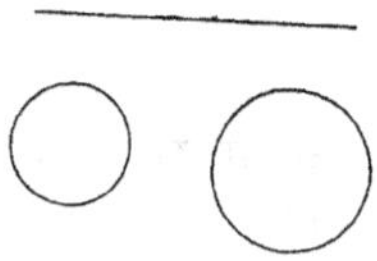	No. 9. To draw a circle tangent to a given right line and to two given circles. Number of solutions, eight.
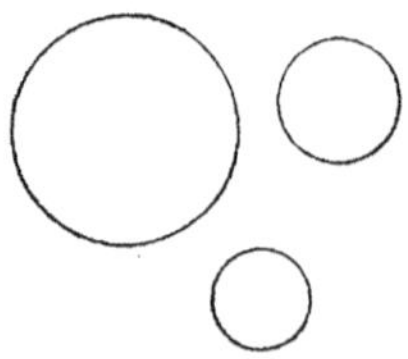	No. 10. To draw a circle tangent to three given circles. Number of solutions, eight.

In the above table, we have added the number of solutions of which each problem is susceptible, or the number of different tangent circles which fulfil the conditions. This number can, of course, be reduced in each case by particular suppositions, but the number given above refers to the general problem. Particular suppositions can also be made in which some of the cases would become impossible, or the circles become straight lines, or circles with infinite radii. This table exhibits all the problems which occur in the tangencies of circles, the geometrical elements being the point, the right line, and the circle—all being in the same plane.

The fact that the *tangent circle is the limit of all secant circles*, leads to the solutions which I shall present, and which will be more fully explained in the solution of Problem 4.

The solutions of Problems 1, 2, 3, 7, and 8 (as see Plate I), are very simple. In Problem 2, extend the line $A\ B$, joining the two given points A and B, until it meets the given line at O. Draw any secant circle, as $A\ B\ M\ N$, through the two given points. Let the radius and position of the centre of this secant circle be changed until the two points of intersection, M and N, come together; then this circle will become the required tangent circle. From O, draw a tangent line, as $O\ E$, to this secant circle. Lay off the distance $O\ E$ in each direction, as $O\ D$ and $O\ D'$, and D and D' are the points of contact of the two circles which will fulfil the conditions. For, as $O\ A \times O\ B = \overline{O\ D}^2$, the circle drawn through the points A, B, and D, will be tangent at D to the given line. The same reasoning applies to the point D'.

In Problem 3, C being the given point, let fall a perpendicular to the line $A\ L$, which is drawn to bisect the angle formed by the two given lines, and lay off $N\ D = N\ C$. The point D will lie on the circumference of the required circle, as $A\ L$ must be an indefinite diameter of that circle. The problem is thus reduced to Problem 2, to draw a circle through the two points C and D, and tangent to the line $A\ E$.

In Problem 8, draw the auxiliary line $L'\ D$ parallel to $L\ I$, and distant from it $D\ F = A\ P$, the radius of the given circle. From A, the centre of the given circle, let fall $A\ B$ perpendicular to $L\ H$ (bisecting the angle), and lay off $K\ B = A\ K$. Then if, through B and A, circles $B\ A\ D$ and $B\ A\ D'$ be described tangent to $L'\ D'$ (by Problem 2), and $O\ D$ and $H\ D'$ be drawn, we have F and I, the points of contact of two of the required circles. For $O\ D = O\ A = O\ N$, and $F\ D = P\ A = M\ N$; therefore, $O\ F = O\ P = O\ M$, $H\ I = H\ P'$. By drawing an auxiliary parallel line $L''\ S$ within the angle, and distant also the radius of the circle, by a like process, two more tangent circles, $X\ Y$ and $Q\ T$, will be found to fulfil the conditions of the problem. There are thus *four* solutions to the problem; two of the circles convex, and two concave to the given circle.

Problem 4. *To draw a circle through two points, and tangent to a given circle.*—Draw through the two given points B and A (see Fig. 1, Plate II), any circle, as

$B\,A\,C\,D$, secant to the given circle $M\,N\,D$, and cutting it in the two points C and D. *If the radius and position of the centre of this circle be changed until the two points of intersection C and D come together, it will become the required tangent circle.* Join $D\,C$, and extend the line until it meets $B\,A$ prolonged at Z. From Z, draw two lines, $Z\,M$ and $Z\,N$, tangent to the given circle; the points of contact N and M will be the points of contact of the required tangent circles. For $Z\,A \times Z\,B = Z\,C \times Z\,D = \overline{Z\,N}^2 = \overline{Z\,M}^2$; therefore, the circle $B\,A\,N$ will be tangent at N to the line $Z\,N$, and both circles, being tangent to the same right line at the same point N must be tangent to each other. The same course of reasoning applies to the other tangent circle $B\,A\,M$. There are, then, *two* solutions; one tangent circle convex, the other concave to the given circle.

With the use of any other secant circle, as $B\,A\,L\,P$, by a like construction, the same tangent circle $B\,A\,N$ would be obtained, and the same point of contact N. Therefore, the secant line drawn through P and L will pass through the same point Z as in the case of the secant line $D\,C$. Fig. 2 exhibits the case when the two given points are within the given circle.

Therefore, it follows that if, through any two points in the plane of a given circle, any number of secant circles be drawn intersecting said circle, and right lines be drawn through the points of intersection, they will all meet in a common point on the prolongation of the line joining the two first named given points.

This solution of Problem 4 is derived, it will be seen, from the fact that THE TANGENT CIRCLE IS THE LIMIT OF ALL SECANT CIRCLES. The tangent circle $B\,A\,N$ is the limit of all secant circles, as $B\,A\,C\,D$, $B\,A\,L\,P$, &c. This principle, and the construction in this problem, will be found of universal application in all that follows.

PROBLEM 5. *To draw a circle through a given point, and tangent to a given right line, and to a given circle.*—Draw the line $C\,B$ (see Fig. 1, Plate III) through the centre of the given circle, and perpendicular to the given right line $C\,E$. Suppose P is the given point, and, for the purpose of analysis, that $O\,P\,E$ is the required tangent circle. $S\,D$, joining the centres, will pass through the point of contact O. Join $B\,O$ and $O\,E$. $B\,O\,E$ will be one continuous straight line. For, $D\,E$ and $B\,S$ being parallel, the angles $O\,S\,B$ and $O\,D\,E$ are equal, and, the triangles being isosceles, the angles at O are equal. In the similar triangles $B\,A\,O$ and $B\,C\,E$, we have $B\,C \times B\,A = B\,E \times B\,O$. Join $B\,P$, and suppose that P' is the point in which $B\,P$ cuts the required circle. $B\,P \times B\,P' = B\,E \times B\,O$. Therefore, $B\,P \times B\,P' = B\,C \times B\,A$. But $B\,C$, $B\,A$, and $B\,P$ are given distances; therefore, the point P' can be found by taking $B\,P'$ equal to the fourth proportional to $B\,P$, $B\,C$, and $B\,A$. This will readily be done by making the angle $B\,A\,P'$ = the given angle $B\,P\,C$; or, passing a circle through the three given points C, A, and P, it will cut $B\,P$ in the required point P'. Then, by Problem 4, through the two points P and P', draw a circle tangent to the given circle; it will also be tangent to the given right line. This gives two circles, $P\,P'\,O$, $P\,P'\,O'$, fulfilling the required conditions.

Also join $P\,A$. By a similar process, we shall find the triangle $A\,E'\,C$ similar to the triangle $A\,O'''\,B$, and $A\,P \times A\,P'' = A\,E' \times A\,O''' = A\,B \times A\,C$. Find, then, $A\,P''$ a fourth proportional to $A\,P$, $A\,B$, and $A\,C$. This can be done by drawing the line $B\ P''$ so as to make the angle $A\ B\ P''$ = the angle $A\ P\ C$; or, pass a circle through P, B, and C, and it will cut $P\ A$ prolonged at P''. Then, by Problem 4, through P and P'', draw circles $O'''\ P''\ E'$ and $P''\ P\ E''$ tangent to the given circle; they will also fulfil the conditions of the problem.

This makes *four* solutions in all; *two* of the tangent circles convex, and *two* concave to the given circle.

Fig. 2 exhibits the case in which the given right line intersects the given circle, the given point being within the circle. There are only two solutions in this case, each circle being convex to the given circle.

PROBLEM 6. *To draw a circle through a given point, and tangent to two given circles.*—In Fig. 1, Plate IV, let E and F be the two given circles, and A the given point. Find the point O, on the line joining their centres, where the line $T\ T'$, tangent to both on the same side of $E\ F$, will cut it. Suppose, for the sake of analysis, $A\ C\ D$ to be the required circle. Join the points of contact C and D. This line, prolonged, will pass through the point O. For, mark the point L where this line cuts the circle F. The triangles $C\ F\ L$, $D\ D'\ C$, and $M\ D\ E$ will be similar. Therefore, the angles $M\ D\ E$ and $C\ L\ F$ are equal, and the radius $F\ L$ is parallel to the radius $E\ D$. Therefore, the line $D\ C\ L$ passes through the point O, which is the intersection of all right lines passing through the extremities of parallel radii on the same side of $E\ F$. (See Biot's *Analytical Geometry*, Chap. II.)

Join O with the given point A, and suppose A' to be the point in which this line cuts the required circle. The triangle $O\ C\ S$ is similar to the triangle $O\ M\ N$; but $O\ M\ N$ is also similar to $O\ D\ K$. Therefore, the triangle $O\ C\ S$ is similar to the triangle $O\ D\ K$, and $O\ K \times O\ S = O\ D \times O\ C = O\ A \times O\ A'$. Therefore, if we lay off $O\ A'$ equal to a fourth proportional to $O\ A$, $O\ K$, and $O\ S$, we obtain the point A'. This point can be obtained by making the angle $O\ S\ A'$ = the angle $O\ A\ K$. Or, pass through the given points A, K, and S, a circle, it will cut $O\ A$ in the point A'. Then, by Problem 4, drawing, through A and A', the circles $A\ A'\ C$ and $A\ A'\ C'$ tangent to one of the given circles, they will also be tangent to the other. This construction gives two of the required circles.

If, in Fig. 2, the line $T\ T'$ be drawn tangent to the two given circles, the points of contact being on different sides of the line joining their centres, the point O', in which these lines intersect, enjoys properties entirely similar to those found for the point O in Fig. 1. We shall find the triangles $O'\ G\ C''$, $O'\ M\ N$, and $O'\ D\ K$, all similar, and $O'\ K \times O'\ G = O'\ D \times O'\ C'' = O'\ A \times O'\ A''$. Thus, the triangle $O'\ G\ A''$ is similar to the triangle $O'\ A\ K$; and laying off $O'\ A''$ equal to a fourth proportional to $O'\ A$, $O'\ K$, and $O'\ G$, we obtain the point A''.

A'' is easily found in construction by drawing $G\ A''$ so as to make the angle $O'\ G\ A''$ equal to the angle $O'\ A\ K$. Or, passing a circle through A, K, and G, it also should cut the line $A\ O'$ at A''. Then, through A and A'', by Problem 4, pass two circles, $A\ C''\ A''$ and $A\ C'''\ A''$, tangent to the circle F, they will also be tangent to the circle E.

This completes *the four* solutions of this problem; one of the circles being convex to both of the given circles, one concave to both, one convex to F and concave to E, and the fourth concave to F and convex to E.

We shall hereafter name the point O the "*external similar point*," and the point O' the "*internal similar point*" of the two circles.[1]

We will now suppose that one of the given circles encloses the other, as in Fig. 3. If the extremities of *any* two parallel radii $E\,Q$ and $F\,C$, on opposite sides of $E\,F$, are joined, the line $C\,Q$ will cut the line joining the centres at a fixed point O. If the extremities of parallel radii, as $F\,N$, and $E\,Q$, on the same side of the line $E\,F$, be joined by the line $Q\,N$, this line, prolonged, will meet the line joining the centres at a fixed point O'. And it will readily be seen that they are the "similar points" of these circles, and that, by using these points O and O' in the same manner as O and O' in the former cases, the four solutions of the problem (exhibited to the eye in Fig. 3) will be obtained.

It is worthy of note, that in Problem 5 (see Fig. 1, Plate III) we can regard the points B and A as every way analogous to the points O and O' in Problem 6. Regarding the given right line $C\,E$ as the circumference of a circle of infinite radius, $B\,C$ is the line joining the centres of the two given circles, and B and A are the points where the lines $B\,N$ and $A\,M$, tangent to both (and parallel to $C\,E$), intersect the line joining the centres. The points B and A answer precisely, therefore, to the description of the "*external and internal similar points*" O and O' in Problem 6.

PROBLEM 9. *To draw a circle tangent to a given right line and to two given circles.*— In this problem, as see Fig. 1, Plate V, draw the auxiliary line $K\,D$ parallel to the given line, $G\,C$, and at a distance equal to the radius of the smaller of the two given circles, and the auxiliary circle $B\,N$ with a radius equal to the difference of the radii of the circles. Then, by Problem 5, through the point F, draw a circle, as $F\,B\,D$, tangent to the circle $B\,N$, and to the auxiliary line $K\,D$. The centre of this circle will be the centre of the required circle. For, join O, the centre of this tangent circle, with A and F, and let fall $O\,D$ perpendicular to the given line, we shall have $E\,F = C\,D = B\,S$; and, taking these distances from the radius of the circle $F\,B\,D$, we have $O\,S = O\,E = O\,C$. Therefore, a circle passed through S, E, and C will be tangent to the two given circles at S and E, and to the given right line at C. So, by the use of a similar auxiliary line, $T\,P$, on the other side of the given line, the circle $N\,P\,F$ is found, whose centre, L, is the centre of another circle, $M\,R\,E'$, which will fulfil the conditions of the problem.

Thus, in each case, the centre of the required circle is found by obtaining the centre of an auxiliary circle, whose radius differs from the required one (either less or greater) by the radius of the smallest of the given circles.

It will be found that there are *eight* solutions to this problem. They are all

---

[1] These are the names given to these points in the dissertations of the German mathematician Steiner, in the first volume of Crelle. It is proper to add that the writer had made use of said points, and, indeed, arrived at nearly all these solutions, in 1838, and communicated them to his friends at West Point, long before he had seen the very curious German memoir referred to.

exhibited in the two figures of Plate V. They are numbered as the points of contact are numbered in circle *A* in both figures. Nos. 1 and 8 are convex to both circles; Nos. 2 and 7, concave to both; 3 and 6, convex to circle *A* and concave to circle *F;* 4 and 5, concave to *A* and convex to *F.*

PROBLEM 10. *To draw a circle tangent to three given circles.*—In Plate VI, let *A*, *B*, and *E*, be the centres of the given circles. Draw the auxiliary circle *B S*, having the same centre as the largest circle, and a radius equal to the difference between the radii of the largest and of the smallest of the given circles. Draw, also, the auxiliary circle *A G* with a radius equal to the difference between the radii of the given circle *A F* and of *E D*, the smallest of the given circles. Draw through *E*, the centre of the smallest circle, by Problem 6, a circle, as *E S G*, tangent to both these auxiliary circles. The centre, *O*, of this will be the centre of one of the required circles. For $D E = S C = F G$. Therefore, $O D = O C = O F$.

By a construction entirely analogous, all the other solutions of this problem will be readily obtained. Sometimes, the radius of the auxiliary circle is longer than the radius of one of the circles by the radius of the smallest circle.

It will be found that there are *eight* solutions to the problem, and they are all exhibited to the eye in Plate VII. In each case, as in Problem 9, the centre of the required circle is found by obtaining the centre of an auxiliary circle whose radius differs from the required one (either less or greater) by the radius of the smallest of the given circles.

The following statement exhibits the auxiliary circles from which the different solutions are obtained. The numbers refer to the required circle, whose point of contact is numbered in Plate VII.

From the auxiliary circles *A G* and *B S* are obtained, by Prob. 6	Nos. 1 and 2.
From *B S′* and *A G′*	Nos. 3 and 4.
From *A G* and *B S′*	Nos. 5 and 6.
From *B S* and *A G′*	Nos. 7 and 8.

It will be found on examination that the eight solutions are made up by tangent circles, which are situated as follows in reference to the three given circles, viz:—

No. 1, convex to the three circles.
No. 2, enclosing or concave to all.
Nos. 3, 5, and 7, concave to one and convex to the other two.
Nos. 4, 6, and 8, convex to one and concave to the other two circles.

THE TANGENCIES OF SPHERES.

Upon examining the question, How many problems are possible in the tangencies of spheres? I find there are fifteen, which can be classified as follows, viz:—

THE FIFTEEN PROBLEMS IN THE TANGENCIES OF SPHERES.

	No. 1. To draw a sphere through four points given in position. Number of solutions, one.
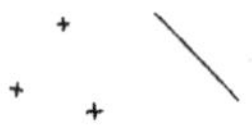	No. 2. To draw a sphere through three points, and tangent to a given plane. Number of solutions, two.
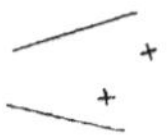	No. 3. To draw a sphere through two points, and tangent to two planes. Number of solutions, two.
	No. 4. To draw a sphere through a point, and tangent to three planes. Number of solutions, two.
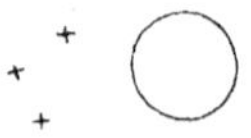	No. 5. To draw a sphere through three points, and tangent to a given sphere. Number of solutions, two.
	No. 6. To draw a sphere through two points, and tangent to a plane and to a sphere. Number of solutions, four.
	No. 7. To draw a sphere through a point, and tangent to two planes and to a sphere. Number of solutions, four.
	No. 8. To draw a sphere tangent to three planes and to a sphere. Number of solutions, four.
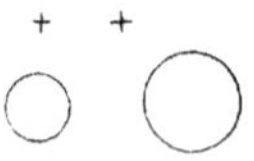	No. 9. To draw a sphere through two points, and tangent to two given spheres. Number of solutions, four.
	No. 10. To draw a sphere tangent to four planes. Number of solutions, eight.

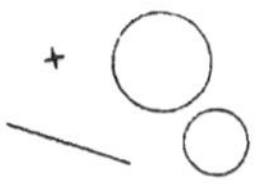	No. 11. To draw a sphere through a point, and tangent to a plane and to two spheres. Number of solutions, eight.
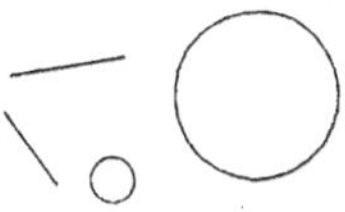	No. 12. To draw a sphere tangent to two planes and to two spheres. Number of solutions, eight.
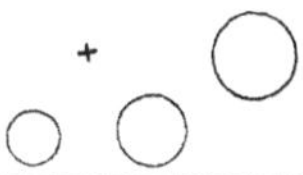	No. 13. To draw a sphere through a point, and tangent to three spheres. Number of solutions, eight.
	No. 14. To draw a sphere tangent to a plane and to three spheres. Number of solutions, sixteen.
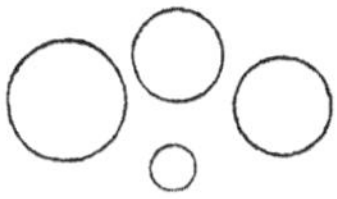	No. 15. To draw a sphere tangent to four spheres. Number of solutions, sixteen.

All of these problems can be solved by the application of the same principle which is employed in the above investigation of the tangencies of circles.

The solutions of Problems 1 and 10 are found in all elementary works on descriptive geometry, and are obvious.

In Problem 2, pass a circle through the three given points, it will be a small circle of the required sphere. Through its centre, pass a plane perpendicular to the given plane, and also to the plane of the circle. It will cut the circumference of the circle in two points, and the given plane in a line which must contain the required point of contact. By Problem 2, in the Tangencies of Circles, through those two points draw a circle tangent to this line, and you will have a great circle of the required sphere, and its point of contact with the plane. It is obvious that there are two spheres which will fulfil the conditions of the problem, as there are two points of contact found by this construction.

In Problem 3, draw a plane bisecting the angle formed by the given planes. It must pass through the centre of the required sphere. Let fall a perpendicular from one of the given points upon said plane, and find on it a point equidistant on the opposite side. The required sphere must pass also through this last point. Therefore, the problem is reduced to Problem 2.

In like manner, PROBLEM 4 can be reduced to Problem 2.

In PROBLEM 5, pass a circle through the three given points. This must be a small circle of the required sphere. Let fall, from the centre of the given sphere, a perpendicular to the plane of this circle. Pass, through this perpendicular and the centre of the small circle, a plane. This will cut the circumference of the small circle in two points (found readily in construction by joining the foot of the perpendicular with the centre of that circle), and it will cut the given sphere in a great circle. Then (by Prob. 4, in Tangencies of Circles) pass through these two points a circle tangent to the great circle. The point of contact will be the point of contact of the required sphere. Two such tangent circles can be drawn, and thus two spheres can be obtained to answer the conditions, viz: one convex and one concave towards the given sphere.

PROBLEM 6. *To draw a sphere through two points tangent to a given sphere and to a given plane.*—Suppose the required point of contact (on the plane) to be known. Through this point, and the centre of the given sphere, pass a plane perpendicular to the given plane, and suppose, for the sake of analysis, that to be the plane of the paper. In Fig. 1, Plate VIII, let A be the given sphere referred to two planes of projection (according to the principles of descriptive geometry), $A' X'$ being the ground line, let the vertical plane of projection be the given plane, and (P, P') (Q, Q') the projections of the given points. Let O and O' be the "similar points," used as in the analogous problem (Prob. 5) in Tangencies of Circles. Suppose, for the purpose of analysis, that Y is the required point of contact on the given sphere and in the horizontal plane, and that $X\ Y$ is the required tangent sphere. Join Y with O and X'. $O\ Y X'$ will be one continuous straight line; see Prob. 5, in Tangencies of Circles. Also, $O\ Y \times O\ X' = O\ A' \times O\ O'$. Join one of the given points (P, P') with O. Let the point whose projections are $M\ M'$ be the point in which this line pierces the tangent sphere. As this line and $O\ Y X'$ are in the same plane, cutting a small circle out of the tangent sphere, we have $O\ M'' \times O\ P'' = O\ Y \times O\ X' = O\ A' \times O\ O'$. Thus, the point whose projections are M, M' will be found by finding $O\ M''$ a fourth proportional to $O\ P''$, $O\ A'$, and $O\ O'$, all these being known distances. We have thus three points (P, P'), (Q, Q'), and (M, M') in the required sphere, and the question is reduced to Prob. 5, Tangencies of Spheres. By this process, two solutions are obtained. By the use of the point O', two more will be obtained; making *four* in all. Two of the required spheres will be convex, and two concave to the given sphere.

In PROBLEM 7, pass a plane bisecting the angle formed by the two given planes. Through the given point, let fall a perpendicular to this plane, and find a point on the opposite side equidistant from the plane. This point must also be found on the required tangent sphere. Then, through these two points, draw a sphere tangent to the given sphere and to one of the given planes; it will be tangent, also, to the other plane. This reduces the problem to Prob. 6.

In Problem 8, pass three auxiliary planes parallel to the three given planes, and distant from each the radius of the given sphere. Through its centre, draw (by Prob. 4) a sphere tangent to these three auxiliary planes. Its centre will be the centre of the required sphere. *Four* solutions will be found; two of the tangent spheres concave, and two convex to the given sphere.

Problem 9. *To draw a sphere through two points, and tangent to two given spheres.*—Let A and B (see Fig. 2, Plate VIII) be the two given spheres, and C and D the two given points; not necessarily in the plane of the paper. Join C with the point O, the "*external similar point*" of the two given spheres. By a method analogous to that explained in Prob. 6 (in Tangencies of Circles), we can find the point, C' in which the line $O\,C$ pierces the required tangent sphere. For, suppose F and F' to be the required points of contact (not necessarily in the plane of the paper). Join $F\,F'$, and the line will pass through the same point O, as seen in the problem just quoted. The lines $F\,F'$ and $C\,C'$, passing through the same point O, are therefore in the same plane, cutting a small circle out of the required sphere. Therefore, $O\,C \times O\,C' = O\,F \times O\,F' = O\,H \times O\,G$. Thus, find $O\,C'$ a fourth proportional to $O\,C$, $O\,G$, and $O\,H$, and you have $O\,C'$. This gives us the point C'. This reduces the problem to that of Prob. 5. By the use of the point O, two of the solutions will be found. By making use of the point O', the "*internal similar point*" of the two given spheres, two other tangent spheres will be obtained; making in all *four* solutions to the problem.

In Problem 11, join the given point with one of the similar points of the two spheres, and, by the method employed in Prob. 9, find another point, which must be on the required sphere. Then, by Prob. 6, through these two points, draw a sphere tangent to the given plane, and to one of the given spheres; it will also be tangent to the other sphere. *Eight* solutions will be found to this problem. Call r and r' the "similar points" of the two spheres, and o and o' of one of the spheres and the plane. Two of the solutions are obtained by the use of o and r, two from o and r', two from o' and r, and two from o' and r'. The *eight* solutions are classified as seen in Prob. 12.

Problem 12. *To draw a sphere tangent to two planes and to two spheres.*—Pass two auxiliary planes parallel to the two given planes, outside of them and distant from each the radius of the smaller of the given spheres. Pass within the larger sphere an auxiliary sphere, having the same centre, and distant from its surface by the above named radius. Through the centre of the smaller sphere, draw (by Prob. 7) a sphere tangent to these two auxiliary planes and to the auxiliary sphere. Its centre will also be the centre of the required sphere. By passing an auxiliary concentric sphere outside the larger sphere, and auxiliary planes on the opposite side of the given planes, other tangent spheres will be found. There are *eight* solutions in all. The classification will be analogous to that in Prob. 9 (in Tangencies of Circles), and the same as in the preceding problem, viz: two of the required spheres convex to the two given spheres, two concave to them, two convex to one and concave to the other, and two concave to one and convex to the other.

PROBLEM 13. *To draw a sphere through a given point, and tangent to three given spheres.*—Let P (see Fig. 1, Plate IX) be the given point, not in the plane of the paper, and A, B, and C, the centres of the three given spheres. Find the points O, M, and N, the "external similar points" of the spheres taken in pairs, and O', M', and N', their "*internal* similar points." The three points O, M, and N, are shown, by a well-known proposition, to be in the same straight line. Join the given point P with each of these points, and, by the principles explained in problem 9, three other points will be found, which must lie on the required sphere. These four points will be in the same plane (as $O\ M\ N$ is a straight line), and on a small circle of the required sphere; and the solution is thus reduced to Prob. 5. By making use of the points O', M', and N', other tangent spheres will be found to answer the conditions of the problem. There are *eight* solutions in all, viz: *one* of the tangent spheres convex to the three spheres; *one*, concave to all; *three*, convex to one and concave to the other spheres; *three*, concave to one and convex to the other spheres.

PROBLEM 14. *To draw a sphere tangent to one plane and to three spheres.*—Pass an auxiliary plane parallel to the given plane on the side farthest from the spheres, and distant the length of the radius of the smallest of the given spheres. Within the two other spheres, pass auxiliary concentric spheres, and distant from their surfaces by the above-named radius. Pass, by Prob. 11, through the centre of the smallest of the given spheres, a sphere tangent to these two auxiliary spheres and to the auxiliary plane. Its centre will be the centre also of one of the required spheres. By passing auxiliary concentric spheres *outside* of the two largest spheres, and another auxiliary plane on the other side of the given plane, other tangent spheres will be found to answer the conditions. The process is analogous to that pursued in Prob. 9, in the Tangencies of Circles. *Sixteen* solutions will be found to this problem, classified as follows, calling the three given spheres A, B, and C:—

Two convex to all the spheres.				
Two concave to all.				
Two convex to	A	and concave to	B and C.	
Two	"	B	"	A and C.
Two	"	C	"	A and B.
Two concave to	A	and convex to	B and C.	
Two	"	B	"	A and C.
And Two	"	C	"	A and B.

PROBLEM 15, AND LAST. *To draw a sphere tangent to four given spheres.*—In Fig. 2, Plate IX, let A, B, C, and D be the centres of the given spheres. The centres A, B, and C may be regarded as in the plane of the paper, D being out of it. Within the three largest spheres, A, B, and C, pass auxiliary concentric spheres $A\ E$, $B\ I$, and $C\ G$, distant from their surfaces by the length of the radius of the smallest of the given spheres. By Prob. 13, pass through D (the centre of the smallest sphere), a sphere tangent to these three auxiliary spheres. Its centre will be the centre of one of the required tangent spheres. Pass three other auxiliary spheres, *A E'*, *B I'*, and *C G'*, outside the same three given spheres, and distant also the length of the radius of the sphere *D*. By combining in all possible ways these six auxiliary spheres, all the solutions, numbering *sixteen*, will be found. The following table classifies the different tangent spheres :—

	No. 1	convex to or inside of all the spheres.
	No. 2	concave to or enclosing all.
Four are convex to one and concave to the other three	No. 3	convex to *A* and concave to the other spheres.
	No. 4	" *B* " " "
	No. 5	" *C* " " "
	No. 6	" *D* " " "
Four are concave to one and convex to the other three	No. 7	concave to *A* and convex to the other spheres.
	No. 8	" *B* " " "
	No. 9	" *C* " " "
	No. 10	" *D* " " "
Six are convex to two and concave to the other two spheres	No. 11	convex to *A* and *B* and concave to the other spheres.
	No. 12	" *B* and *C* " " "
	No. 13	" *A* and *D* " " "
	No. 14	" *C* and *D* " " "
	No. 15	" *A* and *C* " " "
	No. 16	" *B* and *D* " " "

From the auxiliary spheres *A E*, *B I*, and *C G*, are obtained, by Prob. 13, Nos.	1 and 2.
From *A E'*, *C G*, and *B I*	" 3 and 7.
From *A E*, *C G*, and *B I'*	" 4 and 8.
From *A E*, *B I*, and *C G'*	" 5 and 9.
From *A E'*, *C G'*, and *B I'*	" 6 and 10.
From *A E'*, *B I'*, and *C G*	" 11 and 14.
From *A E*, *B I'*, and *C G'*	" 12 and 13.
From *A E'*, *B I*, and *C G'*	" 15 and 16.

If, in this or in any of the previous problems, some of the spheres are enclosed in one of the others, if the problem remains possible, it can be solved on analogous principles, by making use of the "similar points" described in Prob. 6, in Tangencies of Circles, see Fig. 3, Plate IV.

It is interesting to notice that, if these problems had been solved algebraically—as, for instance, by referring the circles, in the last problem in the Tangencies of Circles, to co-ordinate axes, the abscissa of the centre of the required circle being the unknown quantity—the resulting equation would be one of the eighth degree, the eight roots giving the eight solutions. It is not surprising, then, that Descartes should acknowledge (see Montucla's *History of Mathematics*, p. 264) that, in attempting to apply algebraic analysis to this problem, he "obtained, by one process, an expression so complicated that he would not undertake to construct it in a month; and, by another process, one less *embarrassée*, but which was so difficult as to deter him from touching it." If a full analytical expression could be obtained to embrace all cases in Prob. 10, in Tangencies of Circles, the other nine problems could all be solved from it by different suppositions; as, that the radius of one of the circles was zero and the other infinity, which would reduce it to Prob. 5.

If the last problem in the Tangencies of Spheres had been solved algebraically, by referring the spheres to three co-ordinate planes, the resulting equation would be of the sixteenth degree. It will, therefore, be seen that still greater complexity would attend any attempt thus to solve this problem, than was encountered by Descartes in his trial of the questions in the Tangencies of Circles. As the number of solutions, in the separate problems in the Tangencies of Spheres and of Circles, is 16, 8, 4, 2, and 1, all even multiples of 2, I had conjectured that the resulting equation, in either case, might be in the form of a quadratic, but I do not think it has ever been obtained by mathematicians.

But it will be readily admitted that a geometrical solution, generalizing the entire series, such as we have presented, is much more satisfactory than any which could be obtained by the aid of algebra.

Besides the elaborate dissertations referred to on the third page of this paper, frequent geometrical solutions of the problems in the Tangencies of Circles have been given—as in the first book of *Newton's Principia*, in *Leslie's Geometry*, and in the *Geometry* of the "Library of Useful Knowledge"—but none of them reduce the question to the elementary principle above announced.

The author offers this memoir for publication, under the belief that it is one of the highest aims of science to simplify and reduce a complex subject to its elements. An ingenious solution of detached problems would be less valuable, but the elucidation and classification of an entire system, and the development of a principle, however simple, which underlies said system, may be considered worthy of record.

PUBLISHED BY THE SMITHSONIAN INSTITUTION,

WASHINGTON, D. C.

JANUARY, 1856.

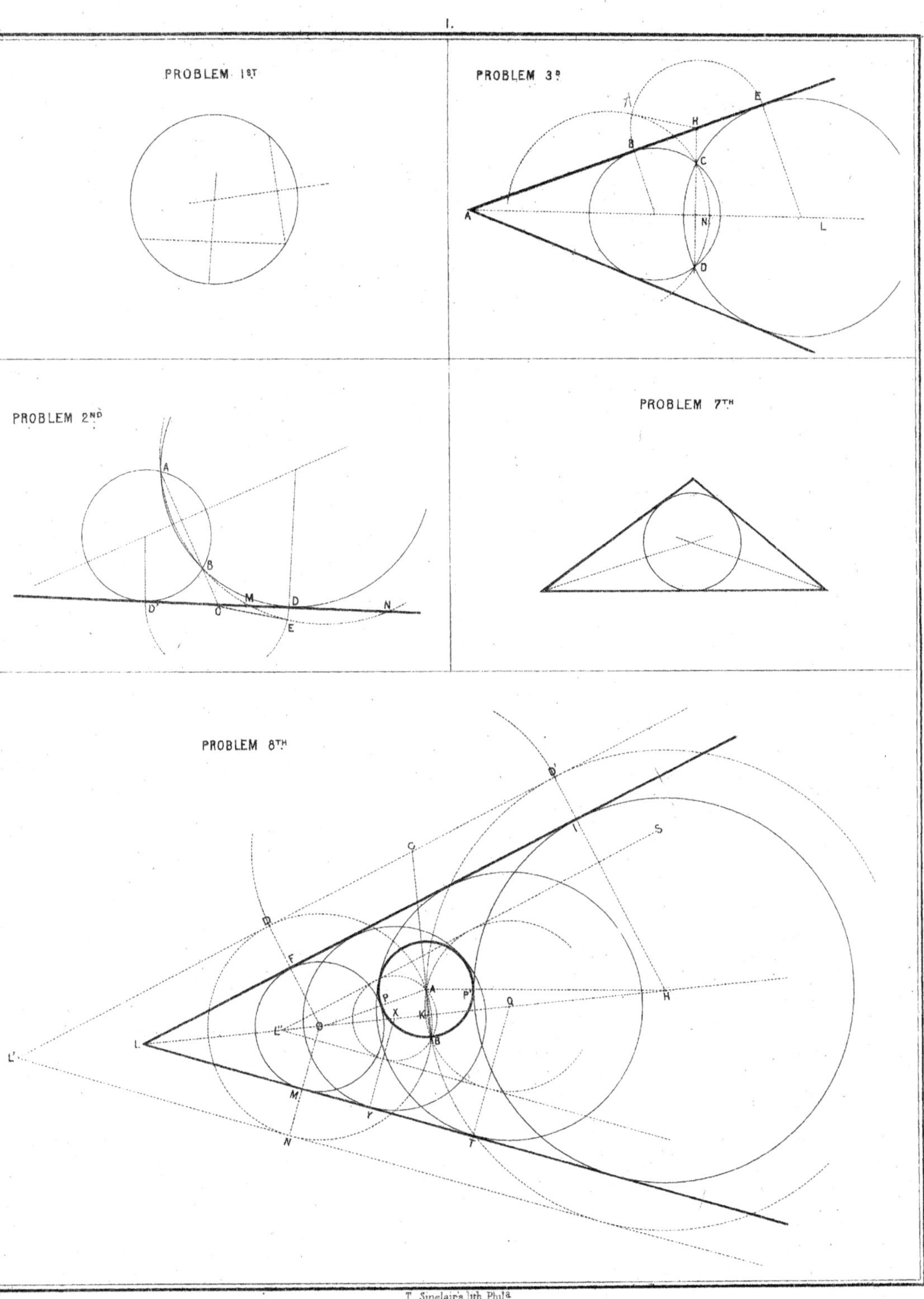
I.
PROBLEM 1ST
PROBLEM 3D
A
B
H
E
C
N
L
D
PROBLEM 2ND
A
B
M
D
D'
O
N
E
PROBLEM 7TH
PROBLEM 8TH
D'
I
S
G
D
F
A
P
P'
Q
H
X
K
L''
O
L
L'
B
M
Y
N
T
T. Sinclair's lith Phil^a

PROBLEM 4TH

To draw a circle through two points and tangent to a given circle.

Fig. 1st

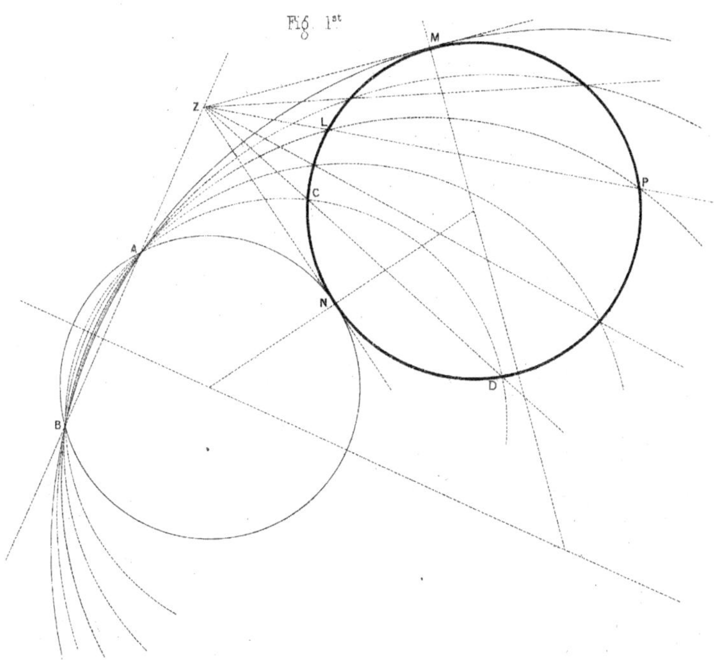

Fig. 2nd

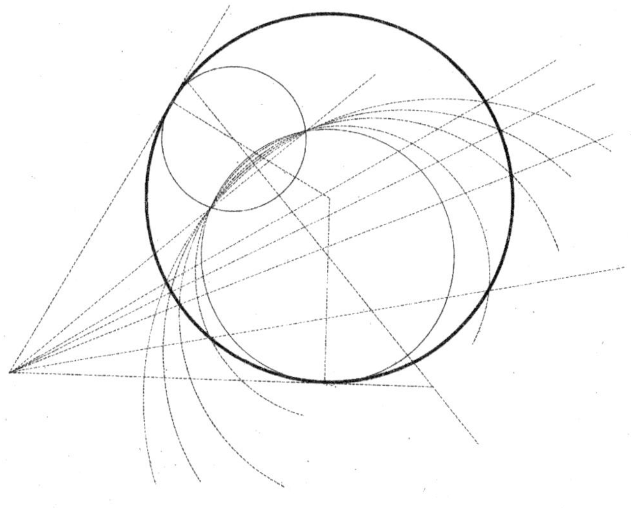

T. Sinclair's lith, Phila

PROBLEM 5TH

To draw a circle through a given point and tangent to a given right line and to a given circle.

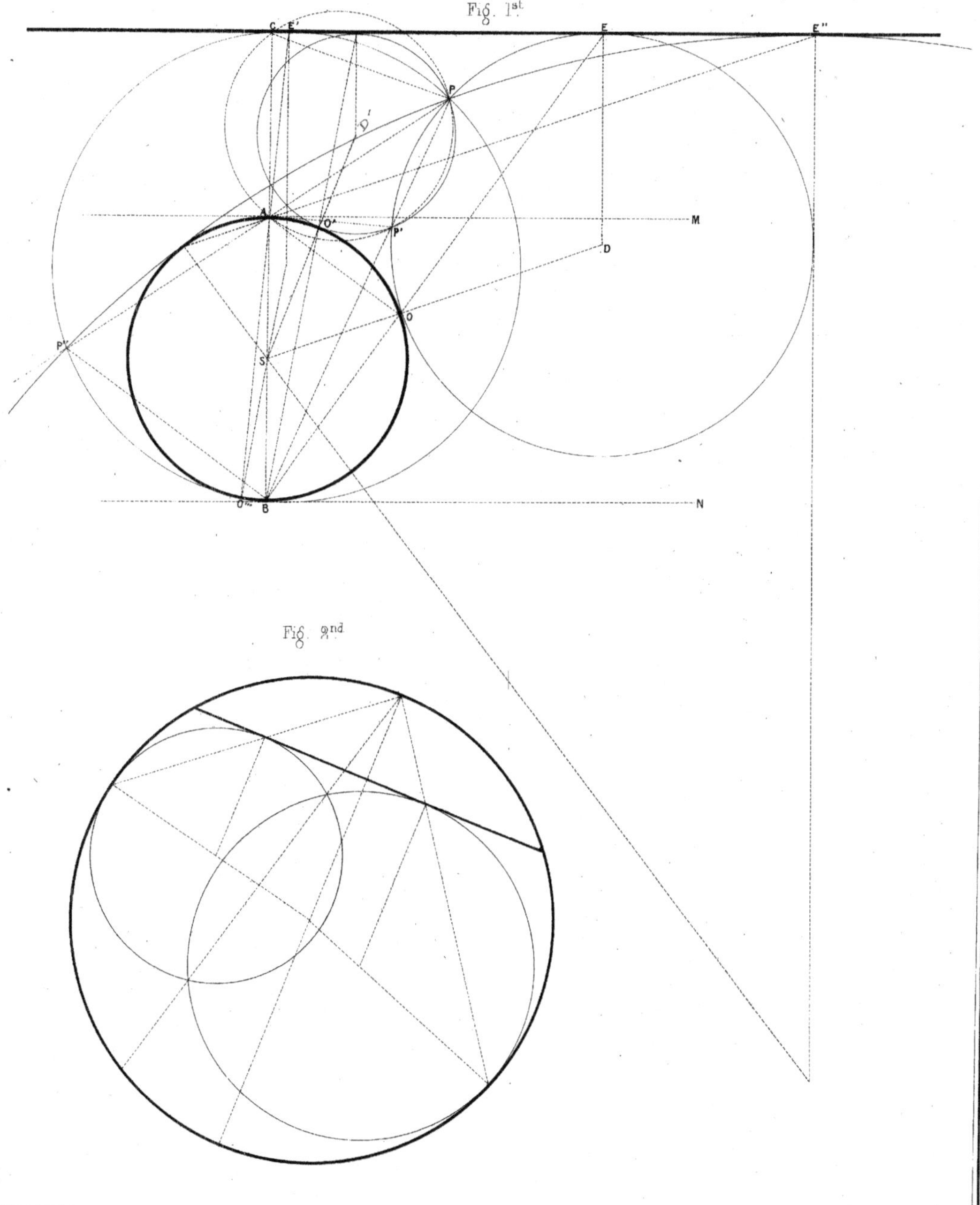

T. Sinclair's lith, Phila

PROBLEM 6TH

To draw a circle through a given point and tangent to two given circles.

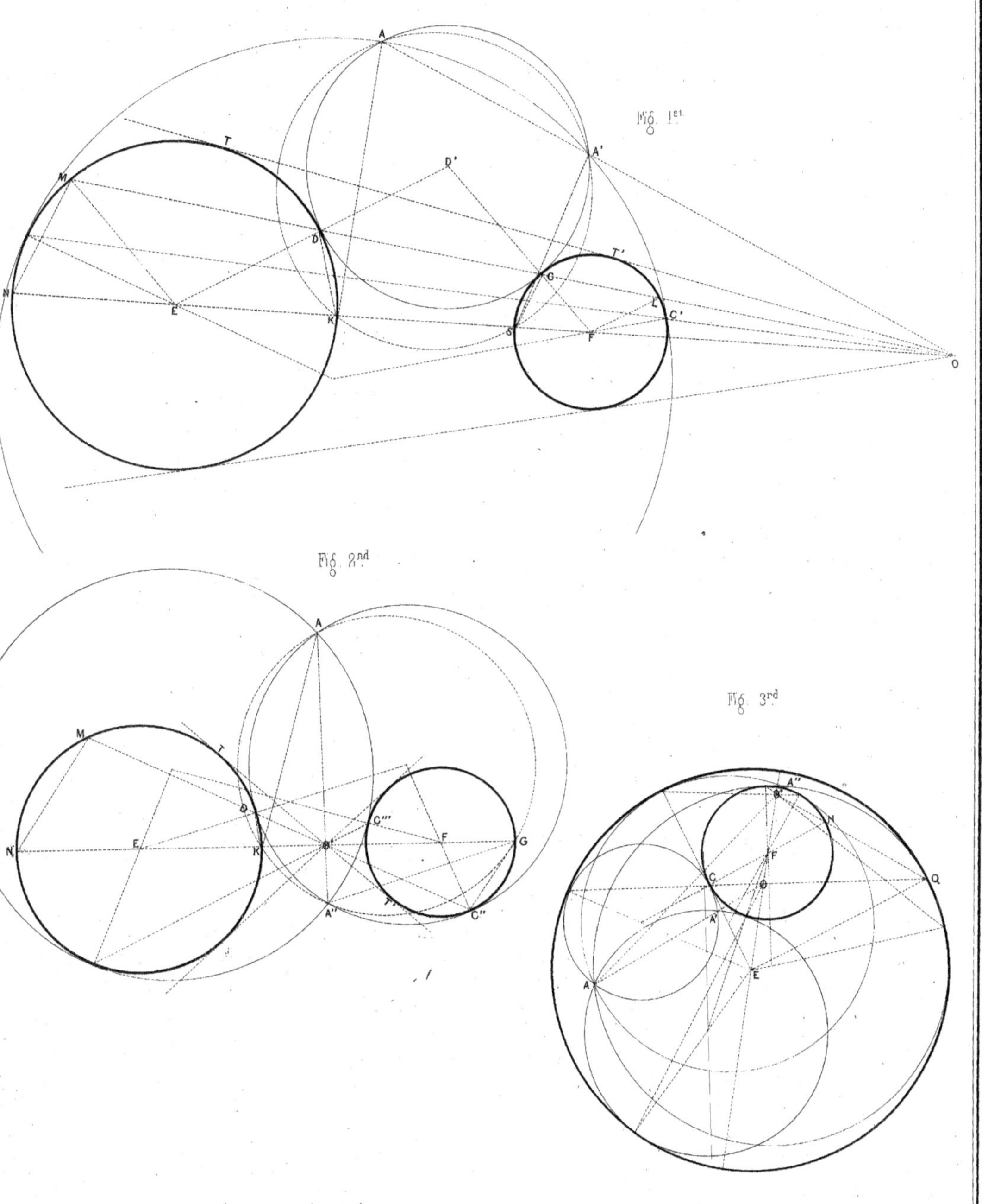

T. Sinclair lith. Phila.

PROBLEM 9TH

To draw a circle tangent to a given right line and to two given circles.

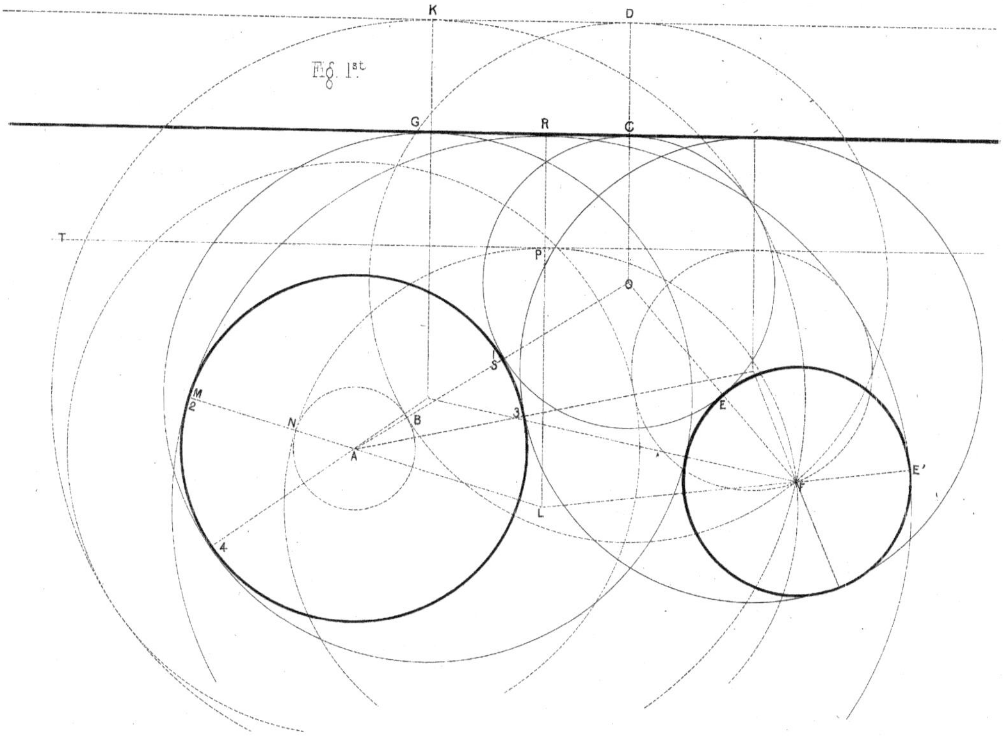

Fig. 1st

Fig. 2nd

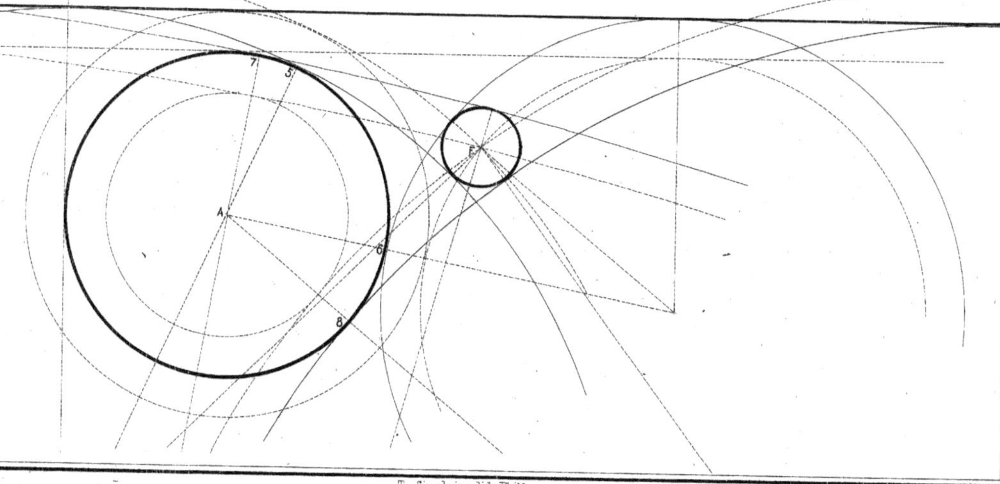

T. Sinclairs lith, Phila

PROBLEM 10TH

To draw a circle tangent to three given circles.

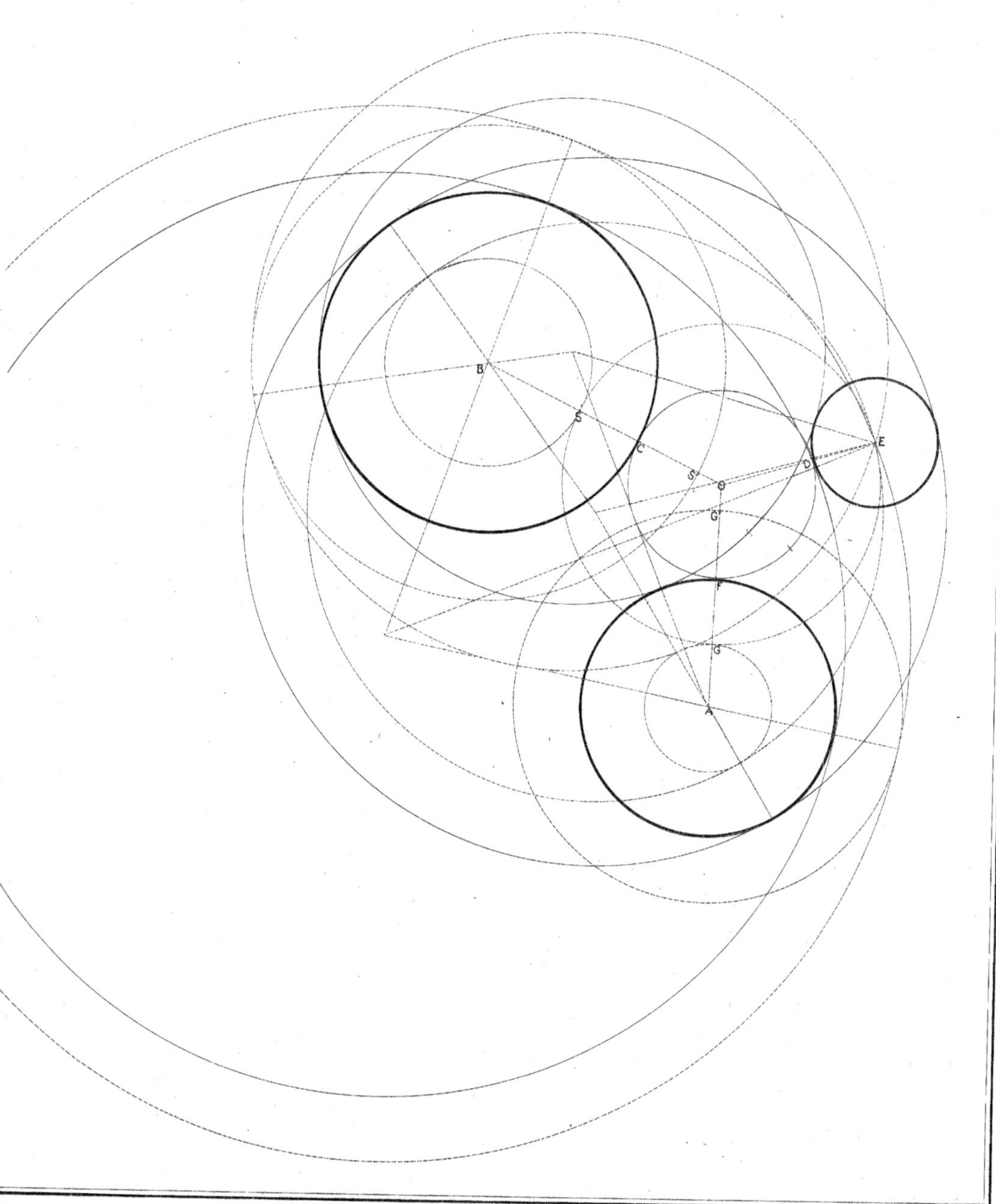

T. Sinclair's lith, Phila

T. Sinclair's lith, Phila.

Fig 1st

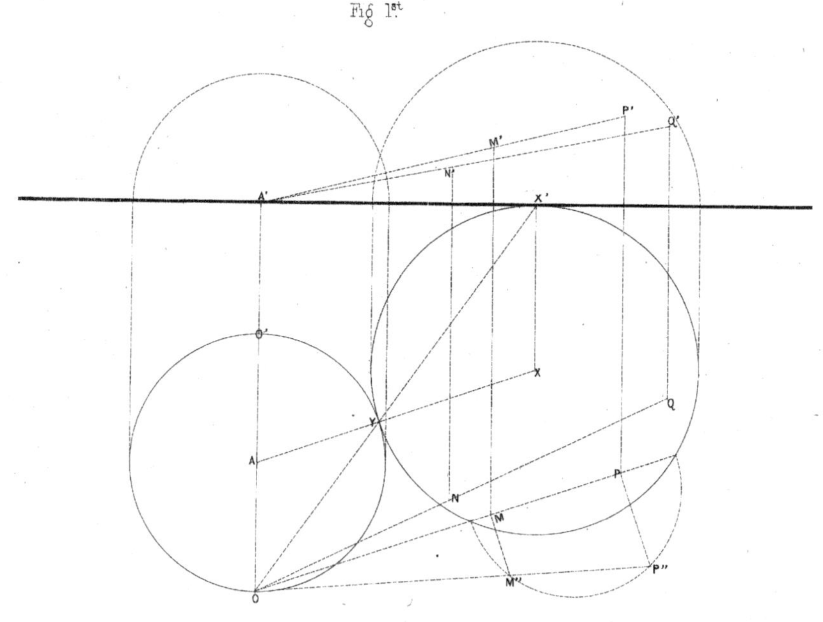

Fig. 2nd

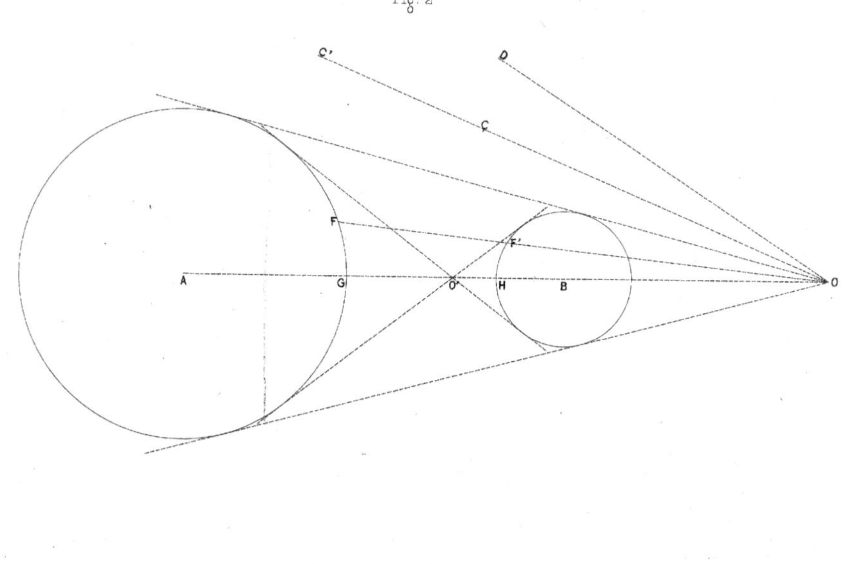

T. Sinclair's lith. Phila

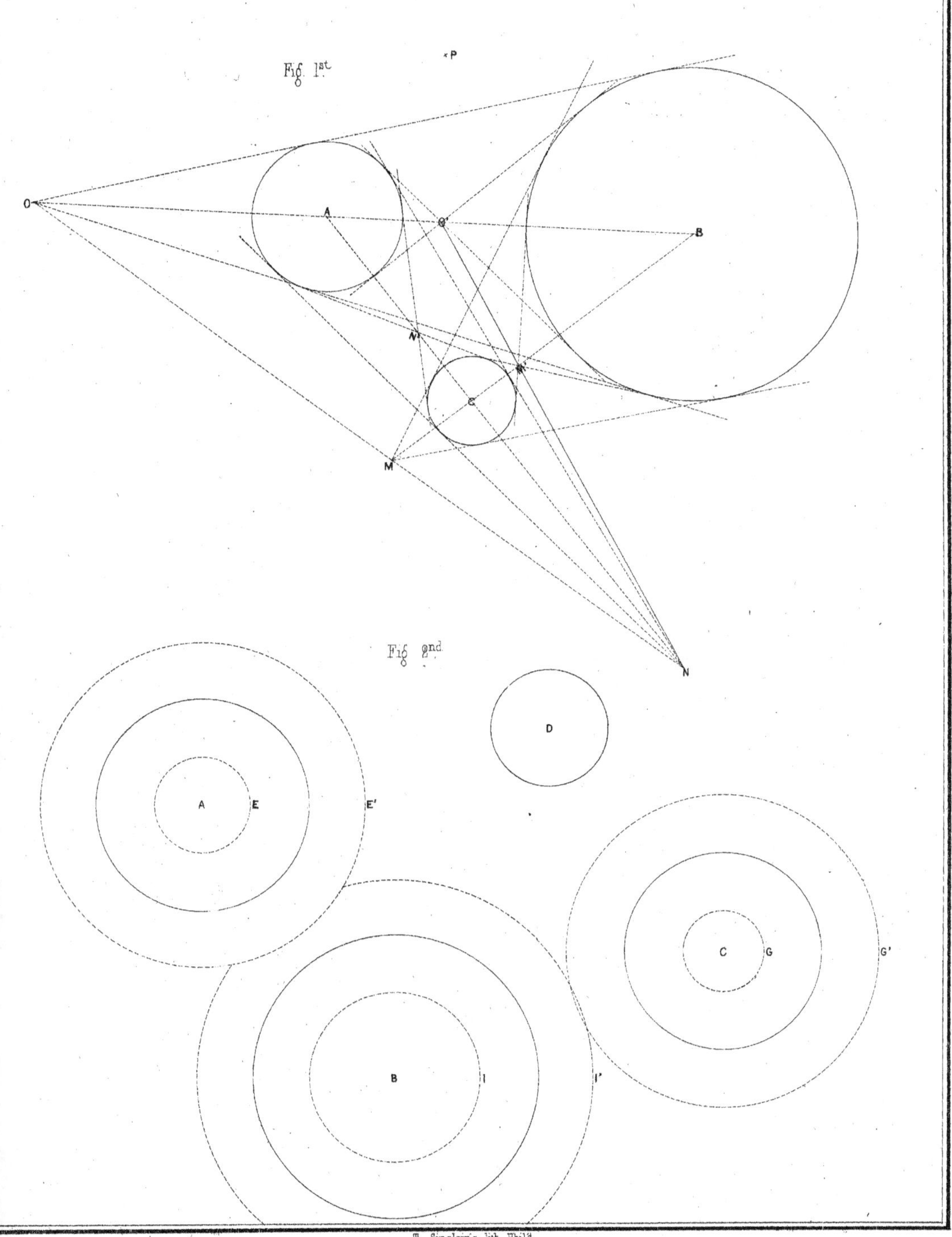

T. Sinclair's lith. Phil[a].

SMITHSONIAN CONTRIBUTIONS TO KNOWLEDGE.

INVESTIGATIONS,

CHEMICAL AND PHYSIOLOGICAL,

RELATIVE TO CERTAIN

AMERICAN VERTEBRATA.

BY

JOSEPH JONES, M.D.,

PROFESSOR OF CHEMISTRY IN THE SAVANNAH MEDICAL COLLEGE.

[ACCEPTED FOR PUBLICATION, MARCH, 1856.]

COMMISSION

TO WHICH THIS PAPER HAS BEEN REFERRED.

Samuel Jackson, M. D.,
Joseph Leidy, M. D.,
Jeffries Wyman, M. D.

Joseph Henry,
Secretary S. I.

T. K. AND P. G. COLLINS, PRINTERS,
PHILADELPHIA.

ANALYTICAL INDEX AND TABLE OF CONTENTS.

CHAPTER III.

CHAPTER IV.

CHAPTER V.

CHAPTER VI.

CHAPTER VII.

CHAPTER VIII.

CHAPTER IX.

CHAPTER X.

LIST OF TABLES.

LIST OF WOOD-CUTS.

INTRODUCTION.

The investigations recorded in the following pages were for the most part conducted in Liberty County, Georgia, where the author had opportunities of obtaining fresh specimens of vertebrata, living and dead, seldom enjoyed by observers. The researches, however, were necessarily attended with great labor and many embarrassments consequent upon the peculiar habits of the animals and the extreme difficulty of access, and miasmatic condition of their localities.

Owing to the extent and complexity of the topics discussed in this Memoir, the results presented must necessarily be very imperfect; and, in fact, are to be considered merely as contributions to science, to be continued and completed hereafter by the author, or by others who may have proper opportunities for so doing.

Whatever may be thought of the deductions and generalizations of the author, he is confident that the experiments which he has presented, and which have been made at so great an expense of time and labor, and which have involved so many sacrifices, will not be considered without value in throwing some light upon the important questions to which they pertain.

CHAPTER I.

METHOD EMPLOYED IN ANALYZING THE BLOOD.[1]

THE blood is a very complex fluid, and owing to the small quantity which, in most cases, can be obtained from the cold-blooded animals, it is difficult to determine all or even a majority of the constituents.

As, however, but little has been done in the study of the circulating fluid of cold-blooded animals, I deemed it important to ascertain even approximately the relative amounts of its principal constituents. The components of the blood which I have endeavored to determine, are the following, viz:—

The Water.
" Solid Constituents.
" Solid Portions of the Serum.
" Moist Corpuscles.
" Solid Parts of Moist Corpuscles.
" Water of Moist Corpuscles.

The Liquor Sanguinis.
" Water of Liquor Sanguinis.
" Solid Constituents of do.
" Albumen and Extractive Matter.
" Fibrin.
" Fixed Saline Constituents.

The following is a brief statement of the method employed in the analysis:—

(*a*.) From twenty-five to fifty grains of blood are received into a porcelain capsule, previously weighed.

(*b*.) A sp. gr. bottle, containing 100 grs. is filled with blood, if the animal be large enough to yield a sufficient quantity for this and other purposes.

(*c*.) The remainder of the blood is received into a porcelain capsule, previously weighed, and capable of containing about 500 grs.

In the majority of experiments with reptiles, small birds and small mammals, the blood is exhausted in filling the last vessel.

TREATMENT OF THE PORTION (*a*).

The weight of the capsule, with the blood, is carefully ascertained by means of a delicate balance, and subtracting from this the weight of the capsule, there remains the weight of the blood.

---

[1] Those who wish to investigate this subject further, will find much useful information in Simon's Chemistry of Man, p. 142, Philadelphia, 1846; Lehmann, Lehrbuch der Phys. Chemie (Lehmann's Physiological Chemistry, translated by G. E. Day, and edited by Prof. R. Rogers, Vol. I, pp. 541–648, Philadelphia, 1855); Bowman's Medical Chemistry, pp. 145–194, Philadelphia, 1850.

The capsule is then placed upon a chloride of calcium bath, and subjected to a temperature of from 220° to 230° F. until it ceases to lose weight. Subtracting the weight of the capsule from the last weight, we obtain the *amount of solid matter in the portion of blood under examination*, and subtracting the solid matter from the amount of blood employed, we ascertain the *amount of water*.

To ascertain the amount of *solid matter in* 1000 *parts of blood*, we use the following proportion :—

Weight of blood employed : Weight of dry residue : : 1000 : Proportion of solid matter in 1000 parts of the blood.

Having ascertained the solid matter in 1000 parts of blood, the amount of water may be determined by simply subtracting the solid matter from 1000.

The solid residue is next incinerated in a porcelain or platinum[1] crucible, until all the carbonaceous portion is consumed, and a light-red or yellow ash remains. A high heat and much care are indispensable in this process.

Another method, recommended by Dr. R. E. Rogers, Professor of Chemistry in the University of Pennsylvania, is to treat the dried residue with nitric acid, and gradually boiling down, incinerate the remainder. The organic matter readily dissolves in the hot nitric acid, and passes off in the form of gas.

The proportion of *fixed saline matter* in 1000 parts of blood may be calculated in the following manner :—

Weight of blood employed : Weight of ash after incineration : : 1000 : Proportion of fixed saline matter in 1000 parts of blood.

From this portion of blood, we have now obtained—

Water in 1000 parts.
Solid matter in 1000 parts.
Fixed saline matter in 1000 parts.

Treatment of the Portion (*b*).

The specific gravity of the blood is determined accurately with the balance. This should be done immediately after the porcelain capsule containing the blood is placed upon the chloride of calcium bath.

Treatment of the Portion (*c*).

The weight of the porcelain capsule, and the blood which it contained, is next ascertained; and, subtracting the weight of the capsule, we have remaining that of the blood. The blood is then to be set aside until it is completely coagulated, and the serum separated from the clot. The length of time required for this varies according to circumstances and the character of the animal.

The specific gravity of the serum is next to be ascertained by means of a specific gravity bottle holding one hundred grains. We then pour into a porcelain capsule (the weight of which has been previously noted), from ten to fifty grains

---

[1] For general purposes, a crucible of porcelain is to be preferred to one of platinum.

of serum, and evaporate upon the chloride of calcium bath until it ceases to lose weight. The *water, solid residue,* and *fixed saline constituents in* 1000 *parts of serum* may be ascertained in a manner exactly similar to that by which these ingredients were determined in 1000 parts of blood.

From the numbers now obtained, the proportion of *solid matters of the serum of* 1000 *parts of the blood* may be calculated in the following manner: Knowing the quantity of water in 1000 parts of blood, and assuming that this water exists wholly in the form of serum; knowing also the amount of water and solid matter contained in a given portion of serum; we may, from the quantity of water in the blood, estimate the quantity of solids held in solution in the serum, thus:—

$$\left\{\begin{array}{c}\text{Weight of water}\\ \text{in the quantity of}\\ \text{serum employed}\end{array}\right\} : \left\{\begin{array}{c}\text{Weight of solid}\\ \text{matter in the quantity}\\ \text{of serum employed}\end{array}\right\} :: \left\{\begin{array}{c}\text{Water in}\\ \text{1000 parts}\\ \text{of the blood}\end{array}\right\} \left\{\begin{array}{c}\text{Solids of serum}\\ \text{in 1000 parts}\\ \text{of the blood.}\end{array}\right.$$

This is not absolutely correct, and all physiological chemists have failed to ascertain, with absolute accuracy, the amount of solid matter in the serum of 1000 parts of blood. The error,[1] in the present state of our knowledge, is unavoidable.

The clot which remains after the removal of the serum, is next cut into thin slices, and inclosed in a muslin bag, and carefully washed under a stream of water until the fibrin remains in the bag free from serum and blood-corpuscles, and becomes almost colorless.

Another method of obtaining the fibrin, is to receive into a small glass bottle (capable of containing from two to four fluidounces) a portion of blood, and then dropping in some dozen small strips of lead, and closing with the stopper, agitate and shake until the fibrin coagulates around the lead strips. Two strong objections lie against the employment of this method in investigations upon cold-blooded animals. 1st. Their blood, in most cases, cannot be obtained in sufficient quantities. 2d. The fibrin, in most individuals, is so soft, that it will not coagulate around the lead strips. Neither of these methods is strictly correct. A portion of the fibrin is necessarily lost during the process of washing, and that which remains always contains colorless blood-cells and remains of colored cells.

The fibrin thus obtained is placed in a small evaporating dish, and dried upon the chloride of calcium bath, until it ceases to lose weight. If we wish still greater accuracy, the fatty and extractive matter may be removed by alcohol and ether, and, after complete drying, its weight is ascertained, and it is finally incinerated and the weight of the ash deducted. The proportion of fibrin in 1000 parts of blood may be determined by a simple proportion.

The amount of albumen and extractive matters in 1000 parts of blood may be determined by subtracting the saline matter of the serum of 1000 parts of blood, from the solid residue of the same.

From the third portion of blood (*c*), we have determined the following constituents:—

---

[1] Several physiological chemists have attempted, without success, to avoid this source of error, by determining absolutely the amount of blood-corpuscles.

Water in 1000 parts of serum.
Solid constituents in 1000 parts of serum.
Solid constituents in serum of 1000 parts of blood.
Albumen and extractive matters.
Fixed saline constituents in 1000 parts of serum.
Fibrin in 1000 parts of blood.

We have now sufficient data from which to calculate the *dried blood-corpuscles, moist blood-corpuscles*, and *liquor sanguinis*.

To ascertain the weight of the *dried blood-corpuscles*, add together the weights of the fibrin and the solids of the serum contained in 1000 parts of blood, and deducting the sum of them from the weight of the entire solid matter, which consists of fibrin, solids of the serum, and blood-corpuscles; the difference will represent the proportion of the latter in 1000 parts of blood.

Another method is founded upon the fact, that a solution of the sulphate of soda possesses the property of rendering the blood-corpuscles capable of being retained upon a filter. This method was first applied by Figuier, and afterwards improved by Dumas and Höfle. Defibrinated blood is treated with eight times its volume of a concentrated solution of Glauber's salts, and filtered, the residue on the filter is rinsed with the same solution, a stream of oxygen is passed through the mass of blood-cells on the filter, and, finally, the mass of blood-cells is either coagulated with hot water, upon the filter, or washed off into tepid water and coagulated by boiling.

This method is not to be depended upon in practice, because some of the blood-corpuscles always pass through the filter, and it is impossible to determine whether all the serum is actually separated in this manner, and also because the solution of the sulphate of soda passes into the corpuscles by endosmosis, whilst the organic constituents of the corpuscles pass out.

F. Simon's method of finding the quantity of the blood-corpuscles directly, is not only tedious, but also wanting in accuracy.

C. Schmidt, to whose intelligence and indefatigable researches physiological chemistry is indebted for many brilliant discoveries, first attempted to determine the relation of the moist blood-cells to the intercellular fluid, or liquor sanguinis. He found that 4 is the constant factor by which we may calculate the moist blood-cells from the dry blood-corpuscles. If we multiply the number of dry blood-corpuscles by 4, we obtain the quantity of fresh blood-cells. Subtracting these from 1000, we have remaining the amount of liquor sanguinis in 1000 parts of blood.

Having briefly described the method by which these important constituents are obtained, we will next state the manner in which the results are exhibited. The constituents of 1000 parts of blood are always presented in two lights.

1st. The fixed saline matter of the dried blood-corpuscles is subtracted from their weight, and we have remaining the dried organic matter of the blood-corpuscles in 1000 parts of blood. In like manner, the fixed saline constituents of the serum of 1000 parts of blood are subtracted from the solid matter of the serum of 1000 parts of blood, and we have remaining the dried organic portion of the albumen and extractive matter. It is evident that, if the analysis has been properly conducted, the sum of the water, dried organic matter of the blood-corpuscles, dried organic matter of the albumen and extractive matters, the fibrin, and fixed saline constituents will equal 1000.

2d. The relation of the moist blood-cells to the intercellular fluid, or liquor sanguinis, in 1000 parts of blood is represented separately.

The exhibition of the constituents of the blood in two different lights, enables us to comprehend more correctly its true constitution, and compare more readily the blood of different animals.

Without stopping to consider the various steps of caution and accuracy which would naturally suggest themselves to every careful observer, we will simply state that the balance used in all these investigations was reliable, and would, with proper care, indicate $\frac{1}{1000}$th of a Troy grain.

CHAPTER II.

BLOOD OF VERTEBRATE ANIMALS IN ITS NORMAL CONDITION.

Blood of Fishes.

1. *Trygon sabina*, Les. (female). Stingray. Aug. 14, 1855.

The appearance of the left uterus of this Ray, indicated that it had been delivered of young ones only a short time before its capture.

The appearance of the viscera and impregnated uterus of one of these fishes is represented in Fig. 19.

The portion of blood first drawn coagulated, in a few moments, into a dense, firm clot, which, in the course of an hour, commenced to dissolve, and in two hours, entirely disappeared. Another portion of blood, drawn subsequently, coagulated imperfectly, allowing the majority of the blood-corpuscles to settle to the bottom of the vessel, and, in the course of half an hour, the fibrin was completely dissolved.

Solid constituents in 1000 parts of blood	115.80

1000 parts of blood contained—

Water	884.20
Solid organic constituents	101.10
Fixed saline constituents	14.70

2. *Zygæna malleus*, Val. Hammerhead Shark. Sept. 10.

The blood coagulated imperfectly, allowing the blood-corpuscles to settle, and the fibrin, in the course of a few hours, was dissolved.

Solid constituents in 1000 parts of blood	138.86
" " " serum	70.96
" " in serum of 1000 parts of blood	65.50
Water in 1000 parts of blood	861.14
" " serum	929.31

1000 parts of blood contained—

Water	861.14
Blood-corpuscles (dried organic constituents)	70.24
Albumen, extractive and fatty matters (dried organic constituents)	60.24
Fibrin	Unstable, coagulating imperfectly, and readily dissolving
Fixed saline constituents	8.38
Fixed saline constituents of blood-corpuscles of 1000 parts of blood	5.26
" " solid matter of serum of 1000 parts of blood	3.12

1000 parts of blood contained—

Moist blood-corpuscles	293.44	Water	220.08
		Organic constituents	68.10
		Fixed saline constituents	5.26
Liquor sanguinis	706.56	Water	641.06
		Organic constituents	62.38
		Fixed saline constituents	3.12

3. *Lepisosteus osseus*, Linnæus. Salt-water Garfish.[1] Aug. 13.

In the southern part of Georgia, we have two species called garfish. The largest inhabits the salt-water rivers and Atlantic ocean, and the other our swamps and fresh-water canals of the rice-fields. The head and jaws of the former are much longer and more slender than those of the latter.

The viscera of the fresh-water species are represented in Fig. 11.

The blood coagulated in an imperfect manner, and, in the course of an hour, the fibrin dissolved and the blood-corpuscles settled to the bottom of the vessel, leaving the clear serum above. In one of the vessels, the blood scarcely coagulated, and the fibrin dissolved in twenty minutes.

It is characteristic of the blood of Fishes, that the arrangement of the atoms of albumen, so as to form fibrin, is very unstable. This instability and imperfection of the fibrin is indicative of a feeble state of the vital force, and, as a necessary consequence, of an imperfect condition of the organs which elaborate the blood.

Solid constituents in 1000 parts of blood	113.30
" " " serum	59.45
" " in serum of 1000 parts of blood	56.05
Water in 1000 parts of blood	886.70
" " serum	940.55

1000 parts of blood contained—

Moist blood-corpuscles	229.00	Water	171.75
		Solid constituents	57.25
Liquor sanguinis	771.00	Water	714.95
		Solid constituents	56.05

1000 parts of blood contained—

Water	886.70
Blood-corpuscles (dried organic constituents)	52.11
Albumen, extractive and fatty matters	50.92
Fibrin	Unstable, being readily dissolved and converted into albumen
Fixed saline constituents	10.27

Blood of Batrachians.

4. *Rana catesboeana*, Shaw. Bullfrog. July 30.

The stomach of this Batrachian contained several Crawfish (*Astacus Bartoni*), and a long slender Grass Snake (*Tropidonotus ordinatus*) about three feet in length. It

[1] This name, as well as some others, is used provisionally until a more critical examination shall have settled its precise synonymy.

had also swallowed, apparently along with the snake, a bunch of shank grass. Although this large frog had been captured for more than seventeen hours, and retained alive in water, the exterior part only of the body of the serpent showed the action of the gastric juice. The stomach contained none of the chyme so often referred to by writers on digestion. We have repeatedly examined the stomachs of Alligators, other Reptiles, and Fishes, and warm-blooded animals, during digestion, and we have never in any instance found a large amount of fluid either in the stomach or intestines. The products of digestion are absorbed almost as fast as they are formed.

The portions of blood first drawn coagulated more slowly than those drawn last. After the blood had flowed for a few moments, it coagulated as soon as it left the wound. The coagulum formed in the different portions of blood embraced most of the blood-corpuscles, and yielded clear serum.

In every instance, after standing for a few hours, the fibrin entirely disappeared, the clot was dissolved, and the blood-corpuscles set free.

The coagulum formed in the blood of the frog was firmer than that of Fishes, but not so firm as that of Serpents and Terrapins and the higher orders of vertebrate animals.

The color of the blood was purplish-red, intermediate between that of venous and arterial blood in Birds and Mammals.

The serum was of a light yellow color.

The strength of the Frog was exhausted more rapidly by the loss of blood than that of Serpents and Chelonians.

Solid constituents in 1000 parts of blood	167.49
" " " serum	61.93
" " in serum of 1000 parts of blood	54.96
Water in 1000 parts of blood	832.51
" " serum	938.07

1000 parts of blood contained—

Water	832.51
Blood-corpuscles (dried organic constituents)	108.68
Albumen, extractive and fatty matters	53.03
Fibrin	Unstable, readily convertible into albumen
Fixed saline constituents	5.78

1000 parts of blood contained—

Moist blood-corpuscles	450.12	Water	337.59
		Solid constituents	112.53
Liquor sanguinis	549.88	Water	494.92
		Solid constituents	54.96

Blood of Ophidians.

5. *Heterodon platyrhinos*, Latreille (female). Hog-nose Viper. June 8.

The alimentary canal was completely empty, and the rectum contained fæcal matter in small amount. All the blood that could be obtained with the greatest care was $33\frac{4}{10}$ grains.

From these facts, it is probable that the serpent had been without food for some days, and perhaps weeks. It had been captured only three days previous to the analysis.

From the small amount of blood yielded by this animal, it was impossible to determine the amount of fibrin.

Solid constituents in 1000 parts of blood	166.76
" " " serum	62.50
" in serum of 1000 parts of blood	55.55
Water in 1000 parts of blood	833.24
" " serum	937.50

1000 parts of blood contained—

Water	833.24
Blood-corpuscles and fibrin	102.22
Albumen, fatty and extractive matter	51.07
Fixed saline constituents	13.47

1000 parts of blood contained—

Moist blood-corpuscles	444.84	Water	333.63
		Solid constituents	111.21
Liquor sanguinis	555.16	Water	499.61
		Solid constituents	55.55

6. *Heterodon niger*, Catesby (female). Black Viper. May 21.
This reptile had been kept without food for more than two weeks.

Solid constituents in 1000 parts of blood	139.43
" " " serum	74.89
" in serum of 1000 parts of blood	69.67
Water in 1000 parts of blood	860.57
" " serum	925.11

1000 parts of blood contained—

Water	860.57
Blood-corpuscles (dried organic constituents)	64.07
Albumen, fatty and extractive matter	66.16
Fibrin	2.16
Fixed saline constituents	7.04

1000 parts of blood contained—

Moist blood-corpuscles	270.40	Water	202.80
		Solid constituents	67.60
Liquor sanguinis	729.60	Water	657.77
		Solid constituents	71.83

Amount of blood obtained . . . . 230 grains

7. *Psammophis flagelliformis*, Catesby (male). Coachwhip Snake. June 13.
This serpent is active and strong, and its movements, like those of the Black Snake (*Coluber constricttor*), are characterized by great swiftness. It had been confined without food for one day. Amount of blood obtained, 480 grains.

Specific gravity of its blood	1036
Solid constituents in 1000 parts of blood	181.70
" " " serum	65.78
" in serum of 1000 parts of blood	57.62
Water in 1000 parts of blood	818.30
" " serum	934.22

1000 parts of blood contained—

Water	818.30
Blood-corpuscles (dried organic constituents)	118.34
Albumen, fatty and extractive matter	55.91
Fibrin	1.88
Fixed saline constituents	5.57

1000 parts of blood contained—

Moist blood-corpuscles	488.80	Water	366.60
		Solid constituents	122.20
Liquor sanguinis	511.20	Water	451.70
		Solid constituents	59.50

8. *Coluber constrictor*, Linnæus (male). Black Snake. May 17.

This snake had been kept without food for ten days.

This is one of the swiftest and strongest of all our North American Ophidians. I have seen it attack the Rattlesnake, and sever the head almost completely from the body. In its habits, food, and swift motions, it resembles very much the Coach-whip Snake (*Psammophis flagelliformis*).

Amount of blood obtained	350 grains
Solid constituents in 1000 parts of blood	211.37
" " " serum	101.42
" in serum of 1000 parts of blood	89.01
Water in 1000 parts of blood	788.63
" " serum	898.58

1000 parts of blood contained—

Water	788.63
Blood-corpuscles (dried organic constituents)	112.22
Albumen, fatty and extractive matter	85.32
Fibrin	5.06
Fixed saline constituents	8.77

1000 parts of blood contained—

Moist blood-corpuscles	469.20	Water	351.90
		Solid constituents	117.30
Liquor sanguinis	530.80	Water	436.73
		Solid constituents	94.07

Blood of Saurians.

9. *Alligator Mississippiensis*, Daudin (female). Alligator. April 30.

The blood was abstracted a short time after the animal was shot in a small stream.

The reptile was remarkably fleshy, and the abdominal cavity, especially about the kidneys, was lined with fat.

The blood was much more abundant than in a male Alligator, which was captured in the same locality in the month of March, and kept without food or drink for three weeks. It also did not coagulate so rapidly.

From the starved Alligator, not more than three fluidounces of blood, with care, could be collected, the veins and arteries of the neck having been opened whilst the animal was living. Although the subject of experiment had been shot for half an hour, still the blood flowed from the jugular veins and carotid arteries in rapid streams, and more than ten fluidounces were readily obtained.

The hole of this Alligator was in the bank of a small stream, which flowed through an extensive salt marsh, abounding with small Fishes and Crustaceans. This reptile, therefore, was abundantly supplied with food.

Specific gravity of defibrinated blood	1046
Solid constituents in 1000 parts of blood	176.14
" " " serum	90.80
" in serum of 1000 parts of blood	82.05
Water in 1000 parts of blood	823.86
" " serum	909.20

1000 parts of blood contained—

Water	823.86
Blood-corpuscles (dried organic constituents)	86.39
Albumen	63.75
Fibrin	3.07
Water and alcohol extractive	9.26
Fatty matter	5.02
Fixed saline constituents	8.65

1000 parts of blood contained—

Moist blood-corpuscles	364.08	Water	273.06
		Solid constituents	91.02
Liquor sanguinis	635.92	Water	550.80
		Solid constituents	85.12

Blood of Chelonians.

10. *Chelonia caretta*, Linnæus. Loggerhead Turtle. July 20.

The blood was examined two days after its capture. During this time, it was kept in a tub of salt water, and supplied with small Fishes.

The blood first drawn coagulated more slowly than that drawn last.

Portions of the blood were placed in several vessels and allowed to coagulate; and, in every instance, the blood-corpuscles settled to the bottom of the vessel, leaving above a transparent clot.

When first abstracted, it was of a dark red color, not so black as venous, but much darker than the arterial blood of warm-blooded animals. This is readily explained when we consider that the venous and arterial blood is mixed in the ventricle of the heart.

The reaction of the blood was slightly alkaline.

Whilst taking the specific gravity of the serum, which had been separated from the clot for several hours, another small clot separated in the specific gravity bottle, having the characteristic appearance of fibrin.

The cavity of the abdomen contained half a fluidounce of clear serous fluid, which coagulated upon standing.

Specific gravity of the blood	1032.5
" " serum	1014.8
Solid constituents in 1000 parts of blood	120.81
" " " serum	49.44
" in serum of 1000 parts of blood	45.82
Water in 1000 parts of blood	879.19
" " serum	950.56

1000 parts of blood contained—

Water	879.19
Blood-corpuscles (dried organic constituents)	69.99
Albumen, fatty and extractive matter	44.63
Fibrin	2.61
Fixed saline constituents	3.58

1000 parts of blood contained—

Moist blood-corpuscles	289.52	Water	217.14
		Solid constituents	72.38
Liquor sanguinis	710.48	Water	662.05
		Solid constituents	48.43

11. *Chelonura serpentina*, Linnæus (male). Snapping Turtle. July 16.

The viscera of this Chelonian are represented in Fig. 8.

This reptile had been captured four days, during the greater portion of which time it was placed in water and supplied with Purslain (*Portulacca oleracea*).

The portions of blood drawn first coagulated more slowly than those drawn last. We have found this phenomenon to occur with all animals whose blood coagulated sufficiently slow to admit of a comparison of the times of coagulation. It appears to be an effort of nature to arrest hemorrhages. The manner in which the albumen of the blood is converted into fibrin is unknown. From the rapidity of the change during bleeding, it appears to have some connection with the nervous system. Whether it be due to nervous influence, or the action of the capillaries upon the albumen, or the mutual reactions between the corpuscular floating glands of the blood, remains to be demonstrated.

The coagulum was small and inconsistent.

The great majority of the blood-corpuscles settled to the bottom of the vessel, and were not included in the clot. In these respects, the blood of the *Chelonura serpentina* resembled that of Fishes and Frogs.

The serum was of a light yellow color, and, when treated with sulphuric acid and gently heated, the characteristic musky odor of the animal was developed.

Specific gravity of the blood	1025.5
" " serum	1013.6
Amount of blood obtained	700 grains

Solid constituents in 1000 parts of blood	105.00
" " " serum	48.68
" in serum of 1000 parts of blood . . .	45.80
Water in 1000 parts of blood	895.00
" " serum	951.32

1000 parts of blood contained—

Water	895.00
Blood-corpuscles (dried organic constituents)	56.37
Albumen, extractive and fatty matter	43.89
Fibrin	.35
Fixed saline constituents	4.39

1000 parts of blood contained—

Moist blood-corpuscles	235.40	Water	176.55
		Solid constituents . . .	58.85
Liquor sanguinis	764.60	Water	718.45
		Solid constituents . . .	46.15

12. *Emys Terrapin*, Schœpff (female). Salt-water Terrapin. July 3. This terrapin had been captured twelve hours.

Specific gravity of its blood	1035.3
" " serum	1012.7

The serum was of a golden color, resembling that of the *Emys serrata* and *Emys reticulata*.

Amount of blood obtained, about	1000 grains
Solid constituents in 1000 parts of blood	154.72
" " " serum	43.83
" in serum of 1000 parts of blood . . .	38.75
Water in 1000 parts of blood	845.28
" " serum	956.17

1000 parts of blood contained—

Water	845.28
Blood-corpuscles (dried organic constituents)	103.82
Albumen, fatty and extractive matter	36.01
Fibrin	4.15
Fixed saline constituents	10.74

1000 parts of blood contained—

Moist blood-corpuscles	447.28	Water	335.46
		Solid constituents . . .	111.82
Liquor sanguinis	552.72	Water	509.82
		Solid constituents . . .	42.90

13. *Emys reticulata*, Bosc. Chicken Tortoise. June 6.

This Chelonian was captured in a pine-barren, and kept without food or drink for thirty-six hours.

The portions of blood first drawn coagulated more slowly than those last drawn. This is universally the case with the blood of cold-blooded animals.

The serum was of a bright orange color.

The alimentary canal was empty as far as the colon. The rectum and colon contained the claws and shells of small crustaceans, and the seeds of berries.

Specific gravity of the blood	1034
Solid constituents in 1000 parts of blood	153.02
" " " serum	63.58
" in serum of 1000 parts of blood	57.51
Water in 1000 parts of blood	846.98
" " serum	936.42

1000 parts of blood contained—

Water	846.98
Blood-corpuscles (dried organic constituents)	88.01
Albumen, fatty and extractive matter	54.71
Fibrin	2.51
Fixed saline constituents	7.79

1000 parts of blood contained—

Moist blood-corpuscles	372.00	Water	279.00
		Solid constituents	93.00
Liquor sanguinis	628.00	Water	567.98
		Solid constituents	60.02

14. *Emys serrata*, Daudin (female). Yellow-bellied Terrapin. May 26.

This terrapin was taken in a swamp and kept out of the water, without food, for three and a half days.

The first portion of blood drawn was placed in a small beaker glass, and coagulated so slowly that the blood-corpuscles sank to the bottom of the vessel, and a transparent clot floated above. This was not the case in the portions abstracted subsequently.

The serum was of a bright golden color, and, when kept for twelve hours, partially coagulated, resembling jelly.

Specific gravity of the blood	1026.5
" " serum	1013.7
Solid constituents in 1000 parts of blood	124.59
" " " serum	43.03
" in serum of 1000 parts of blood	39.36
Water in 1000 parts of blood	875.41
" " serum	956.97

1000 parts of blood contained—

Water	875.41
Blood-corpuscles (dried organic constituents)	80.67
Albumen, fatty and extractive matter	37.66
Fibrin	1.04
Fixed saline constituents	5.22

1000 parts of blood contained—

Moist blood-corpuscles	336.76	Water	252.57
		Solid constituents	84.19
Liquor sanguinis	663.24	Water	622.84
		Solid constituents	40.40

15. *Testudo Polyphemus*, Daudin (male). Gopher. June 23.

This Gopher had been kept for five days, during which time it was abundantly supplied with vegetable food.

When the neck was cut, the blood flowed in a jet with considerable force, as from a severed artery of a warm-blooded animal.

This animal is remarkable for its muscular powers. It required all the force that I could exert with my arms to draw its head out of the shell. The adult will frequently support, and move about with a full-grown man upon their backs.

They live in troops in pine-barren countries, and subsist entirely upon vegetable substances. Their intestinal canal is modified so as to contain large stores of nutritive matters. The appearance of their viscera is represented in Fig. 9. By comparing this with the viscera of a carnivorous Chelonian, as the Snapping Turtle (*Chelonura serpentina*), Fig. 8, we see the modifications by which the alimentary canal is adapted to the habits and food of animals.

The shell of the Gopher is much softer, and its bony structure much thinner and imperfect, even to old age, than that of other Terrapins, as the *Emys serrata*. The shell of young Gophers is composed almost entirely of a material resembling horn, and contains little or no osseous matter. This is due to the character of their food, which contains the fixed alkaline and earthy salts in much less amount than animal food.

The serum was of a light yellow color, differing from the bright golden color of the serum of the *Emys serrata*, *Emys reticulata*, and *Emys Terrapin*. When treated with a drop of sulphuric acid and gently heated, the peculiar smell of the animal, similar to that of a Sheep, was developed.

Amount of blood obtained	2500 grains
Specific gravity of its blood	1030
" " serum	1018
Solid constituents in 1000 parts of blood	156.62
" " " serum	66.41
" in serum of 1000 parts of blood	60.00
Water in 1000 parts of blood	843.38
" " serum	933.59

1000 parts of blood contained—

Water	843.38
Blood-corpuscles (dried organic constituents)	87.28
Albumen, fatty and extractive matter	57.78
Fibrin	5.73
Fixed saline constituents	5.83

1000 parts of blood contained—

Moist blood-corpuscles	393.56	Water	302.67
		Solid constituents	90.89
Liquor sanguinis	606.44	Water	540.71
		Solid constituents	65.73

Blood of Birds.

16. *Ardea Nycticorax*, Linnæus (female). Night Heron. June 12.

This bird had its wing broken, and was also wounded in the neck, where some blood had been extravasated into the cellular tissue. The blood was drawn about two hours after its capture.

Specific gravity of the blood	1028
Solid constituents in 1000 parts of blood	127.11
" " " serum	50.00
" in serum of 1000 parts of blood	45.95
Water in 1000 parts of blood	872.89
" " serum	950.00

1000 parts of blood contained—

Water	872.89
Blood-corpuscles (dried organic constituents)	74.91
Albumen, fatty and extractive matter	43.41
Fibrin	2.20
Fixed saline constituents	6.59

1000 parts of blood contained—

Moist blood-corpuscles	315.84	Water	236.88
		Solid constituents	78.96
Liquor sanguinis	684.16	Water	636.01
		Solid constituents	48.15

17. *Syrnium nebulosum*, Linnæus. Barred Owl. May 14.

This bird had been shot in the eye, wing, and other parts of the body, and kept without food for twenty-four hours.

Solid constituents in 1000 parts of blood	160.34
" " " serum	54.94
" in serum of 1000 parts of blood	48.81
Water in 1000 parts of blood	839.66
" " serum	945.06

1000 parts of blood contained—

Water	839.66
Blood-corpuscles (dried organic constituents)	101.08
Albumen, fatty and extractive matter	46.51
Fibrin	4.69
Fixed saline constituents	8.06

1000 parts of blood contained—

Moist blood-corpuscles	427.36	Water	320.52
		Solid constituents	106.84
Liquor sanguinis	572.64	Water	519.14
		Solid constituents	53.50

18. *Cathartes atratus*, Wils. Black Turkey-Buzzard. Sept. 8.

The blood had a strong, disagreeable, musky odor, similar in all respects to that of the bird itself. When the serum was treated with sulphuric acid and gently heated, this smell was developed with great power.

The odor of the Turkey-buzzard is not only disagreeable in the extreme, but also lasts for a great length of time. It was difficult to remove it from the hands, and my laboratory was fumigated for a considerable length of time after this analysis.

The serum, like that of several Terrapins, was of a bright orange color.

The fibrin was unusually soft and inconsistent, and much of it dissolved during the process of washing.

Solid constituents in 1000 parts of blood	200.83
" " " " serum	51.85
" " in serum of 1000 parts of blood . . .	43.70
Water in 1000 parts of blood	799.17
" " serum	948.15

1000 parts of blood contained—

Water	799.17
Blood-corpuscles (dried organic constituents)	150.47
Albumen, fatty and extractive matters	41.62
Fibrin	.41
Fixed saline constituents	8.33

1000 parts of blood contained—

Moist blood-corpuscles	626.88	Water	470.16
		Solid constituents . . .	156.72
Liquor sanguinis	373.12	Water	329.01
		Solid constituents . . .	44.11

The number of the analyses of the blood of Birds which have been published is very limited. The following analyses of the blood of the Goose and Hen were made by Nasse:—

	Water.	Blood-corpuscles.	Albumen and extractive matter.	Fibrin.	Fat.	Soluble salts.	Insoluble salts.
Goose . . .	814.88	121.45	50.78	3.46	2.56	6.87	1.09
Hen . . .	793.24	144.75	48.25	4.67	2.03	6.97	1.82

The following analyses of the blood of domestic Birds were made by Dumas and Prevost:—

	Water.	Solid constituents.	Blood-corpuscles.	Residue of serum.
Raven	797.0	203.0	146.6	56.4
Heron	808.2	191.8	132.6	59.2
Duck	765.2	234.8	150.1	84.7
Hen	779.9	220.1	157.1	63.0
Pigeon	797.4	202.6	155.7	46.9

Blood of Mammals.

19. *Common Cur-Dog.* June 28.

Previously to this analysis, the dog had been poorly fed, principally upon vegetable food.

The blood coagulated rapidly; the clot was large, and the relative amount of serum small. After standing for several hours, 400 grains of blood yielded not more than 40 grains of serum suitable for analysis.

The serum was transparent, but of a bright red color.

Specific gravity of the blood	1043.6
Solid constituents in 1000 parts of blood	188.13
" " " serum	128.95
" in serum of 1000 parts of blood	120.18
Water in 1000 parts of blood	811.87
" " serum	871.05

1000 parts of blood contained—

Water	811.87
Blood-corpuscles (dried organic constituents)	62.72
Albumen, fatty and extractive matter	116.33
Fibrin	3.04
Fixed saline constituents	6.04

1000 parts of blood contained—

Moist blood-corpuscles	263.64	Water	197.73
		Solid constituents	65.91
Liquor sanguinis	736.36	Water	613.14
		Solid constituents	123.22

20. *Common Cur-Dog*, used in the preceding analysis. August 7th.

For a week previous to this analysis, the dog was supplied with more mutton than he could devour. Upon this diet of animal food, he became very fat and fleshy in a few days.

The blood coagulated in a few moments after it left the body.

Specific gravity of the blood	1045.5
" " serum	1030.5
Solid constituents in 1000 parts of blood	193.48
" " " serum	119.67
" in serum of 1000 parts of blood	109.64
Water in 1000 parts of blood	806.52
" " serum	880.33

1000 parts of blood contained—

Water	806.52
Blood-corpuscles (dried organic constituents)	78.04
Albumen, fatty and extractive matter	106.18
Fibrin	3.15
Fixed saline constituents	6.11

1000 parts of blood contained—

Moist blood-corpuscles	322.76	Water	242.07
		Solid constituents . . .	80.69
Liquor sanguinis	677.24	Water	564.45
		Solid constituents . . .	112.79

Andral, Gavarret, and Delafond, made no less than 222 analyses of the blood of 155 Mammals. The following results of their investigations may be compared with my analyses of the blood of cold-blooded animals.

		Water.	Blood-corpuscles.	Residue of serum.	Fibrin.
Blood of 17 Horses	Mean	810.5	102.9	82.6	4.0
	Maximum	833.3	112.1	91.0	5.0
	Minimum	795.7	81.5	74.6	3.0
Blood of 14 Cattle	Mean	810.3	99.7	86.3	3.7
	Maximum	824.9	117.1	93.6	4.4
	Minimum	799.0	85.1	82.9	3.0
Blood of 19 Sheep (Rambouillet breed)	Mean	815.3	98.1	83.5	3.1
	Maximum	830.3	109.6	96.6	3.8
	Minimum	808.7	82.5	74.7	2.6
Blood of 11 Sheep (cross variety)	Mean	810.8	106.1	80.3	2.8
	Maximum	827.2	123.4	87.7	3.4
	Minimum	789.8	94.6	74.7	2.3
Blood of 13 English Sheep . .	Mean	810.8	95.0	92.4	2.6
	Maximum	822.1	110.4	97.0	3.3
	Minimum	795.3	83.8	82.6	2.0
Blood of 6 English Swine . .	Mean	809.6	105.7	80.1	4.6
	Maximum	816.9	120.6	88.7	5.0
	Minimum	793.9	92.1	73.6	4.1
Blood of 2 Goats	Mean	804.0	101.4	91.4	3.2
	Maximum	809.2	105.7	92.0	3.5
	Minimum	798.8	97.2	90.8	2.6
Blood of 16 Dogs	Mean	774.1	148.3	75.5	2.1
	Maximum	795.5	176.6	88.7	3.5
	Minimum	744.6	127.3	60.9	1.6

The following are the analyses of the blood of different Mammals made by Nasse. The extractive matter and insoluble salts of the blood are included with the albumen.

	Water.	Blood-corpuscles.	Albumen.	Fat.	Fibrin.	Soluble salts.
Horse	804.75	117.13	67.85	1.31	2.41	6.82
Ox	799.59	121.86	66.90	2.04	3.62	5.98
Calf	826.71	102.50	56.41	1.61	5.76	7.00
Goat	839.44	86.00	62.70	0.91	3.90	7.04
Sheep	827.76	92.42	68.77	1.16	2.97	6.91
Rabbit	817.30			1.90	3.80	6.28
Swine	768.94	145.35	72.78	1.95	3.95	6.74
Cat	810.02	113.39	64.46	2.70	2.42	7.01
Dog	790.50	123.85	65.19	2.25	1.93	6.28

Dumas and Prevost analyzed the blood of numerous animals. The method of analysis which they employed was similar, in some respects, to that of Andral,

Gavarret, and Delafond. The fibrin, however, was not determined. The following are the results which they obtained with the blood of the Mammals:—

	Water.	Solid constituents.	Blood-corpuscles.	Solid matter of serum.
Ape (*Simia callitriche*) .	776.0	224.0	146.1	77.9
Dog	810.7	189.3	123.8	65.5
Cat	795.3	204.7	120.4	84.3
Horse	818.3	181.7	92.0	89.7
Calf	826.0	174.0	91.2	82.8
Sheep	829.3	170.7	93.5	77.2
Goat	814.6	185.4	102.0	83.4
Rabbit	837.9	162.1	93.8	68.3
Guinea-pig . . .	784.8	215.2	128.0	87.2

Having examined in detail the blood of cold and warm-blooded animals in a normal condition, we shall next compare the individual results and analyses together, and endeavor to point out the characteristic distinctions of the blood of these two great classes of animals.

Amount of Blood existing in the Bodies of Warm and Cold-blooded Animals in a Normal State.

In determining the amount of blood, several methods have been employed by different chemists and physiologists.

M. Valentin[1] adopted the following ingenious mode:—

Having weighed the animal, he abstracted a definite amount of blood, determined its solid constituents, and then injected a given quantity of distilled water into the bloodvessels. Time was allowed for the diffusion of this by the circulatory apparatus throughout the mass of the blood. A fresh portion of blood was then abstracted, and the amount of solid matters determined. The relation between the amount of solid matters in the blood first drawn and the blood diluted with a given quantity of distilled water, enabled him to calculate the quantity of the entire blood of the animal.

Although this method is sufficiently accurate for general purposes, still the following objections have been urged against it with justice.

The water injected is not diffused uniformly throughout the mass of blood. This is determined by the fact that the blood drawn from different veins yields different proportions of water and solid matters. When an excess of water is injected into the circulatory system, it has a tendency to lodge in certain organs, as the kidneys and spleen, and in a less degree in the lungs. Other circumstances affect the accuracy of the results; as the loss of blood in any of the steps of the operation, the elimination of the water by evaporation from the surface of the lungs and skin, and by the action of the kidneys, and exosmose into the surrounding tissues in the interval of time between the injection of the water and the abstraction of the second portion of blood.

[1] Rept. der Physiol., Bd. s. 281–293.

If, however, the experiment be carefully performed, without allowing any loss of blood, or too great a length of time to elapse between the injection of the water and the abstraction of the second portion of blood, results approaching very nearly to the truth may be obtained.

Another method has been suggested, dependent for its accuracy upon the fact that iron exists only in the blood-corpuscles and hair, and consequently when the latter is shaved off, it will be found only in the former.

A definite portion of blood is abstracted, and the proportion of iron determined. The whole animal is then burned, the ashes collected, and the amount of iron ascertained. By a comparison of this with the amount existing in a definite quantity of blood, the whole amount of blood may be determined. This method, if practicable, promises accurate results.

Another method, proposed by Lehmann,[1] is founded upon the fact that only a definite amount of grape sugar can exist in the blood at any one time, without its elimination by the kidneys.

Having ascertained how much grape sugar the blood may normally contain under favorable circumstances, the quantity of blood contained in an animal may be calculated by ascertaining the quantity of sugar which must be introduced into the circulatory fluid in order to make it pass into the urine.

The methods of Valentin and Lehmann might be applicable to warm-blooded animals, whose circulation is rapid, and whose excretions and secretions are correspondingly abundant. They are, however, wholly inapplicable to cold-blooded animals.

In the first place, the circulation in this class is sluggish, and the blood, owing to the peculiarities of the structure of the circulatory apparatus, is not diffused uniformly to all the organs and tissues, as in the higher animals. In the second place, the secretions and excretions are exceedingly slow, and small in amount. Many animals of this class do not void their urine more than once in a month during starvation, and then in exceedingly small quantities. In many the bladder is absent, and where it does exist, even supposing that the urine was rapidly excreted, owing to the structure and position of the urinary apparatus, it is next to impossible to draw off the contents of the bladder.

From these considerations, then, it would be utterly impossible to determine the amount of blood in cold-blooded animals, by injecting into the circulatory system either water or grape sugar.

The method, also, of determining the quantity of blood from the relative proportion of iron in a definite amount of blood and in the ash of the whole body, would also, in many animals of this class, be absolutely impossible. The Chelonians,

---

[1] Lehmann's Physiological Chemistry, translated by G. E. Day, Amer. edit., Philad., 1855, I, 639.

Other methods of determining the amount of blood have been proposed, but not practised, by the following physiologists: Vogel, Pathol. Anat. des menchl. Körpers, Leipz., 1845, s. 59 (or English translation, p. 84). Dumas, Chim. Physiol. et Med., Paris, 1848, p. 326. Weisz, Zeitsch. d. k. k. Gesellsch. d. Aertze, Dec. 1847, s. 203–229.

are provided with such an enormous external skeleton, that the errors in the calculation of the amount of iron in this would be numerous.

The only practical method which I was able to devise, was, to cut the jugular veins and arteries, and, stretching the neck out, hold the body perpendicular, with the head downwards. The contraction of the heart, bloodvessels, and capillaries, aided by gravity, expelled very nearly all the blood; a fact which was often proved by the thin, watery aspect of the last portions.

This method is more accurate in cold than warm-blooded animals, because their nervous and muscular system, requiring but little nutriment from the blood, the heart continues to beat, and the muscles, bloodvessels, and capillaries to contract, for hours after almost all the blood has been abstracted. In warm-blooded animals, the heart ceases to beat, and the contractility of the muscular system is lost, when not more than one-third of the blood has been abstracted. This method, then, which I employed to determine the amount of blood in cold-blooded animals, should not be condemned because it is not applicable to warm-blooded animals.

Great discrepancies have prevailed amongst physiologists with regard to the amount of blood contained in the bodies of warm-blooded animals.

Blumenbach estimated the quantity in an adult man at 8.5 to 11 pounds, and Reil at 44 pounds.

M. Valentin, by his method of injecting water, arrived at the following results. The numbers represent the relation existing between the quantity of blood and the weight of the body.

Large Dogs (the mean of four experiments)	as 1 : 4.5
A lean, debilitated Sheep	as 1 : 5.02
Cats, female (the mean of two experiments)	as 1 : 5.78
A large female Rabbit	as 1 : 6.20

From these data, he estimated the amount of human blood to be

Male sex	as 1 : 4.36
Female sex	as 1 : 4.93

At the present day, the blood is generally estimated at 22 pounds, which is equal to about the eighth part of the weight of the body.

Lehmann[1] determined the amount of blood in the bodies of two criminals, who were decapitated, to be from 17.5 to nearly 19 pounds, or one-eighth the weight of their bodies.

From numerous careful examinations of cold-blooded animals, by the method previously described, I have arrived at the following results, which must be considered only as an approximation to the truth.

Amount of blood in Serpents . . .	$\frac{1}{18}$ to $\frac{1}{13}$	of the weight of body.	
" *Emys terrapin* . .	$\frac{1}{11}$ to $\frac{1}{14}$	"	"
" *Emys serrata* . .	$\frac{1}{13}$ to $\frac{1}{16}$	"	"
" *Testudo polyphemus* . .	$\frac{1}{14}$ to $\frac{1}{17}$	"	"

[1] Loc. cit., p. 638.

Our investigations have shown that *the blood is far less abundant in cold than in warm-blooded animals.*

This fact is important, because it will aid us in the investigation of many of the phenomena of cold-blooded animals, and in the explanation of the differences which distinguish the two great classes of animals.

Color of the Blood and Serum.

The arterial blood of cold-blooded animals is never of that bright red color of the arterial blood of warm-blooded animals, on account of the mixture of the arterial and venous blood in the common ventricle of the heart. For the same reason, the venous blood is not of so dark a color as that of warm-blooded animals.

The color of the serum in most Reptiles—as Ophidians, Batrachians, Fishes—and some Chelonians—as the Gopher (*Testudo polyphemus*)—is of a light yellow color.

In many carnivorous Terrapins—as the Yellow-belly Terrapin (*Emys serrata*), Chicken Terrapin (*Emys reticulata*), and Salt-water Terrapin (*Emys terrapin*)—the serum is of a golden color.

In most Birds and Mammalia which I have examined, the serum is of a light yellow color. In the Black Turkey-buzzard (*Cathartes atratus*), it is of a golden color.

Odor of Animals.

The strong smell of both cold and warm-blooded animals appears to reside especially in the serum, and may be developed by treating the serum with a little sulphuric acid, and applying a gentle heat. I have demonstrated this fact in numerous instances, and often in the serum of disagreeable animals, with disgusting power. The odor of animals is also due, as in the Alligator and Rattlesnake, to peculiar glands. The secretion of the anal gland of the Rattlesnake emits such a powerful and disagreeable odor, that it may produce giddiness of the head and sickness of the stomach.[1]

Specific Gravity of the Serum and Blood.

These results were accurately determined upon the balance used in all my analyses, which, as we have before stated, was capable of indicating $\frac{1}{1000}$th of a grain.

---

[1] In dissecting a large male Rattlesnake (*Crotalus durissus*), I accidentally cut the anal gland, and the odor was so peculiar, heavy, and disgusting, and exerted such an effect upon the head, that it was with the greatest difficulty that the dissection and drawing were completed.

Table of the Specific Gravities of the Blood and Serum of Animals.

Name of observer.	Name of animal.	Sp. gr. of blood.	Sp. gr. of serum.
Jos. Jones	*Psammophis flagelliformis* (Coachwhip Snake)	1036.0	
"	*Alligator Mississippiensis* (Alligator)	1046.0	
"	*Chelonia caretta* (Loggerhead Turtle)	1032.5	1014.8
"	*Chelonura serpentina* (Snapping Turtle)	1025.5	1013.6
"	*Emys terrapin* (Salt-water Terrapin)	1035.3	1012.7
"	*Emys reticulata* (Chicken Tortoise)	1034.0	
"	*Emys serrata* (Yellow-bellied Terrapin)	1026.5	1013.7
"	*Emys serrata* (Yellow-bellied Terrapin)	1029.6	1014.0
"	*Testudo polyphemus* (Gopher)	1030.0	1018.0
"	*Testudo polyphemus* (Gopher)	1037.0	1017.0
"	Common Cur-Dog	1043.0	
"	Common Cur-Dog	1045.5	1030.5
Becquerel and Rodier	Pregnant Women — Mean	1051.5	1025.5
	Pregnant Women — Maximum	1055.1	1026.8
	Pregnant Women — Minimum	1046.2	1023.6
"	20 human beings, mean	1055.0	1026.1
"	10 human beings, mean	1056.0	
"	11 Men, mean	1060.2	1028.0
"	8 Females, mean	1057.5	1027.4
Lehmann	Human	1057.4	1028.0

From this table we learn that *the blood becomes more concentrated as the organs, and apparatus, and intelligence of animals are developed.*

Table showing the Amounts, in 1000 parts, of the Water and Solid Matters of the Blood and Serum of different Animals.

COLD-BLOODED ANIMALS.

BLOOD OF INVERTEBRATE ANIMALS.

Name of observer.	Name of animal.	Water in 1000 parts of blood.	Solid matter in 1000 parts of blood.	Water in 1000 parts of serum.	Solid matter in 1000 parts of serum.	Solid matter in serum of 1000 parts of blood.
C. Schmidt	*Anodonta cygnea* (Pond Mussel)	999.146	0.854			0.565
Harless & Bibra	*Helix pomatia* (Shell Snail)	985.482	14.518			8.398
" "	*Loligo and Eledone* (Cephalopods)	992.67	7.33			4.70
	BLOOD OF VERTEBRATE ANIMALS.					
	Fishes.					
Jos. Jones	*Trygon sabina* (Stingray)	884.20	115.80			
"	*Zygæna malleus* (Hammerhead Shark)	861.14	138.86	929.31	70.96	65.50
"	*Lepisosteus osseus* (Garfish)	886.70	113.30	945.55	59.45	56.05
J. F. Simon	Carp	872.00	128.00			83.85
"	Tench	900.00	100.00			68.80
Dumas & Prevost	Trout	863.70	136.30			72.50
" "	Eelpout	886.20	113.80			65.70
" "	Eel	846.00	154.00			94.00
	Aquatic Reptiles					
Jos. Jones	*Rana catesbæana* (Bullfrog)	832.51	167.49	938.07	61.93	54.96
Dumas & Prevost	Frog	884.60	115.40			46.40
Jos. Jones	*Chelonia caretta* (Loggerhead Turtle)	879.19	120.81	950.56	49.44	45.82
"	*Chelonura serpentina* (Snapping Turtle)	895.00	105.00	951.32	48.68	45.80
"	*Emys terrapin* (Salt-water Terrapin)	845.28	154.72	956.17	43.83	38.75
"	*Emys reticulata* (Chicken Tortoise)	846.98	153.02	936.42	63.58	57.51
"	*Emys serrata* (Yellow-bellied Terrapin)	875.41	124.59	956.97	43.03	39.36
"	*Alligator Mississippiensis* (Alligator)	823.86	176.14	909.20	90.80	82.05
	Land Reptiles.					
J. F. Simon	*Bufo variabilis*	848.20	151.80			112.33
Jos. Jones	*Heterodon platyrhinos* (Hog-nose Viper)	833.24	166.76	937.50	62.50	55.55
"	*Heterodon niger* (Black Viper)	860.57	139.43	925.11	74.89	69.67
"	*Psammophis flagelliformis* (Coachwhip Snake)	818.30	181.70	934.22	65.78	57.62
"	*Coluber constrictor* (Black Snake)	788.63	211.37	898.58	101.42	89.01
"	*Testudo polyphemus* (Gopher)	843.38	156.62	933.59	66.41	60.00

WARM-BLOODED ANIMALS.

BLOOD OF BIRDS.

Name of observer.	Name of animal.	Water in 1000 parts of blood.	Solid matters in 1000 parts of blood.	Water in 1000 parts of serum.	Solid matters in 1000 parts of serum.	Solid matters in serum of 1000 parts of blood.
Nasse	Goose	814.88	185.12			55.78
"	Hen	793.24	206.76			53.25
Dumas & Prevost	Hen	779.90	220.10			63.00
" "	Pigeon	797.40	202.60			46.90
" "	Duck	765.20	234.80			84.70
" "	Raven	797.00	203.00			56.40
" "	Heron	808.20	191.80			59.20
Jos. Jones	*Ardea nycticorax* (Heron)	872.89	127.11	950.00	50.00	45.95
"	*Syrnium nebulosum* (Hooting Owl)	839.66	160.34	945.06	54.94	48.81
"	*Cathartes atratus* (Black Turkey-buzzard)	799.17	200.83	948.15	51.85	43.70

BLOOD OF MAMMALS.

Name of observer.	Name of animal.	Water in 1000 parts of blood.	Solid matters in 1000 parts of blood.	Water in 1000 parts of serum.	Solid matters in 1000 parts of serum.	Solid matters in serum of 1000 parts of blood.
Andral, Gavarret, and Delafond	17 Horses, Mean	810.50	189.50			82.60
	17 Horses, Maximum	833.30	204.30			91.00
	17 Horses, Minimum	795.70	166.70			74.60
Nasse	Horse	804.75	195.25			70.85
Dumas & Prevost	Horse	818.30	181.70			89.70
Andral, Gavarret, and Delafond	14 Cattle, Mean	810.30	189.70			86.30
	14 Cattle, Maximum	824.90	201.00			93.60
	14 Cattle, Minimum	799.00	175.10			82.90
Nasse	Ox	799.59	200.41			69.90
Dumas & Prevost	Calf	826.00	174.00			82.80
Andral, Gavarret, and Delafond	30 Sheep, mean	813.50	186.50			82.40
Nasse	Swine	768.94	231.06			75.78
"	Rabbit	817.30	182.70			68.30
Dumas & Prevost	Rabbit	837.90	162.10			
" "	Goat	814.60	185.40			83.40
Nasse	Goat	839.44	160.56			65.70
Andral, Gavarret, and Delafond	16 Dogs, mean	774.10	225.90			75.50
Nasse	Dog	790.50	209.50			68.19
Dumas & Prevost	Dog	810.70	189.30			65.50
Jos. Jones	Common Cur-Dog	811.87	188.13	871.05	128.95	120.18
"	Common Cur-Dog	806.52	193.48	880.33	119.67	109.64
Dumas & Prevost	Cat	795.30	204.70			84.30
Nasse	Cat	810.02	189.98			68.46
M. Lecanu	Man, Maximum	853.135	221.37			78.27
	Man, Minimum	778.625	146.86			57.89
	Man, Mean	815.880	184.12			68.08

A careful comparison of these results leads to the following conclusions:—

1. The proportion of water is greatest in the Invertebrata. The blood of these animals has, according to Genth, a specific gravity not many degrees above that of common water.

2. Amongst vertebrate animals, the amount of water existing in the blood is greatest in Fishes and Aquatic Reptiles, and least in Serpents, Birds, and Mammals. As a necessary consequence, the solid matters of the blood are least in the Invertebrata, Fish, and Aquatic Reptiles, and greatest in Serpents, Birds, and Mammalia.

3. *It may be laid down as a general law, that as the organs and apparatus of the animal are developed, and the temperature and intellect correspondingly increased, the blood becomes richer in organic constituents.*

The blood of serpents appears, at first sight, to form an exception. The large amount of solid constituents, however, existing in their blood, is readily accounted for, when we consider their habits. These Reptiles seldom or never drink water; consequently, the fluids of their bodies are derived from the animals which they consume. In all animals, the water of the blood and tissues is continually evaporating from the surface of the lungs and body. The amount of evaporation is in proportion to the structure, habits, and temperature of the animal, and the temperature and moisture of the atmosphere. It is greatest in warm-blooded animals, and in hot and dry climates. Amongst cold-blooded animals, it is greatest in those having naked skins, and least in those covered by scales, bone, and horn. No matter how slow and small this evaporation, if it be not counteracted by a corresponding supply of water, the blood necessarily becomes concentrated, and yields a larger proportion of solid constituents upon analysis.

4. Our knowledge is as yet too limited to develop any laws respecting the amount of water and solid materials which characterize the blood of each species and genus. By comparing the analysis of the blood of the Mammalia, we see that the proportions of its constituents vary as much in individuals of the same species as in individuals of remotely separated genera.

Table of the Moist Blood-corpuscles and Liquor Sanguinis in 1000 *parts of Blood.*

Observer.	Name of animal.	MOIST BLOOD-CORPUSCLES.			LIQUOR SANGUINIS.		
		Blood-corpuscles.	Water.	Solid matters.	Liquor sanguinis.	Water.	Solid matters.
Jos. Jones	*Zygæna malleus* (Shark) . . .	293.44	220.08	73.36	706.56	641.06	65.50
"	*Lepisosteus osseus* (Garfish) . .	229.00	171.75	57.25	771.00	714.95	56.05
Dumas & Prevost	Trout	275.20	206.40	68.80			
" "	Eelpout	192.40	144.30	48.10			
" "	Eel	240.00	180.00	60.00			
Jos. Jones	*Rana pipiens* (Bullfrog) . . .	450.12	337.59	112.53	549.88	494.92	54.96
Dumas & Prevost	Frog	276.00	207.00	69.00			
Jos. Jones	*Heterodon platyrhinos* (Hog-nose Viper)	444.84	333.63	111.21	555.16	499.61	55.55
"	*Heterodon niger* (Black Viper) .	270.40	202.80	67.60	729.60	657.77	71.83
"	*Psammophis flagelliformis* (Coach-whip Snake)	488.80	366.60	122.20	511.20	451.70	59.50
"	*Coluber constrictor* (Black Snake) .	469.20	351.90	117.30	530.80	436.73	94.07
"	*Chelonia caretta* (Turtle) . .	289.52	217.14	72.38	710.48	662.05	48.43
"	*Chelonura serpentina* (Alligator Cooter)	235.40	176.55	58.85	764.60	718.45	46.15
"	*Emys terrapin* (Salt-water Terrapin)	447.28	335.46	111.82	552.72	509.82	42.90
"	*Emys reticulata* (Chicken Terrapin)	372.00	279.00	93.00	628.00	567.98	60.02
"	*Emys serrata* (Yellow-belly Terrapin)	336.76	252.57	84.19	663.24	622.84	40.40
"	*Testudo polyphemus* (Gopher) . .	393.56	302.67	90.89	606.44	540.71	65.73
"	*Alligator Mississippiensis* (Alligator)	364.08	273.06	91.02	635.92	550.80	85.12
Nasse	Goose	485.80	364.35	121.45			
"	Hen	579.00	434.25	144.75			
Dumas & Prevost	Hen	628.40	461.30	157.10			
" "	Duck	600.40	450.30	150.10			
" "	Pigeon	622.80	467.10	155.70			
" "	Raven	586.40	339.80	146.60			
" "	Heron	530.40	367.80	132.60			
Jos. Jones	*Ardea nycticorax* (Heron) . .	315.84	236.88	78.96	684.16	636.01	48.15
"	*Syrnium nebulosum* (Hooting Owl) .	427.36	320.52	106.84	572.64	519.14	53.50
"	*Cathartes atratus* (Black Buzzard) .	626.88	470.16	156.72	373.12	329.01	44.11
Andral, Gavarret, and Delafond	17 Horses { Mean	411.60	308.70	102.90			
	17 Horses { Maximum . . .	448.40	336.30	112.10			
	17 Horses { Minimum . . .	326.00	244.50	81.50			
Nasse	Horse	468.52	351.39	117.13			
Andral, Gavarret, and Delafond	30 Sheep, mean	404.40	303.30	101.10			
Nasse	Sheep	369.68	277.26	92.42			
Andral, Gavarret, and Delafond	14 Cattle { Mean	398.80	299.10	99.70			
	14 Cattle { Maximum . . .	468.40	351.30	117.10			
	14 Cattle { Minimum . . .	340.40	255.30	85.10			
" "	6 Swine, English breed, mean . .	422.80	317.10	105.70			
" "	16 Dogs { Mean	593.20	444.90	148.30			
	16 Dogs { Maximum . . .	706.40	529.80	176.60			
	16 Dogs { Minimum . . .	509.20	387.90	121.30			
Jos. Jones	Common Cur-Dog	363.64	197.73	65.91	736.36	613.14	125.22
"	Common Cur-Dog	322.76	242.07	80.69	677.24	564.45	112.79

The following general facts and conclusions have been derived from a careful comparison of the results contained in this table, and those derived from our previous investigations.

In the Invertebrata, the number of blood-corpuscles is very small in comparison with the number which exists in the blood of the Vertebrata. In this class, we find only colorless corpuscles.

In the *Branchiostoma* or *Amphioxus*, the connecting link between the highest orders, the Mollusca and Fishes, the blood, like that of the Invertebrata, is described as containing only colorless corpuscles, and exceedingly rich in water, and correspondingly poor in solid constituents.

As the organs and apparatus are developed, the blood is correspondingly improved.

The increased development of the cerebro-spinal system, and the organs of vertebrate animals, is attended by a corresponding increase in the solitary gland-cells of the blood.

In this class, the number of blood-corpuscles is, as a general rule, least in cold-blooded animals, and greatest in Birds and Mammals. There are, however, exceptions to this rule. I have found the number of blood-corpuscles in some cold-blooded animals, especially Serpents, higher than that of some Birds and Mammals.

The following table will illustrate this fact:—

Name of observer.	Name of animal.	Blood-corpuscles in 1000 parts of blood.
Jos. Jones	*Rana catesbæana* (Bullfrog)	450.12
"	*Emys terrapin* (Salt-water Terrapin) . . .	447.28
"	*Alligator Mississippiensis* (Alligator) . . .	364.08
"	*Heterodon platyrhinos* (Hog-nose Viper) . .	444.84
"	*Psammophis flagelliformis* (Coachwhip Snake) .	488.80
"	*Coluber constrictor* (Black Snake) . . .	469.20
"	*Ardea nycticorax* (Heron)	315.84
"	*Syrnium nebulosum* (Hooting Owl) . . .	427.36
Andral, Gavarret, and Delafond	Horse	326.20
Dumas and Prevost . .	Horse	368.00
" " . .	Goat	408.00
Nasse	Goat	344.00
Jos. Jones	Cur-Dog	363.64
"	Cur-Dog	322.76
Dumas and Prevost . .	Dog	495.20
" " . .	Calf	364.80

Notwithstanding the differences in the number of blood-corpuscles, the differences of temperature were preserved, not only between the warm and cold-blooded animals, but also between the individual species of each class.

The thermometer indicated a temperature of over 100° in the Heron, having only 364.08 parts of blood-corpuscles, whilst in the Frog, Serpents, and Chelonians, having nearly double the number of blood-corpuscles in a given quantity of blood, the thermometer indicated a temperature several degrees below that of the surrounding medium.

Several physiologists assert that the sole office of the blood-corpuscles is to carry oxygen in, and convey carbonic acid gas out of the animal economy. If this be true, the temperature of an animal would, at first sight, seem to be determined, in great measure, by the number of its blood-corpuscles; but the temperature also depends upon the velocity of transfer of the oxygen, and consequently upon the rapidity of the circulation. Many facts, however, might be brought forward, to prove that the office of the blood-corpuscles is not solely the introduction of oxygen, and the carrying out of carbonic acid. The following facts will show that the liquor sanguinis is also active in the performance of these important offices.

In the capillaries and bloodvessels, the colored corpuscles rush along in the centre of the streams, whilst pure liquor sanguinis alone is in contact with the walls of the vessels. In the capillaries of the lungs, the oxygen, from this arrangement, must necessarily be absorbed first by the liquor sanguinis. Again, in no case do we find the organic cells, the active agents in all secretion and excretion, in immediate contact with the blood-corpuscles. They are separated from them by the coats of the capillaries, and a structureless basement membrane. The same is true of the anatomical elements of the muscular tissue. From whence do they derive oxygen, a continuous supply of which is absolutely necessary for the life and activity of every living molecule of organized beings? The same argument will also prove that the blood-corpuscles are not the sole agents in the conveyance of carbonic acid gas out of the organs and tissues.

These conclusions can be sustained by numerous examples.

Do we find blood-corpuscles in plants? Do we find blood-corpuscles in the lowest orders of invertebrate animals? These bodies absorb oxygen, and give out carbonic acid gas, notwithstanding the absence of blood-corpuscles. Spallanzani[1] has long since demonstrated that all organized bodies, whether living or dead, possess the property of absorbing oxygen and giving out carbonic acid gas.

We do not for one moment deny that one important office of the blood-corpuscles is the absorption of gases, for it has been often demonstrated that blood containing its corpuscles possesses far greater powers of absorbing oxygen, nitrogen, and carbonic acid than pure serum. We wish to show that this is not the sole office of the blood-corpuscle, because it is performed by the liquor sanguinis, and all organic matters, whether living or dead; and respiration is carried on in plants and the lowest animals, which are without blood-corpuscles; and an increase in the number of blood-corpuscles is not necessarily followed by an increase in the temperature.

What, then, are the principal offices of the blood-corpuscles, and what does an increase in their numbers denote?

These questions can only be answered by a consideration of their constitution, and their relations with the liquor sanguinis by which they are surrounded.

Each corpuscle is a cell, resembling, in its nutrition, growth, and general structure, the active agents in the formation, elaboration, and separation of all secretions and excretions. Their cell walls possess the property of separating from the surrounding medium certain peculiar organic and mineral compounds. If a blood-corpuscle be placed in water, it swells up, and finally bursts. If it is placed in a solution denser than its internal contents, they pass out more rapidly than the exterior solution passes in, and the cell wall shrivels up. The same physical laws of endosmose are at work in the animal economy. A mutual action and reaction is incessantly carried on between the interior contents of the blood-corpuscles and the exterior liquor sanguinis. Whenever water, or liquids of low specific gravity,

---

[1] Memoirs on Respiration, by Lazarus Spallanzani. Edited by John Lenebier. London, 1805.

are introduced into the circulatory system, they dilute the serum, and immediately there is an endosmose of the less dense fluid into the denser contents of the corpuscles. Whenever water is withheld, the liquor sanguinis continually loses this element by evaporation from the surface of the lungs and skin, and by the action of the kidneys, becomes denser than the contents of the corpuscles, and exosmose takes place into the surrounding medium. The cell-wall modifies the physical and chemical properties of every molecule of liquor sanguinis that passes through its structure.

The researches of C. Schmidt have shown that the fluid contents of the blood-corpuscles contain, in addition to peculiar organic matters, a preponderance of the phosphates and potash salts; whilst the liquor sanguinis contains the chloride of sodium in large amount, with a little chloride of potassium and phosphate of soda.

In the blood-cells, the fatty acids and globulin are combined both with potash and soda; whilst in the plasma, the organic materials are combined only with soda. The researches of Liebig, confirmed by those of Schmidt, have shown that the fluid contained in the tubules of muscles is, like that of the blood-corpuscles, exceedingly rich in the phosphates and potash salts. The phosphates also exist in large amount in the brain.

These facts render it highly probable that the office of the blood-corpuscles, taken collectively, is that of an immense gland, which separates and elaborates from the liquor sanguinis those organic and inorganic compounds which constitute the most important part of the structure of the muscles and brain.

In the Mammalia, we have an increase not only by weight, but also an immense increase in numbers of the blood-corpuscles, owing to their greatly diminished size, and the amount of secreting surface exposed to the intercellular fluid is correspondingly increased. This being the case, the blood of these animals must be more highly elaborated, and all their organs and apparatus correspondingly developed.

In the present state of our knowledge, notwithstanding the numerous theories which have been ably advocated by different physiologists and anatomists, we are still ignorant of the exact mode of origin of the blood-corpuscles.

Structure of the Blood-corpuscles.

There is a great want of accordance in the descriptions of the structure of the colored blood-corpuscle, and its action under different chemical reagents. Some of the highest authorities are opposed to each other in their statements. I shall confine myself merely to the results of my own observations.

The size and form of the blood-corpuscle vary with the animal. In most of the Mammalia, they are biconcave circular discs.

In Birds, Reptiles, and Fishes, they are biconvex, ellipsoidal, or rounded discs. In the Shovel-nosed Shark (*Zygæna malleus*) and the Loggerhead Turtle (*Chelonia caretta*), they are very nearly of a circular form.

In all adult Mammals—as Dogs, Cats, Raccoons, Squirrels, Deer, Sheep, Moles, &c.—which I have examined, a nucleus is absent.

In Birds, Reptiles, and Fishes, a nucleus is always present. The convexity of the blood-corpuscle in these animals is due to the internal nucleus. When viewed edgewise, as they roll over, this central prominence is rendered evident, standing out from the flattened disc.

The action of acetic acid shows that the exterior cell-wall is connected at the centre with the interior nucleus. The first action of acetic acid, which is almost instantaneous, is to reverse the shape of the blood-corpuscles. They become expanded around the periphery, whilst they remain of the same diameter at the centre, thus forming an hour-glass or dumb-bell figure when viewed in profile. The central portion maintains its diameter, which is that of the nucleus plus the thickness of the attached exterior cell-wall. Generally, the swelling is greatest at the extremities of the ellipsoidal disc. In some cases, the entire circumference of the disc swelled, leaving a central depression, corresponding to the internal nucleus. The next change effected by acetic acid, is to render the exterior cell-wall perfectly transparent, and in some cases to dissolve it completely, thus setting free the nuclei.

Acetic acid renders the nuclei more distinct, and in many instances renders visible a still smaller body, the original rudiment of the blood-corpuscle. The nucleoli are situated sometimes at the centre, and at others attached to the side of the nuclei.

The blood-corpuscles of these animals, then, correspond in structure to many other cells, having a cell-wall, nucleus, and nucleolus.

The best method of viewing the action of acetic acid, is to place a drop of blood upon a glass slide, and, having adjusted it to the focus of the microscope, touch its border with a drop of concentrated acetic acid, and observe, under the microscope, the line where the acetic acid and blood are mingling. Here we will see the blood-corpuscles changing from ellipsoidal, convex discs to hour-glass or dumb-bell figures and biconcave discs, and almost immediately becoming transparent, and exhibiting nothing but the central nucleus with its nucleolus. I have verified these statements by examinations of the blood of numerous Fishes, Batrachians, Ophidians, and Chelonians.

The following figures will represent in a clear light the action of acetic acid. In order properly to illustrate their structure, the blood-corpuscles are represented in a much rougher manner and stronger light than they appear under the microscope.

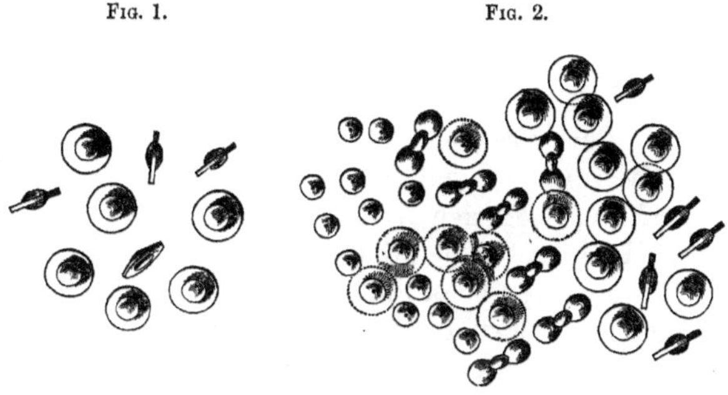

Fig. 1. Fig. 2.

Fig. 1.—Blood-corpuscles of Hammer-head Shark (*Zygæna malleus*) in their normal condition. Mag. 210 diameters.

Fig. 2.—Blood-corpuscles of Hammer-head Shark (*Zygæna malleus*) treated with a drop of acetic acid, showing the different stages of its action. Mag. 210 diameters.

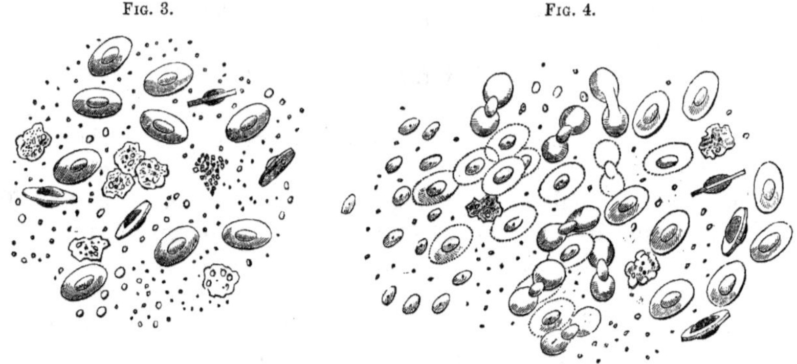

Fig. 3.—Blood-corpuscles of Salt-water Terrapin (*Emys terrapin*) in their normal condition. Mag. 210 diameters.

Fig. 4.—Blood-corpuscles of Salt-water Terrapin (*Emys terrapin*) acted upon by a drop of acetic acid, showing the nuclei, nucleoli, dumb-bell or hour-glass corpuscles, and beyond, where the acid has not extended, the normal corpuscles. Mag. 210 diameters.

Liquor potassa dissolves the cell-walls, nuclei, and nucleoli, alters the color of the blood to a brownish-yellow, and renders it viscid and ropy, like thick mucus. When treated with aqua ammonia, the corpuscles are at first altered in shape, sometimes elongated; and, in many cases, the cell-walls began to swell first toward the periphery, as in the action of acetic acid. In a short time, aqua ammonia, like liquor potassa, completely dissolves the corpuscles.

The colorless corpuscles are more numerous in cold than in warm-blooded animals. Amongst Chelonians, they are most numerous in the Salt-water Terrapins (*Emys terrapin*). In the blood of these Chelonians, numerous minute granules also abound. These minute granules increase during a rapid repair of the elements of the body. They were found to be much more numerous in the blood of Yellow-bellied Terrapins (*Emys serrata*) which had been deprived of food and drink for several weeks, and then transferred to a tub of water and liberally supplied with vegetable food for thirty to sixty days, than in the blood of those Terrapins which had been deprived of food and drink for several weeks.

Effects of Gases upon the Blood of Cold-blooded Animals.

Carbonic Acid Gas.

Salt-water Terrapins (*Emys terrapin*) and Yellow-bellied Terrapins (*Emys serrata*) were placed in large receivers containing this gas. They took long inspirations and expirations, resembling deep sighs. The noise made by the passage of the gas in and out of their lungs, resembled that often made by human beings dying from narcotic poisoning or congestion of the brain. The breathing of the Terrapins became more and more laborious, and less frequent, occurring at intervals of from ten to thirty minutes, and finally ceased in from ten to twelve hours.

The blood was of a much darker color than when the lungs were supplied with atmospheric air, and resembled much the venous blood of the Mammalia. Upon exposure to the air for a length of time, it became, upon its exterior, of a red color. The heart and lungs, and the bloodvessels supplying the intestines, were engorged with black blood. The contractility of the muscles was completely destroyed.

The blood-corpuscles had undergone remarkable changes. They were shrivelled and contorted, presenting innumerable shapes, anything but ellipsoidal. These changes had taken place in the colored corpuscles in all the organs and tissues of the body. The effects of the gas appeared to have been confined principally to the exterior cell wall; for, when they were treated with acetic acid, the nuclei were brought out unchanged. The appearance of the colored corpuscles of a Yellow-bellied Terrapin (*Emys serrata*), which had been kept in the carbonic acid gas until its death, is represented in Fig. 5.

Fig. 5.

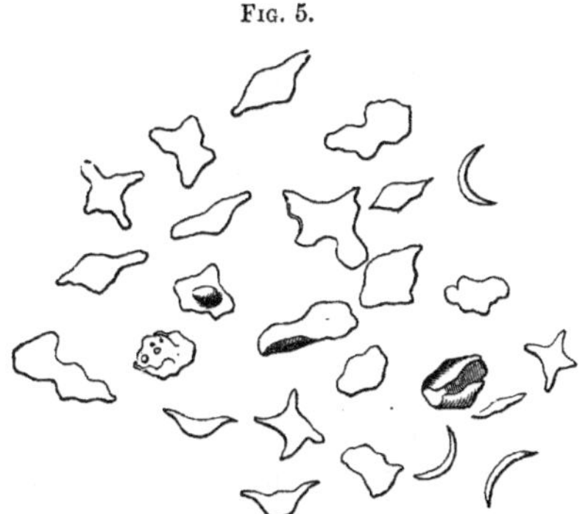

Blood-corpuscles of a Yellow-bellied Terrapin (*Emys serrata*) which had been kept without food or drink for several weeks, and then placed in a tub of water and abundantly supplied with vegetable food for 30 or 40 days, and finally placed in carbonic acid gas.

The urine of all these Terrapins which were confined in carbonic acid gas, contained grape sugar, which is not normally present in the excretions of the kidneys of these animals. The offices of the blood-corpuscles being arrested, oxygen being no longer conveyed into the system, grape sugar, the product of the action of the liver, was not decomposed, and, accumulating in the blood, was eliminated by the kidneys.

When Terrapins were employed which had been starved for a great length of time, the effect of carbonic acid gas upon the blood-corpuscles was not so evident, on account of the concentration of the blood, and the sluggishness of the metamorphoses of their tissues, and the rapidity with which they fell victims to the deleterious influences of this noxious gas. The effects of carbonic acid gas in altering the shape of the blood-corpuscles, were best seen in those Terrapins which had been deprived of food and drink for several weeks, and then transferred to a tub of water, and supplied with vegetable food.

These effects are not produced upon the blood-cells of warm-blooded animals, because they are so rapidly destroyed that the gas has not sufficient time to come in contact, in large quantities, with the corpuscles and materially alter their structure. Cold-blooded animals live much longer in carbonic acid gas than warm-blooded animals, because their muscular and nervous systems are far more independent of the circulatory fluid, and the metamorphoses of the organic and inorganic elements of their fluids and solids are far less rapid.

Carbonic Oxide Gas.

A Corn Snake (*Coluber guttatus*) was placed in a jar of carbonic oxide gas. At first, its efforts to escape were unceasing and violent. Gradually, its respiration became more laborious; it gasped violently for breath; its motions became more spasmodic, and were succeeded by intervals of apparent exhaustion. It died in forty-five minutes after its introduction into the gas.

A Bullfrog (*Rana pipiens*) placed in the carbonic oxide gas presented similar phenomena, but died in a much shorter time, about ten minutes. This difference of time was without doubt due to the difference in the structure of the tegumentary systems of the two Reptiles; the naked skin of the Frog absorbing the gas much more rapidly than the scaly integument of the Serpent.

In both animals (examined immediately after their death), the contractility of the muscular system had been destroyed. The heart was the last portion of the muscular system to yield to the effects of the poison; it continued to beat feebly for a short time.

The blood from all parts of the body was of a brilliant scarlet color, and coagulated into a dense, firm clot, which was unstable and dissolved again. After the dissolution of the fibrin, the blood-corpuscles settled to the bottom, and the serum above was perfectly clear and without any marked color. Under the microscope, the blood-corpuscles presented no unusual appearance when their broad surfaces were turned towards the eye; when, however, they were viewed edgeways, they appeared swollen, and the central nuclei were much less distinct than in their normal condition, being scarcely visible.

Acetic acid exerted its characteristic action, first rendering the blood-corpuscles dumb-bell or hour-glass in shape, when viewed edgeways, and then rendering the exterior cell-wall transparent, and bringing out clearly the nuclei. When the acetic acid was neutralized with diluted liquor potassa, the cell-walls were again brought into view. Concentrated liquor potassa dissolved the blood-corpuscles with no immediate change of color. In a few moments, however, the color changed to a darker red, and gradually assumed a brownish-yellow color, and became, as usual, ropy and viscid.

Vigorous streams of carbonic acid and oxygen gases, passed through separate and the same portions of blood, produced no change whatever in the scarlet color or form of the blood-corpuscles.

Portions of this blood were kept for several weeks, and they still retained their scarlet color, and did not undergo putrefaction.

These reactions show that the change in the color of the blood was due, not to an alteration of the forms of the blood-corpuscles, but to a permanent chemical change of their coloring matter. Another effect of the carbonic oxide gas was to render the fibrin unstable.

This gas arrests oxidation, and the rapidity of its action shows the great importance of this process. The existence of the vital force, and the performance of the functions of the organs and apparatus of the system, are incompatible with the sudden arrest of the chemical changes and metamorphoses of the elements of the solids and fluids. If, however, the process of oxidation be slowly stopped, by a gradual diminution of the temperature of cold-blooded animals, the existence of the vital force is not destroyed, although all the vital, physical, and mechanical functions are suspended.

Hydrogen Gas.

A Yellow-bellied Terrapin (*Emys serrata*), which had been placed in a large receiver of hydrogen gas, died in ten hours.

The blood-corpuscles from all parts of the body presented an altered appearance, similar, in many instances, to that produced by carbonic acid gas. The simple exclusion of the oxygen of the atmosphere, by a harmless gas, produced remarkable alterations in the shape of the corpuscles.

The urine contained grape sugar.

Fig. 6 represents the appearance of the blood-corpuscles of this *Emys serrata*, after it had been confined in hydrogen gas for ten hours.

FIG. 6.

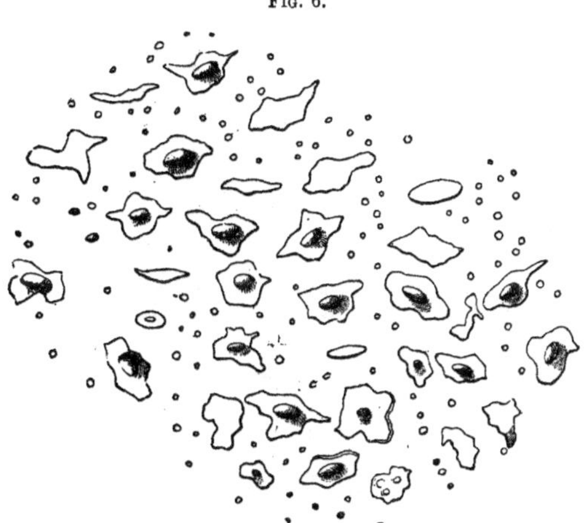

Blood-corpuscles of a Yellow-bellied Terrapin (*Emys serrata*) which had been destroyed in hydrogen gas.

Complete Deprivation of Air.

Ligatures were passed around the tracheas of Yellow-bellied Terrapins (*Emys serrata*) and Salt-water Terrapins (*Emys terrapin*), which had been deprived of food and drink for several weeks, and then transferred to tubs of water, and abundantly supplied with vegetable food. The access of air to the lungs was thus completely cut off.

These Chelonians gave signs of muscular contractility for twelve to twenty hours. In one instance, the stomach and intestines became greatly distended with gas, which consisted partly of carbonic acid.

In all cases, the blood examined after death was of a blackish-red color, and much darker than that of Reptiles in its normal condition. It coagulated when abstracted.

The blood-corpuscles had undergone important modifications. Many of them were shrunken, contorted and contracted; others were swollen, assuming the forms of spheroids, and cubes, and irregular ovoids. The nuclei, which were rendered distinct by the action of acetic acid, in many cases presented corresponding changes. Many of the colorless corpuscles appeared altered in shape.

A stream of oxygen gas, passed through the blood, did not change its color, neither were the forms of the blood-corpuscles altered.

In every instance the urine of these terrapins contained grape sugar.

Figure 7 represents the blood-corpuscles of these terrapins, after they had been deprived of air by a ligature around their windpipes.

FIG. 7.

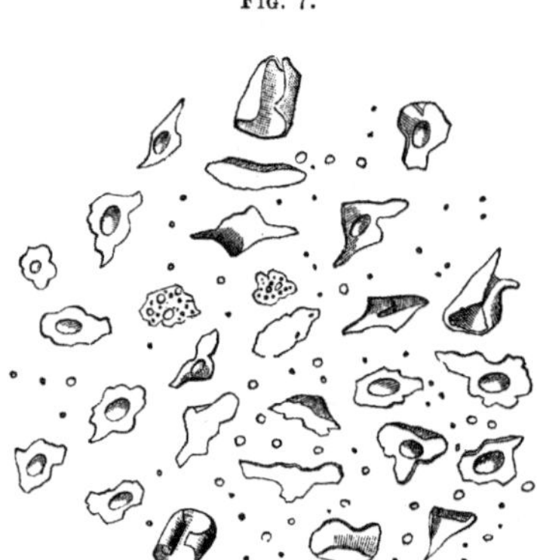

Blood-corpuscles of salt-water Terrapins (*Emys terrapin*) and fresh-water Terrapins (*Emys serrata*), which had been deprived of air by ligatures around their necks.

We will next consider the fibrin and fixed saline constituents of the blood of animals, in its normal condition.

Table of the Fibrin in 1000 parts of the Blood of Animals.

Name of observer.	Name of animal.		Fibrin in 1000 parts of blood.
Jos. Jones	*Trygon sabina* (Stingray)		unstable
"	*Zygæna malleus* (Hammerhead Shark)		unstable
"	*Lepisosteus osseus* (Garfish)		unstable
J. F. Simon	Carp		unstable
"	Tench		unstable
Jos. Jones	*Rana catesbæana* (Bullfrog)		unstable
J. F. Simon	*Bufo variabilis*		unstable
Jos. Jones	*Heterodon niger* (Black Viper)		2.16
"	*Psammophis flagelliformis* (Coachwhip Snake)		1.88
"	*Coluber constrictor* (Black Snake)		5.06
"	*Chelonia caretta* (Loggerhead Turtle)		2.61
"	*Chelonura serpentina* (Snapping Turtle)		0.35
"	*Emys terrapin* (Salt-water Terrapin)		4.15
"	*Emys reticulata* (Chicken Terrapin)		2.51
"	*Emys serrata* (Yellow-bellied Terrapin)		1.04
"	*Testudo polyphemus* (Gopher)		5.73
"	*Alligator Mississippiensis* (Alligator)		3.07
Nasse	Goose		3.46
"	Hen		4.67
Jos. Jones	*Ardea nycticorax* (Heron)		2.20
"	*Syrnium nebulosum* (Barred Owl)		4.69
"	*Cathartes atratus* (Black Turkey-Buzzard)		0.41
Andral, Gavarret, and Delafond	17 Horses	Mean	4.0
		Maximum	5.0
		Minimum	3.0
Nasse	Horse		2.41
Andral, Gavarret, and Delafond	14 Cattle	Mean	3.7
		Maximum	4.4
		Minimum	3.0
Nasse	Ox		3.62
Andral, Gavarret, and Delafond	19 Sheep	Mean	3.1
		Maximum	3.8
		Minimum	2.6
" " "	6 Swine	Mean	4.6
		Maximum	5.0
		Minimum	4.1
Nasse	Swine		3.95
"	Goat		3.90
Andral, Gavarret, and Delafond	16 Dogs	Mean	2.1
		Maximum	3.5
		Minimum	1.6
Nasse	Dog		1.93
Jos. Jones	Common Cur-Dog		3.04
"	Common Cur-Dog		3.15
Nasse	Cat		2.42

From this table we learn that the fibrin constitutes a remarkable index of the vital, organic, and intellectual endowments of animals.

In the whole of the invertebrate kingdom it is absent, except in a few of the most highly organized, in which its presence is accompanied by a corresponding improvement of the cerebro-spinal system, and all the organs.

In the lowest orders of the Vertebrata, as Fishes and Batrachians, it is soft, unstable, and readily convertible into albumen.

In the Ophidians and Chelonians, although it is stable and does not dissolve, still its structure is soft and inconsistent, and resembles, in many respects, the fibrin which is formed when the vital forces of warm-blooded animals have been exhausted by copious and continued bleedings.

Here we have a beautiful demonstration of the fact, that the animal kingdom is constructed upon one great plan. Pathological conditions of the most highly organized animals are found to exist as the normal and permanent conditions of those placed below in the scale of creation. If the forces of a warm-blooded animal be reduced, it presents a condition in many respects similar to that of a cold-blooded animal. We will illustrate this by one other example.

Warm-blooded animals, in health, are able to maintain their temperature at a fixed standard, regardless of that of the surrounding medium. As the surrounding temperature descends, the efforts of nature to sustain a definite degree of heat increase. If, however, the forces of the animal economy be impaired, the efforts of nature are no longer sufficient to keep the body heated to the normal degree, and gradually the body assumes the temperature of the surrounding medium. The intellect and all the organic forces become torpid, the chemical actions cease, or are performed in a feeble or perverted manner; and, finally, the once active and warm-blooded animal is reduced to the condition of a sluggish cold-blooded one.

This table also apparently shows that the fibrin is one of the most variable of all the constituents of the blood. This, however, probably arises in great measure from imperfections in our methods of analysis.

We shall next consider the amount of fixed saline constituents in the blood of different animals.

Table of the Fixed Saline Constituents in the Blood of different Animals.

Name of observer.	Name of animal.	Fixed saline constituents in 1000 parts of blood.	
C. Schmidt	*Anodonta cygnea* (Pond Mussel)	0.256	
Harless and Bibra	*Helix pomatia* (Shell Snail)	6.12	Invertebrate animals.
Bibra	Ascidians and Cephalopods	2.63	
Genth	*Limulus Cyclops*	3.327	
Jos. Jones	*Trygon sabina* (Stingray)	14.70	
"	*Zygæna malleus* (Hammerhead Shark)	8.36	
"	*Lepisosteus osseus* (Garfish)	10.27	Salt-water Fishes and Reptiles.
"	*Emys terrapin* (Salt-water terrapin)	10.74	
"	*Alligator Mississippiensis* (Alligator)	8.65	
"	*Chelonia caretta* (Loggerhead Turtle)	3.58	
"	*Rana catesbæana* (Bullfrog)	5.78	
"	*Chelonura serpentina* (Snapping Turtle)	4.39	Fresh-water Reptiles.
"	*Emys serrata* (Yellow-bellied Terrapin)	5.22	
"	*Emys reticulata* (Chicken Terrapin)	7.79	
"	*Heterodon platyrhinos* (Hog-nose Viper)	13.47	
"	*Heterodon niger* (Black Viper)	7.04	
"	*Psammophis flagelliformis* (Coach-whip Snake)	5.57	Land Reptiles.
"	*Coluber constrictor* (Black Snake)	8.77	
"	*Testudo polyphemus* (Gopher)	5.83	
"	*Cathartes atratus* (Black Buzzard)	8.33	
"	*Ardea nycticorax* (Heron)	6 59	
"	*Syrnium nebulosum* (Owl)	8.06	Birds.
Nasse	Goose	7.92	
"	Hen	8.79	
"	Sheep	7.76	
"	Horse	7.85	
"	Ox	6.95	
"	Calf	7.87	
"	Goat	7.84	Mammalia.
"	Rabbit	6.28	
"	Cat	7.84	
"	Dog	7.33	
Jos. Jones	Common Cur-Dog	6.04	
"	Common Cur-Dog	6.11	

From this table we learn that the proportion of fixed saline constituents in the blood, is remarkably uniform throughout the whole animal kingdom. This fact demonstrates their importance.

In the invertebrata they exist in larger amount relatively to that of the organic constituents of the blood than in vertebrate animals. Thus, in the blood of the Esculent Snail (*Helix pomatia*) there were, according to Harless and Bibra, 6.12 parts of mineral, and only 8.39 parts of organic substances. In the blood of Ascidians and Cephalopods, Bibra found 4.7 parts of organic, and 2.63 parts of mineral substances. When we consider the constitution of the shells of these animals, it is not wonderful that the blood should contain so large a proportion of mineral substances. Schmidt found the albumen of the blood of the Pond Mussel (*Anodonta cygnea*) combined with lime. This fact shows that these mineral bodies are chemically combined with the organic constituents of their bodies.

Amongst vertebrate animals, we find the largest amount of mineral constituents in the blood of Fishes and Reptiles inhabiting the salt water. The only exception to this rule, was found in the blood of the Loggerhead Turtle (*Chelonia caretta*), which had been kept, for forty-eight hours previous to this analysis, in a tub of fresh water. It is possible that an interchange may have taken place between the exterior water and the salts held in solution in the blood. The blood of the Hog-nose Viper (*Heterodon platyrhinos*) yielded a larger amount of ash than that of any other animal. This is accounted for by the fact that the reptile had been starved for a length of time, and the blood was in a concentrated condition. The Alligator is classed amongst the salt-water Reptiles, because it had resided in a small salt-water stream, in a salt marsh. This reptile inhabits, most generally, the brackish and fresh-water rivers, lakes, swamps, and rice-fields.

That the fixed saline constituents are absolutely necessary, not only for the formation of the different structures, but also for the maintenance of life itself, was conclusively demonstrated by a series of experiments performed in France. It was found that when animals were fed upon grain, from which only one element (phosphate of lime) was abstracted, they rapidly lost their forces, and died in the course of a few weeks.

Having completed the study of the blood in its normal condition, we are now prepared to investigate the effects of starvation and thirst.

CHAPTER III.

PHYSICAL AND CHEMICAL CHANGES OF THE SOLIDS AND FLUIDS OF COLD AND WARM-BLOODED ANIMALS, WHEN DEPRIVED OF FOOD AND DRINK.

SERIES I.—EFFECTS OF STARVATION AND THIRST UPON THE FLUIDS AND SOLIDS OF ALLIGATORS (*Alligator Mississippiensis*).

21. *Blood of a small female Alligator, in its normal condition.*

Although this reptile had been shot for half an hour, the blood flowed from its arteries in rapid streams, and twelve fluidounces were collected without any special care.

This alligator had been well fed, and was in good condition; the abdominal cavity, especially in the region of the kidneys, was lined with fat.

Specific gravity of defibrinated blood	1046.
Solid constituents in 1000 parts of blood	176.14
" " " serum	90.80
" in serum of 1000 parts of blood	82.05
Water in 1000 parts of blood	823.86
" " serum	909.20

1000 parts of blood contained—

Water	823.86
Blood-corpuscles (dried organic constituents)	86.39
Albumen	63.75
Fibrin	3.07
Water extract and alcohol extract	9.26
Fatty constituents	5.02
Fixed saline constituents	8.65

1000 parts of blood contained—

Moist blood-corpuscles	364.08	Water	273.06
		Solid constituents	91.02
Liquor sanguinis	635.92	Water	550.80
		Solid constituents	85.12

22. *Blood of a small male Alligator.* April 4.

The subject of these investigations was kept for two weeks and a half, without food or drink. It lived in the same stream with the one used in the preceding analysis, and was in all probability its mate.

This reptile was captured in a novel manner. The ear of the Alligator is provided with a lid which completely covers the *meatus auditorius externus.* When this lid is closed, it is impossible to discover the position of the ear without close inspection. When I fired at the reptile, this lid was raised, and a single small buck-shot passed into the *meatus auditorius externus*, glanced against the bones, and ranging forwards, lodged against the eyeball. The lid was immediately shut down, and remained thus during his confinement. The only evidence of any injury, was a few drops of blood issuing from the corner of his eye; and, although I saw him every day, the true nature of the wound was not ascertained until after his death. The injury was productive of no serious consequences whatever, and only produced a temporary paralysis, just long enough to effect his capture.

In confinement he was exceedingly fierce, when disturbed, opening his jaws and drawing in his breath, making a hissing noise, and swelling out his body, like some Ophidians. When touched or approached, he would throw his head and body completely around—his head occupying the position of his tail. Simultaneously with this movement, the tail was brought violently towards the distended jaws.

During two and a half weeks, he passed no fecal matters, and discharged his urine but once, in quantity about two fluidounces. The urine consisted of a fluid, and a solid, chalk-like portion, composed of innumerable globules of the urate of ammonia.

The blood flowed slowly, and was much less in quantity than that of the female alligator, examined in its normal condition. It coagulated into a dense, coherent clot, immediately after its abstraction from the body.

Specific gravity of defibrinated blood	1056.
Solid constituents in 1000 parts of blood	196.57
" " " serum	90.80
" in serum of 1000 parts of blood	80.24
Water in 1000 parts of blood	803.43
" " serum	909.20

1000 parts of blood contained—

Water	803.43
Blood-corpuscles (dried organic constituents)	106.80
Albumen, and water extractive	74.02
Fibrin	3.41
Fatty constituents and alcoholic extract	2.00
Fixed saline constituents	10.34

1000 parts of blood contained—

Moist blood-corpuscles	451.68	Water	338.76
		Solid constituents	112.92
Liquor sanguinis	548.32	Water	464.67
		Solid constituents	83.65

By comparing the results obtained from the female alligator, in a normal condition, with those obtained from its mate—which had been kept without food and drink for seventeen and a half days—we see that the most obvious effects of starvation and thirst were the diminution of its blood and the consumption of the fat deposited in its tissues. In the normal subject, twelve fluidounces of blood were, with ease, obtained; whilst from the one deprived of food and drink for seventeen and a half days, not more than one-third of this amount could with difficulty be collected. The changes in the relative amounts of the different constituents of the blood will be seen in the following tables:—

Specific Gravities, Water, and Solid Constituents of the Blood.

	Specific gravity of blood.	Water in 1000 parts of blood.	Water in 1000 parts of serum.	Solid constituents in 1000 parts of blood.	Solid constituents in 1000 parts of serum.	Solid constituents in serum of 1000 parts of blood.
Alligator not starved . .	10.46	823.86	909.20	176.14	90.80	82.05
Alligator starved . . .	10.56	803.43	909.20	196.57	90.80	80.24

Moist Blood-Corpuscles and Liquor Sanguinis in 1000 *parts of Blood.*

	Moist blood-corpuscles.	Water in moist blood-corpuscles.	Solid constituents in moist blood-corpuscles.	Liquor sanguinis.	Water in liquor sanguinis.	Solid constituents in liquor sanguinis.
Alligator not starved . .	364.08	273.06	91.02	635.92	550.80	85.12
Alligator starved . . .	451.68	338.76	112.92	548.32	464.67	83.65

Organic and Inorganic Constituents in 1000 *parts of Blood.*

	Water in 1000 parts of blood.	Dry organic constituents of the blood-corpuscles in 1000 parts of blood.	Albumen and extractive matters.	Fat.	Fibrin.	Fixed saline constituents.
Alligator not starved . .	823.86	86.39	73.01	5.02	3.07	8.65
Alligator starved . . .	803.43	106.80	74.02	2.00	3.41	10.34

If we assume that the blood of both alligators had originally the same relative amounts of organic and inorganic constituents, we may note the following changes during abstinence from food and drink :—

The amount of water in the blood was diminished, and the solid constituents relatively, not absolutely, increased.

The number of blood-corpuscles in 1000 parts of blood had increased, whilst in the whole amount of blood originally possessed by the animal they had diminished.

The relative amount of solid constituents in the serum of 1000 parts of blood, had neither increased nor diminished; whilst two-thirds of the amount originally existing in the blood of the reptile had been consumed. Therefore, the constituents of the serum wasted more rapidly than the blood-corpuscles.

The fats and extractive matters were diminished.

The amount of fibrin was relatively increased from 3.07 to 3.41. Its relative increment did not correspond with the concentration of the blood. It was consumed more rapidly than the blood-corpuscles, and not so rapidly as the solid constituents of the serum.

The relative increase in the fixed saline constituents correspond, in part, with the concentration of the blood.

In comparing the blood of one animal with that of another, we determine the influences of starvation and thirst, relatively and not absolutely. If our facts and conclusions were drawn from a few isolated instances, we would be liable to error.

Sources of error, however, have been avoided, as far as possible, by first investigating the blood of cold-blooded animals in a normal state, and then performing an extensive series of experiments upon the effects of a deprivation of food and water. It would have, undoubtedly, added to the accuracy of these experiments, if we could have noted the changes, from time to time, going on in the blood of the same animal. This would have been practicable with the alligators, if they could have been obtained alive. These animals are found in our swamps, marshes, lagoons, and rivers. Their place of habitation is often of difficult access, and very unhealthy in the summer season to the white man, and the reptiles themselves are shy, and can therefore but rarely be obtained in a living state. A shot, from a rifle, in the head (the only vital part), destroys the life, and before they can be carried home, the blood is unfit for analytical examination. In a morning's hunt I have mortally wounded five or six without obtaining a single one, for they all sank in deep water.

With reference to the Terrapins, they are generally so small that the extraction of the amount of blood requisite for only two analyses, would materially affect the final result. We have, accordingly, been compelled to choose between two evils.

By multiplying these observations, as accurate results, we think, have been obtained as if the same cold-blooded animal had been used during the investigation.

We hope that those who may have occasion to follow us in our researches, will make due allowance for the difficulties with which we have had to contend.

SERIES II.—EFFECTS OF STARVATION AND THIRST UPON THE BLOOD OF THE SALT-WATER TERRAPINS (*Emys terrapin*).

23. Blood of an *Emys terrapin*, in a normal condition, having been captured only twelve hours. July 3.

The serum was of a golden color, resembling that of the *Emys serrata*, *Emys reticulata*, and *Cathartes atratus*.

Amount of blood obtained, about 1000 grains.

Solid constituents in 1000 parts of blood	154.72
" " " " serum	43.83
" " in serum of 1000 parts of blood	38.75
Water in 1000 parts of blood	845.28
" " serum	956.17

1000 parts of blood contained—

Water	845.28
Blood-corpuscles (dried organic constituents)	103.82
Albumen, fatty and extractive matter	36.01
Fibrin	4.15
Fixed saline constituents	10.74

1000 parts of blood contained—

Moist blood-corpuscles	447.28	Water	335.46
		Solid constituents	111.82
Liquor sanguinis	552.72	Water	509.82
		Solid constituents	42.90

24. Blood of a Salt-water Terrapin (*Emys terrapin*), which had been kept without food and drink for forty days. July 23.

Weight, June 16	14.285 grains.
" July 23	11.400 "

In thirty-eight days this terrapin had lost 2.885 grains, a little more than one-fifth of its whole weight.

The amount of blood obtained was not more than one-third as much as that procured from terrapins, a short time after their removal from the water.

The blood coagulated rapidly, especially the portions drawn last, which coagulated almost as soon as they reached the bottom of the vessel.

The serum was of a bright, golden color. It was difficult to obtain any amount of it perfectly free from the coloring matter of the blood-corpuscles. When treated with sulphuric acid and a gentle heat, the characteristic odor of the animal was developed.

The blood-corpuscles presented no unusual appearance under the microscope, and gave the characteristic reactions with chemical reagents. This fact proves that a free interchange between the exterior liquor sanguinis and the internal fluid contents of the blood-corpuscles must have been carried on without any intermission.

This animal was probably enfeebled, by long fasting, to a less extent than other animals of this class, because it had deposited eggs only a short time before its capture.

Amount of blood obtained, about 400 grains.

Solid constituents in 1000 parts of blood	199.41
" " " serum	79.50
" in serum of 1000 parts of blood	69.15
Water in 1000 parts of blood	800.59
" " serum	920.50

1000 parts of blood contained—

Water	800.59
Blood-corpuscles (dried organic constituents)	118.56
Albumen and extractive matter	64.85
Fibrin	5.26
Fixed saline constituents	10.74

1000 parts of blood contained—

Moist blood-corpuscles	500.00	Water	375.00
		Solid constituents	125.00
Liquor sanguinis	500.00	Water	425.59
		Solid constituents	74.41

400 parts of blood contained—

Water	320.23
Blood-corpuscles (dried organic constituents)	47.43
Albumen, fatty and extractive matter	25.94
Fibrin	2.11
Fixed saline constituents	4.29
Solid constituents in 400 grains of blood	79.76
" in serum of 400 grains of blood	27.66

400 grains of blood contained—

Moist blood-corpuscles	200.00	Water	150.00
		Solid constituents	50.00
Liquor sanguinis	200.00	Water	170.23
		Solid constituents	29.77

If this terrapin had originally an equal amount of blood of the same chemical constitution with that of the terrapin in the normal state, used in the preceding analysis, then it had lost, during forty days, 600 grains of blood, which had the following composition :—

600 grains of blood, consumed during starvation, contained—

Water	525.05
Blood-corpuscles (dried organic constituents)	56.39
Albumen, fatty and extractive matter	10.07
Fibrin	2.04
Fixed saline constituents	6.45
Solid constituents in 600 grains of blood	74.95
" " in serum of 600 grains of blood	11.09

600 grains of blood contained—

Moist blood-corpuscles	247.28	Water	185.46
		Solid constituents	61.82
Liquor sanguinis	352.72	Water	339.59
		Solid constituents	13.13

25. Blood of a female Salt-water Terrapin (*Emys terrapin*), which had been kept without food and drink for fifty-seven days.

Weight of terrapin, June 21	12.280 grains.
" " August 16	9.255 "
Loss of weight during fifty-six days	3.025 "

In fifty-six days this Chelonian had lost one-fourth of its original weight. The loss each hour during its starvation, was $\frac{1}{5458}$ of the original weight of its body.

This terrapin had just deposited its eggs when captured, and this will account for its living so great a length of time without food or drink.

The female terrapins that were captured before their eggs were deposited, refused to lay, in confinement, became feeble, and died in the course of two or three weeks. This was, without doubt, the result of the anxiety and irritation, occasioned and kept up by the eggs within them.

The blood-corpuscles, under the microscope, presented no unusual appearance, showing that a free interchange between the liquor sanguinis and their contents had been carried on continuously.

Amount of blood obtained	200 grains.
Probable amount of blood consumed	800 "
Solid constituents in 1000 parts of blood	255.22
" " " serum	111.96
" in serum of 1000 parts of blood	92.82
Water in 1000 parts of blood	744.78
" " serum	888.04

1000 parts of blood contained—

Water	744.78
Blood corpuscles (dried organic constituents)	156.96
Albumen, fatty and extractive matter	90.87
Fibrin	1.85
Fixed saline constituents	5.52

1000 parts of blood contained—

Moist blood-corpuscles	642.20	Water	481.65
		Solid constituents	160.55
Liquor sanguinis	357.80	Water	263.13
		Solid constituents	94.67

The number of blood-corpuscles appears to be very great, but it is so only in appearance and not in reality; for, the amount of blood in the Chelonian is very small, and the blood-corpuscles correspondingly few in number. The whole amount of blood, obtained with great care, did not exceed 200 grains.

200 grains contained—

Water	148.96
Blood-corpuscles (dried organic constituents)	31.39
Albumen and extractive matter	18.17
Fibrin	.37
Fixed saline constituents	1.11
Solid constituents in 200 grains of blood	51.04
" " in serum of 200 grains of blood	18.56

200 grains of blood contained—

Moist blood-corpuscles	128.44	Water	96.33
		Solid constituents	32.11
Liquor sanguinis	71.56	Water	52.63
		Solid constituents	18.93

If the starved terrapin, and the one in a normal condition possessed originally equal quantities of blood, having the same chemical constitution, then the starved terrapin must have consumed, during fifty-seven days, 800 grains of blood, having the following constitution:—

Solid constituents in 800 grains of blood	103.68 grains.
" " in serum of 800 grains of blood	20.19 "

800 grains of blood contained—

Water	696.32
Blood-corpuscles (dried organic constituents)	72.43
Albumen, fatty and extractive matter	17.84
Fibrin	3.78
Fixed saline constituents	9.63

800 grains of blood contained—

Moist blood-corpuscles	318.84	Water	239.13
		Solid constituents	79.71
Liquor sanguinis	481.16	Water	457.19
		Solid constituents	23.97

In noting the changes of the constituents of the blood of the *Emys terrapin* during starvation, we might be led into error if the relative quantities of the different constituents in 1000 parts of blood, alone, were considered; for the blood-corpuscles and all the organic and inorganic constituents in this case would appear to have increased rather than diminished during starvation. A correct view of the effects of starvation can only be obtained by ascertaining the absolute amounts of blood and its constituents existing in these reptiles during different lengths of starvation.

By comparing these results with the quantity and constitution of blood in animals in a normal condition, not deprived of food or drink, we can calculate, approximately, the amount of blood and its various constituents that have been consumed during starvation, to supply the wastes of the tissues and keep up the animal temperature.

The following tables give a condensed view of the effects of starvation. They must not be considered absolutely correct, but only as an approximation to the truth.

It would be impossible to determine these changes with absolute accuracy, because differences in the amount and constitution of the blood always exist in different individuals.

I.—*Tables showing the Changes in the Relative Amounts of the Organic and Inorganic Constituents of the Blood of Salt-water Terrapins* (Emys terrapin), *during different periods of Starvation and Thirst. The numbers represent the amount existing in* 1000 *parts of blood. The changes, therefore, are relative, and not absolute.*

WATER AND SOLID MATTERS OF BLOOD AND SERUM.

	Period of starvation and thirst.	Water in 1000 parts of blood.	Water in 1000 parts of serum.	Solid constituents in 1000 parts of blood.	Solid constituents in 1000 parts of serum.	Solid constituents in serum of 1000 parts of blood.
1st female terrapin	12 hours	845.28	956.17	154.72	43.83	38.75
2d " "	40 days	800.59	920.50	199.41	79.50	69.15
3d " "	57 "	744.78	888.04	255.22	111.96	92.82

CONSTITUENTS OF 1000 PARTS OF BLOOD.

	Period of starvation and thirst.	Water.	Blood-corpuscles (dried organic constituents).	Albumen, fatty and extractive matters.	Fibrin.	Fixed saline constituents.
1st female terrapin	12 hours	845.28	103.82	36.01	4.15	10.74
2d " "	40 days	800.59	118.56	64.85	5.26	10.74
3d " "	57 "	744.48	156.98	90.87	1.85	5.52

MOIST BLOOD-CORPUSCLES AND LIQUOR SANGUINIS.

	Period of starvation and thirst.	MOIST BLOOD-CORPUSCLES.			LIQUOR SANGUINIS.		
		Moist blood-corpuscles in 1000 parts of blood.	Water of moist blood-corpuscles.	Solid constituents of moist blood-corpuscles.	Liquor sanguinis in 1000 parts of blood.	Water of liquor sanguinis.	Solid constituents of liquor sanguinis.
1st female terrapin	12 hours	447.28	335.46	111.82	552.72	509.82	42.90
2d " "	40 days	500.00	375.00	125.00	500.00	425.59	74.41
3d " "	57 "	642.20	481.65	160.55	357.80	263.13	94.67

II.—*Tables showing the Actual Amounts of Blood and its Constituents in Salt-water Terrapins, during different periods of Starvation and Thirst.*

WATER AND SOLID CONSTITUENTS OF BLOOD AND SERUM.

	Period of starvation and thirst.	Amount of blood obtained.	Water of blood.	Solid constituents of blood.	Solid constituents of serum.
1st female terrapin	12 hours	1000 grains	845.28	154.72	38.75
2d " "	40 days	400 "	320.23	79.76	27.66
3d " "	57 "	200 "	148.96	51.04	18.56

CONSTITUENTS OF BLOOD.

	Period of starvation and thirst.	Water.	Blood-corpuscles (dried organic constituents).	Albumen and extractive matter.	Fibrin.	Fixed saline constituents.
1st female terrapin	12 hours	845.28	103.82	36.01	4.15	10.74
2d " "	40 days	320.23	47.43	25.95	2.11	4.29
3d " "	57 "	148.96	31.40	18.17	.37	1.10

MOIST BLOOD-CORPUSCLES AND LIQUOR SANGUINIS.

		MOIST BLOOD-CORPUSCLES.			LIQUOR SANGUINIS.		
	Period of starvation and thirst.	Moist blood-corpuscles.	Water of moist blood-corpuscles.	Solid constituents of moist blood-corpuscles.	Liquor sanguinis.	Water of liquor sanguinis.	Solid constituents of liquor sanguinis.
1st female terrapin	12 hours	447.28	335.46	111.82	552.72	509.82	42.90
2d " "	40 days	200.00	150.00	50.00	200.00	170.23	29.77
3d " "	57 "	128.44	96.33	32.11	71.56	52.63	18.93

III.—*Table of the Actual Loss of Weight and Blood, by the Emys Terrapin, during different periods of Starvation and Thirst, in Troy grains.*

	Period of starvation and thirst.	Weight before starvation.	Weight after starvation.	Loss of weight during starvation.	Loss of weight compared to weight of body.	Loss of weight each hour.	Loss of weight per hour, compared to weight of body.	Loss of blood during starvation.
		Grains.	Grains.	Grains.		Grains.		Grains.
2d female terrapin	38 days	14,285	11,400	2,885	$\frac{1}{5}$th	3.317	$\frac{1}{4306}$th	600.
3d " "	56 "	12,280	9,255	3,025	$\frac{1}{4}$th	2.25	$\frac{1}{5458}$th	800.

IV.—*Tables showing the Actual Losses of Blood and its Constituents by Emys terrapin, during different periods of Starvation and Thirst.*

WATER AND SOLID CONSTITUENTS OF BLOOD AND SERUM.

	Period of starvation and thirst.	Amount of blood lost.	Water of blood.	Solid constituents of blood.	Solid constituents of serum.
		Grains.	Grains.	Grains.	Grains.
2d female terrapin	40 days	600	525.05	74.95	11.09
3d " "	57 "	800	696.32	103.68	20.19

CONSTITUENTS OF BLOOD.

	Period of starvation and thirst.	Amount of water lost.	Blood-corpuscles.	Albumen and extractive matters.	Fibrin.	Fixed saline constituents.
		Grains.	Grains.	Grains.	Grains.	Grains.
2d female terrapin	40 days	525.05	56.39	10.07	2.04	6.45
3d " "	57 "	696.32	72.42	17.84	3.78	9.63

MOIST BLOOD-CORPUSCLES AND LIQUOR SANGUINIS.

		MOIST BLOOD-CORPUSCLES.			LIQUOR SANGUINIS.		
	Period of starvation and thirst.	Moist blood-corpuscles.	Water of moist blood-corpuscles.	Solid constituents of moist blood-corpuscles.	Liquor sanguinis.	Water of liquor sanguinis.	Solid constituents of liquor sanguinis.
		Grains.	Grains.	Grains.	Grains.	Grains.	Grains.
2d female terrapin	40 days	247.28	185.46	61.82	352.72	339.59	13.13
3d " "	57 "	318.84	239.13	79.71	481.16	457.19	23.97

These tables show that, during starvation, the water wasted more rapidly than any of the other constituents of the blood, which became more and more concentrated as starvation advanced, and hence the apparent increase in its solid constituents in 1000 parts. The blood-corpuscles wasted as well as the albumen, fibrin, and fixed saline constituents. This fact proves that the blood-corpuscles have important offices to fulfil, in supplying the tissues and organs with nutriment, and replacing the organic and inorganic constituents thrown off and consumed.

SERIES III.—EFFECTS OF STARVATION AND THIRST UPON THE FLUIDS AND SOLIDS OF YELLOW-BELLIED TERRAPINS (*Emys serrata*).

26. Blood of a Female *Emys serrata,* which had been kept without food or drink for three and a half days. May 26th.

Weight of terrapin, May 25th	33.417 grains.
" " twelve hours afterwards	33.258 "
Loss of weight in twelve hours	159 "

In twelve hours it had lost $\frac{1}{210}$th of its whole weight, or $\frac{1}{2520}$th per hour.

The portions of blood drawn first coagulated much more slowly than those drawn last. The first portion drawn, coagulated so slowly that the corpuscles sank to the bottom of the vessel, and a transparent clot was left above. This takes place in a less degree in the blood of females during pregnancy, in that of puerperal fever, acute rheumatism, and inflammations generally.

The serum was of a bright golden color; and, when kept for several hours, partially coagulated.

Specific gravity of the blood	1026.5
" " " serum	1013.7
Solid constituents in 1000 parts of blood	124.59
" " " serum	43.03
" in serum of 1000 parts of blood	39.36
Water in 1000 parts of blood	875.41
" " serum	956.97

1000 parts of blood contained—

Water	875.41
Blood-corpuscles	80.67
Albumen, fatty and extractive matter	37.66
Fibrin	1.04
Fixed saline constituents	5.22

1000 parts of blood contained—

Moist blood-corpuscles	336.76	Water	252.57
		Solid constituents	84.19
Liquor sanguinis	663.24	Water	622.84
		Solid constituents	40.40

Amount of blood obtained from this terrapin, 2000 grains.

Solid constituents in 2000 grains of blood	249.18
" " " serum	86.06
" in serum of 2000 grains of blood	78.72
Water in 2000 grains of blood	1750.82
" " serum	1913.94

2000 grains of blood contained—

Water	1750.82
Blood-corpuscles (dried organic constituents)	161.34
Albumen, fatty and extractive matter	75.32
Fibrin	2.08
Fixed saline constituents	10.44

2000 grains contained—

Moist blood-corpuscles	673.52	Water	505.14
		Solid constituents	168.38
Liquor sanguinis	1326.48	Water	1245.68
		Solid constituents	80.80

27. Blood of a female Yellow-belly Terrapin (*Emys serrata*), which had been kept without food or drink for seventeen days. June 8.

Weight, May 25	20.873 grains.
" June 8	18.756 "
Loss of weight in fourteen days	2.117 "

In fourteen days this Chelonian lost a little more than one-tenth of its whole weight.

Specific gravity of its blood	1040.5
Solid constituents in 1000 parts of blood	178.11
" " " serum	64.51
" in serum of 1000 parts of blood	56.68
Water in 1000 parts of blood	821.87
" " serum	935.49

1000 parts of blood contained—

Water	821.89
Blood-corpuscles (dried organic constituents)	115.75
Albumen, fatty and extractive matters	54.68
Fibrin	1.68
Fixed saline constituents	6.00

1000 parts of blood contained—

Moist blood-corpuscles	478.00	Water	358.25
		Solid constituents	119.75
Liquor sanguinis	522.00	Water	463.64
		Solid constituents	58.36

Amount of blood obtained, 800 grains.

Solid constituents in 800 grains of blood	142.55
" " serum of 800 grains of blood	45.26
Water in 800 grains of blood	657.51

800 grains of blood contained—

Water	657.51
Blood-corpuscles (dried organic constituents)	92.60
Albumen, fatty and extractive matter	43.75
Fibrin	1.34
Fixed saline constituents	4.80

800 grains contained—

Moist blood-corpuscles	383.80	Water	287.85
		Solid constituents	95.95
Liquor sanguinis	416.20	Water	369.60
		Solid constituents	46.60

By comparing the size and amount of blood of this terrapin with that of the terrapin in a normal condition, we obtain, as its probable loss of blood during seventeen days of starvation and thirst, 700 grains.

Solid constituents in 700 grains of blood consumed	44.40
Solid constituents in serum of 700 grains "	13.78
Water in 700 grains of blood	655.60

700 grains of blood contained—

Water	655.60
Blood-corpuscles (dried residue)	28.41
Albumen, fatty and extractive matter	12.74
Fibrin	0.22
Fixed saline constituents	3.03

700 grains of blood contained—

Moist blood-corpuscles	121.60	Water	91.20
		Solid constituents	30.40
Liquor sanguinis	578.40	Water	564.40
		Solid constituents	14.00

28. Blood of a Female Yellow-belly Terrapin (*Emys serrata*), which had been kept without food and drink for twenty-four days. May 23.

This terrapin was captured in the act of excavating a hole in which to deposit its eggs. As usual, they were not deposited during its captivity, but remained in the ovaries and oviducts for twenty-four days.

Solid constituents in 1000 parts of blood	206.28
" " " serum	88.67
" in serum of 1000 parts of blood	77.49
Water in 1000 parts of blood	793.72
" " serum	911.33

1000 parts of blood contained—

Water	793.72
Blood-corpuscles (dried organic constituents)	122.26
Albumen, fatty and extractive matter	74.49
Fibrin	1.68
Fixed saline constituents	7.85

Amount of blood obtained, 500 grains.

Solid constituents in 500 grains of blood	103.14
" " in serum of 500 grains of blood	38.74

500 grains of blood contained—

Water	396.88
Blood-corpuscles (dried organic constituents)	61.12
Albumen, fatty and extractive matter	37.24
Fibrin	0.84
Fixed saline constituents	3.92

1000 parts of blood contained—

Moist blood-corpuscles	508.44	Water	381.33
		Solid constituents	127.11
Liquor sanguinis	491.56	Water	412.39
		Solid constituents	79.17

500 grains of blood contained—

Moist blood-corpuscles	254.22	Water	190.67
		Solid constituents	63.55
Liquor sanguinis	245.78	Water	206.20
		Solid constituents	39.58

Probable amount of blood consumed during twenty-four days of starvation and thirst, 1500 grains.

Solid constituents in 1500 grains of blood	146.04
" " serum of 1500 grains of blood	39.98

1500 grains of blood contained—

Water	1353.96
Blood-corpuscles (dried organic constituents)	100.21
Albumen, fatty and extractive matter	38.08
Fibrin	1.24
Fixed saline constituents	6.52

1500 grains of blood contained—

Moist blood-corpuscles	419.28	Water	314.46
		Solid constituents	104.82
Liquor sanguinis	1080.72	Water	1039.50
		Solid constituents	41.22

29. Blood of Female Yellow-bellied Terrapin (*Emys serrata*), which had been kept without food or drink for twenty-six days.

Weight, May 26	34.155 grains.
" June 14	28.675 "
Loss of weight during twenty days	5.480 "

In twenty-six days this terrapin had lost from one-fourth to one-fifth of its whole weight. Loss of weight each hour, $11\frac{41}{100}$ grains, $= \frac{1}{2994}$th the original weight of its body.

This Chelonian was in a feeble state, and in all probability would not have lived many days.

When its tissues and organs were examined it was found that the yellow fat, which is so abundant in these animals, had disappeared, having been consumed for the maintenance of the animal function, and in the supply of the wastes of the tissues and organs. The destruction of the fat was observed to be one of the constant effects of starvation.

The amount of blood obtained was not more than one-half as much as that obtained from a much smaller terrapin, which was killed only a few days after its removal from the water.

Specific gravity of its blood	1043.
Solid constituents in 1000 parts of blood	198.66
" " " serum	95.48
" " serum of 1000 parts of blood	84.59
Water in 1000 parts of blood	801.34
" " serum	904.52

1000 parts of blood contained—

Water	801.34
Blood-corpuscles (dried organic constituents)	102.97
Albumen, fatty and extractive matter	80.09
Fibrin	4.15
Fixed saline constituents	11.45

1000 parts of blood contained—

Moist blood-corpuscles	439.68	Water	329.76
		Solid constituents	109.92
Liquor sanguinis	560.32	Water	471.58
		Solid constituents	88.74

Amount of blood obtained, 450 grains.

Solid constituents in 450 grains of blood	89.40
" " serum of 450 grains of blood	38.06

450 grains of blood contained—

Water	360.60
Blood-corpuscles (dried organic constituents)	46.34
Albumen, fatty and extractive matter	36.05
Fibrin	1.86
Fixed saline constituents	5.15

450 grains of blood contained—

Moist blood-corpuscles	197.92	Water	148.44
		Solid constituents	49.48
Liquor sanguinis	252.08	Water	212.16
		Solid constituents	39.92

Calculated amount of blood consumed during twenty-six days of starvation and thirst, 1550 grains.

Solid matter in 1550 grains of blood	159.78
" " serum of 1550 grains of blood	40.66

1550 grains of blood contained—

Water	1390.22
Blood-corpuscles (dried organic constituents)	115.00
Albumen, fatty and extractive matter	39.27
Fibrin	0.22
Fixed saline constituents	5.29

1550 grains of blood contained—

Moist blood-corpuscles	475.60	Water	356.70
		Solid constituents	118.90
Liquor sanguinis	1074.40	Water	1033.52
		Solid constituents	40.88

30. Blood of a Female *Emys serrata*, which had been kept without food and drink for thirty-one days.

Weight, May 25	41.086 grains.
" June 13	34.960 "
Loss of weight in twenty days	6.126 "

Loss of weight, each hour, $12\frac{76}{100}$ grains = $\frac{1}{2994}$th of the weight of its whole body. In thirty one days this terrapin lost from one-fourth to one-fifth of its whole weight.

On the day of the analysis the terrapin was found to be completely exhausted by starvation and thirst, and had scarcely strength to move its muscles.

Owing to the feeble state of its circulatory apparatus, and the rapidity of the coagulation of its blood, only a small quantity was collected, insufficient for a complete analysis.

Solid constituents in 1000 parts of blood	222.22
Water in 1000 parts of blood	777.78

1000 parts of blood contained—

Water	777.78
Dried organic constituents	209.66
Fixed saline constituents	12.56

31. Blood of a Female *Emys serrata,* which was kept without food and drink for thirty-eight days.

Weight, May 25	38.540	grains.
" June 28	30.142	"
Loss of weight in thirty-four days	8.398	"

Loss of weight each hour $10\frac{29}{100}$ grains $= \frac{1}{3754}$th of the weight of the whole body. The loss of weight during thirty-eight days of starvation and thirst equalled one-fourth of the original weight of its body.

With the greatest care not more than two hundred grains of blood could be obtained, and the terrapin was weak from long fasting.

The fat of the body had in a great measure disappeared.

The clot formed in the blood was large, and the proportion of serum small. Not more than ten grains of serum could be obtained from $76\frac{65}{100}$ grains of blood, although it had stood for twelve hours. The clot showed little or no disposition to contract. The serum was colored red by the hæmatin of the blood.

The ovaries and oviducts contained twelve hard, and a multitude of soft yellow eggs.

Solid constituents in 1000 parts of blood	226.62
" " " serum	155.00
" " serum of 1000 parts of blood	141.86
Water in 1000 parts of blood	773.38
" " serum	845.00

1000 parts of blood contained—

Water	773.38
Blood-corpuscles (dried organic constituents)	72.91
Albumen, fatty and extractive matter	134.49
Fibrin	6.52
Fixed saline constituents	12.70

1000 parts of blood contained—

Moist blood-corpuscles	312.96	Water	234.72
		Solid constituents	78.24
Liquor sanguinis	687.04	Water	538.66
		Solid constituents	148.38

Amount of blood obtained, 200 grains.

Solid constituents in 200 grains of blood	45.32
" " serum of 200 grains of blood	28.37

200 grains of blood contained—

Water	154.68
Blood-corpuscles (dried organic residue)	14.58
Albumen, fatty and extractive matter	26.90
Fibrin	1.30
Fixed saline constituents	2.54

200 grains of blood contained—

Moist blood-corpuscles	62.60	Water	46.95
		Solid constituents	15.65
Liquor sanguinis	137.40	Water	107.73
		Solid constituents	29.67

Calculated amount of blood lost during thirty-eight days of starvation and thirst, 1800 grains.

Solid constituents in 1800 grains of blood	203.86
" " serum of 1800 grains of blood	62.69

1800 grains of blood contained—

Water	1596.14
Blood-corpuscles (dried organic constituents)	146.76
Albumen, fatty and extractive matter	48.42
Fibrin	0.78
Fixed saline constituents	7.90

1800 grains of blood contained—

Moist blood-corpuscles	561.56	Water	421.17
		Solid constituents	140.39
Liquor sanguinis	1238.44	Water	1174.97
		Solid constituents	63.47

32. Blood of a Male *Emys serrata,* which had been kept without food and drink for forty-nine days.

Weight, May 25	17.797 grains.
" June 9	14.400 "
Loss of weight in forty-five days	3.397 "

In forty-nine days this Chelonian lost one-fifth of its original weight. Loss of weight daily, $75\frac{44}{100}$ grains. Loss of weight hourly, $3\frac{14}{100}$ grains = $\frac{1}{5667}$th of original weight of its body.

All the terrapins (*Emys serrata*) heretofore examined were females, whose ovaries and oviducts contained from eight to twelve hard, and innumerable soft eggs.

The development and nourishment of these eggs consumed the blood, and, consequently, they sank more rapidly under starvation and thirst than this male, which had nothing to support but his own body.

The desire to deposit their eggs induced restlessness. They were continually endeavoring to escape from their confinement. This is in conformity with a law of the animal economy that the exertion of force is always attended by a simultaneous chemical and physical change of the organic elements of structure and nutrition. The amount of these changes corresponds with the force exerted.

The altered materials, which are no longer fit for nutrition or the formation of structure, are eliminated by the lungs and kidneys. The loss of weight by an animal during starvation and thirst should, therefore, correspond entirely with the physical and chemical changes of its organic elements, whatever may be the product of these changes, heat, nervous force, or muscular power.

This principle was strikingly verified by the results of these experiments.

The restless females lost from $\frac{1}{2728}$th to $\frac{1}{3313}$th of their weight hourly, whilst the quiet, composed, indolent male lost $\frac{1}{5667}$th of its weight hourly.

The waste of the blood and tissues was twice as rapid in the females, which corresponds to their greater exertions of muscular and nervous power.

Many of the females grew weak and died in two or three weeks, whilst this male remained active and fierce, apparently without any great diminution of strength and vitality during forty-nine days of starvation and thirst. That this endurance was not due to the peculiar constitution of this male, is proved by a reference to the experiments with the salt-water terrapins (*Emys terrapin*). Those that had deposited their eggs before their capture lived for fifty or sixty days, and their loss of weight corresponded with that of the male *Emys serrata.*

The amount of blood obtained without any difficulty, was 500 grains.

By comparing this with the amount obtained from females, under different periods of starvation and thirst, we see that the blood was consumed to a much less extent in the male.

Specific gravity of its blood	1048.7
Solid constituents in 1000 parts of blood	199.06
" " " serum	108.90
" in serum of 1000 parts of blood	97.88
Water in 1000 parts of blood	800.94
" " serum	891.10

1000 parts of blood contained—

Water	800.94
Blood-corpuscles (dried organic constituents)	92.29
Albumen, fatty and extractive matter	93.38
Fibrin	4.34
Fixed saline constituents	9.05

1000 parts of blood contained—

Moist blood-corpuscles	387.36	Water	290.52
		Solid constituents	96.84
Liquor sanguinis	612.64	Water	510.42
		Solid constituents	102.22

Solid constituents in 500 grains of blood	99.53
" serum of 500 grains of blood	48.94

500 grains of blood contained—

Water	400.47
Blood-corpuscles (dried organic constituents)	46.15
Albumen, fatty and extractive matter	46.69
Fibrin	2.17
Fixed saline constituents	4.52

500 grains of blood contained—

Moist blood-corpuscles	193.68	Water	145.26
		Solid constituents	48.42
Liquor sanguinis	306.32	Water	255.21
		Solid constituents	51.11

Calculated amount of blood consumed during 49 days of thirst and starvation. 1000 grains.

Solid constituents in 1000 grains of consumed blood	87.36
" serum of 1000 grains of consumed blood	10.10

1000 grains of consumed blood contained—

Water	912.64
Blood-corpuscles (dried organic constituents)	74.85
Albumen, fatty and extractive matter	9.80
Fibrin	.61
Fixed saline constituents	3.31

1000 grains of consumed blood contained—

Moist blood-corpuscles	309.04	Water	231.78
		Solid constituents	77.26
Liquor sanguinis	690.96	Water	680.86
		Solid constituents	10.10

The examination of the blood of this male *Emys serrata* completes the series of experiments upon the influence of starvation and thirst upon the constitution and amounts of blood in these Chelonians.

A comparison of these analyses with each other, shows that, in every instance, the water of the blood wasted more rapidly than the other constituents. The rapidity of this consumption of the water, and the consequent concentration of the blood, depended, therefore, upon the length of starvation, and the sex of the reptile.

In females whose ovaries and oviducts were filled with eggs, the anxiety to deposit these, conjoined with their development and nutrition, produced a more rapid consumption of the fat of the body and all the constituents of the blood than in the male. The effects of this anxiety and demand, for the nutrition and development of the eggs, was manifested also in a more rapid destruction of the nervous and vital forces.

The females became weak and exhausted, and several died in two or three weeks, whilst the males retained their usual activity and strength up to their destruction or removal to a tub of water, a period of time varying from three weeks to fifty days.

Tables showing the actual and relative amount of blood, also the actual losses of blood by Yellow-bellied Terrapins (*Emys serrata*), will be given in conjunction with others of a similar character, after the completion of our investigations upon the changes of the blood of different animals when deprived of all food and drink.

SERIES IV.—EFFECTS OF THIRST AND STARVATION UPON THE FLUIDS AND SOLIDS OF GOPHERS (*Testudo polyphemus*).

33. Blood of a male Gopher which had been captured for five days, and abundantly supplied with vegetable food.

Weight of this gopher, 45,500 grains.

When the arteries of the neck were cut, the blood flowed out in a jet, with considerable force, as from the severed artery of a warm-blooded animal.

The serum was of a light yellow color. It was not of such a golden color as that of the *Emys serrata*, or *Emys reticulata*, or *Cathartes atratus*. Heat and sulphuric acid developed in the serum the characteristic odor of the animal, which was similar to that of its urine, and the odor of grass contained in its colon resembled closely that of a sheep.

Amount of blood readily obtained	2500 grains.
Specific gravity of its blood	1030
" " serum	1018
Solid constituents in 1000 parts of blood	156.62
" " " serum	66.41
" in serum of 1000 parts of blood	60.00
Water in 1000 parts of blood	843.38
" " serum	933.59

1000 parts of blood contained—

Water	843.38
Blood-corpuscles (dried organic constituents)	87.28
Albumen, fatty and extractive matter	57.78
Fibrin	5.73
Fixed saline constituents	5.83

1000 parts of blood contained—

Moist blood-corpuscles	393.56	Water	302.67
		Solid constituents	90.89
Liquor sanguinis	606.44	Water	540.71
		Solid constituents	65.73

34. Blood of a male Gopher which was kept without food or drink for thirty days. July 11.

Weight, June 16	18.368 grains.
" " 28	17.919 "
" July 11	16.922 "
Loss of weight from June 16–28 (12 days)	449 "
" " " 28–July 11 (13 days)	997 "

In twenty-five days the loss of weight equalled 1446 grains. In twenty-five days this Gopher had lost $\frac{1}{12}$th of its original weight. Loss of weight each hour, grs. $2\frac{41}{100} = \frac{1}{7621}$th of the original weight of its body. Loss of weight each day—57.8 grains.

The increased loss of weight after June 28, was due to the passage of excrement at various times, and to the elevation of the temperature of the atmosphere. As the temperature is elevated, the wastes of the tissues and chemical and physical changes in the organic molecules of cold-blooded animals are correspondingly increased. In a normal state, the converse of this proposition is true for warm-blooded animals. When, however, the forces are impaired, the warm-blooded animal is governed, in a great measure, by this law.

The serum resembled, in color and smell and relative amount, that of the former Gopher in a normal condition.

The amount of blood readily obtained, was more than 1000 grains. Although this Gopher had been deprived of food and drink for thirty days, still the blood did not appear to have been diminished in quantity. The reason of this will be seen in a few moments.

Specific gravity of its blood	1037
" " serum	1017
Solid constituents in 1000 parts of blood	147.23
" " " serum	61.16
" in serum of 1000 parts of blood	55.55
Water in 1000 parts of blood	852.77
" " serum	944.45

1000 parts of blood contained—

Water	852.77
Blood-corpuscles (dried organic constituents)	84.76
Albumen, fatty and extractive matter	53.17
Fibrin	2.99
Fixed saline constituents	6.31

1000 parts of blood contained—

Moist blood-corpuscles	355.76	Water	267.07
		Solid constituents	88.69
Liquor sanguinis	644.24	Water	585.70
		Solid constituents	58.54

By comparing this analysis with the preceding one, we see that the blood of the Gopher, unlike that of the carnivorous Chelonians, has remained unaltered, both in quantity and the relative proportions of its several ingredients, during a period of thirty days of starvation and thirst.

Upon an examination of its intestinal canal, and the exterior covering of its body, this remarkable power to resist the effects of starvation and thirst will be explained.

The colon of the Gopher enlarges into a receptacle, for food, thirty inches in length and three and a half to four inches in circumference (see Fig. 8). The contents of this consist of grass and leaves, resembling, both in odor and appearance, the contents of the stomach of herbivorous animals. After thirty days of starvation, the undigested vegetable contents of the intestinal canal amounted to 1460 grains.

The skin of the Gopher is almost completely covered with horny excrescences, which prevent all exhalation of water from the surface of the legs, head, and neck, and all those portions of the body not covered by the shell. Hence the loss of water is very small in comparison with that of other terrapins. A large proportion of the weight of these animals, which is lost during starvation, is pure water.

These are wonderful and manifest provisions of the Great Architect, adapting this reptile for habitation in a barren, sandy country, where it is often impossible to obtain water, and where vegetation is scarce. The colon contains a store of vegetable food, which replaces the wastes of the blood and tissues during long seasons of drought. The vegetable matters of the colon also supply the place of the masses of fat found in the abdominal cavities of many Chelonians, Ophidians, and Saurians. We have never noticed this in the Gopher (*Testudo polyphemus*).

35. Blood of a male Gopher (*Testudo polyphemus*), which had been deprived of food and drink for fifty-one days. September 15.

Weight, August 9	21.485 grains.
" September 15	18.127 "
Loss of weight in thirty-seven days	3.358 "

Loss of weight daily, $90\frac{75}{100}$ grains. Loss of weight hourly, $\frac{1}{7821}$th of its original weight. During 51 days of thirst and starvation, this Gopher lost from one-fourth to one-fifth of its original weight.

During this time it discharged several excrements, but no urine. The Terrapins were usually kept in boxes, and examined daily, so that any discharge from the rectum or bladder could not pass unnoticed. During our experiments, not one of the Chelonians voided their urine, so that all these weights represent only the amounts of organic matters and water thrown off by the lungs and the surface of the body.

At the end of fifty-one days of starvation, this Gopher, with several others confined for a similar length of time, still possessed life and activity, and were capable of considerable muscular effort.

The quantity of blood had not diminished to any great extent.

Solid constituents in 1000 parts of blood	170.23
" " " serum	99.50
" in serum of 1000 parts of blood	91.68
Water in 1000 parts of blood	929.77
" " serum	900.50

1000 parts of blood contained—

Water	829.77
Blood-corpuscles and fibrin	78.55
Solid constituents of serum	91.68

1000 parts of blood contained—

Moist blood-corpuscles	314.20	Water	235.65
		Solid constituents	78.55
Liquor sanguinis	685.80	Water	594.12
		Solid constituents	91.68

The colon was occupied by a considerable amount of vegetable matters saturated with juices, and incompletely digested. Hence it appears that the Gopher has the power of retaining, in its intestines, vegetable food for months, without either digesting it or allowing it to ferment or putrefy. When this vegetable food is removed from the intestinal canal, it putrefies in the course of one or two days.

By comparing this analysis with that of the blood of the Gopher in a normal condition, and the blood of the Alligator, *Emys terrapin*, and *Emys serrata* during starvation, we see that the blood of the Gopher is slowly affected by starvation and thirst. This endurance of abstinence from food and drink is a consequence of the following conditions:—

1. The large supply of vegetable food in the great intestine, which continually replaces the wastes of the blood, organs, and tissues.

2. The body is covered, in all parts exposed, with horny excrescences, which prevent the escape of moisture. These are especial provisions of nature, adapting this animal to a barren and dry country.

SERIES V.—EFFECTS OF THIRST AND STARVATION UPON THE SOLIDS AND FLUIDS OF A WARM-BLOODED ANIMAL.

36. Blood of a Cur-Dog in a normal condition.

For a week previous to this analysis, the dog was supplied with more mutton than he could devour. Upon this diet he became very fat and fleshy. On the day previous to the analysis, all food was discontinued.

Weight of dog, 6½ o'clock P. M., August 7, 23¾ lbs.

The blood for analysis was abstracted at 9 o'clock P. M. It coagulated in a few moments after it left the body.

The serum was clear.

Specific gravity of the blood	1045.5
" " serum	1030.5
Solid constituents in 1000 parts of blood	193.48
" " " serum	119.67
" in serum of 1000 parts of blood	109.64
Water in 1000 parts of blood	806.52
" " serum	880.33

1000 parts of blood contained—

Water	806.52
Blood-corpuscles (dried organic residue)	78.04
Albumen, fatty and extractive matter	106.18
Fibrin	3.15
Fixed saline constituents	6.11

1000 parts of blood contained—

Moist blood-corpuscles	322.76	Water	242.07
		Solid constituents	80.69
Liquor sanguinis	677.24	Water	564.45
		Solid constituents	112.79

37. Four o'clock P. M., August 11, fourth day of starvation.

The blood coagulated in a few moments after it was drawn.

Specific gravity of blood	1054.5
" serum	1036.8
Solid constituents in 1000 parts of blood	229.10
" " " serum	134.45
" in serum of 1000 parts of blood	117.18
Water in 1000 parts of blood	770.90
" " serum	865.55

1000 parts of blood contained—

Water	770.90
Blood-corpuscles (dried organic constituents)	102.55
Albumen, fatty and extractive matter	112.53
Fibrin	4.92
Fixed saline constituents	9.10

1000 parts of blood contained—

Moist blood-corpuscles	428.00	Water	321.00
		Solid constituents	107.00
Liquor sanguinis	572.00	Water	449.90
		Solid constituents	122.10

38. Nine o'clock P. M., August 13, sixth day of starvation and thirst.

The blood from the vein was black, flowed with difficulty, and resembled tar. It coagulated immediately after it left the bloodvessels into a firm clot. The blood flowed so slowly, and in such a small stream, that it was difficult to obtain a sufficient quantity for analysis. It had been consumed in supplying the waste of the system.

The dog, during the greater portion of the day, and while the blood was abstracted, lay in a comatose condition. It was completely exhausted, and showed, in its skeleton-like form, the ravages of hunger and thirst. By an unfortunate accident, my last specific gravity bottle was broken, and consequently the specific gravity of its blood and serum was not taken.

The serum was in small amount, relatively to the size of the clot, and was colored red by the hæmatin of the blood.

Many of the blood-corpuscles appear to have undergone partial decomposition. A similar condition of the blood and serum was observed previously in a large female *Emys serrata* during starvation.

Solid constituents in 1000 parts of blood	233.84
" " " serum	144.87
" in serum of 1000 parts of blood	129.80
Water in 1000 parts of blood	766.16
" " serum	855.13

1000 parts of blood contained—

Water		766.16
Blood-corpuscles (dried organic constituents)		96.76
Albumen, fatty and extractive matter		126.32
Fibrin		2.92
Fixed saline constituents of blood corpuscles	4.36	7.84
" " serum	3.48	

1000 parts of blood contained—

Moist blood-corpuscles	402.64	Water	301.98
		Solid constituents . . .	100.66
Liquor sanguinis	597.36	Water	464.64
		Solid constituents . . .	132.72

The dog died at eight o'clock A. M., August 14.

Weight when the experiment was commenced .	23¾ lbs. = 161,326 grains.
Weight after death	16⅛ " = 112,055 "

In 158 hours (6 days and 14 hours) this dog had lost 49,271 grains; one-third to one-fourth of its original weight. Loss of weight during twenty-four hours, 7,476 grains. Loss of weight during one hour $311\frac{5}{10}$ grains = $\frac{1}{517}$ of the weight of its whole body before starvation. During 158 hours of starvation, each pound Avoirdupois (7,000 grains) lost 2,078 grains.

The liver was tested the next morning for grape sugar, but the tests of Trommer and Moore failed to indicate its presence.

The substance of this organ, under the microscope, contained innumerable oil-globules of various sizes. All the fat throughout the body appeared to have been completely consumed. The only source of this fat was the nitrogenized elements of the blood and tissues, which were acted upon by the cells of the liver.

It is stated by physiologists that, after prolonged starvation, the amount of urea formed in the system is increased. The reason of this is obvious. The fat stored up in various parts of the body is first consumed to sustain animal temperature. As long as it supplies the demands of nature, urea, a product of the metamorphoses of the nitrogenized elements of the blood and tissues, is found in normal amount. When, however, the fat is consumed, the nitrogenized elements of the blood and tissues are attacked. The carbon unites, ultimately, with oxygen, forming carbonic acid, whilst the nitrogen is conjoined with oxygen and carbon, and is thrown off as urea. We have, then, in addition to the amount of urea normally formed, that which results from the combustion of the nitrogenized compounds.

The dense and dry condition of the muscular system of the dog, showed that the juices of the muscles must have passed into the blood. This results as a necessary consequence of the physical law of endosmosis.

During starvation and thirst, the blood becomes denser than the surrounding fluids, owing to the evaporation of water which goes on continually in the lungs. The less dense juices of the body necessarily flow into the circulatory system. The object of all endosmotic action is the restoration of an equilibrium, and the rapidity of that action will be determined, in great measure, by the differences of the densities of the exterior and interior solutions.

It is probable that the death of this dog occurred sooner than should have been anticipated, on account of the heat. During the middle of the day, the thermometer generally stood as high as 94°. This heated atmosphere promoted evaporation of the watery elements of the blood and tissues, both from the surface of the body and lungs.

These experiments complete our investigations upon the effects of thirst and starvation upon the blood of different animals. We will now arrange the results in tables, and study them collectively.

I. *Tables showing the Changes in the Relative Amounts of the Organic and Inorganic Constituents of the Blood of Warm and Cold-blooded Animals, during different periods of Starvation and Thirst. The numbers represent the amounts existing in* 1000 *parts of blood. The changes, therefore, are relative and not absolute.*

(*a.*) SPECIFIC GRAVITIES, WATER, AND SOLID CONSTITUENTS OF BLOOD AND SERUM.

Name of animal.	Period of starvation and thirst.	Specific gravity of blood.	Specific gravity of serum.	Water in 1000 parts of blood.	Water in 1000 parts of serum.	Solid constituents in 1000 parts of blood.	Solid constituents in 1000 parts of serum.	Solid constituents in serum of 1000 parts of blood.
Female Alligator . .		1046.0		823.86	909.20	176.14	90.80	82.05
Male Alligator . .	17½ days	1056.0		803.43	909.20	196.57	90.80	80.24
1st female *Emys terrapin* .	12 hrs.	1035.3	1012.7	845.28	956.17	154.72	43.83	38.75
2d " " .	40 days			800.59	920.50	199.41	79.50	69.15
3d " " .	57 "			744.78	888.04	255.22	111.96	92.82
1st female *Emys serrata* .	3½ "	1026.5	1013.7	875.41	956.97	124.59	43.03	39.36
2d " " .	17 "	1040.5		821.89	935.49	178.11	64.51	56.68
3d " " .	24 "			793.72	911.33	206.28	88.67	77.49
4th " " .	26 "	1043.0		801.34	904.52	198.66	95.48	84.59
5th " " .	31 "			777.78		222.22		
6th " " .	38 "			773.38	845.00	226.62	155.00	141.86
7th male " .	49 "	148.7		800.94	891.10	199.06	108.90	97.88
1st male *Testudo polyphemus*		1030.0	1018.0	843.38	933.59	156.62	66.41	60.00
2d " "	30 days	1037.0	1017.0	854.77	938.84	147.23	61.16	55.55
3d " "	51 "			829.77	900.50	170.23	99.50	91.68
1st Cur-dog . . .		1045.5	1030.5	806.52	880.33	193.48	119.67	109.69
2d " . . .	96 hrs.	1054.5	1036.8	770.90	865.55	229.10	134.45	117.18
3d " . . .	158 "			766.16	855.13	233.84	144.87	129.80

(*b.*) CONSTITUENTS OF 1000 PARTS OF BLOOD.

Name of animal.	Period of starvation and thirst.	Water.	Blood-corpuscles (dried organic constituents).	Albumen, fatty and extractive matters.	Fibrin.	Fixed saline constituents.
Female Alligator . .		823.86	86.39	78.03	3.07	8.65
Male Alligator . .	17½ days	803.43	106.80	76.02	3.41	10.34
1st female *Emys terrapin*	12 hours	845.28	103.82	36.01	4.15	10.74
2d " "	40 days	800.59	118.56	64.85	5.26	10.74
3d " "	57 "	744.78	156.98	90.87	1.85	5.52
1st female *Emys serrata*	3½ "	875.41	80.67	37.66	1.04	5.22
2d " "	17 "	821.89	115.75	54.68	1.68	6.00
3d " "	24 "	793.72	122.26	74.49	1.68	7.85
4th " "	26 "	801.34	102.97	80.09	4.15	11.45
5th " "	31 "	777.78				12.56
6th " "	38 "	773.38	72.91	134.49	6.52	12.70
7th male "	49 "	800.94	92.29	93.38	4.34	9.05
1st male *Testudo polyphemus*		843.38	87.28	57.78	5.73	5.83
2d " "	30 "	852.77	84.76	53.17	2.99	6.13
3d " "	51 "	829.77	78.55			
1st Cur-dog . . .		806.52	78.04	106.18	3.15	6.11
2d " . . .	4 "	770.90	102.55	112.53	4.92	9.10
3d " . . .	158 hours	766.16	96.76	126.32	2.92	7.84

(c.) MOIST BLOOD-CORPUSCLES AND LIQUOR SANGUINIS.

Name of animal.	Period of starvation and thirst.	MOIST BLOOD-CORPUSCLES.			LIQUOR SANGUINIS.		
		Moist blood-corpuscles in 1000 parts of blood.	Water in moist blood-corpuscles.	Solid constituents in moist blood-corpuscles.	Liquor sanguinis in 1000 parts of blood.	Water in liquor sanguinis.	Solid constituents in liquor sanguinis.
Female Alligator . .		364.08	273 06	91.02	635.92	550.80	85.12
Male Alligator . .	17½ days	451.68	338.76	112.92	548.32	464.67	83.65
1st female *Emys terrapin*	12 hours	447.28	335.46	111.82	552.72	509.82	42.90
2d " "	40 days	500.00	375.00	125.00	500.00	425.59	74.41
3d " "	57 "	642.20	481.65	160.55	357.80	263.13	94.67
1st female *Emys serrata*	3½ "	336.76	252.57	84.19	663.24	622.84	40.40
2d " "	17 "	478.00	358.25	119.75	522.00	463.64	58.36
3d " "	24 "	508.44	381.33	127.11	491.56	412.39	79.17
4th " "	26 "	439.68	329.76	109.92	560.32	471.58	88.74
6th " "	38 "	312.96	234.72	78.24	687.04	538.66	148.38
7th male "	49 "	387.36	290.52	96.84	612.64	510.42	102.22
1st male *Testudo polyphemus* (Gopher)		393.56	302.67	90.89	606.44	540.71	65.73
2d " "	30 "	355.76	267.07	88.69	644.24	585.70	58.54
3d " "	51 "	314.20	235.65	78.55	685.80	594.12	91.68
1st Cur-dog . . .		322.76	242.07	80.69	677.24	564.45	112.79
2d " . . .	4 "	428.00	321.00	107.00	572.00	449.90	122.10
3d " . . .	158 hours	402.64	301.98	100.66	597.36	464.64	132.72

II.—*Tables showing the Actual Amounts of Blood and its Constituents existing in Animals during different periods of Starvation and Thirst.*

(e.) WATER AND SOLID CONSTITUENTS OF BLOOD AND SERUM.

Name of animal.	Period of starvation and thirst.	Amount of blood obtained.	Water of blood.	Solid constituents of blood.	Solid constituents of serum.
		Grains.			
1st female *Emys terrapin* . .	12 hours	1000	845.28	154.72	38.75
2d " " . .	40 days	400	320.23	79.76	27.66
3d " " . .	57 "	200	148.96	51.04	18.56
1st female *Emys serrata* . . .	3½ "	2000	1750.82	249.18	78.72
2d " " . . .	17 "	800	657.51	142.48	45.26
3d " " . . .	24 "	500	396.86	103.14	38.74
4th " " . . .	26 "	450	360.60	89.40	38.06
6th " " . . .	38 "	200	154.68	49.32	28.37
7th male " . . .	49 "	500	400.47	99.53	48.94

(f.) CONSTITUENTS OF BLOOD.

Name of animal.	Period of starvation and thirst.	Amount of blood obtained.	Water.	Blood-corpuscles	Albumen, fatty and extractive matter.	Fibrin.	Fixed saline constituents.
		Grains.					
1st female *Emys terrapin*	12 hours	1000	845.28	103.82	36.01	4.15	10.74
2d " "	40 days	400	320.23	47.43	25.95	2.11	4.29
3d " "	57 "	200	148.96	31.40	18.17	.37	1.10
1st female *Emys serrata*	3½ "	2000	1750.82	161.34	75.32	2.08	10.44
2d " "	17 "	800	657.51	92.60	43.75	1.34	4.80
3d " "	24 "	500	396.86	61.13	37.24	.84	3.92
4th " "	26 "	450	360.60	46.34	36.05	1.68	5.15
6th " "	38 "	200	154.68	14.58	26.90	1.30	2.54
7th male "	49 "	500	400.47	46 15	46.69	2.17	4.52

(*g.*) MOIST BLOOD-CORPUSCLES AND LIQUOR SANGUINIS.

Name of animal.	Period of starvation and thirst.	Amount of blood obtained.	MOIST BLOOD-CORPUSCLES.			LIQUOR SANGUINIS.		
			Moist blood corpuscles.	Water of moist blood corpuscles.	Solid constituents of moist blood-corpuscles.	Liquor sanguinis.	Water of liquor sanguinis.	Solid constituents of liquor sanguinis.
		Grains.						
1st female *Emys terrapin*	12 hrs.	1000	447.28	335.46	111.82	552.72	509.82	42.90
2d " "	40 days	400	200.00	150.00	50.00	200.00	170.23	29.77
3d " "	57 "	200	128.44	96.33	32.11	71.56	52.63	18.93
1st female *Emys serrata*	3½ "	2000	673.52	505.14	168.38	1326.48	1245.68	80.80
2d " "	17 "	800	383.80	387.85	95.95	416.20	369.60	46.60
3d " "	24 "	500	254.22	190.67	63.55	245.78	206.20	39.58
4th " "	26 "	450	197.92	148.44	49.48	252.08	212.16	39.92
6th " "	38 "	200	62.60	46.95	15.65	137.40	107.73	29.67
7th male "	49 "	500	193.67	145.26	48.42	306.32	255.21	51.11

The following tables have been constructed by calculations based upon careful comparisons of the blood of starved animals with the blood of those in a normal condition. They are, therefore, not absolutely correct, but are the nearest approximation to the truth that can at present be obtained.

III.—*Tables showing the Losses of Blood and its Constituents by Animals during different periods of Starvation and Thirst.*

(*m.*) WATER AND SOLID CONSTITUENTS OF BLOOD AND SERUM.

Name of animal.	Period of starvation and thirst.	Amount of blood consumed.	Water of blood.	Solid constituents of blood.	Solid constituents of serum.
		Grains.			
2d female *Emys terrapin* . .	40 days	600	525.05	74.95	11.09
3d " "	57 "	800	696.32	103.68	20.19
2d female *Emys serrata*	17 "	700	655.60	44.40	13.78
3d " "	24 "	1500	1353.96	146.04	39.98
4th " "	26 "	1550	1390.22	159.78	40.66
6th " "	38 "	1800	1596.14	204.86	62.69
7th male "	49 "	1000	912.64	87.36	10.10

(*n.*) CONSTITUENTS OF BLOOD CONSUMED.

Name of animal.	Period of starvation and thirst.	Amount of blood consumed.	Blood-corpuscles consumed.	Albumen, fatty and extractive matter.	Fibrin.	Fixed saline constituents.	Water of blood consumed.
		Grains.					
2d *Emys terrapin*	40 days	600	56.39	10.07	2.04	6.45	525.05
3d "	57 "	800	72.42	17.84	3.78	9.63	696.32
2d female *Emys serrata*	17 "	700	28.41	12.74	0.22	3.03	655.60
3d " "	24 "	1500	100.21	38.08	1.24	6.52	1353.96
4th " "	26 "	1550	115.00	39.27	0.22	5.29	1390.22
6th " "	38 "	1800	146.76	48.42	0.78	7.90	1596.14
7th male "	49 "	1000	74.85	9.80	.61	3.31	912.64

(*o.*) MOIST BLOOD-CORPUSCLES AND LIQUOR SANGUINIS.

Name of animal.	Period of starvation and thirst.	Amount of blood consumed.	MOIST BLOOD-CORPUSCLES.			LIQUOR SANGUINIS.		
			Moist blood-corpuscles.	Water of moist blood-corpuscles.	Solid constituents of moist blood-corpuscles.	Liquor sanguinis.	Water of liquor sanguinis.	Solid constituents of liquor sanguinis.
		Grains.						
2d female *Emys terrapin*	40 days	600	247.28	185.46	61.82	352.72	339.59	13.13
3d " "	57 "	800	318.84	239.13	79.71	481.16	457.19	23.97
2d female *Emys serrata*	17 "	700	121.60	91.20	30.40	578.40	564.40	14.00
3d " "	24 "	1500	419.28	314.46	104.82	1080.72	1039.50	41.22
4th " "	26 "	1550	475.60	356.70	118.90	1074.40	1033.52	40.80
6th " "	38 "	1800	561.56	421.17	140.39	1238.44	1174.97	63.49
7th male "	49 "	1000	309.04	231.78	77.26	690.96	680.86	10.10

A careful review of the results of these analyses and experiments leads to the following conclusions:—

1. In every instance, during abstinence from food and drink, the water of the blood diminished more rapidly than the solid constituents.

The evaporation from the surface of the body and lungs, and the supply of a solvent for the excretions of the kidneys, were more rapid than the consumption of the solid organic, and inorganic constituents of the blood for the regeneration and maintenance of the tissues and organs.

2. The rapidity of this consumption of the watery element, and consequent concentration of the blood depends upon the vital and physical constitution of the animal, and is most rapid amongst warm-blooded ones.

Amongst cold-blooded animals it is slowest in the gopher. The physical constitution of the epidermis of this animal prevents evaporation from its surface. Its tissues, also, are more compact than those of other Chelonians.

The character of the food of this animal, and the structure of its alimentary canal, are such, that it is able to withstand the effects of hunger without any physical or chemical change in the amount and constitution of its blood, or diminution of its powers, much longer than the Chelonians which inhabit the water.

3. During thirst and starvation, the rapidity of the consumption of the constituents of the blood, organs, and tissues, is in proportion to the temperature, intelligence, vital force, and the amount of muscular and nervous force expended by the animals.

4. The blood-corpuscles waste during starvation, as well as the other constituents of the blood, thus proving that they have important offices to fulfil in the support of the tissues and organs of the living animals, and the maintenance of the vital, nervous, physical, and chemical phenomena.

5. The fibrin decreases during starvation and thirst.

Had we considered the amount of fibrin only in 1000 parts of blood, we would have fallen into an error committed by several observers. The increment of the fibrin in 1000 parts was only apparent, and corresponded in a great measure to the concentration of the blood by the rapid evaporation of its water from the surface of the body and lungs.

6. During long-continued starvation and thirst, the stomach and intestines of cold-blooded animals do not become inflamed and ulcerated, as is almost universally the case with warm-blooded animals.

7. The fat of the body wastes more rapidly than any of the tissues. The manner in which it re-enters the circulation is unknown.

The following tables will serve to elucidate phenomena which have been but imperfectly studied by naturalists and physiologists.

Table of the Temperatures of Warm and Cold-Blooded Animals.

	Temperature of Atmosphere.	Temperature of box or medium in which the animal was kept.	Temperature of region of	Temperature of region of
Micropogon undulatus (Croker Fish)		Water, 84°		Viscera, 84°
Heterodon platyrhinos (Hognose Viper)	75½°	Box, 73½°		Heart, 73°
Heterodon niger (Black Viper)	80½°		Tail, 74°	" 76°
Psammophis flagelliformis (Coachwhip Snake)	72°		" 73½°	" 74°
Alligator Mississippiensis (Alligator, starved 17 days	69°		Surface of body, 65°	" 69°
Chelonura serpentina (Snapping Turtle)	90°	" 85°	Muscles of thigh, 81°	" and Liver, 82°
Chelonia caretta (Loggerhead Turtle)	90°	Water, 81½°		" " 81°
Emys terrapin (Salt-water Terrapin)	78°	Box, 78°	" " 80°	" " 80¼°
Emys serrata (Yellow-bellied Terrapin) deprived of food and drink 3½ days	86½°	" 74°		" " 73½°
Emys serrata, deprived of food and drink 17 days	74½°	" 76°		" " 77°
Emys serrata, deprived of food and drink 21 days	86°	" 84°		" " 75½°
Emys serrata, deprived of food and drink 49 days	85°	" 81°	" " 80°	" " 80½°
Emys reticulata	86°	" 80°		" " 80°
Testudo polyphemus (Gopher)	82°		" " 80°	" " 80½°
Corvus ossifragus (Fish Crow)	80½°		" " 104°	" " 108°
Ectopistes Carolinensis (Turtle Dove)	66°		Intestine, 106°	Pec. maj. muscle, 106½°
Syrnium nebulosum (Barred Owl)	76°			" " 102°
Ardea nycticorax (Night Heron)	78°½			" " 104°
Carduelis tristis (May Bird)	82¾°			" " 105°
May Bird	82¾°			" " 106°
May Bird, which had lost much blood from a bad wound	82¾°			" " 98°
May Bird, which had lost much blood from a wound	82¾°			" " 100¼°
May Bird, which had lost much blood	82¾°			" " 101°
Mammalia generally				Heart, 100°

Table showing the Relation between the Temperature and the Chemical Changes of the Molecules of the Solids and Fluids of Warm and Cold-Blooded Animals.

Name of Animal.	Temperature of the atmosphere and box in which the animal was kept.	Temperature of the region of	Temperature of the region of	Loss of weight each hour.	Loss of weight each hour expressed in a fraction of the original weight of the animal.	Amount of urine excreted hourly.	Amount of urine excreted hourly, expressed in a fraction of the original weight of the animal.	Amount of solid constituents in the urine excreted hourly.
	Fahr.	Fahr.	Fahr.	Grains.		Grains.		Grains.
Emys terrapin .	78°	Muscles of thigh, 80°	Heart and liver, 80¼°	5.18	$\frac{1}{3633}$	.032	$\frac{1}{446406}$	.00114
Emys serrata . .	74°		" 73½°	6. 3	$\frac{1}{3313}$	1.315	$\frac{1}{13865}$	.0034
Emys serrata . .	76°		" 77°	10. 5	$\frac{1}{2870}$	0.357	$\frac{1}{846500}$	.00166
Emys serrata . .	84°		" 75½°	10.29	$\frac{1}{3734}$	1.09	$\frac{1}{34357}$	.00437
Emys serrata . .	81°	" 80°	" 80½°	3.14	$\frac{1}{5667}$	.0277	$\frac{1}{642130}$	.0012
Testudo polyphemus	82°	" 80°	" 80½°	2.41	$\frac{1}{7621}$			
Cur-dog . . .	86°		" 100°	311.84	$\frac{1}{517}$			

These tables show that, although the union of the oxygen of the atmosphere with the elements of the solids and fluids of cold-blooded animals is so slow that their temperature changes with that of the surrounding medium, still they generate within themselves a certain amount of heat. This is proved by the fact, that, the interior of their bodies in the region of the heart and liver generally has a temperature a fraction of a degree higher than that of the parts nearer the surface.

The fact that the temperature of their bodies is often several degrees below that of the surrounding medium is readily explained by a reference to our investigations upon the effects of thirst and starvation upon the solids and fluids. The loss of weight is due, in a greater degree, to the evaporation of the water of the solids and fluids than to the metamorphosis and final elimination of the organic elements in the maintenance of animal temperature. The amount of solid matters consumed in the maintenance of the temperature of cold-blooded animals is not always sufficient to supply the heat abstracted by evaporation.

Losses in the Weights of Animals during different periods of Thirst and Starvation.

Name of animal.	Period of starvation and thirst.	Weight before starvation.	Weight after starvation.	Loss of blood during starvation.	Loss of weight during starvation.	Loss of weight compared to weight of body.	Loss of weight each hour.	Loss of weight per hour, compared to weight of body.
		Grains.	Grains.	Grains.	Grains.		Grains.	
Female *Emys terrapin*	38 days	14,285	11,400	600	2,885	$\frac{1}{5}$	3.317	$\frac{1}{4366}$
" "	56 "	12,280	9,255	800	3,025	$\frac{1}{4}$	2.25	$\frac{1}{5458}$
Female *Emys serrata*	12 hours	33,417	33,258		159	$\frac{1}{200}$	13.25	$\frac{1}{2728}$
" "	14 days	20,873	18,756	700	2,117	$\frac{1}{10}$	6.3	$\frac{1}{3313}$
" "	20 "	34,155	28,675	1500	5,480	$\frac{1}{6}$	11.41	$\frac{1}{2994}$
" "	20 "	41,086	34,960	1550	6,126	$\frac{1}{7}$	12.76	$\frac{1}{3298}$
" "	39 "	38,590	30,142	1800	8,398	$\frac{1}{4}$—$\frac{1}{5}$	10.29	$\frac{1}{3754}$
Male *Emys serrata*	45 "	17,797	14,400	1000	3,397	$\frac{1}{5}$	3.14	$\frac{1}{5667}$
6 *Emys serrata*	27 "	104,698	85,573		19,125	$\frac{1}{5}$—$\frac{1}{6}$	27.97	$\frac{1}{3743}$
Testudo polyphemus (Gopher)	25 "	18,368	16,922		1,446	$\frac{1}{13}$	2.41	$\frac{1}{7621}$
4 *Testudo polyphemus* (Gophers)	37 "	98,280	86,696		11,582	$\frac{1}{9}$	13.04	$\frac{1}{7336}$
Cur-dog	6 d'ys, 14 hours	161,326	112,055		49,271	$\frac{1}{3}$	311.84	$\frac{1}{517}$

A careful consideration of these tables, in connection with previous researches, will tend to support the following conclusions:—

1. The intellect, temperature, nervous and muscular forces, and organic development of animals, are in proportion to the rapidity of the changes of the elements.

In warm-blooded animals, which are endowed with intellect of a high order, and possess great nervous and muscular force, and correspondingly developed organs, the changes in their elements are incessant. When starved, they lose weight rapidly.

In cold-blooded animals, the temperature of which is often below that of the surrounding medium, and whose nervous system and intellect are feebly developed, the changes in their elements are correspondingly slow.

The Cur-dog lost, in six days and fourteen hours, one-third of its original weight, whilst the Chelonians lived from thirty to sixty days without losing more than from one-fourth to one-thirteenth of their original weight. The loss in the former was from six to fifteen times more rapid than in the latter.

2. The loss of weight at the time of death was very nearly equal in warm and cold-blooded animals. The maintenance of the short, vigorous life of the former, required as large a supply of organic and inorganic materials as the prolonged and sluggish existence of the latter. What the warm-blooded animal gained in intensity and power, it lost in duration.

3. The length of life of an animal during starvation and thirst, is proportional to the rapidity of the changes of its elements, and, as a necessary consequence, stands in direct relation to its temperature, intellect, and organic development.

The Cur-dog wasted more rapidly, lived more energetically, and died in a correspondingly shorter time, than the cold-blooded Chelonians.

Amongst cold-blooded animals, the Terrapins which were most active in their movements, and whose nervous system was the most excited, lived during a time corresponding with their increased nervous and muscular exertions.

The female Terrapins, whose ovaries and oviducts were filled with hard and soft eggs, lost from $\frac{1}{2728}$th to $\frac{1}{3313}$th of their weight hourly, and died in the course of twenty-five or thirty-five days; while the females which had deposited their eggs, and the males, which were free from these anxieties, wasted only one-half as much per hour—$\frac{1}{4366}$th to $\frac{1}{5667}$th of their whole weight—and lived twice the length of time—from fifty to seventy days.

We may infer from these facts, as far as they extend, that the acts of life are carried on upon the same general plan, no matter what be the physical or vital constitution of an animal.

4. In cold-blooded animals, the organs, tissues, and apparatus are far more independent of the blood than in warm-blooded ones.

This fact will explain the phenomena of the prolonged contraction of the heart and muscles, and the action of the nervous system, and the continuance of life, for a great length of time after the almost complete removal of the blood. These functions are attended with so little waste, and consequent demand for a fresh supply of nutriment, that a very small amount of the circulatory fluid will suffice to keep them in action for a great length of time.

In warm-blooded animals, on the other hand, the maintenance of the nervous and vital forces, and of a definite temperature, and the exercise of the intellect, involve more decided and constant changes in their elements.

The circulatory apparatus filled with blood is the great laboratory in which these physical and chemical changes of the elements are carried on and the results distributed to every living molecule of matter. According, then, to the perfection of an animal, and the rapidity of these changes, will be the dependence of the organs and apparatus upon the circulatory fluid. It follows as a necessary consequence that the deprivation of this fluid will prove fatal in a length of time inversely proportional to the development and perfection of an animal.

The question now presents itself: Why is the life of cold-blooded animals so sluggish, and all the physical and chemical changes of their elements so tardy, and their temperature and intellect so low? Can Nature be said to be uniform in her operations when all the phenomena of life are so dissimilar in these two classes of animals?

A consideration of the important differences existing between the structure and functions of their respiratory and circulatory systems may serve to settle definitely this question, as will be seen in the course of this chapter.

The principal or only heart in many fishes, has but one auricle and one ventricle, and is traversed by venous blood alone, and corresponds with the right heart of the higher vertebrata.

Although the circulatory apparatus is more highly developed in the reptiles, still a mixture of venous and arterial blood always takes place in the ventricle.

As our experiments have been confined almost exclusively to the higher orders of cold-blooded animals, we shall consider briefly the circulatory and respiratory systems of the Ophidia, Sauria, and Chelonia.

The ventricle of the heart in these higher orders is generally divided by an imperfect septum, which, in the heart of the alligator, is very strong and almost complete. Just at the outlet of the ventricle, however, we find a communication established between the two, and thus the venous and arterial blood are mixed together, and the similarity to the heart of the rest of the reptiles, and the fœtus of birds and mammals, is preserved. The venous blood from all parts of the body is returned to the right auricle of the heart through the venæ cavæ, the terminations of which are guarded by strong valves. The left auricle is appropriated exclusively to the lungs, from which it receives the aerated blood through the pulmonary veins. From the single ventricle two sets of vessels are sent off, the pulmonary and the aortic. The pulmonary artery divides into two branches, one for each lung. The aorta, immediately after its origin, divides into two trunks, which, winding backwards, join and form a large vessel, the branches of which distribute the blood to all parts of the system. The contraction of the right auricle forces the venous blood into the ventricle, whilst the contraction of the left auricle transmits the aerated blood from the lungs into the same common cavity. The contraction of the ventricle distributes a portion of the mixed blood into the lungs through the pulmonary artery, and the remainder to all parts of the body through the aorta and its branches.

From this arrangement it is evident, that not only is partially aerated blood diffused throughout the system, but, also, that a moiety only of the whole amount of blood is sent to the lungs and exposed to the action of the atmosphere at each contraction of the ventricle of the heart.

From the consideration of the heart and circulatory apparatus of the Chelonia and Sauria, we pass very naturally to that of warm-blooded animals.

The circulatory apparatus differs in no essential respect in the two great classes of warm-blooded animals, birds and mammals.

In these higher animals we have a double heart, and two distinct and complete circulations of the blood. Each portion of blood which has passed through the capillaries of the system and become vitiated, is aerated in the lungs before its distribution over the body. This is one of the most important of all distinctions between warm and cold-blooded animals.

The right heart is devoted to the circulation of venous blood, and the left heart to the circulation of oxygenated or aerated blood.

The auricle and ventricle of one heart have no communication with the auricle and ventricle of the other except through the bloodvessels and capillaries. The vessels of each heart are distinct, and perform distinct offices.

The right auricle receives the venous blood from all parts of the system and transmits it to the right ventricle. The contraction of the right ventricle distributes the venous blood to the lungs. The oxygenated or arterial blood is conveyed from the lungs to the left auricle, and thence to the left ventricle, and the contractions of this distributes it throughout all parts of the system.

As the circulatory apparatus is developed, the influence and importance of the nervous system are increased, and corresponding arrangements established for its perfect preservation.

Another consideration to be taken into account is the relative size of the heart and the rapidity of its action in different animals.

I obtained the following results by carefully weighing the entire body of an animal, and then ascertaining the weight of its heart upon a delicate balance capable of turning to the $\frac{1}{1000}$th part of a grain.

Comparative Weights of the Hearts of Fishes.

	Proportion to weight of entire animal.
Weight of the heart of female *Trygon sabina* (Stingray) . . .	$\frac{1}{1012}$
" " fœtus of *Trygon sabina* (Stingray) . . .	$\frac{1}{1070}$
" " *Zygæna malleus* (Hammerhead Shark) . . .	$\frac{1}{1136}$
" " *Zygæna malleus* (Hammerhead Shark) . . .	$\frac{1}{899}$
" " female *Lepisosteus osseous* (Garfish) . . .	$\frac{1}{965}$

Comparative Weights of the Hearts of Reptiles.

	Proportion to weight of entire animal.
Weight of the heart of *Rana catesbæana* (Bullfrog)	$\frac{1}{576}$
" " *Heterodon niger* (Black Viper)	$\frac{1}{496}$
" " *Coluber constrictor* (Black Snake) . .	$\frac{1}{425}$
" " *Coluber guttatus* (Corn Snake)	$\frac{1}{400}$
" " *Psammophis flagelliformis* (Coachwhip Snake) . .	$\frac{1}{354}$
" " *Crotalus durissus* (Rattlesnake)	$\frac{1}{441}$
" " *Chelonura serpentina* (Snapping Turtle) . .	$\frac{1}{403}$
" " *Chelonia caretta* (Loggerhead Turtle) . . .	$\frac{1}{480}$
" " *Emys reticulata* (Chicken Terrapin) . . .	$\frac{1}{420}$
" " *Emys serrata* (Yellow-bellied Terrapin) . .	$\frac{1}{592}$
" " *Emys serrata* (Yellow-bellied Terrapin) . .	$\frac{1}{577}$
" " *Emys serrata* (Yellow-bellied Terrapin) . .	$\frac{1}{543}$
" " male *Testudo polyphemus* (Gopher) . . .	$\frac{1}{453}$
" " male *Testudo polyphemus* (Gopher) . . .	$\frac{1}{470}$
" " female *Alligator Mississippiensis* (Alligator) . .	$\frac{1}{398}$

Comparative Weights of the Hearts of Birds.

	Proportion to weight of entire animal.
Weight of the heart of *Meleagris gallopavo* (Wild Turkey)	$\frac{1}{279}$
" " *Meleagris gallopavo* (Wild Turkey)	$\frac{1}{275}$
" " *Syrnium nebulosum* (Barred Owl)	$\frac{1}{220}$
" " *Cathartes atratus* (Turkey-buzzard)	$\frac{1}{113}$
" " *Tantalus loculator* (Wood Ibis)	$\frac{1}{108}$
" " *Tantalus loculator* (Wood Ibis)	$\frac{1}{100}$

Comparative Weights of the Hearts of Mammals.

	Proportion to weight of entire animal.
Weight of the heart of Common Sheep	$\frac{1}{256}$
" " *Sciurus Carolinensis* (Gray Squirrel)	$\frac{1}{261}$
" " *Didelphis Virginianus* (Opossum)	$\frac{1}{280}$
" " Common Cat	$\frac{1}{275}$
" " *Procyon lotor* (Raccoon)	$\frac{1}{164}$
" " *Procyon lotor* (Raccoon)	$\frac{1}{140}$
" " young *Procyon lotor* (Raccoon)	$\frac{1}{142}$
" " Pointer Dog	$\frac{1}{128}$.

By comparing these tables, we see that the heart is proportionally smallest in Fishes and largest in Birds.

As the organs and apparatus of the animal economy are developed and perfected, the circulation of the nutritive materials becomes more vigorous.

As the temperature, intelligence, and activity of animals, with their corresponding physical and chemical metamorphoses of the elements of organic structure increase, there is a correspondingly rapid supply of those materials by which the wastes may be repaired, and from which the various secretions and excretions may be elaborated and separated.

The next consideration is the rapidity of the circulation in different animals.

The action of the heart may be taken as a general index of this. The following table has been drawn up from the researches of Dumas, Prevost, Müller, and Simon.

Rapidity of Circulation in Different Animals.

	Number of beats per minute.
In the *Amphioxus*	1
" Carp	20
" Fishes generally	20—24
" Green Toad	77
" Frogs generally	about 60
" Pigeon	136
" Common Hen	140
" Duck	110
" Raven	110
" Heron	200
" Birds generally	100—200
" Ox	38
" Horse	56
" Sheep	75
" Goat	84
" Hare	120
" Guinea-Pig	140
" Dog	90—95
" Cat	100—110
" Ape (*Simia Callitriche*)	90
" Human embryo	150
" " just after birth	130—140
" Human being during first year	130—115
" " during second year	115—100
" " during third year	100—90
" " about seventh year	90—85
" " about fourteenth year	85—80
" " in the middle period of life	75—70
" " in old age	65—50
" Mammals generally	38—140

This table shows that the rapidity of the circulation corresponds with the structure, habits, age, and development of animals.

If the vital forces are of a low grade, either from original conformation or the depressing influences of old age, the circulation is correspondingly sluggish and feeble.

As the fluids and solids of animals become more highly elaborated and developed, the action of the heart and circulation of the blood become more rapid and vigorous.

The next consideration is that of the structure of the respiratory system in the different orders of animals.

One of the essential conditions of the life of all organized beings, whether vegetable or animal, is a supply of oxygen. The modes in which oxygen is brought in contact with the fluids and solids of organized structures, vary with the development and peculiar manner of life of the different classes of animals.

In the lowest classes of the Invertebrata, in which the digested matters pass directly from the stomach into the different structures of the body, and become integral parts of the animal, we find no special circulatory system, and respiration is carried on by the whole surface of the body which is bathed by the water. In animals still more highly developed, we find canals carrying water into all parts of the system. In many individuals, bloodvessels accompany these canals, and ramify around their walls. An incessant motion through this aquiferous respiratory system is maintained by cilia lining their interior. These canals open upon the exterior of the body and into the visceral cavity. In many animals of this class, the digestive cavity, which is bathed continually by fresh portions of water, performs the function of respiration.

In the higher orders of the Invertebrata, the respiratory system is confined to a definite portion of the exterior or internal membrane, which is developed within a small space into a great extent of surface, so as to render the contact with the air or water as extensive as possible without any loss of room or power.

According as the fluids are elaborated, and the solids correspondingly developed, the respiratory system becomes more condensed and perfected.

In the *Amphioxus*, or the pulmonary apparatus corresponds with the degraded type of the cerebro-spinal system and all the organs, and, like that of many invertebrate animals, is lodged in the same cavity with the liver, generative apparatus, kidneys, and the greater portion of the alimentary canal. In the Invertebrate animals and the *Amphioxus* amongst the Vertebrate, the circulation of the water through the branchiæ is maintained principally by ciliary action.

In Fishes, however, of higher organization, whose blood is more highly elaborated and circulates with greater rapidity, mere filamentous tufts hanging to the side of the neck will not suffice for the aeration of the blood. It is necessary that large streams of water be constantly and forcibly propelled through the branchial apparatus, in order that the blood may be exposed as much as possible to the action of the air so scantily contained in the water. This is accomplished by the connection of the gills with the cavity of the mouth, the muscles of which send rapid currents of water through the branchial passages. The structure and position of the heart, also, is such that it propels all the venous blood through the branchiæ before its distribution to the body generally.

At first sight, the circulation and respiration of Fishes appear to be more perfect than that of Reptiles. This, however, is not the case. By a reference to the table of the comparative weights of the heart in different animals, it will be seen that the heart of Fishes is about $\frac{1}{1000}$th, whilst that of Reptiles is about $\frac{1}{450}$th of the weight of the entire body.

The heart of Reptiles is relatively more than twice as large as that of Fishes.

The table of the comparative rapidity of the heart's action in different animals, showed that the circulation of Fishes is much slower than that of Reptiles.

The aeration of the blood, also, is much slower and less perfect in Fishes, from the fact that the amount of air contained in the water is infinitely less than that of the atmosphere.

In several remarkable Fishes having strongly marked reptilian characters, as the Garfish (*Lepisosteus osseus*) and the common Mudfish (*Amia calva*) of our southern swamps and ricefields, we find both gills and a pulmonary organ. The lung of these Fishes has been considered by many physiologists and anatomists as analogous to the swimming-bladder of other Fishes. This organ is absent in some individuals, and its presence or absence in those which possess it, appears to make no material difference; in some, it communicates externally, whilst in others again it is completely closed, and all its offices are unknown. It is, therefore, impossible, with our present knowledge, to decide whether the air-bladder of Fishes should be considered as a rudimentary lung.

The lung of the Garfish (*Lepisosteus osseus*) is a capacious sac, which opens by a short trachea high up in the throat, and, extending nearly the whole length of the abdominal cavity, terminates within a short distance of the anus. It lies between the posterior surface of the liver and the anterior surface of the kidneys. When removed from the abdominal cavity and inflated, its diameter is nearly equal to two-thirds of that of the fish. Its structure resembles that of the *Amphiuma means* and other doubtful Reptiles. The bloodvessels ramify upon the walls of this sac, the internal surface of which is increased by the development of numerous sacculi.

This increased development of the respiratory system is attended by corresponding improvements in the structure and functions of the solids.

The Gar is a destructive and active pirate, and consequently needs great muscular power to outstrip and capture the swift inhabitants of the watery element. It is a very difficult matter to hold a recently captured Gar, two or three feet in length, even with both hands, on account of the vigor and rapidity of its motion. In the possession of a lung, and in the general form and appearance of the viscera, this fish bears a strong resemblance to Reptiles. Fig. 11 represents the viscera of the fresh-water Garfish.

In the Congo Snake of our southern swamps and ricefields, and the Hellbender (*Menopoma Alleganiensis*), we find branchial arches without any development of the gills.

The lungs of the Congo Snake (*Amphiuma means*) communicate with the exterior through a short trachea, which opens by a slit in the pharynx, just opposite to the base of the cranium. The trachea passes down between the divisions of the *bulbus arteriosus*, and, a short distance below the position of the heart, divides into two short branches which open into the lungs. The lungs are long slender sacs, having the general structure of these organs in the Batrachia. The diameter of the lungs, even in their inflated condition, is very small, being about half an inch, whilst their length is very great in full-grown individuals, being about eighteen inches. Notwithstanding the absence of gills, the lungs are far smaller than the pulmonary organs of the Garfish (*Lepisosteus osseus*), which has also a large and well developed branchial apparatus. This may be due in part to the fact that its naked skin, as in Frogs and naked animals generally, whether vertebrate or invertebrate, performs the office of a lung.

The chief cause, however, of these discrepancies in the development of the respiratory organs of the two animals is to be found in their habits and vital endowments.

The Gar is active and powerful, whilst the *Amphiuma* is sluggish and degraded in habits and appearance. This is one of numerous instances which might be adduced to show that the consumption of oxygen, and the corresponding waste of the tissues, corresponds exactly with the development, habits and temperature of animals. The viscera of this animal, reduced to one-half their diameter, are represented in Fig. 20.

The lungs of the several orders of reptiles are formed upon one type, being capacious sacs, whose walls are divided into sacculi, and supplied with bloodvessels according to the perfection of the organs and apparatus, and the habits of the animal.

From the internal surface membranous septa project inwards, dividing the interior of the organ into numerous polygonal cells, which are themselves subdivided into smaller compartments. The bloodvessels are distributed over the internal walls of the lungs and over the sides of the pulmonary cells.

In serpents one lung only is developed, and the pulmonary cells are most numerous in the superior portion, whilst the inferior part of the long cylindrical lung is a mere membranous sac with few or no bloodvessels ramifying upon its walls. (See Figure 21.)

We find the greatest number of the polygonal cells and the greatest distribution of the bloodvessels in the pulmonary organs of the Chelonia and Sauria, thus foreshadowing the condition of the lungs in birds and mammals.

In these orders the lungs are filled, more or less, by a coarse and fine network or areolar tissue, forming angular or rounded meshes, which rest partly upon the walls of the lungs, and enclose lesser meshes or air-cells. The bloodvessels ramify over the meshes as well as over the walls of the lungs. The sacculi thus formed communicate with each other, and can all be inflated from any one point.

The size of the lungs differs in the different orders according to their structure and habits. Amongst the Chelonians, we find the most capacious lung in the gopher (*Testudo Polyphemus*). These animals burrow deeply in the ground, and need large lungs as a reservoir of air. In aquatic serpents which remain under the water for a great length of time, the lungs are capable of holding a greater quantity than those of land serpents.

In mammals and birds the blood is abundant, and the circulation rapid, and the wastes and metamorphoses of the tissues correspondingly great, and the lungs are composed of an infinitude of minute cells containing air, and surrounded by a capillary network.

The respiratory system of birds is far more highly developed than that of reptiles, but not so concentrated as that of the mammals. In this class the lungs are no longer closed bags like those of reptiles, but are spongy masses of great vascularity communicating with numerous air-sacs and the cavities of the bones. The main trunks of the bronchial tubes pass through the lungs and open into the cavity of the thorax. The whole thoracico-abdominal cavity is divided by bands of serous membrane into numerous cells communicating with each other and the cavities of the hollow and spongy bones.

In many birds, especially those of powerful flight, the air is admitted into the interspaces between the muscles, and between the skin and muscular system. By this arrangement, which reminds us of the tracheal system of insects, the air penetrates almost every part of their bodies, bathes all their viscera, and fills the cavities of the hollow and spongy bones. It follows as a necessary consequence, that the actions between the oxygen of the atmosphere and the organic elements of their bodies should be rapid and incessant, and the temperature correspondingly high.

The minute structure of the lungs of birds resembles, in many respects, that of reptiles; the cells, however, are infinitely more numerous and minute, and the surface exposed to the action of the atmosphere correspondingly more extensive.

The entire mass of each lung is divided into innumerable lobules or lunglets, the walls of which are formed by a cartilaginous network derived from the bronchial tubes, and by the ramifications of the capillary vessels. From this arrangement, it is evident that the bloodvessels are suspended in air and exposed to its influence on every side. These cells or sacculi are never terminal cells, as in the mammalia, but open parietal cells, communicating freely with each other through the meshes of the capillary and cartilaginous network.

In the mammalia the abdominal cavity is completely separated from the thoracic cavity by the diaphragm, the great muscle of respiration. The lungs are closed bags situated in the cavity of the thorax, and are surrounded by a serous membrane, which, after lining the ribs and intercostal muscles and thoracic surface of the diaphragm, is reflected on the lungs from the point occupied by the pulmonic vessels.

They are composed of innumerable cells communicating with the terminal branches of the bronchial tubes, around which ramify a delicate and closely woven network of bloodvessels. Collectively, these cells present an immense surface, over which the blood circulates and is exposed to the action of the atmosphere. It has been calculated that the number of these air-cells grouped round the termination of each bronchial tube is about 18,000, and that the total number in the lung of the human being is not less than 600,000,000.

In the Amphibia and Batrachia, the lungs are filled by an action that resembles swallowing. In the Ophidia and Sauria, respiration is assisted by the ribs and abdominal muscles. In all cold-blooded animals the mechanism of respiration corresponds with the simple structure of their lungs and the sluggish metamorphoses of their tissue.

The mechanism of respiration in birds is more complete than that in reptiles, but not so perfect as that of the mammalia. From the elastic character of the cartilaginous and bony framework, surrounding the thoracico-abdominal cavity, the natural condition of the lungs is that of inflation. The air is expelled by the action of those muscles which bring the sternum nearer to the vertebral column. When these muscles cease to act, the extended sternum, attached to the elastic thorax, springs outwards, and the air rushes into the lungs to fill the vacuum thus formed.

In the mammalia, the inspiration and expiration of the air are effected by the alternate movements of the diaphragm and the walls of the thoracic cavity.

The relation which exists between the number of the respirations and the rapidity of the circulation of the blood will be seen in the following table drawn up from the researches of Dumas, Prevost, and Simon:—

	Number of the beats of the heart in one minute.	Number of respirations in one minute.
Horse	56	16
Hare	120	36
Goat	84	24
Cat	100	24
Dog	90	28
Guinea-pig	140	36
Ape (*Simia Callitriche*)	90	30
Man	72	18
Heron	200	22
Raven	110	21
Duck	110	21
Common Hen	140	30
Pigeon	136	34

This table shows, that, as a general rule, the activity of the respiratory function corresponds with the rapidity of the circulation.

We are now prepared to understand the results of our experiments, and to show that the operations of nature are carried on upon the same great plan, however simple or complex the animal.

Cold-blooded animals are such, not from any peculiar chemical or physical endowments of the organic and inorganic molecules of their bodies, but from the peculiarity of the structure of their circulatory and respiratory systems.

The perfection of these two systems may be taken as the index of the rapidity of the physical and chemical changes of the molecules of their fluids and solids, and the facts we have presented lead to the conclusion, that the intelligence and activity of the vital actions are exactly proportional to the rapidity and amount of the physical and chemical changes of the organic and inorganic molecules.

Our investigations show that the heart of warm-blooded animals is from two to five times as heavy as that of reptiles, and is far more rapid and powerful in its actions, and, as a necessary consequence, that the blood circulates with much greater rapidity.

The respiratory system of reptiles is imperfectly developed, and its functions imperfectly performed. Only from one-sixth to one-ninth as much blood passes through their lungs, and is exposed to the action of the atmosphere, as circulates through the pulmonary organs of warm-blooded animals.

The blood-corpuscles, the active agents in the elaboration of many of the constituents of the blood, are much less numerous, and the whole amount of blood existing in their bodies is much less abundant in cold than in warm-blooded animals.

The nervous system, the great apparatus for the generation of the excitor-motive power of the animal economy, is imperfectly developed in cold-blooded animals.

From these data we are able to calculate, with almost absolute certainty, that the vital actions of cold-blooded animals should be from one-ninth to one-fifteenth as rapid as those of warm-blooded animals. Here we have a conclusive demonstration that modifications in vital phenomena are accomplished by peculiar modifications of the structure and arrangements of the various organs and apparatus, and by peculiar applications of the forces, and not by a suspension or alteration of the physical and chemical laws which govern all matter.

CHAPTER IV.

EFFECTS OF STARVATION AND THIRST, COMBINED WITH A CHANGE OF DIET, UPON THE FLUIDS AND SOLIDS OF CARNIVOROUS CHELONIANS.

SERIES I.—EXPERIMENTS UPON THE YELLOW-BELLIED TERRAPIN (*Emys serrata*).

39. Examination of a female *Emys serrata* which was starved four weeks, and then transferred to a tub of water, and abundantly supplied with Purslain (*Portulacca oleracea*).

It remained in the tub of water for forty-two days.

Weight, May 25	23.696	grains.
" June 21	19.472	"
Loss of weight in twenty-seven days—during which period it was deprived of all food and drink	4.224	"
Weight, August 2, after remaining forty-two days in the tub of water	25.333	"
Increase of weight in the forty-two days	5.861	"
Gain above the original weight of May 25, ...	1.637	"

The color of the blood was intermediate between arterial and venous.

The serum was of a light yellow color, resembling that of the Gopher (*Testudo polyphemus*) which subsists entirely upon vegetable food. The serum of the *Emys serrata* supplied with animal food, is always of a bright orange color. Here we see that the color had been changed from orange to light yellow by a change of diet.

In one portion of blood which was set aside, the fibrin did not coagulate until nearly all the blood-corpuscles had settled to the bottom, thus affording a transparent clot.

The portions of blood drawn last, coagulated much more rapidly than those drawn first.

The cellular tissue in all parts of the body of this Terrapin, was permeated by a limpid albuminous fluid, which coagulated when removed from the body. The coats of the peritoneum, the cavity of the abdomen and the pleura, contained large quantities of this fluid. The amount of this serous fluid, collected without any special care, was more than five fluidounces, equal to 2420 grains. Its specific gravity, 1005.9. As the blood flowed from the wound in the neck, this serous fluid passed into the bloodvessels, to supply the loss. This was shown by the change in the specific gravity of the serum. That obtained from the portions of blood first drawn, gave a specific gravity of 1014, whilst that of a latter period, containing numerous blood corpuscles, gave a specific gravity of only 1012.9.

The arteries and veins had lost their elasticity, owing to the great pressure caused by the unusual amount of blood which they contained. After its removal they were unable to contract, and were found distended with air throughout all portions of the body. Even the heart contained air in its cavities. This phenomenon has never been witnessed in Terrapins fed upon animal food.

The tissues generally were relaxed, resembling those of a dropsical patient.

The shell had become much softer in its texture, the necessary amount of earthy salts not having been supplied by the Purslain (*Portulacca oleracea*).

The whole amount of blood obtained was much greater than that of Terrapins which were examined immediately after their capture, and which had been living in a normal manner.

Amount of blood obtained, about	2000	grains.
" " serous fluid from the tissues	2420	"
Specific gravity of the blood	1029.6	"
" " first portions of serum	1014	"
" " last " "	1012.9	"
" " serous fluid from tissues	1005.9	"

The bladder contained a large quantity of light yellow transparent urine, having a specific gravity not much higher than that of water.

Solid constituents in 1000 parts of blood	122.35
" " " serum	51.14
" " serum of 1000 parts of blood	47.30
Water in 1000 parts of blood	877.65
" " serum	948.86

1000 parts of blood contained—

Water	877.65
Blood-corpuscles (dried organic constituents)	70.53
Albumen, fatty and extractive matter	45.38
Fibrin	1.64
Fixed saline constituents	4.80

1000 parts of blood contained—

Moist blood-corpuscles	293.64	Water	220.23
		Solid constituents	73.41
Liquor sanguinis	706.36	Water	657.42
		Solid constituents	48.94

40. Examination of a female *Emys serrata*, which was starved and deprived of water twenty-eight days, and then transferred to a tub of fresh water and abundantly supplied with Purslain (*Portulacca oleracea*) eighty-eight days.

Weight, when it was first captured, May 25	20.372	grains.
" after starvation, June 21	15.797	"
Loss of weight during twenty-seven days of thirst and starvation	4.575	"

Weight, September 17, after removal from the tub . .	27.125 grains.
Gain in weight during eighty-eight days subsistence upon vegetable food	11.328 "

The serum was of a light-yellow color, and the clot was large.

The tissues of this terrapin did not present the dropsical appearance of those of the former terrapin.

The bladder was distended with light-yellow limpid urine, having a specific gravity only a few degrees above that of water.

The pleura and cellular tissue, along the side of the back, contained two fluid-ounces of a clear albuminous fluid, which coagulated when allowed to stand, and a well-defined soft clot was formed.

The intestines were much enlarged and distended, resembling those of Chelonians which live exclusively upon vegetable substances. The intestines of carnivorous terrapins in their normal condition are always contracted. This change was observed in the intestines of all those carnivorous terrapins which had been kept for a length of time upon vegetable food, and was, without doubt, due to the character of the food.

The stomach was filled with the buds and leaves of the Purslain, which gave an acid reaction.

The contents of the small intestines were neutral to test-paper.

The colon and rectum were filled with undigested vegetable matter, acid in its reaction.

The pancreas was diseased in this and many other carnivorous terrapins which had been fed entirely upon vegetable food. The diseased portion consisted of black and brown hard masses which could be squeezed out of the substance of the pancreas.

When subjected to the microscope, these masses were found to consist of numerous large yellow cells, with divisions and nuclei, resembling certain cancer cells; also oil-globules, and octohedral and columnar crystals. When the diseased portion was pressed upon the glass the crystals produced a grating noise. The cancer-like cells were found only in the diseased portion, whilst the crystals were found in other parts of the pancreas. We have never noticed this disease of the pancreas in terrapins in a normal condition, and the only cause which can be assigned for this degeneration of structure is the character of the food.

Solid constituents in 1000 parts of blood	115.84
" " " serum	50.00
" in serum of 1000 parts of blood . . .	46.53
Water in 1000 parts of blood	884.16
" " serum	950.00

1000 parts of blood contained—

Water	884.16
Blood-corpuscles (dried organic constituents)	66.88
Solid constituents of serum	46.53
Fibrin	2.43

1000 parts of blood contained—

Moist blood-corpuscles	267.52	Water	200.64
		Solid constituents	66.88
Liquor sanguinis	732.48	Water	683.52
		Solid constituents	48.96

Other terrapins which had been treated in a similar manner were examined, and the results, in every instance, corresponded with those detailed above.

We shall next compare these analyses with those of the *Emys serrata* in its normal condition, and when deprived of food and drink. The following tables will give a condensed view of the changes in the amounts and chemical constitution of the blood of the *Emys terrapin* during thirst, starvation, and a change of diet.

(a). *Specific Gravities and Water in 1000 parts of Blood and Serum.*					*Solid Constituents of Blood and Serum; Fibrin and Fixed Saline Constituents in 1000 parts of Blood.*			
	Specific gravity of blood.	Specific gravity of serum.	Water in 1000 parts of blood.	Water in 1000 parts of serum.	Solid constituents in 1000 parts of blood.	Solid constituents in serum of 1000 parts of blood.	Fibrin.	Fixed saline constituents.
(1). Female *Emys serrata* in a normal condition, having been captured 3½ days	1026.5	1013.7	875.41	956.97	124.59	39.36	1.04	5.22
(2). Female *Emys serrata*, which had been kept without food and drink 26 days.	1043.		801.34	904.52	198.66	84.59	4.15	11.45
(3). Female *Emys serrata*, which was kept without food and drink 28 days, and then transferred to a tub of water and abundantly supplied with vegetable food 42 days.	1029.6	1014.	877.65	948.86	122.35	47.30	1.64	4.80
(4). Female *Emys serrata*, which was kept without food and drink 28 days, and then transferred to a tub of water and abundantly supplied with vegetable food 88 days			884.16	950.00	115.84	46.53	2.43	

(b.) *Amount of Blood existing in these Terrapins.*	Weight of Terrapin.	Amount of blood.
	Grains.	Grains.
(1). Female *Emys serrata* in a normal condition	33.258	2000
(2). Female *Emys serrata* deprived of food and drink 26 days	28.675	450
(3). Female *Emys serrata* deprived of food and drink 28 days, and then transferred to a tub of water and abundantly supplied with vegetable food 42 days	25.333	2000

(c). *Moist Blood-Corpuscles and Liquor Sanguinis in* 1000 *parts of Blood.*

	MOIST BLOOD-CORPUSCLES.			LIQUOR SANGUINIS.		
	Moist blood-corpuscles.	Water of moist blood-corpuscles.	Solid constituents of moist blood-corpuscles.	Liquor sanguinis.	Water of liquor sanguinis.	Solid constituents of liquor sanguinis.
(1). Female *Emys serrata* in normal condition	336 76	252.57	84.19	663.24	622.84	40.40
(2). Female *Emys serrata* starved 26 days	439.64	329.76	109.92	560.32	471.58	88.74
(3). Female *Emys serrata* deprived of food and drink 28 days, and then transferred to a tub of water and supplied with vegetable food 42 days	293.64	220.23	73.41	706.36	657.42	48.94
(4). Female *Emys serrata* deprived of food and drink 26 days, and then transferred to a tub of water and supplied with vegetable food 88 days	267.52	200.64	66.88	732.48	683.52	48.96

Series II.—Experiments upon the Salt-Water Terrapin (*Emys terrapin*).

41. Examination of a female *Emys terrapin* which had been starved twenty-one days, then placed in fresh water, and abundantly supplied with Purslain.

It consumed large quantities of this vegetable, and was kept in the water for four weeks, Sept. 9.

The blood appeared thin and watery.

The portions drawn last coagulated much more rapidly than those drawn first. The former coagulated almost immediately after its removal from the body, whilst the latter required for its coagulation about thirty minutes.

The Fibrin was much softer than that of Terrapins in the normal condition.

Amount of blood obtained, about	1200 grains.
Solid constituents in 1000 parts of blood	114.56
" " " serum	34.90
" in serum of 1000 parts of blood	32.02
Water in 1000 parts of blood	885.44
" " serum	965.10

1000 parts of blood contained—

Water	885.44
Blood-corpuscles (dried organic constituents)	78.16
Albumen, fatty and extractive matter	30.48
Fibrin	0.83
Fixed saline constituents	5.09

1000 parts of blood contained—

Moist blood-corpuscles	326.84	Water	245.13
		Solid constituents	81.71
Liquor sanguinis	673.16	Water	640.31
		Solid constituents	32.85

The bladder contained two fluidounces of clear, light yellow urine, having a slightly acid reaction. Specific gravity, 1002.

The amount of the urine had been greatly increased, and its character also chemically and physically, had been decidedly changed.

This subject will be more fully considered hereafter. The stomach was filled with vegetable food, which gave a slightly acid reaction.

42. Examination of a female salt-water Terrapin (*Emys terrapin*) which was deprived of food and drink for twenty-one days, then placed in a tub of fresh water, and abundantly supplied with Purslain (*Portulacca oleracea*), for thirty-three days, Sept. 17.

The serum was of an orange yellow color.

The clot was small, and like that of the blood of Terrapins under the same circumstances, soft.

The bladder contained about half a fluidounce of clear, light yellow urine, neutral to test paper and of low specific gravity.

The stomach and intestine presented the usual appearance of those of Terrapins which had been treated in a similar manner.

Solid constituents in 1000 parts of blood	113.92
" " " serum	28.97
" in serum of 1000 parts of blood	26.49
Water in 1000 parts of blood	886.08
" " serum	971.03

1000 parts of blood contained—

Water	886.08
Blood-corpuscles	87.43
Solid constituents of serum	26.49

1000 parts of blood contained—

Moist blood-corpuscles	349.72	Water	262.29
		Solid constituents	87.43
Liquor sanguinis	650.28	Water	623.79
		Solid constituents	26.49

Several other salt-water Terrapins which had been starved, and then transferred to fresh water, and supplied with vegetable food, were examined, and in every instance the results were similar to those recorded above. The following tables will give a condensed view of the effects of these experiments upon the constitution of their blood.

(a). *Water and Solid Constituents in* 1000 *parts of Blood and Serum, and Amount of Blood obtained.*					*Fibrin and Fixed Saline Constituents.*		
	Water in 1000 parts of blood.	Water in 1000 parts of serum.	Solid constituents in 1000 parts of blood.	Solid constituents in 1000 parts of serum.	Amount of blood obtain'd.	Fibrin.	Fixed saline constituents.
					Grains.		
(1). Female *Emys terrapin* in normal condition having been captured twelve hours . .	845.28	956.17	154.72	43.83	1000.	4.15	10.74
(2). Female *Emys terrapin* deprived of food and drink 40 days	800.59	920.50	199.41	79.50	400.	5.26	10.74
(3). Female *Emys terrapin* which was deprived of food and drink twenty-one days, and then placed in fresh water and supplied with vegetable food 28 days	885.44	965.10	114.56	34 90	1200.	0.83	5.09
(4). Female *Emys terrapin* which was deprived of food and drink twenty-one days, and then placed in fresh water and supplied with vegetable food 33 days	886.08	971.03	113.92	28.97			

(b.) *Moist Blood-corpuscles and Liquor Sanguinis in* 1000 *parts of Blood.*						
	MOIST BLOOD-CORPUSCLES.			LIQUOR SANGUINIS.		
	Moist blood-corpuscles.	Water of moist blood-corpuscles.	Solid constituents of moist blood-corpuscles.	Liquor sanguinis.	Water of liquor sanguinis.	Solid constituents of liquor sanguinis.
(1). Female *Emys terrapin* in normal condition	447.28	335.46	111.82	552.72	509.82	42.90
(2). Female *Emys terrapin* deprived of food and drink 40 days	500.00	375.00	125.00	500.00	425.59	74.41
(3). Female *Emys terrapin* deprived of food and drink 21 days, and then placed in fresh water and supplied with vegetable food 28 days	326.84	245.13	81.71	673.16	640.31	32.85
(4). Female *Emys terrapin* deprived of food and drink 21 days, and then placed in fresh water and supplied with vegetable food 33 days	349.72	262 29	87.43	650.28	623.79	26.49

By a careful comparison of the results of these experiments upon the Yellow-bellied Terrapins (*Emys serrata*) and the Salt-water Terrapins (*Emys terrapin*), we discover the following effects of starvation, thirst, and a change from animal to vegetable food.

The blood lost during starvation was rapidly restored, in amount, upon a vegetable diet.

The proportion between the moist blood-corpuscles and liquor sanguinis was not altered in any great degree.

In most instances, the solid constituents of the blood were less under a vegetable than under an animal diet.

The fixed saline constituents were diminished, because they do not exist in so large an amount in the Purslain (*Portulacca oleracea*) as in the Small Reptiles, Fishes, Crustaceans, and Mollusca, which constitute the ordinary food of these Chelonians.

In many instances, the shells of the Terrapins suffered from the deprivation of the fixed saline constituents. They were rendered much softer.

A deprivation of these constituents would prove much less injurious to cold-blooded animals than to warm-blooded.

In the latter, all the vital and chemical actions are rapid and incessant, and the integrity of the nervous and muscular systems depends in a great measure upon the supply of certain inorganic salts, as the phosphate of lime, which enter into their anatomical composition, and are absolutely essential to their existence and the performance of their functions. The action of the nervous system is always attended with a corresponding consumption of the inorganic as well as the organic elements.

In cold-blooded animals, the nervous system, circulatory and respiratory apparatus, are feebly developed, and the metamorphoses of the organic and inorganic elements of the tissues and organs are correspondingly slow.

The effects of a change of diet were strikingly exhibited in the alterations of the digestive apparatus.

The intestines of carnivorous Chelonians are small and contracted. See Fig. 8, which represents the digestive apparatus of the Snapping Turtle (*Chelonura serpentina*). In frugivorous Chelonians, as the Gopher (*Testudo polyphemus*), they are large and capacious. (See Fig. 9.)

This is not surprising, since vegetable substances are much more bulky, contain much less nutriment, and are much more slowly digested than an equal amount of animal food; and hence we might infer that the small intestines would be enlarged, so as to render them suitable for the digestion of vegetables.

In many cases, as already stated, the pancreas was affected with a cancerous disease. One of the principal offices of the pancreatic fluid, is to form an emulsion with fats, and I have found the pancreas to be always of a much smaller size in frugivorous animals than in the carnivorous. It is probable that the gland, not being normally exercised, degenerated in structure.

Another marked effect in a change of diet, was the production of dropsical effusions into the cellular tissue, the pleural and abdominal cavities. The vegetable albumen of the Purslain was in a much more diluted form than that derived from flesh, consequently a much larger amount of water was thrown into the circulation than with a diet of animal food. The kidneys, called upon to perform an unusual amount of work, were unequal to the task. Water, holding albumen in solution, accumulated in the cellular tissues and serous cavities. Gradually, however, the kidneys became accustomed to the change, and threw off more perfectly the large amounts of liquid. The Terrapins examined shortly after their removal to the tub of water, contained much more fluid in their tissues and serous cavities than those examined after the lapse of some time. This shows us the manner in which the characters of the blood are preserved. The watery elements absorbed along with the Purslain did not accumulate in the bloodvessels, but were thrown off into the cellular tissue and serous cavities, and discharged by the kidneys. This shows that there is a tendency to a definite standard of concentration of the blood, and also to a definite proportion of its organic and inorganic constituents, which nature endeavors to maintain, however varied the conditions.

The effects of a change of diet upon the quantity, and chemical and physical constitution of the excretions of the kidneys, were strikingly illustrated in these experiments. The following table will present this in a clear light.

	Period of starvation and thirst.	Amount of urine excreted.	Specific gravity of urine.	Solid constituents of urine.	Reaction of urine.	Color of urine.
	Days.	Grains.		Grains.		
Female *Emys serrata*	17	442.3	1011.	11.33	Acid.	Turbid yellow.
" "	26	113.	1033.5	9.	"	Clear yellow, with chalky precipitates.
" "	29	223.1	1020.	10.396	"	Clear yellow, with precipitates.
" "	31	741.5	1017.5	29.36	"	Limpid yellow.
" "	38	890.6	1017.6	37.34	"	Yellow, with heavy precipitates.
Male "	49	300.	1019.4	13.02	"	Yellow, with precipitates.
Female *Emys terrapin*	40	300.	1015.	10.4	"	Clear yellow.
" "	43	70.			"	Cream-colored like pus.
" "	57	130.		8.05	"	Clear yellow.
Female *Emys terrapin*, deprived of food and drink 21 days, and then placed in fresh water and supplied with vegetable food 28 days. . . .		840.	1002.	3.40	Slightly acid.	Limpid light-yellow.
Emys serrata, starved 30 days, and then supplied with water and vegetable food 42 days. . .		2150.	1000.	5.	Neutral.	Limpid light-yellow.
Emys serrata, starved 30 days, and then supplied with water and vegetable food 60 days. . .		2160.	1004.	18.64	Neutral.	Limpid light-yellow.
Emys serrata, starved 30 days, and then supplied with water and vegetable food (purslain) 88 days.		2000.	1000.	1.	Neutral.	Limpid light-yellow.

From this table we see that the effect of the change of diet was to render the urine much more abundant, and to alter entirely its specific gravity and chemical reactions.

This subject, however, will be considered in its important bearings, when we come to the investigation of the kidneys and their excretions.

CHAPTER V.

OBSERVATIONS UPON THE ALIMENTARY CANAL AND DIGESTION OF ALBUMEN AND FLESH.

In many cartilaginous fishes, as the Stingray (*Trygon sabina*), the extent of surface over which the digested aliment is spread, is increased by a spiral valve which winds in close turns, from the pyloric to the anal extremity of the capacious intestine. By this remarkable arrangement, the apparently short intestine possesses an exceedingly enlarged surface of mucous membrane.

Fig. 19 represents the viscera and impregnated uterus of a Stingray (*Trygon sabina*), reduced to half its diameter.

The intestinal canal of Ophidians, is but slightly convoluted; its length is generally about equal to that of the body.

Fig. 21 represents the viscera of the Corn Snake (*Coluber guttatus*), reduced to half its diameter.

Fig. 8.

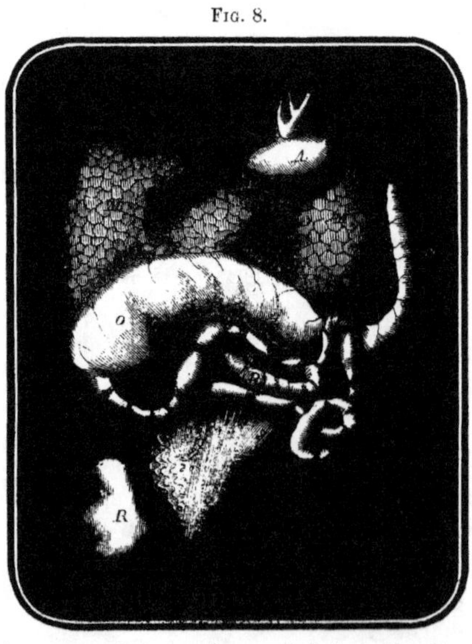

Viscera of Snapping Turtle (*Chelonura serpentina*), a carnivorous chelonian, reduced to one-half diameter. A. Ventricle of heart. B. Auricle of heart. M, M. Liver. N. Stomach. G. Duodenum; a small portion of the pancreas is seen in contact with the superior surface of the duodenum. P, P, P. Small intestines, which suddenly expand into the large intestine. O. Large intestine, filled with shells of crustacea, and fragments of grass and leaves. T. Rectum, S, S. Testicles. Q, Q. Kidneys. R. Bladder, partially filled with light yellow urine; the bladder communicates with the cloaca. X. Divided extremity of the large intestine, called, at this position, the cloaca.

The intestinal canal of the Congo Snake (*Amphiuma means*) resembles, in many respects, that of Ophidians (see Fig. 20).

The intestinal canal of carnivorous chelonians, as the Yellow-bellied Terrapin (*Emys serrata*), Chicken Terrapin (*Emys reticulata*), Salt-water Terrapin (*Emys terrapin*), and Snapping Turtle (*Chelonura serpentina*), is shorter and much less capacious than that of the graminivorous Gopher (*Testudo polyphemus*).

A comparison of the viscera of a carnivorous chelonian, as the Snapping Turtle (*Chelonura serpentina*) (Fig. 8), with the viscera of a graminivorous chelonian, as the Gopher (*Testudo polyphemus*) (Fig. 9), shows the modifications by which the alimentary canal is adapted to the habits and food of animals.

FIG. 9.

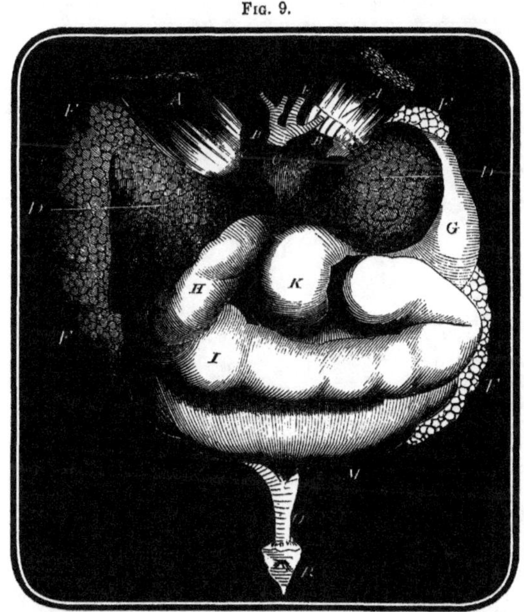

Viscera of the Gopher (*Testudo polyphemus*), a graminivorous chelonian, reduced to one-half diameter. A, A. Muscles. B, B. Auricles of heart. C. Ventricle of heart. F, F, F, F. Lungs; the lungs of this chelonian are very extensive. D, D. Liver. G. Stomach. H. Inferior portion of the small intestine. I, K. The large intestine, filled with grass and vegetable matters. M. Bladder: the bladder of the Gopher is capacious, and in medium-sized individuals of this species, often contains five fluid ounces of urine; the bladder empties its contents into the lower portion of the large intestine, or cloaca. O. Cloaca. R. Tail and anus: the tail is remarkably small and short in the *Testudo polyphemus*.

In all the gophers that I have examined, the stomach and small intestines were completely empty; while the colon and rectum, which are developed to an enormous extent, were packed with grasses and leaves. The vegetable food contained in the colon and rectum of medium-sized gophers, often amounted to several thousand grains.

These animals are able to do without food and drink much longer than carnivorous chelonians, because the wastes of the solids and fluids are supplied from this capacious storehouse of nutritive materials.

When carnivorous terrapins were starved for a length of time, and then fed upon vegetable food (purslain), the intestinal canal gradually became much enlarged, and resembled, in some respects, that of the gopher.

The colon and rectum of carnivorous chelonians generally contain the shells of invertebrate animals, and parts of leaves and grasses. During starvation, all the organic constituents of the shells gradually disappear, and nothing remains in the colon but white chalk-like masses, which I determined, in several instances, to be carbonate and phosphate of lime. The intestines, from the stomach to the anus, never contained any large amount of bile, showing that it was absorbed.

The stomach of cold-blooded animals gives an acid reaction during starvation and digestion. During starvation, the small intestines give, in many places, a feeble acid, and in others a neutral reaction. When fed upon vegetable substances, the reaction from the stomach to the anus was acid.

Table showing the length of the Alimentary Canal in various Animals.

	Weight of the body.	Length of the alimentary canal.
FISHES.	Grains.	Inches.
Trygon sabina (Stingray)	16,400	12
Zygæna malleus (Hammerhead Shark)	54,350	28
Lepisosteus osseus (Garfish)	22,303	30
Lepisosteus osseus (Garfish)	52,110	28¾
REPTILES.		
Menopoma Alleghanensis		24
Rana catesbæana (Bullfrog)	9,800	34
Heterodon niger (Black Viper)	4,620	26
Psammophis flagelliformis (Coachwhip Snake)	5,141	42
Coluber guttatus (Corn Snake)	9,600	54
Coluber constrictor (Black Snake)	5,100	36
Crotalus adamanteus (Rattlesnake)	6,180	42
Alligator Mississippiensis (Alligator), female	211,940	147
Alligator Mississippiensis (Alligator), male	76,507	60
Chelonia caretta (Loggerhead Turtle)	36,985	102
Chelonura serpentina (Snapping Turtle)	16,235	46
Emys reticulata (Chicken Terrapin)	8,400	38
Emys serrata (Yellow-bellied Terrapin)	27,172	66
Emys serrata (Yellow-bellied Terrapin)	14,400	54
Emys serrata (Yellow-bellied Terrapin)	23,100	60
Trionix ferox (Soft-shelled Turtle)		48
Testudo polyphemus (Gopher)	45,500	78
Testudo polyphemus (Gopher)	18,368	54
BIRDS.		
Tantalus loculator (Wood Ibis)	39,375	84
Tantalus loculator (Wood Ibis)	37,625	84
Ardea nycticorax (Night Heron)	10,095	90
Cathartes atratus (Black Turkey-Buzzard)	31,937	60
Syrnium nebulosum (Barred Owl)	10,580	36
Ortyx Virginiana (Quail)	2,760	40
Meleagris gallopavo (Wild Turkey)	36,312	72
Meleagris gallopavo (Wild Turkey)	28,875	68
MAMMALS.		
Didelphis Virginianus (Opossum)	18,812	51
Common Cat	35,000	64
Pointer Dog	247,126	138
Procyon lotor (Raccoon)	47,787	216
Procyon lotor (Raccoon)	54,735	180
Procyon lotor (Raccoon)	59,110	180
Sciurus Carolinensis (Gray Squirrel)	6,960	120
Sciurus capistratus (Black Fox Squirrel)	14,710	123
Cervus Virginianus (fœtus of Deer)	26,935	234
Common Sheep	385,000	1,056

Length of the Stomach, Small Intestines, Colon, and Rectum.

	Length of stomach.	Length of small intestines.	Length of colon and rectum.
	Inches.	Inches.	Inches.
Trygon sabina (Female Stingray)	3½	8½	
Zygæna malleus (Hammerhead Shark)	10	28	
Menopoma Alleghanensis (Hellbender)	3½	16	6
Rana catesbæana (Spring Frog)	4	30	
Chelonura serpentina (Snapping Turtle)	4	32	10
Testudo polyphemus (Gopher)	8	24	46
Testudo polyphemus (Gopher)	6	18	30
Common Cat		54	10
Didelphis Virginianus (Opossum)		38	18
Common Sheep		864	192

Length of the Bodies and Alimentary Canals of Ophidians.

	Length of animal.	Length of the alimentary canal.
	Inches.	Inches.
Heterodon niger (Black Viper)	32	26
Psammophis flagelliformis (Coachwhip Snake)	68	42
Coluber guttatus (Corn Snake)	54	54
Coluber constrictor (Black Snake)	54	36
Crotalus adamanteus (Rattlesnake)	48	42
Water Snake	40	50

Digestion of Albumen and Flesh.

The process of digestion has been the subject of numerous careful and laborious investigations, and after the researches of Spallanzani, Magendie, Tiedemann, Gmelin, Prout, Beaumont, Mulder, Dumas, Liebig, Blondot, Bernard, Lehmann, Bidder and Schmidt, and many others, it seems impossible that it should still remain in obscurity.

It has been the prevailing opinion of authors, that flesh, and the protein bodies generally, are digested entirely in the stomach. This fact, however, has lately been denied by physiologists of the highest authority. By recent experiments, Bidder and Schmidt have convinced themselves, that one of the important offices of the intestinal juice, is to dissolve and render fit for absorption, not only starch, but also flesh and other protein bodies. They assert that the intestinal juice not only metamorphoses starch with as great rapidity as the salivary and pancreatic fluids, but also that the intestine exerts as powerful a digestive influence on flesh and albumen as the stomach. Frerichs, on the other hand, has been unable, in his experiments, to detect any change exerted by the intestinal juice upon the protein elements of the food. Protein bodies, gelatinous substances, fat and starch, remained unchanged, and he denies positively that the intestinal juice has any action as a direct digestive agent.

Professor Lehmann, in a series of experiments upon the intestinal fluid collected from a loop of a gut in a human being with a fistulous opening into the small intestine, found that it possessed in a high degree, the power of converting starch into sugar; whilst protein bodies and fats were not affected in any appreciable manner. Professor Lehmann, however, attaches little importance to these experiments performed by himself, from the fact that the fistulous opening was in the lower portion of the ileum, and probably near the cæcum. He adopts the experiments of Bidder and Schmidt, and by an argument drawn from the amount of gastric juice secreted in a given length of time, and the amount of protein substances which it is capable of digesting, concludes that a large portion of flesh and albumen, and the other protein bodies, pass out of the stomach undigested, and are finally dissolved by the intestinal fluid. According to Professor Lehmann, the amount of gastric fluid secreted by a dog in 24 hours, equals one-tenth the weight of the whole body. 100 grains of recent gastric juice are capable of dissolving from 3 to 5 grains of coagulated albumen. A dog needs daily, for the perfect maintenance of all the physiological functions, 50 grains of flesh (containing 10 grains of albuminates) for every 1000 grains of its weight. It secretes, however, only 100 grains of gastric juice for every 1000 grains of its weight, only one-half the amount capable of dissolving the albuminates of the flesh. Hence a large portion of the protein bodies must pass out of the stomach undigested.

Careful experiments have shown that the gastric juice is deprived in the duodenum, of its free acid; and, with it, of its power of digestion by the bile and pancreatic fluid. Hence other fluids must flow into the intestines, which are capable of dissolving the protein bodies.

The only method of deciding accurately upon the truth of these conclusions, drawn by Prof. Lehmann from the preceding argument, is to appeal to the physico-chemical process of digestion, as it is performed in a normal condition in the animal economy.

I have enjoyed numerous opportunities of examining the contents of the stomachs of Fishes, Reptiles, Birds, and Mammals in every stage of the digestive process, and have never discovered undigested particles of flesh in the small intestines. The following observations were made during the prosecution of various researches upon the blood, urine, relative weights of the organs, comparative anatomy and minute structure of the organs of different animals, without any reference whatever to the maintenance of an hypothesis.

The stomach of an Alligator (*Alligator Mississippiensis*) contained the bones, teeth, hoofs, and hair of a pig. The flesh had been entirely digested, leaving the bones as clean as those of a prepared skeleton.

In the stomach of other alligators, we have found fishes, snakes, crabs, &c., in different stages of digestion—some but slightly acted upon by the gastric juice, others partially dissolved; whilst of others, little more than their bones remained.

The stomach of a Bullfrog (*Rana catesbæana*), which had been captured twenty-four hours, contained several Crawfish (*Astacus Bartoni*), and a slender Grass Snake (*Tropidonotus ordinatus*), about three feet in length. Although this food had been swallowed for more than twenty-four hours, only the exterior parts of the body of the serpent showed the evidences of the action of the gastric juice, and the shell of the invertebrate animals was of a red color, resembling that which they assume after they have been acted upon by boiling water.

In the stomachs of serpents we have found smaller serpents, lizards, and mice in all stages of digestion, whilst the small intestines contained not a particle of flesh.

These observations were also verified by an examination of the contents of the stomachs of fishes, carnivorous birds—as buzzards, hawks, cranes, herons, &c.; and also of carnivorous mammals—as raccoons and dogs.

If one-half of all the flesh received into the stomach passes into the small intestines, and if the process of digestion is, according to the statement of Bidder and Schmidt, as slow as that in the stomach, why is it that its presence always eluded observation when the intestinal canal was laid open? Especially in the case of animals which swallow their prey whole, without any mastication, it is difficult to see how portions of flesh could pass out of the capacious stomach into the contracted intestine, without being evident to the observer? All the observations I have thus far made, convince me that flesh is entirely digested in the stomach.

Another fact worthy of note is, that in the stomach of all animals, whether cold or warm-blooded, which I have examined whilst the process of digestion was going on, the amount of fluid containing the digested matter in solution, was exceedingly small, oftentimes amounting to only a few drops, and in many cases, especially amongst cold-blooded animals, it appeared to be almost entirely absent. This proves that, in the normal process of digestion, the matter dissolved by the gastric juice is almost immediately absorbed or passes into the duodenum.

As far as my observations have extended, a solution of the albuminous matters (chyme) does not often accumulate in the stomach. This accords with the results of the experiments of Dr. Samuel Jackson, Professor of the Institutes of Medicine in the University of Pennsylvania.

This fact shows the fallacy of the inference founded on the amount of flesh which can be digested by a given quantity of gastric juice out of the body. The natural process is far different from the artificial. A portion of gastric juice dissolves a definite amount of flesh, and the solution is then absorbed, or passes out into the small intestines. Another portion of gastric juice is secreted, and acts upon the fresh exposed surface of the flesh, and the products are in turn absorbed. It is evident that this process is far more energetic than that of artificial digestion, and consequently the one cannot be the measure of the other.

Even granting that artificial and normal digestion are precisely similar as far as the rapidity of their actions is concerned, how is it possible to determine the amount of gastric juice secreted by the stomach in a given time, when absorption is almost as rapid as secretion. In the consideration of the digestion of protein bodies, this fact has been left entirely out of view.

The absorption and passage of the digested matters, out of the stomach, immediately after their solution, is true also of graminivorous and frugivorous animals. I have examined the stomachs of numerous squirrels, rats, and birds fed upon grain, acorns, nuts, and berries, and in almost every instance there was no fluid that corresponded to the chyme. Even in those animals which subsist upon grasses and green buds and leaves, which contain a larger amount of fluid, the contents of the stomach are comparatively dry. Almost every one has it in his power to verify these observations, by simply visiting the butcher pens, and examining the contents of the stomachs of cows, sheep, &c.

Amongst cold-blooded animals, the only frugivorous species which I was able to examine, was the Gopher (*Testudo polyphemus*). In this the grasses and vegetable matters appear to be principally digested in the colon, which is enlarged into a receptacle for food, thirty inches in length and four inches in circumference. (See Fig. 9.) In one instance, after starvation for thirty days, the undigested vegetable contents of the colon and cæcum amounted to 1460 grains. The Gopher, as we have said in a previous chapter, has the power of retaining in its intestines vegetable food, which neither digests nor putrefies, though it rapidly decomposes when removed from the body.

CHAPTER VI.

COMPARATIVE ANATOMY AND PHYSIOLOGY OF THE PANCREAS.

AMONG the invertebrates no lymphatic system has been discovered, and the existence of a pancreatic gland has not as yet been satisfactorily shown.

Siebold considers two thick walled cæca, lined with ciliated epithelium, and opening into the beginning of the stomach, in many Rotatoria, a rudimentary pancreas. Hunter, Grant, Owen, Siebold, and Rymer Jones, consider the pale-yellow ramified tubes, which, in many species of Cephalopoda, are appended to the hepatic ducts as true representatives of the pancreatic glands of the higher animals. These, however, have not been definitely proved to be pancreatic glands, for no comparative anatomist or physiologist has as yet described the special character and offices of their secretion.

In the four great classes of vertebrate animals the circulatory system is completely separated from the digestive cavity, all the organs are highly developed, and the existence of a special system of absorbents appears to be absolutely necessary for the preservation of the integrity of the animal fluids, and also for the absorption of fatty matters, which are of great importance in the maintenance of animal temperature.

In Fishes, the development and perfection of the pancreas corresponds in no degree with the position occupied by different individuals in the classification of naturalists. The most superficial examination of the gland under consideration will show that many animals, of an exceedingly simple structure, often have individual organs more highly developed than those which stand far above them in physical and mental constitution. Thus in the lowest orders of the cartilaginous fishes, the Cyclostomi and Plagiostomi, this gland resembles, in all respects, that of the more highly organized mammals. In the Sturiones, its structure is somewhat simplified, and, in the majority of Osseous Fishes, it is reduced to its rudimentary form, consisting of cæca, varying in number in different species, and opening into the duodenum below the circular valve of the stomach, whilst in others, as observed by Cuvier in the Conger Eel, Pike, and Carp, and by Müller in the *Ophisurus serpens*, it is intimately associated with the internal mucous membrane, consisting of simple follicular depressions lined with the peculiar cells constituted to secrete the pancreatic fluid. It cannot, therefore, be asserted as a universal rule, without any exception, that there is a regular progression in the development of the different organs in animals, corresponding to the position which they occupy in the scale of creation. This may be illustrated by comparing together the rudimentary pancreas of the Plaice, Fig. 10; the pancreas of the Stingray (*Trygon sabina*), Fig. 13; the pancreas of the Hammerhead Shark (*Zygæna malleus*), Fig. 22; and the pancreas of the Garfish (*Lepisosteus osseus*), Fig. 11.

It matters not whether we view the pancreas in its earlier stages of development in the higher animals or in its permanent condition in many of the Osseous Fishes, its structure is the same. By classifying this organ according to its development in fishes we have an exact history of the changes which occur during its development in the higher animals. The permanent forms of the pancreas of the former are but transitory conditions, forming the stages in the development of this organ in the latter. According to Müller, Weber, and Wharton Jones, in higher animals which have a perfect pancreas, its development, like that of the salivary glands, commences by a simple diverticulum, or cæcum, from the walls of the duodenum. This subdivides into bud-like processes. As the development of the gland advances, the canal and its branches become more and more ramified and subdivided, until the compound racemose lobulated gland is formed. Precisely the same stages of development in a permanent form are discernible in the different orders, genera, and species of fishes.

Mere cells or follicular depressions in the mucous membrane of the small intestines, according to the observations of Cuvier, Müller, and Solly, perform the offices of the pancreas in several species, as the *Hippoglossus rondeletus*, Conger Eel, Pike, and Carp, and *Ophisurus serpens*.

In the *Ammodytes tobianus* there is a single cæcum prolonged into a pouch, representing this gland in its rudimentary condition. Several species of Plaice have two, whilst others have three, like the River Perch and Common Loach, whilst the *Platessa oblonga* has four of these cæcal pouches, which open into the pylorus and duodenum. This form of the pancreas is seen in the following figure:—

Fig. 10.

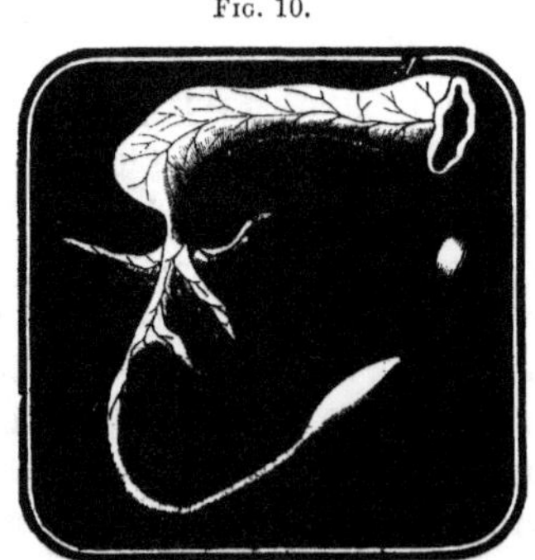

Rudimentary pancreas of the Plaice (*Platessa oblonga*) reduced to one-half diameter. A. Stomach. B. Pyloric extremity of stomach. C, C, C, C. Pancreatic cæca opening into the small intestine below the pyloric valve of the stomach. F. Small intestine. G. Large intestine. S. Spleen.

Five of these cæca occur in *Salmo spirlingulus*, six in *Perca lucioperca* and *Sargus annularis*, seven to eight in the Bass (*Corvina ocellata*), and ten to thirty or more in many Salmons and Herrings, and from eighty to ninety in the Common Salmon.

In *Gadus* and *Scomber*, the number is greatly augmented, and the complexity of the gland increased by the division of the cæca. In *Scomber thynnus* four large trunks arise from the intestine, and divide into branches, each of which subdivide and terminate at length in a tuft-like fasciculus of narrow tubular cæca.

In the salt-water Garfish (*Lepisosteus osseus*) of Georgia, the pancreas is situated with its superior convex border in contact with the inferior concave border of the liver, which resembles in shape and appearance this organ in serpents. The inferior border is in contact with the spleen. Upon the exterior it consists of numerous short cæca, which radiating inwards unite together forming several branches, which again unite and constitute one short duct, having a diameter almost equal to that of the small intestine into which it opens.

The duct branches of cæca generally contain, especially after a meal of fish, a cream-like fluid, which, under the microscope, is found to be a true emulsion, containing innumerable minute globules of oil in a transparent fluid. The large opening of the duct of the pancreas is so situated, just at the bend of the duodenum, that all the digested food, after passing the stomach, must be submitted to the influence of its secretion and much passes into the duct and cæca. All the oleaginous matter must, therefore, be brought into contact with the pancreatic juice, and in this manner an emulsion is formed and prepared for absorption. The emulsion is not found in the stomach above the opening of the duct of the pancreas, but exists in greatest abundance in its immediate vicinity and within the cæca.

The structure of this gland in the fresh-water Garfish of the swamps of Georgia, is constructed on a similar plan; its cæca, however, are longer, and the branches more distinct. The duct, branches, and cæca, contained, in every instance after a full meal, a similar fatty emulsion.

Fig. 11 represents the viscera, with the structure and position of the pancreas of the fresh-water Garfish.

This organ is very large in the Swordfish (*Ziphias gladius*). Professor Grant states, in his *Lectures upon Comparative Anatomy*, that, in the Swordfish, this organ is very large, and that it consists of innumerable small cæca connected together by cellular tissue, in which ramify the capillary vessels. These cæca form a reniform mass which is surrounded with a muscular tunic and the peri-

Fig. 11.

Viscera of a Fresh-Water Garfish reduced one-half diameter. B. Rough outline of the head. C, C. Pectoral fins. A. Heart. F. Superior portion of the lung. M. Lung. T. Inferior portion of the lung. The lung of the Garfish is a capacious fibrous sac which opens by a short trachea, high up in the throat, and extending nearly the whole length of the abdominal cavity, terminates within a short distance of the anus. It lies between the posterior surface of the liver and the anterior surface of the kidneys. When removed from the abdominal cavity, and fully inflated, its diameter is about equal to one-half of that of the fish. In many respects its structure resembles that of the *Amphiuma means* and other doubtful reptiles. L. Liver. N. Stomach. P. Pancreas composed of numerous cæca. S. Spleen situated in a convolution of the small intestines. In many individuals I have found two spleens. R. Inferior portion of intestinal canal. K Anus. X. Anal fin.

toneum. When opened, the innumerable component cæca are found to be formed by the successive divisions of the single great duct into which they all pour their secretions into the duodenum immediately below the pyloric valve.

In the Sturgeon, the structure of the pancreas is similar to that of the *Ziphias gladius.* The hundreds of cæca ramified from one common duct are inclosed in a muscular and peritoneal coat. The contraction of the muscular tunic compresses the cæca and forces their secretion into the intestinal canal. The excretory duct opens close to the pyloric valve and the termination of the *ductus communis choledochus.*

In the Eel, Pike, and fresh-water Trout, we find a yellowish-white compact glandular pancreas, having from two to three excretory ducts, which are frequently accompanied in their course to the intestine by the biliary ducts. In the Trout and some others there exist both pyloric appendages and a compact pancreatic gland.

In the Hammerhead Shark (*Zygœna malleus*), we find an elongated, narrow, flattened, light yellow, compact pancreas, with little lobulation. (See Fig. 22.)

In the Stingray (*Trygon sabina*), this organ is of a yellow color, and well defined, lobulated form, resembling in all respects the perfectly-developed pancreas of the Mammalia and other vertebrates.

The following figures represent the position and appearance of the pancreas of the Stingray (*Trygon sabina*).

FIG. 12. FIG. 13.

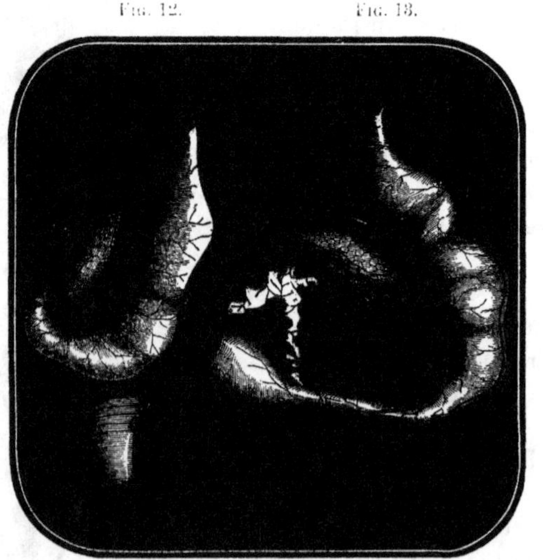

FIG. 12.—Position of the stomach, spleen, and intestine of the Stingray (*Trygon sabina*) after the removal of the liver. Reduced one-half diameter.—A. Inferior portion of the œsophagus expanding into the stomach. B. Stomach. S. Spleen. C. Duodenum, or commencement of small intestine. R. Intestine with spiral valve; the dark lines mark the turns of the valve.

FIG. 13 represents the stomach and spleen of the *Trygon sabina* turned over to one side, thus exposing the pancreas. Reduced one-half diameter.—A. Inferior portion of the œsophagus expanding into the stomach. B. Stomach. C. Small intestine, or duodenum. S. Spleen. P. Pancreas, presenting the appearance of this organ in the higher animals.

The pancreas of the Doubtful Reptiles assumes the appearance presented by that of the Stingray, Shark, and warm-blooded animals.

In the *Menobranchus maculatus*, it is an irregularly-shaped gland, having four principal lobes diverging from each other at right angles, thus presenting a stellate arrangement.

FIG. 14.

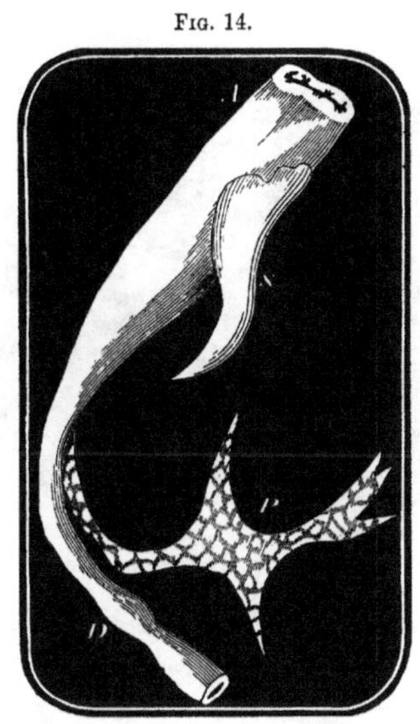

Stomach, spleen, and pancreas of the *Menobranchus maculatus*. Reduced one-half diameter.—A. Stomach. S. Spleen. P. Pancreas. D. Small intestine.

The pancreas of the Hellbender (*Menopoma alleghanensis*) is a long, delicate, light yellow gland, which commences near the pyloric extremity of the stomach, and extends down along the duodenum and small intestine for about three inches. Its inferior portion is more expanded than the superior. (See Fig. 24.) The pancreas of the Congo Snake (*Amphiuma means*) is similar in structure and appearance to that of the *Menopoma alleghanensis*, with the exception that it is broader and thicker. (See Fig. 23.)

In the Batrachia, the pancreas presents a developed appearance, and generally commences by a small slender lobe at the pyloric extremity of the stomach, and, passing downwards and forwards, expands into a broad lobulated mass. As in many other cold-blooded animals, it is not in contact with the spleen.

I have examined many American Ophidians,[1] and in each the pancreas is a compact, ovoid gland, often kidney-shaped, situated in contact superiorly with the

[1] For example, Banded Rattlesnake (*Crotalus durissus*), the Water Rattlesnake (*Crotalus adamanteus*), Ground Rattlesnake (*Cratalophorus miliarius*), Water Mokeson (*Trigonocephalus piscivorus*), Copperhead (*Trigonocephalus contortrix*), Hog-nose Viper (*Heterodon platyrhinos*), Black Viper (*Heterodon niger*), Grass Snake (*Tropidonotus ordinatus*), Water Snake (*Tropidonotus fasciatus*), Green Snake (*Leptophis æstivus*), Coachwhip Snake (*Psammophis flagelliformis*), Indigo Snake (*Coluber couperi*), Chicken Snake (*Coluber quadrivittatus*), Corn Snake (*Coluber guttatus*), Black Snake (*Coluber constrictor*).

gall-bladder, and inferiorly attached to the duodenum. The spleen, which is very small in these animals, is attached to the antero-superior surface of the pancreas. The hepatic and cystic ducts perforate the substance of the pancreas, and, uniting with its duct, enter the duodenum.

The following figure represents the position and appearance of these viscera in the Water Snake (*Tropidonotus sipedon*).

Fig. 15.

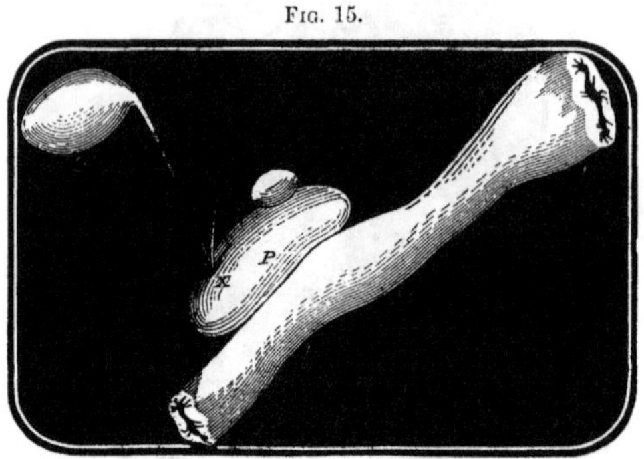

Spleen and pancreas of Water Snake (*Tropidonotus sipedon*). Natural size.—A. Inferior portion of the stomach contracting into the duodenum. R. Small intestine. P. Pancreas, a compact ovoid gland. S. Spleen attached to the anterior superior surface of the pancreas. By comparing the spleen of this serpent with those of other animals (as in Figs. 10, 12, 13, 14, 16, 17, 18, 22, 23, and 24), we see that this organ is remarkably small in Serpents. O. Gall-bladder. N. Cystic duct passing down and joining the hepatic duct, M, just where it perforates the pancreas. M. Inferior portion of the hepatic duct. X. Point at which the cystic and hepatic ducts perforate the pancreas.

In the carnivorous Chelonia, the pancreas is a large, well-developed, light-yellow, lobulated gland.

In the Soft-shelled Terrapin (*Trionyx ferox*), it commences opposite the pyloric valve of the stomach. The principal lobe extends down along the small intestine about three inches. At the inferior portion it sends off two lobes—the inferior one short and broad, the superior longer—and, passing downwards, comes in contact with the spleen, and passes along the anterior surface of this organ.

Fig. 16.

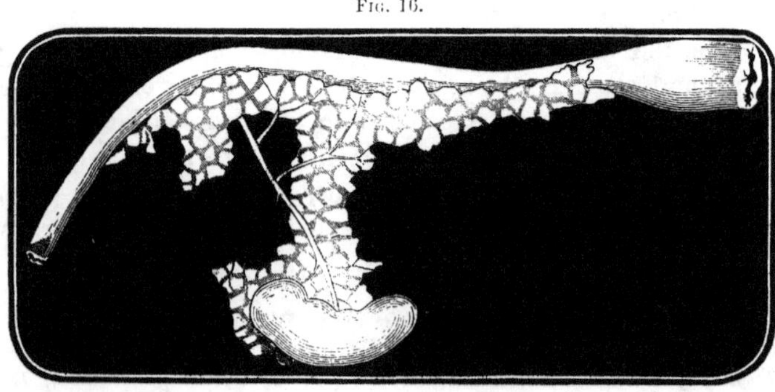

Pancreas of a carnivorous Chelonian (*Trionyx ferox*), Soft-shelled Turtle. Reduced one-half diameter.—A. Inferior portion of stomach contracting into small intestine. P, P, P. Pancreas composed of numerous lobules. S. Spleen. R. Small intestine.

The structure, position, and appearance of this gland do not differ in any essential respect in the Alligator Cooter (*Chelonura serpentina*), Loggerhead Turtle (*Chelonia caretta*), Salt-water Terrapin (*Emys terrapin*), Chicken Terrapin (*Emys reticulata*), Yellow-bellied Terrapin (*Emys serrata*), and other carnivorous Terrapins. The following figure represents the pancreas of the Yellow-bellied Terrapin (*Emys serrata*).

Fig. 17.

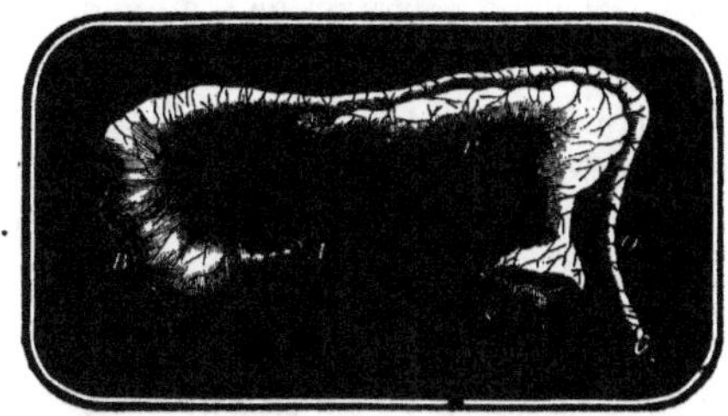

Pancreas of a carnivorous Chelonian (*Emys serrata*). Reduced one-half diameter.—A. Inferior portion of the œsophagus expanding into the stomach. B. Stomach. P. Pancreas. S. Spleen. O. Small intestine.

In the Gopher (*Testudo polyphemus*), which is the only graminivorous Chelonian in Georgia, the size and appearance of the pancreas are far different.

It is a long, slender, delicate gland, consisting of several thin slender lobes, subdivided into numerous small lobules. Its size is far smaller than that of carnivorous Chelonians. The reason of this will be readily understood when we consider the functions of the gland.

Fig. 18.

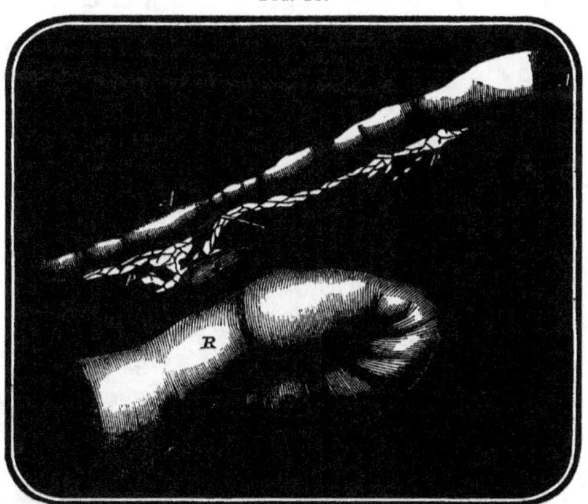

Pancreas of a graminivorous Chelonian (*Testudo polyphemus*), Gopher. Reduced one-half diameter.—A, A. Inferior portion of stomach and small intestine. P, P. Pancreas. S. Spleen. R. Large intestine, which contains grass.

A comparison of Figs. 16, 17, and 18, illustrates the fact that the pancreas of carnivorous Chelonians is larger than that of the graminivorous ones.

In Birds, the pancreas is a conglomerate gland, generally of large size, invariably lodged within a loop formed by the duodenum, and generally consists of two portions or lobes, united by a slender isthmoid portion. In some individuals it is single, and in others consists of three lobes. From each lobe an excretory duct is given off, which terminates separately in the intestine near the opening of the biliary canals. The color and appearance are similar to those of the well-developed pancreas in all animals, cold or warm-blooded, and so constant in this respect are the different glands in vertebrate animals that any one familiar with comparative anatomy and physiology can distinguish them at a glance.

The pancreas of the omnivorous and carnivorous Mammalia resembles, in appearance and structure, that of Man; its secretion enters the duodenum at the same point as that of the liver. In the Apes, the Ruminantia, and most Carnivora and Rodentia, it has but one duct which usually unites with the biliary. In some animals—as the Horse, Hog, Otter, and Beaver—it has two ducts, one of which unites with the biliary duct, and the other enters by itself, further behind, into the duodenum. In the Rabbit, the biliary and pancreatic ducts are separated from each other by a considerable interval.

The pancreas of all the carnivorous Mammalia which I have thus far examined is much larger than that of the frugivorous ones. This illustrates an important physiological fact, which will be shown by numerous comparative weights of the organ accurately ascertained.

Having considered the development, structure, and comparative anatomy of the pancreas in the four great classes of vertebrate animals, we shall next consider its use in the animal economy.

Although Mayer, Magendie, Tiedemann, Gmelin, Leuret, Lassaigne, and other physiologists and chemists had investigated the physical and chemical properties of the pancreatic fluid, still one of its important offices was entirely unknown until the researches of M. Cl. Bernard[1] demonstrated that it is indispensable for the formation of chyle and the absorption of fatty matters. Previous to this discovery, it was considered similar to the fluid secreted by the salivary glands, and its principal use was affirmed to be the conversion of starch into glucose. The investigations of M. Cl. Bernard demonstrated that the limpid chyle (formerly called vegetable chyle) is the product of the digestion of materials which contain no fatty matters, and the white chyle (called formerly animal chyle) contains fatty matters in the state of an emulsion, and the lymphatics of the mesentery are found to contain a white milky fluid only after the absorption of fatty matters, and that this emulsion and modification of the fatty matters were effected by the agency of the pancreatic juice. These conclusions were derived from the results of numerous ingenious experiments.

If Dogs are fed upon oleaginous matters, and killed at different periods, oil will be found unaltered until it comes in contact with the pancreatic fluid, and if the pancreatic ducts be tied, all alteration is prevented, and the oil remains transparent.

The most conclusive and beautiful of all Dr. Bernard's experiments were performed upon the Rabbit. In this animal, the pancreatic duct opens into the intes-

---

[1] Annales des Sciences Natur. Sept. 1848.

tine very low down, from six to fourteen inches below the hepatic duct, and if fatty matter be introduced into the stomach, and the animal killed in three or four hours, it will be found to have become an emulsion, and the lymphatics of the mesentery filled with white chyle only below the opening of the pancreatic duct. M. Cl. Bernard further showed that if fatty bodies be exposed to the pancreatic fluid, out of the body, a complete emulsion is formed, and, if it be allowed to remain long enough, the fatty substances will be decomposed into glycerine and fatty acids, and, in the case of butter, butyric acid. Parallel experiments instituted with other fluids—as bile, saliva, gastric juice, serum of the blood—produce no such effects on fatty bodies.

It was probably supposed that fat was, in the animal economy, resolved into glycerine and fat acids. This process, however, would be very complicated, and involves many difficulties, and it is more reasonable to conclude that the action of the pancreatic juice is limited to the formation of an emulsion, which is nothing more than the mechanical division of the fat into minute globules, coated with a thin film of the albuminoid elements of the pancreatic juice. That this is really the case in living animals, I enjoyed many opportunities of rendering apparent, whilst examining the pancreas of the Garfish (*Lepisosteus osseus*). In this fish, the duct of the pancreas has a diameter almost equal to that of the intestine, and is so situated that all the digested matters which pass out of the stomach must come in contact with its secretion, and often pass, in considerable amount, into the duct and cæca of the gland. When the emulsion is squeezed out, and subjected to the microscope, it is found to consist of innumerable minute globules of oil, surrounded by a transparent fluid.

The correctness of M. Bernard's observations has been called in question by Drs. Bence Jones, Lenz, Frerichs, Bidder, Schmidt, Lehmann, Donders, and Herbert. It is asserted that the bile and intestinal juice are even more active and efficient than the pancreatic juice, in the preparation of fatty matters for absorption. It is objected to Bernard's experiments, that he delayed his examination of the animals too long, and allowed the emulsion, formed with the bile, to pass down and be absorbed, before inspecting the viscera of the rabbits.[1]

Dr. Samuel Jackson, Professor of the Institutes of Medicine in the University of Pennsylvania, has recently examined this subject carefully, and repeated the experiments of Bernard, avoiding every source of error, and especially that of time, by causing oleaginous matters to enter the digestive apparatus, constantly, until the moment of observation. In every instance the results of his experiments confirmed the correctness of Bernard's conclusion, that the emulsion of fatty matters is produced by the action of the pancreatic juice. The doctor concludes his valuable paper by the following summary of the present state of our knowledge on this point:—

"1. Liquid fats are not miscible with the aqueous albumino-saline fluid—liquor

---

[1] American Journal of the Medical Sciences, October, 1854, p. 307.

sanguinis—with which all the vascular tissues are saturated; it cannot enter their pores, and consequently cannot be absorbed.

"2. Liquid fats, when emulsified by albumen, are reduced to minute particles, each coated with albumen. In this state they are miscible with the liquor sanguinis, moistening the tissues, can enter their pores, and are then capable of absorption. This is the sole condition requisite for the absorption of fats.

"3. The white milk-like fluid, named chyle, is this emulsion of the fatty matters of the food, mixed with the ordinary lymph, always contained in the lymphatics of the alimentary canal, and other abdominal organs and mesentery. The molecular base of Gully is the microscopic appearance in the chyle, of the minute globules of fat coated with albumen.

"4. Albumen forms a perfect and persistent emulsion with oils. The pancreatic fluid is a saturated albuminous solution, and forms with oils an emulsion equally as perfect and permanent as that of albumen.

"5. The pancreatic juice is the only highly albuminous fluid in the alimentary canal, and can accomplish the formation of a perfect emulsion; and the opinion of M. Cl. Bernard, that this process is one of its functions, is, it appears to me, sustained.

"6. The observations of M. Cl. Bernard, that the formation of the emulsion of fats in rabbits is at and below the pancreatic duct, and not above it, is confirmed by the experiments reported in this communication. And further, that the experiments on rabbits are the most reliable, as being a true exemplification of the natural process, unattended with violence and torture to the animals, more or less disturbing in their effects.

"7. That M. Cl. Bernard's view of the decomposition of fats by the pancreatic juice is not proved, is opposed by the nature of the process, and by analogy with other emulsions; it is unnecessary to the accomplishment of the absorption of fats, and introduces other and complicated processes, that are unknown to exist, and are mere hypotheses."

Whilst engaged, last summer, in the investigation of the physical and chemical constitution of the fluids and the comparative anatomy and physiology of cold-blooded animals, it occurred to me that the pancreas of carnivorous animals should be larger than that of the frugivorous or granivorous animals, because it is much more incessantly exercised in the secretion of a fluid for the emulsifying of fats. Accordingly, I ascertained accurately the weights of the body and pancreas of every animal that came into my possession. Dividing the weight of the former by that of the latter, we obtain the weight of the pancreas in relation to that of the body, and the relative size of this organ in different animals is thus ascertained.

The weights of the animals were obtained with a pair of scales capable of turning to half a grain, and the weights of the organs with a delicate balance, capable of turning to $\frac{1}{1000}$th of a grain. The following table exhibits the most important results thus found.

Comparative Weights of the Pancreas of Carnivorous Fishes and Reptiles.

	Number of times the weight of its pancreas.
Weight of *Trygon sabina* (Female Stingray)	1071
" *Zygæna malleus* (Hammerhead Shark)	1045
" *Zygæna malleus* (Hammerhead Shark)	1563
" *Lepisosteus osseus* (Female Garfish)	193
" *Lepisosteus osseus* (Garfish)	272
" *Rana catesbæana* (Bullfrog)	1088
" *Heterodon niger* (Black Viper)	537
" *Psammophis flagelliformis* (Coachwhip Snake)	1353
" *Coluber guttatus* (Corn Snake)	1371
" *Coluber constrictor* (Black Snake)	472
" *Crotalus durissus* (Banded Rattlesnake)	965
" *Chelonia caretta* (Loggerhead Turtle)	518
" *Chelonura serpentina* (Snapping Turtle)	630
" *Emys terrapin* (Salt-water Terrapin)	994
" *Emys reticulata* (Chicken Terrapin)	763
" *Emys serrata* (Yellow-bellied Terrapin)	1067
" *Emys serrata* (Male Yellow-bellied Terrapin)	1200
" *Emys serrata* (Female Yellow-bellied Terrapin)	1343

Comparative Weights of the Pancreas of Frugivorous Chelonians.

	Number of times the weight of its pancreas.
Weight of *Testudo polyphemus* (Male Gopher)	3500
" *Testudo polyphemus* (Male Gopher)	3061

Comparative Weights of the Pancreas of Carnivorous Mammals.

	Number of times the weight of its pancreas.
Weight of *Procyon lotor* (Female Raccoon)	241
" *Procyon lotor* (Female Raccoon)	155
" *Procyon lotor* (Female Raccoon)	259
" *Procyon lotor* (fœtus of Raccoon)	583
" Common Cat	402
" Pointer Dog	337
" *Didelphis Virginianus* (Opossum)	192

Comparative Weights of the Pancreas of Frugivorous and Granivorous Mammals.

	Number of times the weight of its pancreas.
Weight of common sheep	1125
" *Sciúrus Carolinensis* (Gray Squirrel)	3026

By comparing these numbers, we arrive at the following conclusions:—

1. The pancreas of the Garfish (*Lepisosteus osseus*), a powerful, voracious and active fish, is much larger than that of more sluggish species. The Garfish consumes large numbers of small fishes, which it readily captures with its long and well armed jaws. The tissues and organs, especially the liver of fishes, contain much oil, and consequently a large gland is needed to afford a sufficient amount of the peculiar substance absolutely requisite for the preparation of the oleaginous

matter for absorption. We have previously stated that, in the pancreas of this remarkable fish we have conclusive proof of the function of this gland.

2. The pancreas of carnivorous fishes and reptiles is relatively much larger than that of frugivorous Chelonians. This difference in the relative size of this organ in these two classes, is evident at a glance. In the Ophidians it is a compact, ovoid gland, and in the carnivorous Chelonians it is a broad, lobulated, well developed, conspicuous gland; whilst in the frugivorous Gopher (*Testudo polyphemus*) it is a thin, delicate, obscure gland, composed of several slender lobes, subdivided into numerous lobules.

3. The pancreas of carnivorous Mammalia is much larger than that of the frugivorous or granivorous. The principal exception to this assertion appears in the Beaver, which is stated to have an unusually large pancreatic gland. A consideration, howver, of the character of the food of this animal will, we think, explain this anomaly. The stomach, and more especially the cæcum of the Beaver, is stated by observers to be filled up with fragments of bark and wood, which appear to constitute its chief aliment. The experiments of Mitscherlich have shown that alkaline solutions are capable of converting cellulose into starch, even more readily than concentrated acids. It is, therefore, highly probable that the great office of the alkaline pancreatic fluid in this animal is the preparation of cellulose for absorption, by converting it into starch.

4. The pancreas of carnivorous fishes and reptiles is larger than that of frugivorous and granivorous mammals, notwithstanding that the digestion of the former is much slower than that of the latter, and the amount of nutritive matters necessary to sustain the economy much less.

5. The pancreas of carnivorous mammals is larger than that of carnivorous cold-blooded animals; the digestive process is much more rapid, and correspondingly larger glands are needed to supply the secretions necessary for the proper preparation of the food for absorption.

The difference between the weights of the organ in these two classes of animals, does not correspond exactly with the disparity of their respective digestive processes, probably because the sluggish circulation and aeration of the blood, and the small amount of nervous force possessed by cold-blooded animals, require much larger organs to accomplish precisely the same results. As circulation and respiration are developed and perfected, and all the acts of life rendered correspondingly active, the more perfect and condensed become the organs and apparatus.

These results were shown, as far as simple dissection and inspection, upon other animals killed in swamps and woods, and at periods when it was impossible to ascertain their weights.

Our investigations upon birds have not been sufficiently extended to warrant general conclusions.

Whilst experimenting upon the effects of starvation and a change of diet upon the blood of carnivorous terrapins I found, as stated in a previous chapter, that the pancreas of many of those which had been deprived of food and drink for a length of time, and then placed in a tub of water and liberally supplied with vegetable food was diseased. Parts of the gland were of a black color and hard texture, and under the microscope contained cancer-like cells and crystals which resembled in appearance those of the triple phosphate. It is probable that the gland, not being normally exercised, degenerated in structure.

In the first of a series of experiments which have not as yet been completed, I ascertained the correctness of M. Cl. Bernard's statement that fatty substances are not altered in the stomach or intestines of dogs if the pancreatic duct be tied.

The abdominal cavity of a remarkably large and voracious pointer dog, noted for his powerful digestive powers, was opened along the linea alba, and two fluidounces of lard oil secured in the stomach by ligatures above and below, and one fluidounce was injected and secured in the same manner in the intestines. The viscera were then carefully returned and the wound sewed up.

At the expiration of six hours the dog was killed, and the contents of the stomach and intestines had neither increased nor diminished, and were changed neither in physical or chemical properties, and the lymphatics of the mesentery did not appear to contain any milky emulsion. Under the microscope, the lard oil presented an appearance differing in no respect from that of ordinary oil.

Lard oil was inclosed separately in the stomach and intestines of a dog, and immersed for eighteen hours in the serum of this animal. At the end of this time neither endosmose of the serum nor exosmose of the oil had taken place. In the living dog the bloodvessels of the stomach and intestines retained their natural size and appearance. When saline solutions of high specific gravity were enclosed in a similar manner in the stomach and intestines of dogs and cats, the bloodvessels were congested with blood, and the internal surface of the mucous membrane presented a pinkish-purple color.

The following general conclusions have been drawn from this study of the comparative anatomy and physiology of the pancreas:—

1. In the Invertebrate Animals, this gland and the lymphatic system do not exist, because the character of the circulatory system, and the manner in which it receives the digested matters from the visceral cavity, are such, that the conditions requiring their presence are wanting.

2. In Fishes we may study the development of the pancreas, the permanent forms being but the transient conditions in the development of this gland in the higher animals.

3. The assertion of M. Cl. Bernard, that the chief office of the pancreas is to prepare fatty matters for absorption, is sustained by the following facts:—

a. In the Garfish (*Lepisosteus osseus*), the emulsion of the fatty matters takes place in the duct and cæca of the pancreas and their immediate vicinity, and nowhere else in the alimentary canal.

b. The pancreas of carnivorous animals is relatively much larger than that of frugivorous and granivorous ones. The amount of oil consumed by the former is much greater than that consumed by the latter. It may be inferred from these data, that the principal office of the pancreatic juice is the preparation of fats for absorption. This is farther sustained by the fact that the size of the pancreas amongst carnivorous animals is in a measure proportional to the amount of oleaginous matters consumed. The pancreas of the active, voracious Garfish, which destroys large numbers of small fish, is larger than that of the more sluggish fishes.

c. The pancreas of carnivorous Chelonians fed upon vegetable matters, degenerated in its structure.

CHAPTER VII.

OBSERVATIONS UPON THE LIVER.

THE form and appearance of the liver vary greatly in different animals. The shape and number of the lobes, and the general color, appear to follow no special law. The following observations, however, will show that its general form is often determined by that of the animal and its abdominal cavity.

The following figure represents the viscera of the Stingray (*Trygon sabina*).

FIG. 19.

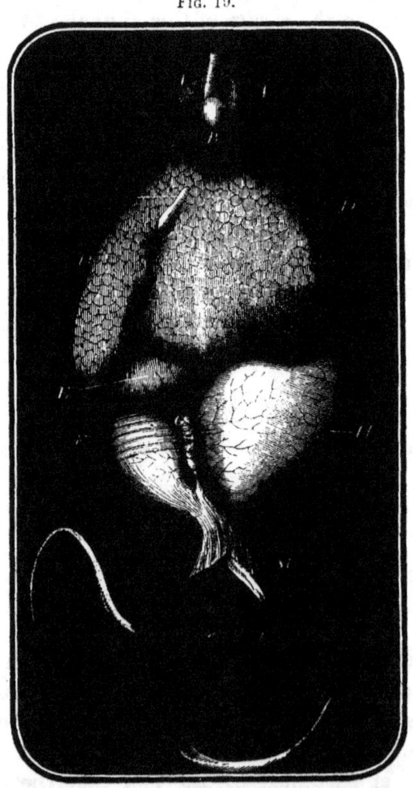

Viscera and impregnated uterus of the Stingray (*Trygon sabina*), reduced to one-half diameter. A, A. Auricle of the heart. B. Ventricle of the heart. D, D. Liver. C. Gall-bladder. E. Stomach. F. Intestine with spiral valve, which increases the extent of surface over which the digestive aliment is spread. The dark lines indicate the position and turns of the valve. H. Impregnated uterus. The tails of the Fœtal Stingrays are seen projecting out of the anus. G. Unimpregnated uterus and ovaries communicating with the cloaca. M. Cloaca. R, S. Tails of Fœtal Stingrays. X. Anus.

In many short, stout, and broad fishes, as the Stingray and Plaice, this organ is broad and thick.

Fig. 20 represents the viscera of the Congo Snake (*Amphiuma means*).

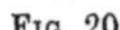

FIG. 20.

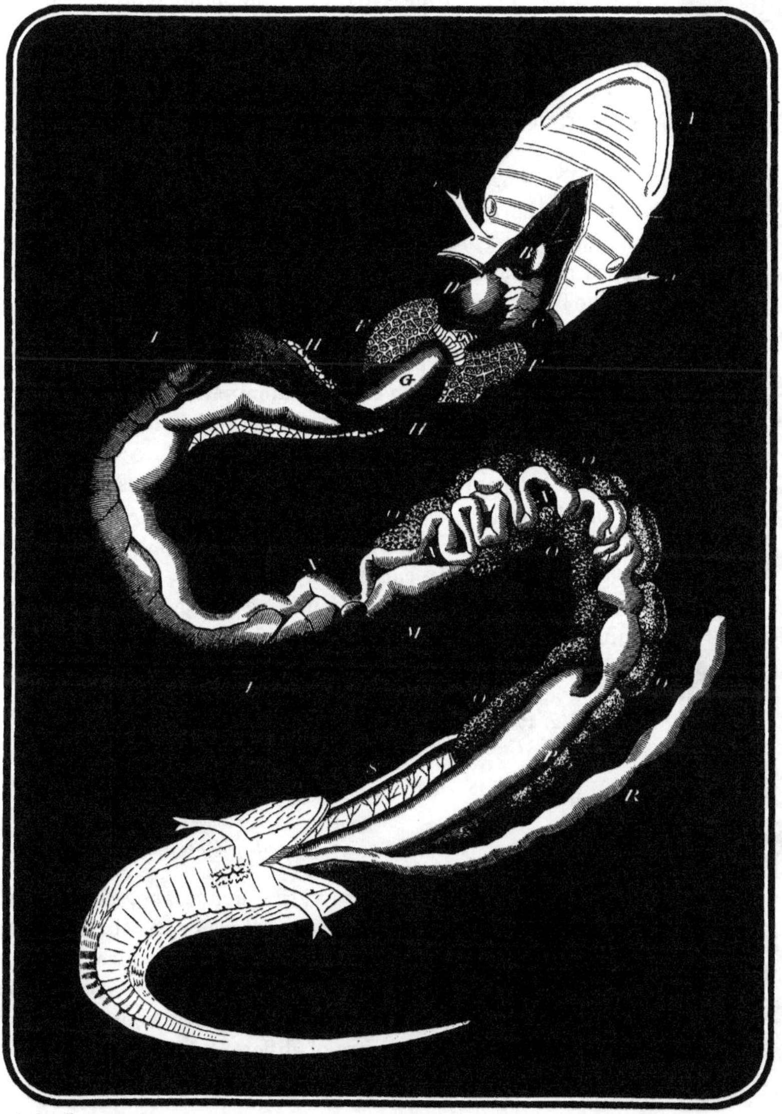

Viscera of the Congo Snake (*Amphiuma means*), reduced one-half diameter. A. Rough outline of head. B. Bulbus arteriosus, dividing into two principal branches. C. Auricle of heart. D. Ventricle of heart. E. Trachea, dividing and entering the lungs. F, F. Superior portions of the lungs slit open, showing their structure. G. Œsophagus and superior portion of stomach. H, H. Exterior surface of the lungs not slit open. I, I. Liver. M. Gall-bladder. N, N, N. Small intestines. O, O, O, O. Ovaries. P. Large intestine filled with claws of crustaceans and shells of molluscous animals, and particles of grass and leaves. R. Urinary bladder, remarkably long. Its contents are poured into the cloaca. S, S. Kidneys, flattened ribbon-like bodies. The lower portion of the figure is a rough sketch of the tail.

FIG. 21.

The general shape of the liver and viscera corresponds with that of the abdominal cavity and the fish.

In the Garfish, a long round fish having a correspondingly long and round abdominal cavity, the liver is elongated and resembles in appearance that of the doubtful reptiles and Ophidians. See Figure 11, representing the liver and viscera of the salt-water Garfish (*Lepisosteus osseus*).

In the Congo Snake (*Amphiuma means*) (Fig. 20), a long, slender, doubtful reptile, with an elongated narrow abdominal cavity, the general form of the liver is that of a long irregularly-shaped prism.

In the shorter and stouter Hellbender (*Menopoma Alleganensis*) and *Menobranchus maculatus*, this organ is correspondingly broad and short.

The liver of Batrachians generally consists of three lobes, and occupies the superior middle portion of the abdominal cavity.

This organ in serpents is narrow and much elongated, corresponding to the shape of the abdominal cavity, whilst in the round, thick-set Chelonians, it consists of two principal lobes extending across the abdominal cavity. These lobes in the Chelonia are united by a small isthmus, and resemble a pair of saddlebags.

Fig. 21 represents the viscera of a Corn-Snake (*Coluber guttatus*) This may be compared with Figs. 8, 9, 11, 19, and 20.

These differences corresponding to the general form of the animals, will be readily comprehended by comparing together the following figures:—

Fig. 19.	Viscera of	Stingray (*Trygon sabina*).
" 11.	"	Garfish (*Lepisosteus osseus*).
" 20.	"	Congo Snake (*Amphiuma means*).
" 21.	"	Corn Snake (*Coluber constrictor*).
" 8.	"	Snapping Turtle (*Chelonura serpentina*).
" 9.	"	Gopher (*Testudo polyphemus*).

The size of the liver also varies much, and, as far as my observations have extended, the difference can be accounted for neither by the habits, nor by the vital, chemical, or physical constitution of animals. The truth of this assertion will be readily verified by a reference to the following table of the relative weights of the livers of different animals, which were carefully ascertained upon delicate balances.

Viscera of Corn Snake (*Coluber constrictor*), reduced one-half diameter. C. Trachea or windpipe. A. Auricles of heart. B. Ventricle of heart. F. Superior vascular portion of the lung. D. Œsophagus. G, G. Liver. S. Stomach. M. Gall-bladder. N. Spleen. The hepatic duct is seen passing over the spleen and perforating the pancreas. P. Pancreas, compact ovoid gland attached to the small intestine. R. Divided end of small intestine.

Comparative Weights of the Liver of Animals.

	Number of times the weight of its liver.
FISHES.	
Weight of the body of *Trygon sabina* (Stingray) female	18
" " *Trygon sabina* (Stingray fœtus)	16
" " *Zygæna malleus* (Hammerhead Shark)	25
" " *Zygæna malleus* (Hammerhead Shark)	41
" " *Lepisosteus osseus* (Garfish)	75
" " *Lepisosteus osseus* (Garfish)	62
REPTILES.	
" " *Rana catesbiana* (Bullfrog)	55
" " *Heterodon niger* (Black Viper)	26
" " *Psammophis flagelliformis* (Coachwhip Snake)	71
" " *Coluber guttatus* (Corn Snake)	64
" " *Coluber constrictor* (Black Snake)	57
" " *Crotalus adamanteus* (Rattlesnake)	55
" " *Alligator Mississippiensis* (Alligator), male	73
" " *Chelonia caretta* (Loggerhead Turtle)	47
" " *Chelonura serpentina* (Snapping Turtle)	42
" " *Emys terrapin* (Saltwater Terrapin)	53
" " *Emys reticulata* (Chicken Terrapin)	18
" " *Emys serrata* (Yellow-bellied Terrapin)	36
" " *Emys serrata* (Yellow-bellied Terrapin)	25
" " *Emys serrata* (Yellow-bellied Terrapin)	48
" " *Testudo polyphemus* (Gopher)	50
" " *Testudo polyphemus* (Gopher)	45
BIRDS.	
" " Turtle Dove, male	77
" " *Meleagris gallopavo* (Wild Turkey)	70
" " *Meleagris gallopavo* (Wild Turkey)	67
" " *Picus erythrocephalus* (Redheaded Woodpecker)	33
" " Night Heron	22
" " *Tantalus loculator* (Wood Ibis)	68
" " *Tantalus loculator* (Wood Ibis)	64
" " *Syrnium nebulosum* (Barred Owl)	56
" " *Cathartes atratus* (Black Buzzard)	47
MAMMALS.	
" " *Didelphis Virginianus* (Opossum)	26
" " Common Sheep	61
" " *Sciurus Carolinensis* (Gray Squirrel)	43
" " *Sciurus capistratus* (Fox Squirrel)	48
" " *Cervus Virginianus* (Fœtus of Deer)	35
" " *Cervus Virginianus* (Fœtus of Deer)	42
" " *Mus rattus* (Rat just born)	39
" " *Mus rattus* (Rat just born)	36
" " *Mus rattus* (Rat half grown)	20
" " *Procyon lotor* (Raccoon), female	25
" " *Procyon lotor* (Raccoon), female	19
" " *Procyon lotor* (Raccoon), female	23
" " *Procyon lotor* (Raccoon, just born)	24
" " Pointer Dog, female	32
" " Common Cat, female	36

M. Cl. Bernard and other physiologists consider one essential function of the liver to be the elaboration of the blood. Chemical analyses have shown that the blood-corpuscles are more numerous in the blood after passing out of this organ than when entering into it. It is, therefore, reasonable to believe that the blood-corpuscles have their origin in the liver. If the main offices of the liver be the elaboration of the albumen, and the formation of the blood-corpuscles, we might infer that it should be larger in warm than in cold-blooded animals, because in the former the blood is more abundant and much more rapidly formed and consumed in supplying the wastes of the tissues than in the latter.

Another function of the liver is the production of grape sugar. Physiologists of high reputation suppose that this is used in the production of animal temperature. If the supply of grape sugar corresponds to the temperature, the liver should be largest in warm-blooded animals.

These are the considerations which led me to investigate the relative size of this organ in different animals. But it must be stated, decidedly, that these views have not been sustained by my researches. A reference to the table shows us that the liver is smaller in Birds than in many Fishes, Reptiles, and Mammals, while the former have the highest temperature and the greatest number of blood-corpuscles.

Notwithstanding these results we need not abandon the preceding physiological doctrines, as no organ in the bodies of animals is so liable to alterations in its weight, unconnected with its secretory or excretory apparatus, as the liver. Fishes especially contain an extraordinary amount of oil. I have detected the presence of oil under the microscope, in the form of innumerable small globules in the livers of all animals, and even in the livers of cold-blooded animals which had been starved for sixty days, and warm-blooded animals which had been starved to death. In the cold-blooded animals, although every particle of fat had disappeared from their tissues, and the animals had died from starvation, still oil globules were found in considerable numbers in their livers. Again, the structure of the liver in cold-blooded animals, and fishes especially, is much softer and less compact than in the warm-blooded ones. These facts show that the weight of the liver is not a true exponent of that portion of the gland which is devoted to the elaboration and formation of the constituents of the blood.

The livers of all animals, cold or warm-blooded, always, as far as my observation has extended, yield grape sugar. I have detected its presence by various tests in the livers of numerous Fishes, Batrachians, Ophidians, Chelonians, Birds, and Mammals. I have found it in the livers of cold-blooded animals at all periods of starvation, and even after death from a deprivation of food and drink. In the liver, however, of a dog which was starved to death, I failed to discover any of it.

These facts show that, during starvation, grape sugar must be formed in the animal economy in part, from the nitrogenized elements.

One of the most prominent effects of starvation in all animals is the consumption of the fatty matters. Fat is found in considerable quantities in the livers of all animals, whether supplied with, or deprived of food and drink; and a universal accompaniment of this fat is grape sugar, a substance closely allied to it in chemical constitution. A relation, therefore, appears to exist between the consumption of fat in the animal economy and the production of grape sugar; but what this relation is, and whether grape sugar is formed from fat, has never been determined.

After its production in the liver, grape sugar passes into the circulation and disappears in the lungs as long as a normal respiration is maintained. I demonstrated by numerous careful[1] experiments upon cold-blooded animals the following facts:—

1. Grape sugar is never normally a constituent of the urine.
2. If the supply of oxygen be cut off from cold-blooded animals by placing them in carbonic acid or hydrogen gas, or by closing the trachea completely, grape sugar accumulates in the blood and is eliminated by the kidneys. The disappearance of this substance in the lungs depends, therefore, upon the introduction of oxygen.
3. In cold-blooded animals the function of the liver in producing sugar continued after the exclusion of the oxygen.
4. The appearance of grape sugar in the urine was accompanied in every instance by remarkable alterations in the forms and appearance of the blood-corpuscles under the microscope.

---

[1] The excretions of the kidneys in cold-blooded animals, generally, are scanty. Chelonians are the best adapted for such experiments on account of their capacious bladders. They were prepared by being starved for a length of time, and then transferred to a tub of water and abundantly supplied with vegetable food (*Portulacca oleracea*). The excretions of the kidneys were thus rendered copious.

CHAPTER VIII.

OBSERVATIONS UPON THE SPLEEN.

THE spleen is absent from all invertebrate animals without exception. It is also wanting in the *Amphioxus*, the connecting links between Fishes and the higher forms of the Mollusca.

In the Cyclostomi and *Lepadogaster*, it is said to be of such small size as to be readily overlooked.

It varies much in size, form, and position, in different fishes. In the Stingray (*Trygon sabina*) it is large and oval (Figs. 12 and 13). In the Hammerhead Shark (*Zygœna malleus*) it is narrow and much elongated, as in the following figure:—

FIG. 22.

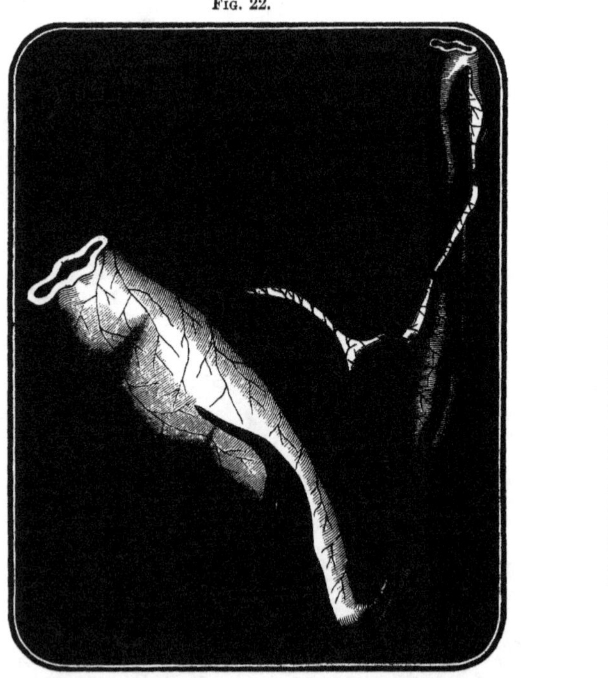

FIG. 23.

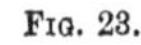

Fig. 22. Stomach, spleen, and pancreas of the Hammerhead Shark (*Zygœna malleus*) reduced one-half diameter. A. Superior portion of stomach. B. Stomach. C, C. Spleen. D, D, D. Small intestine. P, P, P. Pancreas.

Fig. 23. Stomach, spleen, and pancreas of Congo Snake (*Amphiuma means*) reduced one-half diameter. A. Stomach. S. Spleen. D. Small intestine. P. Pancreas.

In the Plaice (*Platessa oblonga*) it is small and oval. See Fig. 10.

The Garfish has frequently two large spleens situated in contact with the inferior surface of the pancreas.

In both the salt and fresh-water Garfishes, this organ is of large size, and often varies in its form in individuals belonging to the same species.

The form of the spleen varies much in the doubtful reptiles. It is elongated and ribbon-like in the Congo Snake (*Amphiuma means*, Fig. 23), and flatter, broader, shorter, and more oval in the Hellbender (*Menopoma Alleganensis*) and Proteus of the Lakes (*Menobranchus maculatus*). In these reptiles the spleen lies upon the left side. The following figures will illustrate these differences:—

FIG. 24.

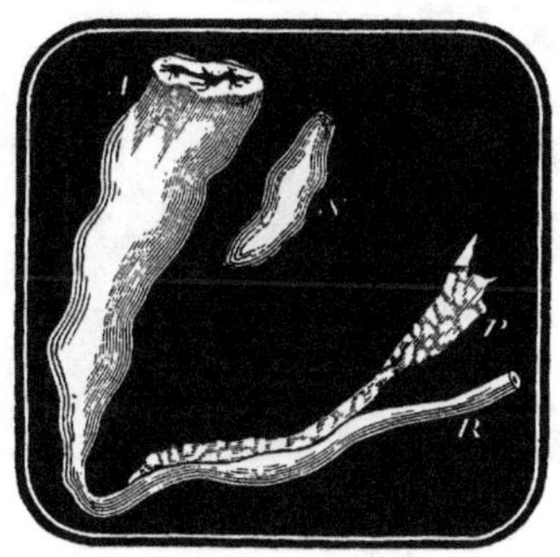

Stomach, spleen, and pancreas of the Hellbender (*Menopoma Alleganensis*) reduced one-half diameter. A. Stomach. S. Spleen. P. Pancreas. R. Small intestine.

The spleen of Batrachians is generally oval or kidney-shaped, and of small size, and occupies a position near the median line of the body.

The spleen of Ophidians is a small oval body, firmly attached to the superior and anterior surface of the pancreas, from which it is readily distinguished by its color. This is true of this organ in the Hognose Viper (*Heterodon platyrhinos*), Black Viper (*Heterodon niger*), Grass Snake (*Tropidonotus ordinatus*), Green Snake, (*Leptophis aestivus*), Coachwhip Snake (*Psammophis flagelliformis*), Pine Snake, (*Pituophis melanoleucus*), Indigo Snake (*Coluber couperi*), Chicken Snake (*Coluber quadrivittatus*), Corn Snake (*Coluber guttatus*, Fig. 25), Black Snake (*Coluber con-*

FIG. 25.

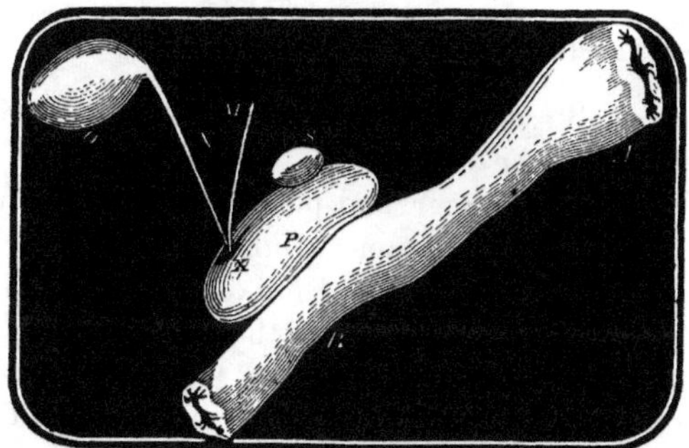

Spleen, pancreas, and gall-bladder of Corn Snake (*Coluber guttatus*), natural size. A. Inferior portion of stomach. R. Small intestine. P. Pancreas. S. Spleen. O. Gall-bladder. N. Cystic duct. M. Hepatic duct.

strictor), Water Mokeson (*Trigonocephalus piscivorus*), Copperhead (*Trigonocephalus contortrix*), Ground Rattlesnake (*Crotalophorus miliarius*), Banded Rattlesnake (*Crotalus durissus*), and Water Rattlesnake (*Crotalus adamanteus*). (*See* Figs. 21 and 25.)

In the Chelonians, the spleen varies much in size and appearance, even in individuals of the same species. In the Soft-shelled Turtle (*Trionyx ferox*), it is of large size, kidney-shaped, and lies a little to the left of the median line of the body, with its anterior concave border in contact with the inferior border of the pancreas. (*See* Fig. 26.)

Fig. 26.

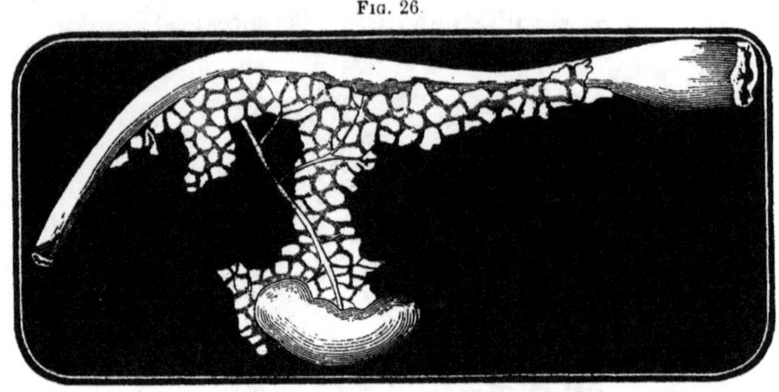

Spleen and pancreas of Soft-shelled Turtle (*Trionyx ferox*). A. Inferior portion of stomach. P, P, P. Pancreas. S. Spleen. R. Small intestine. (Reduced one-half diameter.)

In the Salt-water Terrapin (*Emys terrapin*), Chicken Terrapin (*Emys reticulata*), and Yellow-bellied Terrapin (*Emys serrata*), it is smaller and more oval in shape. (*See* Fig. 27.)

Fig. 27.

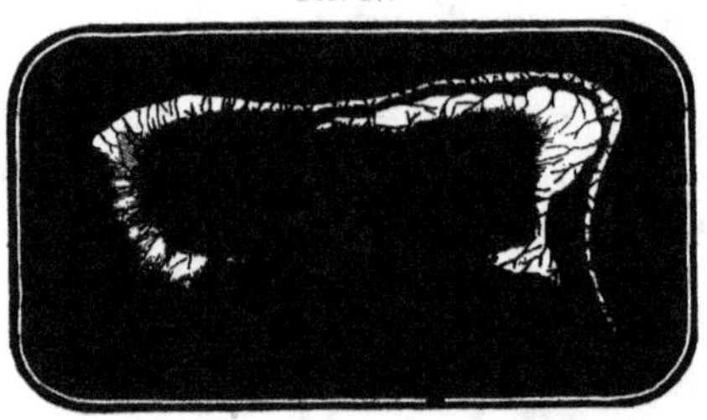

Spleen, pancreas, and stomach of Salt-water Terrapin (*Emys terrapin*), reduced one-half diameter. A. Inferior portion of œsophagus. B. Stomach. O. Small intestine. P. Pancreas. S. Spleen.

The spleen is of very small size in all birds, generally oval in form, and situated near the anterior extremity of the pancreas.

In the Mammalia this organ is larger, and presents manifold diversities of form. In all animals it may be distinguished, almost immediately, by its color alone.

The researches of Professors Ecker and Kölliker, M. Beclard, Dr. Gray, and other physiologists and chemists, have shown that the blood-corpuscles undergo important changes in the spleen.

If the function of the spleen be that of the formation and destruction of the blood-corpuscles, it is reasonable to suppose that it should be much larger in warm than in cold-blooded animals, because the number of the blood-corpuscles is greater, and all the changes of the elements of the fluids and solids much more rapid in the former than in the latter.

To determine this point, I ascertained accurately the weights of the bodies and spleens of cold and warm-blooded animals, contained in the following tables. The first represents the absolute weights of the bodies and spleens, and the last the relative weights of the spleen.

Weights of the Bodies and Spleens of Animals.

Name of animal.	Weight of the body.	Weight of the spleen.
FISHES.	Grains.	Grains.
Trygon sabina (Stingray), female	16,400	56
Trygon sabina (Stingray), fœtus	610	$\frac{6}{10}$
Zygæna malleus (Hammerhead Shark)	54,350	89
Zygæna malleus (Hammerhead Shark)	6,568	14
Lepisosteus osseus (Garfish)	22,303	38
Lepisosteus osseus (Garfish)	52,110	87
REPTILES.		
Rana catesbiana (Bullfrog)	9,800	$4\frac{3}{10}$
Heterodon niger (Black Viper)	4,620	$\frac{18}{100}$
Psammophis flagelliformis (Coachwhip Snake)	5,141	$\frac{8}{10}$
Coluber guttatus (Corn Snake)	9,600	1
Coluber constrictor (Black Snake)	5,100	$\frac{7}{10}$
Crotalus adamanteus (Water Rattlesnake)	6,180	$\frac{4}{10}$
Alligator Mississippiensis (Alligator), male	76,507	58
Alligator Mississippiensis (Alligator), female	211,940	266
Chelonia caretta (Loggerhead Turtle)	36,985	$16\frac{8}{10}$
Chelonura serpentina (Snapping Turtle)	16,235	$20\frac{3}{10}$
Emys terrapin (Salt-water Terrapin)	11,937	$1\frac{5}{10}$
Emys reticulata (Chicken Terrapin)	8,400	$8\frac{7}{10}$
Emys serrata (Yellow-bellied Terrapin)	27,172	$16\frac{8}{10}$
Emys serrata (Yellow-bellied Terrapin)	14,400	$12\frac{8}{10}$
Emys serrata (Yellow-bellied Terrapin)	23,100	$20\frac{3}{10}$
Testudo polyphemus (Gopher)	45,500	18
Testudo polyphemus (Gopher)	18,368	$5\frac{1}{10}$
BIRDS.		
Meleagris gallopavo (Wild Turkey), female	36,312	$23\frac{6}{10}$
Meleagris gallopavo (Wild Turkey), female	28,875	11
Picus erythrocephalus (Red-headed Woodpecker)	1,060	$\frac{2}{10}$
Tantalus loculator (Wood Ibis)	39,375	11
Tantalus loculator (Wood Ibis)	37,625	$18\frac{9}{10}$
Syrnium nebulosum (Barred Owl)	10,580	$7\frac{2}{10}$
Cathartes atratus (Black Buzzard)	31,937	26
MAMMALS.		
Didelphis Virginianus (Opossum)	18,812	45
Common Sheep	385,000	652
Sciurus Carolinensis (Gray Squirrel)	6,960	$10\frac{2}{10}$
Sciurus capistratus (Fox Squirrel)	14,710	16
Cervus Virginianus (Fœtus of Deer)	26,935	95
Cervus Virginianus (Fœtus of Deer)	26,953	77
Mus rattus (Rat just born)	$99\frac{7}{10}$	$\frac{2}{10}$
Mus rattus (Rat just born)	$84\frac{2}{10}$	$\frac{1}{6}$
Mus rattus (Rat half grown)	1,063	$2\frac{1}{10}$
Lepus sylvaticus (Common Rabbit)	20,928	14
Procyon lotor (Raccoon), female	47,787	139
Procyon lotor (Raccoon), female	54,735	391
Procyon lotor (Raccoon), female	59,110	203
Procyon lotor (Raccoon just born)	1,750	$11\frac{3}{10}$
Pointer Dog (male)	247,126	428
Common Cat (female)	35,000	67

Comparative Weights of the Spleens of Animals.

	Number of times the weight of its spleen.
FISHES.	
Weight of the body of *Trygon sabina* (Stingray), female	292
" " *Trygon sabina* (Stingray fœtus)	1,016
" " *Zygæna malleus* (Hammerhead Shark)	601
" " *Zygæna malleus* (Hammerhead Shark)	443
" " *Lepisosteus osseus* (Garfish)	587
" " *Lepisosteus osseus* (Garfish)	599
REPTILES.	
" " *Rana catesbiana* (Bullfrog)	2,279
" " *Heterodon niger* (Black Viper)	25,666
" " *Psammophis flagelliformis* (Coachwhip Snake)	6,426
" " *Coluber guttatus* (Corn Snake)	9,600
" " *Coluber constrictor* (Black Snake)	7,285
" " *Crotalus adamanteus* (Rattlesnake)	15,450
" " *Alligator Mississippiensis* (Alligator), male	1,319
" " *Alligator Mississippiensis* (Alligator), female	798
" " *Chelonia caretta* (Loggerhead Turtle)	2,201
" " *Chelonura serpentina* (Snapping Turtle)	800
" " *Emys terrapin* (Salt-water Terrapin)	7,958
" " *Emys reticulata* (Chicken Terrapin)	965
" " *Emys serrata* (Yellow-bellied Terrapin)	1,618
" " *Emys serrata* (Yellow-bellied Terrapin)	1,125
" " *Emys serrata* (Yellow-bellied Terrapin)	1,138
" " *Testudo polyphemus* (Gopher)	2,527
" " *Testudo polyphemus* (Gopher)	3,600
BIRDS.	
" " *Meleagris gallopavo* (Wild Turkey), female	1,538
" " *Meleagris gallopavo* (Wild Turkey), female	2,625
" " *Picus erythrocephalus* (Red-headed Woodpecker)	2,120
" " *Tantalus loculator* (Wood Ibis)	3,579
" " *Tantalus loculator* (Wood Ibis)	2,044
" " *Syrnium nebulosum* (Barred Owl)	1,470
" " *Cathartes atratus* (Black Buzzard)	1,228
MAMMALS.	
" " *Didelphis Virginianus* (Opossum)	418
" " Common Sheep	590
" " *Sciurus Carolinensis* (Gray Squirrel)	682
" " *Sciurus capistratus* (Fox Squirrel)	919
" " *Cervus Virginianus* (Fœtus of Deer)	283
" " *Cervus Virginianus* (Fœtus of Deer)	350
" " *Mus rattus* (Rat just born)	498
" " *Mus rattus* (Rat just born)	505
" " *Mus rattus* (Rat half grown)	506
" " *Lepus sylvaticus* (Common Rabbit)	1,494
" " *Procyon lotor* (Raccoon), female	343
" " *Procyon lotor* (Raccoon), female	292
" " *Procyon lotor* (Raccoon), female	391
" " *Procyon lotor* (Raccoon just born)	156
" " Pointer Dog (male)	577
" " Common Cat (female)	522

These tables show that the spleen is smallest in Birds and Ophidians, and largest in Fishes and Mammals. The temperature of Birds is high, their blood-corpuscles numerous, their life-actions vigorous, and the physical and chemical changes of the elements of their fluids and solids correspondingly rapid. In Fishes, circulation and respiration are sluggish, the blood-corpuscles few in numbers, the temperature low, the metamorphosis of the elements of their structure slow, and the intellect and all the life actions correspondingly feeble.

If the function of the spleen be the construction, destruction, and elaboration of some of the important elements of the blood, why is it so small and insignificant in birds, and of such great relative magnitude in many cold-blooded animals? Is it possible that an organ, which, in many Ophidians, Chelonians, and Birds, weighs only a few grains or a small fraction of a grain, can exert any important influence upon the physical properties and chemical constitution of the blood? Do not these facts show conclusively that we do not understand the functions of the spleen?

Mr. Gray[1] supposes that one office of the Malpighian corpuscles is to store up nutritive matter when there is a surplus of alimentary materials; to be restored again to the blood when there is a deficiency of these elements. It is, however, difficult to conceive, how nutritive matter of any importance could be stored up in the Malpighian corpuscles of organs, weighing a few grains or only fractions of a grain. The amount accumulated in such organs would be microscopic in its character, and not much more than the hundredth part of a grain.

Even in warm-blooded animals the amount of albuminous compounds contained in the Malpighian corpuscles of the spleen is insignificant, and unworthy of notice when compared with that contained in the circulatory apparatus, the capacious reservoir of the nutritive materials. The circulatory apparatus of an adult man contains, according to the most recent and reliable calculations, about twenty-two pounds of blood, whilst the Malpighian corpuscles of the spleen are capable of containing only a few grains.

Would nature construct an organ, an important office of which would be to store up a few grains of nutritive matter, whilst the circulatory system contains more than ten thousand times the amount?

Mr. Gray instituted a valuable series of researches upon the effects of diet upon the spleen of Cats, Rabbits, and Rats, and found that this organ increases during active nutrition. As far as my observations have extended this phenomenon does not occur in cold-blooded animals.

The spleens of Salt-water Terrapins (*Emys terrapin*) and of Yellow-bellied Terrapins (*Emys serrata*), which had been starved and deprived of water for a great length of time, and then transferred to a tub of water and abundantly supplied with vegetable food, did not exhibit any increase in weight. I have also observed, in numerous instances, that the spleen of cold-blooded animals does not act as a diverticulum for any surplus water or nutritive materials in the circulatory apparatus.

The spleens of many carnivorous Chelonians, whose circulatory apparatus was so filled with blood consequent upon a change of diet, that aqueous albumino-saline effusions took place into the cellular tissue, and all the cavities, presented no increase in size or weight.

The spleens of Ophidians, which are voracious and swallow large masses of flesh,

---

[1] The Structure and Use of the Spleen, by Henry Gray, F. R. S. London, 1854.

were not enlarged, notwithstanding the large amount of nutritive substances which were received into their circulatory apparatus.

That the spleen is an organ of subordinate importance in the animal economy will be shown by the following facts:—

It is absent from all invertebrate animals without exception. It is also absent from the *Amphioxus*, the connecting link between fishes and the higher forms of the mollusca.

In the *Amphioxus* and Invertebrate animals the blood-corpuscles are always colorless. The occurrence of the spleen is accompanied by a change in the color of the blood.

Has the spleen anything to do with the production of the red blood-corpuscles of vertebrate animals? The blood of the invertebrata, with its corpuscles, exists before the formation of any special organs. The same fact is noticed in the development of the fœtus of warm-blooded animals.

A vascular system circulating a fluid containing colored blood-corpuscles exists before the formation of any special organs, and hence it is probable that the spleen has little to do with the formation of the corpuscles and the production of their red color. This conclusion is farther sustained by the fact that the amputation of the spleen of Dogs and other animals is not followed by any alteration in the amount or character of the blood and its constituents, and they enjoy very good health, and there is no sensible difference between them and those that have not undergone the operation. From these investigations we may draw the following conclusions:—

1. The spleen of Birds and many Reptiles is too small to exert an important influence in the animal economy.

2. Its size corresponds in no manner with the number of blood-corpuscles, or the rapidity of the composition and decomposition of the organic and inorganic elements of the fluids and solids of animals.

3. Of the real office of the spleen in the animal economy we are still ignorant.

4. The function of the spleen is not indispensable to the maintenance of life.

CHAPTER IX.

OBSERVATIONS UPON THE KIDNEY.

In the present chapter we do not propose to treat of the comparative anatomy and physiology of this organ in general, but simply to record a few observations which we consider of importance.[1]

June 27. The kidneys of a small Chicken Snake (*Coluber guttatus*), about two and a half feet in length, and those of a large Coachwhip Snake, were carefully amputated. The bloodvessels were secured and the wounds closed. The Chicken Snake was placed in a glass jar and remained in confinement for three and a half days, when it pushed off the top and made its escape, although this was held down by a pound weight. The serpent, therefore, must have been strong and active at the time of its escape.

The Coachwhip Snake died at the end of three and a half days. Its viscera presented remarkable appearances. The lung contained considerable quantities of coagulated blood effused into the air-cells. The blood contained numerous minute white particles. The exterior serous covering of the lungs, the internal surface of its air-cells and coats of its bloodvessels, the serous covering of the intestines, abdominal cavity, and surface of the liver, were covered with small white granules, appearing as if fine white sand had been sprinkled over them. The deposit was in all cases most abundant in the course of the bloodvessels. When the internal structure of the liver was cut or torn it was found to be completely impregnated with these small white masses which could be readily squeezed out, and appeared to occupy principally the neighborhood of the bloodvessels.

At the lower portion of the abdominal cavity, where the kidneys had been amputated, the blood effused, and the peritoneum, with the internal surface of the epidermis, where it had been removed from the muscles, were completely covered with large numbers of these white granules having the appearance to the sight and touch of grains of sand. This increased deposition in the region of the wound was without doubt due to the more active determination of blood towards this part. The intestines were found to contain the same deposit, none of it, however, was found in the humors of the eye and muscular tissue.

These granular masses from all parts of the abdominal cavity, and its viscera and peritoneal coverings, and from the exterior and interior of the lungs were carefully

[1] See Observations by the Author upon the Kidney and its Excretions in Different Animals, American Journal of Medical Sciences, April, 1855.

examined microscopically and chemically. In every instance under the microscope they were found to be composed of small granules and delicate acicular crystals.

All the characteristic chemical tests gave unequivocal evidence that these granules were composed of uric acid and ammonia. A careful microscopical examination also showed that they were the urate of ammonia, which is the most abundant constituent of the urine of serpents.

From the results of this experiment we may draw the following conclusions:—

1. The kidneys are excreting and not secreting organs. The circulatory apparatus not only carries nutriment to the different organs and tissues, but also removes from them the products of their disintegration and metamorphosis of no further use in the animal economy.

The amount and character of an excretion depends entirely upon the amount and character of the excrementitious materials existing in the blood.

A secretion does not exist in the blood. We do not find the gastric juice or the salivary fluid existing in the blood before they are elaborated by special organs.

2. When the kidneys are amputated, other membranes and organs assume their office of depurating the blood. In like manner, if the function of the skin be checked it will be assumed by the kidneys. The act, then, of separating certain materials from the blood can be transferred from one excretory organ to another. This, however, is not true of secretions. Each secretion must have a special set of cells, which alone can produce the peculiar material.

We never find one organ elaborating the secretion of another distinct organ. This is a general law. The salivary gland never secretes gastric juice, nor the mammillary gland, bile. The stomach of a Rattlesnake never secretes the deadly fluid of its poison gland. Thus, in two essential respects, a secretion differs from an excretion.

3. It is probable that in the lower animals which are without kidneys, the office of the latter is carried on by the mucous membrane of the stomach and intestinal canal.

We will next consider the relative size of the kidneys in the four great classes of vertebrate animals.

Comparative Weights of the Kidneys of Animals.

	Number of times the weight of its kidneys.
FISHES.	
Weight of the body of *Trygon sabina* (Stingray), female	188
" " *Trygon sabina* (Stingray) fœtus	93
" " *Zygæna malleus* (Hammerhead Shark)	346
" " *Zygæna malleus* (Hammerhead Shark)	335
REPTILES.	
" " *Rana catesbiana* (Bullfrog)	515
" " *Heterodon niger* (Black Viper)	177
" " *Psammophis flagelliformis* (Coachwhip Snake)	88
" " *Coluber guttatus* (Corn Snake)	152
" " *Coluber constrictor* (Black Snake)	76
" " *Crotalus adamanteus* (Rattlesnake)	131
" " *Alligator Mississippiensis* (Alligator), male	135
" " *Alligator Mississippiensis* (Alligator), female	145
" " *Chelonia caretta* (Loggerhead Turtle)	368
" " *Chelonura serpentina* (Snapping Turtle)	249
" " *Emys terrapin* (Salt-water Terrapin)	775
" " *Emys reticulata* (Chicken Terrapin)	280
" " *Emys serrata* (Yellow-bellied Terrapin)	409
" " *Emys serrata* (Yellow-bellied Terrapin)	416
" " *Emys serrata* (Yellow-bellied Terrapin)	495
" " *Testudo polyphemus* (Gopher)	322
" " *Testudo polyphemus* (Gopher)	360
BIRDS.	
" " *Ectopistes Carolinensis* (Turtle Dove), female	182
" " *Ectopistes Carolinensis* (Turtle Dove), male	237
" " *Ortyx Virginiana* (Quail)	125
" " *Meleagris gallopavo* (Wild Turkey)	204
" " *Meleagris gallopavo* (Wild Turkey)	206
" " *Picus erythrocephalus* (Redheaded Woodpecker)	81
" " *Ardea nycticorax* (Night Heron)	97
" " *Tantalus loculator* (Wood Ibis)	168
" " *Tantalus loculator* (Wood Ibis)	171
" " *Buteo borealis* (Hen Hawk)	141
" " *Syrnium nebulosum* (Barred Owl)	176
" " *Cathartes atratus* (Black Turkey-Buzzard)	132
" " *Ardea candidissima* (Snowy Heron)	86
MAMMALS.	
" " *Didelphis Virginianus* (Opossum)	131
" " Common Sheep	350
" " *Sciurus Carolinensis* (Gray Squirrel)	175
" " *Sciurus capistratus* (Fox Squirrel)	147
" " *Lepus sylvaticus* (Common Rabbit)	186
" " *Mus rattus* (Young Rat), just born	90
" " *Mus rattus* (Young Rat), just born	105
" " *Mus rattus* (Rat), half grown	92
" " *Procyon lotor* (Raccoon), female	66
" " *Procyon lotor* (Raccoon), female	57
" " *Procyon lotor* (Raccoon), female	61
" " *Procyon lotor* (Raccoon), just born	68
" " Pointer Dog	178
" " Common Cat	142

The following conclusions may be derived from this table:—

1. The kidneys of Ophidians and Saurians are much larger relatively than those of the Chelonians. This difference will be readily understood by a comparison of the habits and vital and physical constitution of these two classes.

Serpents take their food in large quantities, often swallowing animals heavier and larger than themselves. All this animal matter is capable of digestion and absorption into the blood, a large portion of which is superfluous, and must be eliminated by the kidneys. The carnivorous Chelonians, on the other hand, are much more moderate, and slow in the indulgence of their appetites. This arises from necessity rather than choice. Their motions are so slow, their disposition to shut themselves up in their shells so great, and their mouth so small, that their appetites are not indulged to such an extent as to burden the kidneys, and call for an increase in their size.

The rapidity of the wastes of the tissues, as we have previously shown, is proportional to the rapidity of the vital actions. Hence, the kidneys will have more to do in active animals than in the sluggish. Many serpents, as the black snake and coachwhip snake, are remarkably active, and all Ophidians are more energetic than the proverbially sluggish Chelonians. Here we have another reason why the kidneys should be larger in the former than in the latter. Those Chelonians which inhabit the water should have smaller kidneys than those Ophidians which inhabit the land, because the function of the skin is much more active in the former than in the latter. The skin of most serpents is completely covered by horny scales, and its power of removing fluids, and, the products of the metamorphoses of the tissues must be very feeble.

2. As far as my observations have extended, it may be asserted, as a general rule, that the kidneys are relatively larger in the carnivorous than in the frugivorous or granivorous birds. In the carnivorous birds, the intestinal canal is much shorter than those living upon a vegetable or mixed diet. Their food is capable of more rapid digestion, and introduction into the circulation, and as a necessary consequence, the organ which regulates, in a great measure, the amount of the solid and fluid materials of the blood, and eliminates all waste and useless matters, must be correspondingly large. Carnivorous birds also appear to be more active and energetic than the frugivorous or granivorous.

Another reason is found in the chemical constitution of the food. This, however, will be considered when we come to study the same law in the Mammalia.

3. The kidneys of the carnivorous Mammalia are relatively larger than those of the graminivorous or frugivorous ones. This may be stated to be generally true, as far as our observations have extended.

If the character of the food, the structure and size of the digestive apparatus, and the habits of the two classes of animals, be attentively considered, we will understand at once why this relative difference should exist in organs fulfilling the same office in both.

The food of the Carnivora, as the name implies, consists of flesh and blood, which is capable of ready digestion and absorption, and rapidly supplies the wants of the animal economy. The intestinal canal is in all cases short when compared with that of the Mammalia, which feed on vegetable substances. Carnivorous animals have voracious, and, in most cases, almost insatiable appetites. They gorge themselves with food, which is capable of entering the circulation with little or no alteration, and rapidly supplies the wants of the economy. There must be some organ to act as a safety-valve, and remove quickly the large unnecessary quantities of nutriment, which are so often received into the circulatory system. To accomplish this effectually, there must be correspondingly large organs.

In the Herbivora and Granivora, on the other hand, the intestinal canal is long; in the case of the sheep, it is more than twenty times the length of the body. In this class of animals, the food requires minute subdivision, and the materials which they contain must go through many metamorphoses before they are ready to supply the wastes and wants of the system. Consequently, their introduction into the circulation is gradual; the elimination of the products of the disintegrations of the tissues, whose place they supply, must be correspondingly slow, and a much smaller sized organ will perform the same office in them than in the Carnivora.

Another important cause of this difference between the relative sizes of the kidneys of these classes of animals is to be found in the chemical constitution of the food.

The food of the Carnivora contains much nitrogen, and in the processes of its compositions and decompositions, for the production and maintenance of animal heat, is not completely consumed, and the resulting compounds, as uric acid, and urea, and ammonia, are eliminated principally by the kidneys. On the other hand, almost all the food of frugivorous and granivorous animals is capable of being ultimately resolved into water and carbonic acid gas, or of being converted into fat. The amount of nitrogenized elements to be eliminated by the kidneys is on this account greater in the former than in the latter.

The same law applies to the kidneys of cold-blooded animals. It is not, however, so evident at first sight.

The kidneys of Ophidians and Saurians, carnivorous reptiles, are much larger than those of the herbivorous Gopher (*Testudo polyphemus*); but the kidneys of carnivorous Chelonians are far smaller than those of the Gopher. How are we to explain this apparent anomaly? A consideration of the peculiar habits and constitution of these animals will answer the question.

The Gopher lives in a barren and sandy country, and to prevent evaporation from the surface, it is covered with horn at all points where the skin is exposed. The function of the skin is consequently little or nothing, and the kidneys must perform the labor. The carnivorous Chelonians, as the Salt-water Terrapin (*Emys Terrapin*), and Yellow-bellied Terrapin (*Emys serrata*), have a naked skin, and live in the water. The function of the skin in all those reptiles living in the water is far more active than that of those living out of it. That evaporation takes place rapidly through the skin of these Chelonians was conclusively shown by our experiments upon the effects of thirst and starvation upon their blood. These animals also do not consume as much food as the Gopher.

It is evident, from these reasons, that the small size of the kidneys of carnivorous terrapins is connected with their peculiar organization and mode of living; and they cannot be fairly compared with an animal differing totally from them in its physical and vital endowments, and mode of life. The Gopher should be compared with the carnivorous Ophidians and Saurians, because they all live upon the land, and their tegumentary systems are similar. A reference to the tables shows that the kidneys of the former are far smaller than those of the latter, and the truth of the generalization announced is sustained.

CHAPTER X.

URINE OF COLD-BLOODED ANIMALS.

I HAVE always found it very difficult to obtain specimens of the urine of Fishes, for examination. Their bladders are almost always empty. I am enabled, however, to furnish the following qualitative analysis of the urine of the Bass-fish or Red Fish (*Corvina ocellata*):—

Uric acid.	Phosphate of magnesia.
Oxalate of lime.	" of soda.
Phosphate of lime.	Chloride of sodium.
" of ammonia.	

When the urine was spread upon a glass slide, and allowed slowly to evaporate, under a magnifying power of 210 diameters, there appeared lozenge-shaped and hexagonal crystals of uric acid, dumb-bell and octohedral crystals of oxalate of lime, and prismatic crystals of triple phosphate.

The urine of Reptiles resembles that of Birds, not only in appearance, but also in chemical constitution—being only a little more solid when first discharged. Here we have the urine of two wholly dissimilar classes, alike in all respects.

Birds have a high temperature—in many cases 10° above that of Mammals. Their blood circulates with rapidity, and receives an abundant supply of oxygen. They are also very active in their habits.

The temperature of Reptiles is not constant; it varies with that of the surrounding medium. Respiration is imperfect—their lungs being, in most cases, simple sacs—around the walls of which ramify the bloodvessels. Their circulation is sluggish and imperfect, and their habits indolent and inactive. Would any one suppose, *à priori*, that the secretions of these two classes would be similar? If the explanation be true, that the production of urate of ammonia, in serpents, is due to their imperfect respiration and consequent incomplete oxygenation of the blood and tissues, why should we have the same state of things existing in birds, which have oxygen supplied in large quantities, not only by their lungs but also throughout the tissues, by means of their porous bones? It is, however, useless to speculate upon this subject, in the present state of our knowledge.

The following is a qualitative analysis of the urine of the Coachwhip Snake (*Psammophis flagelliformis*), which I made during the month of July.

When the urine was allowed to stand for a short time, it formed a hard, white mass, which might have been readily mistaken for so much chalk. Under a magnifying power of 210 diameters, it was seen to consist of a conglomeration of innumerable globules of the urate of ammonia, resembling, in all respects, the solid portion of the urine of birds. Epithelial cells and fibrinous casts of the urinary tubes, were also found.

The following are the results of the microscopical and chemical examination of the urine of this snake:—

Urate of ammonia, in great abundance.	Phosphate of soda.
Phosphate of lime.	Chloride of sodium.
" of ammonia.	Epithelial cells.
" of magnesia.	Fibrinous casts of urinary tubes.

We were unable to detect the presence of urea. We have, however, found this substance in small amount in the urine of other serpents.

The urine of the Black Viper (*Heterodon niger*), Hognose Viper (*Heterodon platyrhinos*), Indigo Snake (*Coluber couperi*), Corn Snake (*Coluber guttatus*), Chicken Snake (*Coluber quadrivittatus*), Rattlesnake (*Crotalus adamanteus*), and others yielded similar results upon a qualitative examination.

In the kidneys of the Indigo Snake (*Coluber couperi*), several pyriform calculi were found imbedded in their substances, extending from their anterior surfaces to the uterus. These calculi were found to consist, in large measure, of the oxalate of lime. Other substances were also present—as urate of ammonia and the phosphates of lime, ammonia, and magnesia.

The amount of urine excreted by the kidneys of Ophidians, during starvation, is exceedingly small. I have kept them, without food or drink, for several weeks, and the amount excreted during this time, often did not amount to more than 20 or 50 grains.

A male Alligator (*Alligator Mississippiensis*), which weighed 76,507 grains, was starved and deprived of water for eighteen days, and during that time it discharged its urine but once, in quantity about two fluidounces. This consisted, as in Ophidians and Birds, of a fluid and a solid, chalk-like portion, composed of minute globules of the urate of ammonia.

We shall next consider the urine of Chelonians. In these animals the bladder is large, and the urine resembles, in many respects, that of the Mammalia. The following table represents the specific gravities of the urine in its normal condition, and during starvation and a change of diet:—

Name of animal.	Specific gravities.	
Snapping Turtle (*Chelonura serpentina*)	1005.7	
Salt-water Terrapin (*Emys terrapin*)	1009.	
Emys terrapin, deprived of food and drink 40 days	1015.	
Emys serrata " " " 17 "	1011.	
" " " " 26 "	1033.5	
" " " " 29 "	1020.	
" " " " 31 "	1017.5	
" " " " 38 "	1017.6	
" " " " 49 "	1019.4	
Emys serrata, deprived of food and drink 28 days, and then transferred to a tub of water, and abundantly supplied with vegetable food (*Portulacca oleracea*)	999.26	81° F.
Emys serrata, deprived of food and drink 28 days, and then abundantly supplied with water and vegetable food	999.9	90° F.
Emys serrata, deprived of food and drink for 28 days, and then placed in a tub of water, and supplied with vegetable food	1004.	
Emys terrapin, deprived of food and drink 21 days, and then placed in fresh water, and supplied with vegetable food (*Portulacca oleracea*) .	1002.	
Gopher (*Testudo polyphemus*). The urine consists of two portions: 1. Fluid. 2. Semi-solid. . . . . Sp. gr. of fluid	1004.	
Sp. gr. of semi-solid	1095.5	
Gopher (*Testudo polyphemus*), deprived of food and drink 30 days. Sp. gr. of fluid portion of urine	1008.9	

This table shows that the specific gravity of the urine of Chelonians was increased, during starvation and thirst, and also, that when carnivorous Chelonians were fed upon purely vegetable diet, the specific gravity of the urine was greatly diminished.

From numerous examinations, which I made last summer, the following are selected as affording the best view of the physical and chemical properties of the urine.

Urine of a Yellow-bellied Terrapin (*Emys serrata*), which had been deprived of food and drink for 29 days. June 20.

Weight of terrapin, May 25th	30,132 grains.
" " June 19th	22,760 "
" lost in twenty-six days	7,372 "

Loss of weight each hour, $10\frac{5}{10}$ grains = $\frac{1}{2870}$th the original weight of the body. The bladder had not been emptied during its confinement, and contained four fluidounces of urine. Sp. gr. 1020. The urine was of a transparent yellow color, and contained white and yellow chalk-like masses, which, under the microscope, were found to consist of numerous minute globules of the urate of ammonia, and hexagonal and lozenge-shaped crystals of uric acid. The presence of ammonia and uric acid was determined by all the characteristic tests. The transparent portion of the urine was ropy, resembling mucus. When treated with *aqua ammoniæ*, a copious precipitate of triple phosphate was thrown down.

1000 parts of the urine contained—

Water	947.19
Solid constituents	52.81

A microscopical and chemical examination, revealed the following ingredients:—

Uric acid, in lozenge-shaped and hexagonal crystals.
Urate of ammonia, in minute globules.
Triple phosphate, prismatic and stellate crystals.
Phosphate of lime.
Phosphate of ammonia.
" of magnesia.
Carbonate of lime in stellate crystals.
Albumen in small quantity.
Mucus.

If urea was present, it must have been in very small quantities, for nitric acid and the microscope failed to reveal its presence.

Urine of a male Yellow-bellied Terrapin, which had been kept without food and drink for 49 days. July 9.

Weight of terrapin, May 25th	17,797 grains.
" " July 9th	14,400 "
" lost during forty-five days	3,397 "

Loss of weight each hour, $3\frac{14}{100} = \frac{1}{5667}$th of weight of body.

The bladder had not been emptied during its confinement, and held six fluidrachms of yellow-colored urine, which contained a small, white deposit of the urate of ammonia.

Amount of the urate of ammonia, thirty minims. Sp. gr. of urine, 1019.4.

1000 parts contained—

Water			954.65
Alcohol extract, and urea in small amount	29.26	Solid constituents	45.35
Uric acid and vesical mucus	4.91		
Fixed saline constituents	11.18		

The extractive matters were viscid, gummy, of a red color, and exceedingly difficult to evaporate to complete dryness. The uric acid was combined with ammonia and other alkalies. The amount of urea present was very small.

Urine of a Salt-water Terrapin (*Emys terrapin*), which had been kept without food and drink for 40 days. July 23.

Weight of terrapin, June 16th	14,285 grains.
" " July 23d	11,400 "
" lost during thirty-eight days	2,885 "

Loss of weight during each hour, grs. $3\frac{317}{1000} = \frac{1}{4366}$ of original weight.

The bladder contained six fluidrachms of clear, limpid urine, having a decided acid reaction. Sp. gr. 1015. Whole amount of urine excreted during thirty-eight days, about 300 grains.

1000 parts contained—

Water	965.34
Urea and alcohol extract	15.27
Water extract	4.56
Uric acid and vesical mucus	3.27
Soluble fixed saline constituents	8.50
Insoluble fixed saline constituents	3.06

300 grains contained—

	Grains.
Water	289.60
Urea and alcohol extract	4.58
Water extract	1.37
Uric acid and vesical mucus	0.98
Soluble fixed saline constituents	2.55
Insoluble fixed saline constituents	.92
Solid constituents in 300 parts of urine	10.4
" " 1000 " "	34.66

When the alcohol extract was treated with concentrated nitric acid, crystals of the nitrate of urea made their appearance in great numbers. Oxalic acid added to the alcoholic extract, gave a precipitate of the oxalate of urea. Aqua ammonia added to the urine, precipitated stellate crystals of the triple phosphate in considerable numbers. After standing for an hour or two, uric acid was precipitated from the urine, in the form of an orange-colored sediment, which, under the microscope, was composed of lozenge-shaped crystals.

Urine of a Salt-water Terrapin, which had been kept without food and drink for 37 days. Aug. 16.

Weight of terrapin, June 21st	12,280 grains.
" " Aug. 16th	9,255 "
" lost in fifty-six days	3,025 "

Loss of weight hourly, grs. 2.25 = $\frac{1}{5458}$th of original weight.

The bladder contained two fluidrachms of clear yellow urine, having a decidedly acid reaction; also, a considerable quantity of gas. After standing for a short time, a white deposit of the urate of ammonia, and lozenge-shaped and acicular crystals of uric acid settled to the bottom of the vessel.

When the fluid portion of the urine was allowed slowly to evaporate upon a glass slide, under the microscope, numerous crosslets of the chloride of sodium, and stellate, plumose and irregular crystals of the phosphate of soda and fixed alkaline salts gradually made their appearance. When treated with aqua ammonia, numerous delicate, plumose, penniform, and stellate crystals of the triple phosphate were precipitated. When concentrated and treated with nitric acid, crystals of the nitrate of urea made their appearance. The whole amount of urine excreted by the kidneys of this terrapin, in fifty-seven days, 130 grains.

Solid constituents in 130 grains of urine	8.05 grs.

130 grains contained—

Water	121.95
Organic constituents, uric acid, urea, ammonia, &c.	6.45
Fixed saline constituents	1.60
Solid constituents in 1000 parts of urine	61.92

1000 parts contained—

Water	938.08
Organic constituents, uric acid, urea, &c.	49.62
Fixed saline constituents	12.30

We shall now proceed to investigate the effects of a change of diet upon the urine of Chelonians, beginning with the carnivorous.

Urine of a Yellow-bellied Terrapin (*Emys serrata*), which was starved for 30 days, and then transferred to a tub of water, and abundantly supplied with vegetable food (*Portulacca oleracea*) 42 days.

The bladder was distended with five fluidounces of light greenish-yellow limpid urine, neutral to test paper, having a slight smell resembling that of the terrapin.

Amount of urine	2150 grs.
Specific gravity, at 81° F.	999.26
Solid constituents in 2150 grains	5 "

2150 grains contained—

Water	2145
Solid constituents	5

1000 parts contained—

Water	997.7
Solid constituents	2.3

The urine of numerous Yellow-bellied Terrapins (*Emys serrata*), and Salt-water Terrapins (*Emys terrapins*) treated in a similar manner, yielded results similar in all respects.

In every instance the amount of urine excreted by the kidneys was greatly increased, its specific gravity diminished—being often the same as that of pure water—and the reaction was changed from acid to neutral. Hippuric acid was never detected.

The important results of this series of experiments will be given in a table.

We next come to the examination of the urine of herbivorous Chelonians.

Urine of a male Gopher, examined four days after its capture.

The bladder contained five fluidounces of urine, having an odor similar to that of the leaves and grasses in the rectum, and also resembling that of the sheep. Four fluidounces of this was a brownish-yellow fluid. Sp. gr. 1004. The remaining fluidounce was a semi-solid, grayish chalk-like precipitate, having a sp. gr. of 1095.5, and consisting, under the microscope, entirely of minute globules of the urate of ammonia. Urea and hippuric acid could not be detected by microscopical or chemical tests, in either the fluid or semi-solid portion of the urine. Aqua ammonia failed to precipitate the triple phosphate.

1000 parts of the fluid portion of the urine contained—

Water	972.75
Solid constituents	27.25

1000 parts of the semi-solid portion contained—

Water	806.31
Solid constituents	193.67
Amount of semi-solid portion	400 grs.

400 grains contained—

Water	322.52
Solid constituents	77.48

The estimate of the solid parts is below the truth, because some of the ammonia must necessarily have been driven off during the process of drying.

Urine of a Gopher (*Testudo polyphemus*), which was kept without food and drink for 28 days, was as follows:—

Weight of Gopher, June 16th	18,368 grs.
" " July 11th	16,922 "
Loss of weight in 25 days	1,446 "

Loss of weight each hour, $2\frac{41}{100} = \frac{1}{7621}$ of the original weight.

Amount of urine	2 fluidounces.
" of fluid portion	$1\frac{1}{2}$ "
" of semi-solid portion	$\frac{1}{2}$ "
Specific gravity of fluid portion	1008.9

The semi-solid portion was very compact, and composed almost entirely of the urate of ammonia.

Weight of the fluid portion	764 grs.
" " semi-solid portion	236 "
Whole amount of urine	1000 "
Amount of solid constituents, uric acid and urate of ammonia, in 236 grs. of semi-solid matters	$42\frac{7}{10}$
Amount of uric acid in this	37.46

The urate of ammonia must unavoidably have lost some of its ammonia during evaporation.

Amount of solid constituents in 764 grs. of the fluid portion of the urine	21.71
Solid matters in 1000 grains of urine	64.41 grs.

1000 grains contained—

Water	935.59
Urate of ammonia	42.70
Extractive matters, and urea in small amount	15.72
Urates of soda and potassa and mucus	5.99

When the extractive matters were treated with nitric acid, effervescence took place, and crystals of the nitrate of urea made their appearance, under the microscope, in small numbers. Hippuric acid was present in the urine of this animal in small amount. The urine of all Gophers, which I have thus far examined, resembled in all respects that of those just described.

The urine of Chelonians was frequently tested for grape sugar. This substance was absent from the urine of all Chelonians, in a normal condition, except in the case of a Gopher, and its presence in this individual might be accounted for by a suppression of the respiration consequent upon several severe blows upon its head.

Whenever the respiration was suspended, by placing the animals in hydrogen and carbonic acid gases, or by passing a ligature around the windpipe, sugar accumulated in the blood, was eliminated by the kidneys, and appeared in the urine.

The following tables will present a condensed view of all the important results obtained in these investigations :—

Table showing the Loss of Weight, and the Amount of Urine Excreted by Chelonians deprived of Food and Drink.

Name of animal.	Duration of starvation and thirst.	Weight before starvation and thirst.	Weight after starvation and thirst.	Loss of weight during starvation and thirst.	Loss of weight expressed in a fraction of the original weight of animal.	Loss of weight each hour.	Loss of weight each hour, expressed in a fraction of the original weight.	Amount of urine excreted during thirst and starvation.	Amount of urine expressed in a fraction of the original weight.	Amount of urine excreted hourly.	Amount of urine excreted hourly, expressed in a fraction of the original weight of animal.	Amount of solid constituents of urine excreted hourly.
	Days.	Grs.	Grs.	Grs.		Grs.		Grs.		Grs.		Grs.
Emys serrata	14	20,873	18,756	2,117	$\frac{1}{10}$	6.3	$\frac{1}{3313}$	442	$\frac{1}{47}$	1.315	$\frac{1}{15865}$	.0034
Emys serrata	20	34,155	28,675	5,480	$\frac{1}{6}$	11.41	$\frac{1}{2994}$	113	$\frac{1}{302}$	.0235	$\frac{1}{145340}$	.00187
Emys serrata	20	41,086	34,960	6,126	$\frac{1}{7}$	12.76	$\frac{1}{3298}$	741	$\frac{1}{55}$	1.543	$\frac{1}{26627}$	.00611
Emys serrata	26	30,132	22,760	7,372	$\frac{1}{4}$	10.5	$\frac{1}{2870}$	223	$\frac{1}{135}$	0.357	$\frac{1}{846500}$	.00166
Emys serrata	34	38,590	30,142	8,398	$\frac{1}{4}$	10.29	$\frac{1}{3754}$	890	$\frac{1}{44}$	1.09	$\frac{1}{35357}$	.00457
Emys serrata	45	17,797	14,400	3,397	$\frac{1}{5}$	3.14	$\frac{1}{5667}$	300	$\frac{1}{59}$	.0277	$\frac{1}{642130}$	.0012
Emys terrapin	38	14,285	11,400	2,885	$\frac{1}{5}$	3.317	$\frac{1}{4366}$	300	$\frac{1}{47}$	.032	$\frac{1}{446406}$	.00114
Emys terrapin	43	18,832	13,485	5,347	$\frac{1}{3}$–$\frac{1}{4}$	5.18	$\frac{1}{3635}$	70	$\frac{1}{269}$	.0067	$\frac{1}{2810731}$	
Emys terrapin	56	12,280	9,255	3,025	$\frac{1}{4}$	2.25	$\frac{1}{5458}$	130	$\frac{1}{4}$	.0096	$\frac{1}{1279166}$	.00059

These Chelonians were kept in boxes, and were carefully and frequently examined, and it was found that they never discharged their urine. The amounts, therefore, noted in the table, represent all that was excreted during the period of their confinement.

This table shows the slow waste of the tissues of cold-blooded animals, and the small amount of work performed by their kidneys.

When these animals were deprived of food and drink, the loss of weight was chiefly due to the evaporation from their lungs and skin, and also to the combination of the elements of their fluids and solids with the oxygen of the atmosphere, and their final elimination as carbonic acid gas.

The researches of Winter, Scherer, and Lehmann have shown that a man, for every kilogramme (15,444 grains) of his weight discharges, on an average in the twenty-four hours, about 26 grammes (400 grains) of urine. From these data we may calculate that the amount discharged per hour, for every kilogramme of the weight of a man, equals 16.76 grains. According to this calculation, the amount of urine discharged by a man, hourly, equals $\frac{1}{919}$th the weight of his body. It is probable that, during thirst and starvation, the amount would be much less.

By comparing this with the results which I obtained from cold-blooded animals we see that the amount of urine excreted by a warm-blood animal is from forty to several hundred times more abundant than that excreted by a cold-blooded animal. This is true of all cold-blooded animals.

An Alligator, weighing 76,507 grains, was kept for eighteen days without food and drink, and excreted during this time only two fluidounces of urine.

I have kept Ophidians for two and three weeks, and during this time they voided their urine not more than once or twice, and then in small quantities.

The results of these experiments demonstrate conclusively that, as the solids and fluids of the animal economy are developed, the temperature elevated, and intellect perfected, the compositions, decompositions, and metamorphoses of the organic and inorganic elements become more rapid and abundant.

When we compare the relative size of the kidneys, and the amounts of their excretions in different animals, the question immediately arises: Why should cold-blooded animals, whose circulation is sluggish, which eat but seldom, often abstaining from food for months, whose habits are indolent, and whose excretions and secretions are exceedingly small, be provided with large urinary organs?

In warm-blooded animals it is natural to suppose that an elevated temperature, rapid circulation, and active energetic mode of life, should call for large organs capable of removing in an efficient manner from the blood the products of the disintegrations of the system; but why should we have in a condition of things directly contrary, in every respect, as large organs, to perform the same office in a much feebler degree.

In attempting to explain this phenomenon we must consider the following facts and laws of the animal economy:—

The blood contains a definite amount of materials to be eliminated by the kidneys, diffused throughout its entire mass. That all these materials should be separated, the entire mass of the blood must be presented to the kidneys, and the rapidity of the elimination will depend upon the rapidity of the circulation, and the activity of the excreting cells and the size of the organs.

Temperature also exerts a great influence upon all the actions of the animal economy.

If the temperature of cold or warm-blooded animals be reduced much below the normal standard their functions will gradually become more feeble, and finally cease.

It may be stated, as a general law, that the lower the temperature of any organ the more feeble will be its action.

Nervous force exerts a great influence upon the circulation, and, through it, upon secretion and excretion.

It is known to every naturalist that cold-blooded animals have much less muscular and nervous power in proportion to their size than the warm-blooded ones.

From these considerations, then, it is evident that to perform the same office, to excrete precisely the same amount, larger organs are required in the cold than in the warm-blooded animals.

In Ophidians which have relatively larger kidneys than the other cold-blooded animals, in addition to the reasons stated above, the character of their alimentary canal and their habits render the existence of large kidneys necessary.

These animals are carnivorous and have a short alimentary canal, which, in many instances, is almost completely straight.

They take their food in large quantities, often swallowing animals heavier and larger than themselves. All this animal matter is capable of digestion and absorption into the blood, a large portion of which is superfluous.

The great channel for the elimination of this is through the kidneys; the lungs being mere sacks, and performing the function of respiration in an imperfect manner.

The kidneys, therefore, must be correspondingly large to remove rapidly the large and unnecessary quantities of nutriment which are often received into the circulatory system.

The following table will give a condensed view of the effects of starvation and thirst, and also of a change of diet upon the blood of cold-blooded animals:—

Table Showing the Effects of Starvation and Thirst, and also of a Change of Diet upon the Urine of Chelonians.

Name of Animal.	Length of starvation and thirst.	Specific gravity of urine.	Amount of urine excret'd	Solid constituents of urine excreted.	Water of urine excreted.	Water in 1000 parts of urine.	Solid constituents in 1000 pt's of urine.	Reaction of urine.	Color of urine.
	Days.		Grains.	Grains.	Grains.				
Female *Emys serrata*	17	1011.	442.3	11.33	430.97	974.39	25.61	Acid.	Turbid yellow.
" "	26	1033.5	113.	9.	104.	920.36	79.64	"	Clear yellow precipitate.
" "	29	1020.	223.1	10.396	219.704	947.19	52.81	"	Limpid yellow.
" "	31	1017.5	741.5	29.36	712.14	960.4	39.6	"	Yellow, with precipitate.
" "	38	1017.6	890.6	37.34	853.26	918.08	41.92	"	Yellow, with precipitate.
Male "	49	1019.4	300.	13.02	286.98	954.65	45.35	"	Clear yellow.
Female *Emys terrapin*	40	1015.	300.	10.4	289.6	965.34	34.66	"	Cream-color'd.
" "	43		70.					"	Cream-color'd.
" "	57		130.	8.05	121.95	938.08	61.92	"	Clear yellow.
Female *Emys terrapin*, deprived of food and drink 21 days, and then placed in fresh water and abundantly supplied with vegetable food 28 days. . . .		1002.	840.	3.40	836.60	995.96	4.04	Slightly acid.	Limpid light yellow.
Female *Emys serrata*, deprived of food and drink 30 days, and then supplied with water and vegetable food 42 days. . .		1000.	2150.	5.	2145.	997.67	2.33	Neutral.	Limpid light yellow.
Female *Emys serrata*, deprived of food and drink 30 days, and then supplied with vegetable food and water 60 days. .		1004.	2160.	18.64	2141.36	991.38	8.62	Neutral.	Limpid light yellow.
Female *Emys serrata*, deprived of food and drink 30 days, and then supplied with water and vegetable food 88 days. . .		1000.	2000.	1.	1999.	999.5	.5	Neutral.	Limpid light yellow.
Testudo polyphemus (Gopher). Fluid.		1004.	2000.	54.50	1945.50	972.75	27.25		
Semi-solid.		1095.5	400.	77.48	322.52	806.31	193.67		
Testudo polyphemus (Gopher). Fluid.		1008.9	764.	21.71	742.29	971.59	28.41		
Semi-solid.			236.	42.70	193.30	819.09	180.91		

PUBLISHED BY THE SMITHSONIAN INSTITUTION,
WASHINGTON, D. C.
JULY, 1856.

APPENDIX.

RECORD OF AURORAL PHENOMENA

OBSERVED IN THE

HIGHER NORTHERN LATITUDES.

COMPILED BY

PETER FORCE.

INTRODUCTORY LETTER.

Professor Joseph Henry,

Secretary Smithsonian Institution.

Sir: In compliance with your request, I place in your hands the collection of observations on the Aurora Borealis, which was made in great part while I was engaged, during the evening hours of relaxation, for several years prior to 1851, in the examination of another, and, to me, at the time, a more interesting subject. In the course of this investigation I met with so many notices of the Aurora, that I thought it worth the time it would take, to gather such of them as came within my reach without leaving the path over which I was travelling; it also occurred to me that such a collection, covering so broad a surface, might be useful in any investigation of the phenomenon, in so far at least, as it would furnish the means of a ready reference to many of the observations recorded by careful and competent observers.

The accompanying papers are my original notes, as they were made from time to time, from the later voyages, travels, and explorations in the northern regions, and particularly in the northern portions of North America. A list of the journals, &c., that I have gone over, which is added, will show how far my examination has extended.

You will perceive that very few of the Auroral observations I have given were made south of the fiftieth degree of north latitude.[1] North of that parallel they are quite full, though not entirely complete. Any omissions may, however, be easily supplied, as the name of the observer, the point of the first appearance and

[1] In a work recently published by the State of New York, entitled "Results of a Series of Meteorological Observations made in Obedience to Instructions from the Regents of the University of Sundry Academies in the State of New York, from 1826 to 1850, inclusive, compiled by Franklin B. Hough, M. D., Albany, 1855," will be found a very full record of all auroras noticed in New York within the limits mentioned. I would also refer to various professed treatises on the subject, and especially to the volume on Auroras published in the Reports of the French "Commission Scientifique du Nord en Skandinavie, Laponie, &c."

the direction of the Aurora, the time of observation, and the locality, by parallel and meridian, are stated in every instance where it was found possible to do so.

I may venture to add that the observations here given, go far, as it appears to me, to establish the following points in regard to the Aurora Borealis:—

1. That in the higher northern latitudes it frequently first appears to the eastward, or to the westward, or to the southward of the observer, and hence is not strictly a north polar light.

2. That it is often at a low elevation, and sometimes near the surface of the earth, within the range of the vision of the observer.

3. That north of the 70th degree of north latitude it is less frequent and less brilliant than to the southward of that parallel.

4. That on and in the vicinity of the Atlantic Ocean and other open waters, it is most frequent and most brilliant.

5. That the season for its appearance is mostly between the autumnal and the vernal equinox.

6. That the time of its appearance is in most cases from six o'clock P. M. to midnight.

PETER FORCE.

WASHINGTON, May 1, 1856.

RECORD OF AURORAL PHENOMENA

OBSERVED IN THE

HIGHER NORTHERN LATITUDES.

Hartford, Ct.—Lat. 41° 45′ 50″ N. Long. 72° 40′ 45″ W. 1835, 1836. A. C. Twining.
New Haven, Ct.—Lat. 41° 18′ 30″ N. Long. 72° 56′ 45″ W. do.

"The height of auroral phenomena is a subject which has divided philosophers. Some consider them as lying in the lower regions of the atmosphere; while others would elevate them beyond its supposed limits, or at least into its extreme upper regions.

It is my intention to prove, in three instances of late occurrence, that the latter opinion is the true one."—Am. Journ. Sc., XXXII, 217.

Auroral Cloud of December 10, 1835.—"Height above the surface of the earth, forty-two miles and one-third."—Ibid., p. 220.

Auroral Arch of August 12, 1836.—"Height above the surface of the earth, one hundred and forty-four and a half miles."—Ibid., p. 224.

Auroral Arch of May 8, 1836.—"Height, one hundred and sixty miles."—Ibid., p. 227.

N. B.—Height of aurora, December 10, 1835, 42⅓ miles.
Do. August 12, 1836, 144½ miles.
Do. May 8, 1836, 160 miles.

Columbia Co., N. Y.—Lat. 42° 30′ N. Long. 73° 20′ W. Autumn of 1806. W.

"*To the Editor of the American Magazine.* Sir: I do not recollect to have read, or heard, that any person had ever witnessed the exhibition of an *aurora borealis in the daytime*, and when the air was perfectly clear and the sky unclouded.

It is some years since I witnessed this, in company with many other persons; and having spoken of it to some friends, lately, in New York, I have been solicited to communicate the facts to the public. If you think them worth publishing, they are at your service.

I do not now precisely recollect the year, but it was about 1806, that I was employed, during several successive days, in surveying some lands near the northeast extremity of the County of Columbia, in the State of New York. The lands, comprising three or four farms, were to be subdivided among the heirs of a person then lately deceased, and were situated on some of the highest hills of that county. I was, of course, constantly attended by some eight, ten, and even twenty persons of the parties concerned, who all witnessed what I am going to relate.

It was late in autumn, and so cold that ice formed every night, and hardly all disappeared during the day. The air was very transparent, and, so far as I now recollect, none or but very few clouds to be seen. For several nights in succession, the *Northern Lights* shone pretty bright, in the valley where I slept, but disappeared in the morning.

On mounting these hills, at about 11 o'clock, we were surprised to witness the *streaks and flashes of the aurora borealis,* occupying the same place that they had done the night before, and so bright and luminous as to command our astonishment and admiration. The streaks were as clearly defined as during the night, and very considerably brighter than the field of the surrounding sky.

Not a cloud was to be seen, at least during two or three hours, while we narrowly watched the exhibition of this splendid phenomenon.

On the next and two or three of the succeeding days, we saw the same appearances at intervals; and through the intervening nights the aurora was quite bright.

I inquired at the time, and frequently afterwards, and could find no person who had noticed it in the day time, excepting those who had been on the hills in our party. Probably others may have observed it, and I regret that I had not sooner made public the result of our observations.

I know that these appearances could not be discovered from the valleys around us, at the time we saw them, because several of our party made the experiment.

I have only further to observe that, during this exhibition, the air was very clear and uncommonly bright for several days.

The streams of light from the north frequently shot up quite over our heads, and seemed to diverge every way, as from a point situated a very little below the visible horizon.

I shall be glad to learn if others have ever observed similar appearances under such circumstances, and to see the observations of the learned on this singular and interesting occurrence."—Spafford's Am. Mag., I, No. 10, March 1816, p. 359.

N. B.—Streaks and flashes of the aurora at noonday. Not a cloud to be seen.

Albany, N. Y.—Lat. 42° 39′ 3″ N. Long. 73° 44′ 49″ W. April 19, 1831. Prof. J. Henry.

"On the 19th of April, 1831, at 12 o'clock at noon, an observation was made with the Hansteen needle, the result of which differed only the fractional part of a second from the usual mean rate of this needle.

At 6 o'clock p. m. the same day, another observation was made with the same needle, and apparently under the same circumstances; but a remarkable change was now observed in the time of its making three hundred vibrations, indicating a great increase in the magnetic intensity of the earth. It was at first supposed that the needle had accidentally been placed contiguous to ferruginous substance; but, on a most careful investigation, nothing could be discovered which would tend in the least degree to explain the cause of the phenomenon.

At about 9 o'clock in the evening, or three hours after the above observation, an unusual appearance was noticed in the *southern part of the heavens,* which was shortly afterwards recognized as an arch of the aurora. It was about nine degrees in breadth, with the vertex of the arch twenty degrees above the horizon.

At this time, the northern part of the sky was covered with light fleecy clouds. At forty-five minutes past nine the clouds partially disappeared, and disclosed *the whole northern hemisphere entirely occupied with coruscations* of the aurora, shooting up past the zenith, and apparently all converging to the same point. The actual formation of a corona might probably have been observed, but for a dark cloud which remained stationary a little south of the zenith."—Am. Journ. Science, XXII, 146.

N. B.—At 9 p. m., noticed in the southern part of the heavens. At 9h. 45m. p. m., whole northern hemisphere entirely occupied with coruscations of aurora.

Toronto, C. W.—Lat. 43° 39′ 35″ N. Long. 79° 21′ 33″ W. May 8, 1836. R. H. Bonnycastle.

"At a quarter past nine o'clock on Sunday night, the eighth day of May (1836) in the present year, my attention, whilst regarding the heavens, was forcibly attracted to the sudden appearance *due east,* of a shining, broad column of light.

At first, as my window overlooks the Bay of Toronto and the low island which separates it from the lake, I took this singular *pillar of light* for the reflection from some steamboat on the clouds; but, having sought the open air on the gallery, which commands a full view of the bay and of Ontario, I was convinced that the meteor was an effluence of the sky, as I now saw it extend upwards, from the *eastern* water horizon line to the zenith, *in a well-defined, equal, broad column of white, strong light,* resembling in some degree that of the aurora, but of a steady brightness and unchanging body, whilst there were few or no clouds.

There was no moon, as on that day it rose at 2h. 4m., consequently it was dark, and, as the sky was not very cloudy, the meteor was seen to the greatest advantage as the night wore on.

It passed very slowly and bodily to the westward, continuing to occupy the space from the horizon to the zenith, until the upper part first faded slowly, and then the whole gradually disappeared, after it had reached nearly to *due northeast.*

The weather was cold, and there was no wind.

At twenty minutes past nine o'clock the pillar of light had vanished, but it immediately afterwards reappeared slightly in the horizon where it had been last seen [due N. E.], and in the mean time the constant auroral arch of the halos I have before mentioned, in Vol. XXX, 131, became visible in the northern horizon, and increased very rapidly in brilliancy, and at ten minutes to ten, gave so intense a glow to the sky that it was light enough to enable me to see the objects around distinctly as in pale moonlight. It was, in short, equal to the light of the moon at the end of the second quarter.

The auroral arch rose very high on this occasion, and then flattened, and at ten the double arch I have already described was peculiarly beautiful, the darkness under it being singularly grand."—Am. Journ. Sci., XXXII, 393.

N. B.—A well-defined, equal, broad column of white, bright light. Appeared due east.

Port Henry, two miles north of Crown Point, Lake Champlain.—Lat. 44° 5′ N. Long. 73° 30′ W. August 13, 1836. W. C. Redfield.

"On the evening of the 13th (of August, 1836), we were entertained with a brilliant exhibition of the Aurora Borealis, which, between 7 and 8 p. m., shot upward in rapid and luminous coruscations from *the northern half of the horizon,* the whole converging to a point apparently fifteen degrees *south of the zenith.*

This appearance was succeeded by luminous vertical columns or pencils, of the color, alternately, of a pale red and a peculiar blue, which were exhibited in great beauty."—Am. Journ. Sci., XXXIII, 302.

N. B.—Rapid and luminous coruscations from the northern half of the horizon. Succeeded by luminous vertical columns or pencils, colored, alternately, with red and a peculiar blue.

St. John's, Newfoundland.—Lat. 47° 33′ 33″ N. Long. 52° 45′ 10″ W. Bonnycastle.

"This phenomenon, but little investigated, and less known, is generally supposed to be the most perfect the nearer we approach the arctic circle in our hemisphere; but I have long doubted that popular opinion.

It may be more permanent in the higher latitudes, compensating for the single night of half a year's duration; but I believe, for I have seen it in very high latitudes, when a young man, in the Northern Seas, that it is more splendid in Western Canada and in Newfoundland, than nearer to the pole. There are circumstances connected with its appearance in the latter country, which tend to upset another generally received notion.

It has been seen here, at St. John's, visibly close to the observer. One gentleman saw it *between his house and Quiddy-Biddy Pond,* a lake about a mile long, *near the south bank of which his dwelling* is erected, on a slope of Signal Hill.

Another gentleman, equally to be depended upon, and very fond of noticing extraordinary appearances, saw it in another situation, near the quarters I occupy, *equally close to him;* and it always appears to me here, as if it was not very far off.

The peculiar humid atmosphere of the east coast, and the vicinage of the ocean, between which and the city there is a lofty barrier of rocky hills, all conduce to render the belief in this new appearance reasonable."—Bonnycastle, I, 359.

N. B.—It has been seen at St. John's visibly close to the observer.

Cedar Lake.—Lat. 53° 12′ 59″ N. Long. 100° 10′ 49″ W. October 13, 1819. FRANKLIN.

"Cross Lake is extensive, running towards the N. E., it is said, for forty miles. We crossed it at a narrow part, and, pulling through several winding channels, formed by a group of islands, entered Cedar Lake, which, next to Lake Winnipeg, is the largest sheet of fresh water we had hitherto seen. Ducks and geese resort hither in immense flocks in the spring and autumn. These birds were now beginning to go off, owing to the muddy shores having become quite hard through the nightly frosts.

At this place the Aurora Borealis was extremely brilliant in the night, its coruscations darting, at times, *over the whole sky*, and assuming various prismatic tints, of which the violet and yellow were predominant."—Franklin, I, 46.

N. B.—Extremely brilliant. Over the whole sky.

Lake Winnipeg.—Lat. 53° 45′ 58″ N. Long. 98° 49′ 58″ W. October 8, 1819. FRANKLIN.

"We left Norway House soon after noon, and the wind being favorable, sailed along the northern shore of Lake Winnipeg the whole of the ensuing night; and on the morning of the 8th landed on a narrow ridge of sand, which, running out twenty miles to the westward, separates Limestone Bay from the body of the lake.

From Norwegian Point to Limestone Bay the shore consists of high clay cliffs, against which the waves beat with violence during strong southerly winds. When the wind blows from the land, and the waters of the lake are low, a narrow sandy beach is uncovered, and affords a landing place for boats. The shores of Limestone Bay are covered with small fragments of calcareous stones.

During the night the Aurora Borealis was quick in its motions, and various and vivid in its colors."—Franklin, I, 44.

N. B.—Quick in its motions. Various and vivid in its colors.

Cumberland House.—Lat. 53° 56′ 40″ N. Long. 102° 16′ 41″ W. Nov. 15, 1819. FRANKLIN.

"The sky had been overcast during the last week; the sun shone forth once only, and then not sufficiently for the purpose of obtaining observations.

Faint coruscations of the Aurora Borealis appeared one evening, but their presence did not in the least affect the electrometer or the compass."—Franklin, I, 50.

November 24, 1819.—"The Aurora Borealis had been faintly visible for a short time the preceding evening."—Ibid., 51.

November 28, 1819.—"The Aurora Borealis was twice visible, but faint on both occasions. Its appearance did not affect the electrometer, nor could we perceive the compass to be disturbed." Ibid., 51.

Cumberland House.—Lat. 53° 56′ 40″ N. Long. 102° 16′ 41″ W. October 23, 1819, to June 13, 1820. Hood.

"The most material information we had obtained at this period regarded the height of the aurora from the earth.

The following is the result of the observations that were made at the Basquiau Hill, and at the same time, by Dr. Richardson, at Cumberland House. The instruments used for the purpose were two small wooden quadrants, revolving on pivots and furnished with plummets. Our chronometers were previously regulated; though great accuracy was not necessary in this particular, as the arches of the aurora are sometimes stationary for many minutes.

On the 2d of April, the altitude of a brilliant beam was 10°, at 10h. 1m. p. m., at Cumberland House. Fifty-five miles S. S. W., it was not visible. As the trees at the latter station rose about 5° above the horizon, it may be estimated that the beam was *not more than seven miles from the earth*, and twenty-seven from Cumberland House.

On the 6th of April, the aurora was, for some hours, in the zenith at that place, forming a confused mass of flashes and beams; and in lat. 53° 22′ 48″ N., long. 103° 7′ 17″ W., it appeared in the form of an arch, stationary about 9° high, and bearing N. by E. It was therefore *seven miles from the earth.*

On the 7th of April, the aurora was again in the zenith, before 10 p. m., at Cumberland House, and in lat. 53° 36′ 40″ N., and long. 102° 31′ 41″ W. The altitude of the highest of two concentric arches at 9h. p. m. was 9°; at 9h. 30m. p. m. it was 11° 30′; at 10h. p. m., 15°—its centre always bearing N. by E. During this time, it was *between six and seven miles from the earth.* After 10h. p. m., it covered the sky at Cumberland House, and passed the zenith at the other place.

These observations are opposed to the general opinion of meteorologists; they are nevertheless facts. We have sometimes seen an attenuated aurora *flashing across* 100° *of the sky in a single second;* a quickness of motion inconsistent with the height of sixty or seventy miles, the least which has hitherto been ascribed to it. This kind of aurora is not brighter than the Milky Way, and resembles sheet-lightning in its motions.

For the sake of perspicuity, I shall describe the several parts of the aurora, which I term beams, flashes, and arches.

The *Beams* are little conical pencils of light, ranged in parallel lines, with their pointed extremities towards the earth, generally in the direction of the dipping needle.

The *Flashes* seem to be scattered beams approaching nearer to the earth, because they are similarly shaped and infinitely larger. I have called them flashes because their appearance is sudden, and seldom continues long.

When the aurora first becomes visible, it is formed like a rainbow, the light of which is faint, and the motion of the beams undistinguishable. It is then in the horizon.

As it approaches the zenith, it resolves itself at intervals into beams, which, by a quick undulating motion, project themselves into wreaths, afterwards fading away, and again brightening, without any visible expansion or concentration of matter. Numerous flashes attend in different parts of the sky.

That this mass, from its short distance above the earth, would *appear like an arch to a person situated at the horizon,* may be demonstrated by the rules of perspective, supposing its parts to be nearly equidistant from the earth. An undeniable proof of it, however, is afforded by the observations of the 6th and 7th of April, when the aurora which filled the sky at Cumberland-House, from the northern horizon to the zenith, with wreaths and flashes, assumed the shape of arches at some distance to the southward.

But the aurora does not always make its first appearance as an arch. It sometimes rises from a confused mass of light in the east or west, and crosses the sky towards the opposite point, exhibiting wreaths of beams, or coronæ boreales, in its way.

An arch, also, which is pale and uniform at the horizon, passes the zenith without displaying any irregularity or additional brilliancy; and we have seen three arches together, very near the northern horizon, one of which exhibited beams and even colors, but the other two were faint and uniform.

On the 7th of April, an arch was visible to the southward, exactly similar to that in the north, and it disappeared in fifteen minutes. It had probably passed the zenith before sunset.

The motion of the whole body of aurora is from the northward to the southward, at angles not more than 20° from the magnetic meridian. The centres of the arches were as often in the magnetic as in the true meridian.

The colors do not seem to depend on the presence of any luminary, but to be generated by the motion of the beams, and then only when that motion is rapid, and the light brilliant. The lower extremities quiver with a fiery red color, and the upper with orange. We once saw violet in the former."—Franklin, I, 541.

N. B.—Height of the aurora.

Cumberland House.—Lat. 53° 56′ 40″ N. Long. 102° 16′ 41″ W. Winter of 1819–20. HOOD.

"The number of auroræ visible in September was 2; in October 3; in November 3; in December 5; 1819: in January 5; in February 7; in March 16; in April 15; in May 11; 1820.

Calm and clear weather was the most favorable for observation; but it is discernible in cloudy weather, and through mists. We could not perceive that it affected the weather. The *magnetic needle, in the open air, was disturbed by the aurora,* whenever it approached the zenith. Its motion was not vibratory, as observed by Mr. Dalton; and this was, perhaps, owing to the weight of the card attached to it. It moved slowly to the east or west of the magnetic meridian, and seldom recovered its original direction in less than eight or nine hours. The greatest extent of its aberration was 45′.

A delicate electrometer, suspended at the height of fifty feet from the ground, was never perceptibly affected by the aurora, nor could we distinguish its *rustling noise,* of which, however, such strong testimony has been given to us, that no doubt can remain of the fact.

The conclusions to be drawn from the above will be found in the observations for the winter of 1820."—Franklin, I, 543.

(At Cumberland House, the aurora always to the north of east and west.)

N. B.—Number of auroræ noticed. Magnetic needle disturbed. Electrometer never affected. No rustling noise distinguished.

Cumberland House.—Lat. 53° 56′ 40″ N. Long. 102° 16′ 41″ W. Variation 17° 17′ 31″ E. October 23, 1819, to June 30, 1820. HOOD.

"From the 23d of October to the 25th of November, the aurora was not visible, or it did not appear before 1 a. m.

November 26th. At 1 a. m., an aurora, arched like a rainbow, about 20° high; centre bearing north; color pale yellow, faint. At 8 p. m., a very faint arch, centre north.

December 6th. At 10 p. m., a faint-arched aurora, centre north by east.

8th. A similar aurora, centre north, at 10 p. m.

9th. At 11 p. m., an arched aurora, centre north; color light yellow, very bright.

12th. At 8 p. m., an arched aurora, centre north; color light yellow, faint."—Franklin, I, 543.

Upper Portage, near Knee Lake.—Lat. 55° 14′ 2″ N. Long. 94° 21′ 54″ W. September 24, 1819. FRANKLIN.

"At seven in the morning of the 24th, we crossed the Long Portage, where the woods, having caught fire in the summer, were still smoking.

We afterwards crossed the Second, or Swampy Portage, and in the evening encamped on the Upper Portage, where we were overtaken by an Indian bringing an answer from Governor Williams to a letter I had written to him on the 15th, in which he renewed his injunctions to the gentlemen of the boats accompanying us, to afford us every assistance in their power.

The Aurora Borealis appeared this evening in a *N. W. and S. E.* direction."—Franklin, I, 35.

Fort Isle la Crosse.—Lat. 55° 25′ 35″ N. Long. 107° 51′ W. March 4, 1820. FRANKLIN.

"We witnessed the Aurora Borealis very brilliant for the second time since our departure from Cumberland" (on the 18th of January, 1820).—Franklin, I, 126.

N. B.—Very brilliant for the second time since 18th January.

Off Cape Farewell.—Lat. 56° 17′ N. Long. 42° 51″ W. October 21, 1852. INGLEFIELD.

"Weather exceedingly disturbed. Aurora Borealis frequently most brilliant."—Inglefield, p. 205.

Methye River.—Lat. 56° 26′ 30″ N. Long. 109° 52′ 54″ W. January 23, 1837. SIMPSON.

"On the 23d, we started at 3 a. m. Some time before daylight there was a magnificent display of the *Aurora Borealis*, commencing with an arch of singular lustre *in the north*, which suddenly flashed up towards the zenith, and represented the interior of a stupendous cone, the apex and upper part being of a bright yellow hue, while the lower assumed a very rich carmine color. I had scarcely time to admire this resplendent phenomenon when it disappeared."—Simpson, p. 57; Ibid., Life, p. 210.

N. B.—1. Arch of singular lustre in the north.
2. Suddenly flashed up towards the zenith.
3. Represented the interior of a stupendous cone.

At Sea.—Lat. 57° N. Long. 49° W. Monday, October 2, 1820. PARRY.

"After 10 p. m. this night, the Aurora Borealis appeared at times in almost every part of the heavens, but *most constantly in the southern quarter.*

It consisted of no distinct figure, either arch or pencils, but of a generally diffused white light, illuminating the atmosphere at times quite as much as the moon does when six or seven days old.

This phenomenon occurred almost every night during our passage across the Atlantic, rendering them extremely light, even when the weather was cloudy; just in the same manner that the moon does although her disk is not visible. When the weather was clear, it most frequently resembled the light of that luminary when issuing from behind a dark cloud."—Parry, I, 306.

N. B.—1. At times, in almost every part of the sky.
2. Most constantly in southern quarter.
3. Consisted of no distinct figure.
4. But of generally diffused white light.

Near York Fort, Hudson's Bay.—Lat. 57° 2′ N. Long. 93° W. February, 1747. CLERK OF THE CALIFORNIA.

"When we came into the winter harbor, and during the winter, the Aurora Borealis seldom appeared from the northwest or northeast, but *generally from the northward of our zenith* shooting south, and at the same time another light, *from the southwest*, streaking towards the zenith; *the former from the bay, the latter over and according to the course of Port Nelson River.*

There was for several successive nights, and at various times in the winter, over Hay's Island, a broad, settled gleam of light, much resembling the Milky Way (only of a brighter color and somewhat broader), that reached from the northward of our zenith, and seemingly joined almost with the horizon.

The Auroræ Boreales were something more frequent in the winter than in the summer months, but were not in winter always apparent on every clear or starlight night."—Voyage to Hudson's Bay, II, 11.

N. B.—1. Seldom appeared from the N. W. or N. E., but generally from the N.
2. At the same time, another light from the S. W., streaking towards the zenith.
3. Aurora something more frequent in winter than the summer months.

Near York Factory.—Lat. 57° 2′ N. Long. 93° W. Winter of 1746–7. ELLIS.

"The air of this country is never, or, at least, is very seldom clear. In the spring and fall of the year there are heavy wet fogs, and in the winter the air is full of an infinite number of icy spicula, that are visible to the naked eye, especially if the wind be northerly or easterly, and the frost severe; the reason of it is this, wherever the water is clear of ice; in the winter there arises a very thick vapor, commonly called frost smoke; this vapor freezing is driven by the wind in the form we see it.

All the beginning of winter, Port Nelson River was unfroze in the stream; this lying to the northward of us, the wind blowing from that point, constantly brought with it showers of these icy particles, which disappeared when it was froze.

Hence, also, frequent mock suns and halos about the moon and sun, very luminous and beautifully tinged, with all the colors of the rainbow, are very common. Six of these parhelia, or mock suns, I have seen at one time, which to us was very surprising."—Ellis, p. 171.

"The true sun also rises and sets there with a large cone of yellow light, perpendicular to it; and no sooner does it disappear than the *Aurora Borealis* spreads a thousand different lights and colors over the whole concave of the sky, with so resplendent a beauty that even the full moon does not efface their lustre. But, if the moon does not shine, these lights are much more apparent, for *one may then read distinctly by them, and the shadows of objects are seen upon the snow, tending to the southeast*, as the light shines brightest in the opposite quarter where it rises, and whence the rays thereof are propagated over the whole face of the sky, with a waving kind of motion.

The stars seem in this country to burn with a fiery redness, especially those near the horizon, which strongly resemble a fire, or a ship's light at a distance."—Ibid., p. 172.

N. B.—1. One may read distinctly by the aurora, when the moon does not shine.
2. The light shines brightest in the N. W.
3. Whence rays are propagated over the sky.

York Fort.—Lat. 57° 2′ N. Long. 93° W. 1772–1780. UMFREVILLE.

"[York Fort, where I resided eight years, lies in the lat. of 57° 2′ N., long. 93° W. from London, as determined by Mr. Philip Turner, a gentleman employed by the company to make astronomical observations within the limits of Hudson's Bay. Page 11.]

In the coldest weather, the atmosphere is the most serene. Throughout the day, the air is generally filled with icy particles, which are small beyond conception. These are driven about in the direction of the wind, and adhere to everything which happens to be in the way of their progress.

In the evening, the stars begin to shine with refulgent lustre, and the contemplative mind is struck with reverence and awe to see the *Aurora Borealis* darting, with inconceivable velocity to all parts of the heavens.

Very few winter nights pass in Hudson's Bay without this phenomenon making its appearance. Sometimes the irradiations are seen of a very bright red, at other times of a pale, milky color, undulating with every beauty it is possible to conceive or describe."—Umfreville, p. 23.

N. B.—1. In coldest weather, atmosphere most serene.
2. Very few winter nights without the aurora.

York Factory.—Lat. 57° 2′ N. Long. 92° 40′ W. Aug. 31 to Sept. 28, 1814. CHAPPELL.

"During our stay in Hudson's Bay, and upon our voyage home from thence, our nights were constantly illuminated by the most vivid and brilliant coruscations of the Aurora Borealis.

Its appearance was very different from that which I have seen in more southern latitudes; resembling continual jets of meteoric fire from the *northern part of the horizon*, which, after darting upwards in long streamers towards the zenith, suddenly collapsed and receded, falling back, in zigzag serpentine lines, with diminished splendor; and ultimately dying away and vanishing from the sight, being succeeded by other jets as beautiful as the first."—Chappell, p. 136.

N. B.—1. Nights constantly illuminated by most brilliant coruscations.
2. Very different from that seen in more southern latitudes.

At Sea.—Lat. 57° 30′ N. Long. 45° W. Tuesday, October 3, 1820. PARRY.

"On the 3d, we observed a more brilliant display than usual of this phenomenon. It appeared at nine p. m. in various parts of the heavens, *from E. N. E., round by S., to W. by N.*, principally consisting at first of many detached luminous patches like clouds, irregularly scattered about, and shifting frequently, though not very rapidly, from place to place. From W. by N. over to the S. S. E., and passing a few degrees to the southward of the zenith, there soon appeared a broad band of light, having a tendency to arch; and the light of which this consisted appeared to come from the west towards the east.

In the E. N. E. quarter, there was a luminous appearance, distinct from the rest, at about 15° or 20° of altitude, exactly resembling the light of the moon behind a dusky cloud, except that at times vivid coruscations shot upwards from it towards the zenith.

At a quarter past ten the phenomenon suddenly became much more brilliant, its general position and character remaining, however, nearly as before. It still appeared chiefly to the southward of the zenith, the arch-like appearance continuing with increased splendor, and accompanied for about a quarter of an hour by a beautifully waving light, of the rapidity and magnificence of which it is impossible to convey any adequate idea. The motion of this light reminded me of the contortions of a snake, except that its velocity was often so great that the eye could with difficulty follow it. The most intense part was of a pale greenish color; the rest nearly white.

The arch, which before had been stationary, at one time shifted its position, by appearing, as it were, to turn up its legs so as to form a part of a circle seen in perspective in the south, parallel to the horizon. The luminous patch, or cloud, in the E. N. E. increased also very much in brightness at the same time, emitting more vivid coruscations, but continuing, as before, quite distinct from the rest of the phenomenon.

This Aurora, when brightest, gave nearly as much light as that of a full moon. There could not be the smallest doubt that it *dimmed*, and even sometimes *altogether obscured, the stars* over which it passed. We particularly remarked that, wherever there was a broad stream of its light stationary for some time in any part of the heavens, it produced exactly the effect of a curtain; for we could only distinguish stars of the first and second magnitude *through* it, while those of inferior brilliancy were visible in great numbers by the side of it.

In this, as in several previous instances, the Aurora appeared very near us, though it was evidently higher than some clouds which were passing, as might readily be distinguished by the latter intercepting a part of its light.

The electrometer was tried during the most brilliant part of the phenomenon, but neither on this or on any other occasion, in crossing the Atlantic, did the gold leaf give any indication of electricity; nor was the *magnetic needle* in the slightest degree affected.

The arch-like appearance above described was not bisected by the magnetic meridian, but by magnetic N. E. and S. W.

At a quarter before eleven, the light became less brilliant, and spread more to the northward, and then gradually disappeared before midnight."—1 Parry, 306.

N. B.—1. Gave nearly as much light as that of a full moon.
2. Dimmed, and sometimes almost obscured the stars.
3. It appeared generally to the south of the zenith.
4. Did not affect the magnetic needle.
5. Appeared very near.

At Sea.—Lat. 57° 30′ N. Long. 45° W. Tuesday, October 3, 1820. FISHER.

"The Aurora Borealis appeared very beautifully from nine till eleven o'clock this evening, forming an arch extending from east to west across the zenith; almost the whole of the *south side* of the hemisphere was indeed illumined by it, but it was not seen to the northward, except near the zenith.

It presented at different times a beautiful display of some of the prismatic colors, particularly the red, orange, yellow, and green; lake was also a predominant color in some parts occasionally.

With respect to the different forms that it assumed, and its various movements, I consider it impossible to give a correct idea of them by words. It appeared sometimes in immense sheets of light, moving rapidly along the surface of the sky; and at other times it darted in straight columns, from different parts of the sky towards the zenith. The most remarkable appearance, however, that it presented, was a sort of serpentine motion that it had at one time, from west to east, across the zenith.

The electrometer was tried, but it *was not affected, nor did we hear any noise* such as has been said to be produced by this phenomenon.

Whether the Aurora Borealis *dims the light of the stars or not,* I can hardly pretend to say; but I can affirm this much, that I *could see very plainly,* in the thickest part of it, the four small stars forming the diamond-shaped figure in the constellation of the Dolphin, from which I imagine that a great part of the dimness that appears to be occasioned, is owing to the stars and Aurora Borealis being nearly of the same color."—Fisher, pp. 288–89.

N. B.—1. Whole southern hemisphere illuminated.
2. At times, displayed prismatic colors.
3. Electrometer not affected.
4. Heard no noise.
5. Small stars seen plainly through thickest part of it.

At Sea.—Lat. 58° 12′ N. Long. 49° 15′ W. June, &c., 1746. CLERK OF THE CALIFORNIA.

"We had the Aurora Borealis some nights this month, as we had had at times from the 28th of June, when to the *westward and southward of Farewell.*

The Aurora Borealis in June was from the *southeast, then shifting round to the east.* Its appearance was like to that of a small yellow cloud, about forty degrees above the horizon, which soon shot out a stream towards the zenith, which stream consisted of a variety of colors—black, blue, flame-color, &c.—continually vibrating; and, after several emanations, which lasted for a small time, would collect and fold itself into the cloud, and then shoot out again.

The color of the others, in general, which we saw both in the bay and also after our arrival in Hays's River, was a yellow or buff color, with large streams shooting out, and then contracting, as we often see them in England, excepting some in the beginning of November, which were like that in June.

The radii of the Auroræ Borealès which we had in the bay, shot from *the southward.*"—Voyage to Hudson's Bay, II, 11.

At Sea: Atlantic.—Lat. 58° 30′ N. Long. 44° 30′ W. September 24, 1825. PARRY.

"The next brilliant display of this beautiful phenomenon which we now witnessed, and which far surpassed anything of the kind observed at Port Bowen, occurred on the night of the 24th of September, in latitude 58½°, longitude 44½°.

It first appeared in a (true) *east* direction, in detached masses, like luminous clouds of yellow or sulphur-colored light, about three degrees above the horizon. When this appearance had continued for about an hour, it began, at nine p. m., to spread upwards, and gradually extended itself into a narrow band of light, passing through the zenith and again downwards to the western horizon.

Soon after this the streams of light seemed no longer to emanate from the eastward, but from a fixed point about one degree above the horizon on a true west bearing. From this point, as from the narrow point of a funnel, streams of light, resembling brightly-illuminated vapor or smoke, appeared to be incessantly issuing, increasing in breadth as they proceeded, and darting with inconceivable velocity, such as the eye could scarcely keep pace with, upwards towards the zenith, and in the same easterly direction which the former arch had taken. The sky immediately under the spot from which the light issued, appeared, by a deception very common in this phenomenon, to be covered with a dark cloud, whose outline the imagination might at times convert into that of the summit of a mountain, from which the light proceeded like the flames of a volcano. The streams of light, as they were projected upwards, did not consist of continuous vertical columns or streamers, but almost entirely of separate though constantly-renewed masses, which seemed to *roll* themselves laterally onward, with a sort of undulating motion, constituting what I have understood to be meant by that modification of the Aurora called the 'merry dancers,' which is seen in beautiful perfection at the Shetland Islands. The general color of the light was yellow, but an orange and a greenish tinge were at times very distinctly perceptible, the intensity of the light and colors being always the greatest when occupying the smallest space. Thus the lateral margins of the band or arch seemed at times to roll themselves inwards so as to approach each other, and in this case the light just at the edges became much more vivid than the rest. The intensity of light during the brightest part of the phenomenon, which continued three-quarters of an hour, could scarcely be inferior to that of the moon when full.

We once more remarked, in crossing the Atlantic, that the Aurora often gave *a great deal of light at night*, even when the sky was entirely overcast, and it was *on that account* impossible to say from what part of the heavens the light proceeded, though it was often fully equal to that afforded by the moon in her quarters.

This was rendered particularly striking on the night of the 5th of October, in consequence of the frequent and almost instantaneous changes which took place in this way, the weather being rather dark and gloomy, but the sky at times so brightly illuminated, almost in an instant, as to give quite as much light as the full moon similarly clouded, and enabling one distinctly to recognize persons from one end of the ship to the other.

We did not, on any occasion, perceive the compasses to be affected by the Aurora Borealis."—3 Parry, 170–71–72.

N. B.—1. First appeared in the (true) east.
2. Very brilliant.
3. On no occasion perceived the compasses affected.

Fort Chippewyan.—Lat. 58° 42′ 38″ N. Long. 111° 18′ 20″ W. April, 1820. FRANKLIN.

"The month of April commenced with fine and clear, but extremely cold weather; unfortunately, we were still without a thermometer, and could not ascertain the degrees of temperature.

The coruscations of the Aurora were very brilliant almost every evening of the first week, and were generally of the most variable kind.

On the 3d they were particularly changeable. The first appearance exhibited three illuminated beams issuing from the horizon in the *northeast and west points*, and directed towards the zenith;

in a few seconds these disappeared, and a complete circle was displayed, bounding the horizon at an elevation of fifteen degrees.

There was *a quick lateral motion* in the attenuated beams of which this zone was composed. Its color was a pale yellow, with an occasional tinge of red."—1 Franklin, 143.

"On the 17th and 19th the Aurora appeared very brilliant in patches of light, bearing *N. W.*"—Ibid., p. 144.

May 2, 1820.—"On the 2d the Aurora faintly gleamed through very dense clouds."—Ibid., p. 145.

June 16, 1820.—"On the evening of the 16th the Aurora Borealis was visible, but after that date the nights were too light for our discerning it."—Ibid., p. 162.

N. B.—1. Three illuminated beams in the N. E. and W. points.
2. A complete circle bounding the horizon, 15° high.
3. A quick lateral motion.

At Sea: Atlantic Ocean.—March 29, 1817. O'Reilly.

March 29, 1817.—"At 8 p. m., *the electric coruscations* suddenly appeared, running about at thirty degrees above the horizon, ascending in a perpendicular direction from a base in a rapid succession of brassy-yellow flames, *from W. to E.*, and soon died away.

Immediately after, from the westward there slowly extended upwards to the zenith four faintly-marked radii, which diverged as they ascended; two, more approximating to each other and nearly of equal breadth throughout. One only remained, stretching in a magnificent arch over the zenith, embracing the horizon east and west, and of a splendor exceedingly faint: it might, on hasty observation, be supposed a cirrus."—O'Reilly, p. 28.

N. B.—1. First appearance—yellow flames from W. to E.
2. Magnificent arch over the zenith embracing the horizon E. and W.

March 30.—"At 9¾ p. m., the coruscations appeared again from *northwest;* and, in the midst of the stunning hurly, I could not resist noticing their activity. Imagination would say, that truly the spirit of the storm was abroad in all his majesty. The account of the lights, immediately noted, may be of interest to some of my readers."—Ibid., p. 29.

N. B.—Coruscations from northwest.

Near Davis's Strait.—April, 1817. O'Reilly.

April 8, 1817.—"Lights very vivid, restless, and playing from every point towards the star Benetnach, as to a centre of afflux."—O'Reilly, p. 31.

April 16.—"The lights, between 10 and 11 p. m., were exceedingly splendid, and seemed to make Benetnach a centre, but moving to N. E."—Ibid., p. 33.

At Sea.—Lat. 59° N. Long. 50° W. October 8, 1818. Robertson.

"At eight in the evening, observed the Aurora very bright on the *true east* quarter, shooting beautiful rays in bundles from the horizon to the altitude of 60°; this was soon obscured by squalls of snow and sleet. From nine to twelve the Aurora was seen in every part of the heavens shooting streams of light in every direction; the most luminous appearing from *north by west* to *west by north,* true bearings."—1 John Ross (Robertson), App., cxxii.

N. B.—1. At 8 p. m., very bright in true E. quarter.
2. From 9 to 12, in every part of the heavens; the most luminous appearing from N. by W. to W. by N.

At Sea.—Lat. 59° 58′ N. Long. 59° 53′ W. August 4, 1819. FRANKLIN.

"At nine p. m., brilliant coruscations of the Aurora Borealis appeared, of a pale ochre color, with a slight tinge of red, in an arched form—crossing the zenith from *N. W. to S. E.*, but afterwards they assumed various shapes, and had a rapid motion."—Franklin, I, 12.

N. B.—1. Arch crossing zenith from N. W. to S. E.
2. Various shapes; rapid motion.

Hoarak (Greenland).—Lat. 59° 59′ N. Long. 44° 36′ W. March 27, 1829. GRAAH.

"At eight o'clock this evening, we saw an Aurora Borealis in the form of a luminous arch stretching from *N. E.* to *S. W.*, 30° high; and, shortly after, three others, stretching from *E. S. E.* to *W. S. W.*, the loftiest of which reached nearly to the zenith."—Graah, p. 60.

N. B.—1. Luminous arch, N. E. to S. W., 30° high.
2. Three others, from E. S. E. to W. S. W.

At Sea.—Lat. 60° N. Long. 56° W. October 6, 1818. ROBERTSON.

"Strong gales and squally, with snow and sleet. Observed the whole sky suddenly illuminated, which lasted five or six minutes. *This might be aurora in the zenith.* Wind N. N. W., moderating towards noon."—1 John Ross (Robertson), App., cxxii.

N. B.—1. Whole sky suddenly illuminated.
2. This might be aurora in the zenith.

Kikkertak (Greenland).—Lat. 60° 4′ N. Long. 43° 2′ W. April 12, 1829. GRAAH.

"In the evening of the 12th, some unusually brilliant coruscations of the Aurora Borealis were seen in the *E.* and *N. E.* They seemed to proceed from out of a thick bank of fog, about 6° or 8° above the horizon; and, after passing the zenith, appeared to be transformed into light clouds, for such were seen to flit past the moon in the southwesterly region of the heavens, while the northern was without a cloud.

They had no sensible effect on the magnetic needle."—Graah, p. 63.

N. B.—1. Brilliant coruscations in the E. and N. E.; seemed to proceed from a thick bank of fog.
2. After passing zenith, appeared to be transformed into light clouds.
3. No sensible effect on the magnetic needle.

Davis's Strait.—Lat. 60° 10′ N. Long. 49° 40′ W. August 2, 1852. INGLEFIELD.

"A good deal of ice encountered off Capes Farewell and Desolation. Aurora in yellow and reddish coruscations on the western sky, extending near the zenith."—Inglefield, p. 201.

At Sea.—Lat. 60° 30′ N. 25° W. Friday, October 13, 1820. PARRY.

"At seven p. m. on the 13th, the wind being squally from the N. N. W., the Aurora Borealis began to display itself in a bright luminous patch in the *northeast*, resembling, as usual, the light of the moon behind a dark cloud.

From this point, faint and narrow coruscations shot upwards, passing a little to the northwestward of the zenith, and appearing to come down *to the W. by S.*

The blue sky between these streams of light looked at first like so many dark streaks or clouds, until the eye had become accustomed to it, and the clearness of the stars in them explained the deception.

In half an hour after, a bright arch, 34° high in the centre, and about 2° in breadth, extended *from the luminous patch in the N. E. over to the W. S. W.*, so that the magnetic meridian would nearly bisect it. This part of the phenomenon remained about an hour, and then became faint; but the Aurora continued to give considerable light, as usual, during the rest of the night."—1 Parry, 307.

N. B.—1. At 7 p. m., a bright luminous patch in the N. E.
2. From this point, faint coruscations, passing a little to the N. of zenith, appeared to come down to the W. by S.
3. Half an hour after, a bright arch, 34° high in the centre, from N. E. over to W. S. W.
4. This remained almost an hour.

At Sea.—Lat. 61° N. Long. 25 W. October 17, 1818. ROBERTSON.

"At eight p. m., observed the Aurora to begin in two concentric arches, the greatest arch from *true east to west*, passing through the zenith; the smaller arch south of the large one, at an altitude of 45°, shooting fine rays from all parts of the arches, but most brilliant from the western part.

At half-past eight, these arches disappeared, and another most brilliant one was seen *north of the zenith*, the centre passing through the pole star, the extremities touching the eastern and western horizons, emitting fine rays having all the prismatic colors. This arch was soon broken, and the Aurora flitted about in beautiful coruscations in the northwestern part of the heavens, shifting round to the *southward*. The moon shone unclouded at the time, and the Aurora was sometimes seen passing her, *eclipsing her in splendor*.

At 9h. 30m. p. m., the Aurora disappeared, the weather moderate at the time, with some light fleecy clouds in the sky, which had a dark appearance when passing under the Aurora."—1 John Ross (Robertson), App., cxxii.

N. B.—1. At 8 p. m., two concentric arches, from true E. to W., passing through the zenith.
2. At half-past 8, an arch N. of the zenith, the centre passing through the pole star; extremes touching E. and W. horizons.
3. Shifted round to the S.
4. Eclipsed the moon in splendor.
5. At 9h. 30m., disappeared.

At Sea.—Lat. 61° 4′ N. Long. 49° 50′ W. August 4, 1852. INGLEFIELD.

"An Aurora Borealis was observed at midnight of the 4th, which illumined the whole of the southern sky with its variegated coruscations of brilliant light.

During the following day, we stood in to within eight miles of the shore, and it was supposed that we were off Omenarsuk."—Inglefield, p. 13.

Moose-Deer Island.—Lat. 61° 18′ 8″ N. Long. 113° 51′ 35″ W. 1822. FRANKLIN.

"Observations were made on the Aurora Borealis, in 1822, at Moose-Deer Island, lat. 61° 18′ 8″ N., long. 113° 51′ 35″ W., variation 25° 40′ 47″ E. Being unwilling, however, to swell the Appendix more than necessary, I shall not insert the tables, but merely remark, that—

Although the Aurora was frequently seen there, the coruscations were seldom either brilliant or of the variable kind. They caused but little alteration in the position of the needle, the greatest deviation observed being 18′, and did not furnish grounds for any additional inferences to those which were drawn from the observations on the Aurora made at Fort Enterprise.

The display of light was generally confined to the *northern part of the sky*, between the true N. E. and S. W. points, usually at a low altitude; and the Aurora was observed extending to the *southward on four occasions* only. This, as well as the circumstance of the magnetic needle being but slightly affected by the presence of the Aurora during the winter at that place, appears to me to be deserving of notice, as affording an indication that *the seat of the phenomenon lies more to the northward;* and were I to venture an opinion as to its probable situation, I should say between the latitudes 64° and 65° N., or about the position of Fort Enterprise [lat. 64° 28′ 24″ N., 113° 6′ W.], because the coruscations were *as often seen there* in the southern as in the northern parts of the sky, and I should consider that latitude the most favorable in this part of the globe for making good observations on this interesting phenomenon."—1 Franklin, 553.

N. B.—1. Had but little effect on the needle.

2. Generally confined to the northern part of the sky, between the true N. E. and S. W. points.
3. Extended to the *southward on four occasions* only.
4. *Seat of the phenomenon* more to the northward.
5. Its situation probably between 64° and 65°.
6. At Fort Enterprise, coruscations seen as often in the south as the north parts of the sky.
7. That latitude most favorable for observations on the aurora.

Davis's Strait.—Lat. 61° 37′ N. Long. 52° W. August 26, 1851. Dr. SUTHERLAND.

"In the evening the wind veered round to N., and freshened up from almost a perfect calm to a smart breeze. The spars of the 'Sophia' again began to feel it, as she scudded before it at the rate of five or six miles an hour.

At midnight, the whole sky was one living fire of Aurora Borealis. It far exceeded anything that we had seen in much higher latitudes during winter. The surface of the sea was sometimes illuminated so much, that had there been objects on the horizon at a distance of several miles, they would have been plainly visible."—Dr. Sutherland, II, 346.

Davis's Strait.—Lat. 61° 58′ N. Long. 54° 40′ W. August 25, 1851. Dr. SUTHERLAND.

"The temperature of the water was increasing almost hourly as we came down the Strait, and now it was up so high as 47°, while that of the air was only 48°. In the evening, there was much rain, and the sky was densely overcast.

There were all the indications of a southwesterly storm; but towards midnight they all disappeared, the blue sky opened out, and a most brilliant Aurora Borealis danced from the horizon to the zenith.

It was really pleasant to behold the broad gleaming bands folding like curtains of the richest and finest woven silken fabric. The color varied every moment from red to white, and from yellow to a slight tinge of green, verging into purple, which became lost in the red.

From the sudden appearance of this beautiful phenomenon, we hardly expected fine weather or a favorable wind, more especially as the barometer was too high for westerly winds."—Dr. Sutherland, II, 345.

Faroe Islands.—Lat. 62° N. TREVELYAN.

"Mr. Trevelyan observed, that the Aurora Borealis in Faroe and Shetland was often seen very low, not more than *forty or fifty feet* above the level of the sea; and he learned that in both countries *it is frequently heard.*

In Faroe, Mr. Trevelyan met one person who stated that, when the color of the Aurora Borealis is dark red, and extends from west to east with a violent motion, he had experienced a smell similar to that which is perceived when an electric machine is in action."—Am. Journ. Sci., VIII, 392; *from* Edinb. Phil. Journ., Vol. VII.

Hudson's Bay.—Lat. 62° 18′ N. Long. 87° 12′ 12″ W. September 18, 1824. LYON.

"Running till 10 p. m., we lay to for the night, as I had reason to suppose we were to the southward of Cape Southampton, and was more particularly confirmed in this opinion from the compasses having all again become restless.

This agitation having frequently been observed on other nights, between the hours of nine and eleven, had always been the cause of great anxiety to me, while endeavoring to steer a course after dark, unless the moon or stars were clearly visible; and it is well worthy of consideration whether this wildness of motion in the compasses is at all caused by the *absence* of the sun, or is in any way occasioned by the *presence* of the Aurora, which phenomenon was rarely seen earlier than 9 p. m., and the time when it was most vivid was generally at about 10. At this hour, on one occasion, Mr. Kendall observed, that during the prevalence of an unusually brilliant Aurora, the larboard binnacle compass would remain stationary at no particular point, while the starboard one, by a bearing of the pole star, had lessened its accustomed error two points.

By a bearing of the sun, on the following morning, it was found to have resumed its original position."—Lyon, pp. 118–19.

"At 10 p. m., I hove to, in consequence of the compasses becoming greatly agitated. This had frequently been observed on other nights, between the hours of nine and eleven, and had always been the cause of great anxiety to me while endeavoring to steer a course after dark.

It is well worthy of consideration, whether this agitation of the compasses is at all to be attributed to the *absence* of the sun, or is in any way occasioned by the *presence* of the aurora, which phenomenon was rarely seen earlier than 9 p. m., and its greatest brilliancy was generally at about 10, although the sun had then been set some hours.

On one occasion, during the prevalence of an unusually brilliant aurora, at 10 p. m., Mr. Kendall observed that the larboard binnacle compass would not remain steady at any point, while the starboard one, by a bearing of the pole star, had decreased its accustomed error two points; but on the following morning, by a bearing of the sun, it was found to have resumed them.

N. B.—Up to this period, the error on this bearing had been eight points E."—Lyon, p. 167.

N. B.—Agitation of the compasses.

At Sea.—Lat. 62° 30′ N. Long. 63° W. October 1, 1818. ROBERTSON.

"At eight in the evening the Aurora was seen in the true *S. S. W.* to *S. S. E.* At nine, the luminous appearance spread from S. W., round by the S. E. quarter, to *N. E.*, in an arched form; the centre of the arch 18° high, the luminous part of arch 3° broad. There was a very dark appearance under the arch, through which the stars appeared with the same *glimmering* light that they shone with through the luminous parts. Small bundles of sharp pointed rays were shot perpendicular from all parts of the arch to the altitude of 40°. About ten the arch shifted more to the westward, and soon disappeared; fresh breezes from W. S. W."—1 John Ross (Robertson), App., cxxi.

N. B.—1. At 8 p. m., seen in true S. S. W. to S. S. E.

2. At 9 p. m., from S. W. by S. E. to N. E., in an arch.

3. Dark appearance under the arch.

4. At 10 p. m., arch shifted more to W., and soon disappeared.

Near Rankin's Inlet.—Lat. 62° 35′ 47″ N. August 22, 1847. RAE.

"The Aurora was very bright last night. It appeared first to the S. S. E., moved rapidly northward, spreading all over the sky, and finally disappeared in the north.

This agrees with what Wrangel asserts, 'that the Aurora is affected by the wind in the same way as clouds are.'"—Rae, p. 188.

Hudson's Bay.—Lat. 62° 45′ 44″ N. Long. 72° 24′ W. September 29, 1824. LYON.

"At noon we obtained observations, and in the evening made the coast, which we neared sufficiently before dark to discern to be the North Bluff, from whence at 8 p. m. we took a departure and steered southeast.

Along the shore, a great number of very large bergs were observed, apparently aground, as if driven to the northern land by the recent southerly winds.

We sailed past several during the night, which was exceedingly bright and fine, the stars shining with uncommon brilliancy, and the Aurora being unusually splendid."—Lyon (Voyage), p. 134.

N. B.—Aurora unusually splendid.

Fort Reliance.—Lat. 62° 46′ 29″ N. Long. 109° 00′ 38″ W. 1833–34, 1834–35. BACK.

"The observations on this phenomenon [the Aurora Borealis] were made, without interruption, during six months in the years 1833–34, and five months in the years 1834–35; but, as their entire insertion would occupy too much space here, I have selected chiefly the instances possessing the greatest interest from the effect produced by them on the needle, and from the brilliancy and eccentric motions of the coruscations.

That the needle was constantly affected by the appearance of the Aurora, seems evident from the facts thus stated; and, on one occasion, indeed, this effect exceeded eight degrees. I abstain, however, from drawing any inferences on this subject, and merely note down carefully, and with as much precision as possible, the whole of the phenomena.

Brilliant and active coruscations of the Aurora Borealis, when seen through a *hazy atmosphere*, and exhibiting the prismatic colors, almost invariably affected the needle. On the contrary, a very bright Aurora, though attended by motion, and even tinged with a dullish red or yellow, in *a clear blue sky*, seldom produced any sensible change, beyond, at the most, a tremulous motion.

A *dense haze or fog*, in conjunction with an active Aurora, seemed uniformly favorable to the disturbance of the needle; and a low temperature was favorable to brilliant and active coruscations. On no occasion, during two winters, was any *sound* heard to accompany the motions.

The aurora was frequently seen at twilight, and as often to the eastward as to the westward. *Clouds*, also, were often perceived in the daytime, in form and disposition very much resembling the Aurora."—Back, p. 595.

N. B.—1. Needle constantly affected by appearance of the Aurora.
2. Aurora frequently seen at twilight; as often to the eastward as westward.
3. Clouds often seen in daytime in form of Aurora.

Fort Reliance.—Lat. 62° 46′ 29″ N. Long. 109° 00′ 38″ W. October 28, 1833. BACK.

"At 5h. 30m. p. m., while occupied in taking the transit of a star, I perceived the coruscations streaming from behind a detached and oblong dark *cloud* in a vertical position at *E. by S.* [magnetic bearing]. They issued along an undulating arch 38° high, and spread themselves laterally in beams north and south. Another arch, brighter and narrower than the former, suddenly emerged from *W. by N.*, and passed between a nearly horizontal black cloud and the stars, which were then not visible through the Aurora. I immediately looked at the needle, and found it slightly agitated, but not vibrating; on returning, I was surprised to see the *dark horizontal cloud* to the westward not in the same shape as before. It had now taken a balloon form, and was evidently fast spreading towards the zenith. On looking to the eastward, I perceived that a *dark cloud* there also was rapidly altering its appearance.

So unusual a sight induced me to call my companions, Messrs. King and McLeod, and we saw the dark broad mass from the westward gradually expand itself, so as to meet the other, which was likewise rising, at or near the zenith. The effect of the junction was a dark gray arch, extending from *E. by S. to W. by N.* across the zenith, and completely obscuring the stars, though at each side of the arch they were particularly clear and twinkling.

In the mean time, the Aurora assumed every variety of form; such as undulating and fringed arches, 30° to 50° high and more or less broad, with flashes and beams at right angles to them. The cloudy arch, too, was illuminated at and around its N. W. edges near the horizon, while rays and beams played round its eastern extremity. In a few seconds, the part of this nearest the horizon assumed a zigzag form, like forked lightning; and immediately the western extremity sympathized, undergoing momentary transitions which defy description. Such convulsions at the extremes soon affected the centre of the arch, which, becoming gradually fainter and fainter, at last vanished entirely, leaving the stars to shine forth in all their brilliance. The detached masses yet remained, though under various forms, and the Aurora nimbly played round and through them, especially the eastern one, until not the slightest vestige of them remained."—Ibid., p. 200.

N. B.—1. At 5½ p. m., coruscations from a dark cloud, E. by S.
2. Stars not visible through the Aurora.
3. Needle slightly agitated.
4. Dark clouds—one E., one W.
5. Meet at or near the zenith.
6. Form an arch from E. by S. to W. by N.

Fort Reliance.—Lat. 62° 46′ 29″ N. Long. 109° 00′ 38″ W. 1833–34. KING.

"The Aurora Borealis, as soon as evening sets in, overspreads the ethereal space, as if intended by Providence to cheer the hours of darkness by its beautiful and varied coruscations. For about two hours after midnight, it was invariably observed by us to be most brilliant and active; passing from east to west, or *vice versâ*, and *northerly;* sometimes appearing in the form of a splendid arch flitting across the heavens with inconceivable velocity, and resembling the spiral motions of a serpent. Then, suddenly disappearing, the veil of night would be at once diffused around; when, as quick as the flash of a star, a thousand dancing lights would again be seen playing mysteriously through the sky, assuming a variety of forms and diversity of motion, of which it is too difficult for an inanimate description to convey any idea.

It seldom appeared *southerly,* as if there was something in that part of the heavens which it dare not approach; but, commencing in the *eastern* or *southeastern* horizon—in which particular it coincides with the remarks of Parry and Crantz—would shoot across the zenith to the west, and descend in a variety of forms to the *northern* part of the earth, covering the whole of *that portion* of the concave with a brilliant light, while the opposite quarter of the hemisphere was enveloped in darkness.

Notwithstanding the Aurora is most frequent in the severest weather during a calm, yet I have seen equally vivid coruscations when the wind was blowing a stiff breeze; and although directly opposed to its motions, far from being in any way affected, it continued uninterruptedly on in its accustomed eccentricity. At times there would appear two currents in active motion from opposite points, approaching the zenith, where they formed a corona, presenting the appearance of so many snakes twisting with amazing swiftness; while at the same time a fringed, undulating arch, composed of numberless bright rays, would be seen flitting with inconceivable velocity from the horizon towards the zenith. Among them might be frequently observed streams of light perpendicular to the horizon, collected together, and moving with even greater velocity than the rest; which from their peculiar appearance have acquired the name of 'merry dancers.'

The appearance of the Aurora is not confined to an unclouded sky; it was frequently observed by us in active motion when the heavens were partially obscured by a hazy atmosphere, and occasionally perceived emerging from behind a *black cloud.*

Capell Brooke observed this peculiarity at Hammerfest; and we had an opportunity of witnessing the same strange phenomenon at Fort Reliance in November, 1833; at which time there were *two dark clouds* in opposite directions, and the coruscations brilliantly streaming in a variety of fantastic figures from behind them. The *clouds* in detached masses remained for some time assuming various forms, while the Aurora nimbly played round and through them until not the slightest vestige of their presence remained. We had also frequent opportunities of observing the appearances described by Parry, of long horizontal separations of the Aurora, resembling so many dark parallel streaks lying over it; which was evidently the dark indigo sky only, as the stars were plainly visible.

I have often observed a *gray haze*, effectually obscuring the sky, suddenly give way to a mass of light that illumined the whole face of the heavens, as if the atmosphere had instantaneously taken fire, leaving the sky, after it vanished, of a dark blue color, and studded with twinkling stars; while, on the contrary, the same *gray mist* has been noticed to take place on the subsidence of the Aurora, which was especially the case on the 4th of April, 1834.

There cannot be a doubt but that this meteor, from the intensity of its light, *dims* the stars; and from the following fact it is equally certain, that it *obscures the sky also in the form of white clouds during the day*, when its luminous appearance is eclipsed by the brightness of the sun.

A mass of *white cloud* was observed at 10 a. m. of the 28th of October, precisely similar in shape to an Aurora of the previous evening, and situated in the same place, at which time the sun was shining brightly. Captain Back having placed himself in the shade of a fir-tree, imagined that he saw a faint filmy arch of pale white issuing from it; and after watching more attentively, a pale yellow arch was seen shooting from the mass of cloud to the westward, and extending *southerly to S. E. by S.* at an angle of 30°. Afterwards several detached radial clouds became visible in the same point, which he more than once thought differed much in brightness.

Clouds were often observed by us in the daytime, in form and disposition very similar to the Aurora, especially on the 25th of last December [1833], when an arch of streaky and filmy clouds exactly resembling its coruscations extended from east to west across the zenith. Captain Parry was also 'struck with the general resemblance to the form of the Aurora assumed by the clouds, in the polar regions, at particular seasons.'

It has always been an interesting question with those who attempt to ascribe this beautiful phenomenon to electrical causes, whether the Aurora be attended with any *sound or noise;* and although many accurate observers have paid particular attention to this subject in various parts of the northern hemisphere, yet the point is far from being settled."—King, II, 90–95.

"On no occasion, during two winters, was any *sound* heard to accompany the motions of the Aurora by either Captain Back or myself. Once or twice I thought a sound was audible, but afterwards ascertained it to be the hissing noise produced by the sudden condensation of my breath into icy particles; and Captain Back several times positively declared he heard a whizzing noise during the rapidity of the motion, until he convinced himself it was the faint murmuring only of Anderson's Fall that had deceived him.

That a *change of color is perceptible in the Aurora*, is admitted by almost every author who has described its appearance. I believe it, however, to be *of rare occurrence;* for, *during two winters of five months each*, notwithstanding scarcely a night passed away without our observing this beautiful phenomenon, Captain Back and I only witnessed it vary from the flame or straw color eight times; five of which it appeared of a red, and the remaining three respectively of an indigo, lake, and orange color. In about the same lapse of time also it was noticed by Parry to vary three times only, of which it appeared twice of a lilac, and once of a green tint.

Whether the magnetic needle be affected by the appearance of the Aurora or not, still remains in doubt. There are different opinions upon the subject, and the observations taken by Captain Back and myself have not yet been reduced by the Professor who has undertaken to work them." —King, II, 96.

"In my humble opinion, *there are not sufficient facts yet collected to justify us in coming to any conclusions*, either as to the effect of the Aurora on the magnetic needle, *or as to the most favorable situation for solving that problem.*

According to Captain Back, who witnessed the Aurora at Forts Franklin and Enterprise, that meteor was not only more brilliant, but the streams of light more rapid, at Fort Reliance than he had observed it at either of the former places; from which circumstance it might be inferred that the 62*d parallel of latitude is even more favorable* for the appearance of this phenomenon than the 65th. If, as has been stated, 'a low temperature is favorable to brilliant and active coruscations' of the Aurora, it is to the eastern extremity of Great Slave Lake that observers should direct their course to further this very interesting inquiry, as in that situation a more intense cold was experienced by ten degrees than had ever before been registered."—King, II, 98.

Fort Reliance.—Lat. 62° 46′ 29″ N. Long. 109° 00′ 38″ W. Winters of 1833–34 and 1834–35. KING.

"It fell to my share, during the two winters the expedition remained at Fort Reliance, to register the position of the needle one thousand and fifty times; but, as the subject will shortly be brought before the Royal Society, I shall offer only a few remarks.

I have sometimes observed the *needle quite stationary*, when the whole concave has been illumined with brilliant and active coruscations; and at other times witnessed it *moving horizontally* several degrees, without the least appearance of an Aurora, although, from the deep indigo color of the sky, it must have been seen had it been present. The same anomaly was remarked in a hazy atmosphere.

During the prevalence of counter currents, the needle was observed to dip, by estimation, at least ten minutes. On one occasion, however, the same action was apparently caused by applying the finger to the front glass of the frame containing the needle."—King, II, 101.

Thermometer at Fort Reliance, January, 1834.

Day.	Highest.	Lowest.	Day.	Highest.	Lowest.
11	—32.00	—47.00	17	—45.00	—70.00
12	—41.00	—56.25	18	—38.00	—45.00
13	—50.00	—59.50	19	—35.00	—54.00
14	—47.00	—59.00	20	—22.00	—50.00
15	—44.25	—52.00	21	—36.00	—49.75
16	—52.50	—68.00	22	—25.00	—48.00

Back, p. 568.

Hudson's Bay (Rowe's Welcome).—Lat. 63° 15′ 44″ N. Long. 89° 3′ 30″ W. September 5, 1824. LYON.

"In the evening, a bright arch rose in the *northwest*, and we quickly found that the gale had shifted with increased violence to that quarter. By night, not a cloud was to be seen, and there was every indication of a decided northwest gale."—Lyon (Voyage), p. 85.

N. B.—Bright arch in northwest.

Southern Greenland.—Winter of 1828–29. GRAAH.

"The northern lights (Aurora Borealis), a remarkable and beautiful phenomenon of which the inhabitants of the greater part of Europe can form no adequate conception, are in Greenland and Iceland a thing of every day occurrence, and serve materially to indemnify the Polar regions for the want of solar light experienced by them, in consequence of the long absence of the sun below their horizon.

It may be said to be of two kinds; the one appearing uniformly between the magnetic E. S. E. and S. W., or, W. S. W., in the form of a luminous arch, shining with a steady and more or less vivid light, its highest being, in the magnetic South, from 10° to 20° above the horizon, and its legs seeming to rise out of the ocean. From this arch usually diverge rays towards the zenith, or a point in its vicinity. This description of Northern Light is colorless; and I think I have observed that it usually precedes, but still oftener follows after, some great change of temperature, especially from thaw to frost.

The other sort of Northern Light, which, still more than the former, seems to stand in connection with barometrical changes, flits from place to place in the semblance either of light luminous clouds agitated by the wind, and through which the light appears to diffuse itself with a sort of undulating motion, or of flaming rays, flashing, like rockets, across the firmament, most commonly upwards in the direction of the zenith, or, finally, like a serpentine or zigzag belt of vivid, undulating light, frequently colored, which at one moment is extinguished, and the next relit. The most beautiful of this class of phenomena, meanwhile, is the *Corona*, a luminous ring near the zenith, of from 2° to 3° in diameter, with rays diverging in every direction, like prolonged radii, from its centre. This highly interesting phenomenon seldom lasts longer than a few seconds, at the expiration of which an explosion, as it seems, takes place, scattering the luminous matter in every direction, and extinguishing it. The centre of the Corona I found to be invariably situated to the east of the meridian, at an elevation of from 81½° to 82½° above the horizon.

When the Aurora displays itself in all its splendor, its light is brighter than that of the full moon. It has been asserted, that this phenomenon is sometimes accompanied by a low, hissing noise. I myself, in fact, have often heard the sound, but am satisfied it has nothing to do with the Aurora, but proceeds partly from the ice, partly from the wind sweeping over the snow and ling-clad hills.

Whenever a more than usually vivid Aurora displayed itself, I made a point of taking measures to observe its effect on a magnet suspended by a silken fibre, but never detected any agitation or alteration in the direction of the latter, that could be attributed to this cause; though, I must add, that in making some like experiments, in the years 1823–24, at the Colony of Good Hope, situated in lat. 69° 14′, I did think that some such effect was perceptible.

That the substance-matter of the Aurora Borealis is liable to being acted on by the winds prevailing in different atmospheric strata seems evident, from the phenomenon itself, and as the changes of the weather depend again, in some degree, upon the winds, it is probable that a connection exists between them and the phenomenon of the Aurora. Many have hence inferred, that the appearance of the latter may safely be regarded as a prognostic of the former. This opinion, however, is, as far as I am aware, by no means well founded; and, in fact, all that may be securely relied on, with reference to this subject, is what follows:—

1. When the Aurora Borealis is vivid, and displays a variety of colors, boisterous or bad weather may be expected, and the wind may be looked for from that quarter where the Aurora has disappeared, or been extinguished.
2. When, after a long absence, an Aurora Borealis appears between S. W. and S. E. in the form of an arch, from 10° to 20° high, and glowing with a steady light, it is a prognostic of approaching frost.

The Greenlanders have a singular superstition connected with the phenomenon of the Aurora Borealis. They conceive it to be the spirits of the dead, playing at ball with the head of a walrus, and fancy that it draws nearer to them when they whistle,—a superstition at all events not more absurd than the idea long, and, indeed, still, prevalent in some parts of Europe, of its being ominous of war, pestilence, or famine."—Graah, p. 52.

Beresov (Russia).—Lat. 64° N. Long. 65° W. December 1, 1828. Erman.

"In order to determine the magnetic declination, I observed, about eight o'clock in the evening, the passage of the pole-star through the transit instrument. A few minutes after the observation was concluded, the clouds, which had hitherto obscured the lower part of the northern sky, disappeared, and we saw in their stead, a brilliant Auroral light.

Towards the horizon there was still some darkness, but above that there was bright light, which rose highest at a point about 27° west of the astronomical, 38° west of the magnetical, north; the greatest elevation being about 6° above the horizon; and from that point an irregular arch of light extended downwards on both sides of the horizon. Extremely vivid bands of light, from half to three quarters of a degree in breadth, shot up frequently from different points of the arch. I could not perceive, however, that these radiations converged towards the zenith: on the contrary, those from the eastern side of the arch seemed decidedly to tend towards points east of the zenith; those from the western side, in like manner, to lean westwards, just as if they had all diverged from a point below the horizon and within the arch.

These phenomena continued, without any change of character, the whole night, till near sunrise, when the sky became clouded. In every part of the fixed arch, the light was in unceasingly tremulous motion; its brightness increased from time to time, and at those moments the radiated pillars of light also rose higher and brighter than usual. The color of the light was yellow-red, and underwent but little change. About twenty-five minutes past ten, the apparent width of the region of the heavens filled with light was measured, and was ascertained to lie within the vertical circles of N. 15° E., and N. 30° W.

* * * * * *

The fact that, in the present instance, neither the middle of the coruscating area, nor the point of the heavens from which proceeded the attraction for the south end of the needle, lay in the vertical plane of the magnetic meridian; but that while the polar light inclined to the west of that plane, the attracting point was distant about 25°.3 from it towards the east, acquires importance from the unanimous and distinct assurance of the people of Beresov, that they are accustomed here to distinguish between two kinds of Polar Light. The one, like that seen to-day, which appears on the western side of the sky, is always fainter and lower than that which shows itself east of the meridian. The latter, which is sometimes observable for months together throughout the night, begins regularly about the time of the greatest cold, and is often so elevated and so bright, as to frighten the animals in the sledges.

December 2.—The people of Beresov all maintained that the Polar Light of yesterday announced the return of the regular cold, and this prediction was confirmed to-day in a remarkable manner."—Erman, I, 351–353.

Good Hope (Greenland).—Lat. 64° 10′ N. Long. 51° 42′ W. August 1, 1761—August 21, 1765. CRANTZ.

"And even if the moon does not shine in the winter, the northern lights, with their sportive streams of variegated colors, often supply its place still better. I will not enter into the illustration of the origin of this wonderful phenomenon, but only observe so much, that neither I nor those that have lived many years in this country, have ever seen the true Aurora Borealis, or Northern Lights, make their appearance in the north or northwest (except a faint blue glance over the horizon, which might arise from the reflection of the sun), but they have always sprung up in the east and southeast; from whence they have often, if not always, extended over the whole horizon as far as the northwest; and sometimes they may be seen in all the four quarters of the sky at once. Consequently, they have a quite different situation to those that are observed in Norway, Lapland, Russia, and all the other countries of Europe."—Crantz, I, 48.

N. B.—1. Aurora never makes its appearance in N. or N. W.
2. It always springs up in E. or S. E.

Reykiavik (Iceland).—Lat. 64° 10′ N. Long. 21° 25′ W. Winter of 1814–15. HENDERSON.

"The most striking aerial phenomenon exhibited by an Icelandic winter, is doubtless the Aurora Borealis, or northern lights, which are here seen in all their brilliancy and grandeur. I had an opportunity of contemplating them almost every clear night the whole winter, sometimes shooting across the hemisphere in a straight line, and presenting to the view, for a whole evening, one vast steady stream of light; but more commonly they kept dancing and running about with amazing velocity, and a tremulous motion, exhibiting, as they advanced, some of the most beautiful curvated appearances. On gaining one point of the hemisphere, they generally collected as if to muster their forces, and then began again to branch out into numerous ranks, which struck off to the greatest distances from each other as they passed the zenith, yet so as always to preserve the whole of the phenomenon in an oval shape; when they contracted nearly in the same way as they expanded; and, after uniting in a common point, they either returned in the course of a few minutes, or were lost in a stream of light, which grew fainter and fainter, the nearer it approached the opposite side of the heavens.

They were mostly of a dunnish yellow, yet often assuming mixtures of red and green. When they are particularly quick and vivid, a crackling noise is heard, resembling that which accompanies the escape of the sparks from an electric machine.

They almost always took their rise from the summit of Mount Esian, which is about due *northeast* from Reykiavik, and proceeded in a *southwest* direction. When visible the whole length of the hemisphere, they were uniformly *strongest* towards the north and northeast, and were always sure to be seen in that quarter, when they appeared nowhere else. Once or twice I observed them in the south, but they were very faint and stationary."—Henderson, p. 277.

N. B.—1. Aurora always took its rise in N. E.
2. And proceeded in S. W. direction.
3. Always to be seen in N. or N. E. when they appeared nowhere else.
4. Once or twice observed it in S., but they were very faint and stationary.

Iceland.—1820–21. THIENEMANN.

"Dr. L. Thienemann, who spent the winters of 1820 and 1821 in Iceland, made numerous observations on the *Polar Lights*. He states the following as some of the general results of his observations:—

1. The Polar Lights are situated in the lightest and highest clouds of our atmosphere.
2. They are not confined to the winter season or to the night, but are present, in favorable circumstances, at all times, but are distinctly visible only during the absence of the solar rays.
3. The Polar Lights have no determinate connection with the earth.
4. He never heard any noise proceed from them.
5. Their common form, in Iceland, is the arched, and in a direction from *N. E. to W. S. W.*
6. Their motions are various, but always within the limits of the clouds containing them."—Am. Journ. Sci., X, 187.

North End of Hunter's Portage.—Lat. 64° 6′ 47″ N. Long. 113° 23′ 9″ W. August 14, 1820. FRANKLIN.

"At eight p. m., a *faint Aurora Borealis* appeared *to the southward.* The night was cold, the *wind strong from N. W.*"—1 Franklin, 219.

N. B.—1. Faint Aurora to the southward.
2. The night cold.
3. Wind from northwest.

Near Fort Enterprise.—Lat. 64° 15′ 17″ N. Long. 113° 2′ 39″ W. Aug. 18, 1820. FRANKLIN.

"At ten p. m., the Aurora Borealis appeared very brilliant in *an arch* across the zenith, *from northwest to southeast*, which afterwards gave place to a beautiful *corona borealis.*"—1 Franklin, 221.

N. B.—1. At ten p. m., Aurora very brilliant in an arch across the zenith, from N. W. to S. E.
2. Gave place to a beautiful corona borealis.

Rowe's Welcome.—Lat. 64° 15′ 27″ N. Long. 87° 43′ 46″ W. September 9, 1824. LYON.

"Rain fell heavily with the gale, and our prospects were most unpromising, when, at ten p. m., a low red line was observed to *the westward.*

It slowly arose as an arch, and the whole of the black clouds began to recede from our heads. A blue and transparent sky in the west, soon discovered a few stars shining, and, in half an hour, the gloom which had shadowed us fell like a dark curtain to the eastward. As it sank, the full moon burst from behind it with the greatest brilliancy; and, in less than an hour from the first welcome appearance of the fiery streak on the horizon, not an angry cloud was to be seen.

A magnificent Aurora, composed of all the prismatic colors, flashed wildly and beautifully for a short period, and, *as we expected,* a heavy northwest gale succeeded to that from the southward."—Lyon (Voyage), p. 91.

N. B.—1. At ten p. m., a low red line to the W.
2. It slowly arose as an arch.
3. All the clouds went to eastward.
4. In an hour from the appearance of the fiery streak, not a cloud to be seen.
5. Magnificent Aurora composed of all the prismatic colors.
6. And, as we expected, a heavy N. W. gale succeeded to that from S.

Fort Enterprise.—Lat. 64° 28′ 24″ N. Long. 113° 6′ W. December, 1820. FRANKLIN.

"The Aurora appeared with more or less brilliancy on twenty-eight nights of this month, and we were also gratified by the resplendent beauty of the moon, which, for many days together, performed its circle round the heavens, shining with undiminished lustre, and scarcely disappearing below the horizon during the twenty-four hours."—1 Franklin, 257.

N. B.—Aurora appeared with more or less brilliancy twenty-eight nights of the month.

Fort Enterprise.—Lat. 64° 28′ 24″ N. Long. 113° 6′ W. January—May, 1821. FRANKLIN.

"*General Remarks.*—So few observations of the Aurora Borealis in high northern latitudes have been recorded, that I trust a minute account of the various appearances it exhibits, will not be thought superfluous or uninteresting.

The remarks of the late Lieutenant Hood are copied verbatim from his journal. They speak sufficiently for themselves to render any eulogium of mine unnecessary.

To this excellent and lamented young officer, the merit is due of having been, I believe, the first who ascertained, by his observations at Basquiau Hill (combined with those of Dr. Richardson at Cumberland House), that *the altitude of the Aurora upon these occasions was far inferior to that which had been assigned to it by any former observer.*

He also was the *first who satisfactorily proved,* by his observations at Cumberland House, *the important fact of the action of the Aurora upon the compass needle.*

By his ingenious electrometer, invented at Fort Enterprise, he seems also to have *proved the Aurora to be an electrical phenomenon,* or at least that it induces a certain unusual state of electricity in the atmosphere.

The observations of Dr. Richardson, independent of their merit in other respects, point peculiarly to the *Aurora being formed at no great elevation,* and that it is dependent upon certain other atmospheric phenomena, such as the formation of one or other of the various modifications of cirro stratus.

With respect to my own observations, they were principally directed to the effects of the Aurora upon the magnetic needle, and the connection of the amount, &c., of this effect with the position and appearance of the Aurora.

I have been anxious to confine myself to a mere detail of facts, without venturing upon any theory.

My notes upon the appearances of the Aurora coincide with those of Dr. Richardson in proving that the phenomenon is frequently seated within the region of the clouds, and that it is dependent, in some degree, upon the cloudy state of the atmosphere.

The manner in which the needle was affected by the Aurora will need some description. The motion communicated to it was neither sudden nor vibratory. Sometimes it was simultaneous with the formation of arches, prolongation of beams, or certain other changes of form, or of activity of the Aurora; but generally the effect of these phenomena upon the needle was not visible immediately, but in about half an hour, or an hour, the needle had attained its maximum of deviation. Its return to its former position was very gradual, seldom regaining it before the following morning, and frequently not until the afternoon, unless it was expedited by another arch of the Aurora operating in a direction different from the former one.

The bearings of the terminations of the arches are to be taken with considerable allowance. They were estimated by the position of the Aurora, with respect to the sides of the house, the angles of which had been previously determined. The bearings given in the whole of my observations refer to the magnetic meridian, and are reckoned from the magnetic North, towards the East, round the whole circle, which it is conceived will afford a means of more readily computing the horizontal extent of the arches.

It is to be noticed, that the bearings given by Dr. Richardson and Lieutenant Hood are true, and not magnetic."—1 Franklin, 539.

N. B.—1. Altitude of Aurora far inferior to that assigned to it by former observers.
2. Action of the Aurora on the compass needle.
3. Aurora an electrical phenomenon.
4. Aurora formed at no great elevation; dependent on formation of cirro stratus.

Fort Enterprise.—Lat. 64° 28′ 24″ N. Long. 113° 6′ W. January—May, 1821. FRANKLIN.

"*Observations on the Aurora* at Fort Enterprise, extracted from the Journal of Captain Franklin.—The forms of the Aurora Borealis, during the winter, have been so various and fleeting, that it is impossible to comprehend them in a general outline; and the inferences I have drawn on a subject, respecting which I had not prepared my mind by previous study, are offered with diffidence."—1 Franklin, 549.

"Before adverting to the effect of the Aurora on the needle, I must premise that the arch-like appearance of the Aurora, noted in the daily remarks, did not always resemble a portion of a great circle; but, on the contrary, frequently crossed the zenith, without originating and terminating in opposite points of the horizon; and although the general arrangement of the parts gave the idea of an arch, yet this arch was frequently broken, and its portions disconnected.

The color of these arches varied from gray to a lively yellow, and in clear weather the light emitted was generally observed to be more brilliant and dense than when an opposite state of the atmosphere existed.

The horizontal bands or masses of light mentioned in the notes, appeared indiscriminately in every quarter of the sky, and at different elevations; they more frequently originated or terminated in the magnetic east or west, but not invariably so; and we have seen them on more than one occasion begin and end in the magnetic meridian. Their light varied much in density, and was generally of a yellowish hue.

The arches and horizontal bands of Aurora occasionally separated into parts or beams, which had a quick lateral motion. At such times the colors were generally most vivid, and now and then prismatic. The extremities of these beams did not appear to point uniformly to any particular part of the sky, but to depend entirely upon the direction of the arch which they composed.

The term 'beam,' used in the notes, does not always allude to the appearances just mentioned, but is also applied to the commencement of an arch when it appears in an uniform stream of light, issuing from the horizon, and before it has attained an altitude sufficient to give it an arched form.

The arches of the Aurora most commonly traversed the sky nearly at *right angles to the magnetic meridian*, but the *deviations from this direction*, as has been already stated, *were not rare;* and I am inclined to consider that *these different positions* of the Aurora *have considerable influence upon the direction of the needle*."—1 Franklin, 550.

"In one instance only, a complete arch was formed in the magnetic meridian; in another, the beam shot up from the magnetic north to the zenith; and, *in both these cases, the needle moved towards the west.*

The needle was most disturbed on February 13, p. m., and at a time when the Aurora was distinctly seen passing *between a stratum of clouds and the earth*, or at least illuminating the face of the clouds opposed to the observer.

This and several other appearances, recorded in the accompanying notes, induced me to infer that *the distance of the Aurora from the earth* varied on different nights, and produced a proportionate effect on the needle.

When the light shone through a dense hazy atmosphere, when there was a halo round the moon, or when a small snow was falling, the disturbance was generally considerable; and on certain hazy, cloudy nights, the needle frequently deviated in a considerable degree, although the Aurora was not visible at the time.

Our observations do not enable us to decide whether this ought to be attributed to an Aurora concealed by a cloud or haze, or entirely to the state of the atmosphere. Similar deviations have been observed in the daytime, both in a clear and cloudy state of the sky, but more frequently in the latter case.

Upon *one occasion, the Aurora was seen immediately after sunset*, whilst the bright daylight was remaining.

A circumstance to which I attach some importance must not be omitted. *Clouds* have been *sometimes observed during the day to* assume the forms of the Aurora, and I am inclined to connect with the appearance of these *clouds* the deviation of the needle, which was occasionally remarked at such times.

An Aurora sometimes approached the zenith *without producing any change* in the position of the needle, contrary to the general effect, whilst at other times *a considerable alteration* took place, although the beams or arches did not come near the zenith. The Aurora was frequently seen without producing any perceptible effect on the needle. At such times its appearance was that of an arch or an horizontal stream of dense yellowish light, with little or no internal motion."—1 Franklin, 551.

"I *have not heard the noise* ascribed to the Aurora, but the uniform testimony of the natives and of the residents in this country induced me to believe that it is occasionally audible. The circumstance, however, must be of rare occurrence, as is evidenced by our having witnessed the Aurora upwards of two hundred times without being able to attest the fact. I was almost inclined, last year, to suppose that unusual agitations of the Aurora were followed by storms of wind; but the more extended opportunities I enjoyed of observing it in 1821, at Fort Enterprise, have convinced me that no such inference ought to have been drawn."—1 Franklin, 552.

Fort Enterprise.—Lat. 64° 28′ 24″ N. Long. 113° 6′ W. January—May, 1821. FRANKLIN.

"*Notices of the Appearances of the Aurora* at Fort Enterprise, extracted from Captain Franklin's Journal.—The following appearances of the Aurora Borealis were noted at the times when the position of the horizontal needle was observed. They have been described as they appeared to the eye, without any regard to perspective. The bearings of the terminations of the arches or beams, are reckoned from the magnetic north towards the east and south, round the whole circle.

Jan. 12, 1821, midnight. A very faint arch in the zenith, lying 324° and 144°. The sky cloudless.

14th. At 7h. 30m. p. m., the Aurora first appeared in a patch bearing 279°, from which darted a slender faint beam, that passed about 4° east of the zenith and then instantly disappeared. A horizontal stream extended from 279° to 54°, elevated about 20°. At 8h. 20m., a faint coruscation across the zenith. At 11h. 20m., a brilliant, irregular, wreathed arch across the zenith, from 279° to 99°, the interior motion passing rapidly from the horizon at the former bearing to the latter. Soon afterwards, this arch twisted round, so that its extremities were directed to 122° and 234°; the internal motion very rapid. At 11h. 30m., the coruscation had removed from the zenith, and appeared in a line parallel to the horizon, extending from 99° to 234°. At midnight, horizontal streams from 99° to 234°, and from 279° to 234°; but the latter had the greater elevation. The needle drawn considerably to the westward. Just as I had left the instrument, a flash darted from a beam 113° towards the zenith, and instantly a different Aurora appeared tinged with the prismatic colors, having an agitated circular motion. A few seconds afterwards, a beam flashed from 279°, and united with that which shot from bearing 113°; and then a continuous though irregular arch was formed from the one horizon to the other, and the interior motion passed rapidly from both these extremities towards the zenith. As long as the arch continued in that direction, the needle pointed as at midnight; but in about two minutes, the arch descended towards the east, and then the needle gradually returned eastward to its zero, in which position it remained until the coruscation had disappeared.

At 1h. a. m., Aurora visible in patches 279° and 99°, and a beam 346°; the needle then stood at 348° 16′, having moved eastward 34′ since midnight. At 9h. p. m., January 15th, the needle had attained the usual position at that hour; the Aurora then appeared in the zenith. At midnight, a waving irregular arch continued across the zenith from 279° to 99°, and a rapid interior motion passed from the former to the latter direction. Motion of the needle westward.

16th. At 12h. 20m., faint streams from 99°, inclining to the westward.

20th. At 11h., an arch crossed the zenith; and at midnight, a patch appeared 54° lying parallel to the horizon.

21st. An arch from 99° to 212°, elevation about 10°. At midnight, a broad patch in the zenith. Slender beams rose from 234° and 31°, which were prolonged to the zenith, and came almost in contact with this patch; at the same time, a low arch proceeded from 279° to 54°. Between nine and midnight, the needle moved westward 32 minutes.

22d. At 9h. p. m., an arched horizontal stream from 110° to 54°. At midnight no Aurora perceptible, yet the needle had changed its position.

23d, 9h. p. m. A brilliant arch across the zenith, from 279° to 99°, composed of slender beams lying parallel to each other. The motion passed from 99° to the zenith. This arch separated in the zenith. The westward part disappeared entirely, but a column of light remained at 99°. Motion of the needle westward. At 12h., thick hazy weather; no Aurora visible. Needle had moved eastward.

24th, 9h. p. m. Two low arches extending from 99° to 178°. At midnight, the coruscations were generally diffused over the upper part of the sky; but the streams traversed the zenith in a different direction from the course they more frequently take, and their extremities were at 54° and 234°. The most conspicuous beam, rising 245°, proceeded to the zenith, and curled round so as to point towards 335°. The next in brilliancy came from bearing 76°, which also crossed the zenith, but did not unite with the other beam. There were two other streams of light running in the same direction. The needle had moved 48′ eastward since nine, and in a contrary way to the course it usually followed when vertical arches crossed the zenith at about 279° or 324°.

25th, 9h. p. m. A brilliant curve; terminations 324° and 76°, elevation about 50°. Several beams jutted from this curve, pointing towards the horizon. At 11h., a beam rose at 279°, passed over the zenith to 99°, then ran horizontally, and formed an irregular band from 99° to 171°. The portion of light at 99° was stratified by intervening layers of clouds.

27th. A beam elevated about 13° at midnight whilst snow was falling.

28th, 9h. p. m. An arch from 99° to 349°. At 11h., the coruscation generally diffused over the south and eastern parts of the sky, which seemed to have proceeded from a slender beam bearing 99°, from whence a flash darted to the zenith, which instantly dilated into a broad mass of light.

At midnight, an elevated arch and a low convex stream extended from 99° to 200°. A beam at 94° pointing towards the zenith. Needle stationary.

29th. At 11¼h., a broad arch across the zenith from 99° to 257°, and a horizontal fringed belt from 99° towards the east, at a low elevation. At midnight, the S. E. portion of the sky was occupied by a dense mass of light, which resembled an open fan branching upwards. A stream shot from the eastern part of it, and proceeded in an arch to 290°, the centre being elevated 70°. Several patches in the zenith parallel to this arch. In two minutes afterwards the fan disappeared, and a brilliant curved stream darted forth at 110°, and shot to the westward; its centre bore 133°, elevated 25°.

30th. An arch across the zenith from 302° to 121°, but the extremities did not approach either horizon by 20°.

31st. At 9h. p. m., two horizontal bands of light extended from 99° to 212°, the lowest being elevated 8°. The S. E. end was wavy, and it appeared as if several beams had been twisted together. There was also a beam at 302°, directed towards the zenith. At midnight, an elliptical arch proceeded from 99° to 279°, by the south and westward, at a low elevation. Several streams issued from this band between 279° and 245°, each pointing towards the zenith. This arch separated after a few minutes, and then two parallel arches were displayed having the same direction. Slight motion of the needle eastward.

February 1st. At 11h., an arch across the zenith from 279° to 99°, for a considerable time stationary. This arch descended to the westward a few minutes before midnight, and when at an elevation of 20° it disappeared. The stars were perfectly visible through the column of light. Needle stationary.

2d. At midnight, a stream spread from 110° to 267°, ascending gradually from the horizon to an elevation of 30°. The stars appeared through the light with undiminished brilliancy.

3d. At 9h. p. m., Aurora commenced by a brilliant arch across the zenith, from 279° to 99°, extending to each horizon, which remained stationary and motionless for several minutes. By midnight, the coruscation was generally diffused over the sky. A broad brilliant band, elevated 10°, extended from 99° to 200° through an arch of about 279°. An illuminated curve branched from the latter termination, which pointed to 245°, and from this bearing a beam shot across the zenith towards the opposite direction; but it had not proceeded above five degrees eastward of the zenith, when it suddenly turned to the north and assumed a scroll shape. The needle immediately moved eastward, which is the same direction it had been observed to follow on January 14th, when the streams of light appeared in nearly a similar position in the zenith, namely, lying east and west true, or about 54° and 234° magnetic bearings, but in a contrary direction to that in which it had been observed to move when the arches crossed the zenith, having their extremities at 279° and 99°, or at 324° and 144°. This coruscation remained for several minutes, when the vertical arch disappeared, and a band was presented lying parallel to the horizon from 212° to 279°. Shortly afterwards, a similar band of light proceeded from 76° to 324°, and the horizon was almost encompassed with a brilliant zone; color pale yellow. No motion of the Aurora perceptible.

4th. At midnight, a faint slender beam arose at 290°, and flashed to the zenith; at the same instant, another proceeded from 99° to an elevation of 50°. A broad low stream of light from 76° to 346°, and a faint belt from 189° to 234°. No change was perceived in the needle.

5th. The atmosphere very dense and hazy. The needle had been disturbed in the night, and showed this morning a considerable change of position. At midnight, Aurora gleamed through the haze in two arches, the extremities 54° and 234°, and they passed the zenith. One of them turned towards the north, and the other towards the south. The needle moved to the eastward, as on February 3d and January 14th, when the Aurora appeared in a similar position.

6th. At midnight, Aurora was perceived across the zenith, 279° and 99°, gleaming through a very dense atmosphere, and when snow was falling. Two stars only were visible. Motion of the needle since 9h. p. m., 28′ westward.

8th. A faint stream at 99° towards the zenith.

9th. At 9h. p. m., a beam at 290°. At 11h., a broad arch traversed the zenith from 290° to 110°, which remained until 45 minutes after midnight, and then disappeared at bearing 99°. Motion of the needle westward.

10th. At midnight, an arch resembling a horse-shoe, the extremities of which bore 99° and 76°. From each of these points streams were projected across the zenith towards 290°, but they did not reach the opposite horizon. They were of a faint grayish-yellow color. The stars shone brilliantly through the columns of light. Moon very bright. The needle was not the least affected. I have observed that the needle is usually most disturbed by the appearance of the Aurora in dense hazy weather.

11th. At 3h. p. m., a cloud extended in an arch from 99° to 279°, elevated 30°, which bore a strong resemblance to the Aurora, particularly at the end at 279°, from whence some beams were projected towards the zenith. The needle was not affected.

12th. At 8h. 30m. p. m., faint curved streams in the zenith. At 9h., an arch from 99° to 279°, exactly similar in shape to the cloud seen yesterday. The color resembled the halo round the moon. The needle was not affected. At 11h. 40m., the coruscations occupied a considerable portion of the northern part of the sky, lying in parallel arches from 76° to 279°. The centre one was brilliant, and the motion, resembling a volume of smoke, passed from the former bearing towards the latter. Some arches appeared in the zenith lying 65° and 245°, and flashes darted with instantaneous motion from these towards the point to which their extremities were directed. The needle betrayed a slight motion eastward. At 12h., a broad band of light from 302° to 54°, elevated 20°.

13th. The atmosphere was so dense this night that the stars were completely obscured, and the edges of the moon could only be faintly traced through the haze. At 9h. p. m., there was not any appearance of the Aurora, and the needle rested at 348° 30′, its usual position at this hour when undisturbed by the Aurora. At 11h. 30m., faint streams of light gleamed through a large portion of the heavens, both in the zenith and near the horizon, and immediately afterwards brilliant coruscations burst forth of the most agitated kind. At 11h. 40m., a horizontal stream extended from 279° to 31°, and the anterior motion, similar to rolling smoke, passed from the first point to the latter. The needle was now drawn 3° 30′ to the eastward, or as far as 345° 00′. At 11h. 50m., there appeared another stream of irregular shape, which proceeded from 279° in a line nearly parallel to the horizon, until it curled round at 9°, or near the direction of the magnetic meridian. The interior motion flashed along this stream with the utmost rapidity. The needle moved now to 343° 50′, or 4° 40′ eastward of its first position; and, during the appearance of this coruscation, I perceived the needle to oscillate between 343° 50′ and 344° 40′; and it may be remarked this was the only occasion on which a vibratory motion was observed. On the disappearance of this display, brilliant semicircular curves were presented in the same quarter, ornamented with all the prismatic colors. At 11h. 55m., the needle had receded westward as far as 347° 00′. The important fact of the existence of the Aurora at a less elevation than that of dense clouds, was evinced on two or three occasions this night, and particularly at 11h. 50m., when a brilliant mass of light, variegated with the prismatic colors, passed between an uniform, steady, dense cloud and the earth; and, in its progress, completely concealed that portion of the cloud which the stream of light covered until the coruscation had passed over it, when the cloud appeared as before.

The observations of this evening seem to corroborate the remark which I had previously made, that the direction in which the needle moves appears to depend on the position in which streams of Aurora are placed, and the quantity of the effect upon its proximity to, or distance from, the earth. When the extremities of arches lay near the bearings of 234° and 54°, the needle moved eastward; and when near the bearings 324° and 144°, or 279° and 99°, the motion of the needle was westward. Both of these facts were shown to-night. At the first display, when the extremities of the arches pointed near 234° and 54°, and the interior motion followed the same direction, the needle moved eastward as far as 345° 00′; but after midnight, the coruscations ceased to appear in that direction, and, at 12h. 10m., were presented in three arches, traversing the zenith, whose extremities pointed 121° and 302°; the needle then receded towards the west, and rested at 349° 30′, having varied its position 5° 40′ in the course of twenty minutes.

14th. At 11h. 30m., a faint low band proceeded from 110° to 178°, elevated 8°, and another at a higher elevation from 121° to 212°. These streams crossed each other in the bearing 155°; and it may be remarked that this is the only occasion on which I have seen the streams to cross each other. They separated before midnight; the eastern one ascended some degrees higher, but the other remained in the same state. Cloudless sky.

15th. At 9h. p. m., Aurora crossed the zenith from 257° to 76°. None visible at midnight, yet the needle had moved forty minutes westward.

18th. At 9h. p. m., Aurora gleamed through the horizon in a continuous arch from 279° to 99°.

19th. At 8h. p. m., Aurora appeared to the eastward in five arches, having the same extremities at 88° and 279°. The upper arch crossed the zenith, and the others were elevated between 15° and 20°. At midnight, two concentric arches appeared through the haze, lying across the zenith; their extremities bore 65° and 245°. The needle then pointed to 348° 5′, having moved 40° eastward. At 12h. 25m., a broad and more brilliant arch crossed the zenith, from 133° to 313°; the needle then moved westward 1° 5′, to 349° 10′. This change is a further confirmation of the observations on February 13th.

20th. At 9h. p. m., beams of light issued at 99° and pointed towards the zenith. At 10h. 30m., a brilliant arch from 99° to 279°, elevated 80°, a small arch in the zenith, and several beams at 279°. At midnight, several beams arose parallel to each other between 335° and 349°. In a few seconds, flashes were emitted from them, which first darted to the zenith, and then, twisting round, shot towards a stream that had proceeded at the same instant from 212°, which they joined. The coruscation now resembled an irregular horse-shoe, composed of many slender beams of brilliant light. This display soon passed off to the eastward, having descended to the horizon before it disappeared. The needle was not in any way disturbed after nine, from which circumstance I am induced to suppose that the Aurora was very distant. We seldom witnessed a greater variety of arches, beams, and flashes than were displayed this night, both in the horizon and zenith. If these coruscations had passed as near to the earth as they appear to have done at other times, some effect, I conceive, would have been produced on the needle. The sky was cloudless.

On the following morning, it was perceived that the needle had receded two degrees eastward, and it did not regain its usual position before 4h. p. m. At 8h. p. m., a horizontal band of faint light extended from 88° to 245°, elevated 7°, which remained almost stationary until midnight, at which hour two brilliant arches appeared, whose united extremities bore 279° and 76°; and a faint broad arch traversed the zenith from 279° to 88°. Needle moved eastward. Shortly afterwards, the horizon was encircled with an illuminated zone, and the northern part of the sky covered with Aurora.

22d. At 9h. p. m., a continuous arch across the zenith from 279° to 99°; the color pale yellow. Needle moved westward.

23d. At 9h. p. m., a low band, parallel to the horizon, extending from 302° to 346°, patches at 76°, and some faint streams in the zenith pointing to 234° and 54°. The needle had moved eastward. At 11h. 15m., a broad brilliant arch extended from 29° to 99° across the zenith, reaching to each horizon. The needle had, since 9h., receded 24′ westward. At midnight, two arches appeared; one from 54° to 324°, elevated 50°, the other from 234° to 144°, elevated 12°.

24th. At 9h. p. m., a continuous arch, through which the stars were distinctly visible, passed from 99° to 279° across the zenith, and a beam appeared parallel to this, proceeding from 99°, which terminated in the zenith. At midnight, two belts of brilliant light extended from 99°—one by the south and west, the other by the north—which encircled the horizon at an elevation of 20°, except between the points 324° and 322°. No perceptible disturbance of the needle.

26th. At midnight, a brilliant arch issued from 313° and reached to 99°, the centre being elevated 20°. At the latter point, the coruscation curved upwards, and was then prolonged across the zenith to 200°. The stars shone through this stream with undiminished brilliancy. The needle moved a few minutes westward.

27th. At 9h. p. m., two arches crossed the zenith from 76° to 279°, very broad and brilliant; the stars were distinctly visible through them. At midnight, the Aurora was diffused over a great portion of the sky. Three arches appeared parallel to each other in the zenith, whose extremities pointed to 54° and 234°, and a horizontal stream about 30° high, reaching from 302° to 31°, along which the interior motion was extremely rapid. Soon afterwards, some dense clouds overspread the sky, but the Aurora gleamed through. The needle moved near two degrees eastward after nine. It kept an easterly position until after 2h. p. m. on the next day, and then it receded 40′ in the course of an hour. The clouds were of a fleecy kind, which sailors denominate a mackerel sky. At midnight, an irregular band extended from 88° to 200°, at an elevation of 15°. A beam at 324° pointing towards the zenith.

March 1st. At 9h. p. m., an arch stretched from 99° to 155°. At 11¼h., when the snow was falling heavily, and a dense atmosphere obscured the stars, the Aurora appeared in an arch across the zenith, having its extremities 88° and 200°, but did not extend to either horizon. This stream disappeared before midnight. The atmosphere was then more dense, and the snow descended in larger flakes. Between midnight and the following morning, the needle was drawn 45′ to the eastward, and it did not recover its usual position before 9h. p. m. on March 2d.

2d. At 8h. 30m. p. m., Aurora appeared in a broad arch from 279° to 99°, and continued without any alteration until nine, when the needle had moved 32 minutes westward. The breadth of the arch then increased considerably, and a dark cloud passing along its middle gave an appearance of two arches. At midnight, the coruscations occupied many parts of the sky. Two faint arches crossed the zenith from 99° to 279°. A more brilliant arch extended from 76° to 290°, at an elevation of 60°. Several patches between 54° and 346°, and a broad band from 279° to 223.° The needle did not evince any material change.

3d. At midnight, a slender beam at 76°, and a patch at 279°. Needle had moved 10 minutes westward since nine.

4th. At midnight, an arch across the zenith, 54° and 234°, in which the interior motion ran swiftly from the former to the latter bearing. A low band extended from 279° to 346°. Motion of the needle 10 minutes eastward since nine.

5th. A low stream from 121° to 189°, at an elevation of 10°. No change in the position of the needle.

6th. The atmosphere very hazy, and snow fell. No Aurora visible, but the needle moved 30 minutes westward between nine and midnight.

8th. At 6h. 30m. p. m., Aurora appeared, whilst the western horizon was tinged with the rays of the recently-departed sun, in two beams from 99° extended to the zenith. At 9h. p. m., a brilliant stream from 121° to 212°, elevated 10°. A beam, having a wavy form, ascended from 99° to the zenith; its color a bright yellow; the stars were seen distinctly through it. No change in the needle. At midnight, Aurora was diffused over a great portion of the sky. A broad arch crossed the zenith, whose extremities were at 88° and 200°, but they did not reach either horizon. A band stretched from 279° to 76°, elevated 12°, from which three beams were prolonged nearly to the zenith, between 302° and 335°. Needle moved 1° 5′ westward.

9th. At nine, Aurora brilliant and variable; the interior motion passed rapidly from 234° to 54°. An arch across the zenith, extremities 279° and 99°. A horizontal band from 245° to 76°. No change in the needle. At midnight, some patches bearing 324°. An arch was instantly projected from that, bearing across the zenith to 144°. This arch separated in the zenith, and both parts passed off against the wind to the westward. The needle moved 30 minutes westward between nine and 11h. 30m.

11th. At 9h. p. m., a waving arch passed from 290° to 88°, about 2° east of the zenith, and reached from one horizon to the other. An elliptical arch from 313° to 76°, elevated about 50°. At 11h., two waving streams stretched from 279° to 43°, and some beams shot from both these extremities towards the zenith, but more numerously from 279°. The needle had moved 1° 8′ westward, between nine and eleven. Whilst I was looking at the instrument, a flash darted towards the zenith from a low beam bearing 9°, and the needle immediately moved 8′ westward; but the arch having in a few seconds passed over to the south, the needle returned eastward to its first position. At midnight, a beam arose at 54°, darted to the zenith, and then the upper extremity turned so as to point to 144°. Another beam darted from 257° and joined the former one. The arch thus formed descended gradually against the wind. There was only a slight lateral motion perceptible while it remained across the zenith, but when it had sunk to about 60° from the horizon, an interior motion rushed from each of the extremities towards the middle, and, at the place of contact, the greatest commotion was excited, and the prismatic colors were exhibited. The motion of the needle 8 minutes eastward. This arch disappeared at an elevation of 25°. Between 11h. and midnight, sounds were repeatedly heard resembling the hissing of a musket-ball or the shaking of a thin pliant stick in the air, which were at first supposed to have been occasioned by the motion of the Aurora. Mr. Wentzel, however, who assured us that he had often heard the noise of the Aurora, said these sounds were very dissimilar to that which the Aurora makes, and that he supposed the noise to be occasioned by the cracking of the snow, in consequence of a great decrease in temperature immediately after the two preceding days of mild weather. I was of the same opinion, from the circumstance of a similar noise having been heard after midnight coming from the eastward, in which quarter there was not the least appearance of Aurora, and when only a faint motionless beam was visible to the eastward. This opinion was further confirmed on the following morning, when similar sounds were distinctly heard at the time the sun was shining bright and there was not any symptom of Aurora.

12th. At midnight, faint streams from 88°, directed towards the zenith. Some patches visible in other parts of the sky.

13th. At midnight, a beam shot from 302° across the zenith to 88°. Another extended to the zenith, whose lower extremity bore 290°. A horizontal band from 234° to 257°. The needle, since nine, moved 1° 25′ westward.

14th. At 9h. p. m., a faint beam at 99° pointing towards the zenith. At midnight, a faint low stream from 76° to 110°. No change in the needle.

15th. At midnight, waving streams from 110° to 144°, and from 189° to 212°, elevated 20°. No change in the needle.

16th. At 3h. p. m., some clouds appeared about 279° which bore a strong resemblance to the Aurora, particularly one of the beams, which extended 40° towards the zenith. The needle moved 18′ westward between 3h. and 5h. p. m. At midnight, a faint stream of Aurora reached from 65° to 279°, elevation 25°. No change in the needle.

19th. At 9h. p. m., a faint arch from 121° to 212°, elevated 25°. At midnight, low streams from 144° to 324°, which nearly encircled the horizon. Seven beams were projected upwards from different parts of this zone. Their points did not meet in the zenith, but terminated about 3° short of that part. The whole appearance strongly resembled an artificial globe, the zone being the equator, and the beams the meridian lines. The needle moved 25′ eastward between nine and midnight, but I observed it to move gradually westward as these beams were disappearing. Immediately after they had ceased to be visible, an arch was exhibited crossing the zenith in the direction of the magnetic meridian. The needle still continued to recede westward, until it rested nearly in the position at which it was at 9h. p. m.

20th. At 9h., an arch from 99° to 279°. A beam at 99° pointing towards the zenith. A stream from 257° to 290°. At midnight, a low stream from 302° to 54°, along which the interior motion passed very rapidly. The needle moved 1° westward. The sky was overspread with fleecy clouds.

21st. At 11h. a. m., some clouds lying parallel to the horizon, between 346° and 76°, strongly resembled the Aurora. At 9h. p. m., Aurora in a bright arch from 99° to 280°, passing within 3° of the zenith. This descended to the eastward against the wind. At midnight, two beams darted from 144°; one shot across the zenith to 290°, the end of the other curved round just beyond the zenith, and, in a few minutes, both of them rushed back to 144°, and then disappeared. A waving stream reached from 279° to 99°, elevated 12°; several beams were projected upwards from this stream. A beam darted from 54° across the zenith, and, immediately after this flash, the lower extremity of the beam moved round to 99°, and an arch was formed from 99° to 279°. The needle moved nearly 2° westward, between nine and midnight. At 12h. 30m., Aurora generally diffused over the sky. A brilliant arch crossed the zenith from 279° to 110°. This soon afterwards separated, so as to form three arches parallel to each other. Some beams laid at right angles to this arch, which had come from the eastern horizon or bearing 54°. No motion in the needle perceptible.

22d. At 9h., Aurora in an arch from 290° to 88°; a bright band from 88° to 65°. At midnight, the following appearances of the Aurora were visible through a very dense atmosphere. A beam at 324°, elevated 15°; an arch from 234° to 121°, and some short beams at 76°.

23d. At 9h., two parallel arches from 313° to 76°, supported on buttresses at both extremities. The appearance resembled a bridge of light. At 11h. 30m., the northern and eastern parts of the sky were entirely free from Aurora. Some irregularly-curved streams extended from 99° to 234°, and dark clouds intervened between them. At midnight, three arches from 110° to 234°, the upper one most brilliant. No perceptible interior motion of the Aurora. The needle moved 10° westward after nine.

24th. At 9h. p. m., Aurora appeared through the clouds and snow, traversing the zenith in the direction of 65° and 245°. The needle moved eastward 1° 5′. At midnight, a beam from 99°, of slender breadth, when near the horizon, dilated considerably in its ascent, and at its termination in the zenith spread so as nearly to cover the upper part of the heavens. Another beam arose from the same point, curved several degrees to the westward, and then proceeded to the zenith. These beams quickly disappeared, but a low arch, extending from 279° to 65° remained stationary. The needle moved westward, between nine and midnight, 1° 22′.

25th. At 9h. p. m., faint beams at 324° and 144°. At midnight, a horizontal stream from 133° to 223°, some beams at 324°, and patches in several other parts; all very faint.

26th. At 9h. p. m., a faint Aurora at 99°. At midnight, a mass of dense light burst forth, bearing 65°, at an elevation of 20°, which presently curved round, and assumed the shape of a horseshoe. At that instant, a beam flashed from 324° to the nearest part of the curve, and immediately an arch proceeded upwards, and passed about 3° eastward of the zenith. The needle moved eastward 12′.

28th. At 8h. p. m., when daylight was perceptible to the westward, a stream of Aurora issued from a dark mass of cloud bearing 110°, and proceeded upwards in the direction of 346°; but, when it reached the zenith, the upper part inclined to the westward, and an arch was formed from 110° to 290° reaching from one horizon to the other. Some smaller streams appeared about 189°, lying parallel to a range of clouds which resembled it in color, both being a steel-gray. The extremities of these streams pointed 121° and 257°. At 9h. p. m., clear weather. Three arches appeared; one from 94° to 290°, elevated 80°, the other from 290°, passing about 2° east of the zenith, and the third went parallel to this, and united in the same points in the horizon, but they were separated in the zenith by a stream of cloud. In two minutes afterwards, the first arch disappeared, and the two others, closing in the zenith, formed one broad stream, and passed off to the westward. Stars were faintly seen. At midnight, a very dense atmosphere obscured the sky; neither stars nor Aurora visible. The needle, however, moved 35′ westward between nine and midnight.

29th. A faint gleam of Aurora fringed the upper part of some dark clouds between 133° and 155°.

30th. At 9h., a broad arch across the zenith from 88° to 290°, and the interior motion was rapid. At midnight, an arch from 110° to 257°, elevated 20°. It separated in the zenith, and then the light passed instantaneously down to each horizon. Needle moved westward.

April 1st. The changes in the position of the needle this morning deserve some notice. At 8h. a. m. it was nearly in the same position as at midnight; an hour afterwards it had moved 12′ eastward, and by eleven 10′ more. At 8h. a. m., there was a mackerel sky to the north, the strata of the clouds being vertical. Near the west horizon there was a layer of dense clouds, which soon spread over the whole sky. At 11h., these dark clouds gave place to a thin fleecy sky, and many blue portions were seen. The needle then returned towards the westward, and by four had reached within two minutes of the point at which it stood at 9h. a. m. At 9h. 30m. p. m., the Aurora appeared through a hazy atmosphere, in an arch from 99° to 234°.

5th. An arch passed from 88° to 178°, at a low elevation. At midnight, an arch, composed of several streams apparently blended together, issued from 110°, and passed about 10° west of the zenith to the horizon at 279°. This arch separated in the zenith, and then each part passed over to the horizon at 279°. A very slender faint arch remained from 9° to 189°. The needle moved a little westward.

6th. At 9h., masses of light of irregular breadth fringed the upper part of a range of clouds extending from 99° to 212°. At midnight, a waving low stream from 99° to 212°, of dense light, the motion rapid, going towards the latter bearing. Motion of the needle westward.

7th. At 9h. p. m., an arch stretching from 279° to 110°; motion of the needle westward. At 10h. 30m., a very irregular arch from 99° to 234°. The interior motion darted rapidly in opposite directions, and the red, purple, and violet colors were exhibited. Numerous slender beams, in which there was a quick lateral motion, shot from this arch; some of them were projected to the zenith. The arch separated at 121°, and the western portion immediately rushed towards the north, preserving the same elevation. At this instant, the wind changed from the north to the opposite direction, south. At midnight, a horizontal band appeared from 99° to 234°, and several beams to the southward. The needle moved eastward 27′ between nine and midnight.

8th. At 11h. 10m. p. m., various streams appeared, stratifying a dense mass of clouds. In two parts of this coruscation, the motion darted from 144° and 324° towards the zenith; in another, from 76° to the horizon at 144°. The needle had moved westward 2° 19′ since nine. At midnight, a beam rose at bearing 65°, and darted to an elevation of 30°. Nearly at the same instant, another beam issued from 9° and joined this, and then an arch was formed terminating in these bearings. Several other masses of light were seen to the eastward. The needle had moved eastward 1° 55′ since the last observation. Heavy dark clouds spread over a large portion of the sky.

11th. At midnight, a faint gleam of Aurora appeared through a very dense atmosphere, and when there was a halo round the moon.

13th. Atmosphere hazy; no Aurora or stars were visible, yet there was a motion of the needle 7° to the westward between nine and midnight.

14th. A faint arch from 313° to 133° at midnight.

15th. At 9h., several brilliant beams bearing 54°, in which there was much lateral motion and a variety of colors. An arch crossed the zenith from 313° to 133°. Needle moved westward 9′. At midnight, an arch across the zenith from 290° to 110°. Another from 65° to 313°, the motion passing rapidly from the latter to the former horizon. Needle moved a little more westward.

18th. At midnight, a faint patch bore 144°.

19th. At midnight, streams of a dense pale yellow light, at a low elevation, nearly parallel to the horizon, and extending from 99° to 200°. These were stationary for some hours; dark clouds lay between them.

20th. Whilst daylight remained, the Aurora was perceived fringing the upper part of a mass of dense cloud, in shape like the festoons of a curtain. It extended from 99° to 200°. At midnight, a waving arch of low elevation from 76° to 212°. Needle had moved 45° westward since nine.

21st. At 7h. p. m., some streams of cloud which resembled the Aurora in shape and color, crossed the zenith; but when the daylight disappeared, no Aurora was visible.

23d. At 10h. 30m. p. m., Aurora first appeared in an arch from 279° to 189°, elevation 12°. Needle moved westward 1° 11′.

27th. At midnight, aurora appeared through the haze in two low arches from 99° to 189°.

29th. Aurora beamed through the haze in low streams of faint yellow color.

30th. At 11h. 40m., some patches of Aurora at 144°, elevated 20°. No motion perceptible in the needle.

May 1st. The coruscations were very agitated and brilliant between 11h. and midnight, but they did not produce any change in the needle.

3d. At midnight, Aurora proceeded from a mass of dense cloud bearing 99°; passed near the zenith to 257°. The attenuated beams of which this arch was composed had a quick lateral motion. Little change in the needle. Daylight in the eastern part of the sky.

5th. A faint stream proceeded from 144° to an elevation of 45°. Needle moved westward.

I did not observe any Aurora after this day, but Mr. Hood saw it on the 6th, 10th, 11th, 12th, and 13th, after which date there was constant daylight, which prevented us from seeing it."—1 Franklin, 554–569.

Fort Enterprise.—Lat. 64° 28′ 24″ N. Long. 113° 6′ W. January—May, 1822. FRANKLIN.

"The appearance of the Aurora, and the *disturbance it occasioned* on the motion of the needle at Fort Enterprise, was so frequent, that the mean monthly variation must have been deduced from but few observations if they had been rejected.

The circumstance of the mean variation being least at midnight there, and at Moose-Deer Island, was evidently caused by *the frequent disturbance* in the motion of the needle *which the Aurora occasioned;* for on those days when it was not visible, the mean diurnal variation followed the course Mr. Hood had observed it to do at Cumberland House, being most easterly at the time of the first observation in the morning, and least between three and four in the afternoon.

The change in the diurnal variation in these parts of North America seems to be governed by the same law as that in England, as the decrease in easterly variation between the morning and afternoon is in fact a motion of the needle to the westward."—1 Franklin, 629.

N. B.—1. Motion of the needle frequently disturbed by the appearance of the Aurora.

2. Mean variation being least at midnight, evidently caused by the frequent disturbance in the motion of the needle which the Aurora occasioned.

Fort Enterprise.—Lat. 64° 28′ 24″ N. Long. 113° 6′ W. Winter 1820–21. HOOD.

"*Appearances of the Aurora at Fort Enterprise.* Extracted from the Journal of Lieutenant Hood, R. N.—January 10, 1821. At 8h. p. m., an arched Aurora N. N. W. to N. N. E. At 11h. p. m., a double arch, much broken but not bright, from N. W. to S. E.

11th. At midnight, faint Aurora from west to east.

14th. At midnight, five arches of Aurora from N. W. to S. E. A large Corona Borealis."—1 Franklin (Hood), 588.

Fort Enterprise.—Lat. 64° 28′ 24″ N. Long. 113° 6′ W. 1820–21. HOOD.

"*On the Aurora Borealis at Fort Enterprise.* Extracted from the Journal of Lieutenant Robert Hood, R. N.—During the summer of 1820, the Aurora was only once visible before the month of August, when the nightly temperature of the air was generally below 50°. The late continuance of daylight, and the few opportunities which we had of making observations at the most favorable hours, render it possible that the Aurora may have sometimes appeared in this long interval without our knowledge. But those opportunities were sufficiently numerous to convince me that it is actually very seldom present in these regions during the summer.

The number of Auroræ visible in August, 1820, was ten; in September, six; in October, seven; in November, eight; in December, twenty; in January, 1821, seventeen; in February, twenty-two; in March, twenty-five; in April, eighteen; and in May the brightness of twilight prevented us from seeing more than nine.

The whole amount is more than double the number of our observations at Cumberland House.

It is worthy of remark, that the number of Auroræ in each month of both the winters, bears some proportion to the thermometrical range."—1 Franklin (Hood), 580.

N. B.—1. Number of appearances of Aurora at Fort Enterprise.

2. More than double the number of observations at Cumberland House.

"The shapes of the Aurora at its entry into the horizon and progress through the sky, may be reduced under two general descriptions.

In the first, I shall class those which are formed like rainbows or arches, in the earliest stage of their appearance.

They rise with their centres sometimes in the magnetic meridian, and sometimes several degrees to the eastward or westward of it.

The number visible at the same time seldom exceeds five, and is seldom limited to one. The altitude of the lowest, when first seen, is never less than 4°. As they advance towards the zenith, their centres (or the parts most elevated) preserve a course nearly in the magnetic meridian or parallel to it. But the eastern and western extremities vary their respective distances, and the arches become irregularly broad streams in the zenith, each dividing the sky into two unequal parts, but never crossing one another till they separate into parts.

Those arches which were bright at the horizon increase their brilliancy in the zenith, and discover the beams of which they are composed when the interior motion is rapid.

This interior motion is a sudden glow, not proceeding from any visible concentration of matter, but bursting out in several parts of the arch, as if an ignition of combustible matter had taken place, and spreading itself rapidly towards each extremity."—1 Franklin (Hood), 580.

N. B.—*Shapes of the Aurora at its entry into the horizon; First Class.*

1. Those which are formed like rainbows or arches.
2. Rise with their centres sometimes on magnetic meridian; sometimes E. or W. of it.
3. Number visible at same time seldom exceeds five; seldom limited to one.
4. Rise towards zenith, with their centres nearly in magnetic meridian.
5. But the E. and W. extremities vary their respective distances.
6. Arches bright at the horizon, increase in brilliancy in the zenith.

"The second general class of Auroræ are those which propagate themselves from different points of the compass, between north and west, towards the opposite points; sometimes, also, originating in the S. E. quarter, and extending themselves towards the N. W.

They may be subdivided, like the former, into the distant arches, which pass to the southward without much visible change in their appearance; and those which discover beams, and separate at intervals into wreaths, flashes, and irregular segments, exhibiting all the phenomena described above.

In explaining the mode by which the two general classes of Auroræ are conducted into the horizon, I shall call the motion of the arches (which is in a plane seldom deviating more than two points from the magnetic meridian) *the direct motion*, and that by which the Auroræ propagate themselves nearly at right angles to the magnetic meridian *the lateral motion*.

Let us suppose a mass of Aurora to be modelled at its birth *in a longitudinal form, crossing the meridians* at various angles, the whole to be impelled with a direct motion towards the magnetic south, but the parts having different velocities, and each extremity continually removing itself, by a lateral motion, from the centre, so as *to increase the length of the mass.*

If the centre enter the northern horizon, *it will appear like an arch*, the real extremities being invisible; and its direct motion will carry it to the southward in that form.

But if one extremity first enter the horizon, it will extend itself, by its lateral motion, to the opposite point, passing at the same time, by its direct motion, to the southward."—1 Franklin (Hood), 582.

N. B.—*Second General Class of Aurora.*

1. Those which propagate themselves from different points of the compass.
2. Direct motion.
3. Lateral motion.
4. Longitudinal form.

Fort Enterprise.—Lat. 64° 28′ 24″ N. Long. 113° 6′ W. March 8, 1821. HOOD.

"On the 8th of March, 1821, at 5h. 30m. p. m., immediately after sunset, an arched Aurora was visible, extending from *N. W. to S. E. by S.* This was the earliest period of the day at which we saw it; for although it might, from the shortness of the days in December and January, have been seen at 3h. p. m., if present, it seldom appeared before 7h. p. m., and was usually most brilliant at midnight.

On the 11th of February, the clouds formed a regular arch, extending N. N. W. to E., and the needle of a compass, fixed in the house for the purpose of making observations, receded 20′ from the magnetic meridian to the westward. I saw these clouds disperse, and afterwards collect in a different form. The disturbance of the compass is another proof of the presence of the Aurora during the day; but, on the whole, there is reason to conclude that such is not often the case."—1 Franklin (Hood), 583.

N. B.—1. Arch from N. W. to S. E. by E. (immediately after sunset), at 5h. 30m.
2. In January and December, it could have been seen at 3h. p. m.
3. Yet seldom appeared before 7h. p. m.
4. And was most brilliant at midnight.

Fort Enterprise.—Lat. 64° 28′ 24″ N. Long. 113° 6′ W. March 13, 1821. Hood.

"On the 13th of November (1820), *the Aurora was seen between the clouds* and the earth, by Mr. Franklin and Dr. Richardson.

On the 13th of March (1821), I saw an Aurora, which was emanating in wreaths from the *N. W.*, *pass over the lower surface of a stratum of white clouds.* The upper edge of the clouds was 80 feet distant from the lower, and its azimuth S. 35° W. The Aurora passed at the altitude of 70°, and, therefore, *could not have been more than two miles from the earth*, supposing that the elevation of the clouds was two and a half miles. The wind was west, and the temperature of the air 36°.

Another circumstance, which twice came under my observation, is too remarkable to be omitted. The Aurora was very brilliant near the zenith, the sky perfectly clear, and the wind moderate, when a discharge took place of small flakes of snow, which continued during several minutes. In both instances, showers of snow had fallen about half an hour before; but, at the precise period of these phenomena, no clouds were visible 10° above the horizon. To account for them on any known principles, we must wholly abandon Euler's theory of the zodiacal light and Dr. Halley's circulation of magnetic effluvia."—1 Franklin (Hood), 583.

N. B.—Aurora between the clouds and the earth.

Fort Enterprise.—Lat. 64° 28′ 24″ N. Long. 113° 6′ W. April 27, 1821. Hood.

"On the 27th of April, 1821, at 10h. 30m. p. m., a single column of Aurora rose *in the north*, and traversed the zenith towards the south; another column appearing N. E. by E., and taking a parallel direction. The first was slightly agitated, and the beams momentarily visible. It passed to the western horizon in ten minutes, and was followed by the other, which became brighter as it approached the zenith.

I am now convinced they were borne away by the wind, because the columns preserved exactly their distance from each other during their evolution, and some detached wreaths, projected from them, retained the same relative situations of all their parts; which never happens when the Aurora is carried through the air by its own direct motion. The wind was E. by N., a strong gale, and the temperature of the air 9°.

It must be admitted that *the influence of the wind upon the Aurora was never suspected until the 27th of April.* However, there are several particulars connected with the subject, which may have prevented such an influence from manifesting itself on former occasions.

1st. When the coruscations were rapid and brilliant, they forced themselves against the wind, or in a contrary direction, without any perceptible difference of speed; from which circumstance

I was led to suppose that they were not in any degree affected by the wind, and did not afterwards pay sufficient attention to discover my error.

2d. The prevalent winds were from the eastward and westward; and the arches usually extending from N. W. to S. E., the influence of the wind might have been mistaken for their lateral motion.

3d. The northerly winds, acting from the same quarter as the direct motion, were confounded with it.

Lastly. The southerly winds, which were not common, always filled the atmosphere with clouds, so that the Aurora was not visible.

Perhaps, after all, the Aurora of the 27th of April was nearer to the earth than any other which we saw."—1 Franklin (Hood), 584.

N. B.—Aurora borne away by the wind.

Fort Enterprise.—Lat. 64° 28′ 24″ N. Long. 113° 6′ W. March 11, 1821. Hood.

"On the 11th of March, at ten p. m., a body of Aurora rose *N. N. W.*, and after a mass of it had passed to *E. by S.*, the remainder broke away in portions consisting each of several beams, which crossed about 40° of the sky with great rapidity.

We repeatedly heard a *hissing noise*, like that of a musket-bullet passing through the air, and which seemed to proceed from the Aurora; but Mr. Wentzell assured us that this noise was occasioned by severe cold succeeding mild weather, and acting upon the surface of the snow previously melted in the sun's rays. The temperature of the air was then —35°, and on the two preceding days it had been above zero. The next morning it was —42°, and we frequently heard a similar noise.

Mr. Hearne's description of the noise of the Aurora agrees exactly with Mr. Wentzel's, and with that of every other person who has heard it. It would be an absurd degree of skepticism to doubt the fact any longer, for our observations have rather increased than diminished the probability of it.

We were informed by the natives that the Aurora indicated, by peculiar appearances, the state of the atmosphere which was to follow on the ensuing day.

For instance, when it is bright and the motion rapid, it will be succeeded by a strong wind; but when attenuated and expanded over the sky, by mild and cloudy weather.

A careful examination of the meteorological journal does not furnish sufficient foundation for these conclusions. But, although the influence of the Aurora upon the weather has been deemed insignificant, it is by no means improbable that the latter considerably affects the former.

To suppose a luminous body, floating in the air and sometimes situated near the clouds, is within the bounds of the ordinary atmospherical changes, and may announce those changes by assuming a form which must be in some measure determined by the circumambient pressure, is not, I should think, inconsistent with any philosophical principles.

If we had not, unfortunately, lost the only instrument calculated for the purpose, we might at least have ascertained what relation the weight of the air bears to this interesting meteor."—1 Franklin (Hood), 585.

N. B.—1. Noise supposed to proceed from the Aurora.
2. Is occasioned by severe cold, succeeding mild weather, acting on the surface of the snow.

Fort Enterprise.—Lat. 64° 28′ 24″ N. Long. 113° 6′ W. Winter of 1820–21. Richardson.

"*Remarks on the Aurora Borealis at Fort Enterprise.* Extracted from Dr. Richardson's Journal.—The account of the Aurora Borealis in the following pages is an exact transcript of notes taken at the moment of the appearance of the different phenomena.

To place a connected view of the appearances before the reader, the whole of the observations in the month of December, 1820, have been given, to which a few remarkable nights in the other months have been added.

The altitudes and dimensions of the different masses of light were ascertained merely by the eye, and, therefore, have no pretensions to accuracy; and it is only the *apparent* shapes that are described, the effect of perspective not being taken into account.

The bearings given of the Aurora are also to be taken with some latitude, but they are more likely to be generally correct than the altitudes, as they were ascertained by the different angles of our buildings; or, in some cases, when the masses of light *were near the horizon,* by their relations to distant trees and peaks of hills, whose bearings from the spot of observation were known.

To reduce the bearings given to magnetic bearings, the easterly mean variation of the compass at Fort Enterprise, amounting to 36° 20′, is to be applied.

The dip of the needle there was 86° 59′.

To show the condition of the atmosphere with regard to the transmission of sound, and its capacity for moisture, the state of a rapid about a quarter of a mile from the house, which continued open all the winter, has been occasionally mentioned.

The forms of the Aurora are described in such language as occurred at the time, without any regard whatever to theory; but it may be proper to remark that, in reference to Mr. Dalton's opinions, detailed in *Rees's Cyclopedia* (which comprised the whole of my limited reading upon the subject up to the time of observation), I have been more particular in noting the directions of the small slender beams of light of which the masses were sometimes composed, than I should otherwise have thought necessary.

It will be seen that the following observations do not accord with the positions he lays down; that, contrary to his statement, the beams would not always meet in a point if prolonged upwards; that they do not always converge to the place in the heavens to which the south pole of the dipping needle points; and that the rainbow-like arches do not invariably cross the magnetic meridian at right angles.

But, independent of all theory, I think the following notes will at least serve to prove that the Aurora is occasionally seated in a region of the air below a species of *cloud which is known to possess no great altitude.* I allude to that modification of cirro-stratus which, descending low in the atmosphere, produces a hazy continuity of cloud over head, or fog bank in the horizon. Indeed, I am inclined to infer that the Aurora Borealis is constantly accompanied by, or immediately precedes, the formation of one or other of the various forms of cirro-stratus.

On the 13th of November and 18th of December, its connection with a cloud intermediate between cirrus and cirro-stratus is mentioned; but the most vivid coruscations of the Aurora were observed when there were only a few thin attenuated shoots of cirro-stratus floating in the air, or when that cloud was so rare that its existence was only known by the production of a halo round the moon.

The bright moonlight of December was peculiarly favorable for observations of this kind. Had the nights been dark, many of the attenuated streaks of cloud hereafter mentioned would have been totally invisible.

The natives of this country pretend to foretell wind by the rapidity of the motions of the Aurora, and say that when it spreads over the sky in an uniform sheet of light, it is followed by fine weather, and that the changes thus indicated are more or less speedy, according to the appearance of the meteor early or late in the evening. Our observations were not continued long enough to confirm or contradict these notions; but it may be perhaps worthy of notice that certain kinds of cirro-stratus are also regarded by meteorologists as sure indications of wind and rain.

In reference to Mr. Dalton's opinion that the arches of the Aurora always cross the magnetic meridian at right angles, it may be observed that there is very often an apparent convergence of the parts of the Aurora towards the magnetic east and west, or to some point in their neighborhood; but the light in its passage across the sky, even when it traversed the zenith, very seldom appeared to the eye to describe the segment of a circle, but was either elliptical or formed various irregular curves and flexures.

I think I have on some occasions discerned a polarity in the masses of cloud belonging to a certain kind of cirro-stratus which approaches to cirrus, by which their long diameters, having all the same direction, were made to cross the magnetic meridian nearly at right angles. The apparent convergence of such masses of cloud towards opposite points of the horizon, which has been frequently noticed by meteorologists, is, of course, an optical deception, produced when they lie in a plane parallel to that on which the observer stands.

These circumstances are here noticed, because if it should be hereafter proved that the Aurora depends upon the existence of certain clouds, its apparent polarity may, perhaps with more propriety, be ascribed to the clouds themselves which emit the light; or, in other words, the clouds may assume their peculiar arrangement through the operation of one cause (magnetism for instance), while the emission of light may be produced by another, a change in their internal constitution perhaps, connected with a motion of the electrical fluid. These crude opinions are offered with diffidence, and my knowledge on these subjects is so limited, that I attach no importance to them; but it appears to me that they would be strengthened were the attempts now making to excite magnetism, by the electrical or galvanic fluid, to prove successful.

Generally speaking, the Aurora appeared in small detached masses for some time before it assumed that convergency towards opposite parts of the horizon which produced the arched form. An observation that I would connect with the previous remarks, by saying that it was necessary for the electric fluid (or the Aurora, if they are the same) to operate for some time before the polarity of the thin clouds in which it has its seat is produced.

This part of the subject, however, is more intimately connected with the interesting observations made on the variation of the magnetic needle by Captain Franklin and Mr. Hood. The object of my notes was merely to record the optical appearances of the meteor.

An electrometer, constructed upon Saussure's plan, placed in an elevated situation out of doors, exhibited no signs of a change from the atmosphere at any time during the winter. The electricity of our bodies, however, at times was so great, that the pith balls instantly separated to their full extent upon approaching the hand to the instrument, and our skins were, in the middle of winter, so dry that rubbing the hands together considerably increased their electricity, and, at the same time, produced a smell similar to that which is often perceived when the cushion of an electrifying machine rubs hard against the cylinder.

The same thing was observed more sensibly in some stuffed quadrupeds that hung in our apartments. Their furred skins, whether rubbed or not, often accumulated such a charge of the electrical fluid, that, when the knuckles were presented to them, they gave a smart shock, which was felt as far as the elbow.

The Aurora *did not often appear immediately after sunset. It seemed that the absence of that luminary for some hours was in general required for the production of a state of atmosphere favorable to the generation of the Aurora.* On one occasion only (March 8, 1821), did I observe it distinctly previous to the disappearance of daylight.

By the way of more perfectly describing one form of the Aurora, rather than with a view of drawing any inference, I shall state that the slender beams of light which compose the Aurora when its motions are rapid, are exactly similar to what would be produced by a quick succession of electric sparks, elicited from a charged cylinder by a body, studded with a row of points, moved rapidly to and fro before it.

Or, supposing a long range of cloud were to commence at one end to impart, from successive points of its surface, its charge to a similar parallel mass, a current of light would be produced, apparently consisting of parallel beams, lying at right angles to its line of direction, as described on the night of the 29th–30th December at 2h. a. m.

Were the clouds supposed to lie in different planes, and to be bounded by curved edges, every variety of form which that species of Aurora assumes might be produced.

The color of the light of the Aurora is not always noted in the following pages, but, when faint, it was generally steel-gray or that of the galaxy.

When the low hazy modification of cirro-stratus appeared in the sky, the light, for the most part, was a gold-yellow color, more or less deep; and when the sky was clear, or when only a few fine threads or thin shoots of cloud were visible, the colors were vivid and prismatic.

I have never heard *any sound* that could be unequivocally considered as originating in the Aurora;

but the uniform testimony of the natives—both Crees, Copper Indians, and Esquimaux—and of all the older residents in the country, induce me to believe that its motions are sometimes audible. These instances are, however, rare, as will appear when I state that I have now had an opportunity of observing that meteor for upwards of two hundred different nights."—1 Franklin (Richardson), 599.

NOVEMBER 13, 1820.

"In the evening the sky was covered by a stratum of fleecy clouds, their forms generally orbicular and texture rare. They were separated from each other by intervals of clear blue sky of various extent, but in some points came in contact.

The Aurora was observed to move along these clouds, *strongly illuminating their faces next to the earth*, and very seldom passing across the blue sky, but spreading from cloud to cloud by their points of contact, sometimes slowly, more often with considerable rapidity.

The light was generally brightest in the centre of the cloud, and it often originated simultaneously in various parts of the heavens, more or less distant from each other.

At some moments the whole sky was illuminated.

No distinct beams were seen, and the light had uniformly a grayish color, with a light tinge of yellow.

Thermometer at noon +10°, in the evening +8°."—Ibid., p. 600.

N. B.—1. In the evening the sky was covered by a stratum of fleecy clouds.

2. Aurora was observed to move along these clouds, strongly illuminating their faces next the earth.

3. The light was generally brightest in the centre of the cloud.

NOVEMBER 24, 1820.

"A bright moonlight evening, cloudless sky, with a slight breeze from W. N. W.

An arch-formed Aurora, extending *from S. E. to N. W.* This arch was composed of several disunited portions of arches, every succeeding one having a higher commencement and termination than that which preceded it, reckoning from the horizon to the zenith.

Their altitude near the centre of the imperfect arch which they formed by their arrangement was from 40° to 60°.

One of these portions presented a smooth edge inferiorly, or towards the south, but its northern border was fringed with long falcate pointed rays, whose bases appeared to twist together to form the southern edge.

It had a striking resemblance to a shoot of the moss called dicranum scoparium majus."—Ibid., p. 600.

N. B.—1. Clear moonlight.

2. An arch-formed Aurora extending from S. E. to N. W.

NOVEMBER 26, 1820.

"Thermometer at noon —13°; in the evening —25°. Sky cloudless, and of a pretty deep blue.

An Aurora appeared in the early part of the night, having a general direction from *N. W. to E. S. E.* It consisted of several concentric but irregular arches, all of which, without changing their position, occasionally assumed the falcate form observed on the 24th. The uppermost arch nearly reached the zenith. The smaller stars *became invisible* when the brighter parts of the Aurora passed over them.

Although the air appeared perfectly clear during the time the Aurora was visible, yet there was a fall of very small snow. Its particles were so minute as to be scarcely visible to the naked eye, and were most readily detected by their melting upon the skin. The same phenomenon of an almost imperceptible snow falling from a clear sky, had been before observed in a bright sun, which rendered visible a great number of icy spiculæ floating in the air."—Ibid., p. 600.

N. B.—1. Sky cloudless.

2. An Aurora early in the evening from N. W. to E. S. E.

3. It consisted of several concentric but irregular arches.

4. The smaller stars became invisible when the brighter parts of the Aurora passed over them.

DECEMBER 1, 1820.

"During the day the sky kept tolerably clear, a slight appearance only of the stratus being visible near the horizon; but a snow, whose particles were so minute as to be discerned only in the sunshine, fell at intervals during the forenoon. At noon the snow was more apparent, and a bow was produced in the neighborhood of the sun's place in the heavens. At 8 p. m., wind E. N. E., light, with a very clear sky.

The Aurora commenced by a beam shooting up *from the northern horizon;* afterwards, masses of light appeared in various parts of the sky, particularly *in the eastern quarter;* and at length *an arch was formed from S. E. to N. W.*

The centre of the arch, when it was first formed, lay to the northward of the zenith, but afterwards passed gradually to the southward.

When about 60° above the southern horizon, it assumed the falcate appearance described on the 24th of November, the pointed tails directed towards the north. The falciform processes sometimes separated laterally, so as to appear like parallel beams crossing the line of direction of the arch obliquely. Their altitude was not altered at the moment of their separation.

At times the general arch was dispersed, and a number of small arches formed whose ends occasionally rolled inwards upon themselves in form of a scroll.

The whole body of light ultimately descended below the southern horizon and disappeared. Not a cloud was visible during the evening."—Ibid., p. 601.

DECEMBER 4, 1820. Temp. —25°.

"The Aurora forming a *broad arch* of bright light; its centre about 45° *south of the zenith*, and its extremities bearing *S. E. and N. W.* respectively.

It *passed gradually to the southward* and disappeared."—Ibid., p. 602.

DECEMBER 5, 1820. Temp. —26°.

"The Aurora to-night had its light disposed in large masses, having indefinite shapes, situated in various parts of the sky, but most crowded in *the southern quarter.*

There were several layers of dark clouds near the horizon.

The Aurora was visible in various spots where no stars were to be seen, but several of the larger stars were visible through a bright arch which at one time crossed the zenith *having a direction from north to south.*"—Ibid., p. 602.

DECEMBER 6, 1820. Temp. —14°.

"Aurora in an arch form *passing from S. E. to N. W.* over the zenith, broad towards its middle, but narrow and spirally twisted near the horizon. Stars appeared through it without any perceptible diminution of their brilliancy."—Ibid., p. 602.

DECEMBER 7, 1820. Temp. —26°.

"At ten p. m., the Aurora formed an arch, broader towards its middle, and emitting a denser light from its southern edge, but becoming fainter by imperceptible degrees towards its northern edge, until it disappeared altogether. Its upper or northern edge lay near the zenith.

As its limbs approached the horizon, they became more slender, and assumed a twisted appearance. The *stars appeared very dimly through the more dense parts of the Aurora.*"—Ibid., p. 603.

N. B.—The stars appeared very dimly through the more dense parts of the Aurora.

DECEMBER 8, 1820. Temp. —30°.

"At 11h. p. m., sky very clear, and the stars brilliant. A well-formed arch of light crossed the zenith, *extending from N. W. to S. E.*

It *moved slowly to the southward*, broke up into several irregular masses of light, and disappeared. At midnight, there was no appearance of Aurora."—Ibid., p. 603.

DECEMBER 9, 1820. Temp. —36°.

"The Aurora made its first appearance at nine o'clock p. m. near the horizon, *in the N. W. by N.*, and shot over to the *S. W.*, forming several concentric arches, the uppermost of which *passed a little to the southward* of the zenith.

As the limbs of these arches approached the horizon, they seemed to be twisted together, and terminated on each side in a single, suddenly acuminated point, about seven or eight degrees high. These extremities emitted a more dense light than the middle parts of the arches, which were rare, and permitted *the stars to be seen clearly through them.*

At 9h. 30m., the moon arose, and the Aurora now formed broken, irregular masses *near the southern horizon.*

At 10h. 30m., a depressed arch of the Aurora was formed, its extremities terminating in the opposite points of the horizon, or in the *N. W. and S. E.*, and its centre *scarcely rising ten degrees above the southern horizon.* It was more brilliant than the former arch, and *completely hid the stars.*

Half an hour after midnight, there were several large masses of light *in the eastern and N. E.* quarters of the sky. The arch had disappeared, but a luminous point remained *in the N. W.*, the quarter from whence it originally sprung.

About 1h. a. m. (10th), several portions of light were arranged so as to form an interrupted arch from *E. to the N. W.* The masses of light before noticed in the *E. and N. E.* had now united, and spread *along the horizon to the S. E.*"—Ibid., p. 603.

DECEMBER 10, 1820. Temp. —43°.

"At half past six p. m., an arch of the Aurora appeared having an elevation of 30° and *a direction from W. N. W. to S. S. E.* It was irregularly elevated and depressed in various parts, and its breadth, which was in general about 6°, occasionally expanded so as to occupy thrice that space.

These dilatations were effected with a slow motion, and were partial, seldom including more than 10° or 15° of the arch at a time. The centre of the dilating part was more brightly illuminated than the other parts of the arch. The return of the arch to its former dimensions was equally gradual with its dilatation.

The arch was occasionally divided into five parallel beams, which, having *a direction nearly from north to south,* traversed it obliquely.

These beams had a *quick lateral motion,* and were sometimes gathered into masses that receded so far from each other as to break the arch into several portions, which had pointed extremities, arising from the obliquity of the beams which composed them.

The length of the beams was sometimes considerably increased by their northern extremities shooting up whilst their lower ends remained stationary. These appearances were but of momentary duration, the beams rapidly reuniting to form a homogeneous arch.

After the Aurora had continued for about half an hour to display a succession of the above forms, the arch totally disappeared, and a horizontal mass of light was observed in *the southern quarter of the sky,* having its face longitudinally barred by several thin strata of clouds.

At 10h. 30m., there were various irregular masses of light scattered over the sky, but *most luminous in the north.*

The Aurora had appeared early in the night in the *west;* afterwards, its most luminous parts were collected in the *south.* About nine, it shone most brightly in the *eastern quarter* of the sky, and now, as we have just mentioned, its principal seat was in the north."—Ibid., p. 604.

N. B.—1. The beams had a quick lateral motion.

2. Aurora early in the night in the *west;* then its most luminous parts were collected in the *south;* at nine, it shone most brightly in the *eastern* quarter; at 10h. 30m., its principal seat was in the north.

DECEMBER 11, 1820. Temp. —31°.

"At 5h. p. m., several *broad arches of rare light* appeared, extending from *N. W. to S. E.* At 6h. they disappeared, no change in the weather having occurred in the interim, the sky remaining clear, with a bright moon.

At 9h. an arch was formed *in the east,* broad, irregular, and rather faint. Its extremities bore *N. and S. E.*, and were spirally twisted near the horizon.

At 10h. 30m , there was an arch *in the southern quarter* of the sky, 40° high. Its extremities had an equal breadth with its centre, and bore *N. W. and S. E.* respectively. Wind a little more northerly; sky clear.

At 11h., two bright arches passed near the zenith in a direction *from N. W. to S. E.;* one complete, extending from horizon to horizon, the other reaching one-half way across the sky, *the west end being deficient.* The edges of both arches were well defined, their apparent acuteness throwing the clear blue sky far back.

The arches were broadest near the zenith; and, when most bright, appeared to consist of several streams of light, nearly but not exactly parallel to each other, and having the same direction with the arch.

These streams receded from each other by a *lateral motion,* leaving interstices, sometimes of a fainter light, sometimes of a clear blue sky; and they were at times gathered together toward one side of the arch, which then shone with a very dense light. The S. E. extremities of the two arches were united near the horizon, and, bending to an angle, ran *horizontally to the northward* for a considerable distance.

After the arches had continued for some time, they moved *slowly to the southward,* became rarer and broader, were blended into each other, and finally broke into several irregular masses of light.

During the evening, many of the meteors termed falling stars were observed. The Rapid was very loud."—Ibid., p. 605.

N. B.—At 5h. p. m., several broad arches of rare light appeared extending from N. W. to S. E.

DECEMBER 12, 1820. Temp. —40°.

"At 9h. p. m., there was a broad, faint, irregular arch of light, whose extremities bore *N. N. W.* and *S. E. by S.*

At 11h., weather rather hazy, a bur or halo closely encircling the moon. A low arch of light *from E. to S. E.*, and *a broad horizontal mass in the north.*

At midnight, there were two faint but distinct arches whose extremities, originating and terminating in consort, bore *N. N. E.* and *S. E.* The upper arch had of course a greater curvature. It nearly reached the zenith; the other was about 70° high.

At the same time, many faint and irregular masses of light existed in other parts of the sky. After the circles had remained stationary for a short time, they broke in the middle. The *S. E.* ends disappeared; whilst the remainder, separating laterally into several long streaks of light, shot quickly up in flashes *from the N. W. to S. E.*, crossing the zenith. Sky moderately clear.

About 1h. a. m. (13th), there were many masses of light in various parts of the sky, which bore a strong resemblance to assemblages of the clouds denominated cirro-cumuli.

At one time, a remarkable body of light appeared *in the N. N. E.*, which occasionally split into detached parts by a lateral recession, but its general *motion was directly to the S. W.* It obscured the smaller stars, but did not completely hide those of the first magnitude."—Ibid., p. 606.

N. B.—1. At 9h. p. m., a broad, faint, irregular arch, N. N. W. to S. E. by S.
2. It obscured the smaller stars, but did not completely hide those of the first magnitude.

DECEMBER 13, 1820. Temp. —34°.

"At 1h. a. m. (14th), a broad arch of faint light, crossing the zenith, extended from horizon to horizon, its *extremities bearing E. and W.*

A meteor, termed a falling star, was observed at this time. It remained luminous until it came below the near side of a tree-top at no great distance.

When the arch broke up, its west end disappeared entirely, but its eastern extremities assumed for some time the semblance of a group of cirro-cumuli."—Ibid., p. 607.

DECEMBER 14, 1820. Temp. —16°.

"At midnight, a faint arch extended from the horizon *in the S. E. by E. to the N. W. by W.*, its centre passing *to the southward of the zenith.* Bright moonlight."—Ibid., p. 607.

DECEMBER 17, 1820. Temp. —30°.

"At 1h. 30m. a. m. (18th), a number of detached irregular masses of light were so arranged as to form an arch 30° high, having a direction from *N. W. to S. E.* Weather clear, strong wind."—Ibid., p. 608.

DECEMBER 18, 1820. Temp. —37°.

"At 11h. 30m. p. m., the sky, which had previously been clear, was covered by a thin stratum of clouds belonging to that modification of cirrus which forms the mackerel sky of sailors, conjoined with small portions of what are termed by the same people mares'-tails. Between the bars of the former and the long fringes of the latter, streaks of deep-blue sky appeared.

These clouds were not dense enough to hide the larger stars completely, and from their first appearance until they spread entirely over the sky, not more than a quarter of an hour elapsed.

On attentively regarding the sky for some time, the more rounded parts of the mackerel sky were observed to send shoots across the blue spaces to unite with similar processes of the neighboring masses. At the moment of junction, a yellowish light, with a slight tinge of red, was emitted most brightly from the centres of the two clouds, but extending, though more faintly, to their margins. A longer space of time had not elapsed than was required to note down these appearances, when an arch of light was observed to cross the zenith, its extremities bearing east and west, and terminating about 50° from the horizon. It was from 3° to 4° broad, and had a pale gold-yellow color. When it ceased to emit light, its site was seen to be occupied by a range of small fleecy clouds, similar to those already described, but more closely aggregated. The moon now bore nearly south, and shone brightly, strongly illuminating the arch-formed range of clouds just mentioned; but their rarity was such that they showed no dark sides. Winds very variable from S. W. to W.

About a quarter of an hour after the last observation, a round mass of cloud in the S. E. was observed to assume, suddenly, an appearance of greater density, at the same time emitting from its centre a yellowish light. Immediately after which, it shot forth towards the S. E. several bright parallel horizontal streaks of light, which, crossing the near face of a neighboring mass of clouds, became slightly curved from the south. They were about 8° or 10° above the horizon, and were prolonged after passing before the clouds, through a portion of clear sky. A few degrees beneath them, there were two or three dark layers of cirro-stratus.

The clouds, in their general arrangement at this period, had that appearance of convergency in opposite points of the horizon which has been frequently noticed in a sky covered with cirri. In the present instance, these points were at right angles to the magnetic north and south. In the zenith, the mackerel sky prevailed; but in the S. E. and N. W. (true), the clouds were more dense, and presented various depending fringes towards the points of the horizon already mentioned. The magnitudes of the masses, too, in different parts of the sky, diminished so regularly, as they receded from the zenith, as to convey an idea that their long sides were seen in the N. E. and S. W. quarters of the sky, but their ends only in N. W. and S. E. quarters.

At midnight, several of the cirriform clouds, which were in the neighborhood of the moon's place, reflected her light strongly, and hence appeared to have a pretty dense structure; but when they passed before the face of that luminary, they became nearly invisible, producing only a slight halo or bur, but not sensibly diminishing the light.

At 20m. after midnight, the northern quarter of the sky became perfectly clear to the height of 35°, the rest of the heavens being overspread by small fleecy clouds, separated by narrow intervals. The edge of cloud bordering on the clear sky was well defined, ran east and west, and was made up of the ends of small and rather broad parallel bars, having a direction from north to south; a very common modification of cirrus. The moon was at this time wading through a collection of small clouds, and was surrounded, at the distance of 10°, by a faint though distinct halo. In the S. W., in a clear part of the sky, there existed a small spot of yellowish-white light, which, for a few seconds, gradually increased in brightness, and then sent forth suddenly a luminous beam, which, crossing a portion of the deep-blue sky, passed over the well-marked edge of cloud above described, continued its course in front of the clouds, brightly illuminating their faces, and terminated to the southward of the zenith, near the moon's place in the heavens.

When this beam had attained its extreme length, it formed a half-arch concave to the westward. It was scarcely formed, however, before it divided into a number of small parts, which, being segments of circles and rising successively one above the other, formed a kind of tiled arch. It disappeared altogether in three or four minutes, leaving the clouds unaltered in appearance.

At 12h. 40m., the sky had become clear as far as the zenith. The edge of the clouds, which were now overhead, was still composed of parallel bars directed to the north and south. Under these bars, a few streaks or threads of very rare cloud were seen floating, and at times emitting a faint orange-colored light. The clouds in the southern part of the sky, although they appeared pretty dense in the bright moonlight, were yet rare enough to allow the larger stars to appear through them.

By one o'clock, the whole mass of cloud had gathered together towards the south, and disappeared in the horizon; but, at the same time, a few long and very rare threads of cloud, which were at intervals faintly luminous, shot athwart from east to west in the deep blue of the northern part of the sky. On former occasions, the Aurora had been observed to illuminate the face of the clouds next the earth; but the present night was remarkably favorable for the observance of that phenomenon, the brightness of the moonlight, and the clearness of the sky, rendering the clouds very visible and well defined."—Ibid., p. 609.

DECEMBER 19, 1820. Temp. —38°.

"At midnight the sky cleared up, a few cirro-strati were seen to the southward, and there was a slight bur round the moon. The rest of the sky was of a grayish blue color.

At this time, a broad bank of the Aurora appeared in the north, lying horizontally, at an elevation of 25°. There were also a few long parallel streamers to *the westward*, flashing in the direction of their lengths *from W. by N. to E. by S.* They disappeared suddenly, leaving in their site a faint yellowish light."—Ibid., p. 611.

DECEMBER 20, 1820. Temp. —46.6°.

"At 10h. 45m., bright moonlight. The sky, which had previously been very clear, was suddenly overspread by a thin stratum of fleecy clouds. They were in general orbicular, but were much crowded, so as to leave only small interstices of clear blue sky. A few stars were visible through the rarer parts. About 7° or 8° above the northern horizon, there existed a mass of cloud rather more dense, which began soon after its formation to emit a faint yellowish light. In two minutes, the light became brighter, and spread towards the S. W. by a slow waving motion, like an increasing volume of smoke rolling parallel to the horizon. It continued sweeping round the sky in this manner until the produced end bore N. W., and then became irregularly elevated in the middle, assuming an arched form. At the instant at which this elevation took place, a stream of light, issuing from the S. W., formed an arch about 2° higher than the other, and parallel to it. The second arch exhibited nearly the colors of the rainbow.

The red color occupied its under edge, and it darted down towards the inferior arch a number of light-red, fringe-like processes. The two arches were scarcely formed when they disappeared, but instantly appeared again, and continued to do so, in rapid succession, for a minute or two; the upper one retaining its prismatic tints, and the under one an uniform pale-yellow color. The motion of the light by which the arches were reproduced was sometimes from right to left, sometimes in the opposite direction. The upper arch, too, was occasionally split into narrow parallel beams, which had not only a rapid lateral motion in the direction of the arch, but were also lengthened out, both upwards and downwards, by sudden flashes. At such moments, the colored tints were most vivid; the red always predominating.

About five minutes after the first appearance of the Aurora, a bright mass of light was observed bearing N. N. W., from which a column, possessing prismatic tints, shot up as high as the zenith; a similar column at the same time springing to meet it from the site of the two arches which had now disappeared. A brilliant arch was thus formed, whose extremities bore W. N. W. and S. S. E. In an instant thereafter, the whole sky was covered with small arcs and irregular masses of light, mostly composed of short parallel beams. These masses moved rapidly from the horizon towards the zenith, and back again. The duration of this phenomenon was about seven or eight minutes, when the light wholly disappeared.

The colors of the arches, in their general appearance and arrangement, resembled those of the rainbow; but the blue, green, or violet, were not distinctly visible. The yellow ray occupied most space and was the faintest, whilst the orange was the brightest. The red was nearly as abundant as the yellow, and approached in its hue to lake-red. The moon shone brightly all the time. After the disappearance of the Aurora, the sky remained as before, covered with a thin stratum of clouds, but their texture had become more rare, their edges worse defined, and their masses more blended into each other. In short, they answered the description of the cirro-stratus in the first stage of its change from the cirrus. The moon had a bur or halo round it; and a candle, both in the open air and the house, was also surrounded by a halo.

At 11h. 30m., there was a faint mass of light in the S. S. W., about 20° high, occasionally fading away, and allowing a body of dark cloud to appear in its site. The light reappeared first in the centre of the cloud of a gold-yellow color, but became fainter as it spread outwards.

At midnight, the weather was rather hazy, and there was very little blue sky to be seen. A few minutes before twelve, a portion of cloud in the S. E. was faintly illuminated; and, at the same instant, a luminous spot made its appearance in a clear blue space in the north, about 15° high. From this spot, an arch shot up which, passing to the eastward of the zenith, joined the luminous cloud in the S. E. The arch was scarcely formed when it disappeared, but was as speedily formed again by a mass of light rising in the S. E., and rolling to the north like a volume of smoke from a chimney, increasing in dimensions as it rose. Immediately after the second formation of this arch, it assumed that appearance of a shoot of the moss alluded to in the notes on November 24th, and which is termed by botanists *falcato-secund.* The points of the rays or streams were directed to the south. In a short time, the arch separated into small curved segments, which vanished in their turn; and the attention was next directed to the formation of a long range of prismatic light about 60° high, its extremes bearing west and north. This light had a pale gold-yellow color, and was attenuated towards the north, its southern or upper edge being brightest. When this passed away, a number of irregular masses appeared in various parts of the sky. At 1h. a. m. (21st), the sky was obscured by a fog."—Ibid., p. 612.

DECEMBER 21, 1820. Temp. —42°.

"During the early part of the evening, there were a few thin horizontal clouds in the N. E., but the sky in general had a clear grayish-blue color. Some streaks of cirrus were faintly visible in the east. The moon shone brightly, but was surrounded by a bur, as was also the candle. Rapid noisy.

At 10h. 20m., the Aurora rose in the S. S. E., and, proceeding across the sky, divided into several broad arches, which terminated about 30° from the western horizon. The common stem in the S. S. E. appeared as if formed by the twisting of the ends of the different arches together, and had a waving irregular motion, sometimes apparently doubling upon itself; and once or twice it separated into small parallel portions, having a lateral motion in the direction of the arch, but with their ends pointing north and south. The arches were three, and at one time four, in number, and gradually diverged more and more from each other towards their western ends. The uppermost passed a little to the southward of the zenith, and they were each about 4° or 5° broad. The spaces between them were sometimes faintly illuminated. After they had continued stationary for about ten minutes, the S. S. E. common stem moved slowly round the horizon until it bore south, leaving a streak of light behind it, whilst the truncated ends, or those which were directed towards the western horizon, approached each other, and were lengthened out to the horizon in the W. N. W. by the rolling motion of smoke. Contemporaneously with these motions, the centre of the arch moved up and down, so as to appear undulated and even contorted; the moving parts frequently dilating considerably, and always becoming brighter in the centre, at the commencement of their motion. The light had a pale yellow hue, and, when brightest, was not sufficiently dense to hide the larger stars. Its motions were in general slow, and unattended by flashes.

At 11h., a bright arch extended across the zenith from E. by S. to N. W. by W.; the S. W. quarter of the sky being at the time occupied by a homogeneous mass of light, which had a crescentic edge turned towards the east, and there was a similar mass in the north concave towards the south. The arch at first exhibited a vermicular motion from east to west, then split into parallel beams, possessing, as usual, a rapid lateral motion; and, in a short time, the Aurora in every part of the sky began to move with such velocity, and to assume such a variety of forms, as to defy description. The central arch more than once exhibited two distinct currents, or motions of its parts, flowing from one end to the other in opposite directions at the same instant; and at one time all the detached parts of the Aurora appeared to collect together to form a beautiful circle or corona, which surrounded the zenith at the distance of 45°, and in which the rapid lateral motion of the beams was very apparent, having a direction from north, round by the south, west and east. The beams, in this case, were apparently perpendicular to the earth's surface in every part of the luminous ring which they formed. In a half arch, which rose immediately afterwards from the northern horizon to the zenith, the extremities of the beams were directed from east to west, and the ranges of beams which formed, in rapid succession, masses of light of various shapes in every part of the sky, had no certain direction. The general color of the Aurora was a pale yellowish-gray; but when the beams moved with a rapidity that could scarcely be followed with the eye, they emitted a pale but bright red light, slightly tinged with purple or violet. These beams sometimes lengthened and shortened themselves with extreme rapidity, and the prolonged extremities emitted a light equally brilliant, and of the same hue, with the rest of the beam. In about fifteen minutes, the whole of these beautiful phenomena vanished, leaving behind only a few faint masses of light. The moon was still surrounded by a slight bur, and the wind had changed to the west.

At midnight, the southern quarter of the sky was occupied by a broad horizontal mass of light. At 1h., there was no appearance of the Aurora whatever. Sky cloudless, but rather hazy; minute crystals of snow falling. During the evening, the wind was very variable, but light."—Ibid., p. 614.

DECEMBER 22, 1820. Temp. —43°.

"At 4h. 30m. p. m., dark and rather cloudy. A faint mass of the Aurora in the *E. S. E.*, about 20° high.

At nine o'clock p. m., the sky being of a pretty deep-blue color, except in the S. E., where there was a mass of white clouds near the horizon, the Aurora appeared in the form of an arch of yellowish-gray light, about 70° broad in the centre, where it reached from the zenith to within 29° of the southern horizon. Its limbs were spirally twisted and tapered, touching the horizon in the S. E. by S. and N. W. by W. The light of this arch was arranged in longitudinal bands, having different densities, and varying in length from 20° to 80°. These long portions of light occasionally receded laterally from each other, and then formed a series of arches or parts of arches, the upper ones including those beneath them. Whilst the arches were thus separated, some of them exhibited a waving lateral motion, the others remaining stationary, and sometimes, one end of an arch moving more than the other, it was carried obliquely across the general line of direction of the parts of the large arch. The arches approached each other by an irregular, slow, lateral motion, occurring simultaneously in the different arcs, and again formed a continuous body of light, varying in density in different parts.

At 11h., a beam of light rose from the southern horizon to the height of 45°, where it terminated, that end then bearing N. W. by N. It was about 10° broad, and gradually attenuated from its centre outwards.

At 11h. 30m., there was a long luminous bank in the south, nearly of equal dimensions throughout. Its centre was slightly elevated, and about 40° high. Its extremities faded imperceptibly away in the S. S. E. and western parts of the sky. It was about 6° broad, and emitted a greenish-yellow light. The sky near its extremities was dark, and completely hid the stars. Five or six degrees below this nearly horizontal mass, a smaller but similar one appeared for a short time. Neither continued above two or three minutes, and they exhibited no quick motions, but merely brightened a little, undergoing at the same time a slight dilatation. They appeared, however, and disappeared at intervals until 2½h. a. m. (23d), when a haziness overspread the sky."—Ibid., p. 616.

DECEMBER 23, 1820. Temp. —45°.

"At 11h. p. m., a faint arch of pale greenish light, about 10° broad, rose to the height of 30°. One of its limbs, bearing *S. E. by S.*, sprung from a collection of whitish clouds (cirri) situated about 10° above the horizon. The other, bearing *W. by N.*, faded away imperceptibly in a dark part of the sky, where there were neither clouds nor stars visible.

The moon was surrounded by a bur, and did not give much light.

At 12h., the arch was still visible, but several strata of pretty dense white clouds now occupied *the southern part of the sky* to the height of 20°, and the extremities of the arch, which were broader and fainter than before, bore *S. by E.* and *W. N. W.*

In the middle of the arch, there were several gentle elevations and depressions; but, although the light occasionally brightened up in some spots, there were no quick motions amongst its parts.

The state of the atmosphere continued, as before, pretty clear in the zenith; but the bur round the moon, of a faint gray color, with a slight tinge of orange on its outer edge, remained. A similar bur was formed round a candle, its diameter enlarging rapidly as the observer receded from it."—Ibid., p. 617.

DECEMBER 25, 1820. Temp. —28°.

"At 1h. a. m. (26th), the Aurora appeared for the first time this night, in form of a faint arch, extending from the altitude of 40° *in the N. W.* to a spot near the zenith, bearing *S. E.*

It was composed of longitudinal bands or streams of light, connected with each other by a faint luminousness.

A little snow was falling at this time in minute crystals, and there was a slight haziness in the sky."—Ibid., p. 618.

DECEMBER 26, 1820. Temp. —32°.

"At 10h. 30m., an arch-formed Aurora, about 8° broad, appeared a little to the southward of the zenith. Its extremities descended to within 15° of the horizon, and terminated in the S. E. and N. W. At one time, the light of the arch appeared of uniform density throughout; at other times, it was most intense along its southern or lower edge, and became gradually fainter upwards until it disappeared.

The stars were seen obscurely through the denser light; in other parts of the sky they shone brightly. At the same time, there appeared in the E. S. E., parallel to the horizon, a mass of bright light with two or three dark horizontal streaks across its face, produced apparently by intervening layers of cloud. The arch continued for a considerable time without undergoing any material alteration in its appearance, except that it occasionally brightened up and faded away again. Once, indeed, for a few moments, it separated into portions parallel to each other, but having about 11° of obliquity with respect to the arch. These portions emitted a bright light, and were separated by faintly luminous spaces.

At 11h., the arch, having nearly the same direction as before, was composed throughout the greater part of its length by two parallel portions, each gradually fading away towards their edges; and the S. E. end of the arch was also lengthened out and bent towards the east, so as to come in contact with the mass of light noticed above as bearing E. S. E. This bent portion of the arch was composed of several bars nearly of equal length, and arranged so that every succeeding one lay to the north of that which preceded it in their approach to the horizon. The whole were connected together by a faint diffused light; and from the same body of light in which that end of the arch now terminated, a column of faint beams rose perpendicularly to the height of 15°.

At 11h. 20m., the arch had increased its breadth to 20°, its northern edge being very near the zenith. Its extremities, bearing S. E. and N. W., were composed of irregular and somewhat detached roundish masses, but its centre consisted of five bright longitudinal bands, connected by a faint diffused light. The mass of light formerly bearing E. S. E. had now moved round towards the south, and, still resting in the horizon, formed the S. E. end of the arch.

At midnight, a great number of detached masses of light occupied the sky from 20° south to 10° north of the zenith. These masses of light varied in shape, but the greater number had somewhat of an oblong form. They were separated in some places by clear blue sky, in others they were connected by a diffused light. They lay in various directions in the zenith, but towards the horizon they had an appearance of convergency to the N. W. and S. E., and thus formed in the aggregate an arch 30° high in the middle, and tapering towards its extremities.

At 1h. 30m. (27th), the centre part of the above-mentioned arch, or aggregated masses of light, had dilated so as to occupy the whole sky, except a clear blue space of 20° from the northern horizon. The shapes of its component parts had undergone a material alteration, and were now so arranged and blended together as to bear a striking semblance to an immense double curtain with its ends gathered together, in the N. W. by W. and S. E., at about 10° above the horizon, the space beneath being of a clear blue. From the zenith, to carry on the similitude, the folds of the curtain proceeded in several beautiful festoons towards the north and south, and had occasionally a slow motion, as if it were folding and unfolding again and again. The moon at this time shone with a bright light, and illuminated several layers of cloud (cirro-stratus) in the N. E., every other part of the sky being unclouded.

At 2h. a. m., a large homogeneous sheet of rare light was spread over 20° on each side of the zenith, and near the horizon there were many layers of cirro-stratus, some of them pretty dense, so as to obscure the moon when they passed over its face. The Rapid was quite inaudible at this time."—Ibid., p. 618.

DECEMBER 27, 1820. Temp. —45°.

"At 11h. p. m., the sky clear, the moon not yet risen, but many stars visible. A beam of light, about 8° broad, rose from 10° above the horizon in the S. E. by S., and, gradually becoming fainter upwards, disappeared a little south of the zenith. After continuing stationary for some time, it sent forth a beam of light from its southeast end, which extended 11° more to the northward, whilst its fainter end was at the same instant prolonged so as to form a complete arch, terminating in the N. W. by W. horizon. A little haze was visible at this time in the southern horizon.

At midnight, the Aurora formed a somewhat interrupted circle round the sky, about 15° high, which sent down, from its N. W. by W. and S. E. points, several pointed processes which nearly touched the horizon. Some large flexuous streaks, and masses of light traversing the zenith, connected the northern with the southern part of the circle; and there were also a few detached irregular masses of light in other parts of the sky. The best-defined part of the circle was in the N. E. quarter, and here a quick lateral motion to and fro was produced, as if by its separation into perpendicular bars. It was about 8° broad at this place. During the continuance of this phenomenon, many beams of light rose perpendicularly from the upper margin of the circle, but, before they reached the zenith, their extremities were bent from their course so as to make various curves sideways, or even to appear as if rolled up upon themselves.

When the Aurora had exhibited itself in this form for a considerable space of time, the whole mass of light suddenly appeared in motion, and, sweeping round on each side, was gathered together to the southward of the zenith. Immediately thereafter, a large portion of it was seen in the S. E., assuming an exact resemblance to a curtain suspended in a circular form in the air, and hanging perpendicularly to the earth's surface. The lower edge of this curtain was very luminous, and had a waving motion; and the illusion was further heightened by the momentary appearance of perpendicular dark lines or breaks in the light, in rapid succession round the circle, exactly as the waving of a curtain would cause the dark shades of its folds to move along it. This beautiful curtain of light was about 40° high, of a pale yellowish color, and sent forth on the one side a process which approached the S. E. by E. point of the horizon, and on the other was connected with a long regular arch, terminating in the N. W. horizon, similarly constructed, and having the same waving motion with the curtain itself. All this time the sky was perfectly clear, except in the southern quarter, which, to the height of 4° or 5°, was occupied by dark clouds, apparently intermediate between stratus and cirro-stratus.

Half an hour after its first appearance, this curtain-formed Aurora was resolved into a number of detached irregular portions, which sometimes increased rapidly in every direction until they met with other masses, either before existing or appearing at the instant, and formed an uniform sheet of light which covered the whole sky. The formation of this great sheet of light was so rapid, that the eye could only trace its progress partially; and its dissolution and reappearance were equally sudden.

At 2h. p. m., the moon arose. A clear sky. The Aurora fainter and further to the southward than before."—Ibid., p. 620.

DECEMBER 28, 1820. Temp. —49°.

"At 6h. p. m., the Aurora, in an arched form, extended from the S. E. horizon to the N. W., across the zenith. This arch was at one time composed of a bright homogeneous stream of light about 8° broad; at other times, it split into parallel beams, their ends directed to the east and west. These beams receded from each other laterally, until they were separated by a space of clear blue sky more than twice their breadth, speedily reuniting again, however, to form the uninterrupted arch. A fainter arch appeared to the northward of the other, springing from, and terminating at, the same points in the horizon, but having an apparent curvature so much greater as to keep their centres 5° or 6° apart.

At 8h., the low fog to the southward had increased, and minute crystals of snow were falling, but the zenith remained clear.

At this time, there existed a zone of light in the north, about 20° high, whose extremities, united with those of a similar zone in the south, dipped suddenly down to the horizon in the S. E. and N. W. points.

At 9h., in a calm and clear atmosphere, there were five arches, each about 4° broad; one crossed the zenith, another was elevated about 60° above the northern horizon, and there were three in the southern half of the sky, at elevations of 45°, 6°, and 80°. Their light was faint, and their extremities converged so as to terminate conjointly in the N. W. by N. and S. E. by S. points.

At 10h. 30m., columns of faint light rose perpendicularly from the horizon in the N., S. E., and S. W. points, to the height of 20°.

At midnight, there was an arch of light in the south, about 15° high, having its lower edge, throughout its whole length, resting upon a fog-bank; and there were also two or three faint beams rising from the horizon in the S. E., across a portion of clear sky, and a beam lying midway between the zenith and horizon, about 20° long, and pointing north and south.

At 1h., the sky in the zenith was clear, and was occupied by an arch tending from N. W. to S. E." —Ibid., p. 622.

DECEMBER 29, 1820. Temp. —52°.

"At 6h. p. m., there appeared an arch of yellowish-gray and pretty dense light, about 10° broad and 25° high, which in a few minutes began to increase in breadth, and at length separated into two parallel arches, whilst at the same time a fainter beam sprung from its northern end, taking a direction towards the S. by E., but, becoming more diffuse as it rose, it disappeared in the zenith. The brighter part of the light obscured the stars. The united limbs of the two arches in the N. by W. were divided by perpendicular dark spaces so as to appear to be composed of oblique bars.

About 10m. after these appearances were noted down, the sky was occupied, for about 70° to the northward of the zenith, by large masses of light, arranged so as to converge towards the N. W. by N. and S. E. by S. points of the horizon. Near these points, long slender processes of light descended, and united so as to form a common stem on each side similar to the limbs of an arch of the common dimensions of 2° or 3° in breadth. The internal movements of the Aurora at this time were sluggish, but large masses of light were frequently generated almost instantaneously.

At 7h. 30m., a number of arches sprung from the horizon in the N. W. by N., and, sweeping across the sky in various directions, suddenly curved in to terminate in the S. E. by S. The arches were in general about 6° broad, and their middles were distant enough from each other to spread on each side of the zenith to the distance of 50°.

From 9h. to midnight, the Aurora formed many arches of light, very various in breadth and density, all having a common origin and termination in the N. W. and S. E., but crossing the heavens in a variety of directions, so as to occupy about three-fourths of the space on each side of the zenith.

The middle portions of some of these arches ran horizontally across the sky, whilst their extremities, making sudden curves, arrived at the common origin and termination of all the arches, which were seated for the greater part of the night about 4° above each horizon. At one time, the light was arranged in a series of curves, including each other and having their convexities turned towards the north on both sides of the zenith. In short, their arrangement was continually varying, but the breadth of the arches at all times was greater in the zenith. Large and diffuse columns of light sometimes shot up at right angles from the convex side of the arches, and portions of broken arches were occasionally seen in various parts of the sky, lying obliquely across the general line of direction. The changes of form were not produced by a quick flashing motion, but by the different parts of a new arch appearing simultaneously but faintly, then gradually brightening up in a manner that could be traced only by keeping the eye steadfastly fixed on a clear part of the sky and watching the evolution of the light there.

At midnight, a clear blue sky surrounded the zenith to the distance of about 20°. The rest of the sky had a light-grayish appearance, resembling the light of the milky way; many stars shining brightly at the time. In some spots this diffused light brightened up for a moment or two, assuming at the same time a yellowish hue.

At 12h. 30m., there was an arch in the south about 15° high, and various irregular masses of light in the north, the rest of the sky being of a deep blue.

At 2h., the sky very clear. At this time the Aurora was very brilliant, and its motions so rapid that it was impossible to record them in the order of their occurrence with anything like accuracy.

At one period, the S. W. part of the sky was occupied by a mass of dense light, which was connected with a similar mass in the east by a current of light about 4° broad, moving with extreme velocity from W. to E. This stream of light bore a stronger resemblance to a cascade of water than to anything else I can liken it to; and it in general flowed from the one mass of light to the other, but sometimes its eastern extremity curled back in various directions, forming, as it were, beautiful eddies. The dark lines or spaces, whose instantaneous appearance and disappearance evinced the motion of the light, lay perpendicular to its line of direction, or pointing to the north and south.

For an instant, when the motions were most rapid, the light became very vivid, and assumed a reddish hue. At this moment, a loud crash was heard, similar to what is produced by a large piece of ice floating down a river and crushing against a stone.

This noise was not repeated, and, as it appeared to come from the river, would not have been noticed unless for its contemporaneous occurrence with the brightening of the Aurora. The air at this time was rather favorable for the transmission of sound, the Rapid being distinctly heard."—Ibid., p. 623.

December 30, 1820. Temp. —48°.

"At 5h. p. m., an arch-formed Aurora extended completely across the sky *from the N. W. by N. to the S. E. by E.* From the N. W. end of this arch, a pencil of light rose perpendicularly, and terminated at the zenith. Its hue and brightness were equal to that of the milky way, which was distinctly visible at the time.

At 8h. p. m., two columns of light rose perpendicularly from the horizon, in the *N. W.* and *S. E.*, to the height of 10°. Their summits being connected by a nearly horizontal beam of light, a depressed arch was formed to the northward of the zenith, from various parts of which pencils of light shot up directly towards the south, and rising 40° or 50°. Portions of two smaller and concentric arches were occasionally seen under the other.

At 9h. the Aurora continued to exhibit modifications of the appearances above described.

At midnight, an irregular mass of light, having a spirally-twisted form, rose in the horizon in the *N. W. by N.* to the height of 60°, apparently perpendicularly; then, turning to the northward, it continued its course horizontally across the sky; and, lastly, bent suddenly and obliquely to terminate in the *S. E. horizon.*"—Ibid., p. 625.

DECEMBER 31, 1820. Temp. —40°.

"At 6h. 35m. p. m., an arch-formed Aurora 15° high, extremities bearing *N. by W.* and *E. by S.* From its north end, several rays rose to the height of 10° or 12°, having a direction *to the south.*

At 9h., a zone of light, rising from the horizon in the *N. E.*, swept round the horizon to the eastward and southward, with a gradual ascent, until it bore S. W. and had an elevation of 35°; from thence it gradually descended, and finally terminated in the *N. W. by N.* point of the horizon.

Near the eastern horizon, this zone was continuous, but towards the south it was composed of thin and parallel layers.

At midnight, the Aurora covered the sky in fleecy masses, having the same apparent convergence to the *N. W.* and *S. E.* points that has been described on former occasions."—Ibid., p. 626.

FEBRUARY 13, 1821.

"At midnight, several layers of cirro-stratus in the northern half of the sky with clear blue intervals.

A zone of light existed in the north, its extremities bearing *N. W.* and *E. N. E.* It was composed of parallel beams pointing *to the southward*, and having a quick lateral motion. The *eastern* extremity of the zone was the most brilliant, and it sometimes rolled back upon itself, producing various curtain-like appearances, during which motions *it passed in front of the neighboring clouds and completely hid them.*

The *southern half* of the sky was overspread with thin white clouds, through which a few stars appeared. When these clouds passed over the face of the moon, they produced a bur immediately around it, and a halo at the distance of 15°. The northern edge of the halo was occasionally illuminated with the yellowish-red light of the Aurora, which gradually faded away into the white moonlight reflected from the cloud.

The zone in a short time broke up, and its parts approached the zenith, often in their course whirling into a circular form with an extremely rapid motion. At those times, the beams of light appeared to be perpendicular to the horizon, and emitted various prismatic rays, of which yellow and pale violet were the most conspicuous. Sometimes the violet merely tipped the beams; at other times it appeared throughout their whole length. When these beams were arranged in the circular form, so as to form a ring, their length varied from 2° to 4°.

The light appeared this evening, to the eye, *to be near the earth, a thin white haze evidently floating behind or above it*, in some places near the moon's situation in the sky.

The needle, by Mr. Franklin's observations, diverged very much to-night.

A very short time after these observations were made, the whole sky was overspread by a tolerably dense, uniform, hazy white cloud, which hid the stars and considerably obscured the moon. The Aurora shot across this cloud from *N. N. W. to S. S. E.*, in the form of parallel arches which emitted a bright yellowish-white light.

The arches were of short duration, and when they disappeared their site was observed to be occupied by the unaltered stratum of cloud."—Ibid., p. 627.

MARCH 8, 1821.

"At 6h. p. m., before the daylight was gone, the Aurora appeared *in the S. E.*, stretching up towards the zenith.

At 7h., two faint arches crossed the zenith.

Twilight. The Aurora was bright and copious all the evening.

At 1h. a. m. (9th), it was extremely beautiful and brilliant, but its changes were too various and rapid to be described. Its intestine motions were curved, waved, and serpentine.

Sometimes it appeared in large masses, like the modification of cloud termed the cumulus; at other times it assumed the curtain-like appearance formerly described; and occasionally it split into beams varying much in altitude, but generally perpendicular to the horizon.

One of its forms was very remarkable. It was a hollow truncated cone of light, formed of rays originating about 20° about the horizon, *on every side*, and terminating about 3° or 4° from the zenith. These rays had much *lateral motion*, and emitted a most brilliant green light, intermixed with a bright purple. Their convergence was very regular, and, had they been prolonged, they would have terminated in the zenith. The cone was, in fact, the phenomenon we have termed *Corona Borealis*, with beams longer than usual."—Ibid., p. 627.

MARCH 11, 1821.

"At midnight, a zone of light was observed extending *from the E. to the N. W.*, lying about 20° above the horizon, and emitting a yellowish-gray light. This zone exhibited some intestine motion, but it was faint, and consisted rather of a brightening up and fading away again of the light than of flashes.

At this time, sounds were heard at intervals of from five to ten minutes to a few seconds, resembling the noise of a wand waved smartly through the air. The *sounds* appeared to issue from various parts of the sky, and as they were frequently simultaneous with a brightening of the Aurora, I was at first inclined to regard them as *reports of its motions*, but Mr. Wentzel *stated them to arise from the contracting of the snow upon the sudden increase of cold*, and his opinion was further supported by the same sounds being heard next morning.

We heard in the evening from 50 to 100 of these reports, and they continued nearly as frequent after the Aurora had almost faded away as when it was brightest.

The air was not very favorable for the transmission of sound, as the Rapid was scarcely audible." —Ibid., p. 628.

Cape Lavenorn (Greenland).—Lat. 64° 30′ N. Long. 39° 30′ W. August 23, 1829. GRAAH.

"This evening, for the first time since April last, we saw the Northern Lights."—Graah, p. 103.

[Graah remained at Nukarbik from October 1, 1829, to April 5, 1830, but does not mention a single appearance of the Aurora.

Nukarbik is in lat. 63° 21′ 38″ N., long. 40° 50′ W.]

Fort Norman.—Lat. 64° 40′ 38″ N. Long. 124° 44′ 47″ W. October, 1849. Lieut. HOOPER.

"16th. At 11h. p. m., a fine Aurora extended in a broad undulating curve from N. E. to W. S. W. The sky was clear; temperature considerably below freezing.

22d. At 11h. p. m., I observed a dim Aurora extending in a segment from N. N. W. to W., at about 45° of elevation.

23d. At midnight, Aurora was visible spanning the sky in a broad belt, passing through Orion in the E. and the Pleiades at S. E., and continuing to W. and N. W. Night clear and stars brilliant.

25th. At 7h. 20m. p. m., I saw a very fine Aurora forming a brilliant arch from E. to N. by W. (true), the centre being about 20° in altitude. At N. N. W., a column rose from the visible horizon to the zenith, very fine below, and widely outspread above, somewhat in the shape of an open fan which has been much torn in the web. At ten, the Aurora had shifted in position and form, being now extended from S. S. E. through the zenith towards the western horizon, where it formed a magnificent scroll at about 40° elevation. It was a most superb spectacle.

The rays of both of these were uncolored, except that they seemed to possess a more brightly golden hue than usual, the moon being nearly at the full and very bright, and the stars brilliantly displayed. The moon went down about eleven, when also the Aurora disappeared, and the sky became entirely overcast.

26th. At 8h. 30m., I observed an Aurora nearly similar in form and position to that first seen last night, but not nearly so brilliant, and of greater altitude, as the inner line of curve was now just above the Pleiades; whereas, in that of last night, at an earlier hour, the upper edge intersected that constellation.

29th. A faint Aurora visible, very nearly in the form and position of that of the 26th instant, with an additional column, irregular and uncertain in form and place.

31st. A fine clear and cold day; a light air from southward, with an almost cloudless sky. The night one of the most lovely I have seen here; perfectly cloudless; the moon high, and, with the stars, very bright; and a beautiful Aurora, in waving tremors, all over the sky; its hue a pale and somewhat yellowish green."—Hooper's Journal, 156.

NOVEMBER, 1849.

"3d. The night very fine and clear, and freezing intensely; a slight Aurora to the northwestward.

12th. A fine Aurora visible, principally in the south and west quarters.

13th. A fine Aurora at night, extending from east, through the zenith, to west, in an irregular curve."—Ibid., p. 158.

MARCH, 1850.

"1st. Cloudy; very mild weather; wind moderate, from south. In the early evening, the Aurora was dully displayed from *S.* to *S. W.* by *W.*, in a segment of about 25° altitude at the centre; vertical short thick rays proceeding from its upper edge. About 11h., the sky cleared, and wind came from E. S. E. moderate.

3d. About 10h. p. m., a beautiful broad streak of Aurora extended from N. W., through the zenith, towards *S. E.*, of a pale yellowish green and very bright. Later, it spread all over the sky, and, moving incessantly, threatened *an increase of wind.*

5th. A cold breeze from N. W.; weather cloudy. The night clear and cold. In the early part, an arch of Aurora was visible from *S. E.* to *E. N. E.*, of inconsiderable altitude and little brilliance; the rays colored pale yellowish green.

6th. Rather sharp in the morning. A fine sunny day, with a fresh breeze from S. S. W. The night very clear and nearly calm. A light vein of Aurora at E. S. E.

7th. Very fine and clear; a fresh breeze from the southward. The morning cold. The night fine, clear, and cold. Midnight, a broad wave of Aurora from east, through the zenith, to west.

8th. Night fine and clear; a slight Aurora to the eastward. At 10h. p. m., a broad arch of Aurora from E. to N. N. W.; altitude at centre about 30°. Calm.

10th. In the evening there were visible three bright rays of Aurora, all proceeding from the east; later the Aurora spread all over the sky.

11th. The wind has been very unsteady during the day, but blew principally from N. E., especially when strongest. The weather has been exceedingly mild, and even oppressive, despite the strong breeze. At 9h. p. m., the sky was still overcast. There was a dull but distinct arch of Aurora from *E.* to *S. W.*, the centre having about 35° of altitude.

13th. At 2h. a. m., there was a fine Aurora spread over the sky, and in particular a *large mass* about 20° N. E. of the zenith; the wind was also gentle from N. E., and the sky cloudless; a great deal of *rime* was falling, apparently from the *large mass* before mentioned.

The day fine and rather cold. At 10h. p. m., a broad and bright irregular arch of Aurora extended from S. E. to W. N. W., the centre having about 60° of altitude. There was at this time a gentle westerly breeze, from which quarter the wind has been all day, light, and a *rime* fell, as last night, and again, as it seemed to me, proceeded from the Aurora.

14th. About 11h. p. m., there was an Aurora visible of a pale green hue, extending from S. E. towards W. S. W. in a regular arch, thence swerving to W. N. W.

15th. At 1h. a. m., the Aurora changed its position and appearance greatly, now proceeding from *E. S. E.*, in two branches, towards north and west. These united at about 50° altitude, N. W. of the zenith, and a large body of light between them passed through the zenith and joined the main branch or stem at their junction, thence a beautiful stream led nearly down to the horizon at N. W.

A fine Aurora at 10h. p. m. from *E. S. E.*, through the zenith, to W. N. W., in two broad streams, in vertical waves like a heavy curtain; the lights and shades beautifully alternating, and, as last night, the rays of a pale yellowish green hue.

16th. A very fine cold day; wind blowing strongly from N. N. W. until the afternoon, when it moderated. The evening calm, mild, and overcast. A very faint appearance of Aurora at midnight to the *S. E.*

17th. A little snow fell in the small hours, but the day became very fine, sunny, cloudless, and calm. The night fine and very clear. A beautiful pale-green 'curtain' Aurora from east, through the zenith, to west.

21st. A very little thin snow was falling this morning when we rose, but it soon ceased, and the day became fine and clear, a moderate breeze blowing from the N. W. The night calm and clear, with a light bank of clouds on the horizon at south and west; weather very mild. About 11h. p. m., a bright and extensive Aurora displayed itself, in the 'falling drapery form,' spreading from S. E. in a broad path, and passing about 20° west of zenith to west; the weather also became colder.

22d. A very beautiful day, but much colder than it has been of late. The evening very fine and cold. An Aurora visible at midnight, similar in position and appearance to that seen last night." —Ibid., pp. 171–72.

April, 1850.

"2d. At 10h. p. m., a bright Aurora visible from east to west.

3d. At 11h. p. m., a fine Aurora from E. by N. to W. by N.; centre about 70° altitude.

4th. At 10h. 30m. p. m., a firm but not brilliant Aurora visible, in parallel arcs, from E. N. E. to N. N. E.; centre of highest about 25°.

6th. At 11h. 30m. p. m., calm and very mild. From east up to the zenith a fine Aurora displayed, spread out above like a 'sea anemone.'

I have generally found the weather calm when the Aurora is thus shown in the zenith.

8th. An Aurora at 10h. p. m., similar to that of the 6th.

28th. At 9h. 30m. p. m., there were a few beautiful patches of Aurora to the eastward, colored pale yellowish-green, like the autumnal tint of the fading leaf.

30th. At 10h. 30m., a very faint ray of Aurora, of a pale green hue, extended from the visible horizon at east, towards the zenith, to about 40° of altitude."—Ibid., p. 173.

At Sea.—Lat. 65° N. Long. 63° W. September 28, 1818. Robertson.

"At 11h. p. m., observed the Aurora very brilliant *from S. by E. to S. by W.* It first appeared from behind a cloud at the altitude of 5°, shining with a silvery light; shortly after darting up small bundles of rays to the altitude of 16°.

There was no appearance of the Aurora in any other part of the heavens. Weather calm and clear at first appearance; a breeze soon sprung up from west, which shifted to S. W. Moderate weather."—1 John Ross (Robertson), App. 121.

N. B.—1. At 11h. p. m., very brilliant.
2. First appearance from behind a cloud.
3. No appearance of Aurora in any other part of the heavens.
4. Weather calm and clear.

At Sea.—Lat. 65° N. Long. 63° W. September 29, 1818. Robertson.

"At ten in the evening, the Aurora was seen very brilliant from *S. W. to S. E.*, true bearings, shooting rays to the altitude of 15°. In the morning of the 30th, the Aurora was spread all over the heavens.

Strong breezes from westward with clear weather, continuing to blow fresh from that quarter till past noon."—1 John Ross (Robertson), App. 121.

N. B.—1. At 10h. p. m., very brilliant.
2. A. M. 30th, spread all over the heavens.
3. Strong breezes from west; clear weather.

Fort Franklin.—Lat. 65° 12′ N. Long. 123° 12′ W. December, 1825. Franklin.

"The length of our shortest day did not exceed five hours, but the long nights were enlivened by most brilliant moonlight, and we had frequent and very fine appearances of the Aurora Borealis

The latter phenomenon made some of its grandest displays on the 26th of October, the 2d of November, and the 7th of December.

On all these occasions, the *disturbed motions of the magnetic needle were very remarkable*, and a most careful series of observations convinced the party that they had a close connection with the direction of the beams of light of which the Aurora was composed.

My observations also led me to conclude that the deviations of the needle were, in a certain degree, connected with *changes in the weather;* for, previous to a gale or a snow storm, the deviations were always considerable, but, during the continuance of the gale, the needle almost invariably remained stationary."—2 Franklin, 66.

N. B.—1. Grandest displays of Aurora.
2. Disturbed motions of the needle on these occasions very remarkable.
3 Deviations of the needle connected with changes in the weather.

Fort Franklin.—Lat. 65° 11′ 56″ N. Long. 123° 12′ 44″ W. February 14, 1826. FRANKLIN.

"On the 14th, at 45m. after nine a. m., the arched form of the *clouds*, and the appearance of a collection of rays projected from the sun's disk in the shape of a fan, strongly resembled the coruscations of the Aurora. The atmosphere was misty; temperature in the shade +8° 5′, and when the thermometer with a blackened bulb was exposed to the sun's rays, it rose to +43°.

The *magnetic needle*, at nine a. m., was perceived to have made a greater deviation to the westward than usual at that hour, and I imagine that the cause of this increase probably arose from the atmosphere being then in a state of electricity, similar to that in which it is when the Aurora appears in hazy weather; on which occasions we have observed that its coruscations have the strongest effect in causing aberrations of the needle."—2 Franklin, 72–3.

N. B.—1. Arched form of clouds noticed at 9h. 45m. a. m.
2. At 9h. a. m., magnetic needle was perceived to have made a greater deviation than usual.

Fort Franklin.—Lat. 65° 11′ 56″ N. Long. 123° 12′ 44″ W. 1825–26–27. FRANKLIN.

"The results of the observations on this phenomenon made during the present expedition coinciding with the remarks on the same subject given at much length in the Appendix to my former Narrative, I shall here confine myself to the mention of a few brief deductions from a careful examination of our registers at Bear Lake.

A careful review of the daily registers of the appearance of the Aurora, has led me to form the following general conclusions:—

1. That brilliant and active coruscations of the Aurora Borealis cause a deflection of the needle almost invariably, if they appear through a hazy atmosphere, and if the prismatic colors are exhibited in the beams or arches. When, on the contrary, the atmosphere is clear, and the Aurora presents a steady dense light of a yellow color, and without motion, the needle is often unaffected by its appearance.
2. That the Aurora is generally most active when it seems to have emerged from a cloud near the earth.
3. When the Aurora is very active, a haziness is very generally perceptible about the coruscations, though the other parts of the sky may be free from haze or cloud.
4. That the nearest end of the needle is drawn towards the point from whence the motion of the Aurora proceeds, and that its deflections are greatest when the motion is most rapid. The effect being the same whether the motion flows along a low arch or one that crosses the zenith.
5. That a low state of temperature seems favorable for the production of brilliant and active coruscations; it being seldom that we witnessed any that were much agitated, or that the prismatic tints were very apparent, when the temperature was above zero.
6. That the coruscations were less frequently visible between the first quarter and the full moon,

than in any other period of the lunation, and that they were most numerous between the third quarter and the new moon.

7. That the appearance of the Aurora was registered at Bear Lake, in 1825–26, 343 times, without any sound having been heard to attend its motions.

8. The height of the Aurora was not determined by actual observation; but its having been seen, on several occasions, to illuminate the under surface of some dense clouds, is conclusive that its elevation could not have been very great. When Dr. Richardson and Mr. Kendall made their excursion on Bear Lake, in the spring of 1826, the former saw the Aurora very brilliant and active, displaying the prismatic colors, in a cloudless sky (on the 23d of April); while Mr. Kendall, who was watching at the time, by agreement, for its appearance, did not see any coruscation, though he was only twenty miles distant from Dr. Richardson.

9. The gold-leaf electrometer, which was kept in the Observatory, was never affected by the appearance of the Aurora.

10. On four occasions, the coruscations of the Aurora were seen very distinctly before the daylight had disappeared, and we often perceived the clouds in the daytime disposed in streams and arches such as the Aurora assumes.

The opinions I have ventured to advance above, are at variance with the conclusions drawn by Captains Parry and Foster from their observations at Port Bowen; those officers inferring that the Aurora does not influence the motion of the needle. But the discrepancy may be perhaps explained by the difference in activity and altitude of the Aurora at the two places.

I have stated that the needle is most affected when the Aurora is very active and displays the prismatic colors. Captains Parry and Foster have informed me that the Aurora seen at Port Bowen was generally at a low altitude, without much motion in its parts, and never exhibiting the vivid prismatic colors, or the rapid streams of light, which are so frequently recorded in our registers of its appearance at Fort Enterprise and Fort Franklin. *At both these places, we as often witnessed the coruscations crossing the zenith* as at any other altitude, and under such a variety of forms, and in such rapid motion as to baffle description.

From the difference in the appearance and activity of the Aurora at Port Bowen and Forts Enterprise and Franklin, an inference may be deduced that *the parallel of 65° N. is more favorable for observing this phenomenon,* and its effect on the needle, than a higher northern latitude."—2 Franklin, cxlv–cxlvii.

N. B.—1. Brilliant coruscations cause a deflection of the needle.
2. Aurora most active when it emerges from a cloud near the earth.
3. When the Aurora is very active, a haziness is very perceptible about the coruscations.
4. The nearest end of the needle is drawn towards the point whence the motion of the Aurora proceeds.
5. A low state of temperature is favorable for the production of active coruscations.

Fort Franklin.—Lat. 65° 11′ 56″ N. Long. 123° 12′ 44″ W. October 26, 1825. FRANKLIN.

"An arch of 20° elevation, extending from *W. N. W. to E. N. E. by the north.* The motion of the light rushed at the first from the former to the latter point, and then backwards and forwards, and ultimately passed off to the southward. Needle stationary a few seconds. A beam shot along the arch from west by north, to east. Beam from north, across the zenith, to south horizon. Motion of light from W. N. W. along the arch. Motion from N. W. to N. E. at an elevation of 8°. Beam from north to the zenith. Needle stationary, the Aurora having disappeared. Interval of time—between 10h. 10m. and 10h. 30m. p. m.

Remarks on the 26th.—These coruscations were extremely brilliant, and in continual motion.

The principal feature was a broad band of light that extended along the northern part of the sky, *from W. N. W. to E. N. E.*, at an elevation of 20°, from which beams of a less intense light were frequently projected across the zenith *from north to south,* or in the contrary direction; and they sometimes reached the opposite horizon before they disappeared.

The band, as well as the beams, seemed to be composed of an infinite number of slender rays, which were highly inclined and exhibited the prismatic colors, the strongest tints being red, yellow, and green.

The whole of these coruscations appeared to be interposed between the spectator and a thin filmy mass of cloud."—2 Franklin, cxlviii.

October 27, 1825.

"A stream of light extending from E. N. E. to the north, at an elevation of 15°. The motion of its parts very rapid.

A beam from north to the zenith. On reaching that part, it instantly spread across the zenith, and its extremities were pointed S. W. by W. and E. N. E.

Another beam from north, which spread across the zenith as the former had done, having its points directed W. by S. and E. by N.

The whole coruscation then disappeared, and the needle gradually recovered its usual position. Interval of time—from midnight to ten minutes after that hour.

Remarks on the 27th.—It should be observed that there were two distinct issues of light from E. N. E. along the above-mentioned stream, which, on reaching the north point, rushed towards the zenith; and, in both instances, similar arches were formed across the zenith.

The needle betrayed the same course of deviation in both cases.

The motion of the light was extremely rapid."—Ibid., p. cxlix.

November 2, 1825.

"Motion of the Aurora rapid from S. S. E. to N. N. W. across the zenith. Arch the same; direction of motion not noted.

Arch across zenith from south to north; motion rapid.

Arch across zenith from N. N. W. to S.; motion N. N. W. to S. Aurora gradually disappearing, and needle stationary at the last position. Interval of time—between 10h. 30m. and 10h. 45m. p. m.

Remarks on the 2d.—The Aurora this night was extremely brilliant and active, and exhibited the prismatic tints.

The coruscations commenced with a highly illuminated arch, spreading *from S. E. to N. W.* across the zenith, in which part it formed a corona, from whence slender rays were projected *perpendicularly downwards*, giving to the coruscation the appearance of a globe with the meridians marked upon it.

This Aurora originally sprung *from a mass of cloud bearing S. S. E.*, which gradually changed its position to the eastward; and, on its reaching the east point, a band of light, resembling the fringe of a curtain, rushed forth and extended round the northern horizon at an elevation of 8°.

The corona disappeared at the time this latter change took place, and arches were projected in rapid succession from *S. S. E.* to *N. N. W.*, *S.* to *N.*, and from *N. N. W.* to *S.;* all of them displaying the most brilliant colors.

The needle betrayed its greatest deviation during the projection of the last-mentioned arches, and was, in fact, kept in a state of vacillation for about five minutes, approaching towards, or receding from, the true north, according to the apparent motion of the rays of light."—Ibid., p. cl.

December 7, 1825.

"A bright beam darted from an elevated arch towards the horizon at the N. N. W. point. A stream from E. S. E. to N. W., with a rapid vibratory motion in its parts. Coruscations in the form of a horseshoe; motion following that shape. Interval of time, between 11h. and 11h. 25m. p. m.

Remarks on the 7th.—The Aurora this night was very generally diffused, and extremely active and brilliant.

The most remarkable part of the coruscation was three perfect arches, at the several altitudes of 40°, 50°, and 90°, having the same points in the horizon. From the lowest of these arches, a beam flashed towards the horizon to N. N. W., which produced a change in the needle of 2° 45′, as above noted.

When these arches became faint, a mass of light rushed from E. S. E., and in its progress to the

N. W., in an horizontal direction, the rays of light of which the stream was composed were seen vibrating backwards and forwards, between the two extremes, in the most rapid manner.

During this commotion, which lasted ten minutes, the needle deviated between 39° 15′ and 41° 15′. It afterwards continued stationary for three minutes at 40° 45′, though the Aurora was violently agitated; but the motion of the light was then nearly circular, or in the form of a horseshoe, and confined to the zenith. The color of the light was faint red.

In a few seconds afterwards, the whole body of the light, being concentrated in the W. N. W. point, darted in an instant across the zenith to E. S. E., exhibiting in its progress a similar agitation in its rays to that already described.

The coruscation then branched off to the north, forming a broad band of light about 20° high, reassumed the horseshoe form at the latter point, and its rays undulated through every part of this figure like the waves of the sea or a rolling volume of smoke.

During these last-mentioned changes, the needle retraced its course, as shown in the last three notices, and remained stationary at 38° 5′, while the Aurora formed a zone that encircled the horizon at an elevation of 30°, in which shape it remained a few minutes and then disappeared."—Ibid., p. cli.

DECEMBER 8, 1825.

"Aurora visible. Motion from N. W. by N. along a band of light stretching to the eastward, elevated 15° and about 2° broad. The colors very vivid; motion rapid. Needle stationary for five minutes at this position. Motion returning from the eastward, along the band, to N. W. by N. The needle stationary at this position for five minutes, during which interval the light was rushing from each extreme of the band, meeting in the N. by E. point. There was but little display of color. The motion from the N. W. prevailed. A stream of light about 20° broad darted across the zenith from N. W. by N. to S. S. E. A beam darted from the zenith to N. W. by N., followed by the whole mass that had ascended from this point. Motion along the first-mentioned band from N. W. by N. to the eastward. A stream from N. W. by N. to the zenith. A beam from zenith to N. by E. Needle stationary for some minutes, the motion rolling from opposite directions of the arch that extended from N. W. by N. to east, and clashing in the centre. Motion from N. W. by N., in nearly a horizontal direction, to W. S. W. Stationary for five minutes. A stream of an irregular shape darted from N. W. by N. to S. S. E. across the zenith. Aurora generally diffused in filmy streams without motion. Motion from E. S. E. to N. W. by N. in a band similar to that first described. Interval of time, between midnight and 25 minutes after that hour.

At 1h. 20m. a. m., the Aurora appeared in an arch from N. E. to north, but motionless.

General Remarks.—The changes in the coruscations were so various and rapid as to render their description impossible. The band of light first mentioned as extending horizontally from N. W. by N. to the eastward, remained nearly the whole time."—Ibid., p. clii.

Fort Franklin.—Lat. 65° 11′ 56″ N. Long. 123° 12′ 44″ W. November, 1849. HOOPER.

"20th. The day pretty fine and calm. A fine Aurora in the night.

21st. Very fine, clear, and cold. A most splendid Aurora at night, spreading in waved lines all over the sky."—Hooper's Journal, p. 161.

DECEMBER, 1849.

"4th. Weather stormy, wind strong and squally from N. W. Late in the evening it cleared up a little, and a curious appearance of Aurora was visible to the northward, fringing the upper edge of a heavy 'nimbus.'

5th. Clear, very fine, and cold. Calm until towards sunset, when the wind rose from N. E. and increased much and quickly, coming in smart squalls, no doubt blowing with great force in an open space, our position being greatly sheltered.

The night fine and very cold; a few windy clouds in the sky. Fantastically flitting rays and streaks of Aurora visible, darting hither and thither through the heavens like lightning flashes. The stars very bright.

7th. A fine day, calm and very cold. A most lovely Aurora at night, extending from east, through north, to west, with coruscations towards the zenith.

8th. As I have generally observed to be the case, the Aurora of last evening was followed by a strong breeze, the weather completely changing during the night; the clear starlit sky becoming overcast with a heavy drift of clouds from N. E., from which quarter the wind was strong, accompanied by thickly falling and driving snow. The weather continued thus all day, and was, moreover, bitterly cold, but improved a little towards night, the wind and snow ceasing, and a few stars peeping out.

9th. The night was very fine; a gentle breeze from west, a cloudless sky, and a beautiful Aurora; which latter first formed in an arch from N. N. E. to N. N. W., but later appeared similar to that of the seventh, in broken and vertical rays, coruscating towards the zenith. The stars visible in myriads, and very bright.

11h p. m. I have just come in from viewing (aye, and listening to) the Aurora, which now presents a gorgeous spectacle. It has shifted from its first position, and now covers one-half of the heavens, from east, through south, to west. Oh, it is exquisite! I cannot describe it, for it is too splendid for description, even if viewed by a Byron, but I will try to set down an idea of it, although it can be but a faint one.

Orion is now bearing about S. S. W., and on each side of that constellation to about four points rays are converging very nearly to the zenith, while they are perfectly regular in distance one from the other, and in form remind me of the lines of longitude on a globe, like which, also, they are cut just below the zenith. Around and about them are wreaths and rolls, lines and curves, masses and skirmishers of the luminous fluid, never still for an instant, but waving and rolling, advancing and retiring, folding and unfolding, fast and changeful as thought can fly; never twice alike, but, like the fickle kaleidoscope, ever presenting some new appearance, beautiful and wondrous as those already seen and vanished. The converging curved rays before mentioned are just in shape, &c., as we see in those pictures where the Spirit of God is represented descending upon the Saviour in the form of a dove. I do not think nor write this with levity, for the phenomenon is too awe-inspiring to excite mirth or ridicule.

As the heavy curtain in a theatre is drawn up or let down, so are some of the flying lines expanding and contracting incessantly; others, again, seem heavy breakers, curling and turning under and about. There was one large mass, a perfect blaze of light, which seemed to be not twenty feet above me; others with less body appearing far, far away. It was a glorious sight, and I stood gazing in rapture, although not very poetical, until I found myself chilled throughout; but one who is privileged to view a scene like this can have little soul, little of the spirit contemplative, an he feel not his very heart-strings thrill with solemn joy at the sight.

And now, too, a question long doubted is by me doubted no more. I have *heard* the Aurora; not once, nor twice, merely, but many times; not faint nor indistinct, but loud and unmistakable; now from this quarter, now from that; now from on high, and again from low down. At first it seemed to be like a field of ice cracking, then like the distant stroke of an axe; again it resembled the noise of pile driving by a monkey, and at last like the whirring of a cannon-shot when heard from a short distance. Once, three like this followed in rapid succession, and I thought I could see the mass whence the sounds proceeded tumbling or vibrating.[1]

The night is intensely cold, the sky perfectly clear, the stars showing as brilliantly through the illumined fluid as where the 'lights' are not; the wind is moderate from N. N. W. I have no doubt that we shall have heavy weather after this display. I have read that in other northern voyages, the sound of the Aurora resembles the cracking of a whip, but to-night I heard nothing like this, to my idea.

In a few minutes, the character of the phenomenon changed, the tremors and rays all disappearing, and nought now appeared to view but a long low arch from E. S. E. to S. W., banking a rising

---

[1] This error respecting the Aurora's sound affords a curious indication of the power of imagination in assisting delusion.

mass of clouds, but I still heard occasionally the sounds as before, now much subdued and less frequent. The night continued calm, but became cloudy.

11th. Snowing and blowing hard all day. The sky clearing a little at night, a fine Aurora was visible, and the wind increased to a strong gale, in which the squalls were very violent.

12th. Still blowing hard all day from the same quarter, N. W., as yesterday; the snow driving fast and furious. The Aurora at night was very fine, the wind having gradually decreased from sunset, and the night became very calm and fine. We again heard the cracking sounds, and our fisherman had a fine laugh at my sounding Aurora, saying that the noise is only that of the ice cracking on Bear Lake; but this solution of the question was not at all to my taste, and I retired to rest perfectly satisfied that it was caused by the Aurora, and not the ice.

13th. Fine and cold, with little wind. All my enthusiastic ideas respecting the Aurora's sound are dispelled, and I find that I have, to use a vulgar phrase 'found a mare's nest,' for those noises which I before heard with so much rapture, as belonging to an exquisite and wondrous phenomenon, were this morning repeated in broad daylight, and are, I now see, unmistakably caused by the ice cracking. A moderate breeze in the evening from N. E.; weather cloudy.

17th. A moderate breeze from N. W.; cloudy and cold. The night set in pretty clear, but with the wind strong and squally from N. W. Late in the night, a fine Aurora was visible to the *southward.*

18th. Very fine and clear weather; breeze moderate from W. N. W. Towards evening the sky became cloudy, but in the night was clear, and displayed the 'merry dancers' to advantage; the wind being then fresh from westward.

19th. Colder by far than yesterday; very fine, and, in the morning, calm. About midday, a moderate breeze sprung up from N. E., but the night was calm, fine, and clear.

Aurora was visible in, at first, thin bright streaks, and later in a long arch from *E. S. E.* to *S. W.;* and *another*, with less length and of greater altitude, from N. N. W. to N. E. The stars brilliant as gems.

20th. The day was very fine and calm, but the cold penetrated through all covering; even our fisherman was forced to return before his usual time.

At night we saw a lovely Aurora. At one time it was like this , the point being to the eastward, and the flourish reaching half way down to the western horizon, breaking at the extremity into perpendicular lines. The night calm and very fine.

22d. Light mizzling snow during the day, with a light air from the westward. Last night we observed a fair Aurora; masses of light rolling and tumbling over each other incessantly, and apparently very low. The weather has completely changed since yesterday, being now cloudy and very mild. A slight Aurora to the westward visible this evening.

27th. Very fine, clear, and cold; a fresh breeze from W. N. W. The night like that of yesterday; wind light from west. Our breath was distinctly audible out of doors, and our fisherman got frostbitten on the cheek on returning from the nets. Some time about midnight, a pretty but not brilliant Aurora was visible, of a pale green hue.

30th. Cloudy and mild; a light breeze from the N. W. Read prayers to the party. The evening fine; a moderate breeze from the west. A bright Aurora visible, extending in an irregular semicircle, of considerable altitude at the vertex, from east towards west.

31st. Very fine and not very cold. A fresh breeze from W. N. W. in the morning; the remainder of the day and the evening calm.

A fine Aurora visible this evening, extending from the horizon at N. N. W. to E. by N., its altitude in the centre about 15°, with vertical coruscations."—Ibid., pp. 162–65.

JANUARY, 1850.

"1st. The Aurora seen last evening changed its position as the moon neared the horizon, progressing before she appeared regularly and gradually towards *south.*

3d. The breeze continued all day, but with less violence than yesterday. The weather still cloudy and mild. At night, before the moon rose, I observed an Aurora from N. E. by E. to N. by W., over a heavy 'incubus,' at about 15° altitude.

4th. The day cloudy and mild. In the evening, an Aurora visible from N. by W. to N. E., of which I give one phase; but it was ever changing in appearance.

8th. About an hour before daybreak, there was a curious Aurora visible. Late in the day, the wind became fresh, and, accompanied by a fine driving snow, made the weather very cold. The evening was cold, with a little snow; and moderate wind from west. Aurora showing all night, flying about all over the sky.

9th. The night was at first very cold, the breath being slightly audible, but later the weather became calm, misty, and much milder. A fine Aurora was visible.

10th. At night the wind was fresh, a little snow fell, and the temperature was very low. A faint Aurora visible, similar in form and position to that of last night.

11th. The night calm and cold. Aurora during the night to the northward.

12th. Before daylight, a fine Aurora was displayed to the *southward*, afterwards shifting to the north. A moderate breeze from the west.

13th. A fine Aurora was visible about three hours before daybreak to the southward; the sky clear. The day very fine, calm, and tolerably mild; a haze on the horizon. Read prayers. The night fine and cold; the breath being audible. Beautiful phases of the Aurora visible during the night in all parts of the sky.

14th. Here it was quite calm, but on the Lake there was a very fresh breeze from the west. Very fine appearances of the Aurora all night; uncolored, and inconstant in position.

15th. Last night and this morning there fell a sort of rime, which was in so minute particles as to be almost invisible. I fancy this must be frozen dew; perhaps it is this which forms the Auroræ by reflection from the snow. The night fine and very cold. Beautiful Auroras throughout.

16th. We consider this the coldest day we have had here, the wind being strong and squally from N. E. In the sunshine to-day, I observed the atmosphere crowded with frozen particles sparkling brilliantly, like motes in a sunbeam. All night, beautiful phases of Aurora visible.

17th. The night was cold and clear; Auroras showing all night. It is impossible to picture them, so various and inconstant were their positions and forms.

18th. Very fine; not a speck in the sky. The sun's warmth is now beginning to be perceptible, but the air is, notwithstanding, very cold. A light breeze from the west.

The night fine and cold; Aurora displayed in a very beautiful manner; all the sky from *E. S. E.*, through north, to west, was covered with broken vertical lines in waves coruscating towards the zenith, and in slight motion. To the *southward*, was a long low arch, of perhaps 15° altitude at the centre. There was a light northwesterly air.

22d. Just after sunset, the wind increased greatly, becoming also squally, and the weather getting correspondingly cold. Beautiful Auroras during the night.

25th. Very fine and clear; wind N.W., moderate; the same on the Great Bear Lake; the weather mild. The night very fine, and, late, cold.

Beautiful Auroras visible, one of which, extending from E. N. E. to N. W., was shaped like a huge mustache, its centre about 20° north of the zenith. Another appeared as below attempted.

27th. The night very fine and very cold, the breath being again audible. Calm on Bear Lake.

When the moon had risen to about 12′ of altitude, there was a very pretty Aurora about her; the rays tinted pale yellowish-green, which hue I have always observed them to take when the moon is near the full.

Beautiful 'tremors' all night, moving rapidly over the heavens, and of the same pale-green hue. Whenever I have seen these rapid movements of the Aurora, *wind* has shortly followed."—Ibid., p. 167.

FEBRUARY, 1850.

"1st. Last night was very cold, and Aurora was displayed in a beautiful manner from N. E. to N. in 'tremors' and rolling folds.

The evening was very cold, fine, and clear. About 10h. p. m., we viewed one of the most exquisite spectacles we ever beheld. The Aurora had been for some time visible, and it now spread over all the sky, excepting to the southward, and kept an incessant motion, whirling, dancing, and darting around with lightning-like rapidity. All the colors of the rainbow were displayed by turns, visible at one instant, and in the next succeeded by another hue. There was a perpetually shifting fringe, at one moment of an exquisite violet, and then again of a grass-green tint; these were the predominant colors, but all others, in every variety of shade, were here and there shown. A more exquisite or more gorgeous spectacle cannot be imagined. I shall never again begrudge the time spent in our exile here, since in it I have been privileged to enjoy so perfect a specimen of the king wonder of natural phenomena.

We knew very well that this appearance betokened wind, and this rose with the moon about three hours later, the Aurora of course becoming faint as the darkness decreased.

2d. The wind blew freshly all night from the N. E., and did not abate any with sunrise. In the afternoon, it increased considerably, and the sky became covered with clouds; 'cumulus' above, and 'stratus' on the horizon. The weather clear; a slight snow drift.

I am more than ever confirmed in my conviction that the *Aurora is frozen dew or vapor*, illumined by, or rather reflecting, the light of the frozen masses round the pole, or perhaps only by that from the surrounding snow-clad earth. That it must be congealed vapor suspended in the atmosphere and existing in atomic particles, I hold to more than all, from its instant motion with the slightest breeze, and from the resemblance of that motion, when the mass is strongly excited, to that of a cloud of dust raised by a strong breeze; the same eddy-like twisting, the same rolling and folding motion, and of one volume into and over another, &c.

7th. Late last night there were beautiful 'tremors' visible, principally displayed near the zenith. A fresh breeze set in from the N. E., but declined at daybreak.

12th. The Aurora was finely displayed last night in 'tremors,' and this morning there was a strong breeze from the west, with a heavy snow drift.

13th. A strong breeze all day from westward, and a heavy drift, moderating at night, which was fine. Aurora dully displayed in two long arches, one to the *north* and the other to the *southward.*

14th. Pretty fine; a fresh breeze from west both here and on the lake; weather not very cold; the night mild and rather cloudy. Aurora displayed in much the same manner as last night, and, towards morning, brightly and in various directions.

15th. Very fine and very mild. The night calm and fine, displaying Aurora as in the early part of last night.

16th. A most lovely day; clear, warm, and sunny, thawing in the sun. A light northerly air here; calm on the Great Lake. In the evening, the clouds gathered over to the east and south, threatening wind. In the night, there was a beautiful Aurora all over the sky, in vertical short rays, rolling and folding over each other, while at *W. by S.* a segment commenced, leading towards the zenith eastward, but breaking and mingling with the mass of Aurora at about 60° altitude."—Ibid., pp. 168–70.

Duke of York's Bay (Southampton Island).—Lat. 65° 28′ 13″ N. Long. 84° 40′ 07″ W. August 15, 1821. PARRY.

"The Aurora Borealis was visible during the whole of the night, consisting of many luminous patches or nebulæ, having, when viewed together, a tendency to form an arch, and extending from *south by east to southwest, and sometimes to west,* its height in the centre being 15°. From this arch, pencils of rays shot upwards towards the zenith.

It differed from any other phenomenon of this kind that I have seen, in being at times of a beautiful orange color."—2 Parry, 39.

At Sea.—Lat. 65° 50′ N. Long. 61° W. September 26, 1818. ROBERTSON.

"About nine in the evening, the Aurora Borealis was seen very brilliant in every point of bearing, shooting bundles of rays of unequal length to the zenith.

This Aurora was first seen through *a thick mist in the zenith;* as the mist passed away the Aurora increased in brilliancy; the stars shone bright; not a cloud to be seen. At eleven, the Aurora became less brilliant, and the sky again obscured with mist. The horizon continued hazy till two next morning, when the Aurora was again seen very brilliant in *the zenith.*"—1 John Ross (Robertson), App. 120.

Winter Island.—Lat. 66° 11′ 25″ N. Long. 83° 10′ W. December, 1821. LYON.

"As we now had seen the darkest, although not by many degrees the coldest, season of the year, it may not be irrelevant to mention the beautiful appearance of the sky at this period.

The Aurora Borealis does not appear affected by the brilliancy even of the full moon, but its light continues still the same. The first appearance of this phenomenon is generally in showers of falling rays, like those thrown from a rocket, although not so bright. These, being in constant and agitated motion, have the appearance of trickling down the sky. Large masses of light succeeded next in order, alternating from a faint glow, resembling the milky way, to the most vivid flashes, which stream and shoot in every direction with the effect of sheet lightning, except that after the flash the Aurora still continues to be seen.

The sudden glare and rapid bursts of these wondrous showers of fire render it impossible to observe them without fancying that they produce a rushing sound; but I am confident *there is no actual noise attending the changes, and that the idea is erroneous.* I frequently stood for hours together on the ice, to ascertain this fact, at a distance from any noise but my own breathing, and thus I formed my opinion.

Neither did I observe *any variety of color* in the flashes, which were to my eye always of the same shade as the milky way and vivid sheet lightning.

The stars which gleam through the Aurora certainly emit a milder ray, as if a curtain of the finest gauze were interposed.

It is remarkable that *whenever the weather is calm,* the Aurora has a tendency to form an arch at whatever position it may occupy in the heavens.

On the 29th of this month, we were particularly gratified by a beautiful exhibition of this kind at near midnight. A perfect arch was formed to the *southward, stretching from east to west;* its centre elevated about 2° above the horizon.

The night was serene and dark, which added considerably to its effect, and the appearance continued unchanged for about a quarter of an hour; *but, on a slight breeze springing up,* small rays shot occasionally to the zenith, and the arch became agitated with a gentle and undulating motion, after which it spread irregularly, and, separating into the usual streamers, soon diffused itself over the whole sky.

In stormy weather, the Northern Lights fly with the rapidity of lightning, and with a corresponding wildness to the gale which is blowing, giving an indescribable air of magic to the whole scene." —Lyon, pp. 99–101.

MAY 30, 1822.

"In the afternoon, a most singular phenomenon was observed in the heavens. The western sky was blue and cloudless, while overhead it was hazy, and abounding in what sailors call 'mackerel and mares' tails.' The division of colors was by a most perfect arch, the legs of which stood in the N. E. and S. W. A strong breeze from the westward did not in any way affect the edge of the bow, which was clearly defined.

With the legs stationary, the whole clouded part receded, or fell slowly to the eastward, in the same manner as the hood of a carriage is thrown back, until by degrees, and after the expiration of two hours, the sky was all of the same pure azure as had at first been seen in the west. A strong wind continued blowing all night."—Ibid., p. 204.

Winter Island.—Lat. 66° 11′ 25″ N. Long. 83° 10′ W. November 15–16, 1821. Parry.

"At thirty minutes past nine a. m. on the 15th, the weather being rather cloudy and a light breeze blowing from the southward, the electrometer was tried, and again at nine p. m. on the 16th, at which time the *Aurora Borealis*, consisting of a stationary white light near the horizon, was visible in the *S. by E.* quarter of the heavens; but in neither case was the gold-leaf in the slightest degree affected."—2 Parry, 133.

N. B.—1. At 9h. 30m. a. m. electrometer tried, and again on the 16th at 9h. p. m.;
2. At which time Aurora Borealis was visible in the S. by E. quarter—stationary light;
3. But in neither case was the gold leaf affected.

November 17–18, 1821.

"At 8h. p. m. of the 17th, the Aurora Borealis was seen, consisting of *a stationary light* occupying a very small portion of the heavens *in the S. E. by E. quarter*, and close to the horizon, from which, at times, vivid flashes shot across the zenith nearly to the opposite horizon.

After ten p. m., the stationary light shifted more to the southward, and then gradually disappeared.

At ten p. m. on the 18th, this phenomenon assumed a similar appearance in the S. by W. quarter." —Ibid., p. 133.

November 23–24, 1821.

"On the evening of the 23d, the Aurora Borealis made its appearance in the *northwest*, vivid coruscations shooting at times *across the zenith to the opposite horizon.* The gold leaf of the *electrometer* was not perceptibly affected by it.

On the morning of the 24th, it was again faintly seen in irregular streams of white light, extending from the *western horizon to the zenith.* For several hours the same night, also, this extraordinary phenomenon was visible from the *southeast, round by south, to west,* being principally confined to a space about five degrees above the horizon.

The magnetic needle, which was attentively watched, *was not at all affected by any of these phenomena.*"—Ibid., p. 135.

N. B.—1. Gold leaf of electrometer not affected.
2. Magnetic needle not at all affected.

November 26–28, 1821.

"On the 26th, both in the morning and evening, the Aurora again appeared from *S. E. to S. W.*, the brightest part being about ten degrees above the horizon, and with pencils of rays shooting upwards towards the zenith. In *almost every instance*, it is observable that the light, however irregularly disposed in other respects, has *a tendency to assume an arch-like* form; but I think a plane bisecting the arch would more generally have *coincided with the true than the magnetic meridian* in the phenomena we had here an opportunity of observing. This was particularly the case on the morning of the 27th, when, at 6h. a. m., the Aurora formed *one broad, continuous, and well-defined arch*, its centre passing rather to the southward of the zenith, and its legs appearing to rest upon *the horizon at east and west.*

For several hours on the evening of the 28th, it was seen *in the S. E.* with rays darting rapidly up nearly as high as the zenith. There is almost always *one stationary patch of light* near the horizon, appearing, as it were, *the source* whence the shifting or variable part of the phenomenon proceeds.

It will be seen from about this period, *how much more frequently* the Aurora seemed to issue *from the southeastern quarter than from any other* during the rest of the winter."—Ibid., p. 135.

N. B.—1. Appeared from S. W. to S. E. (26th).
2. However irregularly disposed in other respects, has a tendency to assume an arch-like form.
3. Plane bisecting the arch generally coincided with the true meridian.
4. Evening of 28th, seen in S. E.
5. Almost always a stationary patch of light near the horizon.
6. From about this period, Aurora seemed to issue more frequently from S. E. quarter than from any other.

DECEMBER 2–3, 1821.

"The concluding month of this year presented more frequent as well as more brilliant displays of the Aurora Borealis than we had noticed at an earlier period of the winter.

On the evening of the 2d, we observed it constantly appearing, from five till ten o'clock, in one quarter of the heavens or another, but *entirely confined to the southern side of the zenith.* It consisted sometimes of luminous blotches or small clouds; at others, of coruscations shooting upwards, and a stationary light always perceptible near the horizon from *S. S. E. to S. W.* The light was white or yellowish-white, and the compass was not affected.

On the evening of the 3d, it also appeared in little white spots, *resembling the nebulæ* in the heavens, as viewed by a telescope, or the milky way on a very clear night.

I may here remark, by the way, that this last beautiful feature of the heavens very seldom appeared here, for, notwithstanding the notion generally entertained of *the extreme clearness* of the atmosphere under a polar sky, *we have always found the very reverse to be the fact.* It is true, indeed, that, with a northerly or westerly wind, the sky was generally what *would be called clear; but there is scarcely one night in twenty* when the heavenly bodies, if viewed through a telescope, do not appear surrounded with more or less haze. Indeed, it very seldom happens that a considerable deposition of minute snow may not be observed to take place, even in the clearest nights, in these regions."—Ibid., p. 141.

N. B.—1. Aurora entirely confined to the south side of the zenith.
2. Appeared in little white spots resembling the nebulæ.
3. Instead of the extreme clearness of atmosphere under a polar sky, we have always found the very reverse to be the fact.

DECEMBER 4, 1821.

"While making lunar observations on the evening of the 4th, Mr. Ross and myself remarked a meteor falling from the S. E. to N. W., being about 40° high when it disappeared. It fell so slowly as to be visible for four or five seconds, but was in every other respect like the falling stars, as they are called, seen in other parts of the world.

At 11h. p. m., the Aurora was seen forming an arch, about 5° high in the centre and extending *from S. S. W. to S. E.* The magnetic needle of Alexander's compass was not perceptibly affected during its continuance."—Ibid., p. 142.

DECEMBER 14, 1821.

"On the afternoon of the 14th, the Aurora began to show itself as soon as it was dark, consisting principally of rays shooting up from the horizon, *in the E. by N.*, towards the zenith, and sometimes passing through but very little beyond it towards the opposite side of the heavens. Just before ten o'clock, however, a much finer display of this phenomenon presented itself than we had yet seen this season.

There still remained a place near the horizon at *E. by N.*, whence a bright light seemed constantly to issue; and if any part of the phenomenon could be said to continue uniformly the same, it was the leg of a broadish arch in that point, which scarcely ever changed its place or the intensity of its light.

The arch was at times completed, or thrown over to the *W. S. W.*, being 15° high in the centre and generally about 2° broad, though in this respect it was irregular and somewhat variable. The lower part of the arch was always well defined, the space under it appearing dark, as if a black cloud had been there, which, however, was not the case, as we saw the stars in it unobscured except by the light of the *Aurora.* The upper side of the arch was never well defined, but its light was gradually softened off so as to mingle with the azure of the sky, and often sent up coruscations towards the zenith.

Thus far description may give some faint idea of this brilliant and extraordinary phenomenon, because its figure here maintained some degree of regularity; but during the most part of its continuance it is, I believe, almost impossible to convey to the minds of others an adequate conception of the truth. It is with much deference, therefore, that I offer the following description, the only recommendation of which, perhaps, is, that it was written immediately after witnessing this magnificent display.

Innumerable streams or bands of white and yellowish light appeared to occupy the greater part of the heavens *to the southward of the zenith, being much the brightest in the S. E. and E. S. E.,* from whence it had, indeed, often the appearance of emanating. Some of these streams of light were in right lines like rays; others crooked, and waving in all sorts of irregular figures and moving with inconceivable rapidity in various directions. Among these might frequently be observed those shorter collections or bundles of rays which, moving with even greater velocity than the rest, have acquired the name of the 'merry dancers,' which, if I understand aright the descriptions given of them by others, I do not think I ever saw before.

In a short time, the Aurora extended itself *over the zenith about half way down to the northern horizon, but no farther, as if there was something in that quarter of the heavens which it did not dare to approach.* About this time, however, some long streamers shot up from the horizon in the N. W., which soon disappeared.

While the light extended over part of the northern heavens, there were a number of rays assuming a circular or radiated form near the zenith, and appearing to have a common centre near that point, from which they all diverged. The light of which these were composed appeared to have inconceivably rapid motion in itself, though the form it assumed, and the station it occupied in the heavens, underwent little or no change for perhaps a minute or more.

Suppose, for instance, a stream of light to have occupied a space between any two of the stars, by which its position could be accurately noticed, the light appeared to pass constantly and instantaneously from one to the other, as if, when a portion of the subtle fluid of which it is composed had made its escape and vanished at the end next one of the stars, a fresh supply was uninterruptedly furnished at the other. This effect is a common one with the Aurora, and puts one in mind, as far as its motion alone is concerned, of a person holding a long ribbon by one end, and giving it an undulatory motion through its whole length, though its general position remains the same. One of the most striking of the various locomotive properties of the Aurora is that which it often has laterally, by which I mean in the direction perpendicular to its length. This motion, when compared with the other, is usually slow, though still very rapid in the 'merry dancers,' which seem to observe no law with regard to the rest of the phenomenon. When the streams or bands were crooked, the convolutions took place indifferently in all directions.

The Aurora did not continue long to the north of the zenith, but remained as high as that point for more than an hour; after which, on the moon rising, it became more and more faint, and at half past eleven was no longer visible. The color of the light was most frequently yellowish-white, sometimes greenish, and once or twice a lilac tinge was remarked when several strata, as it were, appeared to overlay each other by very rapidly meeting, in which case the light was always increased in intensity.

The *electrometer* was tried several times, and two of Kater's compasses exposed upon the ice during the continuance of this Aurora, but neither was perceptibly affected by it.

We listened attentively for any *noise* which might accompany it, *but could hear none;* but it was too cold to keep the ears uncovered very long at one time.

The intensity of the light was something greater than that of the moon in her quarters. Of its dimming the stars, there cannot, I think, be a doubt. We remarked it to be, in this respect, like drawing a gauze veil over the heavens in that part, the veil being most thick when two of the luminous sheets met and overlapped.

The phenomenon had all the appearance of being full as near as many of the clouds commonly seen, but there were none of the latter to compare them with at the time.

I may, in conclusion, remark that, notwithstanding the variety and changeableness displayed by this Aurora, there was throughout a perceptible inclination in the various parts of it to form an irregular arch from E. by N. over to S. W. by W."—Ibid., pp. 142–144.

N. B.—1. Magnificent display.

2. Electrometer not affected.

3. Listened attentively, but could hear no noise.

4. Intensity of light greater than that of the moon in her quarters.

5. Aurora appeared to be fully as near as many of the clouds commonly seen.

DECEMBER 20, 1821.

"From 7h. till 10h. p. m. on the 20th, while engaged in making observations upon the ice, we observed the *Aurora* almost constantly appearing, though varying in its form and situation. It commenced with a number of vertical coruscations *from the S. E., S., and N. W.* horizons, darting nearly as high as the zenith. This being discontinued after half an hour, the leg of an arch appeared at *E. S. E.* inclining towards the south, which remained nearly unaltered for three-quarters of an hour, its light being of a yellow cast and remarkably brilliant. After this an arch was gradually formed by the light extending over to *W. N. W.*, the brightest portion of it being still that in the eastern quarter. The arch was irregular, and sometimes not continuous, but divided into a number of luminous patches like *nebulæ.*

We also noticed, and now remembered to have done so *once before*, that there were in some places narrow but long horizontal separations of the light, appearing like so many dark parallel streaks lying over it, which, however, they were not, as the stars were here most plainly visible.

The *magnetic needle was not affected.*

This night was one of the clearest we had during the winter, the milky way appearing unusually bright and well defined."—Ibid., p. 144.

N. B.—1. From 7h. till 10h. p. m., Aurora constantly appearing.
2. Commenced with vertical coruscations from the S. E., S., and N. W. horizons.
3. Arch from E. S. E. to W. N. W.
4. The magnetic needle was not affected.
5. One of the clearest nights of the winter.

DECEMBER 22, 1821.

"On the 22d, the electrometer was tried, the wind being light from the N. W., with overcast weather, and some very small snow falling; but no perceptible effect was produced upon the gold leaf.

In the evening, the *Aurora* appeared like a white cloud in the E. S. E. At half past nine, an irregular arch extended from that point of the horizon to the S. W., the breadth being from one to two degrees, though constantly varying, and its height in the middle ten degrees.

When this kind of arch appears most perfect, it is less frequently than any other kind attended with coruscations or very rapid motion in the light. When these do accompany it, they are almost invariably observed to proceed from the upper side of the arch only."—Ibid., p. 145.

N. B.—1. Electrometer tried; no effect on the gold leaf.
2. Aurora appeared like a white cloud in the S. E.

DECEMBER 23, 1821.

"In the evening of the 23d, though the wind was from the N. W., a number of small roundish clouds, very unusual here at this season, rose from *the S. E.*, and the sky was very prettily illuminated in the intervals by the Aurora. These clouds remaining quite dark in their appearance, except about their edges, even during the most brilliant display of the Aurora, seemed to indicate that the latter phenomenon was the most distant of the two. The light of the Aurora was, *as usual, much the brightest in the S. E. quarter.*

This phenomenon again made its appearance very beautifully on the 24th, resembling, in most particulars, that described on the 14th. It was principally confined to the *southern half* of the heavens, and the streamers and coruscations, though almost infinitely varied, had an evident tendency to arch from E. by S. over to the opposite horizon.

The 'merry dancers' were also playing about with indescribable rapidity, and many of the sheets of light, when they overlapped in meeting, had a very perceptible lilac tinge."—Ibid., p. 145.

DECEMBER 28, 1821.

"On the morning of the 28th, the Aurora Borealis appeared faintly to the *westward* from four to six o'clock. Early on the following morning, it was observed to form an arch of very bright light *from S. E. to S. S. W.*, its centre being 30° high. In its general form it was quite stationary, as, indeed, the more perfect arches usually are, but varied occasionally in the intensity of the light and also in its continuity.

From the time that the daylight began to leave the heavens in the afternoon, the *Aurora* again appeared, commencing in the *S. E. by E.* with very long coruscations or streamers, which afterwards shot past the zenith over to the N. W.

At nine o'clock, the light had become concentrated into a low arch, 4° high in the centre, well defined at the lower edge, but not so at the upper. The legs were at first situated in the E. S. E. and S. W. by W. quarters, but the former gradually shifted about two points more to the south.

At one time in the evening, and before the phenomenon had assumed the more regular arch-like form above mentioned, we observed for the space of a few minutes together the same radiated appearance about the zenith as that described on the 14th. This changed pretty suddenly into an irregularly circular band of light, like a ribbon, and then again returned to the radiated form, but neither of these appearances continued very long. There was a great deal of lilac tint observable this evening, and the effect of the sheets of light in obscuring the stars was again too evident to admit a doubt.

The frequency and ill success with which we had tried the electrometer made us almost despair of ever detecting any electricity in the atmosphere, but on the evening of the 13th, the chain being observed to tremble very much, we thought the motion might have been occasioned by this cause. On applying the electrometer, however, the gold leaf was not in the slightest degree affected. We afterwards found it to have arisen from the wind acting upon the plank at the masthead in a certain angle, the same effect being once or twice afterwards produced with a breeze in the same direction."—Ibid., pp. 145–146.

JANUARY 14, 1822.

"There was to-day a very thick deposit of snow almost constantly occurring, though the weather might very well be called clear. The winter atmosphere of these regions is, indeed, seldom or never free from it, as may readily be seen by placing an instrument in the open air for an hour or two. That of to-day only differed from the usual deposit in the degree in which it took place.

At one p. m., a thermometer on the north side of the post, on the ice, stood at —32°, and the other, exposed to the sun's rays on the south side, only indicated a temperature one degree higher."—Ibid., p. 153.

JANUARY 13, 1822.

"The appearances of the Aurora Borealis during January were generally more distinguished for their frequency than their brilliancy or for any extraordinary forms which this phenomenon presented.

Towards midnight on the 13th, the weather being clear, it appeared in a very bright arch from *S. to N. E.*, being 10° to 15° higher in the centre. It afterwards assumed a wavy or serpentine form, which constantly varied; and smaller streams of light seemed to be continually meeting the larger from near the zenith.

From midnight till 2h. a. m. (on the 14th), it continued very bright, and generally extended *from east, where it was most brilliant, to W. N. W.*"—Ibid., p. 155.

JANUARY 15, 1822.

"The following evening [the 15th], an arch of the Aurora assumed the most perfect bridge-like form I ever saw. It extended *from S. E. to N. W., on the southern side of the heavens;* both its edges being well defined, which is very rarely the case.

At 7h. a. m. on the following morning, it appeared again in a form still more novel, *three complete arches* being now visible; the middle one, which was the brightest, passing through the zenith, and the others, which were in the centre, about 20° distant from it on each side, gradually closing till they joined it at the east and west points of the horizon.

It was impossible not to be struck with the general resemblance in the form of this phenomenon to that I have frequently mentioned as assumed by the *clouds* in the polar regions at particular seasons.[1] *This coincidence may possibly serve to throw some light on the nature and peculiarities of the Aurora.*

---

[1] Account of the Voyage of 1819–20, pp. 141, 144, 164.

For several hours on the same night, this meteor formed a tolerably well-defined *arch from E. S. E. to W. N. W.*, being 6° high in the centre, reaching from one horizon to the other, and *confined entirely to the southern side of the heavens.*

Early on the morning of the 16th, it was seen for an hour and a quarter much in the same situation, and on the following evening it appeared faintly *in almost every part of the heavens.*"—Ibid., pp. 155–56.

N. B.—Resemblance in form of Aurora; this coincidence may possibly serve to throw some light on the nature and peculiarities of the Aurora.

JANUARY 18, 1822.

"From 11h. p. m. till past midnight, on the 18th, it once more appeared very bright from *W.* to *S. E.*, having at times a very rapid and irregular motion. Whenever the light was most concentrated it was also the brightest, and almost always in that case we observed it to assume an arch-like form in the southern part of the heavens.

This was particularly the case on the evening of the 19th, when there appeared two concentric though not altogether continuous arches, extending from *S. E. by E.* to *W. S. W.*, the highest being 8° to 10° above the horizon, but in this respect at times slowly varying. At 11h. p. m., after thus remaining, without any very remarkable alteration, for above two hours, it suddenly became extremely variable, shifting its place *laterally* with a prodigously rapid motion, but still keeping within the general limits above mentioned both in bearing and altitude. In this lateral motion, which was somewhat of the kind I have endeavored to describe on the 14th of December, it seemed, as it were, to *roll* over from one end of the arch to the other, while at the same time numberless lighter and less brilliant coruscations were emitted from its upper margin.

Whenever the phenomenon occupied the smallest space in the heavens, the light was invariably the most intense, and often when several sheets of it appeared to unite, in the manner before explained, the lilac tint was quite vivid; in general its color was yellowish. Stars of the second magnitude were almost obscured by it.

Towards the end of January, this phenomenon appeared frequently in the *S. E.* and *E. S. E.*, but it was generally faint, and unmarked by any peculiarity requiring further notice.

The electrometer was frequently applied to the mast-head chain, and the magnetic needle constantly watched during all these appearances, but neither of these was on any one occasion sensibly affected."—Ibid., pp. 156–57.

MARCH, 1822.

"The appearance of the Aurora Borealis was less frequent during March than in the preceding winter months, in consequence of the increased duration of daylight at this period. Whatever slight variations might exist in these appearances, it still continued a matter of constant remark to us, that the phenomenon almost invariably commenced in the *southeastern* quarter of the heavens; and it is perhaps worthy of notice, that the same thing was observed by Crantz in Greenland (whose very words would truly describe what we so frequently noticed during this winter).

The arch-like form assumed by the Aurora was also one of its almost invariable peculiarities; the legs of the arch being usually situated somewhere between the east and west points of the horizon, and almost always occupying the *southern side* of the heavens.

The only instance of this phenomenon during the month of March deserving particular description, occurred on the evening of the 30th, when it made its appearance as usual in the *southeastern* horizon, from whence it soon diffused itself in a low but tolerably regular arch extending to the *W. S. W.* Again, at times, it altogether vanished, and then as suddenly reappeared much in the same situation as before.

We often fancied that this phenomenon exhibited a light of greater actual intensity when the moon was above the horizon than at other times, though its appearance was of course less splendid on that account. Whether this was in reality the case or not, we had no means of correctly judging; but some idea of its brightness may be formed from the circumstance of its being very often distinctly visible when the moon was between her quarters and the full.

The electrometer was tried during the continuance of this evening's Aurora, but no effect was perceptible either on that or a Kater's compass."—Ibid., p. 200.

April 4, 1822.

"The phenomenon frequently observed at Melville Island in the spring, of the white *clouds* assuming the form of two continuous arches with their legs meeting near the east and west horizons, was finely displayed on the 4th; the height of the arches in the centre, from the north and south horizons, being from 50° to 70°."—Ibid., p. 206.

April 16, 1822.

"Some hard, well-defined clouds, being nearly the first we had seen this season, appeared for a short time to-day, and were welcomed as the harbingers of returning moisture in the atmosphere.

The Aurora Borealis was seen at night to the southward, and extending at times in a broad band of light across the heavens, but at a low altitude, from east to west."—Ibid., p. 213.

May 2, 1822.

"After sunset on the evening of the 2d, a thin horizontal streak or band of vapor appeared along the lower parts of the land. As the night advanced, it became thicker and more diffused, and at length, for the first time this season, the ships were for an hour or two enveloped in fog."—Ibid., p. 223.

May 16, 1822.

"On the evening of the 16th, something like small rain was falling for a few minutes, being the first we had seen this season; but it soon formed the less equivocal form of sleet, the thermometer being at 31°."—Ibid., p. 228.

June 2, 1822.

"On the 2d, at 3h. p. m., a thin white *cloud* was observed to extend across the northern sky from northeast to southwest, being then about 65° high in the centre. The whole of the heavens to the southward of this was covered with a *similar kind of cloud*, that to the northward exhibiting a clear blue sky. The edge, which was well defined, formed a very perfect arch, and here the *cloud* was much more dense than in any other place, reminding one of a veil of gauze of which there were more folds in that part than elsewhere. Though the wind was, with us, at W. by N., it blew gently over to the S. S. E., still retaining its perfect and continuous arch-like form at the margin. In a quarter of an hour, it had got 20° on the south side of the zenith, in forty minutes was only 25° high, and in an hour and a quarter had totally disappeared beneath the southern horizon, leaving the whole of the heavens perfectly cloudless.

This was the most striking phenomenon of the kind we had ever witnessed, and, while the arch remained near the zenith, this magnificent canopy had a singularly grand and imposing appearance."—Ibid., p. 238.

Duckett's Cove.—Lat. 66° 12′ 36″ N. Long. 86° 44′ 45″ W. August 29, 1821. Parry.

"The morning was beautifully clear and tranquil, and the Aurora Borealis was faintly visible at break of day in the *southwest quarter of the heavens*."—1 Parry, 69.

Chamisso Island.—Lat. 66° 13′ 11″ N. Long. 161° 47′ 45″ W. Sept. 28, 1827. Beechey.

"On the 24th and 28th, the nights were clear and frosty, and the Aurora Borealis was seen forming several arches.

On the 28th, the display was very brilliant and interesting, as it had every appearance of being *between the clouds and the earth;* and, after one of these displays, several meteors were observed issuing from parts of the arch, and falling obliquely towards the earth.

This was also one of the rare instances of the Aurora being seen *to the southward of our zenith.*" —2 Beechey, 560.

N. B.—1. Had every appearance of being between the clouds and the earth.

2. This was one of the rare instances of the Aurora being seen to the southward of our zenith.

At Sea.—Lat. 66° 30′ N. Long. 59° W. September 23, 1818. ROBERTSON.

"About ten in the evening, the Aurora Borealis was seen in the *true south horizon.* The horizon was first illuminated like the rising or setting of the moon behind a cloud, or rather like the illumination of the atmosphere caused by great fires. This extended four points of bearings. Rays were soon after darted up perpendicularly in bundles to 20° altitude, The Aurora spread to S. E. without darting rays, and soon after disappeared."—1 John Ross (Lieut. Robertson), App. 120.

Behring's Sea.—Lat. 66° 30′ N., Long. 163° 00′ W., to Lat. 71° 23′ 31″ N., Long. 156° 21′ 30″ W. Autumns of 1826 and 1827. BEECHEY.

"We had frequent opportunities of observing the Aurora Borealis in the Autumns of 1826 and of 1827. From the 25th of August until the 9th of October, about the time of the departure of the Blossom from the northern regions in both years, this beautiful meteor was visible on every night that was clear, or when the clouds were thin and elevated. [In 1826 it was visible on twenty-one nights; in 1827 only eleven.] It is remarkable that, in both years, its first appearance was on the 25th August. The season of 1826 was distinguished by an almost uninterrupted succession of fine weather and easterly winds, and that of the following year by continued boisterous weather and winds from the westward. In the former year, the weather being fine, the Aurora was more frequently seen than in the latter; but in 1827 the displays were brighter, and the light more frequently passed to the southward of the zenith. It never appeared in wet weather.

In 1826, when, as before mentioned, the weather was settled, the Aurora generally *began in the W. N. W. and passed over to the N. E.* until a certain period, *after which it as regularly commenced in the N. E.* and passed to the N. W.; whilst in 1827, the appearance of the meteor was as uncertain as the season was boisterous and changeable.

The period when this change in the course of the light took place, coincided very nearly with that of the equinox; and, as the Aurora Borealis has been supposed to be affected by that occurrence, we imagined that the change might be in some way owing thereto; but the irregularity of the meteor in this respect, in 1827, gave a contradiction to this hypothesis. It was, however, uniform in making its appearance *always in the northern hemisphere*, and generally in the form of elliptical arches from 3° to 7° of altitude, nearly parallel with the magnetic equator.

These arches were formed by short perpendicular rays passing from one quarter to the other with a lateral motion, or by their being met by similar rays from the opposite direction. The arches, when formed, in general remained nearly stationary, and gave out coruscations which streamed towards the zenith. When at rest, the light was colorless; but when any movement took place, it exhibited prismatic colors, which increased in strength as the motion became rapid. The coruscations seldom reached our zenith, and more rarely passed to the southward of it, but when that occurred the display was always brilliant; on one occasion only they extended to the southern horizon.

We remarked that when any material change was about to occur one extremity of the arch became illuminated, and that this light passed along the belt, with a tremulous hesitating movement, toward the opposite end, exhibiting the colors of the rainbow. An idea may be formed of this appearance, from the examination of the rays of some molluscous animals in motion, such as the nereis, but more particularly the beroes. Captain Parry has compared its motion to the waving of a ribbon. As the light proceeded along the arch, coruscations emanated from it; and, as the motion became violent, the curve was often deflected and sometimes broken into segments, which were brightest at their extremities and in general highly colored. When one ray of the Aurora crossed another, the point of intersection was sometimes marked by a prismatic spot, very similar to that which occurs in the intersections of coronæ about the moon, but far more brilliant; and when the segments, which generally *crooked* towards the zenith, were much curved, colors were perceptible in the bend. Generally speaking, after any brilliant display, the sky became overcast with a dense haze or with light fleecy clouds.

The Aurora has been frequently observed to rest upon a *dark nebulous substance*, which some persons have supposed to be merely an optical deception, occasioned by the lustre of the arch; but this appearance never occurs above the arch, which would be the case, I think, if these surmises were well founded. We sometimes saw this *cloud* before any light was visible, and observed it afterwards become illuminated at its upper surface, and exhibit all the appearances above mentioned.

It was the general opinion that the lustre of all the stars *was diminished* by the Aurora, but particularly by this part of it.

Captain Parry, however, observes that the stars in this dark cloud were unobscured, except by the light of the Aurora. He, however, agrees with us in the lower part of the arch being always well defined, and the upper being softened off, and gradually mingled with the azure of the sky. It is worthy of notice, that we never observed any rays shoot downwards from this arch, and I believe the remark will apply equally to the observations of Captains Parry and Franklin."—2 Beechey, 2, 722.

N. B.—1. In 1826, Aurora generally began in the W. N. W. and passed over to the N. E.
2. After a certain period, it as regularly began in the N. E. and passed over to N. W.
3. Whilst in 1827 the appearance of it was uncertain.
4. It was, however, uniform in making its appearance always in the northern hemisphere.
5. It was frequently observed to rest upon a dark nebulous cloud.
6. We sometimes saw the cloud before any light was visible.
7. The lustre of all the stars was diminished by the Aurora.

"We frequently observed the Aurora attended by a thin, *fleecy, cloud-like substance*, which, if not part of the meteor, furnishes a proof of the displays having taken place within the region of our atmosphere, as the light was decidedly seen between it and the earth. This was particularly noticed on the 28th of September, 1827. The Aurora on that night began by forming two arches from *W. by N.* northward *to E. by N.*, and about eleven o'clock threw out brilliant coruscations. Shortly after, the zenith was obscured by a lucid haze, which soon condensed into a canopy of light clouds. We could detect the Aurora above this canopy by several bright arches being refracted, and by brilliant colors being apparent in the interstices.

Shortly afterwards the meteor descended, and exhibited a splendid appearance, without any interruption from clouds, and then retired, leaving the fleecy stratum only visible as at first. This occurred several times, and left no doubt in my own mind of the Aurora being at one time above and at another below the canopy formed about our zenith.

I must not omit to observe here that, on several occasions when the light thus intervened between the earth and the cloud, brilliant meteors were precipitated obliquely toward the south and southwest horizons."—Ibid., p. 723.

N. B.—1. Aurora frequently attended by a fleecy cloud-like substance;
2. Which proves that its displays were within the region of our atmosphere,
3. As the light was decidedly between it and the earth.
4. Aurora at one time above and at another time below a canopy formed about our zenith.
5. On several occasions, when the light intervened between the earth and the clouds, brilliant meteors were precipitated.

"This supposition of the light being *at no great elevation*, is strengthened by the different appearances exhibited by the Aurora at the same times to observers not more than from ten to thirty miles apart, and also by its being *visible to persons on board the ship at Chamisso Island after it had vanished in Escholtz Bay, only ten miles distant,* as well as by the Aurora being seen by the barge detached from the Blossom several days before it was visible to persons on board the ship about two hundred miles to the southward of her."—Ibid., p. 723.

N. B.—1. Aurora at no great elevation.
2. Visible to persons on board the ship after it had vanished in Escholtz Bay, only ten miles distant.

"In Kotzebue's Sound [lat. 66° 30′ N., long. 163° W.], the Aurora *was seldom visible before ten o'clock at night or after two o'clock in the morning.*

We never heard any noise, nor detected any disturbance of the magnetic needle; but here I must observe that Kater's compass was the only instrument employed for this purpose, and then on board the ship only, the exposed situation in which we were anchored not admitting of any establishment on shore, either for this purpose or for astronomical observations."—Ibid., p. 724.

"In considering the subject of the Aurora Borealis, my attention was drawn to a fact which does not appear to me to have been hitherto noticed. I allude to the direction in which the Aurora generally makes it first appearance, or, which is the same thing, the quarter in which the arch formed by this meteor is usually seen. It is remarkable that *in this country the Aurora has always been seen to the northward;* by the expeditions which have wintered in the ice, it was almost always seen to the southward; and by the Blossom, in Kotzebue's Sound, 250 miles to the southward of the ice, it was, as in England, always observed in a northern direction. Coupling this with the relative positions of the margins of the packed ice, and with the fact of the Aurora appearing more brilliantly to vessels passing near the situation of that body than by others entered far within it—as would seem to be the case from the reports of the Greenland ships, and from my own observations at Melville Island and at Kotzebue's Sound—it does appear, at first sight, that that region is most favorable to the production of the meteor."—Ibid., p. 725.

N. B.—1. In Kotzebue's Sound, Aurora seldom visible before 10h. p. m. or after 2h. a. m.
2. Never heard any noise,
3. Nor detected any disturbance of the magnetic needle.
4. Here the Aurora has always been seen to the northward.

Fort Hope (Repulse Bay).—Lat. 66° 32′ 16″ N. Long. 86° 55′ 51″ W. Aug. 15, 1846. RAE.

"This was a beautiful day throughout. In the evening, the sky being clear and cloudless, some stars were visible, and a few streaks of orange-colored Aurora showed themselves to the southward."—Rae, p. 65.

Fort Hope (Repulse Bay).—Lat. 66° 32′ N. Long. 86° 56′ W. Sept., 1846, to April, 1847. From Dr. RAE's Meteorological Register.

SEPTEMBER, 1846.

"22d. Aurora visible to the southward at 8h. p. m.

OCTOBER, 1846.

16th. Faint Aurora to the S. and S. by E.; altitude 12°.
17th. Much drift. Aurora to S. S. E., parallel to the horizon; altitude 12°.
18th. Drift; cirrus. Some faint streaks of Aurora to the west.
21st. Much drift. At 8h. p. m., several streaks of faint Aurora extending across the zenith in a N. W. and S. E. direction; many rays in different parts of the heavens.
27th. Some faint streaks of Aurora in various parts of the sky, bearing for the most part N. N. W. and S. S. E.
28th. A few clouds near horizon; a very faint, light-yellow cloud Aurora to the S. E. and N. W.
29th. Cirrus extending from S. S. E. to N. N. W., resembling much the Aurora.

NOVEMBER, 1846.

5th. Drifting. A faint ray of Aurora to the S. E. extending vertically towards the zenith.

6th. Drifting. Some faint beams of Aurora extending from S. W. to N. W.; altitude 60°. One ray to the S. E. pointing towards the zenith.

14th. Much drift. A faint beam of Aurora to the westward, directed towards the zenith; drifting.

17th. Drifting. Three beams of Aurora pointing towards the zenith; two of them bearing N. N. W., and the other S. E.

20th. At 7h. 30m., a faint Aurora extending from W. to S. E.; altitude 20°; motion rapid, no prismatic colors.

22d. Some faint streaks of Aurora, most of them to the southeastward and pointed towards the horizon.

23d. Some faint rays of Aurora visible this morning at 5h. 30m. in different parts of the heavens; drifting.

25th. Two faint beams of Aurora bearing W. N. W. and pointing towards the zenith; altitude of lower limb 30°.

DECEMBER, 1846.

5th. Parhelia with prismatic colors. Aurora visible to the south in two arches arising from near the horizon to the zenith.

13th. The sky to the north had a beautiful lake-colored tint at sunset; the most brilliant display of Aurora I have observed this winter, the centre being towards the true south, and gradually rising from an altitude of 12° to 70° or 80°. It was of a pale yellowish-green color. Horizontal needle not affected.

14th. Some faint beams of Aurora in different parts of the heavens. A very faint Aurora to the southward.

15th. A very faint Aurora; centre true south.

17th. Wind variable from N. to E. Faint Aurora to the S.; altitude 10°; centre S. S. W. 30°.

18th. Aurora faint to the S. by W.

21st. Arch of Aurora across zenith nearly east and west; brightest at western extremity.

JANUARY, 1847.

2d. Faint Aurora; centre S. W. by S.; altitude 15°. Drifting. Some streaks of Aurora to the southward pointing to the zenith.

3d. A beam of Aurora to the south pointing to the zenith.

4th. Aurora faint; centre of arch S. by W.; altitude 10°. Aurora in a narrow line parallel to horizon; altitude 4°; extent 70°; centre south.

6th. Drifting. A faint Aurora extending from S. S. E. across the zenith.

11th. Much drift. A beam of Aurora S. E.; altitude 25°.

12th. Much drift. Very faint Aurora; centre W. by N.; altitude 10°.

13th. Drifting. A very faint Aurora; centre S. S. W.; altitude 16°; extent 60° or 70°.

14th. Drift. Arch of Aurora faint; altitude 11°; centre S. S. W.; extent 90°.

16th. Drifting, stratus. Arch of Aurora faint; centre south; altitude 18°; extent 60°. Centre S. S. W.; altitude 12°; extent 90°.

17th. Drifting. Aurora visible, faint but brightest to the westward; centre south; altitude 60°.

18th. A very faint arch of Aurora from N. W. by N. extending across zenith.

26th. A faint arch of Aurora across zenith S. W. and N. E.

28th. Drifting; very cold to the sensation; spiculæ of snow falling. A broad band of Aurora, the lower edge having a reddish or lake tint, running parallel to the horizon; altitude 2°; centre S. W.; extent 70°. Some beams of Aurora S. E. pointing towards the zenith.

FEBRUARY, 1847.

9th. Drifting; solar halo with parhelia. A faint arch of Aurora.

10th. Cirrus. Some faint beams of Aurora S. and S. S. W. (say S. W.).

APRIL, 1847.

3d. At 8 p. m., a faint Aurora of an orange color; centre south; altitude 5°."—Rae, pp. 225–239.

"On the 3d of April, the thermometer rose above zero for the first time since the 12th of December. As the Aurora was seldom noticed after this date, I may here make a few remarks on this subject. It was often visible during the winter, and usually made its appearance first to the southward in the form of a faint yellow or straw-colored arch, which gradually rose up towards the zenith.

During our stay at Fort Hope, I never witnessed a finer display of this strange phenomenon than I had done at York Factory, nor did it on any occasion affect the horizontal needle as I had seen it do during the previous winter there.

The Esquimaux, like the Indians, assert that the Aurora produces a distinctly audible sound, and the generality of Orkney men and Zetlanders maintain the same opinion, although, for my own part, I cannot say that I ever heard any sound from it.

A fine display, particularly if the movements are rapid, is very often succeeded by stormy or snowy weather, but I have never been able to trace any coincidence between the direction of its motions and that of the wind."—Ibid., p. 96.

Cape Espenburg (Behring's Sea).—Lat. 66° 34′ 56″ N. Long. 163° 36′ 38″ W. Sept. 22, 1826. BEECHEY.

"On the 22d, the Aurora Borealis was seen in the W. N. W., from which quarter it passed rapidly to the N. E. and formed a splendid arch emitting vivid and brilliantly colored coruscations."—Beechey, 1, p. 329.

SEPTEMBER 25, 1826.

"During the night we had a brilliant display of the Aurora Borealis, remarkable for its masses of bright light. It extended from N. E. to W., and at one time formed three arches."—Ibid., p. 330.

Fort Confidence.—Lat. 66° 53′ 36″ N. Long. 118° 48′ 45″ W. April, 1838. SIMPSON.

"Now that the constant daylight renders the Aurora Borealis no longer visible, I shall make one or two general remarks regarding it. Its most common appearance at Fort Confidence is an arch with little motion, passing through the zenith and spanning the heavens from *northwest to southeast.* Now, since the variation of the compass is here little more than four points easterly, it follows that there is a tendency in this remarkable phenomenon to dispose itself at *right angles to the magnetic meridian.*

In the depth of winter, thin white clouds, seen during the short imperfect daylight, in many instances proved to be the Aurora; which, also, not unfrequently appeared through a hazy sky. Its displays were seldom very brilliant, and it hardly ever exhibited those vivid prismatic tints which I had often admired in lower latitudes."—Simpson, p. 237.

"On the 24th of April, the thermometer rose *at noon* to the freezing point, for the first time since the 17th of October; a period of six months and a week! The mean temperature for the whole of that long and dismal interval is 14° below zero."—Ibid., 236.

MARCH 5, 1839.

"This season, as I have already remarked, was less severe than its predecessor; and, as if it were a consequence of the difference, the Aurora was more brilliant, displaying on several occasions the prismatic hues; but the same arched form *from northwest to southeast* predominated. Every clear night, when not eclipsed by the moon, it was to be seen, but was *brightest and most active in the mornings* some time before daylight.

At a quarter to four a. m., on the 5th of March, Ritch witnessed a most brilliant exhibition. It formed a quadrant issuing from W. N. W. and extending to the zenith. There it doubled on itself, and terminated in a semi-elliptical figure, apparently very near the earth, in rapid motion, and tinged with red, purple, and green. The half ellipse seemed to descend and ascend, accompanied by an *audible sound, resembling the rustling of silk.* This lasted for about ten minutes, when the whole phenomenon suddenly rose upwards and its splendor was gone.

Ritch is an intelligent and credible person, and, on questioning him closely, he assured me that he had perfectly distinguished the sound of the Aurora from that produced by the congelation of his breath—for the temperature at the time was 44° below zero.

I can, therefore, no longer entertain any doubt of a fact uniformly asserted by the natives, and insisted on by Hearne, by my friend Mr. Dease, and by many of the oldest residents in the fur countries; though I have not had the good fortune to hear it myself."—Ibid., p. 330.

Fort Macpherson, on Peel's River.—Lat. 67° N. Long. 135° W. Sept. 1849. HOOPER.

"6th. At 0.20 a. m., witnessed an appearance of the Aurora, a broad blaze of light passing from east, through the zenith, to west; rays uncolored; slight horizontal coruscations and tremors in rapid movement, with occasional light airs from S. E.

7th. At midnight of yesterday, we observed an appearance of the Aurora different in its style to any I have ever before seen. It formed an arc from 5° in elevation at N. E. to about 10° at E. N. E., and presented much the same form and appearance as a lunar rainbow, but did not possess prismatic colors; its hue being grass-green, with vertical light purple rays or stripes, which were not constant. It fringed a heavy 'nimbus,' imparting to it a shade of ultramarine, in which the rolling folds or waves of the cloud were finely marked. It being tolerably close to the moon (rather below and to the eastward of her), I at first imagined it to be a lunar rainbow; she was, however, much obscured, and I am nearly of a decided opinion that it was not such, but an Aurora.

12th. A very mild day; the evening clear and calm. At 11.30 p. m., saw a faint Aurora extending in an arch from S. W. to S. S. W.; centre about 10° altitude; main color pale green, with a few vertical purple rays.

16th. Ten p. m., observed Aurora extending in an arch from S. S. W. to W. by N.; central altitude about 20°.

17th. One a. m., a very beautiful Aurora extending right round the visible horizon in regular vertical rays, extending to, and converging in, the zenith. The weather calm, very fine, and clear. At midnight, a faint Aurora, not having any precise tending, being dispersed in irregular lines all over the heavens.

19th. From about 8 p. m. until midnight, there was a fine display of the Aurora, which appeared in a succession of fretted waves or folds, constantly swaying and shifting about with the light variable airs occasionally springing up."—Hooper's Journal, pp. 148, 151, 152.

Cape Krusenstern.—Lat. 67° 8′ N. Long. 163° 46′ W. August 25, 1827. BEECHEY.

"For the first time since we entered Behring's Straits, the night was clear, and the Aurora Borealis sweeping across the heavens, reminded us that it was exactly on that night twelvemonth that we saw this beautiful phenomenon for the first time in these seas. A short time before it began, a brilliant meteor fell in the western quarter. The Aurora is at all times an object of interest, and seldom appears without some display worthy of admiration, though the expectation is seldom completely gratified. The uncertainty of its movements, and of the moment it may break out into splendor, has, however, the effect of keeping the attention continually on the alert; many of us, in consequence, stayed up to a late hour, but nothing was exhibited on this occasion more than we had already repeatedly witnessed.

We were more fortunate the following night, when the Aurora approached *nearer the southern* horizon than it had done on any former occasion that we had observed in this part of the globe.

It commenced much in the usual manner, by forming an arch from *W. N. W.* to *E. N. E.* and then soared rapidly to the zenith, where the streams of light rolled into each other, and exhibited brilliant colors of purple, pink, and green. It then became diffused over the sky generally, leaving about 8° of clear space between it and the northern and southern horizons.

From this tranquil state it again poured out coruscations from all parts, which shot up to the zenith and formed a splendid cone of rays, blending pink, purple, and green colors in all their varieties. This singular and beautiful exhibition lasted only a few minutes, and then the light became diffused over the sky in a bright haze."—Beechey, 2, 538–39.

Fort Good Hope.—Lat. 67° 28′ 21″ N. Long. 130° 54′ 38″ W. September, 1849. Hooper.

"27th. At night we observed a fine Aurora spreading all over the sky, and having very little movement."—Hooper's Journal, p. 153.

At Sea.—Lat. 68° 19′ 45″ N. Long. 66° 5′ 45″ W. September 12, 1820. Parry.

"Soon after 10h. p. m., the Aurora Borealis made its appearance. I am indebted to Captain Sabine for the following description of this phenomenon :—

'The Aurora was visible for upwards of half an hour, its appearance being comprised within about twelve points of the heavens from *S. E. by E. to W. by N.*, the magnetic north being about N. 76° W.

The character of this phenomenon was peculiar, being distinguished from those which we were accustomed to see at Melville Island, by the far greater rapidity with which it spread and shifted from one part of the heavens to another; by the depth and vividness of the colors, both of red and green, with which its coruscations were tinted; and by its streamers breaking out unexpectedly in places previously obscure, and extending indifferently downwards as well as upwards. The latter distinction was contrasted with the more usual appearance of rays streaming towards the zenith from an arch of faintly brilliant light.'

An Aurora of similar appearance was observed in the Atlantic during the return of the Isabella, in October, 1818, from Davis's Strait to Shetland. The peculiarities of the present phenomenon were more marked in the commencement than towards the conclusion of its appearance."—1 Parry, 291–2.

At Sea.—Lat. 68° 19′ N. Long. 60° 5′ W. September 13, 1820. Fisher.

"The Aurora was seen last night streaming very beautifully from *west to southeast;* in the latter direction its motions were very rapid, and its colors were also very brilliant. The prevailing color was a light yellow; but the outer edge of those coruscations, that streamed towards the zenith, appeared at different times of a light purple hue."—Fisher, p. 285.

Behring's Sea.—Lat. 68° 30′ N. Long. 167° W. August 25, 1826. Beechey.

"The night of the 25th was clear and cold, with about four hours' darkness, during which we beheld a brilliant display of the Aurora Borealis, which was the first time that phenomenon had been exhibited to us in this part of the world. It first appeared in an arch extending from W. by N. to N. E. magnetic (by the north).

The arch, shortly after it was formed, broke up; but united again, threw out a few coruscations, and then entirely disappeared. Soon after, a new display began in the direction of the western foot of the first arch, preceded by a bright flame, from which emanated coruscations of a pale straw color. An almost simultaneous movement occurred at both extremities of the arch, until a complete segment was formed of waving perpendicular radii. As soon as the arch was complete, the light became greatly increased; and the prismatic colors, which had before been faint, now shone forth in a very brilliant manner. The strongest colors, which were also the outside ones, were pink and green; the centre color was yellow, and the intermediate ones, on the pink side, purple and green, on the green side purple and pink; all of which were as imperceptibly blended as in the rainbow. The green was the color nearest the zenith. This magnificent display lasted a few minutes, and the light had nearly vanished, when the S. E. quarter sent forth a vigorous display, and nearly at the same time a corresponding coruscation emanated from the opposite extremity. The western foot of the arch then disengaged itself from the horizon, crooked to the northward, and the whole retired to the N. E. quarter, where a white spot blazed for a moment, and all was darkness.

I have been thus particular in my description, because the appearance was unusually brilliant, and because very few observations on this phenomenon have been made in this part of the world.

There was *no noise* audible during any part of our observations, nor were the compasses *perceptibly affected*."—Beechey, 1, 281–82.

N. B.—1. There was no noise audible during any part of our observations,
2. Nor were our compasses perceptibly affected.

Nijnei Kolymsk.—Lat. 68° 31′ 53″ N. Long. 160° 56′ E. November 22, 1820. VON WRANGELL.

"The polar night had set in on the 22d of November (1820), and the beauty of the varied forms of the Aurora, seen on the deep azure of the clear *northern sky*, was a source of unwearied enjoyment to us almost every evening."—Von Wrangell, p. 83.

Nijnei Kolymsk.—Lat. 68° 31′ 53″ N. Long. 160° 56′ E. 1820–21. VON WRANGELL.

"The general characteristics of the Aurora Borealis are so well known that it is unnecessary to describe them here; I will, therefore, confine myself to the following particulars, which appear to deserve a special notice.

1. When the streamers rise high, and approach the full moon, a luminous circle of from 20° to 30° is frequently formed round it; the circle continues for a time and then disappears.
2. When the streamers extend to the zenith, or nearly so, they sometimes resolve themselves into small, faintly luminous, and cloud-like patches, of a milk-white color, and which not unfrequently continue to be visible on the following day in the shape of *white wave-like clouds.*
3. We often saw on the *northern horizon,* below the auroral light, dark blue clouds, which bear a great resemblance in color and form to the vapors which usually rise from a sudden break in the ice of the sea.
4. Even during the most brilliant Auroras, we could never perceive *any considerable noise*, but in such cases we did hear a slight hissing sound, as when the wind blows on a flame.
5. The Auroras seen from Nijnei Kolymsk (lat. 68° 32′) usually commence in the *northeastern quarter* of the heavens; and the middle of the space which they occupy in the northern horizon is generally 10° or 20° east of true north. The magnetic variation at this place is about 10° east.
6. Auroras are more frequent and more brilliant on the sea-coast than at a distance from it. The latitude of the place does not otherwise influence them. Thus, for example, it would seem from the accounts of the Tchuktches, that in Koliutchin Island (in 67° 26′ latitude), Auroras are much more frequent and more brilliant than at Nijnei Kolymsk, in latitude 68° 32′. On the coast, we often saw the streamers shoot up to the zenith; whereas this was rarely the case at Nijnei Kolymsk; nor was the light nearly so brilliant at the latter place.
7. The inhabitants of the coast affirm, that after a brilliant Aurora they always have a strong gale from the quarter in which it appeared; we did not observe this to be the case at Nijnei

Kolymsk. The difference, however, may proceed from local circumstances, which often either prevent the sea-winds from reaching so far inland, or alter their direction. For example, it often happens that there is a strong northerly wind at Pochodsk, seventy wersts north of Kolymsk, while at the latter place the wind is southerly.

8. The finest Auroras always appear at the *beginning of strong gales* in November and January; when the cold is most intense, they are more rare.
9. A remarkable phenomenon which I often witnessed deserves to be recorded; *i. e.*, when shooting stars fell near the lower portion of an auroral arch, fresh kindled streamers instantly appeared, and shot up from the spot where the star fell.

From some of the above remarks, it may be inferred that the freezing of the sea may be connected with the appearance of Auroras. Perhaps a great quantity of electricity may be produced by the suddenly rising vapors, or by the friction of large masses of ice against each other.

The Aurora does not always occupy the higher regions of the atmosphere; it is usually nearer the surface of the earth, and this is shown by the visible influence of the lower current of the atmosphere on the beams of the Aurora. *We have frequently seen the effect of the wind on the streamers as obvious as it is on clouds; and it is almost always the wind which is blowing at the surface of the earth.*"—Von Wrangell, p. 506.

N. B.—1. We have frequently seen the effect of the wind on the streamers as obvious as it is on the clouds;

2. And it is almost always the wind that is blowing on the surface of the earth.

"There is a remarkable phenomenon known here by the name of Teploi Weter (the warm wind), blowing from the S. E. by S. It sometimes begins suddenly, when the sky is quite clear, and in the middle of winter raises the temperature, in a short time, from —47° to +35°; so that the plates of ice which are the substitute for glass in the windows begin to melt. In the valleys of the Aniui, the warm wind is frequently felt; its influence does not extend to the west of Cape Tchukotski. It is seldom of longer continuance than twenty-four hours."—Ibid., p. 49.

"*Northeast wind*, or more often E. N. E., is seldom of long continuance and violent. It usually clears the atmosphere from mist, and thus causes the thermometer to rise in summer and to fall in winter. *Auroras often accompany this wind in winter.*

Southeast wind drives away mist, and may be regarded as the prevailing wind in autumn and winter. Sometimes, in the middle of winter, a wind from the S. E. by E., or S. E. ½ E., causes the temperature to rise suddenly from —24° to +25°, or even to 32°; previously to this, the barometer sinks as much as four-tenths of an inch in the course of eight hours. The S. S. E. wind has no particular influence either on the barometer or thermometer. S. E. winds, but more particularly E. by S. and E. winds, *are frequently accompanied by Auroras.*"—Ibid., p. 513.

Nijnei Kolymsk.—Lat. 68° 31′ 53″ N. Long. 160° 56′ E. March 1, 1821. COCHRANE.

"The only meteorological phenomenon which occurred during my stay at the Kolyma, was the Aurora Borealis. The scene fell far short of my expectations. I understood, however, that the months of October and November are the most proper to view them in their greatest splendor.

Those which appeared during my stay were generally from the north, and consisted of columns of fire moving in an horizontal direction, and generally disappearing in the southwest; the height of the columns being from 50° to 60°.

At times, an immense illuminated space from north to east would advance very close to us, and throwing up rays or rockets of fire, and, forming into concave arches, approached us so near as apparently to endanger our situation, exhibiting at the same time every color of the rainbow.

The most beautiful Aurora which I saw was at midnight of the 1st of March, 1821. The wind was from the N. N. W., and the glass at 36° of cold. The Aurora occupied the whole circle of the heavens, at an elevation of 28° or 30°, and, gradually rising, disappeared in the zenith. The figure was as an illuminated tent, with festoons or fringes at the lower part, and which had an appearance as if constantly receiving accessions of fire, which were equally distributed to it from every part of the foundation of the tent. The illuminated part gradually diminished in splendor as it approached the zenith.

It lasted about two hours, and did a little affect the electrometer."—Cochrane, p. 184.

Virchni Kovima.—Winter of 1786–87. Billings.

"The effects of the cold are wonderful. Upon coming out of a warm room, it is absolutely necessary to breathe through a handkerchief; and you find yourself immediately surrounded by an atmosphere, arising from breath and the heat of the body, which incloses you in a mist, and consists of small nodules of hoar ice. Breathing causes a noise like the tearing of coarse paper or the breaking of thin twigs, and the expired breath is immediately condensed in the fine substance mentioned above.

The Northern Lights are constant and very brilliant; they seem close to you, and you may sometimes hear them shoot along; they assume an amazing diversity of shapes; and the Tungoose say that they are spirits at variance fighting in the air."—Sauer (Billings), p. 57.

Hearne's Sea, north of Coppermine.—Lat. 68° 48′ 27″ N. Long. 115° 31′ W. September 9–16, 1839. Simpson.

"Stress of weather sadly retarded our return. The last of the Canada and snow geese quitted the shores of the Polar Sea, and our deer hunters' excursions were fruitless, the animals having already made a move inland.

One night there was a most *superb display of the Aurora without the prismatic tints;* and on another, that was pitch dark, the flashing of the sea almost rivalled that strange lustre of the heavens.

We pursued our way unremittingly night and day, fair and foul, whenever the winds permitted; and on the 16th, in a bitter frost, and the surrounding country covered with snow, we made our entrance into the Coppermine, after by far the longest voyage ever performed in boats on the Polar Sea, the distance we had gone not being less than 1,408 geographical, or 1,631 statute miles."—Simpson, p. 388.

Igloolik.—Lat. 69° 15′ N. Long. 81° 45′ W. 1822–23. Parry.

November 7, 1822.

"The appearances of the Aurora Borealis were neither frequent nor brilliant during this month.

On the 7th, near midnight, this phenomenon appeared from *E. S. E. to S. W.*, forming an irregular arch of white light, not continuous in every part, and about 8° high in the centre. From the upper margin of this arch, coruscations now and then shot upwards towards the zenith."—2 Parry, 381.

November 21, 1822.

"On the morning of the 21st, Mr. Ross remarked a bright arch of the *Aurora* passing *through the zenith from east to west*, and meeting the horizon at each end. Besides this, two smaller, and apparently concentric arches, were visible to the southward; the higher arch being in the centre about twenty degrees above the horizon, and the other about ten degrees.

An arch of the same kind appeared at night in the *southwest* quarter of the heavens."—Ibid., p. 381.

December 13, 1822.

"Between one and two a. m. on the 13th, while Messrs. Ross and Bushnan were employed in taking some observations alongside the Fury, they saw a vivid flash of light, which it afterwards occurred to them must have come down the electric chain attached to the masthead, directly under which they happened to be standing at the time.

As soon as Mr. Fisher was acquainted with this circumstance, he applied the electrometer to the chain, but, as usual, without any perceptible effect on the gold leaf.

The Aurora Borealis had been visible to the *southward* for some hours during the night, but had disappeared for half an hour before the flash was seen."—Ibid., p. 386.

FEBRUARY 15, 1823.

"On the 15th, some remarkable *clouds* were hanging over the open water to the eastward, appearing like vast volumes of smoke curling into rounded and almost circular forms. This peculiarity we never observed at any other time, though there was constantly a 'water-sky' in that direction, consisting of a general and diffused darkness, varied occasionally by numerous vertical columns of 'frost smoke.'"—Ibid., p. 407.

N. B.—1. Remarkable clouds hanging over the open water to the eastward.
2. Constantly a water-sky in that direction.

MARCH, 1823.

"At the close of the month of March, we were glad to find that its mean temperature, being —19.75°, when taken in conjunction with those of January and February, appeared to constitute a mild winter for this latitude. There were, besides, some other circumstances which served to distinguish this winter from any preceding one we had passed in the ice. One of the most remarkable of these was the frequent occurrence of *hard and well-defined clouds;* a feature we had hitherto considered as almost unknown in the winter sky of the polar regions.

It is not improbable that these may have in part owed their origin to a large extent of sea keeping open to the southeastward throughout the winter, though they not only occurred with the wind from that quarter, but also with the colder weather usually accompanying northwesterly breezes." —Ibid., p. 418.

N. B.—Hard and well-defined clouds were of frequent occurrence; a feature hitherto considered as almost unknown in the polar regions.

"Another peculiarity observed in this winter was the *rare occurrence* of the Aurora Borealis, and the *extraordinary poorness* of its display whenever it did make its appearance.

It was almost invariably seen to the *southward, between an E. S. E. and a W. S. W.* bearing, generally low, the stationary patches of it having a tendency to form an irregular arch, and not unfrequently with coruscations shooting towards the zenith. When more diffused, it still kept, in general on the *southern side* of the zenith; but never exhibited any of those rapid and complicated movements observed in the course of the preceding winter, nor, indeed, any feature that renders it necessary to attempt a particular description.

The *electrometer was frequently tried* by Mr. Fisher, at times when the state of the atmosphere appeared the most favorable, *but always without any sensible effect being produced on the gold leaf.*"—Ibid., p. 420.

N. B.—1. Another peculiarity observed in this winter was the rare occurrence of the Aurora Borealis, and the poorness of its display.
2. It was almost invariably seen to the southward.
3. Electrometer frequently tried,
4. But always without any effect on the gold leaf.

Igloolik.—Lat. 69° 15′ N. Long. 81° 45′ W. March, 1823. LYON.

"During the dark season, I mean the time that we did not at all see the sun, it was remarked with astonishment that the Aurora Borealis was very rarely seen, in fact only once or twice, and then so faintly as scarcely to call our attention."—Lyon (Private Journal), p. 306.

At Sea (Davis's Strait).—Lat. 69° 30′ N. September, 1825. PARRY.

"In running down Davis's Strait, as well as in crossing the Atlantic, we saw on this passage, as well as in all former autumnal ones, a good deal of the Aurora Borealis.

It first began to display itself on the 15th of September, about the latitude of 69½°, appearing in the (true) *southeast* quarter as a bright luminous patch five or six degrees above the horizon, almost stationary for two or three hours together, but frequently altering its intensity, and occasionally sending up vivid streamers towards the zenith.

It appeared in the same manner, on several subsequent nights, *in the southwest*, west, and east quarters of the heavens; and on the 20th, a bright arch of it passed across the zenith *from southeast* to northwest, appearing to be *very close to the ship*, and affording so strong a light as to throw the shadow of objects on the deck."—3 Parry, 170.

N. B.—Very close to the ship.

On the Ice.—Lat. 69° 43′ N. Long. 168° 4′ E. March 1, 1821. Von Wrangell.

"The thermometer was at —25° throughout the day.

In this day's journey we saw an unusual phenomenon: in the *N. E. horizon* there appeared an insulated dark-gray cloud, from which white beams streamed to the zenith and across it to the opposite horizon, resembling the beams of the Aurora, but whether luminous or not we could not tell on account of the daylight. The phenomenon lasted about half an hour. One of our Cossacks who had been before on the Polar Sea, maintained that the cloud was occasioned by vapor rising from a sudden crack in the ice.

On the same evening, there was an Aurora extending from *N. E. to N. W.*"—Von Wrangell, pp. 101–2.

N. B.—Preceded by a dark-gray cloud with beams streaming from it to the zenith.

On the Ice.—Lat. 69° 58′ N. 168° 41′ E. March 2, 1821. Von Wrangell.

"We saw this evening an Aurora of extraordinary beauty. The sky was clear and cloudless, and the stars sparkled in their fullest arctic brilliancy. With a slight breeze from the N. E., there rose in the *E. N. E.* a great column of light, from which rays extended over the sky, in the direction of the wind, in broad and brilliant bands, which appeared to approach us, whilst they varied continually in form.

From the rapidity with which the rays shot through the whole space from the horizon to the zenith, in less than two seconds, the Aurora appeared to be *nearer to us than the ordinary height of the clouds*. We could perceive no effect on the compass needle."—Von Wrangell, pp. 103–4.

N. B.—1. Aurora nearer than the ordinary height of clouds.
2. No effect on the compass needle.

Felix Harbor (Gulf of Boothia).—Lat. 69° 59′ N. Long. 92° 1′ 6″ W. Ross.

October 18, 1829.

"It was a beautiful day, with calm weather; the thermometer was between 6° and 8°, but in the evening it fell till it reached 1° only, at seven o'clock. This was by very much the lowest temperature we had yet experienced. Sunday found all our men well, and him who had met with the accident recovered. More than fifty lunar distances were obtained for the longitude. The Aurora was seen in the southeast."—2 Ross, 204.

October 21.

"The Krusenstern was secured yesterday, and at night an Aurora made its appearance."—Ibid., p. 205.

October 31.

"At sunset there was a large halo, being but the second we had seen; it was, however, only a white one. There was afterwards an Aurora to the southward."—Ibid., p. 208.

NOVEMBER 1.

"There was an Aurora at night, but not brilliant."—Ibid., p. 216.

NOVEMBER 21.

"A very faint Aurora was seen in the southeastern horizon."—Ibid., p. 223.

NOVEMBER 24, 25.

"There was a brilliant Aurora to the southwest, extending its red radiance as far as the zenith. The wind vacillated on the following day, and there was a still more brilliant one in the evening, increasing in splendor till midnight, and persisting till the following morning. It constituted a bright arch, the extremities of which seemed to rest on two opposed hills, while its color was that of the full moon, and itself seemed not less luminous; though the dark and somewhat blue sky by which it was backed was a chief cause, I have no doubt, of the splendor of its effect.

We can conjecture what the appearance of Saturn's ring must be to the inhabitants of that planet; but here the conjecture was perhaps verified, so exactly was the form and light of this arch what we must conceive of that splendid planetary appendage when seen crossing the Saturnian heavens. It varied, however, at length, so much as to affect this fancied resemblance; yet with an increase of brilliancy and interest. While the mass, or density, of the luminous matter was such as to obscure the constellation Taurus, it proceeded to send forth rays in groups, forming such angular points as are represented in the stars of jewelry, and illuminating the objects on land by their coruscations. Two bright nebulæ of the same matter afterwards appeared beneath the arch, sending forth similar rays, and forming a still stronger contrast with the dark sky near the horizon. About one o'clock it began to break up into fragments and nebulæ; the coruscations becoming more frequent and irregular until it suddenly vanished at four."—Ibid., p. 223–4.

DECEMBER 2.

"A black cloud in the southern horizon would have prevented the sun from being seen, though it had still risen above that line, as it did the day before. The magnetic observatory was erected, and the other one commenced. At midnight there was a magnificent arch of an Aurora, but it was only five degrees high. The color was a light yellow, and it emitted rays; finally breaking up and disappearing about one o'clock."—Ibid., p. 227.

DECEMBER 9.

"The temperature fell to 26° minus in the evening, and there was an insignificant Aurora."—Ibid., p. 228.

DECEMBER 18.

"There was another beautiful Aurora this day."—Ibid., p. 229.

DECEMBER 19.

"Clouds obscured the Aurora of yesterday, though it was still partially visible, as if occupying the whole space from east to west."—Ibid., p. 229.

DECEMBER 20.

"The Aurora still continued; and, in want of other variety, it afforded us amusement amid this wearisome uniformity.

After the Aurora had ceased, it recommenced at night in a more brilliant form, with bright flashes amid its other varieties, disappearing a little after midnight. The clearness of the sky overhead was such, that we could see perfectly well in the cabin at midday, even through the double skylight, though it was covered with snow. Outside the ship, the smallest print could be read distinctly."—Ibid., p. 230.

DECEMBER 24.

"There was again an Aurora; another to add to a succession of these appearances more regular and durable than any which had been experienced in the former voyage to this climate."—Ibid., p. 231.

DECEMBER 25.

"It was Christmas day. There are few places on the civilized earth in which that day is not, perhaps, the most noted of the year; to all, it is at least a holiday, and there are many to whom it was somewhat more. The elements themselves seemed to have determined it should be a noted day to us, for it commenced with a most beautiful and splendid Aurora, occupying the whole vault above. At first, and for many hours, it displayed a succession of arches, gradually increasing in altitude as they advanced from the east and proceeded towards the western side of the horizon; while the succession of changes were not less brilliant than any that we had formerly witnessed."—Ibid., p. 231.

DECEMBER 30.

"There was very good light during the day from ten till half after three, and, in the course of it, the temperature rose to minus 20°. There was also a faint Aurora; and some transits of the stars were observed."—Ibid., p. 233.

DECEMBER 31.

"On the Aurora Borealis which we had so often seen, no experiments could be made, from the state of the weather, and the force of the winds, at those times." Ibid., p. 234.

JANUARY 6, 1830.

"Another obscure Aurora made its appearance in the zenith."—Ibid., p. 241.

Sheriff Harbor (Gulf of Boothia).—Lat. 70° N. Long. 91° 53′ W. Ross.

JANUARY, 1831.

"There were many gales, as the Journal has shown; and on all those days the barometer fell and the temperature rose. But it was an invariable remark that, when the gale was from the northward, the former fell less, and the thermometer rose more, than when it was from any other quarter; as this was also most striking when the wind was from the southward. The Auroræ were very inconspicuous; but the halos were of a very striking character."—2 Ross, 503.

FEBRUARY 7, 8.

"The cold weather continued through the two following days, in which there was nothing remarkable but a slight Aurora."—Ibid., p. 504.

MARCH 1.

"There was a bright Aurora, which agitated the magnetic needle in the manner that has been often observed. Such light as I could collect from it by means of a large reading lens, had no effect on the differential thermometer."—Ibid., p. 506.

MARCH 9.

"Sunday (March 6) was somewhat warmer, the temperature rising in the day to 28° for two hours. It was 40° on Monday night, and a hare was killed on that day. The two following days (8th and 9th) were little noticeable for anything but a general continuance of the same weather and temperature; except that, on the last of those, there was a bright Aurora."—Ibid., p. 506.

Baffin's Bay.—Lat. 70° 03′ 33″ N. [Long. 63° 20′ W.] April 6, 1851. KANE.

"At 1 a. m., faint and fleeting Aurora visible to the S. E. At 9 p. m., an Aurora to the south (true)."—1 Kane, p. 530.

Sheriff's Bay (850 feet north of Felix Harbor).—Lat. 70° 1′ N. Long. 91° 54′ W. Ross.

NOVEMBER 14, 1830.

"A bright Aurora Borealis was the only noticeable event. They had been rare or absent for a long time."—2 Ross, 485.

DECEMBER 16, 1830.

"There was little to note this day but a splendid Aurora."—Ibid., p. 494.

JANUARY, 1831.

"The Auroræ were very inconspicuous; but the halos were of a very striking character."—Ibid., p. 503.

FEBRUARY, 1831.

"7th and 8th. There was nothing remarkable but a slight Aurora."—Ibid., p. 504.

MARCH, 1831.

"1st. There was a bright Aurora.
2d. There was a bright Aurora."—Ibid., p. 506.

"As the expedition which I commanded in 1818 did not winter in the arctic regions, my observations during that voyage were confined to the months of September and October, during which time the ships were moving in a southerly direction from the latitude of 74° to 58° N.; when it was observed that from the latitude of 74° until 66° the phenomenon was seen to the *southward*, particularly at midnight; but that when the ship had passed to the southward of the latitude of 66°, it was seen to the *northward*. In several instances, the Aurora was distinctly observed to be between the two ships, and also between the ships and the icebergs; proving unquestionably that it could not be at that time beyond the atmosphere of the earth. This, indeed, was the only fact which I completely established during that voyage."—2 Ross, Appendix, pp. 113–14.

Victoria Harbor (Gulf of Boothia).—Lat. 70° 09′ N. Long. 91° 34′ W. Jan. 8, 1832. ROSS.

"The thermometer came down to 45°, but, being calm, it was not very cold. It is certain, also, that we had now resumed our winter standard of sensation on this subject. The Aurora was again seen on Saturday (the 8th)."—2 Ross, p. 624.

On the Ice.—Lat. 70° 20′ N. Long. 174° 13′ E. March 21, 1823. VON WRANGELL.

"I availed myself of the unavoidable delay to take a meridian altitude, which gave our latitude 70° 20′; the longitude, deduced by angles from points visible on the mainland, was 174° 13′, the variation 21½ E.

We profited by the light of a beautiful Aurora in the *northeast quarter* to continue our march until the night was far advanced, when we had accomplished twenty-four wersts since noon, among old hummocks and loose snow, which afforded comparatively easy travelling."—Von Wrangell, p. 332.

"The winter of 1822–23 was generally considered a very mild one at Nijnei Kolymsk. The temperature was only once as low as —51° (on the 10th of January), and Auroras were rare, and not so brilliant as usual."—Ibid., p. 318.

N. B.—Winter mild. Auroras rare; not brilliant.

Baffin's Bay.—Lat. 70° 43′ 56″ N. Long. 63° 44′ 33″ W. KANE.

"March 26, 1851. At 11 p. m., faint Aurora to southward and eastward.
March 28. At 11 p. m., Aurora to the eastward (true)."—1 Kane, 529.

Middle Ice of Baffin's Bay.—Lat. 71° 20′ N. Long. 62° 28′ W. Sept. 21, 1852. INGLESFIELD.

"A calm, lovely night, with brilliant Aurora and starlit sky, gave symptoms of fine weather, which, in our present position, was much to be desired, although a little wind would be beneficial to keep the ice sufficiently in motion to prevent our being frozen in."—Inglesfield., p. 98.

Moore's Harbor, Point Barrow.—Lat. 71° 23′ N. Long. 156° 20′ W. Winter of 1853–54.

"Compared with the last year, the winter set in with great severity; the ship being frozen in ten days sooner, and the temperature falling below zero on the 28th of September, sixteen days earlier than in the previous season. This winter was altogether colder than the last, with a considerable less fall of snow, and the sky generally clearer; but there is some reason to consider it nearer the mean climate of the place.

Associated with this was a more frequent display of Aurora Borealis, suggesting the idea of this phenomenon being connected with terrestrial radiation."—Maguire's Report.

Baffin's Bay.—[Lat. 72° 10′ 11″ N. Long. 68° 36′ 40″ W.] February, 1851. KANE.

"19th. At 5 a. m., an Aurora visible, passing near the zenith, in a N. N. W. and S. S. E. direction.

21st. At 1 a. m., a faint Aurora to the east. At 4 p. m., an Aurora passing through the zenith, and extending to the horizon in a N. W. and S. E. direction (true).

24th. At 6 a. m., a faint Aurora seen about the zenith in a southward and westward direction.

25th. At 3 p. m., faint Aurora visible, passing through the zenith in a N. W. and S. E. direction. At 10 p. m., several Auroras seen to the northward and westward.

26th. At 1 a. m., an Aurora to the southward and eastward. At 9 p. m., several Auroras visible in different parts of the heavens.

27th. At 3 a. m., Aurora passing through the zenith in an east and west direction."—1 Kane, p. 527.

Baffin's Bay.—[Lat. 72° 15′ N. Long. 68° 40′ 22″ W.] February 13, 1851. KANE.

"A fine, pleasant day. At 7 p. m., faint Aurora visible to the southward (true)."—1 Kane, p. 526.

Baffin's Bay.—Lat. 72° 19′ 40″ N. Long. 68° 55′ 20″ W. February 7, 1851. KANE.

"I have quoted the 'fog or cloud-like segment' as forming a prominent feature in the continental descriptions, for the purpose of introducing from my Journal two anomalous exhibitions of Aurora in the same connection. One was in direct conjunction with the diffracted solar rays; the other, a true daylight Aurora. I give them verbatim from my notes.

'February 7. Cold and clear; thermometer, at 8h. 40m. a. m., at 38°, while on the vessel's stern, and at 42° when freely suspended by the bows outside; my Green's spirit standard, some fifty paces from the vessel, at —48°: one more illustration of the local influence of ship-board, and of the irregularity of our system of registration.

The sun was completely visible at about ten a. m., but his rays were subdued by a slight haziness, caused by myriads of crystallized specks that filled the atmosphere. These, when examined by my travelling Frauenhofer at two hundred diameters, gave in some few cases regular hexagonal prisms, with well-defined terminations; but this symmetry of form was generally obscured by groupings and long oblique truncations. I have now made eight careful examinations of these crystalline spiculæ, at varying temperatures, when they come to us accompanied by parhelia, halos, or anomalous columns proceeding from the sun. In every case, there was a decided approach to the six-sided form.

The sun to-day exhibited an unusual phenomenon. At 10h. 20m., while very low, a column of light was observed stretching from the upper summit of its disk to an approximate height of 15°. This expanded fan-fashion as it rose, and was lost by its pencilled radiations blending with the illuminated sky. Thus far it did not differ materially from the vertical or crepuscular rays accompanying rudimentary forms of parhelia. But, by eleven o'clock, this fan-like column had enlarged to a cloudy shaft of bright yellow light, twenty to twenty-four degrees in height, and proceeding from a complete segment of illumination, which was thickly studded with cirrous clouds. The upper terminus of this column, unlike the parhelia which we had seen before, assumed a curvilinear wedge shape, not unlike the section of a pear, from whose sides rose tangentially a series of pencilled illuminations terminating in streaks of cloud strata.

The feature about this phenomenon of greatest interest, was a distinct play of light, a series of coruscating changes resembling the scintillations of the Aurora. The rays which shot out from the three-curved summit sometimes extended twelve or fifteen degrees, with a sudden movement of increased energy almost resembling ignition; then, again, they retired, until represented by but a few feeble points. The cloud-like segments showed in a lesser degree the same movements; and, at the periods of most active display, the vertical or fan-like shaft flashed up into more intense illumination. The diameter of this shaft at its entering base could not have been less than eighty degrees.'

This singular exhibition recalled irresistibly the analogous phenomena of the Aurora, with those anomalous displays of coronæ which have been referred to diffraction of light by atmospheric vesicles or icy spiculæ. I give it from my notes as a simple detail of facts, without comment or opinion.

A daylight Aurora has been described by other observers. I witnessed several, one of them interesting enough to be worth transcribing.

'About ten o'clock, going out to exercise at foot-ball, I noticed that the usual cloud-bank of the horizon had nearly cleared away at the south. One or two feathery cirri hung about the zenith, and the northern horizon retained its usual deep obscurity. This was in the course of my usual cursory examination for my weather record. Half an hour after, I observed one spot where the banking remained, attracting attention by its nearness to the sun and its well-defined segmentary character. Its margin was distinctly and regularly arched; its tinting a peculiar purple, slightly warmed or bronzed at its margins, but deepening into a heavy brown at the line of the horizon. The centre of the segment bore south twenty degrees west (magnetic); its altitude eight degrees nearly. Smoke and vapor from ship's fires purple tinted; distant objects not very clearly visible; atmosphere filled with ice spiculæ.

Soon from the circumference of this arch proceeded a fimbriated or fringy series of purple cirri, delicately tinted at their edges, increasing with wonderful regularity, and extending in long, ray-like processes of cloud to an altitude of some twenty degrees above the horizon. Before eleven o'clock, these processes had become long, stratiform, illuminated clouds, beautifully marked, of a breadth, measured roughly by the eye, of four or five degrees, interrupted where they crossed the illuminated region of the sun, but everywhere else extending over the heavens to the south and west (true); and, although still diminishing in intensity, extending nearly to the eastern quarter of the sky. By coalescing at their bases, these radiating processes augmented the size of the central segment. The intervals between them appeared, by contrast, to be artificially illuminated.

Till now there had been no movement; but, at 11h. 20m., these cloud-like processes or radiations strikingly resembled the rays or beams of a coruscating Auroral arch. Dr. Vreeland and myself witnessed repeatedly interruptions of their continuity; then suddenly shootings out, or increasings of their length; and then a rapid and momentary formation, followed by a sudden and complete disappearance.

At this time, too, a strange wavy movement was seen about the shorter prolongations in the neighborhood of the vertex of the mass. These resembled the rising wreaths of 'frost-smoke' seen in the Wellington Channel, and had an appearance almost of combustion.

During all these phases, the cloud-like character was singularly preserved; the rays appeared to modify the processes as light would behind our ordinary clouds. The whole exhibition was a daylight one, perfectly cloud-like, differing only in the elements of shape, movement, and radiated illumination. It was a day Aurora.

The appearance continued until twenty minutes of meridian. At 11h. 10m., when it was at its maximum, the rayed prolongations stretched nearly across the sky; and the centre of the mass from which they emanated was fifteen degrees west from the south pole of the needle. At about the same deviation—viz: N. by E. $\frac{1}{2}$ E.—and at a rude altitude of about fifteen or twenty degrees, was an irregular cirro-cumulated cloud of the same purple tint, but not so much illuminated. From its eastern margin, rays or processes were seen stretching as high as fifty degrees, and as far as due east.

Before the sun had reached his meridian altitude, the prolongations had become faint, and passed into detached feathery clouds, when collected at the zenith and lost the radiated arrangement altogether. The mass of cloud stratus to the south (magnetic), also, had blended with the usual bank about the horizon.' "—1 Kane, pp. 319–323.

Baffin's Bay.—[Lat. 72° 30′ N. Long. 69° W.] February, 1851. KANE.

"2d. 1 a. m., Aurora visible to the southward and eastward (true); beams of light covering the whole of the eastern half of the heavens, most of them parallel to the plane of the meridian. Aurora extending to within 30° of the horizon to the N. W."—1 Kane, p. 526.

"Between the hours of six and eight p. m., we had an interesting display of the Aurora. It was of a luminous white, not much more marked than any of the isolated nebulæ seen through a telescope, which it indeed resembled. This white light stretched in cumulated masses from the northwest to the southeastern horizon, forming to the northward an arch of some regularity. From the inner circumference of this great arch proceeded a series of scintillating processes, at apparent right angles to the plane of the horizon, and constantly shifting their positions, so as to produce an effect nearly like that of the 'merry dancers.' To the south, however, the arch became irregular and changing; its diameter varied from five to thirty degrees, the augmentation being a broken series of parallel bands, no one exceeding six or eight degrees.

At the period of its greatest intensity, 7h. 10m., it enveloped Procyon and the Pleiades, obscuring the larger portion of Taurus, and actually hiding Aldebaran. A process extended obliquely from about twelve degrees above the horizon to Castor and Pollux, whose brightness it sensibly dimmed. The zone then narrowed, passing about eleven degrees to the west of Polaris, and ascending in a regular arch to the northwest. It faded gradually, and by 9h. 20m. had disappeared.

Neither a silk-suspended magnetic needle, nor our rude electrometers, detected any disturbance.—Ibid., p. 316.

"5th. Faint Aurora seen to the southward and eastward.

6th. 7 a. m., a faint Aurora to the southward, near the horizon.

7th. 2 a. m., faint Aurora seen to N. N. E. and S. S. W. 7. a. m., Aurora to the S. E. and E. (true)."—Ibid., p. 526.

Somerset House, Prince Regent's Inlet.—Lat. 72° 48′ N. Long. 95° 41′ W. ROSS.

DECEMBER, 1832.

"The Aurora Borealis had been seen but seldom, and was inconspicuous, while its position was generally opposed to that of the sun. But, to end with the summary of this month, the weather, variable and severe as it had been, became calm and clear, though cold; and thus did we terminate the month of December, and the year 1832."—2 Ross, 688.

MARCH, 1833.

"We had taken but three foxes and two hares in the whole month; which, as food, amounted to nothing. At the end of it, after all the changes had taken place under the gales, the ice was so rough that it was impassable on sledges, and even on foot. No Aurora Borealis had been seen; and, indeed, we had scarcely noticed one the whole winter."—Ibid., p. 694.

Baffin's Bay.—Lat. 72° 49′ 15″ N. Long. 70° 59′ 15″ W. January 29, 1851. KANE.

"6 a. m., faint Aurora near the horizon. One-third of the sun's disk visible from the deck. 11 p. m., faint Aurora near the horizon, to the S. W. and N."—1 Kane, p. 525.

Baffin's Bay.—Lat. 72° 52′ 45″ N. Long. 71° 15′ 35″ W. January 28, 1851. KANE.

"1 a. m., light Aurora from W. to S. W. Two arcs of light, the southern being about 10°, the western 20° from the horizon at the middle point. About two-thirds of the sun's disk visible from the topgallant yard."—1 Kane, p. 525.

Baffin's Bay.—Lat. 73° 09′ 13″ N. Long. 72° 02′ 21″ W. January, 1851. KANE.

"26th. Aurora visible to the northward, 9 p. m.

27th. Auroras to the southward and westward, near the horizon, 2 a. m. and 8 a. m."—1 Kane, p. 525.

Port Bowen.—Lat. 73° 13′ 39″ N. Long. 88° 54′ 49″ W. October, 1824—March, 1825. PARRY.

"The Aurora Borealis, which constitutes one of the peculiar features of a polar winter, occurred with nearly the same frequency as on former occasions. The number of nights on which it is registered are—

2 in October,	15 in January,
5 in November,	13 in February,
7 in December,	5 in March;

being, in the whole, forty-seven from October to March.

It may have appeared faintly on a few other occasions, not noticed in our Journals, and unquestionably would have been seen more frequently but for the height of the land on the south side of Port Bowen, which intercepted our view to the altitude of five or six degrees.

By far the greater part of these phenomena assumed one general character, and occupied nearly the same position.

It usually consisted of an arch, sometimes tolerably continuous, but more frequently broken into detached irregular masses or nebulæ of light, extending from about *W. to S. E.* (true); which bearings correspond with *N. E. by N.* and *W. by S.* (magnetic).

It sometimes, however, extended a few points beyond these bearings, *but very rarely occupied any of the northern part of the heavens.*

Its termination to the S. E. was never exactly visible, owing to the height of land in that quarter; but, upon the whole, the arch seems to have been more frequently bisected by the plane of the magnetic, than by that of the true meridian.

The altitude of the upper margin of a permanent arch seldom exceeded ten or fifteen degrees, and from this coruscations were generally observed to be shooting towards the zenith.

In a few instances, the arch itself passed as high as the zenith; and on a single occasion, on the 28th of January, its direction was from true north to south.

The lower edge of the arch was generally well defined and unbroken, and the sky beneath it appeared, by contrast, so exactly like a dark cloud (to me often of a brownish color) that nothing at the time of viewing it could well convince one to the contrary, if the stars shining there with undiminished lustre did not discover the deception."—3 Parry, 59.

N. B.—1. Number of nights on which Aurora was seen.
2. The greater part assumed the same general character.
3. Usually consisted of an arch extending from W. to S. E.
4. Coruscations seldom occupied any of the northern part of the heavens.

DECEMBER 21, 1824.

"This winter certainly afforded but few brilliant displays of the Aurora. The following notice includes all that appear to me to require a separate description.

Late on the night of the 21st of December, the phenomenon appeared partially, and with a variable light, in different parts of *the southern sky* for several hours.

At seven on the following morning, it became more brilliant and stationary, describing a well-defined arch, extending *from the E. S. E. horizon to that at W. N. W.*, and passing through the zenith. A very faint arch was also visible on each side of this, appearing to diverge from the same points in the horizon,[1] and separating to twenty degrees' distance in the zenith.

It remained thus for twenty minutes, when the coruscations from each arch met, and, after a short but brilliant display of light, gradually died away."—Ibid., p. 60.

N. B.—1. This winter afforded very few brilliant displays.
2. This night appeared partially in different parts of the *southern* sky.
3. At 7 next a. m., arch from E. S. E. to W. N. W. passing through the zenith.
4. A very faint arch visible on each side of this.
5. After a short but brilliant display, died away.

JANUARY 15, 1825.

"Early on the morning of the 15th of January *the Aurora broke out to the southward*, and continued variable for three hours between a N. W. and S. E. bearing.

From three to four o'clock, *the whole horizon from south to west* was brilliantly illuminated, the light being continuous almost throughout the whole extent, and reaching several degrees in height. Very bright vertical rays were constantly shooting upwards from the general mass.

At half-past five, it again became so brilliant as to attract particular notice, describing *two arches passing in an east and west direction* very near the zenith, with bright coruscations issuing from it; but the whole gradually disappeared with the returning dawn.

At dusk the same evening, the Aurora again appeared *in the southern quarter*, and continued visible nearly the whole night, but without any remarkable feature."—Ibid., p. 61.

N. B.—1. Early a. m., Aurora broke out to the *southward.*
2. From 3h. to 4h. a. m., whole horizon from S. to W. brilliantly illuminated.
3. Very bright vertical rays shooting upward.
4. At 5h. 30m., again became very brilliant.
5. Describing two arches passing in an E. and W. direction very near the zenith.

JANUARY 27, 1825.

"About midnight on the 27th of January, this phenomenon broke out in a single compact mass of brilliant yellow light, *situated about a S. E. bearing*, and appearing *only a short distance above the land.* This mass of light, notwithstanding its general continuity, sometimes appeared to be evidently composed of numerous pencils of rays, compressed, as it were laterally, into one, its limits both to the right and left being well defined and nearly vertical. The light, though very bright at all times, varied almost constantly in intensity, and this had the appearance (not an uncommon one in the Aurora) of being produced by *one volume of light overlaying another*, just as we see the darkness and density of smoke increased by cloud rolling over cloud.

While Lieutenants Sherer and Ross and myself were admiring the extreme beauty of this phenomenon from the observatory, we all simultaneously uttered an exclamation of surprise at seeing a bright ray of the Aurora shoot suddenly downward from the general mass of light, *and between us and the land*, which was there distant only three thousand yards.

Had I witnessed this phenomenon by myself, I should have been disposed to receive with caution the evidence even of my own senses as to this last fact; but the appearance conveying precisely the same idea to three individuals at once, all intently engaged in looking towards the spot, I have no doubt that the ray of light actually passed within that distance of us."—Ibid., pp. 61, 62.

N. B.—1. About midnight, broke out in a single mass of brilliant yellow light, S. E.
2. Only a short distance from the land.
3. Bright ray of the Aurora shot down from general mass of light *between us and the land.*

---

[1] I am aware that this appearance is usually referred to the effect of viewing the phenomenon in perspective; but I here describe *appearances* only.

FEBRUARY 23, 1825.

"About one o'clock on the morning of the 23d of February, the Aurora again appeared over the hills *in a south direction*, presenting a brilliant mass of light very similar to that just described (27th January).

The rolling motion of the light laterally was here also very striking, as well as the increase of its intensity thus occasioned. The light occupied horizontally about a point of the compass, and extended in height scarcely a degree above the land, which seemed, however, to conceal from us a part of the phenomenon.

It was always evident enough that the most attenuated light of the Aurora *sensibly dimmed the stars*, like a thin veil drawn over them.

We frequently listened for any *sound* proceeding from this phenomenon, but *never heard* any."—Ibid., p. 62.

N. B.—1. Appeared in a south direction; brilliant.
2. Most attenuated light of the Aurora always sensibly dimmed the stars.
3. Frequently listened for sound, but never heard any.

Port Bowen.—Lat. 73° 13′ 39″ N. Long. 88° 54′ 58″ W. Winter of 1824–25. PARRY.

"On several occasions which seemed the most favorable for the purpose, the electrometer, with gold leaf, was applied to the chain, *but without the slightest perceptible effect.*

The chain was attached to the skysail masthead by glass rods, precisely in the manner described on our last voyage, the pointed end of the upper link being considerably above the masthead, and one hundred and fifteen feet from the level of the sea.

That the *atmosphere* during the winter months was *favorable to the excitement of electricity*, appeared from the facility with which a small electrical machine, constructed by Mr. Rowland, was found to act. The sparks given out by this machine, of which the cylinder was only six inches long and five in diameter, Dr. Neill considered as large as are usually elicited from apparatus of much larger dimensions in England.

Our *variation-needles, which were extremely light*, suspended in the most delicate manner, and, from the weak directive energy, susceptible of being acted upon by a very slight disturbing force, *were never in a single instance sensibly affected by the Aurora*, which could scarcely fail to have been observed at some time or other, had any such disturbance taken place, *the needles being visited every hour for several months*, and oftener when anything occurred to make it desirable."—3 Parry, p. 63.

N. B.—1. Not the slightest perceptible effect produced on the electrometer.
2. Variation-needles suspended in the most delicate manner.
3. Were never in a single instance sensibly affected by the Aurora,
4. Though the needles were visited every hour for several months.

"There was no want of well-defined clouds this winter; these were almost entirely of the kind called cirro-stratus, or approaching to that modification. Cumuli and cirro-cumuli occurred only with the advance of spring.

The sky in this respect differed from that of our winter at Melville Island, and also from those at Winter Island and Igloolik, clouds occurring much more frequently than at the former, and more rarely than at the two latter stations.

This difference seems to have coincided nearly with the state of the sea in the offing at each wintering-place, clouds occurring with more frequency in proportion to the extent of open water in our neighborhood.

At Port Bowen, we had occasionally lanes of clear water in the offing as late as the 22d of January, and the ice could be heard in motion till the 11th of February; but the water was of small extent after the first month subsequent to our arrival in winter quarters.

The occasional occurrence of fog, and the appearance of a dark water-sky to the northward, frequently observed from the hills during the winter, render it extremely probable that Barrow's

Strait was never entirely closed; a probability confirmed by the appearance of it at all times of the year in which it is accessible by ships."—Ibid., p. 76.

N. B.—1. No want of well-defined clouds this winter.
2. They were almost entirely cirro-stratus.
3. Cumuli and cirro-cumuli occurred only with the approach of spring.
4. Fogs and dark water-sky.

"Lieutenant Ross tried the thickness of the salt-water ice during different periods of the winter, by digging holes in that formed upon the canal by which the ships had entered, and found it to have increased in the following ratio:—

Date.	Whole thickness in inches.	Thickness above the sea in inches.	Proportion of that above to that below; the latter being = 100.
November 20, 1824	30.5	3.8	14.23
December 13, "	38.5	4.4	12.90
January 1, 1825	45.3	5.2	12.97
February 2, "	55.9	6.0	12.02
March 2, "	73.0	7.1	10.77
April 2, "	82.5	7.8	10.44
May 4, "	86.5	8.0	10.19"

Ibid., p. 77.

N. B.—Thickness of the salt-water ice during different periods of the winter.

Batty Bay.—Lat. 73° 17′ N. Long. 91° W. October 29, 1851. Kennedy.

"The weather has been very boisterous for some time past, with heavy showers of snow falling every day. The sun was for a very short time visible to-day.

The Aurora Borealis bright in the southwest about 9 p. m."—Kennedy, p. 86.

Batty Bay.—Lat. 73° 17′ N. Long. 91° W. December 28, 1851. Bellot.

"The sky has been generally clear these last days, and this evening we have, the first time, a complete *Aurora Borealis*, or *Northern Lights*, as our Shetlanders call them (they also call them *Dancing Lights*).

Great luminous rays like the milky way, but with a slight yellowish tint, divide the vault of the sky, issuing from the zenith, from which they spread like the leaves of a palm, widening at the base.

I do not know that mention has anywhere been made of this singular phenomenon."—2 Bellot, 73.

Lancaster Sound.—[Near Lat. 73° 40′ 40′′ N. Long. 75° 03′ 24′′ W.] Jan. 15, 1851. Kane.

"3 a. m., a faint Aurora to the southward."—1 Kane, p. 524.

Lancaster Sound.—[Near Lat. 74° N. Long. 80° W.] January, 1851. Kane.

"1st. A faint Aurora visible to the southward, 11 p. m.

2d. An Aurora passing near the zenith in an E. and W. direction, 1 a. m. Two Auroras visible (7 a. m.), one passing through the zenith in an E. and W. direction, the other in faint beams radiating from the southward.

3d. An Aurora to the southward, 4 a. m.

4th. 5 a. m., an Aurora visible to the southward and westward."—1 Kane, p. 524.

Captain Austin's Winter Quarters.—Lat. 74° 10′ N. Long. 94° 16′ W.

DECEMBER, 1850.

"The Aurora Borealis, which has hitherto afforded other voyagers so much interest, and which some writers allege to be almost constant in these regions, has not yet presented itself with any striking effect to our notice, except on the night of the 1st of December. A very complete arch in a N. N. W. and S. S. E. (true) direction, passing through the zenith, divided the celestial concave into two equal parts. It measured about 5° in width; it lasted about half an hour, and was of a whitish color. Towards the north, it became tinged with red before it disappeared. The stars were seen through it with great brilliancy; they assumed for the time the same color as the Aurora.

Some bright coruscations were seen on the morning of the 5th, shooting from the S. E. towards the zenith."—Arctic Miscellanies, pp. 113–14.

JANUARY, 1851.

"The Aurora Borealis has been observed eleven times during the month, but generally of a faint tinge. It has appeared in the form of an arch, touching the N. W. and S. E. quarters of the horizon; also in an arc between the S. W. and E. S. E. points, the altitude of the centre being 25°. Coruscations have been seen to cross the sky from various points of the horizon, and diverge in a variety of directions. During its presence, the heavenly bodies were always very bright. Many theories are advanced concerning these phenomena, one of which being that they move in columns parallel with the magnetic meridian, which is at variance with its movement in this locality."—Ibid., pp. 197–98.

FEBRUARY, 1851.

"The Aurora Borealis has been seen more frequently, though never with that brilliancy by which it is often characterized in these regions. The number of observations in the month, of any importance, amounts to twelve. The coruscations, when detached, flitted from various points of the horizon, in light fleecy clouds, towards the zenith, sometimes of a straw color. When it has appeared in an arch, its direction has been nearly north and south, passing across the zenith. On the evening of the 20th, luminous beams of the Aurora were frequent from the southwest to the northwest points, and continued for several hours. On the following day we had fresh winds from the southwest. It has been observed that when this phenomenon appears unusually intense in any particular quarter, that a strong breeze has succeeded it from that particular direction of the compass."—Ibid., pp. 250–51.

MARCH, 1851.

"The Aurora has appeared bright on four occasions; generally in the form of an arch, from the southeast quarter towards the north. On the night of the 25th, it was more brilliant than on any other occasion this season, making an arch from the southeast to the north, with coruscations shooting off laterally from it toward the zenith."—Ibid., p. 291.

Lancaster Sound.—Near Lat. 74° 18′ 08″ N. Long. 82° 10′ 18″ W. Dec., 1850. KANE.

"26th. Faint Aurora at noon, to the southward. An Aurora in form of a bow, passing through the zenith in a N. W. and S. E. direction.

27th. An Aurora visible at 5 a. m.; at 6 a. m., another one. In the afternoon, an Aurora passing through the zenith in a north and south direction, 10 p. m.

28th. Auroras visible; one passing 30° from the zenith, in form of an arch, to the westward, 1 a. m. and 8 a. m.

29th. An Aurora passing near the zenith in an east and west direction, 4 a. m.

31st. Auroras visible; one appeared in the form of an arch, extending to the horizon, in N. N. E. and S. W. direction, passing 15° from the zenith, 10 p. m."—1 KANE, 523.

Lancaster Sound.—[Lat. 74° 30′ N. Long. 90° W.] December 1, 1850. KANE.

"We had an Aurora about 7h. p. m. The thermometer at —33°, and falling. Wind steady, W. N. W. The meteor resembled an illuminated cloud; illuminated, because seen against the deep blue night sky; otherwise it resembled the mackerel fleeces and mares' tails of our summer skies at home.

It began toward the northwestern horizon as an irregular flaring cloud, sometimes sweeping out into wreaths of stratus; sometimes a condensed opaline nebulosity, rising in a zone of clearly-defined whiteness, from 3° to 5° in breadth up to the zenith, and then arching to the opposite horizon. This zone resembled more a long line of white cirro-stratus than the Auroral light of the systematic descriptions. There was no approach to coruscations, or even rectangular deviations from the axis of the zone. When it varied from a right line, its curvatures were waving and irregular, such as might be produced by the wind, but having no relation to the observed air-currents at the earth's surface. It passed from the due northwest, between the Pleiades and the Corona Borealis; the star of greatest magnitude in the latter of these constellations remaining in the centre, although its waving curves sometimes reached the Pleiades. At the zenith, its mean distance from the polar star was 7° south, and it passed down, increasing in intensity near Vega, in Lyra, to the southeast.

There was throughout the arc no marked seat of greatest intensity. Around the corona of the north, its light was more diffused. The zone appeared narrowed at the zenith, and bright and clear, without marked intermission, to the southeast. The frost-smoke was in smoky banks to the northwest; but the Aurora did not seem to be affected by it, and the compass remained constant."—1 Kane, p. 245–46.

Griffith Island.—Lat. 74° 30′ N. Long. 95° 20′ W. Winter of 1850–51. OSBORNE.

"With one portion of the phenomena of the North Sea we were particularly disappointed—and this was the Aurora.

The colors, in all cases, were vastly inferior to those seen by us in far southern latitudes; a pale-golden or straw color being the prevailing hue. The most striking part of it was its apparent proximity to the earth.

Once or twice the Auroral coruscations accompanied a moon in its last quarter, and generally previous to bad weather.

On one occasion, in Christmas week, the light played about the edge of a low vapor which hung at a very small altitude over us; it never, on this occasion, lit up the whole under surface of the said clouds, but formed a series of concentric semicircles of light, with dark spaces between, which waved, glistened, and vanished, like moonlight upon a heaving but unbroken sea.

At other times, a stream of the same colored vapor would span the heavens through the zenith, and from it would shoot sprays of pale-orange color for many hours; and then the mysterious light would again as suddenly vanish."—Osborne, pp. 164–65.

Griffith Island.—Lat. 74° 30′ N. Long. 95° 20′ W. December, 1850. MARKHAM.

"The Aurora Borealis began also to dart its ever-changing rays across the heavens. On the 1st of December [1850], a very complete arch, passing through the zenith, divided the celestial concave into two equal parts, of a whitish color tinged with red. The stars were seen through it with great brilliancy, assuming, for the time, the same color as the Aurora.

On the 5th, also, some very bright coruscations were seen to dart their rays towards the zenith.

Whenever this phenomenon appeared unusually intense in any particular quarter, a strong breeze generally succeeded from the same direction."—Markham, p. 70.

At Sea.—Lat. 74° 31′ N. Long. 111° 38′ W. September 20, 1819. PARRY.

"The wind blew hard from the northward during the night, with a good deal of snow; and the thermometer was at $10\frac{1}{2}$° at midnight.

The Aurora Borealis was seen faintly in the S. S. W. quarter of the heavens."—1 Parry, 93.

Barrow Strait and Lancaster Sound.—Between Lat. 74° 36′ 53″ N., Long. 91° 45′ 45″ W., and Lat. 74° 20′ 06″ N., Long. 86° 26′ 16″ W. December, 1850. KANE.

"3d. Faint Aurora visible for a short time.
5th. A transit Aurora, ending with luminous bands to the S. E.
6th. Faint Aurora, 4 a. m., to the west (true).
8th. Faint Aurora, 3 a. m., to the southward and eastward (true); another, 10 a. m., to the N. W. (true).
11th. An Aurora to the southward, 4 a. m."—1 Kane, p. 522.

Off Beechy Island.—[Lat. 74° 40′ N. Long. 92° W.] November 8, 1850. KANE.

"Aurora to the southward and westward, 5h. a. m. (true).
Ten Auroras observed during the month."—1 Kane, p. 520.

Assistance Harbor (Cornwallis Land).—Lat. 74° 40′ N. Long. 94° 16′ W. SUTHERLAND.

DECEMBER, 1850.

"The Aurora Borealis was frequently observed, but the extent and brilliancy of this beautiful meteoric phenomenon never equalled what had been seen in September and October, while crossing the Atlantic, in the latitude of Cape Farewell."—Sutherland, 1, p. 449.

JANUARY, 1851.

"The sky, during the hours of daylight—which, by this time, were lengthening out very plainly—was frequently spread over with fleecy clouds; and at night the Aurora, of a beautiful golden color, danced from east to west in vivid coruscations, and enlivened our midnight scenes, although, as has been remarked already, they were much less vivid than in more southern latitudes."—Ibid., pp. 457–58.

Barrow Strait (off Griffith Island).—[Lat. 74° 45′ N. Long. 94° W.] September, 1850. KANE.

"12th. A feeble Aurora at midnight.
15th. A feeble Aurora."—1 Kane, p. 516.

Winter Harbor.—Lat. 74° 47′ 13″ N. Long. 110° 49′ W. 1819–20. PARRY.

OCTOBER 13, 1819.

"On the evening of the 13th, the Aurora Borealis was seen very faintly, consisting of a stationary white light *in the southwest* quarter, and near the horizon."—1 Parry, 109.

OCTOBER 20, 1819.

"Between six and eight p. m., we observed the Aurora Borealis, forming a broad arch of irregular white light, extending from *N. N. W.* to *S. S. E.*, the centre of the arch being 10° to the eastward of the zenith. It was most bright near the southern horizon; and frequent, but not vivid, coruscations were seen shooting from its upper side towards the zenith.

The magnetic needle was not sensibly affected by this phenomenon."—Ibid., p. 111.

N. B.—1. Light most bright near southern horizon.
2. Magnetic needle not sensibly affected.

NOVEMBER 9, 1819.

"On the same evening, the weather being fine and clear, the Aurora Borealis was seen for nearly two hours, forming a long, low, irregular arch of light, extending from north to south in the western quarter of the heavens, its altitude in the centre being 3° or 4°. The electrometer-chain was hoisted up to the masthead, and its lower end brought down to the ice, so as to keep it perfectly clear of all the masts and rigging, which method was used throughout the winter; but no sensible effect was produced on the gold leaf. It was tried a second time, after the sky became full of white fleecy clouds, but with as little success."—Ibid., p. 115.

NOVEMBER 12, 1819.

"The thermometer having fallen to —31°, we expected to have seen the sun again, and looked out from the masthead for that purpose, but it did not reappear.

At six p. m., the Aurora Borealis was seen in a broken irregular arch, about 6° high in the centre, extending from N. W. by N. to S. by W., from whence a few coruscations were now and then faintly emitted towards the zenith."—Ibid., 115.

NOVEMBER 13, 1819.

"From eight p. m. till midnight, on the 13th, it was again seen in a similar manner from S. W. to S. E., the brightest part being in the centre, due south."—Ibid., p. 115.

NOVEMBER 15, 1819.

"On the 15th, Lieutenant Beechey informed me that he had seen, *in the N. N. W. and S. E.* quarters, some *light transparent clouds*, from which *columns of light* were thrown upwards, resembling the Aurora Borealis; those to the *S. E.*, being opposed to a very light sky, had a light-brown appearance."—Ibid., p. 115.

N. B.—1. Light transparent clouds N. N. W. and S. E.
2. From which columns of light were thrown upwards.
3. Resembling the Aurora Borealis.

NOVEMBER 16, 1819.

"This phenomenon was again observed on the 16th, consisting of a bright stationary light *from S. S. W. to S. by E.*, and reaching from the horizon to the height of about 6° above it."—Ibid., p. 116.

NOVEMBER 17, 1819.

"At three p. m. a remarkable variety of the Aurora Borealis was seen by several of the officers. Having about this time been confined for a few days to my cabin by indisposition, I am indebted to Lieutenant Beechey for the following description of it:—

'*Clouds*, of a light-brown color, were seen diverging from a point near the horizon, bearing *S. W. by S.*, and shooting pencils of rays upwards at an angle of about 45° with the horizon. These rays, however, were not stationary as to their position, but were occasionally extended and contracted. From behind these, as it appeared to us, flashes of white light were repeatedly seen, which sometimes streamed across to the opposite horizon; some passing through the zenith, others at a considerable distance on each side of it.

This phenomenon continued to display itself brilliantly for half an hour, and then became gradually fainter till it disappeared about four o'clock. The sun, at the time of the first appearance of this meteor, was on nearly the same bearing, and about 5° below the horizon.'"—Ibid., pp. 116–17.

N. B.—1. Remarkable variety of Aurora Borealis.
2. Clouds of a light-brown color.

NOVEMBER 18, 1819.

"The stars of the second magnitude in Ursa Major were just perceptible to the naked eye a little after noon this day, and the Aurora Borealis appeared faintly in the *southwest* at night."—Ibid., p. 117.

NOVEMBER 26, 1819.

"On the 26th, in the morning, some vivid coruscations of the Aurora Borealis were observed *from S. to N. W.*, commencing at 4° or 5° of altitude, and streaming toward the zenith."—Ibid., p. 118.

DECEMBER 14, 17, 1819.

"On the 14th of December, the day was beautifully serene and clear, and there was more redness in the southern sky about noon than there had been for many days before; the tints, indeed, might almost be called prismatic.

At 6 p. m., the Aurora Borealis was seen forming two concentric arches, passing from the western horizon on each side of the zenith to within 20° of the opposite horizon, resting on a *dark cloud* about seven degrees high, from behind which the light appeared to issue, and partially streaming from the *cloud* to the zenith. No effect was produced by it on the electrometer or the magnetic needle.

The appearance I have just described of the light seeming to issue from behind an obscure *cloud*, is a very common one; it is not always, however, easy to tell whether any *cloud* really exists, or whether the appearance is a deception arising from the vivid light of the Aurora being contrasted with the darker color of the sky near it.

On the 17th, in the morning, this phenomenon was again observed, being a stationary faint light from *S. W. to W. S. W.*"—Ibid., p. 121.

N. B.—1. At 6 p. m. Aurora formed two arches.
2. Passing from western horizon on each side of zenith.
3. Resting on a dark cloud,
4. From behind which light seemed to issue.
5. No effect produced on electrometer or needle.
6. The appearance of light seeming to issue from behind a cloud is a very common one.

DECEMBER 19, 1819.

"On the 19th, the weather being fine and clear, the Aurora borealis appeared frequently at different times of the day, generally from the *south* to the *W. N. W.* quarters, and not very vivid. From eight p. m. till midnight, however, it became more brilliant, and broke out in every part of the heavens, being generally most bright from S. S. W. to S. W., where it had the appearance of emerging from behind a *dark cloud* about five degrees above the horizon.

We could not, however, help feeling some disappointment in not having yet witnessed this beautiful phenomenon *in any degree of perfection* which could be compared to that which occurs at Shetland, or in the Atlantic, about the same latitude as these Islands."—Ibid., p. 122.

N. B.—1. Aurora appeared frequently at different times of the day.
2. Generally from S. to the W. N. W. quarters; not very vivid.
3. From 8 p. m. to 12, more brilliant.
4. Most bright from S. S. W. to S. W.,
5. Where it appeared to emerge from behind a dark cloud.
6. We had not yet witnessed this beautiful phenomenon in any degree of perfection.

DECEMBER 20, 1819.

"On the morning of the 20th, the Aurora Borealis again made its appearance in the N. W., which was more to the northward than usual. It here resembled two small bright clouds, the one nearly touching the other, and being about seven degrees above the horizon. These remained quite stationary for half an hour, and then broke up into streamers shooting rapidly towards the zenith."—Ibid., p. 122.

JANUARY 8, 1820.

"At half-past five p. m. on the 8th, the Aurora Borealis was seen forming a broken and irregular arch of white light, 10° or 12° high in the centre, extending from N. by W., round by W., to S. S. E., with occasional coruscations proceeding from it towards the zenith. It continued thus for an hour, and reappeared from eight o'clock till midnight in a similar manner, making, however, but a poor display of this beautiful phenomenon. Neither the magnetic needle nor the gold leaf of the electrometer were, in either instance, in the slightest degree affected by it."—Ibid., p. 133.

JANUARY 11, 1820.

"At eight a. m. on the 11th, faint coruscations of the Aurora Borealis were observed to dart with inconceivable rapidity across the heavens *from W. N. W. to E. S. E.*, from horizon to horizon, and passing about 25° to the south of the zenith.

At noon to-day, the temperature of the atmosphere had got down to 49° below zero, being the greatest degree of cold which we had yet experienced."—Ibid., p. 133.

N. B.—1. At 8h. a. m., faint coruscations,
2. Across the heavens from W. N. W. to E. S. E., from horizon to horizon,
3. Passing 25° to the south of the zenith.
4. At noon to-day, temperature —49°.

JANUARY 15, 1820.

"On the evening of the 15th, the atmosphere being clear and serene, we were gratified by a sight of the ONLY *very brilliant* and diversified display of Aurora Borealis which occurred during the whole winter. I believe it to be almost impossible for words to give an idea of the beauty and variety which this magnificent phenomenon displayed; I am at least certain that no description of mine can convey an adequate description of it, and I therefore gladly avail myself of the following account, by Captain Sabine, which was furnished by my request, at the time, for insertion in my Journal.

'Mr. Edwards, from whom we first heard that the Aurora was visible, described it as forming a complete arch, having its legs nearly north and south of each other, and passing a little to the eastward of the zenith.

'When I went upon the ice, the arch had broken up. Towards the southern horizon was the ordinary Aurora, such as we had lately seen on clear nights, being a pale light, apparently issuing from behind an *obscure cloud*, at from six to twelve degrees of altitude, extending more or less towards the east or west on different nights, and at different times of the same night, having no determined centre or point of bisection, the greater part, and even at times *the whole of the luminous appearance being sometimes to the east, and sometimes to the west of south, but rarely seen in the northern horizon*, or beyond the east and west points of the heavens. This corresponds with the Aurora most commonly noticed in Britain, except that it is there as peculiar to the northern *as here to the southern horizon*, occasionally shooting upwards in rays and gleams of light. It was not distinguished by any unusual brilliancy or extent on this occasion; the splendid part of the phenomenon being detached, and apparently quite distinct.

'The luminous arch had broken into irregular masses, streaming with such rapidity in different directions, varying continually in shape and intensity, and extending themselves from north, by the east, to south. If the surface of the heavens be supposed to be divided by a plane running through the meridian, the Aurora was confined, during the time I saw it, to the eastern side of the plane, and was usually most vivid and in longer masses in the E. S. E. than elsewhere. Mr. Parry and I noticed to each other that, where the Aurora was very brilliant, the stars seen through it were somewhat dimmed; though this remark is contrary to former experience.

'The distribution of light has been described as irregular and in constant change; the various masses, however, seemed to have a tendency to arrange themselves into two arches; one passing near the zenith, and a second about midway between the zenith and horizon, both having generally a north and south direction, but curving towards each other, so that their legs produced a complete ellipse; these arches were as quickly dispersed as formed. At one time, a part of the arch near the zenith was bent into convolutions, resembling those of a snake in motion, and undulating rapidly; an appearance we had not before observed. The end towards the north was also bent like a shepherd's crook, which is not uncommon. It is difficult to compare the light produced by the Aurora with that of the moon, because the shadows are rendered faint and indistinct by reason of the general diffusion of the Aurora; but I should think the effect of the one now described scarcely equal to that of the moon when a week old. The usual pale light of the Aurora strongly resembles that produced by the combustion of phosphorus. A very slight tinge of red was noticed on this occasion, when the Aurora was most vivid, but no other colors were visible, Soon after we returned on board, the splendid part wholly disappeared, leaving only the ordinary light near the horizon; in other respects the night remained unchanged, but on the following day it blew a fresh gale from the north and N. N. W.

'This Aurora had the appearance of being *very near us*, and we listened attentively for the *sound* which is said sometimes to accompany brilliant displays of this phenomenon, but neither on this nor on any other occasion could any be distinguished.'

On the following day, the Aurora was repeatedly seen for an hour or two together, assuming the shape of a long low arch, from 3° to 12° high in the centre, extending from south to N. W."—Ibid., pp. 134–35–36.

N. B.—1. The only brilliant display of Aurora seen during the whole winter.
2. Towards southern horizon, the ordinary Aurora.
3. Apparently issuing from behind a cloud.
4. Aurora seen sometimes east, and sometimes west of south, but rarely seen in the northern horizon.
5. Aurora in Britain as peculiar to the northern horizon as here to the southern.
6. This Aurora appeared to be very near us.
7. Heard no sound, which is said sometimes to accompany brilliant Aurora.

FEBRUARY 3, 1820.

"At six p. m., the Aurora Borealis appeared very faintly in a horizontal line of white light, extending from S. to S. S. W. and about 5° above the horizon. From nine till eleven, it was again seen quite stationary and very faint, from S. S. W. to W. N. W., at three or four degrees of altitude.

Captain Sabine had, for some time past, kept one of the needles used for determining the intensity of the magnetic force, suspended by a silk thread, in the Observatory, for the purpose of remarking more satisfactorily than it could be done on board the ships, whether any effect was produced upon it by the Aurora Borealis.

It might be supposed that in these regions, where the directive power of the needle had almost entirely ceased, it would be more easily disturbed by any adventitious cause than in those parts of the globe where the directive energy was greater; *but we never could perceive the slightest derangement to be produced in it by the Aurora.*"—Ibid., p. 139–40.

N. B.—1. At 6 p. m., appeared very faintly.
2. From 9 till 11, again seen very faint.
3. Could never perceive the slightest derangement of the needle produced by the Aurora.

FEBRUARY 8, 1820.

"On the 8th, at noon and for half an hour after, an appearance presented itself in the heavens which we had not before observed. *A thin fleecy cloud*, of a pale-red color, and shaped like part of an arch, commenced pretty strongly from the top of the land *in the N. W., and ran more and more faintly to N. by W.*, beyond which it could no longer be traced; it was here fifteen degrees above the northern horizon. On looking for a continuation of it in the opposite quarter of the heavens, we perceived a larger portion of another and fainter arch of pale-red or orange, commencing at the horizon in the E. by N., and extending to 60° of altitude in the N. N. E., so as evidently not to form a part of the western arch. Captain Sabine afterwards observed the whole phenomenon to alter its position; the leg of the eastern arch shifting considerably more to the southward. *In the evening*, the Aurora Borealis was seen forming a confused and irregular arch of white light, continually varying in brightness, about 8° high in the centre, and extending from *S. by E., round by the W., to N. N. W.* From the upper part of this arch, coruscations occasionally shot upwards, and a few streamers now and then burst forth also from the horizon in the S. S. E.; these latter went nearly up to the zenith, while the rest were more faint, and did not reach so high. I am confident that Aldebaran and the Pleiades were very sensibly dimmed by the most vivid of the coruscations, which appeared, in this respect, not to differ from any thin vapor or cloud floating in the atmosphere. The gold leaf of the electrometer, as well as the magnetic needle suspended in the Observatory, was carefully attended to, but neither of them suffered any sensible disturbance."—Ibid., pp. 141–42.

N. B.—1. At noon, a thin fleecy cloud.
2. Commenced in N. W., and ran more faintly to N. by W.

FEBRUARY 10, 1820.

"At a quarter past six p. m. on that day, the Aurora began to appear in *the south and S. W.*, in detached and not very brilliant pencils of rays darting upwards from near the horizon.

Soon after, an arch of the usual broken and irregular kind appeared in the western quarter of the heavens, extending from *N. W. to south*, and being from 5° to 8° high in the centre. From the upper part of the arch proceeded a few faint coruscations reaching to no great height.

At a quarter before seven, a second and better-defined arch crossed over *from S. E. to N. W. by N.*, passing on the northern side of the zenith, from which it was distant from 10° to 15° in the centre.

This arch was very narrow, and seemed to be formed of two parts, each shooting with great rapidity from those parts where the legs stood, and joining in the centre. In a short time, this second arch entirely disappeared, and the first became less brilliant.

The phenomenon was then for some minutes confined to some bright pencils of rays *in the south and S. S. E.*, which were generally parallel to each other, but sometimes also diverged at an angle of about 15°.

At a quarter past seven, two long and narrow streams of light crossed over, at 35° to 40° of altitude, on the western side of the zenith, *from the N. W. by N. and south points* of the horizon. Their upper ends did not quite meet in the centre so as to complete an arch, but inclined to the shape of shepherds' crooks, as described on the 15th of January, and often remarked by former observers; but they were neither so brilliant nor so well defined as when we saw them before.

About a quarter before eight, as we were returning on board from the Observatory, the low arch to the westward first described, and which had never altogether disappeared, increased considerably in brilliancy. It was still, however, so irregular as to appear in detached roundish clouds or blotches, from which the pencils, which shot upwards, appeared immediately to proceed. These pencils, which were infinitely varied both in length and breadth, were observed to have also a slow, though very sensible, *lateral motion from north to south and vice versâ;* and we remarked on one occasion that, when two of them met and had the appearance of overlapping, they produced, for about fifteen seconds, the most intense degree of light we had yet seen from the Aurora. *The pencils appeared generally to travel bodily in one direction*, but sometimes to widen out in both at the same time.

We were all decidedly of opinion that the fixed stars were very perceptibly dimmed by this phenomenon, which gradually disappeared by nine o'clock."—Ibid., p. 142.

N. B.—1. At 6 p. m., a very brilliant display S. and S. W.
2. Soon after, an arch from N. W. to S.
3. At a quarter before seven, a second arch, better defined, from S. E. to N. W. by N.
4. Then for some minutes confined to some pencils of rays in S. and S. E.
5. At 7h. 15m., two long streams of light, west side of zenith, from N. W. by N. and S. points of the horizon.
6. Lateral motion from north to south.
7. The pencils appeared to travel bodily in one direction.
8. Disappeared at 9h. p. m.
9. Fixed stars perceptibly dimmed.

FEBRUARY 11, 1820.

"At half-past eight p. m., the Aurora Borealis made its appearance for a short time in an arch, very irregular but at times very bright, *from S. W. to S. S. E.*, at 4° or 5° above the horizon in the centre."—Ibid., p. 144.

FEBRUARY 19, 1820.

"At half-past ten p. m. on the 19th, the Aurora Borealis was seen, as described by Lieut. Beechey, in bright coruscations, shooting principally from the *S. by W. quarter, across the zenith, to N. N. E.*, and partially in every part of the heavens.

The light, when most vivid, was of a pale-yellow, at other times white, excepting to the southward, in which direction a dull red tinge was now and then perceptible. The coruscations had a tremulous waving motion, and most of them were crooked towards the E. N. E.

The fresh gale which blew at the time from the N. N. E. appeared to have no effect on the Aurora, which, as before observed, streamed directly to windward, and this with great velocity.

The brighter part of this meteor *dimmed whatever stars it passed over, even those of the first magnitude;* and those of the second and third magnitude so much as to render them scarcely visible.

The wind blew too strong for the electrometer to be used, but Kater's compass was not in the slightest degree affected.

The whole of the phenomenon disappeared in about three-quarters of an hour."—Ibid., p. 147.

N. B.—Dimmed whatever stars it passed over, even those of the first magnitude.

MARCH 4, 1820.

"The Aurora Borealis was seen faintly near the S. S. W. horizon, for three or four hours before midnight."—Ibid., p. 152.

MARCH 8, 1820.

"From nine p. m. till midnight, the Aurora Borealis appeared faintly in the horizon *to the south*, occasionally streaming towards the zenith in coruscations of pale-white light."—Ibid., p. 156.

APRIL 16, 1820.

"In the afternoon of the 16th, the weather became clear and nearly calm; Mr. Hooper and myself observed a coloring in some light fleecy clouds, which formed one of the most beautiful phenomena that I had ever seen.

These clouds, which were small and white, and almost the only ones in the heavens, assumed, as they approached and passed under the sun, the most soft and exquisite tints of light lake, bluish-green, and yellow about their edges that can possibly be imagined. These tints appeared only when the clouds were within 15° or 20° of the sun, were brightest as they passed under it, which they did as close as 2°, and began to be again indistinct at 10° from it. Some of the clouds remained colored in this way for upwards of a quarter of an hour. There did not seem to be any regular arrangement of tints, as in the prismatic spectrum, but the lake was always next the sun."—Ibid , p. 166.

Winter Harbor.—Lat. 74° 47′ 13″ N. Long. 110° 49′ W. FISHER.

OCTOBER 27, 1819.

"The Aurora Borealis was seen *to the southward*, but it was too faint to deserve any description."—Fisher, p. 150.

NOVEMBER 17, 1819.

"Between three and four o'clock this afternoon, a remarkable *cloud* was observed in the southwest; the centre of it, indeed, bore S. W. by S. (true). It diverged from a centre, at the horizon, in straight lines or columns, which extended to a great distance over the surface of the sky. The lower edge of it, on each side, was very straight and well defined, and formed an angle of about 45° with the horizon. Directly over its centre, instead of straight lines, it had more the appearance of an immense volume of smoke than anything else. The whole was compared by our gunner to a powder magazine in a state of explosion; which those who had an opportunity of seeing such a sight thought a very apt comparison, for the reflected rays of the sun, which illumined that part of the sky behind the cloud, gave it very much the appearance of an immense explosion.

It is probable that this remarkable cloud had some connection with the Aurora Borealis; for after it had vanished, which took place about six o'clock, that phenomenon was seen in the same part of the heavens that the cloud occupied. It made its appearance, indeed, before the cloud disappeared entirely, but not before it had lost its radiated form, and dispersed so much that nothing particular could be seen about it."—Ibid., pp. 156–57.

N. B.—1. Between three and four p. m. remarkable cloud.
2. It is probable that this remarkable cloud had some connection with the Aurora Borealis.

Wellington Channel.—[Lat. 74° 54′ N. Long. 93° W.] October, 1850. KANE.

" 17th. A faint Aurora to the southward (true) at one a. m.
21st. A faint Aurora 8° east of magnetic north.
22d. A faint Aurora, more bright, with segment.
26th. Very faint Aurora.
27th. Bistre-colored auroral segment, 20° east of magnetic axis.
29th. Faint nebulous Aurora.
31st. Observed a small Aurora to the northward (by compass) at one a. m."—1 Kane, p. 519.

Baffin's Bay.—Lat. 75° 12′ N. July 21, 1817. O'REILLY.

"July 21, 1817. Thermometer 34°, 48°, 42°. Wind, a perfect calm.

At three a. m. this morning, a most magnificent display of radiation occurred, of which a sketch has been attempted.

The cirrus radiation here remarked is always observed to issue from a body of detached clouds assuming the form of an arch. Whether this curved arrangement be actually in a portion of a circumference of a circle, or merely an optical delusion, I will not undertake to assert, but the curve invariably appeared to me arched as I have related. The basis arch of the phenomenon which occurred this morning was of amazing span, embracing several leagues of sea, the central radius passing through the horizon in *nearly E. by N. per compass;* which corresponds closely with the point of variation.

The radiation darted rapidly and irregularly towards the opposite point of the sky in pale white spires. The atmosphere in the southern region immediately became suffused with whitish-brown cirro-stratus. Soon afterwards, various beautiful changes to minute cirro-cumulus and comoid cirrus were observable.

Within the arch lay a long linear bed of cirro-stratus, almost black, which preserved a horizontal position and unaltered form during the radiation and the changes mentioned. In the space of three hours from the first appearance, the whole was dissolved and dissipated, leaving the atmosphere free of visible cloud, but not quite clear, being of a milky blue.

I should not have intruded upon the reader's notice the detail of this radiation, had I not been convinced, by repeated observations, that there exists a close, it may be said a direct, correspondence between its appearance and the variation of the needle. From what cause this singular coincidence proceeds, it will still longer, I fear, remain to be explored. The facts, however, which are herein exhibited, may be relied on for the accuracy and faithfulness of report, and may induce some enlightened and able mind to study a satisfactory illustration of the phenomenon.

It is right, also, to inform the reader that, during the formation and continuance of the radiation, no irregular motion of the compass was observable; the entire process appearing to go on at an elevation far too great to admit of any influence on the needle.

The state of the cloud, its being invariably a base of distinct cirro-stratus in a curved chain, the radiation always issuing, as it would appear, from behind the cirro-stratus, and having a cirrous consistence, and all those appearances being usually succeeded by a wind from the opposite point, besides the correspondence with the variation, are circumstances well worthy the philosopher's attention."—O'Reilly, pp. 169–71.

Northumberland Sound (Winter Quarters).—Lat. 76° 52′ N. Long. 97° W. December, 1852. BELCHER.

"On the evening of the 2d of December, about nine p. m., the first well-authenticated Aurora was observed. All our instruments being then available, I was anxious to ascertain its effect on them. Mr. Cheyne was directed to report on the electrometers, and I add his remarks, as I believe he was called in time to see it in part.

'SIR: Last night, at 9.20, I observed an Aurora, a light narrow streak, extend from the summit of the Observatory Hill, passing immediately through the zenith in a direction south by east (true), terminating in a feather about 25° north of the zenith (?). Four cumulous-shaped masses appeared as though only about a couple of hundred feet from the mastheads; these masses lasted about three minutes, and then suddenly disappeared, having apparently shifted their position about twenty feet during that time. The long streak gradually vanished in about eight minutes.

The magnetometer read 116.50°, was perfectly steady; nor was the electrometer in the least affected. The sky was perfectly clear.

(Signed) J. P. CHEYNE, Lieutenant.

December 3, 1852.'

Mr. Cheyne was not an observer; he probably took this 116.50° from the register for nine hours,[1] which is there so recorded, but he could not judge of the steadiness of the magnetometer: at eight it was 117.30°; at ten, 120.60°. But *it is not clear to my mind* that it was not affected, and that the causes which *produced this Aurora* had not been in action the last eight hours; viz: from four p. m. until midnight, when it reached 137.80°, equal to 27.60° of deflection; a disturbance not before recorded. Even between nine and midnight, we have a deflection of 21.30°!

The barometer, during the interval between eight and midnight, suddenly changed from 29.860 to 29.650, regaining its height, and rising to 29.900 when the magnetometer, at sixteen hours, showed 107.90.

I had almost begun to conjecture that we were in too cold a medium, or that it might not extend to so high a latitude. Considering, too, that its first appearance generally occurs with the first shades of winter, I could hardly understand its prolonged absence. I had observed it to the north of Behring's Strait on the 25th August, and continuously up to the 5th October, in its greatest brilliancy; and in Wales, at Swansey, in August. But I notice that Parry, in his first voyage, and nearest to us, did not record it until the 8th of January; on his third, which follows in order of latitude, in October and November; and in his second, in October. I did not witness it myself; indeed, it was not reported. I casually heard of it next day, and issued orders 'invariably to call me.' It was only on perusing the official report called for from Lieut. Cheyne, that I was induced to search the magnetometer records for its motions.

December 5. Another Aurora, noticed this evening, presented vertical shoots or broom-like fasciæ shooting towards the zenith (from behind the hill N. N. W), in pale flame-tinted rays, to an altitude of 20°. No disturbance was recorded, but it is highly probable that the variations registered at nine and ten p. m. are attributable to this influence. It recurred about midnight, but it is not indicated by the magnetometer. At noon, it is suddenly deflected."—Belcher, 1, p. 173.

"On the 6th, 9th, and 10th of December, further exhibitions of Aurora occurred, and some slight deflections of the magnetometer were apparent, but generally preceding or following.

---

[1] All terms of time refer to astronomical periods from noon to noon.

About three a. m. on the 12th, the Aurora was reported by the officer of the watch as very brilliant. But as I was comfortably in bed, and it was beyond my examination, and would vanish before I could possibly be in a proper state to receive such a delicate visitor, I directed Messrs. May and Cheyne to pay every attention. It was Mr. May's guard at the magnetometer, and Mr. Cheyne was excused watch solely to attend to the electrometers, &c. It was asserted that the electric fluid was noticed on the wires *fairly caught; certes* Mr. Cheyne found no disturbance. I am not quite sure that he had his instruments placed in connection with his wires, or that he reached in time, possibly thinking as I did. (?) Mr. May repaired to the Observatory, and, unfortunately, my later orders were not then in force, or we should have had a full history of this visitation. The magnetometer exhibited the most unmistakable signs of disturbance, moving instantaneously from 114° to 128°, and up to 150°, returning at four a. m. to 117.90.

This, then, I consider as strong proof; and, taking into consideration other very decided deflections when no cause was apparent, I am induced to believe that the affection precedes or follows what may be indistinct, or not at all noticed by simple atmospheric observers, and nothing short of very close watching at the magnetometer will indicate the truth. But it must be borne in mind that this extra duty is a delicate service, and, to maintain even moderate interest, I know full well that the greatest tact is necessary to keep up the importance of the operators. No 'soft sawder' will do here; it is only by making the observer feel his importance, and in this aspect his responsibility to the civilized world, that he can be persuaded to extend his labors. Science will never be driven.

This Aurora was reported 'to have been duly captured, but broke the wires;' and as we could not find any of *her* (she has become a female) on the wires, and I could obtain no direct testimony (but the reverse) that Mr. Cheyne's electrometers were not influenced, the question remained *in nubibus.*"—Ibid., p. 178.

At Sea.—Lat. 77° 55′ N. Long. 0° 55′ W. May 20, 1818. SCORESBY.

"The nights being light, the Aurora Borealis could not be seen; but on the evening of the 20th of May, an appearance was observed very much resembling the Aurora Borealis, yet no signs of electricity were observed in the electrometer applied to the conductor."—1 Scoresby, 383.

Van Rensselaer Harbor (N. E. of Smith's Sound).—Lat. 78° 45′ N. Long. 71° W. KANE.

NOVEMBER 13, 1853.

"Three a. m. Nebulous patch to the south by east, closing in S. S. W. with slight illumination.

NOVEMBER 26, 1853.

Nine p. m. Bright belt crossing the zenith from north to south; wavy in outline, but destitute of color or scintillation.

NOVEMBER 28, 1853.

One a. m. Bright auroral light to the southward (S. 14° W.).

Four a. m. Same; west 21° south to south, quite fixed; a nebulous patch of illuminated sky; elevation never exceeding 30°.

NOVEMBER 30, 1853.

Five hours thirty minutes p. m. Aurora of same character but very faint, nearly due east; faded by 7 p. m.

DECEMBER 1, 1853.

Eight p. m. Two horizontal belts to S. W.

DECEMBER 4, 1853.

Two a. m. A very slight illumination noted to S. W.

DECEMBER 8, 1853.

Three a. m. Same, more defined, from N. E., at altitude of 30°, passing through the zenith and lost in diffused light.

DECEMBER 24, 1853.

Four to eight a. m. Bright 'spots' described by watch on the horizon to S. W. Perhaps auroral.

DECEMBER 29, 1853.

Twelve (noon) to four p. m. Light illumination above northern horizon.

JANUARY 27, 1854.

Five a. m. to eight a. m. Brilliant Aurora of same character as that of November 26; no colors; needle undisturbed; altitude 70°.

JANUARY 28, 1854.

Twelve (midnight). A slight auroral light, extending from S. E. to N. in a belt.

FEBRUARY 4, 1854.

Four hours thirty minutes a. m. Bright arch to W. and N. W. extending towards zenith.

FEBRUARY 5, 1854.

Seven p. m. Auroral arc; altitude of centre of segment 35°; direction from N. to E. N. E.

NOVEMBER 13, 1854.

Four p. m. Nebulous patches S. and S. W. (Too light to observe.)

NOVEMBER 18, 1854.

Six p. m. A belt seen to S. W.

NOVEMBER 22, 1854.

Two a. m. Slight approach to arch-like arrangement.

DECEMBER 14, 1854.

Ten p. m. Tolerably defined arc passing through zenith; limbs lost about 40° above horizon; quite anomalous.

JANUARY 7, 1855.

Twelve to two a. m. Bright patch of illumination about 15° above horizon, S. by W., as seen from outside floes.

FEBRUARY 10, 1855.

Two a. m. Diffused light with slight motion, S. by W.

GENERAL REMARKS.—During second winter only were marked exhibitions noted. In but two instances—viz: January 27, 1854, and February 10, 1855—was any motion detected allied to 'merry dancers' of the south. The processes had no apparent connection with the magnetic dip, and in no case did the needle of our unifilar indicate disturbance. The scintillations noted November 26 were very imperfect. The general character of the display was analogous to that of Lancaster Sound, but less intense in illumination, wanting in definition, and having no uniform relation to any quarter of the compass."—Kane's Expedition through Baffin's Bay to the Open Polar Sea, Lat. 82° 30′ N.

[*The following observations were accidentally omitted.*]

Cumberland House.—Lat. 53° 56′ 40″ N. Long. 102° 16′ 41″ W. October 23, 1819, to June 13, 1820. Hood.

"January 14, 1820. At ten p. m., Aurora faintly visible north.

19th. An Aurora, embracing the horizon from N. N. W. to N. N. E., about 12° high, 5° broad; faint, but permanent; twelve p. m.

20th. At eleven p. m., an arched Aurora, centre north, 15° high, and 5° broad.

27th. At ten p. m., an Aurora 40° high and 5° broad; usual color, and faint; centre north.

February 2d. An Aurora very faint; centre north, about 2° high; extending from east to west.

8th. Appearance of an Aurora, at ten p. m., in the northern horizon.

10th. An Aurora arched, centre N. by E., about 4° high and 30° long.

12th. At ten p. m., an arched Aurora, centre north, about 6° high. Between it and the zenith, were sometimes visible several perpendicular streams, with one extremity pointed, and declining nearly in the direction of the dipping needle. They sometimes reappeared in the same place which they had occupied at first. I shall, for the future, call them flashes.

19th. An Aurora across the zenith, cutting the meridian at right angles. That side of it which faced the south was a regular line; but the other streamed at intervals towards the east or west, separating itself into portions resembling the flashes, but much smaller; color as usual; many flashes near the northern horizon. This Aurora was followed, on the 20th, by a storm of snow E. S. E.

29th. An Aurora arched, centre north, extending 60°; height 30°, breadth 5°. Towards the eastern extremity, it was broken, by a quick undulating motion, into those portions described above, which I shall call beams, because they appear to tend towards a common centre, though their direction is sometimes altered when in motion. Color as usual.

March 4th. At twelve p. m., a beautiful and singular Aurora; four regular concentric arches, the outermost extending from N. N. W. to E. N. E., about 30° high, and the others at equal distances within it, the last being 7° high. Each was 3° broad; faint, but visible for three hours.

5th. An appearance of Aurora in the northern horizon.

6th. A large, brilliant, arched Aurora, centre N. N. E., at nine p. m. It advanced rapidly to the southward, separating into beams, and scattering many flashes. The motion of the beams was exceedingly quick, and they were bright, but of the usual color. They ranged themselves in wreaths, forming Coronæ Boreales in the zenith, which faded gradually, leaving a pale undistinguished body of light, out of which they were soon again renovated, without apparent communication with any other body of the Aurora.

7th. At one a. m., the above Aurora spread over the whole sky, except a portion from S. S. E. to S. S. W.

At nine p. m., an arched Aurora, centre N. N. E.; many flashes, which, at twelve p. m., filled the northern half of the sky.

8th. An arched Aurora, centre N. N. E. It did not advance to the zenith, but separated into brilliant beams, and scattered many flashes. The motion of the beams was in wreaths, or segments of circles; rapid, and exhibiting at the lower extremities a red-orange color, and at the upper faint yellow.

9th. At eight p. m., an Aurora consisting of several arches, the highest of which was the faintest. They were almost obscured by flashes between them and the spectator.

10th. At nine p. m., an Aurora, in rapid motion, seen through breaks in the clouds.

11th. An Aurora, in many segments, from E. N. E. to W. N. W.; beams in rapid motion; ordinary color.

12th. At eight p. m., an arched Aurora, centre N. by E. At ten p. m., it approached near the zenith, and broke into beams and flashes. Ordinary color.

14th and 15th. Auroræ just visible through the clouds.

16th. A bright Aurora, but almost hid by the clouds.

17th. Aurora visible through a dense haze.

18th. At twelve p. m., an arched Aurora, centre N. N. E., about 20° high, 6° broad, extending from N. W. to E.

19th. At eight p. m., an appearance of Aurora in the northern horizon.

N. B.—From March 22 to April the 8th, the descriptions of the Auroræ and other observations relative to their height, have been delivered in a separate paper.

April 10th and 12th. Appearance of Aurora north.

14th. At nine p. m., an arched Aurora, about 15° high; centre north.

15th. An arched Aurora, 16° high, centre N. by E.

16th. Appearance of Aurora N. N. E.

19th. At ten p. m., an arched Aurora 25° high, centre N. by E., extending from N. E. to N. N. W. At eleven p. m., it was 35° high, and its eastern extremity turned back upon itself, and appeared to dart a flash perpendicularly towards the earth. At 11h. 30m. p. m., several flashes reached the zenith. Color as usual.

20th. Appearance of Aurora through a thick fog.

27th. At twelve p. m., a segment of an arch, and several flashes, north, and about 30° high.

29th. Several flashes of Aurora bearing north.

30th. At eight p. m., an arched Aurora 30° high; centre bearing N. N. E., extremities N. E. by E. and N. W. by N.

May 1st. A twelve p. m., a remarkable Aurora rose from E. N. E. like the trunk of a tree, and spread forth branches all over the sky, but principally towards the south. They were composed of beams, which always are distinguishable when the Aurora is much agitated. Ordinary color; many scattered flashes round the horizon.

2d. At eleven p. m., an arch across the zenith, 6° broad, and faint; extremes E. by S. and W. by N.

3d. At ten p. m., an Aurora in rapid motion, seen through the clouds.

5th. At eleven p. m., an arched Aurora, very faint; centre N. N. E.

12th. At twelve p. m., the northern half of the sky was filled with a light attenuated Aurora, not more brilliant than the milky way; but flashing with such rapidity that the eye could not follow its motion, nor determine its form.

12th. At eight p. m., appearance of Aurora north.

18. Ditto.

23d. An arched Aurora 15° high; centre N. by E.

28th. Appearance of Aurora in the northern horizon.

N. B.—The above descriptions were taken at the times inserted. The Aurora no doubt often changed its form afterwards. Many of the faint arches, however, altered only their positions in the course of four or five hours, by approaching nearer to the zenith."—1 Franklin (Hood), 543–46.

Christian's Sound.—Lat. 60° 04′ N. Long. 43° 00′ W. October 26, 1828. GRAAH.

"In the evening a beautiful Aurora Borealis displayed itself, in the shape of a bow stretching through the zenith from east to west. It produced no perceptible effect on the magnetic needle."—Graah, p. 48.

Nennortalik (Greenland).—Lat. 60° 08′ N. Long. 45° 16′ W. March 21, 1829. GRAAH.

"Between nine and eleven p. m., we had a brilliant display of the Aurora, which, particularly towards the south and zenith, exhibited a succession of the most vivid colors."—Graah, p. 58.

Off Winter Island (Hudson's Bay).—Lat. 66° 11′ 26″ N. Long. 82° 53′ 45″ W. August 31, 1823. LYON.

"During the night, we saw the Aurora very bright over Winter Island.

It was remarkable that we should have seen it so seldom and faintly at Igloolik, and that now again we should, on returning to Winter Island, find it as brilliant as we had been accustomed to see it at the same place two years before.

The nights were now very cold, long, and dark, and the sea froze thickly when not agitated."—Lyon, pp. 455–56.

LIST

OF

JOURNALS, ETC., REFERRED TO IN THE PRECEDING PAGES.

American Magazine.—A Monthly Miscellany, conducted by Horatio Gates Spafford, A. M., F. A. A. Albany, N. Y., March, 1816.

Arctic Miscellanies.—A Souvenir of the late Polar Search. By the Officers and Seamen of the Expedition. A MS. Newspaper, called "The Aurora Borealis," published on board H. M. S. Assistance, Captain Ommaney, 1850–51. London, 1852.

Austin.—Report of Proceedings of Arctic Searching Expedition, under command of Captain Austin, R. N.

Austin.—Report of H. T. Austin, Captain of her majesty's ship Resolute and in charge of an Expedition to the Arctic Seas in search of Sir John Franklin, 1850–51. Inclosing Reports and Journals of Proceedings of Searching Parties acting under his orders.

Back.—Narrative of the Arctic Land Expedition to the mouth of the Great Fish River, and along the shores of the Arctic Ocean, in the years 1833, 1834, and 1835. By Captain Back, R. N., Commander of the Expedition. London, 1836.

Beechey.—A Voyage of Discovery towards the North Pole, performed in his majesty's ships Dorothea and Trent, under the command of Captain David Buchan, R. N., 1818. By Captain F. W. Beechey, R. N., F. R. S., one of the lieutenants of the Expedition. London, 1843.

Beechey.—Narrative of a Voyage to the Pacific and Behring's Strait, to co-operate with the Polar Expeditions, performed in H. M. ship Blossom, under the command of Capt. F. W. Beechey, R. N., in the years 1825–26–27–28. London, 1831.

Belcher.—Narrative of a Voyage round the world, performed in her majesty's ship Sulphur, during the years 1836–42. By Captain Sir Edward Belcher, R. N., Commander of the Expedition. In two volumes. London, 1843.

Belcher.—Proceedings of the Squadron in the Arctic Seas, under the command of Sir Edward Belcher, C. B. August, 1852, to July, 1853.

Belcher.—Narrative of Sir Edward Belcher; detailing his visit to Jones's Sound, and further proceedings to the 10th of November, 1853, when the "Assistance" was frozen in near Cape Osborn in the Wellington Channel. And his further proceedings to March, 1854, and August, 1854.

Belcher.—The Last of the Arctic Voyages; being a Narrative of the Expedition in H. M. S. Assistance, under the command of Captain Sir Edward Belcher, C. B., in search of Sir John Franklin, during the years 1852–53–54. In two volumes. London, 1855.

Bellot.—Memoirs of Lieutenant Joseph René Bellot, Chevalier of the Legion of Honour, &c. With his Journal of a Voyage to the Polar Seas in search of Sir John Franklin. In two volumes. London, 1855.

Billings.—An Account of a Geographical and Astronomical Expedition to the Northern parts of Russia, performed by Commodore Joseph Billings, in the years 1785, &c., to 1794. Narrated from the original papers by Martin Sauer, Secretary to the Expedition. London, 1802.

Bonnycastle.—Newfoundland in 1842. By Sir Richard Henry Bonnycastle, Knt., Lieutenant-Colonel in the Corps of Royal Engineers. In two volumes. London, 1842.

Cartwright.—A Journal of Transactions and Events, during a residence of nearly sixteen years on the Coast of Labrador. By George Cartwright, Esq. In three volumes. London, 1792. 4to.

Chappell.—Narrative of a Voyage to Hudson's Bay in his majesty's ship Rosamond; containing some account of the Northeastern coast of America, and of the Tribes inhabiting that remote Region. By Lieut. Edward Chappell, R. N. London, 1817.

Cochrane.—Narrative of a Pedestrian Journey through Russia and Siberian Tartary, from the frontiers of China to the Frozen Sea and Kamtschatka, performed during the years 1820, 1821, 1822, and 1823. By Capt. John Dundas Cochrane, R. N. Philadelphia, 1824.

Collinson.—Proceedings of Captain Collinson, C. B. Her majesty's discovery ship Enterprise, Behring's Strait division of Arctic Search, 1851–54.

Cook.—A Voyage to the Pacific Ocean. Undertaken by the command of his majesty for making Discoveries in the Northern Hemisphere. Performed under the direction of Captains Cook, Clerk, and Gore, in his majesty's ships the Resolution and the Discovery, in the years 1776, 1777, 1778, 1779, and 1780. In three volumes. London, 1784. 4to.

Crantz.—The History of Greenland: containing a Description of the Country and its Inhabitants, &c. By David Crantz. In two volumes. London, 1767.

Dixon.—A Voyage round the World; but more particularly to the Northwest Coast of America. Performed in 1785, 1786, 1787, and 1788. By Captain George Dixon. London, 1789. 4to.

Dobbs.—An Account of the Countries about Hudson's Bay, in the Northwest part of America. By Arthur Dobbs, Esq. London, 1744. 4to.

Duncan.—Voyage to Davis's Strait. By David Duncan, Master of the ship Dundee. London, 1827.

Ellis.—A Voyage to Hudson's Bay, by the Dobbs Galley and California, in the years 1746 and 1747, for discovering a Northwest Passage, &c. By Henry Ellis, Gent. London, 1748.

Erman.—Travels in Siberia; including Excursions Northwards, down the Obi, to the Polar Circle, and Southwards to the Chinese frontier. By Adolph Erman. Translated from the German by W. D. Cooley. In two volumes. Philadelphia, 1850.

Fisher.—A Journal of a Voyage of Discovery to the Arctic Regions, in his majesty's ships Hecla and Griper, in the years 1819 and 1820. By Alexander Fisher, Surgeon R. N. Third edition. London, 1821.

Forsyth.—Proceedings of Commander Charles C. Forsyth, R. N., of the "Prince Albert" discovery vessel, in the summer of 1850.

Franklin.—Narrative of a Journey to the Shores of the Polar Sea, in the years 1819, '20, '21, and '22. By John Franklin, Captain R. N., F. R. S., and Commander of the Expedition. London, 1823.

Franklin.—Narrative of a Second Expedition to the Shores of the Polar Sea, in the years 1825, 1826, and 1827. By John Franklin, Captain R. N., F. R. S., &c., and Commander of the Expedition. Including an Account of the Progress of a Detachment to the Eastward. By John Richardson, M. D., &c. London, 1828.

Frederick.—Proceedings of Captain Charles Frederick, Commander H. M. ship Amphitrite, on a visit to Behring's Straits and the vicinity. 1852.

Freminville.—Voyage to the North Pole in the frigate The Syreone; including a Physical and Geographical Notice relative to the Island of Iceland. By the Chevalier de la Poix de Freminville, Lieutenant, Chief of the Brigade of the Marine Cadets, &c. London, 1819.

Goodsir.—An Arctic Voyage to Baffin's Bay and Lancaster Sound, in search of friends with Sir John Franklin. By Robert Anstruther Goodsir, late President of the Royal Medical Society of Edinburgh. London, 1850.

Graah.—Narrative of an Expedition to the East Coast of Greenland, sent, by order of the King of Denmark, in search of the Lost Colonies, under the command of Captain W. A. Graah, of the Danish Navy. London, 1837.

Hearne.—A Journey from Prince of Wales's Fort, in Hudson's Bay, to the Northern Ocean. Undertaken, by order of the Hudson's-Bay Company, for the Discovery of Copper Mines, a Northwest Passage, &c., in the years 1769, 1770, 1771, and 1772. By Samuel Hearne. London, 1795. 4to.

Henderson.—Iceland; or, the Journal of a Residence in that Island during the years 1814 and 1815. By Ebenezer Henderson, Doctor in Philosophy, &c. Second edition. Edinburgh, 1819.

Hooper.—Ten Months among the Tents of the Tuski; with Incidents of an Arctic Boat Expedition, in search of Sir John Franklin, as far as the Mackenzie River and Cape Bathurst. By Lieut. W. H. Hooper, R. N. London, 1853.

Hooper.—Journal of Proceedings of Lieutenant W. H. Hooper, R. N., from Fort Macpherson, on the Peel's River (6th September, 1849), to Winter Quarters on the Bear Lake, and subsequently after he had separated from Commander Pullen.

Inglefield.—Proceedings of Commander E. A. Inglefield, R. N., commanding the screw steam-vessel Isabel (Private Expedition) on a Voyage of Arctic Discovery. 1852.

Inglefield.—Proceedings of Captain E. A. Inglefield, Commander of H. M. steam-vessel Phœnix, by Baffin's Bay to Beechy Island, in search of Sir John Franklin, in the year 1853.

Inglefield.—A Summer Search for Sir John Franklin; with a peep into the Polar Basin. By Commander E. A. Inglefield, R. N. London, 1853.

Jukes.—Excursions in and about Newfoundland, during the years 1839 and 1840. By J. B. Jukes, M. A., &c. In two volumes. London, 1842.

Kane.—The U. S. Grinnell Expedition in search of Sir John Franklin. A Personal Narrative. By Elisha Kent Kane, M. D., U. S. N. New York, 1854.

Kellett.—Narrative of the Proceedings of Captain Kellett, of her majesty's ship Herald, through Behring's Straits, and Discovery of Herald Island, in 1849.

Kellett.—Narrative of the Proceedings of Captain Henry Kellett, of her majesty's ship Herald, from May, 1849, to October, 1850.

Kellett.—Proceedings of Captain Kellett, C. B., of H. M. S. Resolute, and Senior Officer in Barrow Strait. August, 1852, to May, 1853.

Kennedy.—Proceedings of Mr. William Kennedy, commanding the Prince Albert, discovery vessel (Lady Franklin's Private Arctic Expedition), accompanied by Lieutenant Bellot of the French Navy. 1852.

Kennedy.—A Short Narrative of the Second Voyage of the Prince Albert in Search of Sir John Franklin. By William Kennedy, Commander of the Expedition. London, 1853.

King.—Narrative of a Journey to the Shores of the Arctic Ocean in 1833, 1834, and 1835, under the command of Captain Back, R. N. By Richard King, M. R. C. S., &c. In two volumes. London, 1836.

Kotzebue.—A Voyage of Discovery into the South Sea and Behring's Straits, for the purpose of Exploring a Northeast Passage. Undertaken in the years 1815–18, in the ship Rurick, under the command of Lieutenant Otto Von Kotzebue, of the Russian Imperial Navy. In three volumes. London, 1821.

Krusenstern.—Voyage Round the World, in the years 1803, 1804, 1805, and 1806, under the command of Captain A. J. Von Krusenstern, of the Russian Imperial Navy. London, 1813.

Laing.—A Voyage to Spitzbergen; containing an Account of that Country, &c. By John Laing, Surgeon. Third edition. Edinburgh, 1820: 12mo. London, 1815: 8vo.

Langsdorff.—Voyages and Travels in various parts of the World, during the years 1803, 1804, 1805, 1806, and 1807. By G. H. Von Langsdorff. London, 1813.

Lisiansky.—A Voyage Round the World, in the years 1803, 1804, 1805, and 1806; performed in the ship Neva. By Urey Lisiansky, Captain in the Russian Navy. London, 1814.

Lyon.—The Private Journal of Captain G. F. Lyon, of H. M. S. Hecla, during the recent Voyage of Discovery under Captain Parry. London, 1825.

Lyon.—A Brief Narrative of an unsuccessful attempt to reach Repulse Bay through Sir Thomas Rowe's Welcome, in his majesty's ship Griper, in the year 1824. By Captain G. F. Lyon, R. N. London, 1825.

Mackenzie.—Voyages from Montreal, on the River St. Lawrence, through the Continent of North America, to the Frozen and Pacific Oceans, in the years 1789 and 1793. By Alexander Mackenzie, Esq. London, 1801. 4to.

M'Clure.—Proceedings of Captain M'Clure, of her majesty's discovery ship Investigator, in search of the Expedition under Sir John Franklin, from August, 1850, to April, 1853; and reporting the Discovery of the Northwest Passage.

M'Cormick.—Narrative of a Boat and Sledge Expedition up Wellington Channel and round Baring Bay, in search of Sir John Franklin and the crews of the discovery ships Erebus and Terror. By Dr. M'Cormick, of the North Star.

M'Keevor.—A Voyage to Hudson's Bay during the Summer of 1812. By Thomas M'Keevor, M. D., of the Dublin Lying-in Hospital. London, 1819.

Maguire.—Proceedings of Commander Rochfort Maguire, Commanding her majesty's ship Plover in the vicinity of Behring's Straits. With a Journal of Proceedings of Plover's boats on an Expedition to and from Point Barrow, commencing 19th July, and ending 12th August, 1852. And further Report of Proceedings to August, 1853.

Maguire.—Narrative of Proceedings at Moore's Harbor (east of Cape Barrow), September, 1852, to August, 1853. By Rochfort Maguire, Commander of her majesty's discovery ship Plover.

Maguire.—Proceedings of Commander Maguire, her majesty's discovery ship Plover, Behring's Straits division of Arctic Search, during her second winter passed at Point Barrow, 1853–54.

Manby.—Journal of a Voyage to Greenland in the year 1821. By George William Manby, Esq. London, 1822.

Markham.—Franklin's Footsteps: a Sketch of Greenland, along the shores of which his Expedition passed, and of the Parry Isles, where the last traces were found. By Clement Robert Markham, late of H. M. S. Assistance. London, 1853.

Meares.—Voyages made in the years 1788 and 1789 from the Northwest Coast of America. By John Meares, Esq. London, 1790. 4to.

Moore.—General Proceedings of Commander T. E. L. Moore, of her majesty's ship Plover, through Behring's Strait, and towards Mackenzie's River, 1848–49.

Moore.—Narrative of the Proceedings of Commander T. E. L. Moore, of her majesty's ship Plover, from September, 1849, to September, 1850.

Moore.—Proceedings of Captain Thomas Moore, Commanding her majesty's ship Plover, in the vicinity of Behring's Straits, during the winter of 1851–52.

O'Reilley.—Greenland and the adjacent Seas, and the Northwest Passage to the Pacific Ocean; illustrated in a Voyage to Davis's Strait during the Summer of 1817. By Bernard O'Reilley, Esq. London, 1818. 4to.

Osborne.—Stray Leaves from an Arctic Journal: or, Eighteen Months in the Polar Regions, in search of Sir John Franklin's Expedition, in the years 1850–51. By Lieutenant Shevard Osborne. London, 1852.

Parry.—Journal of a Voyage for the Discovery of a Northwest Passage from the Atlantic to the Pacific; performed in the years 1819–20, in H. M. ships Hecla and Griper, under the orders of William Edward Parry, R. N., F. R. S., and Commander of the Expedition. London, 1821.

Parry.—Journal of a Second Voyage for the Discovery of a Northwest Passage from the Atlantic to the Pacific; performed in the years 1821–22–23, in H. M. ships Fury and Hecla, under the orders of Captain William Edward Parry, R. N. London, 1824.

Parry.—Journal of a Third Voyage for the Discovery of a Northwest Passage from the Atlantic to the Pacific; performed in the years 1824–25, in H. M. ships Hecla and Fury, under the orders of Captain William Edward Parry, R. N. London, 1826.

Parry.—Narrative of an Attempt to reach the North Pole, in the year 1827, in boats from the Hecla, under the command of Captain William Edward Parry, R. N., F. R. S., &c. London, 1828.

Penny.—Mr. Goodsir's Narrative of the Voyage of the Advice (whale ship), Mr. Penny Commander, through Lancaster Sound, 1849.

Penny.—Report of Proceedings of Expedition in search of Sir John Franklin, commanded by Captain William Penny.

Penny.—Letter from Mr. William Penny, inclosing Reports of Proceedings of the Travelling Parties from her majesty's ship Sophia, in search of Sir John Franklin, in the Spring and Summer of 1851.

Phipps.—A Voyage to North Pole, undertaken by his majesty's command, 1773. By Constantine John Phipps. London, 1774.

Portlock.—A Voyage around the World; but more particularly to the Northwest Coast of America. Performed in 1785, 1786, 1787, and 1788. By Captain Nathaniel Portlock. London, 1789. 4to.

Pullen.—Proceedings of a Boat Expedition from Wainwright Inlet to Fort Simpson, on the Mackenzie River, July 25 to October 3, 1849. By Commander W. J. S. Pullen, of H. M. brig Plover.

Pullen.—Journal of the Proceedings of the Party from Mackenzie River towards Cape Bathurst, in search of Sir John Franklin's Expedition; thence back again, and on to Fort Simpson. July 17 to October 5, 1850. By W. J. S. Pullen, Commander R. N., commanding the Expedition.

Pullen.—Journal of the Proceedings of her majesty's ship North Star, in Erebus and Terror Bay, Beechey Island. Winter of 1852–53, and to August, 1853. By W. J. S. Pullen, Commander R. N.

Rae.—Narrative of an Expedition to the Shores of the Arctic Sea, in 1846 and 1847. By John Rae, Hudson Bay Company's service, Commander of the Expedition. London, 1850.

Rae.—Narrative of the Proceedings of an Expedition, under the command of Dr. Rae, from Fort Confidence to the Shores of the Arctic Sea, by way of the Coppermine River, in the Summer of 1849.

Rae.—Expedition under Dr. Rae from Fort Confidence, April, 1851, in which he examined the shore of Wollaston Land to the eastward of long. 110°, and westward as far as long. 117° 17′.

Rae.—Proceedings of Dr. John Rae, Chief Factor Hudson's Bay Company, by Repulse Bay to Castor and Pollux River, in 1853 and 1854, during which journey he obtained conclusive information of the fate of a portion of Sir John Franklin's Expedition.

Richardson.—Narrative of the Proceedings of Sir John Richardson to the Shores of the Polar Sea, between the Mackenzie and Coppermine Rivers, in 1848.

Richardson.—Arctic Searching Expedition; a Journal of a Boat-voyage through Rupert's Land and the Arctic Sea, in search of the Discovery Ships under command of Sir John Franklin. By Sir John Richardson, C. B., F. R. S., &c. In two volumes. Published by authority. London, 1851.

Ross, John.—A Voyage of Discovery, made under the orders of the Admiralty, in H. M. ships Isabella and Alexander, for the purpose of Exploring Baffin's Bay, and inquiring into the probability of a Northwest Passage. By John Ross, K. S., Captain Royal Navy. London, 1819.

Ross, John.—Narrative of a Second Voyage in search of a Northwest Passage, and of a Residence in the Arctic Regions during the years 1829, 1830, 1831, 1832, 1833. By Sir John Ross, R. N.

Ross, Sir John.—Proceedings of Sir John Ross in the Felix discovery vessel, 1850–51.

Ross, Sir James.—Narrative of the Proceedings of Captain Sir James C. Ross, in command of the Expedition through Lancaster Sound and Barrow Straits, 1848–49.

Sabine.—The North Georgia Gazette and Winter Chronicle. Edited by Captain Edward Sabine. Melville Island, winter of 1819–20. London, 1821.

Saunders.—Proceedings of her majesty's ship North Star, Mr. James Saunders Master-commanding, on an Expedition to Barrow Straits, in 1849 and 1850.

Scoresby.—An Account of the Arctic Regions, with a History and Description of the Northern Whale Fishery. By W. Scoresby, Jr., F. R. S. E. In two volumes. Edinburgh, 1820.

Scoresby.—Journal of a Voyage to the Northern Whale Fishery; including Researches and Discoveries on the Eastern Coast of West Greenland, made in the Summer of 1822, in the ship Baffin, of Liverpool. By William Scoresby, Jr. F. R. S. E., &c., Commander. Edinburgh, 1823.

Seemann.—Narrative of the Voyage of H. M. S. Herald during the years 1845–51, under the command of Captain Henry Kellett, R. N., C. B.; being a Circumnavigation of the Globe, and three Cruises to the Arctic Regions in search of Sir John Franklin. By Berthold Seemann, F. L. S., &c. In two volumes. London, 1853.

Simpson, A.—The Life and Travels of Thomas Simpson, the Arctic Discoverer. By his brother, Alexander Simpson. London, 1845.

Simpson, T.—Narrative of the Discoveries on the North Coast of America, effected by the Officers of the Hudson's Bay Company during the years 1836–39. By Thomas Simpson, Esq. London, 1843.

Smith.—An Account of a Voyage for the Discovery of a Northwest Passage by Hudson's Straits to the Western and Southern Ocean of America. Performed in the years 1746 and 1747, in the ship California, Captain Francis Smith, Commander. By the Clerk of the California. In two volumes. London, 1748.

Snow.—Voyage of the Prince Albert in search of Sir John Franklin: a Narrative of every-day life in the Arctic Seas. By W. Parker Snow. London, 1851.

Sutherland.—Journal of a Voyage in Baffin's Bay and Barrow Straits, in the years 1850–51, performed by H. M. ships Lady Franklin and Sophia, under the command of Mr. William Penny, in search of the missing crews of H. M. ships Erebus and Terror. With a Narrative of Sledge Excursions on the ice of Wellington Channel. By Peter C. Sutherland, M. D., &c. In two volumes. London, 1852.

Umfreville.—The Present State of Hudson's Bay; containing a full Description of that Settlement and the adjacent Country, &c. By Edward Umfreville. London, 1790.

Vancouver.—A Voyage of Discovery to the North Pacific Ocean, and round the World; in which the Coast of Northwest America has been carefully examined and accurately surveyed, &c. Performed in the years 1790, 1791, 1792, 1793, 1794, and 1795, in the Discovery sloop-of-war, and the armed tender Chatham, under the command of Captain George Vancouver. In three volumes. London, 1798. 4to.

Wrangell.—Narrative of an Expedition to the Polar Sea in the years 1820, 1821, 1822, and 1823. Commanded by Lieutenant, now Admiral, Ferdinand Von Wrangell, of the Russian Imperial Navy. London, 1844.

PUBLISHED BY THE SMITHSONIAN INSTITUTION,

WASHINGTON, D. C.

JULY, 1856.

APPENDIX.

PUBLICATIONS OF LEARNED SOCIETIES AND PERIODICALS

IN THE LIBRARY OF THE SMITHSONIAN INSTITUTION.

PART II.

NOTICE.

The present list completes the European portion of the series intended to show what works have been received in the way of exchange by the Smithsonian Institution, and includes likewise all transactions of learned societies and periodicals which have in any way been added to its library. Part first was published in Vol. VII. of Smithsonian Contributions to Knowledge, and embraced the countries for which Dr. Flügel acted as agent, namely, Sweden, Norway, Denmark, Russia, Holland, Germany, Switzerland, and Belgium. The present or second part includes France, Italy, Spain, Portugal, and the United Kingdom of Great Britain and Ireland, the agents for which countries are Hector Bossange, Paris, and Henry Stevens, London.

The Smithsonian Institution, desirous of collecting together all published transactions of societies and scientific periodicals, will be happy to receive from its correspondents any additions to these lists, especially when such will serve to complete series already in its possession.

JOSEPH HENRY,
Secretary S. I.

Smithsonian Institution, May 1, 1856.

PUBLICATIONS

OF

LEARNED SOCIETIES AND PERIODICALS IN THE LIBRARY OF THE SMITHSONIAN INSTITUTION, MAY, 1856.

PART II.

FRANCE.

Congres Scientifique de France.*

Congrès Scientifique de France. V, 1837. Metz, 1838. X. I & II, 1842. Strasbourg, 1843. 8vo.

AMIENS.

Societe des Antiquaires de Picardie.

Mémoires de la Société des Antiquaires de Picardie. Documents inédits concernant la province. I, 1845; II, 1853; IV, 1855. Histoire générale de la province de Picardie. I & II, 1853. Amiens. 4to.

Mémoires de la Société des Antiquaires de Picardie. Deuxième série. I, 1851; II, 1853; III, 1854. Amiens et Paris. 8vo.

Bulletin de la Société des Antiquaires de Picardie. 1853, I—IV; 1854, I—IV; 1855, I—III. Amiens. 8vo.

Annuaire administratif et historique de la Somme, pour les années 1852 et 1853, publié sous les auspices du conseil général du Départment, par la Société des Antiquaires de Picardie. Amiens, 1852. 8vo.

Séance publique du 29 Juin 1854, et inauguration de la statue de Pierre l'Ermite, à Amiens. Amiens, 1854. 8vo.

Délibération du 23 Décembre 1852, concernant les travaux de la cathédrale d'Amiens. Amiens, 1853. 8vo.

ANGOULEME.

Societe d'Agriculture, Arts et Commerce du Departement de la Charente.

Annales de la Société d'Agriculture, Arts et Commerce du département de la Charente. XXXIV, I & II, 1852. Angoulême. 8vo.

---

* Unless otherwise stated, the works mentioned in this list are a donation or exchange from the address under which they are recorded.

ARCUEIL.

Societe d'Arcueil.

Mémoires de physique et de chimie, de la Société d'Arcueil. I & II, 1807 et 1809. Paris. 8vo.
(*Purchased*).

BEZIERS (*Hérault*).

Societe Archeologique.

Bulletin de la Société Archéologique de Béziers. Livr. I—XIV. 1836—1855. Béziers. 8vo.

BORDEAUX.

Academie des Sciences, Belles-Lettres et Arts de Bordeaux.

Recueil des Actes de l'Académie des Sciences, Belles-Lettres et Arts de Bordeaux. XIII, 1851; XIV, 1852; XVI, 1854. Bordeaux. 8vo.

Societe Linneenne de Bordeaux.

Bulletin d'histoire naturelle de la Société Linnéenne de Bordeaux. Deuxième édition. I (1826), 1830; II, 1845. Bordeaux. 8vo.

Actes de la Société Linnéenne de Bordeaux. V—XIX, 1832—1853. Paris et Bordeaux. 8vo.

Compte-rendu des travaux de la commission instituée par la Société Linnéenne de Bordeaux pour l'étude de la maladie de la vigne pendant l'année 1852 (*Extrait des Actes de la Société Linnéenne de Bordeaux, XVIII*). Bordeaux, 1853. 8vo.

CAEN.

Academie Royale des Sciences, Arts et Belles-Lettres.

Mémoires de l'Académie royale des Sciences, Arts et Belles-Lettres de Caen. 1847; 1849; 1851; 1852; 1855. Caen. 8vo.

Bulletin de l'instruction publique et des Sociétés savantes de l'Académie de Caen. Première année, I & II, 1840—41; Deuxième année, I & II, 1841—42; Troisième année, I & II, 1842—43. Caen. 8vo.

Societe d'Agriculture et de Commerce de Caen.

Précis des travaux de la Société royale d'Agriculture et de Commerce de Caen. I, 1801—1810; II, 1827; IV, 1836. Caen. 8vo.

Societe des Antiquaires de Normandie.

Mémoires de la Société des Antiquaires de Normandie. 2e série. II, 1841; IV, 1844; VI, 1852; VII, 1847; VIII, 1851; IX, 1851; X, 1853. 3e série. I, 1855. Paris. 4to.

Societe de Medecine.

Séance extraordinaire de la Société de Médecine de Caen, tenue le 10 Juin 1853. Caen. 8vo.

CAEN.

Societe Linneenne de Normandie.

Mémoires de la Société Linnéenne de Normandie. V—IX, 1835—1853. Paris. 4to.

Mémoires de la Société Linnéenne du Calvados. 1824 et 1825. Caen. 8vo.

CHERBOURG.

Societe Academique.

Mémoires de la Société Académique de Cherbourg. 1852. Cherbourg. 8vo.

Societe des Sciences Naturelles.

Mémoires de la Société des Sciences naturelles de Cherbourg. I, I, 1852; II, 1854. Cherbourg. 8vo.

DIJON.

Academie des Sciences, Arts et Belles-Lettres.

Mémoires de l'Académie des Sciences, Arts et Belles-Lettres de Dijon. Deuxième série. I & II, 1851—1853. Dijon, 1852 et 1854. 8vo.

EVREUX.

Societe libre d'Agriculture, Sciences, Arts et Belles-Lettres de l'Eure.

Receuil des travaux de la Société libre d'Agriculture, Sciences, Arts et Belles-Lettres de l'Eure. 3e série. II, 1852—1853. Evreux, 1853. 8vo.

LE MANS.

Societe d'Agriculture, Sciences et Arts de la Sarthe.

Analyse des travaux de la Société royale des Arts du Mans, depuis l'époque de son institution, en 1794, jusqu'à la fin de 1819. I, 1820. Au Mans. 8vo.

Bulletin de la Société royale d'Agriculture, Sciences et Arts du Mans. III & IV, 1838—1841. Le Mans, 1840 & 1843. 8vo.

Bulletin de la Société d'Agriculture, Sciences et Arts de la Sarthe. V—VIII, 1842—1849. Le Mans, 1844—1848. 8vo.—IIe série. I & II, 1850—1853. III, I—IV, 1854. Le Mans. 8vo.

Mémoires de la Société d'Agriculture, Sciences et Arts de la Sarthe. I, I, 1855. Le Mans. 8vo.

LILLE.

Societe des Sciences, de l'Agriculture et des Arts de Lille.

Mémoires de la Société royale des Sciences, de l'Agriculture et des Arts de Lille. 1847; 1850; 1851; 1852; 1853. Lille. 8vo.

LYON.

Societe d'Agriculture, Histoire Naturelle et Arts utiles de Lyon.

Compte-rendu des travaux de la Société d'Agriculture, Histoire naturelle et Arts utiles de Lyon. 1812—1813; 1814; 1814—1815; 1817; 1819—1820; 1821; 1822—1823; 1823—1824. Lyon, 1813—1824. 8vo.

Mémoires de la Société d'Agriculture, Histoire naturelle et Arts utiles de Lyon. 1825—1827; 1828—1831; 1832; 1833—1834; 1835—1836. Lyon, 1828—1837. 8vo.

Annales des sciences physiques et naturelles, d'agriculture et d'industrie, publiées par la Société royale d'Agriculture, &c. de Lyon. I, 1838; II, IV, V & VI; III, VI; IV, V & VI; V, I & VI; VI, II, V & VI; VII, 1844; VIII, 1845; IX, 1846; X, 1847; XI, 1848. Deuxième série. I, 1849; II, 1850; III, 1850—51. Lyon et Paris. 8vo.

(*Wanting: livr.* 1, 2 *and* 3 *of vol. II; livr.* 1—5 *vol. III; livr.* 1—4 *vol. IV; livr.* 2, 3, 4 *and* 5 *of vol. V, and liv.* 1, 3 *and* 4 *vol. VI.*)

Rapport à la Société royale d'Agriculture, Histoire naturelle et Arts utiles de Lyon, sur l'essai comparatif des différentes charrues, fait par ordre de la chambre royale d'agriculture de Savoie, par C. GARIOT. Imprimé par ordre de la Société d'Agriculture de Lyon. Lyon, 1831. 8vo.

Notice sur les travaux de la Société royale d'Agriculture, Histoire naturelle et Arts utiles de Lyon, pendant le cours de l'année 1832, lu dans la séance publique du 3 Septembre même année, par L. F. GROGNIER. Lyon, 1832. 8vo.

Rapport fait à la Société royale d'Agriculture, Histoire naturelle et Arts utiles de Lyon, au nom de la commission chargée de proposer des sujets de prix pour être décernés en 1833 et 1837, lu dans la séance du 5 Aout 1832. Commissaires: MM. GENSOUL, BUISSON, JURIE, et BOTTEX, rapporteur. Imprimé par ordre de la Société. Lyon, 1833. 8vo.

Rapport fait à la Société royale d'Agriculture, Histoire naturelle et Arts utiles de Lyon, sur la fête agricole du comice de Meyzieu (Isère), tenue le 27 Mai 1834; par CHARLES GARIOT. Imprimé par ordre de la Société. Lyon, 1834. 8vo.

Société royale d'Agriculture, Histoire naturelle et Arts utiles de Lyon. Séance publique, tenue le 23 Juillet 1835. Lyon, 1835. 8vo.

Academie des Sciences, Belles-Lettres et Arts de Lyon.

Comptes rendu des travaux de l'Académie royale des Sciences, Belles-Lettres et Arts de Lyon. 1824; 1825; 1826; 1835; 1837; 1839; 1841. Lyon. 8vo.

Mémoires de l'Académie des Sciences, Belles-Lettres et Arts de Lyon. Classe des Sciences. II, 1850. Classe des Lettres. I & II, 1848 & 1850. Lyon. 8vo.

Mémoires de l'Académie nationale des Sciences, Belles-Lettres et Arts de Lyon. Nouvelle série. Classe des Sciences. I, 1851. Classe des Lettres. I, 1851. Lyon. 8vo.

Societe Linneenne de Lyon.

Société Linnéenne de Lyon. Compte-rendu des travaux des années 1839 et 1840; 1841; 1842; 1844. Lyon. 8vo.

Annales de la Société Linnéenne de Lyon. Années 1847—1849; 1850—1852. Lyon. 8vo.

MARSEILLE.

Academie des Sciences, Lettres et Arts de Marseille.

Histoire de l'Académie de Marseille depuis sa fondation en 1726, jusqu' en 1826; par Mr. J. B. LAUTARD. I—III, 1826—1843. Marseille. 8vo.

Lettres archéologiques sur Marseille, par M. J. B. LAUTARD. Seconde édition. Marseille, 1844. 8vo.

MENDE.

Societe d'Agriculture, Industrie, Sciences, et Arts, du Departement de la Lozere.

Mémoires et analyse des travaux de la Société d'Agriculture, Commerce, Sciences et Arts de la ville de Mende, chef-lieu du département de la Lozère. 1827; 1828; 1829; 1830; 1831; 1832—33; 1833—34; 1834—35; 1835—36; 1837—38; 1839—40; 1841—42; 1843—44; 1845—46; 1847—1848—1849. Mende. 8vo.

Bulletin de la Société d'Agriculture, Industrie, Sciences et Arts du département de la Lozère. I, 1850; II, 1851; III, 1852; IV, 1853; V, 1854; VI, 1855. Mende. 8vo.

METZ.

Academie de Metz.

Mémoires de l'Académie royale de Metz. Lettres, sciences, arts et agriculture. 1819—1853 (34 vols.). Metz et Paris, 1821—1853. 8vo.

Societe d'Histoire Naturelle du Departement de la Moselle.

Bulletin de la Société d'Histoire naturelle du département de la Moselle. I—VII, 1843—1855. Metz. 8vo.

MONTPELLIER.

Societe Archeologique.

Mémoires de la Société Archéologique de Montpellier. I, 1840; II, 1850; III, 1850—1854. Montpellier. 4to.

Thalamus parvus. Le petit thalamus de Montpellier, publié pour la première fois d'après les manuscrits originaux par la Société Archéologique de Montpellier, 1840. Montpellier. 4to.

Publications de la Société Archéologique de Montpellier. No. 17. Documents historiques. No. 6. Les coutumes de Perpignan. Montpellier, 1848. 4to.

Academie des Sciences et Lettres.

Académie des Sciences et Lettres de Montpellier. Séance publique de l'année 1847.

Académie des Sciences et Lettres de Montpellier. Mémoires de la section des lettres. 1847; 1849; 1850; 1851; 1851. (Suite et compl. du fasc. de 1849.) Mémoires de la section des sciences. I, 1847—1850; II, I, 1851, II, 1852—1853. Mémoires de la section de médecine. I, 1849—1853. Montpellier. 4to.

NIMES.

Academie du Gard.

Mémoires de l'Académie du Gard. 1835—1855. Nîmes. 8vo. (11 vols.)

ORLEANS.

Societe des Sciences, Belles-Lettres et Arts d'Orleans.

Mémoires de la Société royale des Sciences, Belles-Lettres et Arts d'Orléans. I—IX, 1837—1849. Orléans. 8vo.

PARIS.

Institut de France: Academie des Inscriptions et Belles-Lettres.

Histoire de l'Académie royale des Inscriptions et Belles-Lettres, avec les mémoires, de litérature tirés des régistres de cette académie. I—L, 1666—1793. Paris, 1736—1808. 4to.

Tableau général raisonné et méthodique des ouvrages contenus dans le recueil des mémoires de l'Académie royale des Inscriptions et Belles-Lettres, depuis sa naissance jusques et compris l'année 1788, servant de supplément aux tables de ce recueil. Paris, 1791. 4to.

Institut de France: Academie des Sciences.

Regiæ scientiarum academiæ historia, in qua præter ipsius Academiæ originem et progressus, variasque dissertationes et observationes per triginta quatuor annos factas, quàm plurima experimenta et inventa, cùm Physica, tùm Mathematica in certum ordinem digeruntur. Secunda editio priori longe auctior. Autore JOANNE-BAPTISTA DU HAMEL, ejusdem Academiæ socio. Parisiis. 1701. 4to.

Histoire (et Mémoires) de l'Académie royale des Sciences. 1666—1790. Paris, 1733—1797. 4to. (107 vols.)

Mémoires de mathématique et de physique, présentés à l'Académie royale des Sciences, par divers sçavans, et lûs dans ses assemblées. I—XI, 1750—1786; et 1773. Paris, 1776. 4to. (12 vols.)

Machines et inventions approuvées par l'Académie royale des Sciences. I—VII, 1666—1754. Paris, 1735—1777. 4to.

Recueil des pièces qui ont remporté les prix de l'Académie royale des Sciences. I—IX, 1720—1772. Paris, 1721—1777. 4to.

Suites des mémoires de l'Académie royale des Sciences. 1720—1764. Paris. 4to. (7 vols.)

Jugement de l'Académie royale des Sciences et Belles-Lettres sur une lettre prétendue de Leibnitz. Paris. 4to.

Table alphabétique des matières contenues dans l'histoire et les mémoires de l'Académie royale des Sciences, publiée par son ordre, et dressée par M. GODIN, de la même académie. I—IV, 1666—1730. Paris, 1729—1734. 4to.

Table générale des matières, &c. Par M. DEMOURS. V—X, 1731—1790. Paris, 1747—1809. 4to.

PARIS.

Institut de France: Academie des Sciences.—*Continued.*

Nouvelle table des articles contenus dans les volumes de l'Académie royale des Sciences de Paris, dans ceux des arts et métiers publiés par cette académie, et dans la collection académique. I—IV, 1775—1776. Paris. 4to.

Mémoires de l'Institut national des Sciences et Arts. Sciences mathématiques et physiques. I—VI, 1798—1806. Paris. 4to.

Mémoires de la classe des Sciences mathématiques et physiques de l'Institut de France. 1806—1812. Paris, 1806—1820. 4to. (8 vols.)

Mémoires de l'Académie royale des Sciences de l'Institut de France. I—XVI, 1816—1838. Paris. 4to.

Mémoires présentés à l'Institut des Sciences, Lettres et Arts, par divers savans, et lus dans ses assemblées. Sciences mathématiques et physiques. I—II, 1806 et 1811. Paris. 4to.

Mémoires présentés par divers savans à l'Académie royale des Sciences de l'Institut de France et imprimés par son ordre. Sciences mathématiques et physiques. I—VI, 1827—1835; et XIII, 1852. Paris. 4to.

Mémoires de l'Institut national des Sciences et Arts, Litérature et Beaux-Arts. I—V, 1798—1804. Paris. 4to.

Rapports et discussions de toutes les classes de l'Institut de France, sur les ouvrages admis au concours pour les prix décennaux. Paris, 1810. 4to.

Rapport historique sur les progrès des sciences mathématiques depuis 1789—1808 et sur leur état actual. Redigé par M. Delambre. Paris, 1810. 4to.

Base du système métrique décimal, ou mesure de l'arc du méridien compris entre les parallèles de Dunkerque et Barcelone, exécutée en 1792 et années suivantes, par MM. Méchain et Delambre. Suite des mémoires de l'Institut. I—III. Paris, 1807—1810. 4to.

(*All the preceding obtained by purchase.*)

Comptes rendus hebdomadaires des séances de l'Académie des Sciences, publiés conformément à une décision de l'Académie en date du 13 Juillet 1835, par MM. les secrétaires perpétuels. I—XLII, 1835—1855. Paris. 4to.

Institut de France: Academie des Sciences Morales et Politiques.

Mémoires de l'Institut national des Sciences et Arts. Sciences morales et politiques. I, III, IV & V. Paris, 1798—1804. 4to.

Mémoires de l'Académie royale des Sciences morales et politiques de l'Institut de France. Deuxième série. I—VII, 1837—1850. Paris. 4to.

Savans étrangers. I et II, 1841 et 1847. Paris. 4to.

Institut Historique.

Journal de l'Institut historique. I—XII, 1834—1840. Paris. 8vo.

L'Investigateur, Journal de l'Institut historique. IIe série. I—X, 1841—1850. Paris. 8vo.

Congrès historique. 1837; 1838; 1839; 1843. Paris. 8vo.

Congrès historique européen. I & II, 1835 & 1836. Paris. 8vo.

PARIS.

Ministere de la Marine.

Annales hydrographiques, receuil d'avis, instructions, documents et mémoires relatifs à l'hydrographie et à la navigation, publié par le Dépôt général de la marine. III & IV, 1850. Paris. 8vo.

Ministere de l'Instruction Publique.

Annuaire des Sociétés savantes de la France et de l'étranger. Publié sous les auspices du Ministère de l'Instruction publique. I, 1846. Paris. 8vo.

Museum d'Histoire Naturelle.

Archives du Museum d'Histoire naturelle, publiées par les professeurs-administrateurs de cet établissement. I, 1839; II, 1841; III, 1843; IV, 1844; V, 1852; VI, 1852; VII, 1853—1855; VIII, I & II, 1855. Paris. 4to.

Societe d'Histoire Naturelle.

Actes de la Société d'Histoire naturelle de Paris. I, I, 1792. Paris. Folio.

Societe d'Horticulture.

Annales de la Société d'Horticulture de Paris, et journal spécial de l'état et des progrès du jardinage. I—X, 1829—1832; LXII & XLIII, 1851 & 1852; XLIV (except 8th, 9th and Dec. Nos.), 1854. Paris. 8vo.

Societe de Geographie.

Bulletin de la Société de Géographie. I, 1822; III—XX, 1825—1833. Deuxième série. I—XX, 1834—1843. Troisième série. I—XIV, 1844—1850. Quatrième série. I—IX, 1851—1855. Paris. 8vo.

(*Wanting:* tables des matières of vol. I; vol. II; June No. of vol. V; July, August & September No's. of vol. VI.)

Societe Ethnologique.

Mémoires de la Société ethnologique. I & II, 1841 & 1845. Paris. 8vo.

Bulletin de la Société ethnologique. I, 1847. Paris. 8vo.

Societe des Antiquaires de France.

Annuaire de la Société (royale, impériale) des Antiquaires de France. 1848; 1849; 1850; 1851; 1853. Paris. 12mo.

Mémoires de la Société (royale, impériale) des Antiquaires de France. XVII—XX, 1844—1850. Paris. 8vo.

Societe Philomatique de Paris.

Extraits des procès-verbaux des séances. Pendant l'année 1848; 1849; 1850; 1851; 1852; 1853; 1854; 1855. Paris. 8vo.

PARIS.

Societe Zoologique d'Acclimatation.

Bulletin de la Société zoologique d'Acclimatation. I, 1854, & II, I—VII, 1855. Paris. 8vo.

Societe de Biologie.

Comptes-rendus des séances et Mémoires de la Société de Biologie. Deuxième série. I, 1854. Paris, 1855. 8vo.
(*Purchased.*)

Ecole des Mines.

Annales des Mines, ou recueil de mémoires sur l'exploitation des mines et sur les sciences et les arts qui s'y rapportent; redigées par les ingénieurs des mines, et publiées sous l'autorisation du Ministre des travaux publics. Quatrième série. IX—XX, 1846—1851.—Table des matières de la 4e série. 1 vol. 8vo. —Cinquième série. I—IV, 1852—1853.—Partie administrative. Vol. I & II. Paris. 8vo.

Annales de Chimie, ou recueil de mémoires concernant la chimie et les arts qui en dépendent. I—XLVI, 1789—1803; L—XCVI, 1804—1815; tables générales des matières et des auteurs. Paris. 8vo.
(*Wanting XLVII—XLIX.*)

Annales de Chimie et de Physique. I—LXXV, 1816—1838; tables générales des matières et des auteurs. Paris. 8vo.—Troisième série. I—XXXVI, 1841—1852. Paris. 8vo.
(*Wanting XV.*)

Annales des Sciences naturelles, comprenant la zoologie, la botanique, l'anatomie et la physiologie comparées des deux règnes, et l'histoire des corps organisés fossiles. Troisième série. Zoologie et Botanique. XIII—XX, 1850—1853.—Quatrième série. Zoologie et Botanique. I—III, 1854 et 1855. Paris. 8vo.
(*Purchased.*)

Miscellanea.

Magazin de Zoologie. I—VIII, 1831—1838. Paris. 8vo.

Magazin de Zoologie, d'anatomie comparée et de palæontologie. Deuxième série. I—VII, 1839—1843. Paris. 8vo.

Revue zoologique, par la Société Cuviérienne; association universelle pour l'avancement de la zoologie, de l'anatomie comparée et de la palæontologie; Journal mensuel. Publié sous la direction de M. F. E. GUERIN-MENEVILLE. 1838—1848. Paris. 8vo. (11 vols.)

Revue et Magazin de Zoologie pure et appliquée; recueil mensuel destiné à faciliter aux savans de tous les pays les moyens de publier leurs observations de zoologie pure et appliquée à l'industrie et à l'agriculture, leurs travaux de paléontologie, d'anatomie et de physiologie comparées, et à les tenir au courant des nouvelles découvertes et des progrès de la science. Par Messieurs F. E. GUÉRIN-MÉNEVILLE et AD. FOCILLON. 2e série. I—VII, 1849—1855. Paris. 8vo.
(*Purchased.*)

PARIS.

Miscellanea.—*Continued.*

Archives de physiologie de thérapeutique et d'hygiène sous la direction de M. BOUCHARDAT. No. 1, Janvier 1854. Mémoire sur la digitaline et la digitale, par E. HOMOLLE et QUÉVENNE. Paris, 1854. 8vo.
(*From the editor.*)

Bulletin général et universel des annonces et des nouvelles scientifiques; dédié aux savants de tous les pays et à la librairie nationale et étrangère: publié sous la direction de M. le B[on] DE FÉRUSSAC. I—IV, 1823. Paris. 8vo.

Bulletin des Sciences naturelles et de Géologie. Deuxième section du Bulletin universel des sciences et de l'industrie publié sous la direction de M. le B[on] DE FÉRUSSAC. I—XXVII, 1824—1831. Paris. 8vo.
(*Purchased.*)

ROUEN.

Academie des Sciences, Belles-Lettres et Arts de Rouen.

Précis analytique des travaux de l'Académie royale des Sciences, Belles-Lettres et Arts de Rouen. 1842—1848. Rouen, 1843—1854. 8vo. (12 vols.)

SAINT-LO

Annuaire du département de la Manche. IV—IX, 1832—1837; XI & XII, 1839 & 1840; XVI & XVII, 1844 & 1845; XXIII—XXV, 1851—1853 Saint-Lo. 8vo.
(*From Mr. Jules Travers of Caen.*)

SAINT-QUENTIN.

Societe Academique.

Société Académique de Saint-Quentin. Annales agricoles, scientifiques et industrielles du département de l'Aisne. Deuxième série. X, 1852. Saint-Quentin, 1853. 8vo.

STRASBOURG.

Societe des Sciences, Agriculture et Arts de Strasbourg.

Mémoires de la Société des Sciences, Agriculture et Arts de Strasbourg. I & II, 1811 & 1823. Strasbourg. 8vo.

Nouveaux Mémoires de la Société des Sciences, Agriculture et Arts du département du Bas-Rhin. I—III, 1832—1842. Strasbourg. 8vo.

Bulletin agricole de la Société des Sciences, Agriculture et Arts, du département du Bas-Rhin. 1843—1845. Strasbourg. 8vo.

Séance publique de la Société des Sciences, Agriculture et Arts du Bas-Rhin. 1846—1849. Strasbourg. 8vo.

Journal de la Société des Sciences, Agriculture et Arts, du département du Bas-Rhin. 1826. II, III & IV. Strasbourg. 8vo.

STRASBOURG.

Societe du Museum d'Histoire Naturelle.

Mémoires de la Société du Muséum d'Histoire naturelle de Strasbourg. II, 1835; III, 1840—1846; IV, 1850—1853. Strasbourg. 4to.

TOULOUSE.

Academie des Sciences, Inscriptions et Belles-Lettres.

Histoire et Mémoires de l'Académie royale des Sciences, Inscriptions et Belles-Lettres de Toulouse. I, 1782; IV, 1790. Toulouse. 4to.

Histoire et Mémoires de l'Académie royale des Sciences, Inscriptions et Belles-Lettres de Toulouse, depuis son établissement en 1807, pour faire suite à l'histoire et aux mémoires de l'ancienne académie. I—VI, 1827—1843. Toulouse. 8vo.

Mémoires de l'Académie (royale, nationale) impériale des Sciences, Inscriptions et Belles-Lettres de Toulouse. Troisième série. I—VI, 1844—1850. Quatrième série. I—IV, 1851—1854. Toulouse. 8vo.

Annuaire de l'Académie (royale, nationale) impériale des Sciences, Inscriptions et Belles-Lettres de Toulouse pour l'année 1846; 1848; 1849; 1850; 1851; 1854. Toulouse. 32mo.

Statuts et règlements de l'Académie (royale) nationale des Sciences, Inscriptions et Belles-Lettres de Toulouse. 1847; 1849. 32mo.

ITALY.

Riunione degli scienziati Italiani.

Atti della prima riunione degli scienziati Italiani tenuta in Pisa nell' Ottobre del 1839. Pisa, 1840. 4to.—Seconda edizione aumentata dell orazione dell Prof. Rosini per l'inaugurazione della statua del Galileo e della biografia del Cav. Pr. Gerbi. Pisa, 1840. 4to.

Atti della seconda riunione, Settembre, 1840. Torino, 1841. 4to.

" terza " " 1841. Firenze, 1841. 4to.

Il congresso di Pisa, Lettere di Gottardo Calvi. Milano, 1839. 8vo.

Diaro del settimo congresso degli Scienziati Italiani in Napoli dal 20 di Settembre a' 5 di Ottobre dell anno 1845. No. 1—20 di Settembre. 4to.

Dei lavori scientifici dell' VIII congresso Italiano radunato in Genova nel Settembre del 1846. Relazione del Dottore Carlo Lurati. I & II. Lugano, 1847. 8vo.

Alcune osservazioni sopra i congressi scientifici Italiani lettera di Tizio a Sempronio e riposta di Sempronio a Tizio. Milano, 1847. 8vo.

BOLOGNA.

Accademia delle Scienze dell' Istituto di Bologna.

Novi Commentarii Academiae Scientiarum Instituti Bononiensis. I, 1834; II, 1836; III, 1839; IV, 1840; V, 1842; VI & VII, 1844; VIII, 1846; IX & X, 1849. Bononiae. 4to.

Rendiconto delle Sessioni ordinarie dell' Accademia delle Scienze dell Istituto di Bologna. (Extratto dal Bullettino delle Scienze Mediche.). I. Bologna, 1833. 8vo.

Rendiconto delle Sessioni dell Accademia delle Scienze dell' Istituto di Bologna dal Novembre 1837, al Novembre 1838; 1838-39; 1839-40; 1840-41; 1841-42; 1842-43; 1843-44; 1844-45; 1845-46; 1846-47; 1847-48; 1848-49, 1849-50; 1850-51; 1852-53; 1853—1854. Bologna. 8vo.

Memorie della Accademia delle Scienze dell' Istituto di Bologna. I & II, 1850; III, 1851; IV, 1853; V, 1854. Bologna. 4to.

Opere edite ed inedite del Professore Luigi Galvani raccolte e publicate per cura dell' Accademia delle Scienze dell' Istituto di Bologna. Bologna, 1851. 4to.

Osservazioni intorno ad un articolo del chiarissimo signor Professore G. Grimelli sulla collezione galvaniana publicata dall' Accademia delle Scienze dell' Istituto di Bologna e nuove notizie sal Galvani illustrazioni e difese delle opere sue Discorso del Dottor SILVESTRO GHERARDI letto all Accademia nella seduta del 24 Febbrajo 1842 e nella stessa seduta decretato alla stampa in aggiunta alla detta collezione con appendice sopra un' edizione di opere del Cel. P. Beccaria pochissimo conosciuta in cui si fa menzione di un opuscola del Galvani. Bologna, 1842. 4to.

Primo decennio di osservazioni meteorologiche fatte nella specola di Bologna ridotte esposte ed applicate da ALESSANDRO PALAGI. Bologna, 1850. 4to.

Universalità dei mezzi di previdenza, difesa, e salvezza per le calamitá degl' incendi opera premiata in concorso dalla Accademia delle Scienze dell' Istituto di Bologna Sorilta da FRANCESCO DEL GUIDICE. Bologna, 1848. R. 8vo.

Della Instituzione de' Pompièri per Grandi città e terre minori di qualunque stato libri tre ne' quali si tratta, delle regole generali per fonlare compagnie di soccorritori contro gl' incendi; si compendiano, esaminano, e paragonano tra loro molti regolamenti oggi in vigore in Europa; e si propone una nuova forma di statuto per quelli da essere dovunque a datto. Opera premiata in concorso dalla Accademia delle Scienze dell' Istituto di Bologna e scritta dal Cavaliere FRANCESCO DEL GUIDICE. Bologna, 1852. 8vo.

BRESCIA.

Ateneo di Brescia.

Commentari della Accademia di Scienze, Lettere, Agricultura, ed Arti del Dipartimento del Mella per l'anno 1808. Brescia, 1808. 8vo.

"	"	1809.	"	1814.
"	"	1810.	"	1811.
"	"	1811.	"	1812.

BRESCIA.

Ateneo di Brescia.—*Continued.*

Commentari dell'	Ateneo di Brescia	per l'anno	1812.	Brescia,	1814. 8vo.
"	"	"	1813-14 & 15.	"	1818.
"	"	"	1816 & 17.	"	1818.
"	"	"	1818 & 19.	"	1820.
"	"	"	1820.	"	1823.
"	"	"	1821.	"	1824.
"	"	"	1822.	"	1824.
"	"	"	1823.	"	1824.
"	"	"	1824.	"	1825.
"	"	"	1825.	"	1826.
"	"	"	1826.	"	1827.
"	"	"	1827.	"	1828.
"	"	"	1828—40.	"	1829—42.
"	"	"	1842—50.	"	1844—50.

CATANIA.

Accademia Gioenia di Scienze Naturali.

Atti dell' Accademia Gioenia di Scienze naturali di Catania. I—XX, 1825—1843. Messina and Catania. 4to.—Serie seconda. I—VIII, 1844—1853. Catania. 4to.

FIRENZE.

Accademia del Cimento.

Saggi di naturali esperienze fatte nell' Accademia del Cimento terza edizione fiorentina preceduta da notizie storiche dell' Accademia stessa e seguitata da alcune aggiunte. Firenze, 1841. 4to.

Notizie sulla storia delle Scienze fisiche in Toscana cavate da un manoscritto inedito di GIOVANNI TARGIONI-TOZZETTI. Firenze, 1852. 4to.

LUCCA.

Reale Accademia Lucchese di Scienze, Lettere, ed Arti.

Memorie e documenti per servire all 'istoria del principato Lucchese. I, 1813.

Memorie e documento per servire all' istoria della citta e stato di Lucca. II, 1814, III, I, 1816; II, 1817; IV, I, 1818; II, 1836; V, I, 1844; II, 1837; III, 1841; VII, 1834; IX, 1825; X, 1831. Lucca. 4to.
(*Wanting VI & VIII.*)

Atti dell' I. E. R. Accademia Lucchese di Scienze, Lettere ed Arti. I—XIV. Lucca, 1821—1853. 8vo.

MILANO.

Imperiale Regio Istituto Lombardo di Scienze, Lettere ed Arti.

Giornale dell' I. R. Istituto Lombardo di Scienze, Lettere ed Arti. I, 1841; II & III, 1842; IV, 1843; V, 1844; VI, 1845; VII, 1846; VIII, 1847. Milano. 8vo.

MILANO.

Imperiale Regio Istituto Lombardo di Scienze, Lettere ed Arti.—*Continued.*

Giornale dell' I. R. Istituto Lombardo di Scienze, Lettere ed Arti e Bibliotheca Italiana. (Nuova serie.) I, 1847; II, 1850; III, 1851; IV, 1852; V, 1853; VI, 1854. Milano. 4to.

Memorie dell' I. R. Istituto Lombardo di Scienze, Lettere ed Arti. I, 1843; II, 1845; III, 1852; IV, 1854. Milano. 4to.

MODENA.

Societa Italiana delle Scienze.

Memorie di matematica e di fisica della Società Italiana delle Scienze residente in Modena. XXIV, I & II, 1848 & 1850; XXV, I, 1852. Modena. 4to.

NAPOLI.

Reale Accademia delle Scienze, e Belle Lettere.

Atti della Reale Accademia delle Scienze, sezione della Società Reale Borbonica. I, 1819; II, 1825; III, 1832; IV, 1839; V, I, 1843; V, II, 1844. Napoli. 4to.

Rendiconto della Reale Accademia delle Scienze sezione della Società Reale Borbonica. Anno I della nuova serie. I, II, V, VI. Napoli, 1852. 4to.

Relazione sulla malattia della vite apparsa nei contorni di Napoli ed altri luoghi delle provincia fatta da una commissione appositamente nominata e presentata alla Reale Accademia delle Scienze nella tornata de' 12 Novembre 1851. Napoli, 1852. 4to.

PADOVA.

Imperiale Regia Accademia di Scienze, Lettere ed Arti di Padova.

Saggi Scientifici e Letterarj dell' Accademia di Padova. I, 1786; II, 1789; III, I & II, 1794. Padova. 4to.

Memorie della Accademia di Scienze, Lettere ed Arti di Padova. V, 1809. Padova. 4to.

Nuovi Saggi della Cesareo-Regia Accademia di Scienze, Lettere ed Arti di Padova. I, 1817; II, 1825; III, 1831; IV, 1838; V, 1840; VI, 1847. Padova. 4to.

PALERMO.

Accademia Palermitana di Scienze e Lettere.

Atti della Accademia di Scienze e Lettere di Palermo. Nuova serie. I. Palermo, 1845. 4to.

Miscellanea.

Specchio delle Scienze o Giornale enciclopedico di Sicilia deposito Letterario delle moderne cognizioni, scoperte, ed osservazioni sopra le Scienze ed Arti e particolarmenta sopra la Fisica, la Chimica, la Storia naturale, la Botanica, l'Agricoltura, la Medicina, il Commercio, la Legislazione, l'Educazione, &c. Scritto

PALERMO.

Miscellanea.—*Continued.*

dal Signor C. S. RAFINESQUE. Tomo primo. Prima annata e primo semestre. Tomo secondo. Prima annata e secondo semestre, I—XI. Palermo, 1814. 8vo.

ROMA.

Osservatorio Astronomico del Collegio Romano.

Memoria intorno ad alcune osservazioni fatte alla specola del Collegio Romano nel corrente anno 1838. Roma. 4to.

Memoria intorno a parecchie osservazioni fatte nella specola dell' Università Gregoriana in Collegio Romano dagli Astronomi della Compagnia di Gesu l'anno 1839. Publicato il di 31 Gennajo 1840. Roma. 4to.
" Anni 1840–41. Publ. Feb. 1842. "
" Anno 1842. " Lugl. 1843. "

Osservazioni fatte nella specola dell' Università Gregoriana in Collegio Romano diretto dai PP. della Compagnia di Gesu. Anno 1843. Roma. 4to.

Annali dell' Osservatorio Astronomico diretto dai PP. delle Compagnia di Gesu nell Collegio Romano. I. Roma, 1843. 4to.

Memorie dell' Osservatorio dell' Università Gregoriana in Collegio Romano diretto dai PP. della Compagnia di Gesu. Anno 1850. Roma, 1851. 4to.

Stelle del Catalogo di Baily dal Polo boreale fino a 30° di decl. Australe contrassegnate secondo i loro diversi colori asservati nella specola del Collegio Romano. I.

Nuova cometa di Breve periodo ossia Memoria intorno alle perturbazioni cagionate dall' azione di giove nell' orbita d'una delle comete comparse il 1819 creduta identica coll' osservata il 1743, e di cui si attende probabilimente il ritorno verso lafine del presente anno 1836. Roma, 1836. 4to.

Memoria sopra i colori delle stelle del Catalogo di Baily osservati dal P. BENEDETTO SESTINI della compagnia di Gesu. Roma, 1845. 4to.

Memoria seconda intorno al colori delle stelle del Catalogo di Baily osservati dal P. BENEDETTO SESTINI. Roma, 1847. 4to.

Accademia Pontifica dei Nuovi Lincei.

Atti dell' Accademia Pontificia de' Nuovi Lincei publicati conforme alla decisione Accademica del 22 Dicembro 1850, e compilati dal Segretario. I (1847—1848), 1851; IV (1850—51), 1852; V (1851—1852), I—III. Roma. 4to.
(*Wanting II, III.*)

TORINO.

Accademia Reale delle Scienze.

Memorie della Reale Accademia delle Scienze di Torino. Serie II. I, 1839; II, 1840; III, 1841; IV, 1842; V, 1843; VI, 1844; VII, 1845; VIII, 1846; IX, 1848; X, 1849; XI, 1851; XII, 1852; XIII, 1853; XIV, 1854. Torino. 4to.

VENEZIA.

I. R. Istituto Veneto di Scienze, Lettere ed Arti.

Atti delle Adunanze dell' I. R. Istituto Veneto di Scienze, Lettere ed Arti. Dal Marzo 1840, all' Ottobre 1841. I. Venezia, 1841. 8vo.
II, 1841—43. " 1843.
III, 1843—44. " 1844.
IV, 1844—45. " 1845.
V, 1845—46. " 1846.
VI, 1846—47. " 1847.
VII, 1847—48. " 1848.
Serie secunda. I, 1850. " 1850.
II, 1850—51. " 1851.
III, I—IV, 1851—52. " 1852.

VERONA.

Accademia d'Agricoltura, Commercio ed Arti di Verona.

Memorie dell' Accademia d'Agricoltura, Commercio ed Arti di Verona. I & II, 1807; III, 1812; IV, 1813; V, VI & VII, 1815; IX & X, 1824; XI, 1829; XII & XIII, 1831; XIV, 1833; XV, 1834; XVI, 1840; XVII, XVIII & XIX, 1841; XX, 1842; XXI, 1846; XXII, 1848; XXIII, 1849; XXIV, 1850; XXV, 1851; XXVI, 1850; XXVII & XXVIII, 1851. Verona. 8vo. (*Wanting VIII.*)

Storia della Accademia di Agricoltura Commercio ed Arti di Verona pel triennio 1848—49—50. Compilata dal Socio ANTONIO MANGANOTTI. Letta nella tornata 2 Dicembre 1852. Verona, 1853. 8vo.

SPAIN.

BARCELONA.

Academia de Buenas-Letras de la ciudad de Barcelona.

Real Academia de Buenas-letras de la ciudad de Barcelona; origēn, progressos, y su primera Junta general baxo la proteccion de su Magestad, con los papeles que en ella se acordaron. Tomo primo. Parte I & II. Barcelona. 4to.

MADRID.

Real Academia de la Historia.

Historia general y natural de las Indias, islas y tierra-firme del mar oceano, por el Capitan GONZALO FERNANDEZ DE OVIEDO Y VALDÉZ, primer chronista del nuove mundo. Publicala la Real Academia de la Historia, cotejada con el códice original, enriquecida con las enmiendas y adiciones del autor, é ilustrada con la vida y el Juicio de las obras del Mismo-por D. JOSÉ AMADOR DE LOS RIOS. Primera parte. 1851. Tomo primero de la segunda parte, segundo de la obra. 1852. Madrid. 4to.

MADRID.

Real Academia de la Historia.—*Continued.*

Opúsculos legales del Rey don Alfonso el Sabio, publicados y cotejados con varios códices antiguos por la Real Academia de la Historia. Tomo I. El espéculo ó espejo de todos los derechos. 1836. Tomo II. El fuero real, las leyes de los adelantados mayores, las nuevas y el ordinamiento de las tafurerias; y por apendice las leyes del estilo. 1836. Madrid. 4to.

Memorias de la Real Academia de la Historia. VIII. Madrid, 1852. 4to.

Diccionario geográfico-histórico de España, por la Real Academia de la Historia. Seccion II. Comprende la Rioja ó toda la provincia de Logroño y algunos pueblos de la de Burgos. Su autor el individuo del numero Don Angel Casimiro de Govantes. Madrid, 1846. 8vo.

Viage Literario a las Iglesias de España. Su autor Don Jaime Villaneuva. XI—XXII, 1850—1852. Madrid. 8vo.

Memorial histórico español: coleccion de documentos, opúsculos y antigüedades, que publica la Real Academia de la Historia. I & II, 1851; III & IV, 1852. Madrid. 8vo.

Elogio histórico del Excelentísimo Señor Don Antonio de Escano, &c., por Don Francisco de Paula Quadrado y de Roo. Lo publica la Misma Real Academia. Madrid, 1852. 8vo.

Disertacion sobre la historia de la nautica, y de las ciencias matematicas que han contribuido á sus progresos entre los españoles. Obra postuma del Excmo. Sr. Don Martin Fernandez Navarrete: la publica la Real Academia de la Historia. Madrid, 1846. 8vo.

España Sagrada, continuada por le Real Academia de la Historia. XLVII. Tratodo LXXXV. De la Santa Iglesia de Lérida en su estado moderno. Su autor el Doctor Don Pedro Sainz de Baranda. Madrid, 1850. 8vo.

Coleccion de fueros y cartas-pueblas de España por la Real Academia de la Historia. Catálogo. Madrid, 1852. 8vo.

Memoria histórico-crítica sobra el Gran Disco de Theodosio, leida a la Real Academia de la Historia por su anticuario Don Antonio Delgado en la Junta ordinaria de 9 Setiembre de 1848. Madrid, 1849. 8vo.

Discurso leido á la Real Academia de la Historia por su Director el Excmo. Señor Don Martin Fernandez de Navarrete, en Junta de 24 de Noviembre de 1837, al terminar el trienio de su direccion, en cumplimiento de lo mandado en los Estatutos. Madrid, 1838. 8vo.

Discurso leido á la Real Academia de la Historia por su Director el Excmo. Señor Don Martin Fernandez de Navarrete, en Junta de 27 de Noviembre de 1840, al terminar el trienio de su direccion en cumplimiento de lo mandado en los Estatutos. Madrid, 1841. 8vo.

Discurso leido á la Real Academia de la Historia por su Director el Excmo. Señor Don Martin Fernandez de Navarrete, en Junta de 15 de Diciembre de 1843, al terminar el trienio de su direccion, en cumplimiento de lo mandado en los Estatutos. Madrid, 1844. 8vo.

MADRID.

Real Academia de la Historia.—*Continued.*

Discurso leido á la Real Academia de la Historia por su Director el ilmo Señor Don Marcial Antonio Lopez, Baron de Lajoysa, en Junta general de 27 de Noviembre de 1846, al terminar el trienio de la direccion, en cumplimiento de lo mandado en los Estatutos. Madrid, 1847. 8vo.

Discurso leido á la Real Academia de la Historia en Junta de 30 de Noviembre de 1849, por su Director el Excmo. e ilmo Señor Don Marcial Antonio Lopez, Baron de Lajoyosa, al terminar el trienio de su direccion en cumplimiento de lo mandado en los Estatutos. Madrid, 1850. 8vo.

Real Academia de Ciencias de Madrid.

Memorias de la Real Academia de Ciencias. I. Madrid, 1850. 4to.

Resumen de las actas de la Academia real de Ciencias de Madrid en el año academico de 1849—1850, leido en la sesion del dia 11 de Octubre, por el segretario perpetuo Doctor Don Mariano Lorente. Madrid, 1850. 4to.

Memoria que comprende el Resumen de los trabajos verificados en el año de 1852 por las diferentes secciones de la comision encargada de formar el mapa geologico de la provincia de Madrid y el general del Reino, presentada en 11 de Junio de 1853 al Excmo. señor ministro de Fomento por Don Francisco de Lujan. Madrid, 1853. 4to.

Memoria sobre las causas meteorológico-fisicas que producen las constantes sequías de murcia y almeria, señalando los medios de atenuar sus effectos: Premiada por el ministerio dé comercio, instruccion y obras públicas, á juicio de la Real Academia de Ciencias, en el certámen abierto por Real decreto de 30 de Marzo de 1850. Su autor Don Manuel Rico y Sinobas. Madrid, 1851. 8vo.

PORTUGAL.

LISBOA.

Academia Real das Sciencias.

Memorias de Litteratura Portugueza, publicadas della Academia Real das Sciencias de Lisboa. (*Nisi utile est quod facimus, stulta est gloria.*) I, 1792; II, 1792; III, 1792; IV, 1793; V, 1793; VI, 1796; VII. 1806. Lisboa. 8vo.

GREAT BRITAIN AND IRELAND.

British Association for the Advancement of Science.

Reports of the British Association for the Advancement of Science. 1835—1854. London. 8vo.

BATH.

Bath and West of England Agricultural Society.

Journal of the Bath and West of England Society for the encouragement of Agriculture, Arts, Manufactures, and Commerce, established 1777. I—III, 1853—1855. London. 8vo.

BELFAST.

Natural History and Philosophical Society.

Miscellaneous sheets relating to its meetings. 8vo.

The Ulster Journal of Archæology. I—IV, 1853. Belfast. 4to.

BERWICK-ON-TWEED.

Berwickshire Naturalists' Club.

Proceedings of the Berwickshire Naturalists' Club. III, I—V. 8vo.

CAMBRIDGE.

Cambridge Philosophical Society.

Transactions of the Cambridge Philosophical Society. I—VIII, 1822—1849; IX, I & III, 1851 & 1853. Cambridge. 4to.
(*Wanting II,* I; *IX,* II.)

Cambridge Observatory.

Astronomical observations made at the observatory at Cambridge. I—XVII, 1828—1848. Cambridge, 1829—1854. 4to.

DUBLIN.

Dublin University Philosophical Society.

Transactions of the Dublin Philosophical Society. I—V, 1843—1852. Dublin. 8vo.

Geological Society.

Journal of the Geological Society of Dublin. I—IV, 1838—1849; V, I & II, 1850—1852. Dublin. 8vo.

DUBLIN.

Royal Dublin Society.

The Journal of the Royal Dublin Society. Published quarterly. I, I, 1856 Dublin. 8vo.

Royal Irish Academy.

Proceedings of the Royal Irish Academy. I—V, and VI, I & II. Dublin, 1841—1855. 8vo.
(*Wanting IV*, II.)

Transactions of the Royal Irish Academy. I—XXII, 1787—1855. Dublin. 4to.

DURHAM.

Observatory.

Results of astronomical observations, made at the Observatory of the University, Durham, from October, 1849, to April, 1852. Durham, 1855. 8vo.

EDINBURGH.

Botanical Society.

First annual report, laws, and proceedings of the Botanical Society of Edinburgh. Instituted 17th March, 1836. Session 1836—37.—Third, fourth and fifth, sixth, seventh and eighth reports. 1839—44. Edinburgh. 8vo.

Transactions of the Botanical Society. I—III, 1844—1850; IV, I, II, 1850 & 51. Edinburgh. 8vo.

Laws, by-laws, and regulations of the Botanical Society of Edinburgh. Corrected to 1st October, 1841. Edinburgh, 1841. 8vo.

Royal Observatory.

Astronomical observations made at the Royal Observatory, Edinburgh. I—X, 1834—1847. Edinburgh, 1838—1852. 4to.

Royal Scottish Society of Arts.

Transactions of the Royal Scottish Society of Arts. III, I, II, III & V, 1845—51; IV, I & III, 1852—1855. Edinburgh. 8vo.

Royal Society.

Proceedings of the Royal Society of Edinburgh. Session 1851—2; 1853—4; 1854—5. Edinburgh. 8vo.

Transactions of the Royal Society of Edinburgh. IV—XX, and XXI, I & II, 1804—1855. Edinburgh. 4to.

Society of Antiquaries of Scotland.

Proceedings of the Society of Antiquaries of Scotland. I, I, II, III, 1852—1855. Edinburgh. 4to.

EDINBURGH.

Society of Antiquaries of Scotland.—*Continued.*

Archæologia Scotica: or Transactions of the Society of Antiquaries of Scotland. I—IV, 1792—1823. Edinburgh. 4to.

The Bannatyne Club.

Original Letters relating to the ecclesiastical affairs of Scotland, chiefly written by, or addressed to his majesty King James the Sixth, after his accession to the English throne. I & II, 1703—1725. Edinburgh, 1851. 4to.

Historical notices of Scottish affairs, selected from the manuscripts of Sir John Lauder of Fountainhall, Bart., one of the senators of the College of Justice. I—II, 1661—1688. Edinburgh, 1848. 4to.

Historical observes of memorable occurents in church and state, from October, 1680, to April, 1686. By Sir John Lauder, of Fountainhall. Edinburgh, 1840. 4to.

Registrum honoris de Morton: a series of ancient charters of the earldom of Morton, with other original papers, in two volumes. I. Original papers. II. Ancient charters. Edinburgh, 1853. 4to.

Origines Parachiales Scotiæ. The antiquities ecclesiastical and territorial of the parishes of Scotland. I—II, I, II. Edinburgh, 1850—1855. 4to.

Carte monalium de Northberwic prioratus cisterciensis B. Marie de Northberwic munimenta vetusta quæ supersunt. Edinburgi, 1847. 4to.

Descriptive catalogue of impressions from ancient Scottish seals, royal, baronial, ecclesiastical, and municipal, embracing a period from A. D. 1094 to the Commonwealth. Taken from original charters and other deeds preserved in public and private archives. By Henry Laing, Edinburgh. Edinburgh, 1850. 4to.

Liber S. Thome de Aberbrothoc. Registorum Abbacie de Aberbrothoc pars prior. Registrum aetus munimentaque eidem coetanea complectens. 1178—1329. Edinburgi, 1848. 4to.

The Darien Papers: being a selection of original letters and official documents relating to the establishment of a colony at Darien by the company of Scotland trading to Africa and the Indies. 1695—1700. Edinburgh, 1849. 4to.

Registrum S. Marie de Neubotle abbacie cisterciensis beate virginis de neubotle chartarium vetus accedit appendix cartarum originalium. 1140—1528. Edinburgi, 1849. 4to.

Horn et Rimenhild. Recueil de ce qui reste des poëmes relatifs à leurs aventures composés en français, en anglais et en écossais dans les treizième, quatorzième, quinzième et seixième siècles publié d'après les manuscrits de Londres, de Cambridge, d'Oxford et d'Edinburgh par Francisque Michel. Paris, 1845. 4to.

Breviarum Aberdonense. I—II. Londini, 1854. 4to.

The Black Book of Taymouth, with other papers from the Breadalbane Charter room. Edinburgh, 1855. 4to.

The Bannatyne Miscellany; containing original papers and tracts, chiefly relating to the history and literature of Scotland. III. Edinburgh, 1855. 4to.

EDINBURGH.

The Bannatyne Club.—*Continued.*

Album of the Bannatyne Club. No. III. 8vo.

Catalogue of the books printed for the members of the Bannatyne Club since its institution. February, 1854. 8vo.

Thomas Thomson, Esq., Advocate, President of the Bannatyne Club. 4to.

Bannatyne Club. Nos. XXIII, XXIV & XXV. Abstract of the Treasurer's accounts, 1852, 1853 & 1854. 4to.

The Letters and Journals of Robert Baillie, A. M., Principal of the University of Glasgow. 1737—1772. In three volumes. Edinburgh, 1841—1842. 4to. (*Purchased.*)

Miscellanea.

The Edinburgh Philosophical Journal, exhibiting a view of the progress of discovery in natural philosophy, chemistry, natural history, practical mechanics, geography, statistics, and the fine and useful arts. Conducted by Dr. Brewster and Professor Jameson. I—XIV. Edinburgh, 1819—1826. 8vo.

The Edinburgh Journal of Science, exhibiting a view of the progress of discovery in natural philosophy, chemistry, mineralogy, geology, botany, zoology, comparative anatomy, practical mechanics, geography, navigation, statistics, antiquities, and the fine and useful arts. Conducted by David Brewster. I—X, 1824—1829. New series. I—VI, 1829—1832. Edinburgh. 8vo.

The Edinburgh New Philosophical Journal, exhibiting a view of the progressive improvements and discoveries in the sciences and the arts. Conducted by Robert Jameson. I—LVII. Edinburgh, 1826—1854. 8vo.

The Edinburgh Journal of Natural and Geographical Science. Under the direction of William Ainsworth and Henry A. Cheek. I—II. Edinburgh, 1830. 8vo.

The Edinburgh Review or Critical Journal. I—CII, 1802—1855. Edinburgh, 8vo.

Blackwood's Edinburgh Magazine. LXXIV, 1853. Edinburgh. 8vo.

The North British Review. I—XVI, 1844—1851; XX, xl, & XXI—XXIII, XXIV, xlvii, 1854 & 1855. Edinburgh, 8vo. (*Purchased.*)

GREENWICH.

Royal Observatory.

Tables containing the sum of three equations of aberration, solar nutation, and precession, for twenty-three principal fixed stars, for every day in leap year, the first, second, and third years after. Folio.

The sum of three equations of aberration, solar nutation, and precession, of forty principal stars, for every day of the year, in leap year, the first, second, and third years after. Folio.

GREENWICH.

Royal Observatory.—*Continued.*

The sum of three equations of aberration, solar nutation, and precession, for twenty-three principal fixed stars, for every day in leap year, the first, second, and third years after. Folio.

Description of the transit circle of the Royal Observatory, Greenwich. 1852. 4to.

Description of the altitude and azimuth instrument, erected at the Royal Observatory, Greenwich, in the year 1847. 4to.

Description of the instruments and process used in the photographic self-registration of the magnetical and meteorological instruments at the Royal Observatory, Greenwich. London, 1849. 4to.

Regulations of the Royal Observatory, Greenwich. 1852. 4to.

Astronomical observations made at the Royal Observatory at Greenwich. I—IV, I & III; V, I & II, 1811—1820; 1815—1820, & 1822—1826; 1827, I, II, III, IV; 1828, I, II, III, IV; 1829, I, II, III, IV, V; 1830, I, II, III, IV, V; 1831, I, II, III, IV, V; 1832, I, II, III, IV, V; 1833, I, II, III, IV, V; 1834, I, II, III, IV, V; 1835, I, II, III, IV, V. Folio.
(*Wanting IV*, II; *and* 1821.)

Approximate right ascension and north polar distance of 720 stars, from observations made at the Royal Observatory at Greenwich. Folio.

A catalogue of 1112 stars, reduced from observations made at the Royal Observatory of Greenwich from the years 1816 to 1833. London, 1833. Folio.

Astronomical observations made at the Royal Observatory, Greenwich. 1836—1853. London. 4to.

Appendix to Greenwich Observations. 1836; 1837; 1842; 1845. London. 4to.

Reduction of the observations of the moon, made at the Royal Observatory, Greenwich, from 1750—1830. I & II. London, 1848. 4to.

Cancels for the introduction to the reductions of the Greenwich Lunar Observations. 4to.

Reduction of the observations of planets, made at the Royal Observatory, Greenwich, from 1750 to 1830. London, 1845. 4to.

Magnetical and meteorological observations made at the Royal Observatory, Greenwich, in the years 1840 and 1841; 1844; 1845; 1846; 1847. London, 1842—1849. 4to.

Appendix to the Greenwich Observations, including the results of Magnetical and Meteorological Observations. 1848; 1849; 1850; 1851; 1852 & 1853. 4to.

Report of the Astronomer Royal to the Board of Visitors. 1836—1852, and 1854 & 1855. 4to.

KILKENNY.

Kilkenny and Southeast of Ireland Archæological Society.

Proceedings and Transactions of the Kilkenny and Southeast of Ireland Archæological Society. III, 1854 & 1855. Dublin. 8vo.

KILKENNY.

Kilkenny and Southeast of Ireland Archæological Society.—*Continued.*

Proceedings and Papers of the Kilkenny and Southeast of Ireland Archæological Society. New series. I, I, 1856. Dublin, 1856. 8vo.

Transactions of the Kilkenny Archæological Society. II, I & II, 1852 & 1853. Dublin, 1853 & 1855. 8vo.

LEEDS.

Philosophical and Literary Society.

Reports of the Council, on the general state of the Leeds Philosophical and Literary Society. V—VII, 1824—1827; XI—XXX, 1830—1850; XXXII, 1850—1852. Leeds. 8vo.

Laws and regulations of the Leeds Philosophical and Literary Society. (Instituted the 14th of January, 1820.) Revised and corrected to May 7, 1841. Leeds. 8vo.

Transactions of the Philosophical and Literary Society of Leeds, consisting of papers read before the Society. I, I. London, 1837. 8vo.

LIVERPOOL.

Historic Society of Lancashire and Cheshire.

Proceedings and papers. Session I—III, 1848—51; session II, 1849—50. II, I.

Transactions of the Historic Society of Lancashire and Cheshire. VII, 1854—55. London, 1855. 8vo.

LONDON.

Annals and Magazine of Natural History.

The Magazine of Natural History, and journal of zoology, botany, mineralogy, and geology. Conducted by J. C. LOUDON. I—IX, 1829—1836. London. 8vo.

The Magazine of Natural History. Conducted by EDWARD CHARLESWORTH. I—IV. New series. 1837—1840. London. 8vo.

Magazine of Zoology and Botany. Conducted by Sir W. JARDINE, P. J. SELBY, and Dr. JOHNSTON. I & II. London, 1837 & 1838. 8vo.

The Annals and Magazine of Natural History, including zoology, botany, and geology (being a continuation of the "Magazine of Zoology and Botany," and of Loudon and Charlesworth's Magazine of Natural History). Conducted by Sir W. JARDINE, P. J. SELBY, Dr. JOHNSTON, Sir W. J. HOOKER, and RICHARD TAYLOR. I—XX, 1838—1847. Second series. I—XVI, 1848—1855. London. 8vo.

British Government.

Observations made at the Magnetical and Meteorological Observatory at Hobarton, in Van Diemen Land, and by the Antarctic Naval Expedition. I—III, 1841—1846. London, 1850—1853. 4to.

LONDON.

British Government.—*Continued.*

Observations made at the Magnetical and Meteorological Observatory at St. Helena. I, 1840—1843. London, 1847. 4to.

Observations made at the Magnetical and Meteorological Observatory at the Cape of Good Hope. I, 1841—1846. London, 1851. 4to.

Observations made at the Magnetical and Meteorological Observatory at Toronto, Canada. I, 1840—1845. London, 1845—1853. 4to.

Observations on days of unusual magnetic disturbance, made at the British colonial magnetic observatories, under the departments of the Ordnance and Admiralty. I, I, 1840—1841; II, 1842—1844. London, 1843—1851. 4to.

Allelodidactic Society.

Transactions of the Allelodidactic Society. I, I & II. London, 1847 & 1848. 8vo.

Duke of Northumberland.

Results of astronomical observations made during the years 1834, 5, 6, 7, 8, at the Cape of Good Hope; being the completion of a telescopic survey of the whole surface of the visible heavens, commenced in 1825, by Sir JOHN F. W. HERSCHEL. London, 1847. 4to.

Account of the Northumberland equatoreal and dome, attached to the Cambridge Observatory. Cambridge, 1844. 4to.

Archæological Institute of Great Britain and Ireland.

Proceedings at the annual meeting of the Archæological Institute of Great Britain and Ireland, at Winchester, September, 1845. London, 1846. 8vo.

Also—

York meeting,	July,	1846.	London,	1847.
Norwich	"	1847.	"	1851.
Lincoln	"	1848.	"	1850.
Salisbury	"	1849.	"	1851.

British Archæological Association.

The Journal of the British Archæological Association established in 1843, for the encouragement and prosecution of researches into the arts and monuments of the early and middle ages. I—IX. London, 1846—1854. Also No. XXXVII & XXXVIII, 1854. London. 8vo.

The Archæological Journal. Published under the direction of the Central Committee of the British Archæological Association for the encouragement and prosecution of researches into the arts and monuments of the early and middle ages. I—VII. London, 1845—1850. 8vo.

Transactions of the British Archæological Association, at its second annual congress, held at Winchester, August, 1845, consisting of the papers read at the several meetings, together with an account of the exhibitions, and excursions made by the Association. London, 1846. 8vo.

Also—

Third annual congress, held at Gloucester, August, 1846. London, 1848.

LONDON.

Chemical Society.

Memoirs and proceedings of the Chemical Society of London. 1841—1848. London, 1843—1848. 8vo.

The Quarterly Journal of the Chemical Society of London. I—V, 1849—1853; VI, I, III, IV, 1853—1854; VII, I, II, IV, 1854; VIII, I, II, III, 1855. London. 8vo.

Entomological Society.

The Transactions of the Entomological Society of London. I—V. London, 1836—1849. 8vo.

Ethnological Society.

Journal of the Ethnological Society of London. I, 1848; II, 1850; III, 1852; IV, 1856. London. 8vo.

A Manual of ethnological inquiry; being a series of questions concerning the human race, prepared by a sub-committee of the British Association for the Advancement of Science, appointed in 1851, and adapted for the use of travellers and others, in studying the varieties of Man. London, 1852. 8vo.

Address to the Ethnological Society of London, delivered at the annual meeting on the 25th of May 1855, by JOHN CONOLLY, President; and a sketch of the recent progress of Ethnology, by RICHARD CULL. London. 8vo.

Geological Society.

Proceedings of the Geological Society of London. 1826—1842. I—III. London, 1834—1842. 8vo.

Transactions of the Geological Society of London. Second series. II—VI, 1826—1842; & VII, I, II, III, 1845—1846. London. 4to.

The Quarterly Journal of the Geological Society of London. Edited by the Assistant Secretary of the Geological Society. Part the first. Proceedings of the Geological Society. Part II. Miscellaneous. I—XI, 1843—1855; XII, I, 1856. London. 8vo.

The Hakluyt Society.

The history of the great and mighty kingdom of China, and the situation thereof. Compiled by the Padre JUAN GONZALES DE MENDOZA, and now reprinted from the early translation of R. Parke. I. London, 1853. 8vo.

Horticultural Society.

Transactions of the Horticultural Society of London. I—VII. London, 1812—1830. 4to.

Journal of the Horticultural Society of London. I—IX, 1846—1854. London. 8vo.

Charters and by-laws of the Horticultural Society of London. London, 1816. 4to.

LONDON.

Horticultural Society—*Continued.*

Additional by-laws of the Horticultural Society of London. London, 1817. 4to.

List of the Horticultural Society of London. January, 1818; May, 1818; January, 1819; May, 1819; May, 1820; May, 1821; May, 1822; May, 1823; May, 1824; March, 1825; May, 1825; May, 1826. London. 4to.

Horticultural Society of London. Report of the garden committee on the formation and progress of the garden. March 31, 1823; March 31, 1824. London. 4to.

Institute of Actuaries of Great Britain and Ireland.

The Assurance Magazine and Journal of the Institute of Actuaries. IX; XIII & XIV; XV—XXI; XXIII, 1852—1856. London. 8vo.

List of members of the Institute of Actuaries of Great Britain and Ireland. 1853; 1854—55. London. 8vo.

Linnean Society.

Transactions of the Linnean Society. I—XXI, 1791—1855. London. 4to.

Proceedings of the Linnean Society of London. I & II, 1838—1855. London. 8vo.

List of the Linnean Society of London. 1848. 4to.

Museum of Practical Geology and Geological Survey.

Records of the School of Mines and of Science applied to the Arts. I, I—IV. London, 1852 & 1853. 8vo.

Industrial instruction on the continent. (Being the introductory letter of the session 1852—1853.) By LYON PLAYFAIR. London, 1852. 8vo.

Memoirs of the Geological Survey of Great Britain, and of the Museum of practical (economic) Geology in London. I; II, I & II. London, 1846—1848. 8vo.

Memoirs of the Geological Survey of the United Kingdom. Figures and descriptions illustrative of British organic remains. Decade I—VII, 1849—1853. London. R. 8vo.

Numismatic Society.

The Numismatic Chronicle, and Journal of the Numismatic Society. Edited by JOHN YONGE AKERMAN. XL—XLIII, 1848 & 1849. London. 8vo.

Remains of pagan Saxondom, principally from tumuli in England. I—III, VI, VIII, XV—XX. London, 1852—1855. 4to.
(*From John Yonge Ackerman.*)

Philological Society.

Proceedings of the Philological Society. 1842—1852. I—V. London, 1844—1854. 8vo.

LONDON.

Ray Society.

The British species of angiocarpous lichens, elucidated by their sporidia. By the Rev. W. A. LEIGHTON. London, 1851. 8vo.

On the alternation of generations; or, the propagation and development of animals through alternate generations: a peculiar form of fostering the young in the lower classes of animals. London, 1845. 8vo.

Bibliographia zoologiæ et geologiæ: a catalogue of all books, tracts and memoirs on zoology and geology. By LOUIS AGASSIZ. I—III. London, 1841—1852. 8vo.

A monograph of the British nudibranchiate Mollusca: with figures of all the species. By JOSHUA ALDER and ALBANY HANCOCK. I—V. London, 1844—1851. 4to.

A monograph of the British naked-eyed Medusæ: with figures of all the species. By EDWARD FORBES. London, 1848. 4to.

The organization of trilobites, deduced from their living affinities; with a systematic review of the species hitherto described. By HERMANN BURMEISTER. London, 1846. 4to.

Reports and papers on botany. London, 1846 & 1849. (2 vols.) 8vo.

Outlines of the geography of plants. By F. J. F. MEYER. London, 1846. 8vo.

Reports on the progress of zoology and botany. 1841, 1842. London, 1845. 8vo.

Reports on zoology for 1843, 1844. London, 1847. 8vo.

Memorials of John Ray, consisting of his life by Dr. DERHAM; biographical and critical notices by Sir JOHN E. SMITH, and CUVIER and DUPETIT-THOUARS. With his itinerary, &c. London, 1846. 8vo.

The correspondence of John Ray, consisting of selections from the philosophical letters published by Dr. Derham, and original letters of John Ray in the collection of the British Museum. London, 1848. 8vo.

The natural history of the British entomostraca. By W. BAIRD. London, 1850. 8vo.

A monograph on the sub-class Cirripedia, with figures of all the species. By CHARLES DARWIN. The Lepadidæ; or Pedunculated cirripedes. London, 1851. 8vo.

Royal Agricultural Society of England.

The Journal of the Royal Agricultural Society of England. I—XVI, 1840—1856. London. 8vo.

Royal Asiatic Society.

The Journal of the Royal Asiatic Society of Great Britain and Ireland. I—XVI, I, 1834—1855. London, 8vo.
(*Wanting XI*, II, & *XIV*, II.)

Royal Asiatic Society of Great Britain and Ireland. The thirty-second annual Report. 1855. London. 8vo.

Royal Asiatic Society of Great Britain and Ireland. List of members, committees, &c. 1855. London. 8vo.

LONDON.

Royal Astronomical Society.

Monthly notices of the Royal Astronomical Society, containing papers, abstracts of papers, and reports of the proceedings of the Society. I—XV, 1831—1855; XVI, I, II, III, V, VI, 1856. London. 8vo.

Memoirs of the Astronomical Society of London. I—XXIII, 1822—1854. London. 4to.

Royal Geographical Society.

The Journal of the Royal Geographical Society of London. 1830—1831, and I—X, 1831—1841. Index. XI, I, XII, I; XIV—XX, 1844—1851. Index. XXI—XXIV, 1851—1854. London. 8vo.
(*Wanting XI*, II; *XII*, II; *XIII*.)

Addresses at the anniversary meetings of the Royal Geographical Society. 1851—1854. London. 8vo.

Royal Institution of Great Britain.

Notices of the meetings of the members of the Royal Institution of Great Britain. II—V, 1851—1855. London. 8vo.

The Royal Institution of Great Britain. A list of the members, officers, &c., with the report of the visitors for the years 1851, 1852, 1853. London. 8vo.

The Journal of Science and the Arts. Edited at the Royal Institution of Great Britain. Published quarterly. I—VI, 1816—1819. The Quarterly Journal of Literature, Science, and the Arts. VII—XXIX, 1819—1830. London. 8vo.
(*The latter obtained by purchase.*)

Royal Society.

Philosophical Transactions, giving some account of the present undertakings, studies and labors, of the ingenious in many considerable parts of the world. I—LXV, 1665—1775. London. 4to.

Philosophical Transactions of the Royal Society of London. LXVI—CXLV, 1776—1855. London. 4to.
(*Wanting* 1831; 1843; 1845—1848 *inclus.*)

The Philosophical Transactions and Collections, abridged and disposed under general heads. I—XI, 1732—1756. London. 4to.

Diplomata et statuta regalis societatis Londini, pro scientiâ naturali promovendâ: Jussu præsidis et concilii edita. Londini, 1819. 4to.

Abstracts of the papers communicated to the Royal Society of London (*Proceedings*). V, 1843—1850; VI, 1850—1854; VII, I & II, and V—XI; VIII, I, 1855. London. 8vo.
(*Wanting V, pp.* 1—802.)

Addresses read at the anniversary meetings of the Royal Society. 1852 & 1853. London. 8vo.

A History of the Royal Society, with memoirs of the presidents. Compiled from authentic documents, by CHARLES RICHARD WELD. In two volumes. London, 1848. 8vo.

LONDON.

Royal Society.—*Continued.*

A review of the works of the Royal Society of London; containing animadversions on such of the papers as deserve particular observation. In eight parts, under the several heads of arts, antiquities, medicine, miracles, zoophytes, animals, vegetables, minerals. By JOHN HILL. London, 1751. 4to.

Society of Antiquaries of London.

Proceedings of the Society of Antiquaries of London. I, XVI & XVII; II, XVIII—XXXVI; III, XXXVII—XLII. London, 1853—1855. 8vo.

Lists of the Society of Antiquaries of London. 1853; 1854; 1855. London, 8vo.

Letter addressed to the fellows of the Society of Antiquaries, on the objections urged against the proposal of the president and council to reduce the payments to the Society. By JOHN BRUCE, Esq., Treas. S. A. London, 1852. 8vo.

Archæologia: or miscellaneous tracts relating to antiquity, published by the Society of Antiquaries of London. XXXIII—XXXV, XXXVI, I, 1849—1855. London. 4to.

Society for the Encouragement of Arts, Manufactures, and Commerce.

Transactions of the society, instituted at London, for the encouragement of arts, manufactures and commerce; with the premiums offered. 1783—1845. I—LIV, 1806—1845. London. 8vo.

Transactions of the Society of Arts for 1846—7; 1847—8. I & II. London, 1847 & 1849. 4to.

The Journal of the Society of Arts, and of the institutions in union. I—III, 1852—1855; IV, 157—179, 1856. London, 1853—1855. R. 8vo.
(*Wanting of Vol. I, Nos.* 18, 19, 26 *&* 27.)

Catalogue of the Eighth Exhibition of Inventions. London, 1856.

Statistical Society.

Journal of the Statistical Society of London. I—XVIII, 1839—55; XIX, I, 1856. London. 8vo.—General index to the first fifteen volumes. London, 1854. 8vo.
(*Wanting XIII & XVI,* I.)

List of fellows of the Statistical Society of London. Founded in 1834. No. 12, St. James's Square. Session 1854—55; 1856. London. 8vo.

Objects and regulations of the Statistical Society of London. 1855. 8vo.

Twentieth anniversary meeting of the Statistical Society. Session 1853—54. 8vo.

Zoological Society.

Transactions of the Zoological Society of London. I—III, 1835—1849. London. 4to.

Proceedings of the Zoological Society of London. I—XXII, 1833—1854. London. 8vo.

LONDON.

Miscellanea.

The University College, London, calendar for the session 1855—1856. London. 8vo.

The Zoologist: a popular miscellany of natural history. Conducted by EDWARD NEWMAN. IX—XIII. London, 1851—1855. 8vo.

The Archeologist, and Journal of Antiquarian Science. I, 1841—1842. London, 8vo. (Vol. II incompl.)

The Chemical Gazette, or Journal of Practical Chemistry, in all its applications to pharmacy, arts and manufactures. Conducted by WILLIAM FRANCIS. VIII & IX, 1850 & 1851; XII & XIII, 1854 & 1855. London. 8vo.

The Lancet. A journal of British and foreign medicine, physiology, surgery, chemistry, criticism, literature, and news. 1852—1856. London. R. 8vo.

The Philosophical Magazine, or Annals of Chemistry, Mathematics, Astronomy, Natural History, and General Science. By RICHARD TAYLOR and RICHARD PHILLIPS. I—XI. London, 1827—1832. 8vo.

The London and Edinburgh Philosophical Magazine and Journal of Science. Conducted by Sir DAVID BREWSTER, RICHARD TAYLOR, and RICHARD PHILLIPS. I—XVI. New and united series of the Philosophical Magazine and Journal of Science. 1832—1840. London. 8vo.

The London, Edinburgh, and Dublin Philosophical Magazine and Journal of Science. Conducted by Sir DAVID BREWSTER, RICHARD TAYLOR, RICHARD PHILLIPS, and ROBERT KANE. XVII—XXXVII. New and united series of the Philosophical Magazine, Annals of Philosophy, and Journal of Science. 1840—1850. London. 8vo.

The London, Edinburgh, and Dublin Philosophical Magazine and Journal of Science. Conducted by Sir DAVID BREWSTER, RICHARD TAYLOR, RICHARD PHILLIPS, Sir ROBERT KANE, and WILLIAM FRANCIS. Fourth series. I—IX, 1851—1855. London. 8vo.

Annals of Philosophy; or, Magazine of Chemistry, Mineralogy, Mechanics, Natural History, Agriculture, and the Arts. By THOMAS THOMSON. I—XXVIII. 1813—1826. London. 8vo.

The Retrospective Review. I—XIV, 1820—1826.—The Retrospective Review, and Historical and Antiquarian Magazine. Second series. I & II, 1827 & 1828. London. 8vo.

The London Journal of Arts and Sciences; containing reports of all new patents, with a description of their respective principles and properties: also, original communications on subjects connected with science and philosophy; particularly such as embrace the most recent inventions and discoveries in practical mechanics. By W. NEWTON. I—XIV, 1820—1827. Second series. I—IX, 1828—1834. London. 8vo.

The London Journal of Arts and Sciences, and Repertory of Patent Inventions. Conducted by W. NEWTON. Conjoined series. I—XXXIX, 1832—1851. London. 8vo.

A Journal of Natural Philosophy, Chemistry, and the Arts. Illustrated with engravings. By WILLIAM NICHOLSON. I—XXXVI, 1802—1813. London. 8vo.

LONDON.

Miscellanea.—*Continued.*

The Monthly Review, or New Literary Journal. A periodical work, giving an account, with proper abstracts of, and extracts from, the new books, pamphlets, &c. as they come out. By several hands. I—LXXXI, 1749—1789. London. 8vo.

A General Index to the Monthly Review, from its commencement to the seventieth volume. In two volumes. London, 1786. 8vo.

The Monthly Review, or Literary Journal, enlarged. I—LXXXVIII, 1790—1819. London. 8vo.

The Westminster Review. I—XL, 1824—1842. London, 1825—1843. 8vo.

The Westminster Review. New series. I, III & IV, 1852 & 1853; V (except title and index) VI, I, VII, I, VIII, 1854—55. London. 8vo.

The Foreign Review and Continental Miscellany. I—V. London, 1828—1830. 8vo.

The Foreign Quarterly Review. I—XXIII, 1827—1839; XXVII—XXIX; XXXIII—XXXVII, 1841—1846. London. 8vo.

The Westminster and Foreign Quarterly Review. XLVII—XLIX, 1847—1849. London. 8vo.

The Quarterly Review. I—LVIII, 1802—1837, & LXII—XCVI, 1837—1855. London. 8vo.

The Gentleman's Magazine. New series. I—XXVI, 1834—1846; & XXXIV—XLI, 1850—1854. London. 8vo.

The British Quarterly Review. I—XXII, 1845—1855. London. 8vo.

Frazer's Magazine for Town and Country. XLIII—XLVI, & XLVIII, 1851—1853. London. 8vo.

The Banker's Magazine, Journal of the money market, and railway digest. XI—XIV, 1851—1854. London. 8vo.

The Dublin Review. XXVIII—XXXVIII, 1850—1855. London. 8vo.

The Art Journal. New series. XI—XV, 1849—1853. London. 4to.—And Illustrated Catalogue. 1851. 4to.

The Illustrated London News. I, 1843; IV, 1844; VI, 1845; XX & XXI, 1852. London. Folio.

The Spectator. A weekly journal of news, politics, literature, and science. XXIV, 1851. London. Folio.

The Athenæum; Journal of Literature, Science, and the Fine Arts. 1836—1855. London. 4to.

Notes and Queries: a medium of inter-communication for literary men, artists, antiquaries, genealogists, &c. I—VIII, 1849—1853; XI & XII, 1855. London. 4to.

(*Wanting IX & X,* 1854.)

The Architectural Magazine, and journal of improvement in architecture, building, and furnishing, and in the various arts and trades connected therewith. Conducted by J. C. LOUDON. I—V. London, 1834—1838. 8vo.

LONDON.

Miscellanea.—*Continued.*

The Mechanic's Magazine. Edited by R. A. Brooman. LXII (except three first Nos.), LXIII, LXIV. London, 1855. 8vo.

Colburn's United Service Magazine and Naval and Military Journal. 1851—1854. London. 8vo.

The Artizan. A monthly journal of the operative arts. IX—XI, 1851—1854. London. 4to.

The Penny Magazine of the Society for the Diffusion of Knowledge. I—IX, 1832—1840. London. R. 8vo.—New series. I—V, 1841—1845. London. 8vo.

The Penny Cyclopædia of the Society for the Diffusion of Useful Knowledge. I—XXVII, 1833—1843. London. R. 8vo.—Supplement, I—VI.

The Quarterly Journal of Education. I—II. London, 1831. 8vo.

Encyclopædia Metropolitana; or Universal Dictionary of Knowledge, on an original plan: comprising the twofold advantage of a philosophical and an alphabetical arrangement, with appropriate engravings. I—XXVI. London, 1845. 4to.

Encyclopædia Britannica, or Dictionary of Arts, Sciences, and General Literature. Eighth edition. With extensive improvements and additions, and numerous engravings. I—IX, 1843—1855. London. 4to.

Reports of the British and Foreign Bible Society, with extracts and correspondence, &c. I—XII, 1805—1839. London. 8vo.
(*Purchased.*)

MANCHESTER.

Literary and Philosophical Society.

Memoirs of the Literary and Philosophical Society of Manchester. I—V, 1785—1798.—Second series. I—XII, 1805—1855. London. 8vo.

NEWCASTLE-UPON-TYNE.

Natural History Society of Northumberland, Durham, and Newcastle-upon-Tyne.

Transactions of the Natural History Society of Northumberland, Durham, and Newcastle-upon-Tyne. I & II. Newcastle, 1831 & 1838. 4to.

OXFORD.

Radcliffe Observatory.

Astronomical observations made at the Radcliffe Observatory, Oxford, 1840—1854. I—XV. Oxford, 1842—1856. 8vo.

PENZANCE.

Royal Geological Society of Cornwall.

Transactions of the Royal Geological Society of Cornwall. Instituted February 11, 1814. I—VI, 1818—1846. Penzance. 8vo.

PENZANCE.

Royal Geological Society of Cornwall.—*Continued.*

Royal Geological Society of Cornwall. Thirty-fourth annual report of the Council, with the President's Address, and papers and notices read to the Society. Penzance, 1847. 8vo.

Also, thirty-fifth, thirty-sixth, thirty-eighth, and thirty-ninth Reports. 1848—1851.

YORK.

Yorkshire Philosophical Society.

Proceedings of the Yorkshire Philosophical Society. I, I. London & York, 1849. 8vo.

ADDENDA.

LEEDS.

Geological and Polytechnic Society of the West Riding of Yorkshire.

Proceedings of the Geological and Polytechnic Society of the West Riding of Yorkshire. I, 1839—42; II, 1842—48; III, pp. 1—296. Leeds. 8vo. (*Wanting I,* I.)

Reports and proceedings of the quarterly meeting of the Geological and Polytechnic Society of the West Riding of Yorkshire, held December 6, 1839. Leeds, 1839. 8vo.

The Geological and Polytechnic Society of the West Riding of Yorkshire. Established December, 1837. 8vo.

LEICESTER.

Leicester Literary and Philosophical Society.

Leicester Literary and Philosophical Society. Instituted June, 1835. Report of the council presented to the annual general meeting, assembled, June, 1855; and a selection of papers read before the Society since its formation. Leicester, 1855. 8vo.

www.ingramcontent.com/pod-product-compliance
Lightning Source LLC
LaVergne TN
LVHW021225110826
845150LV00002B/245

* 9 7 8 1 4 2 5 5 7 1 9 4 8 *